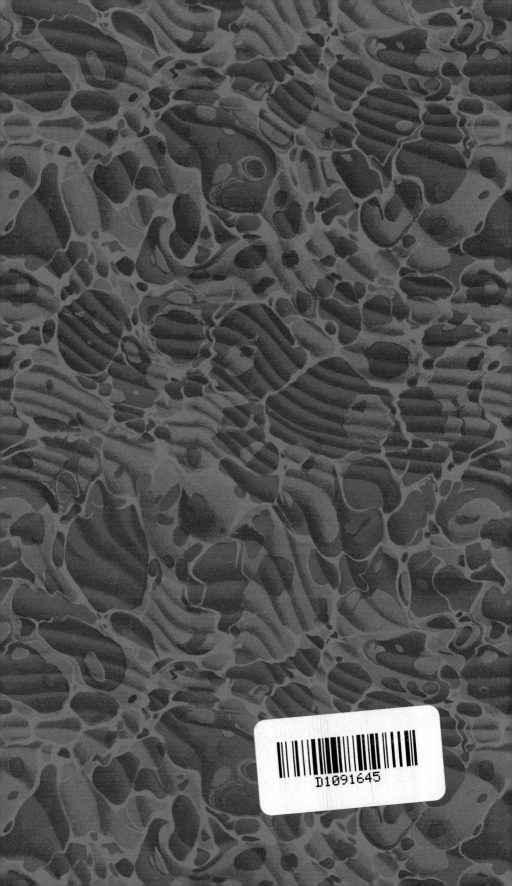

GARFIELD

GARFIELD

A Biography by Allan Peskin

THE KENT STATE UNIVERSITY PRESS

Library of Congress Cataloging in Publication Data

Peskin, Allan.
   Garfield.

   Bibliography: p.
   Includes index.
   1. Garfield, James Abram, Pres. U. S., 1831-1881. 2. Presidents—United
States—Biography. 3. United States—Politics and government—1849-1877.
4. United States—Politics and government—1877-1881.
E687.P47   973.8'4'0924 [B]   77-15630
ISBN 0-87338-210-2

*E
687
. P47*

Library of Congress Catalog Card Number 77-15630
ISBN: 0-87338-210-2
Printed in the United States of America
Designed by Harold M. Stevens

To My Father and Mother

CONTENTS

CONTENTS

PREFACE

Three things, Garfield once said, should be considered in writing the biography of any man. "First, What was he and what were the elements and forces within him? Second, What were the elements and forces of life and society around him? Third, What career resulted from the mutual play of these two groups of forces? How did he handle the world, and how did the world handle him? Did he drift, unresisting, on the currents of life, or did he lead the thoughts of men to higher and nobler purposes?"

Garfield, of course, lived in a day when all literature, including biography, was expected to perform a moral function; when the lives of great men, as the poet said, were designed to teach us that we could make our lives sublime. Living in a different age, I have been unable to follow Garfield's advice to biographers. Instead, I have tried to avoid blatant moralizing and overt analysis, preferring to allow Garfield's story to unfold within its own framework, letting the reader draw his own conclusions about the ultimate meaning of Garfield's career.

I have been occupied with this project for many years (too many, my wife would add) and in that time have accumulated debts which cannot be repaid but only gratefully acknowledged. Cleveland State University (and its predecessor, Fenn College) was generous with summer grants and a sabbatical leave as well as clerical assistance. Of the many libraries whose assistance was so indispensable, three deserve special thanks: the Manuscript Division of the Library of Congress; the Western Reserve Historical Society, whose librarian, Kermit Pike, was always eager to bring fresh Garfield items to my attention; and the Hayes Memorial Library at Fremont, Ohio.

Contrary to the stereotype portrayed in academic novels, the scholarly community can be remarkably unselfish. I have learned much from my friends and colleagues, especially from those who shared with me their own research: Fred Nicklason, Jim Kitson and C. H. Kramer who allowed me to inspect their notes on Dawes, Blaine and Ingersoll. President John S. Millis of Western Reserve University gave me access to the Garfield family of Bratenahl, Ohio, who, in turn, introduced me to Professors Harry Brown and Frederick Williams of Michigan State University. Their generosity in sharing their papers, their office and their immense stock of Garfield lore greatly facilitated the completion of this project. Of my teachers, two should be mentioned: William Best Hesseltine, who taught me something about writing and considerably more about human nature; and Harvey Wish, who introduced me first to historical research and then to my wife. My brother Perry, a stern grammarian and a gentle critic, saved me from numerous solecisms.

Portions of this book first appeared, in considerably different form, in various scholarly journals, all of which have granted me permission to reprint. Much of Chapter 7 was published in *Ohio History*, January and April, 1963; a portion of Chapter 14 appeared in *Public Administration Review*, November/December, 1973; material from various chapters in Section II was published in *Mid-America*, October, 1973 and in *Ohio History*, Spring-Winter-Summer, 1968. Much of Chapter 21 first appeared in *The Wisconsin Magazine of History*, Summer, 1972. Excerpts from Chapters 24 and 25 can be found, respectively, in *The South Atlantic Quarterly*, Winter, 1977 (copyright 1977 by Duke University Press) and in *The Journal of the Illinois State Historical Society*, May, 1977 (copyright 1977). The portrait used for the frontispiece was supplied by the Lake County Historical Society.

Long-standing custom requires that acknowledgements conclude with an affectionate, half-humorous tribute to the author's wife for graciously performing her menial tasks. I find myself unable to strike the proper bantering tone and can only simply, gratefully, and inadequately thank Barbara for everything.

PART ONE

CHAPTER ONE

CHAOS OF CHILDHOOD

Early in March of 1820 Abram Garfield lifted his bride Eliza into a one-horse wagon loaded with their few possessions and set out for the shores of Lake Erie. They were scarcely twenty years old. Ahead of them stretched two hundred miles of jolting roads that wound their way over thickly wooded hills, past isolated cabins and straggling villages, across unbridged streams swollen by the spring rains, through mud sloughs deep enough to swallow the wagon entire, leading at last to a small log cabin on the banks of the Cuyahoga river that was to be their first home together.[1]

For Abram and Eliza Garfield the road to northern Ohio had been a long one. It began, as it had for so many of their Western Reserve neighbors, in New England. As early as 1630 an Edward Garfield had found his way to Massachusetts, where for over a century and a half his descendants would live and work without achieving any noteworthy distinction. Shortly after the Revolution, Solomon Garfield, a giant of a man whose awesome feats of strength would remain a legend for years among his neighbors, joined the tide of restless Americans who set out for the new lands in the West. He settled in Worchester, New York, and it was there, only three days before the dawn of the nineteenth century, that his grandson Abram was born.[2]

Eliza Ballou's parents had been born in Providence, Rhode Island. Obeying the same impulse that had stirred Solomon Garfield, they too had left the Atlantic coast for the foothills of the interior, settling in New Hampshire, where Eliza was born. When Eliza was eight her father died. Her mother, thrown on her own resources, brought her family further west to Worchester, where their lives and that of Abram Garfield's briefly joined. Abram was smitten with Eliza's sister, Mehitabel, but in less than a year they had to part when the Ballous pushed further west, to Muskingum County, Ohio, where they joined Eliza's brother James, fresh from his service in the recently concluded War of 1812. A few years later, Abram Garfield, now an orphan, shook loose from the farmer to whom he had been apprenticed and followed his childhood sweetheart, determined to make her his wife. He was too late. Mehitabel was already married. When he heard the news he turned around and went home. Eliza, however, was still unmarried and when her path again crossed that of Abram's a romance quickly blossomed. They were married in February of 1820 and the next month Abram carried her off to his log cabin in the Cuyahoga valley.[3]

In those days Ohio was just beginning to shake off the crudeness of the frontier. The War of 1812, which eliminated the Indian menace, had removed the last major obstacle to settled life. The new prosperity, however, failed to touch the Garfield's home in northern Ohio. Cut off from the rest of the state by all but impassable roads, with its commerce stifled by lack of cash and its citizens enervated by constant epidemics, this section stagnated. A traveler passing through northern Ohio at this time was struck by the "frequent and great appearances of poverty and distress." He found the settlers "ignorant, unpolished . . . rude and uncultivated."[4] Children commonly roamed barefoot, even in winter. The most typical dwelling was, like the Garfields', a rude log hut, lit and ventilated only through chinks in the walls, its dirt floor often churned to mud, its heat derived from a chimneyless fire, which would sometimes ignite the cabin itself. The nearby village of Cleveland at that time had scarcely six hundred inhabitants, one church, and no public schools. Through it meandered the Cuyahoga River, blocked by sandbars, little more than a stagnant, mosquito-ridden cesspool, useless for commerce, but highly productive of disease.[5]

These primitive conditions took their toll on the Garfields. Shortly after they settled in their "snug log house" they were both struck down by the "Ague" and the "Bilious fever,"

4

which compelled them to abandon their home and move in with relatives until they regained their strength. So long as they continued to live in the malarial Cuyahoga valley the ague was an annual visitor. "We was sick every fall regular," Mrs. Garfield recalled.[6]

In spite of sickness, in spite of hardship and poverty, the family grew rapidly. First to be born was Mehitabel in 1821, named after Eliza's mother. Then, in quick succession, came Thomas in 1822 and Mary in 1824. As Abram's family grew, so did his prospects. Despite his inauspicious circumstances he possessed many of the qualities that led to success on the frontier. His two main drawbacks, humble origins and lack of capital, were but the common lot of his neighbors, while his assets were such as to lend him distinction. Tall and strong, he won fame as the champion wrestler for miles around. "He . . . weighed over two hundred pounds," recalled an admiring nephew, "and could take a barrel of whiskey by the chime and drink out of the bung-hole and no man dared call him coward." His industry was such that, as his proud wife boasted, he could easily do the work of two ordinary men. "Everybody liked him" she recalled, ". . . he had a tolerably quick temper but he could govern it well, he was pleasant in his family, most always cheerful and social, a kind word for everyone . . . I tell you he was a handsome man, he had a noble heart. . . ."[7]

Not even his admiring wife ever claimed that Abram Garfield was in any way remarkable for intellectual brilliance or learning. Nevertheless, he knew an opportunity when he saw one, and that opportunity was not long in coming. By the mid 1820s it was apparent that northern Ohio could never prosper unless better transportation linked its trade to the rest of the nation. Inspired by the example of New York's Erie Canal, Ohioans set to work to build their own network of canals. The Cuyahoga valley provided a natural route. Abram Garfield and two friends pooled their resources and contracted to build a section of the canal along the river. "They made out first rate." Flushed with his success, Abram expanded his operations, but this time his optimism outran his capacity. "We sunk a good deal on the canal," Mrs. Garfield ruefully recalled.[8]

Before the collapse of his canal venture Abram Garfield

5

had been able to save enough money to realize the dream
that had brought him west. He bought a parcel of land and
moved his family into their own house, "the first Land and
House we ever owned." This was in Orange township, on the
edge of a ravine sloping down to the Chagrin river, today the
plush exurbanite community of Moreland Hills, but then the
"hilliest and remotest of townships."⁹ As 1829 drew to a
close the Garfield's friends and neighbors gathered for a
festive roof-raising. Prominent in the celebration were their
neighbors, the Boyntons, doubly close kin, for Amos Boynton
was Abram's stepbrother, and his wife Alpha was Eliza's
sister.

Two years later in this same log cabin, on November 19,
1831, another son was born to the Garfields. As his mother
fondly recalled, he was "the largest Babe I ever had, he
looked like a red Irishman." He was given the name James
Abram Garfield in memory of an earlier son of that name
who had died in infancy.

Despite their joy in their new child, the death of that earlier
James had cast a pall over the Garfield household which
could not be dispelled. Searching their hearts, they came to regard their loss as a judgment from God. Up to this time they
had felt no need for religion, had never, in fact, heard a sermon. But now they were determined to amend their godless
ways. "We resolved to live a different life if we could find the
right way."¹⁰ The way was soon shown them by a wandering
preacher named Murdoch who represented a movement that
was just beginning to take root in the Western Reserve.
Called variously Disciples, Christians, or Campbellites, after
its chief proponent Alexander Campbell, it was a uniquely American answer to the unique religious conditions of the American
frontier.

Reduced to its simplest terms, the religious problem of the
frontier was one of imbalance: the East had the preachers,
while the frontier had the sinners. Educated clergymen were
often reluctant to leave their comfortable Eastern pulpits,
and so such religion as the West did have usually passed by
default into the hands of poorly educated fanatics whose crude
revivalism often aroused passions as violent as the sins it set
out to suppress. In this emotionally heated atmosphere,

6

which encouraged the direct communion of man with his Maker, bitter sectarian antagonisms flourished, with each group convinced that it alone held the true key to salvation.

These were some of the abuses that Alexander Campbell, a western Virginia minister, set out to correct. He believed they could not be resolved until the churches purged themselves of all "man made" creeds and practices, and took for their guide only the plain commandments of the Bible and the primitive purity of Apostolic days. Confident that all Christians could unite on this platform, he looked forward to a new Reformation. At first Campbell had hoped that this Reformation might take place within the Baptist organization, but his followers, impatient with the conservatism of existing churches, began to cut loose from their old affiliations. Tentatively at first, but with gathering confidence, an independent religious movement began to take shape.

On the Western Reserve this movement found a particularly hospitable home. The Reserve was unusually tolerant of religious dissent; within a few miles of the Garfield home could be found the Shaker community of North Union, and only a few miles down another road lay Kirtland, soon to be a rallying point for Joseph Smith and his Mormons. Many Reserve citizens, the sober sons of New England, were repelled by the emotional excesses of Kentucky-style revivalism. Yet, as good democrats, they could not accept New England Calvinism, with its promise of salvation limited to the elect.

Campbell's movement (which in this region usually went under the name Disciples of Christ) proved eminently suitable to their needs. They not only approved of its theology but, even more important, they found its style congenial. The Disciples stressed a sane, educational evangelism that appealed to reason rather than to emotion. By eschewing creeds and formal articles of faith they hoped to avoid the factional squabbles and overly intellectual logic-chopping that plagued the older denominations. The Disciple reliance on lay preachers also proved to be an advantage since it enabled them to spread their message to areas that lacked ordained ministers.[11]

Those who joined with the Disciples found themselves part of a warm, tightly-knit brotherhood. Within its ranks could be found friendship, as well as an uplifting sense of high mission.

7

The older, well-established denominations looked down contemptuously on the Disciples as a faintly radical, somewhat disreputable band, and the Disciples retaliated by gleefully exposing each of their deviations from scriptural precept. All of this rancor was perhaps slightly out of keeping in a movement designed to unite all Christendom under one banner, but the incongruity did not seem to bother anyone.

This was the group to which Abram and Eliza Garfield gave their allegiance, and which was to shape so profoundly the life of their son James. For a while they held back: "We knew our duty, but like a great many postponed it." Early in 1833, all doubts resolved, they at last "obeyed the Saviour," and were baptized. "It then seemed we were perfectly happy."

Their happiness was all too brief. A few months after he had been "delivered to the Saints," Abram Garfield caught a chill from fighting a fire. Under the care of a local quack, he developed complications and, after paying a final farewell to farm, oxen and family, Abram Garfield died at the age of thirty-three.[12]

His widow had little time for grief. Within a few days of the funeral she was in the fields, splitting fence rails to protect the ripening wheat crop. Her twelve-year-old son Thomas, suddenly compelled to be a man, worked at her side. Eliza was determined to keep her family together. She sold some of her land to pay off the most pressing debts, and settled down on her remaining thirty acres. She did not despair. Her situation, though grim, was not hopeless. Many were worse off than she. She owned her farm outright, and her family was healthy and able to work. The Garfields were neither squatters nor paupers, but even with the help of Amos Boynton, the Garfield household lived near the raw edge of poverty. Everyone worked: Thomas in the fields, Mary and "Hittie" at home, while Eliza took in neighbors' sewing.

Only the infant James escaped the grinding struggle for survival. Too young to work, he grew up as the pampered pet of the family. As a child he was bright and restless. "He was a very good-natured Child," recalled his mother,

> he walked when he was nine months old, when ten months old
> he would climb the fence, go up the ladder a dozen times a day

8

he was never still a minute at a time in his whole life. . . .
Always uneasy, very quick to learn, he was rather lazy, did not
like to work the best that ever was.[13]

He displayed a certain precocity. When he was only three his
sister carried him through the woods to the little red district
school house, and soon he was delighting his proud family by
reading from the Bible.

Within the song-filled circle of his family, James passed
a happy childhood. His mother had the gift of banishing care
from her hearth. A bright, cheerful woman who always had
a song on her lips, she raised her children in a sunny atmosphere. Upon her youngest child she lavished particular devotion. James, inclined to be a "stubborn willful boy," required careful handling. One year, for example, tiring of the
weekly three mile tramp through the woods to attend church,
James refused to go. His mother received this rebellion with
unexpected calm, and agreed that he could stay home on Sunday, stipulating only that he was not to leave the house. A
year of this weekly house arrest was too much for James's
restless nature, and when his term was over he docilely returned to church.

In later years Garfield often revisited the site of his boyhood days to refresh the memories of "our Dear Old Home."
Through a haze of nostalgia he tried to recapture the joys of
tramping through the woods, playing with his Boynton cousins,
and reading by the flickering hearth fire. Orange township,
with its forests, creeks, and ravines, had been a good place
in which to be a boy.

But as he grew older not even the warmth of his mother's
home could shield Garfield from the cold reality of his pinched
circumstances. He learned that he was poor and that he was
an orphan. The neighborhood boys cruelly taunted him until
he ran weeping to brother Thomas for comfort. "Cold hearted
men frowned upon me," he recalled, "and I was made the
ridicule and sport of boys that had fathers, and enjoyed the
luxuries of life. . . ."[14] Garfield may have exaggerated these
early humiliations. Throughout his life he was always unduly
sensitive to slights. "Sensitive as a girl;" "the skin of a rabbit;"
"could not face a frowning world;"[15] were some of the judg-

ments of his political associates. Yet even if they were exaggerated, these boyhood wounds left a lasting scar on his personality.

Some of the taunts may have been prompted by a scandal in which Garfield's mother was involved. The whole episode is wrapped in obscurity. None of Garfield's many biographers mention the incident. No hint of it can be found in the otherwise remarkably candid Garfield correspondence. Were it not for an unguarded allusion briefly dropped into Garfield's diary many years later, the affair would have remained entirely hidden. The very fact that so much effort was devoted to covering its traces indicates that the whole business must have left a painful impression. Briefly, what seems to have happened was that Garfield's mother, weary of her single-handed struggle against poverty, remarried in April of 1842. Her new husband was a Warren (or Alfred) Belden of Bedford, Ohio, a nearby village. She and James lived with him for a year, and then, for some reason, Eliza packed her belongings and moved back to Orange. Belden repeatedly begged her to come back, but she refused. Finally, despairing of her return, he instituted proceedings for divorce. Eliza evaded the summons for some years, but finally in 1850 the Cuyahoga Court of Common Pleas judged her "guilty of gross neglect of duty as a wife," and awarded Belden a divorce.[16]

Divorce in those days was a rare and scandalous occurrence. Even a woman who divorced her husband for good cause often found her reputation forever tainted. A woman whose husband divorced her must have been an ideal target for all the malicious gossip so delightful to small towns. What prompted Garfield's mother to leave Mr. Belden's bed and board will probably never fully be known. Garfield himself blamed his stepfather, whom he never forgave. Many years later, even after he had been elected President, and could be expected to view his childhood humiliations with detachment, Garfield received the news of Belden's death with cold satisfaction. "After this long long silence ended in death," he noted in his diary, "it is hard for me to think of the man without indignation."[17] If Garfield, normally a poor hater, could nurse a grudge over all these years undimmed into manhood, what was the impact of the affair upon the twelve year old boy?

As he grew into adolescence, Garfield began to develop traits that disturbed his mother. An "overgrown, uncombed, unwashed boy,"[18] he was moody and belligerent by turns. Frequently he picked fights with the boys who crossed him. More often, however, he withdrew into himself, "framing mighty plans and transactions of which I was always the hero." Even his favorite cousin, Phebe Boynton, could not resist teasing him for "building those lofty 'air castles' and talking it over with yourself." Lost in his private dream world, he often wandered about in an abstracted daze, once plunging heedlessly into a well, other times absentmindedly slashing himself with an axe while chopping wood.[19]

His dreams were fed by books. Next to hunting, reading was his greatest passion. Books were rare, but those he had were devoured over and over until they could be reeled off from memory. He liked history, especially those stirring stories of the American Revolution that reminded him of the ballads his mother loved to sing. Fiction, however, was his chief delight, especially stories of faraway places. While he browsed Uncle Amos's cattle or chopped wood for the neighbors, his imagination was pacing Robinson Crusoe's lonely island and drifting down the Mississippi on a flatboat. Stories of the sea fascinated him most of all. The thought of running away to sea took hold of him with an obsessive grasp. His drab land-locked existence seemed intolerable, but whenever he caught a glimpse of a sail on Lake Erie he would go "almost insane with delight."[20] Whenever he had a free afternoon he would drift down to Cleveland and hang around the wharves, running errands for his heroes, the canal boat captains, and eagerly absorbing their tales of adventures in faraway places.

In the summer of 1848, when he was sixteen years old, he resolved to leave home to make a new life on the open seas. Ignoring the tearful pleas of his distraught mother, he collected his savings and set out for Cleveland. There was one ship in port at the time, and he headed straight for it. With a light heart he bounded up the gangplank and politely asked

11

the captain to take him on. The captain, half drunk, and already in a rage over some earlier harassment, turned on Garfield with a savage oath, and in painfully explicit language told him what he thought of sea-struck adolescents. "Such swearing and cursing as he indulged in," Garfield recalled,

> it had never been my lot to hear before. He did not deign to answer my question. At the close of a time which must have been very short, but which seemed to me very long, I turned upon my heel and left the vessel amid the loud jeers and laughter of the men.[21]

Disappointed and humiliated, Garfield could not return home—not with the sailors' mocking laughter still ringing in his ears—so he decided to settle for half a dream. If he could not enjoy the high adventure of the open sea, he would have to be satisfied with the more prosaic routine of the canal. That same day, August 16, 1848, he shipped aboard the canal boat *Evening Star*, captained by his cousin, Amos Letcher. Garfield was taken on as a driver. "As canaling was at the bottom of sailing, so driving was at the bottom of canaling."[22] His job was to prod the patient dray horses that slowly pulled the barges. Garfield trudged along the towpath, switch in hand, occasionally swatting the horses across their rear ends. The work was as drab as any of the odd jobs he found so distasteful at home, but his irrepressible imagination clothed it with glamour. Lost, as always, in dreams, he fell into the canal fourteen times and, since he could not swim, had to be fished out each time.

Garfield followed the *Evening Star* for six weeks. During that time he made four trips from Cleveland to Pittsburgh. By the end of the first trip he had been promoted from driver to bowman, charged with preparing the locks, trimming the lamps, and other odd duties, for which he was paid $14.00 a month. He liked the life. At first the older hands tried to push him around, but Garfield had inherited his father's strength, and would not be bullied. His fists won him the respect of his rough colleagues. As Amos Letcher remembered it, " . . . the boys all liked him first rate." Before long Garfield began to imagine himself the very picture of a "weatherbeaten boatman."[23]

After six weeks his canal career came to an abrupt end. Early in October he fell sick with the "ague." Too weak to work, he stumbled back to home and mother, and fell into his old bed. There he tossed, his teeth chattering, until the following January, when the fever at last began to break. As she nursed him back to health, Garfield's mother carefully plotted to wean her son from his wanderlust. Her campaign was aided by Samuel Bates, who taught district school that winter. Young and full of enthusiasm, Bates was far more stimulating than the usual stodgy drillmasters Garfield had known. His teacher and his mother convinced Garfield that even a sailor needed an education. Garfield listened to their arguments and agreed to postpone his return to the canal for a year. In the meantime he promised to continue his schooling. In nearby Chester township there was a little school, Geauga Academy, where Bates had once studied and he persuaded Garfield to enroll. On March 6, 1848, accompanied by his friends Orrin Judd and William Boynton, Garfield hiked across the Chagrin valley to Chester, rented a room and signed up for classes. "No greener boy," in his opinion, "ever started out for school."[24]

In later years Garfield's childhood was to become one of his chief political assets. The legend of the boy who rose from the towpath to the White House (as in the title of an admiring biography) seemed to embody the American dream of the self-made man. In sermons and pamphlets, Garfield's early life would be extolled as an illustration of the blessings of adversity, and children were exhorted to follow his example. Garfield himself was not above exploiting his childhood hardships for political gain, but in more candid moments he looked back upon his boyhood days with shame and some regrets. "To some men," he confessed to a friend,

> the fact that they came up from poverty and singlehandedness is a matter of pride. . . . I lament sorely that I was born to poverty . . . and in this chaos of childhood seventeen years passed before I caught up any inspiration which was worthy of my manhood. . . . precious 17 years in which a boy with a father and some wealth might have become fixed in manly ways. . . . Let no man praise me because I was poor and without a helper. It was very bad for my life.[25]

13

CHAPTER TWO

A VERY PULPY BOY

When Garfield set foot in the academy at Chester he found himself, for the first time, in his natural habitat. The next dozen years of his life would be passed almost entirely within the walls of one classroom or another. It would take the shock of war to wrench his life away from its academic bent, but throughout his long career he never entirely shed his scholarly (some would say pedantic) habits. As a friend observed, "He *taught* all his life—in the pulpit, on the platform, and in the halls of Congress."[1]

Geauga Academy, where Garfield first sampled the charms of learning, was not, by objective standards, a particularly impressive school. Founded in 1842 by Free Will Baptists, it offered a level of instruction only slightly more advanced than the rude one-room district school where Garfield had spent his boyhood. Ohio had not, at that time, any general system of public education. Each district taught its children the elements of reading, writing, and calculating as best it could, leaving more ambitious students dependent upon private institutions to continue their education. In the 1840s and 1850s a host of seminaries and academies sprang up to fill the gap between the common school and the college.[2]

Geauga Academy was neither the best nor the worst of these schools. In some respects it was shockingly inadequate. Latin instruction, for example, was confined solely to abstract grammatical principles with scarcely a hint that behind these principles lay a language with a literature. Garfield was the Academy's prize Latin student, but when he transferred to a more advanced school he was barely able to puzzle out the meaning of "Omnia Gallia in tres partes divisa est." In defense of Geauga Academy it must be realized that its pupils were so poorly trained in the common schools that they could scarcely grapple with more advanced subjects. Of the eighteen students who began to study algebra with Garfield, all but three fell by the wayside before the term was over.[3]

Garfield had originally enrolled in Geauga Academy with the intention of whiling away the winter months until the spring thaw would allow him to resume his work on the canal. But (as his mother had cunningly realized) once he plunged into school work, all his seafaring plans were drowned in this new fascination with learning. At the close of the spring term, instead of returning to the canal, he impatiently counted the days until the fall term began. When he returned to Chester that August his diary recorded his elation: "Exercises once again. Welcome the day." A few weeks later his satisfaction was unbounded. "Good times now," he gloated, "good times."[4]

The term passed quickly, with his days occupied with algebra, arithmetic and grammar, and his evenings spent in the pleasant companionship of the Zeletherian Society or the Mystic Ten. In debates and lyceums he and his fellow students earnestly thrashed out such problems as the propriety of disunion, the desirability of universal suffrage, and the natural inferiority of the Negro. All too soon, the term drew to an end. "The thoughts of parting rend my heart," he sadly noted. "We must soon say adieu."[5]

In spite of his best efforts at economy, the seventeen dollars that his mother had given him barely lasted out the first term. When he returned to Chester in August he had only six cents to his name. He threw that in the church collection box "for luck" and settled down to work. He boarded with a local family who charged him one dollar and six and a quarter cents a week for room, board, and washing. To make ends meet he worked on the side at the carpenter's trade.[6]

If he were to afford another year at the academy he would have to earn some money during the long winter vacation. But in winter the canal was frozen solid, the harvests were already

15

gathered, and no one needed a carpenter. The only trade open was schoolteaching. Indeed, it was for this very purpose—to allow its students to teach district school—that the academy closed down for the winter. After a cursory examination Garfield, himself only a year removed from school days, was licensed as a teacher. For a week he made the rounds of the districts near Orange, looking for an opening, but with no success. One evening, after he had returned home, tired, discouraged and resigned to failure, a man from Solon rode up to his door and offered him, unsolicited, a job for four months at twelve dollars a month.[7]

In later years, as he looked back upon this incident, it seemed to Garfield an omen of his future course. "The coming of this man confirmed me in the opinion that place-seeking was not in my line; and I have never asked anybody for a place from that day to this."[8] This was not quite true. The very next year Garfield applied for, and obtained, another teaching job.[9] But over the years Garfield's abhorrence of vulgar "place-seeking" hardened into a fixed habit—almost a superstition. Never to ask for an office became, he declared, "the law of my life," and he firmly believed, "that should I violate that law I would fail."[10] Time after time, in his military and political career, Garfield would let coveted opportunities slip by when they might easily have been his. One exasperated friend wondered, "What is the lack in Garfield? What is the thing wanting?" Some, like John Sherman, attributed these many missed opportunities to a lack of character: "His will power was not equal to his personal magnetism."[11] The real reasons for Garfield's seeming lack of "push," however, were far more complex than Sherman realized, arising from a sense of inadequacy incongruously coupled with an almost mystic sense of destiny, as well as an acute distaste for the more obvious forms of self-aggrandizement—qualities of character just beginning to appear in the raw nineteen-year-old boy who, with some trepidation, began to teach school in November of 1849.

He started the term in a grim mood, expecting trouble. He was not disappointed. His unruly students, some older than he, turned the classroom into a noisy, brawling nightmare. Gar-

16

field had to impose order by brute force. One exceptionally "saucy" boy tried to brain his teacher with a stick of fire-wood. They had "a merry time," but the teacher managed to disarm his assailant. After that, classes went more smoothly. Garfield was a conscientious teacher. Each night, before he allowed himself to fall asleep, he would trace on his bedsheets a diagram of his classroom, and run over in his mind the progress of each pupil.[12]

At the end of the term, with mixed feelings of relief and regret, Garfield said goodbye to his pupils. Time lay heavy on his hands, and he was drawn to a Disciple camp meeting in progress nearby. Up to this time Garfield had paid little attention to religious matters. After his brief childhood rebellion had been quashed, he had dutifully resumed his churchgoing, more to please his mother than out of any deep spiritual hunger. Lately, however, he had been experiencing a vague dissatisfaction with the course of his life. He had recently vowed to abstain from "low vulgar company and expressions," and raise his mind "to noble and sublime thoughts," but the restlessness persisted.[13] In this questing frame of mind he attended the camp meeting. At first he was drawn only by curiosity, but soon he began to enter into the spirit of the occasion. On March 3, 1850 he opened his soul, and allowed the light of the Lord to enter. The next day, to seal his new-found grace, he was immersed in baptism in the ice-cold waters of the Chagrin River. "Buried with Christ," he emerged from the river trembling with cold and exaltation, "to walk [in] newness of life."[14]

Garfield was transformed by his new-found faith. Unlike those of other sects, a Disciple was not converted in the hot blood of passion; his religious experience was deep rather than enthusiastic, but it was no less genuine. From the vantage point of Garfield's fresh enlightenment the very heavens seemed to declare the glory of God. "Month after month rolls round," he solemnly reflected, "the sun annually wheels round in endless cycles and we are carried nearer to eternity at every revolution. What responsibility rests upon us for the way and manner in which we spend our time."[15]

The whole world now seemed an ordered extension of God's will. Even Garfield's studies were suffused with a mystic pur-

17

pose. He perceived new beauties in them all, "especially Botany: which teaches us to 'look through nature up to nature's God' and to see his wisdom manifested in the flowers of the field."[16] Even the course of his own life seemed a striking demonstration of divine providence. He now realized that on the canal he had been "ripe for ruin . . . ready to drink in with every species of vice." But he had been spared—a brand plucked from the burning. "Thus by the providence of God I am what I am and not a sailor. I thank him."[17]

Renouncing his sinful past, he vowed to lead a purer life. On the canal he had often indulged in the casual profanity of sailors. He now put that vice aside and never swore again, not even while he was in the army. Theatrical amusements, which had once delighted him, now seemed grossly immoral, and he determined to avoid them in the future for his soul's sake.[18]

Acceptance of the Disciple communion involved more than just a religious experience. Although the Disciples professed scorn for all man-made creeds, they soon developed (in their own heterodox way) a common set of beliefs that virtually amounted to an orthodoxy. Inspired by the vision of Alexander Campbell, they held fast to the goal of a reformed, united Christianity, purged of all sectarian strife. Following Campbell's formula, "Where the Bible speaks, we speak; where it is silent, we are silent," they held aloof from all purely worldly matters, such as politics. In their contempt for a sinful world they often approached the radical extremes of pacifism, equalitarianism, and semi-anarchy of the more pietistic sects. This was just a passing phase in the development of the Disciples. All too soon, they would find themselves drawn into the conflicts that shook the world around them. The slavery struggle in particular was to divide and embitter the church. And as the passage of time failed to bring the hoped-for Reformation, Disciples began to shed their millennialist, pietistic trappings, and became a denomination more or less like other Protestant bodies.

But when Garfield joined the Disciples, their vision was still fresh and hopeful. With the passion of a true believer, Garfield accepted all Disciple doctrines. He viewed other denominations with indignation for their perverse persistence in unscriptual practices. The tumult of a Methodist camp meeting left him "grieved and disgusted with the shameful proceedings . . . this religion is only adapted to the coarser order of mind, and has more of the animal than spiritual in it." Comparing the Methodists to the Disciples, he piously concluded that "the motives and enjoyment of the Gospel are higher and nobler than this, producing a holy *quiet* of *calm* enjoyment, and not a *furious* piety, and *noisy* zeal." The errors of the Presbyterians left him in dismay. "It pains my heart," he said, after attending their service, "to see the ignorance and bigotry that is abroad in the land. I wish that men would let all human traditions alone and take the Bible alone for their guide." Other sects fared no better; all were "adulterated with sectarianism."[19]

The impressionable Garfield reflected the Disciple influence in his political views. He dismissed the antislavery cause, then sweeping the Western Reserve, as "carnal," for according to his reading of the Bible, "the *simple relation* of master to slave is NOT UNCHRISTIAN." He scorned all politics and politicians. "It looks to me," he declared, "like serving two masters to participate in the affairs of a government which is point blank opposed to the Christian (as all human ones must necessarily be)." A brief view of the Ohio legislature confirmed this prejudice. "Their rubicund bloated faces," he noted with disdain, "spoke plainly of the midnight bowl. . . ." The excitement of politics left him unmoved. "I am profoundly ignorant of its multifarious phases," he boasted, "and am not inclined to study it. I am exceedingly disgusted with all the wire-pulling of politicians and the total disregard of truth in all their operations. Miserable, low ungentlemanly trash fills the columns of the political press, unfit for refined feelings, tender consciences or kind hearts." Each July 4th, while his neighbors were celebrating with patriotic frenzy, Garfield piously withdrew into prayer, puzzled that so many could celebrate independence while still slaves to their appetites and passions.[20]

Garfield's wholehearted commitment to the Disciple movement was a natural development in the course of his life. After drifting through an aimless childhood, he had recently been seized with a burning desire "to make a mark in the world." In a burst of braggadocio, he declared, "I know with-

19

out egotism that there is some of the sleeping thunder in my soul and it shall come out!" But inwardly he lacked confidence in his ability. He needed to immerse his weak, untested self in the reassuring atmosphere of eternity. The Disciples suited his needs in many ways. He had always regretted that his brothers and sisters had been too old to be really close to him. Within the ranks of the Disciples, however, everyone was hailed as Brother or Sister. How satisfying it must have been to be called "Brother James," instead of merely "Widow Garfield's Jimmie."[21]

Imbued as he was with Disciple fervor, Garfield felt increasingly out of place at the Baptist Geauga Academy. By October he was convinced that it was permeated with "a manifest sectarian spirit . . . which I fear will eventually destroy the school," and at the end of the term he left in disgust. His departure was hastened by a clash between the academy's Disciple principal and the Baptist trustees, but doctrinal matters did not completely account for Garfield's unhappiness at Chester. Garfield was a poor boy who had to dispense with the frills and luxuries enjoyed by more fortunate students. For the entire spring term he had to subsist on a meatless diet of milk, bread, and pudding. Despite this Spartan regimen he was unable to make ends meet. He started the fall term penniless and was compelled to work four hours each day for eight cents an hour. His sensitive nature was humiliated by his coarse, homemade clothes: a faded wool shirt, conspicuously patched trousers, and a wide straw hat straight out of Huckleberry Finn. He cringed at the snubs he received, or thought he received, from the better-dressed students. "Some few (the offscourings of creation) publicly sneer at me and many (not a whit better) do the same more slyly by avoiding my company, which to me is very desirable. Alas! How many judge a man by his clothes." A kindly neighbor assured him that when he got to be a United States Senator, no one would care what clothes he wore as a boy, but her motherly advice was scant consolation at the time.[22]

So Geauga Academy was left behind, with few regrets, and Garfield set out to earn enough money to enable him to continue his education in happier surroundings. For almost a year he worked at various jobs around Ohio at the trades he knew best—schoolteaching and carpentry. His experience at a school in Warrensville township of Cuyahoga County was no happier than that at Solon the previous year. The sullen, surly students stubbornly resisted all of Garfield's most ingenious pedagogic devices, and the ceaseless "thump and bang" of the classroom unnerved him. "It is indeed trying to my patience and also to my stomach to have so many little ones about me," he complained. "I believe it is in the province of females to teach little scholars the rudiments of education. . . . I want something that has the *thunder* in it more than this has."[23]

In the spring of 1851, he and his mother paid a visit to their Boynton and Ballou kin in Muskingum County. There for a time Garfield taught in a "miserable old log schoolhouse . . . as smutty as a blacksmith's shop."[24] A similar experience inspired him to verse:

> Of all the trades by men pursued
> There's none that's more perplexing
> Than is the country pedagogue's—
> It's every way most vexing
>
> Cooped in a little narrow cell,
> As hot as black Tartarus,
> As well in Pandemonium dwell
> As in this little schoolhouse.[25]

Educational standards in Southern Ohio were even lower than on the Reserve. Garfield was accounted a wonder because he was the only teacher in two counties able to solve a problem involving long division, but the loose-disciplined children and the tight-fisted parents drove him to resign. He returned to the Reserve and for the rest of the summer worked as a carpenter for Jedidiah Hubbell of Chagrin Falls who remembered him as "a very good hand for the price."[26]

In 1849, Reserve Disciples, disturbed at the prospect of their children being educated by hostile sectarians, resolved to found a school of their own. They chose Hiram, deep in the hills of Portage County, as their site, partly because of its isolation from urban centers of vice and temptation. Amos Sutton Hayden, a self-educated preacher, was induced to serve as

21

president, and the school, ponderously named the Western Reserve Eclectic Institute, opened its doors in November of 1850. Despite Hiram's isolation and lack of boarding facilities, hundreds of Disciple boys and girls, mostly from Ohio but some from distant states, flocked to the Eclectic.[27]

In the fall of 1851, Garfield, accompanied by a quartet of his Boynton cousins, enrolled in the new Disciple school, "to seek the sparkling gems of science." The Eclectic then consisted of little more than "a cornfield with a solid, plain brick building in the centre of it," but in his eagerness for knowledge Garfield overlooked the humble campus and saw only the opportunities before him. Twenty-five years later he still vividly recalled his first impressions. "A few days after the beginning of the term," he remembered, "I saw a class of three reciting in mathematics—geometry I think . . . and regarding both teacher and class with a feeling of reverential awe for the intellectual heights to which they had climbed, I studied their faces so closely that I seem to see them now as distinctly as I saw them then."[28]

Exhilarated by his new surroundings, Garfield plunged into his studies, prodded by a fierce determination to excel. He pursued knowledge not only for its own sake, but also in order to convince himself of his own ability. As he admitted, "If at any time I began to flag in my effort to master a subject . . . I was stimulated to further effort by the thought, 'Some other fellow in the class will probably master it.' " At night, when he studied Latin in his lonely room, he could look across the way to the window of his chief rival. When the light in that window went out, Garfield smiled, knowing that his rival had given up for the night, but he doggedly stuck to his books for at least a quarter hour more.[29]

In the Disciple environment of Hiram, Garfield no longer felt the snubs he had received from the proud Chester Baptists. Although his dress had not improved—he wore rude Kentucky jeans and slipover sleeves of unmatching calico—and his poverty was still apparent, he quickly gained a position of leadership in the student body. He worked for a time as school janitor, charged with sweeping the floors and ringing each hour the bell hanging under the Eclectic's zinc-plated dome, but no true Disciple could scorn him because of his humble duties. His scholastic ability, impressive enough by the standards of the Eclectic, won admiration but his popularity was based on more than intellectual prominence. His commanding physical appearance, almost six feet tall with broad shoulders and a massive head topped by a shock of unruly tawny hair, and his ability to outrun and outwrestle his schoolmates, instilled automatic respect. This, coupled with his serious demeanor, which gave an impression of quiet dignity, and his unaffected friendliness—his heart, said a friend, was "as big as a milk pail"—all contributed to Garfield's popularity. His friends acknowledged his preeminence. "He will distinguish himself, if he lives," predicted one. "I suppose he will be a preacher, and if so he will be a superior one."[30]

In the congenial atmosphere of the Eclectic Institute, surrounded by admiring friends, Garfield blossomed. As he discovered latent talents and unused powers, his confidence in himself and his future grew. In particular, he discovered that he had the power to sway an audience, that he was a natural orator. In the debates of the Philomathean Society, which he and his friend Corydon E. Fuller helped to organize, he learned the oratorical techniques that were to make him one of the most effective stump speakers of his generation. His debating style was pugnacious for, as he admitted, "I love agitation and investigation and glory in defending unpopular truth against popular error."[31]

Early in Garfield's forensic career he had already mastered a favorite weapon of all successful debaters—the plausible non sequitur. In May of 1852 a "strolling lecturer" named Joseph Treat appeared at Hiram to give a series of lectures defending atheism and spiritualism. He challenged the godly to debate and, no other suitable champion being present, Garfield accepted the challenge. He rose and quietly asked Treat what was the present participle of the verb "to be" in Greek. Unable to answer this question, Treat was routed in confusion and the cause of the righteous was sustained.[32]

The most characteristic feature of Garfield's oratory during this period was his love of florid, high-flown rhetoric. Both

23

his speaking and his writing were studded with elegant "literary" flourishes, modeled after the style of currently popular writers, such as the sentimental essayist Donald G. Mitchell ("Ik. Marvel"), a particular favorite of the Hiram set. All of Garfield's schoolmates shared, to some extent, this penchant for lofty prose. In their correspondence, rather than discuss trivial gossip, they grappled with such serious matters as The Progress of the Soul, the Path of Duty, and the Higher Meaning of Life. In doing so they were trying to prove to each other (and to themselves) that they had escaped from a society "where there is no topic for conversation but raising hogs and cattle."[33] They followed literary models because only through literature could they obtain a picture (however distorted) of the larger world that existed beyond their own experience.

Into his diary, his "Journal of Daily Events and Private Cogitations; or his Confidential Friend to Whom he entrusts the secret thoughts of His Heart,"[34] Garfield poured all the restless, surging emotions of adolescence. His prose was compounded of equal parts of piety and romanticism. Scarcely a week passed without evoking some elevated sentiment such as this reflection:

> This is the last day of March, and the blast drives hurriedly along. The storm-king is abroad in his fury, and shrieks and howls fiercely at every opposing obstacle. The dreary outward world causes the mind to retire within itself and contemplate upon the great and wonderful destiny to which we are all hastening, to scan the events of the past, and learn to avoid the errors, and copy the virtues of those who have gone before us.[35]

Like many adolescents of his day, Garfield was stirred by the Romantic impulse. He liked to imagine himself as a solitary Byronic figure inspired to lofty thoughts by the grandeur of nature. "There is a bold lofty point of the hill running near the schoolhouse," he wrote in his diary one spring day,

> whose hoary top I ascend in the morning before I commence school, and there contemplate the surrounding scenery. I there see the lofty peaks whose blue waving lines kisses the cloud in the depths of the blue cerulean. There is the place of meditation and communion with the Creator.[36]

24

A morbid tinge colored his musings. The thought of early death oppressed him and his comrades. When he first visited New York City he paid little attention to the various tourist attractions, preferring to spend his time in "a place to call forth serious meditation and reflection"—Greenwood Cemetery. There he passed the entire afternoon reciting Gray's Elegy to the tombstones.[37]

In after years, when Garfield reread the "gush and slush" of his schoolboy diary, he could barely keep from blushing. "I was," he admitted, "a very pulpy boy till I was at least 22 years old. But with all the rudeness and crudeness of those days, I was very dead in earnest and was working by the best light I had."[38]

Despite his Romantic posturings—or perhaps because of them—Garfield was ill at ease in the company of women. In the coeducational atmosphere of Hiram, increasing contact with the opposite sex began to polish his crudeness. One woman in particular, Almeda A. Booth, took Garfield under her wing. Painfully plain, intensely severe, Almeda Booth was the most commanding personality on the Eclectic campus. "An empress in her power to control, a conqueror of every will that seemed to stand in the way of true progress, she was undisputed mistress of all who came within her sphere of influence." Garfield thought her the equal of Margaret Fuller, and another Hiram student, without the slightest thought of blasphemy, estimated that "her early pupils regarded her with almost as much reverence as the devout Romanist does the Virgin Mary." "Sister Almeda" took Garfield in hand and civilized him. "When I first came here," he admitted,

> I had no correct views of society, as to what it should be and no one was more crude and uninitiated than I was. . . . I can truly say that I never met with any person save my own dear mother who has been of so much advantage to me in thinking reasoning and living as Almeda A. Booth. . . . I have looked up to her as a near and dear elder sister. . . .[39]

Almeda may have been cherished as a beloved sister, but when Garfield fell in love he chose a different sort of girl altogether. The object of his affections, Mary Hubbell, a niece of his former carpentry boss, had once been a pupil of his at Warrensville district school. She was a lively, bubbling, vivacious girl, full of fun and laughter, but not a member of the sternly intellectual circle presided over by Almeda Booth. Garfield, however, did not think Mary too frivolous. During their long walks together he would pour out his heart, while she listened attentively. "She has a good intellect," he concluded after one such monologue.[40]

Their courtship followed the chaste pattern of the day: moonlit strolls, sentimental poetry, anonymous *billets-doux*, and tender handclasps. Before long they had "traded hearts." "To no other being but yourself, upon earth," he swore, "is the fountain of my heart unsealed, and gushes forth with all the ardor of youthful affection, and it causes my heart to thrill with emotion to think that she upon whom I lavish my fondest affections, bestows her warmest love upon a poor, penniless, orphan-boy like myself."[41]

Garfield's friends noted their relationship and silently disapproved, but they held their tongues, since they assumed that the couple was engaged. So, for that matter, did Mary. But Garfield, perhaps mindful of his mother's unfortunate marriage, had refrained from committing himself fully. Suddenly, in late 1852, he realized that what he had begun as an innocent flirtation threatened to get out of hand. An appalling dilemma loomed before him. On the one hand, he believed that "of all characters in society, none is more despicable, heartless, and truly deserving the frown and contempt of all good men and women, than the man who wantonly trifles with the affections of a woman." He was satisfied that his course had been honorable, but "the world," unfortunately "judges by external appearances. . . ." On the other hand, to marry Miss Hubbell would be to "consign myself to a living grave; clip the free wings upon which I have thus far soared and flutter 'unearthly flutterings' and flap my useless pinions, bound to a mate of another species—the eagle with the robin."[42] "Shall the inconsiderate words and actions and affections of thoughtless youth," he asked plaintively, "fasten their sad consequences upon the whole of after life? Or is it right to shake them off and let mature judgement revoke the false decisions of verdant youth?"[43]

The problem was difficult, but in the end, after much soul-searching, the path of honor was forsaken and Garfield broke with Mary. The girl and her "high-spirited" family were outraged, and threatened to make his love letters public. For a season Garfield was the target of gossip and public disapproval, and many Hiram ladies boycotted him out of sympathy with their jilted sister.[44]

The whole affair left Garfield shaken. His former happy view of a world directed by God to the best, now gave way to a cynical, world-weary despondency. "To the first view life—the world and society—seem pleasant and alluring," he reflected, "but when their depths are penetrated, their secret paths trod, they are found hollow, soulless and insipid." Each day convinced him "more *more* and MORE of the utter hollowness of the world and all human affairs." His self-confidence began to ebb. "Can I enter the secret chambers of my own heart and soul," he asked himself, "and there see and know whether real honesty is there?" The bitter answer was not long in coming, for by April he felt "there seems to be a something within me, I cannot name it, that whispers fearful words into my heart. It tells me I'm not honest . . . that there is no such thing as human sincerity or real honesty."[45]

With his customary energy Garfield took up sadness with as much enthusiasm as he had previously displayed in learning Latin or falling in love. Eventually even his sympathetic friends began to weary of his gloomy pose. "If there is anything wrong," burst out an exasperated friend, Charles D. Wilber, "depend upon it, it is you! You do see a great deal of *emptiness*. Yes, and you express some contempt as to the ways and means of life! . . . Now, James, this fantastic leaping up and down—is mere boyishness."[46] Wilber was astute. Before long even the joys of melancholy began to pall on Garfield, and by the summer of 1853, in spite of himself, he began to feel cheerful again.

Chastened by his experience, Garfield plunged into his studies with renewed vigor. His courses included geology, geometry, trigonometry, and penmanship (taught by Platt Spencer of Spencerian fame), but Greek and Latin remained his favorite subjects. "The longer I live," he declared at the age of twenty, "the firmer is my determination to obtain a thorough classical education. There is a path by which young men and young ladies can rise above the groveling herd 'that scarcely know they had a soul within.' '' The path was rocky, but he felt the goal was worth the effort. "I never look for riches, ease and affluence," he declared, "but regard the riches of a well stocked mind as infinitely above all the blessings that wealth can bestow."[47]

When he first began to study Latin at Hiram, Garfield characteristically was filled with misgivings. He was ready to drop the course if he should prove a "drag" on the other students, whom he imagined must be far wiser and better than he. To compensate for his imagined deficiencies he studied up to eighteen hours a day, preparing lessons at least six times longer than the teacher assigned. He admired his teacher, Norman Dunshee, as a "very fine scholar and one of the best men and Christians I know of,"[48] but before long Garfield was too advanced for formal classroom instruction. Undaunted, he and Almeda Booth continued their studies on their own, reading Horace, Virgil, Sallust, Xenephon and the New Testament. Echoes of this classical training were later to resound on the floors of Congress in Garfield's speeches, which were often studded with appropriate Latin tag-lines.

Preoccupied though he was with the literature of pagan antiquity, Garfield did not neglect his Christian duty. In the spring of 1853 he began to preach at neighboring churches. Garfield approached his first full-length sermon in a cold sweat of anxiety. By the end of the year, however, he was preaching almost every Sunday, and receiving a gold dollar for each sermon. He now felt quite sure of himself, and was filled with an almost un-Christian pride at his prowess. "After I get to speaking I feel very calm and collected. . . . I am almost alarmed, fearing it is a kind of self confidence."[49]

Absorbed in his college and church activities, the scars left from the Hubbell affair, which Garfield had feared would pain for the rest of his life, began to fade. After the stormy end of his romance he had vowed to "cut loose from the world of womankind," but inevitably his resolve weakened.[50] As 1853 drew to a close he found his thoughts dwelling increasingly on Miss Lucretia Rudolph, a former Chester classmate, now his star Greek pupil. His courtship began in November with a letter beginning stiffly: "Please pardon the liberty I take in *pointing* my pen towards *your name*. . . ."[51] This inaugurated a lengthy correspondence on "The Study of Dead Languages." With each succeeding letter his tone grew less formal and more familiar, until a time came when Greek and Latin were forgotten entirely.

Lucretia Rudolph ("Crete" to her friends) was the daughter of Zeb Rudolph, a leading Hiram Disciple and a trustee of the Eclectic Institute. A sober, serious, darkly beautiful girl, she conveyed at first an impression of aloofness, but her sincerity, dignity, and quiet charm usually impressed those who knew her well. Although Garfield had known her since Chester days, her seemingly cold manner had discouraged him from considering a close relationship. Garfield preferred friends with whom he could bare his soul and exchange intimate confidences. He had little patience with those who chose to keep their inner feelings to themselves, when he was ready to share his most private sentiments with any sympathetic listener. "I am so constituted that I cannot enjoy a cool formal friend (a misnomer) but must be as a brother or sister to enjoy them."[52]

In spite of her reserve, Lucretia's manifest qualities of mind and character commended her to Garfield, and he determined to know her better. By December 31, he was writing warmly of her in his dairy. His intentions were becoming serious, but he still wondered "whether she has that warmth of feeling that loving nature which I need to make me happy. She is either studiously concealing it or else she does not possess it. . . . For myself, I feel that under the proper circumstances I could love her, and unite my destiny to hers."[53] By spring it was settled: "We love each other, and have declared it." Burned once, however, Garfield proceeded warily this time.

> [We] are both determined to let our judgement rule in the matter. . . . Time which changes all things may make changes in us or our circumstances. . . . I am not certain that I feel just as I ought towards her. . . . there is no delerium of passion

29

nor overwhelming power of feeling that draws me to her irresistably. Now I do not know as there should be, but I feel inclined to be cautious and so does she.[54]

In many ways it was a strange romance. Garfield, normally the most effusive of men, who could shed unabashed tears over a sentimental novel, or compose a rapturous ode to a sunset, found himself for once completely tongue-tied. A stiffly formal note crept into his usually uninhibited diary whenever it touched upon the question of matrimony. Could he have seen Lucretia's diary he would have realized that his fears of her coldness were unfounded. Her nature was there revealed to be much the same as that of her "noble" James. Beneath her formal, reserved manner fluttered an intensely passionate heart. But only to the privacy of her journal would she admit that "when at last he bowed his great noble soul to tell me that he *loved* and with the kiss of affection told me what tongue may never utter, then a willing captive my heart was surrendered. . . ."[55]

To the barrier of mutual misunderstanding that separated the couple was soon to be added he barrier of distance. Garfield had made up his mind to leave Hiram. By 1854 he had exhausted the intellectual offerings of the Eclectic. For some time he had ceased to attend classes, and was now employed as a full-time teacher for three hundred dollars a year. He earned his money. In a typical day he would rise before dawn to meet his five o'clock Virgil class. After breakfast he graded papers until nine. The rest of the morning was spent in teaching grammar, Greek, and algebra. He rushed through dinner in order to prepare his afternoon classes: algebra, Latin, geometry, and Greek once again. His day did not end with supper, for in the evening he taught penmanship for two hours, followed by the Glee Club, after which he might permit himself a brief diversion, such as a lecture on Phrenology, before resuming his work. He studied and graded papers until eleven, and then and only then could he drop into sleep. The sabbath brought no rest, for his preaching services were in such demand that he usually spoke at two or more churches each Sunday.[56]

To a man like Garfield, convinced that "The hand of the

Lord has been with me, and he has preserved me for some *purpose*, I know not what, . . ." such a grinding routine could hardly be satisfying. His friends sensed his discontent. "I know your aspirations—your longing—your thirstings after knowledge," sympathized one. "I know you disdain to be a fisherman in a little pond, while you hear in the distance the rumblings of great Oceans." For over a year Garfield had been toying with vague plans to continue his education in the East, but lack of funds and his deep-rooted aversion to change had kept him at Hiram long after he had outgrown it. By mid-1854 the decision could no longer be put off.[57]

As a good Disciple, Garfield's natural choice should have been the Disciple college at Bethany, in western Virginia, where he could "sit at the feet of our beloved and mighty Brother A. Campbell."[58] In the summer of 1853 he visited Bethany to reconnoiter the college. Campbell himself lived up to his expectations: "he is a living wonder. When in his company you feel the shadow of greatness falling upon you . . . his mind seems to be taking a sweep through the universe and is enlightening new objects at every inch of its orbit."[59] But the college disappointed him. The students seemed poorly trained, and they behaved with a facile politeness which Garfield, who was nothing if not sincere, interpreted as "Southern Dandyism." But what shocked the prudish Garfield most of all was a college theatrical, almost as "obscene" as Shakespeare. "It does not seem much like educating preachers of the Gospel," he muttered sadly.[60]

The question of Bethany plagued him for a year. It was not just a choice of colleges; it represented a basic decision as to the future course of his life. Bethany meant a continuation of his Disciple-centered life, probably leading to a preaching career. Would this satisfy him? He could not tell until he had tasted life more fully. He was, after all, still very much a country boy, innocent of the wider world around him. He was nineteen before he heard a piano, and twenty-three when he ate his first banana. How many other fresh experiences were waiting, just beyond his present range of vision? Possibly (the thought could not be repressed) even his Disciple zeal itself might be only a product of his provincialism.[61]

He wrestled with the problem with an unaccustomed objectivity and sophistication. "I am the son of Disciple parents," he reasoned, "have always lived among Disciples, listened to their preachings, have become one myself. . . . Now I know that every denomination (for even those who oppose sectarianism seem themselves to be a sect) has its peculiar views and distinctive characteristics. Each is accustomed to look at the world . . . from one particular standpoint. Now," he continued, "any person who looks at things from one point of view must have imperfect conceptions and illiberal views of human nature and thought in general." Thus, despite the fact that he could finish Bethany in ten months while a New England college would require two years, Garfield decided to turn his face east, "for the sake of liberalizing my mind."[62]

He sent letters of inquiry to Yale, Brown, and Williams. Yale's reply seemed "aristocratic," and Brown's was coldly formal. But from President Mark Hopkins of Williams College he received a more cordial response. This reply tipped the scales in favor of Williams, and in June of 1854, when his teaching duties were completed, Garfield was ready to leave Hiram's "hallowed ground," to find out what the wider world had to offer.[63]

CHAPTER THREE

ON ONE END OF A LOG

On July 11, 1854 James A. Garfield arrived at Williamstown, a sleepy college town nestled in the Berkshire hills of western Massachusetts. Having recently escaped from a life of drudgery at a small denominational school in Ohio, Garfield was jubilant at the prospect before him. As he viewed his new surroundings, the first mountains he had ever seen, he could scarcely contain his enthusiasm. "Beauty and Sublimity are enthroned upon these hills, and gladness and joy dwell in the valley. Fit place this seems, to give the mind to thought and contemplation of the works of God and the truths of science."[1]

Garfield had been drawn to Williams College by a cordial letter from its president, Mark Hopkins. Upon arriving, he immediately presented himself at President Hopkins's home for an informal entrance examination. Ushered into the study, he was confronted by the president and a few professors who posed him a geometry problem or two, and then pulled some Latin and Greek texts from the shelves and asked him to translate. Satisfied with his performance, the faculty admitted Garfield to the junior class. The exam was cursory and the issue was never really in doubt. Williams College, isolated by mountains from the main currents of New England life, with virtually no endowment nor patronage, could scarcely afford the luxury of high entrance standards. Furthermore, the ranks of the junior class had just been decimated by a mass expulsion of its rowdier students. But even without these practical considerations, President Hopkins would have welcomed Garfield to his college. For many years Hopkins had been fighting a rearguard action in defense of the old New England virtues. Lately he had been disturbed by signs of effeteness in his eastern students, and he always rejoiced at the appearance of a sincere, if rustic, Westerner like Garfield. For his part, Garfield took an instant liking to President Hopkins. "On the whole," he concluded, "I think he is a great man." Garfield never found reason to change this opinion,[2] and years later, his admiration undimmed, he immortalized President Hopkins with the famous aphorism, "The ideal college is Mark Hopkins on one end of a log and a student on the other."[3]

Garfield was eager to begin his college life at Williams but, unaware that Eastern schools closed down for a long summer vacation, he had arrived too early and had to mark time until fall. He spent the rest of the summer studying for the forthcoming year and "reconnoitering the ground." On the whole, he found himself "well pleased—*very well* pleased" with his new surroundings, despite the nearly prohibitive cost of living (almost three dollars a week), and the rowdy student atmosphere, which he blamed on the absence of women with their civilizing influence. But even though he missed the familiar foods of Ohio, and longed to hear once more the old Disciple hymns, he was satisfied with his decision to break away from home influences to try himself in a new environment.[4]

The New England atmosphere was exotic, but it was stimulating. He soon caught a glimpse of a genuine Massachusetts intellectual, and it left him stunned. "On Tuesday evening I listened to an address from Ralph Waldo Emerson of Boston and I must say he is the most startlingly original thinker I ever heard. . . . I could not sleep that night after hearing his thunderstorm of eloquent thoughts. It made *me* feel so small and insignificant to hear him."[5] Years later Garfield claimed that his intellectual life began as he listened to Emerson's speech. It could not have been the contents of the speech that affected him so, for he could barely remember what Emerson had said. Rather it must have been the revelation of a hitherto undreamed of world of mind and spirit which now seemed to lie before him.

Garfield was determined to belong to that world, but he was racked with doubts as to his ability. He had been successful at the Eclectic Institute, a small school without academic traditions or pretensions, where most of the students shared his social and religious background. Could he succeed at Williams? The challenge tormented him. "I lie here alone on my bed at midnight, tossing restlessly while my nerves and sinews crawl and creep, and I almost feel that there are but two tracks before me—to stand at least *among* the first or *die*."[6]

His zeal was intense, but characteristic. Throughout his adolescence and well into manhood, Garfield alternated, sometimes quite rapidly, between ambition and confidence on the one hand, and discouragement and doubt on the other. In spite of his professions of Christian humility, he longed for personal success. Passing through New York City on his way to Williamstown he had stopped at a phrenologist and eagerly asked, "How high a place in the world should I aim for?" He was gratified to hear the reply, "Just as high as you please, for your self-confidence is too small."[7]

The phrenologist was a shrewd judge of character; Garfield *was* unsure of himself. His self-assurance was precariously poised, and the slightest adversity could plunge him into extreme, almost morbid doubts. He blamed this weakness on his childhood humiliations. In times of stress he indulged in fancies of self-pity based on "that long, strange story of my boyhood," while in imagination "the taunts, jeers and cold, averted looks of the rich and the proud, chill me again for a moment as did the real ones of former days." Years later, after he had already achieved considerable success, this same feeling often rose to plague him. "Hardly a day passes . . ." he confided to a friend in 1862, "when some fortunate young son of early opportunities does not make me feel my inferiority to him." He conceded that he did have some ability, "But in the thousand little great things of life . . . how sadly weak and inferior I feel."[8]

Williams was full of "young sons of early opportunities," whose first impulse was to snub this earnest, awkward, ill-tailored Westerner. Garfield's roommate, Charles D. Wilber, an old Hiram friend, looking back on their first days at

35

Williams, recalled that "we were in a focus of not unfriendly but unrelenting criticism." "Their position," according to a classmate, "at first was a very isolated and peculiar one," and was not enhanced by the rumor that they were Campbellites. "Now what that meant, or what tenets the sect held, nobody seemed to know, but it was supposed to mean something very awful."[9]

This snobbery only increased Garfield's fierce determination to excel. "When I am in a class," he said, "I can not bear to be behind." Fortunately, he had several assets in his favor. The most valuable of these was his speaking ability, which had been so carefully cultivated on the rostrums at Hiram and the pulpits of innumerable churches. Before the rise of organized sports, the debating team was the focus of collegiate activity and a good debater was prized for the glory he shed upon his school. When Garfield began to debate at Williams, his talents were immediately appreciated. "He was undoubtedly one of the greatest debaters ever seen at Williams College," testified an awed classmate, who could not forget how "his massive figure, commanding, self-confident manner, and magnificant bursts of fiery eloquence, won and held the attention of his audience from the moment he opened his lips."[10]

Once he had won his debating laurels, Garfield's social difficulties vanished and he found himself the center of a large circle of admiring friends. He was the oldest student at Williams, and his friends paid him the natural deference youth accords to slightly greater age and experience. With his greater maturity went a quiet dignity and self-control that impressed the more flighty youngsters. To them he seemed a figure built on a large and heroic scale. "There was a *good deal of him*—body, soul, and spirit," recalled a college comrade, who concluded, "Garfield's greatness was to our young eyes enigmatical, but it was real."[11]

With his acceptance in Williams society assured, Garfield unbent and began to be more convivial. His exuberant, booming laughter rang often through the college halls, and in later years his classmates would relish the memory of the future statesman "rolling at full length on the campus, con-

vulsed with some newly fledged joke." Garfield carried his
new-found sense of humor into his debates, sometimes causing even stern old President Hopkins to double up in convulsions of laughter, as when, for example, debating an arm-
flailing opponent Garfield compared him to Don Quixote
attacking a windmill. "Or rather," he corrected himself, "it
would be more appropriate to say that the gentleman resem-
bles the *windmill* attacking the knight."[12]

Fortunately, Garfield's debating skill did not usually depend
on this sort of tactics for its effectiveness. His technique
seldom relied on the inspiration of the moment, but was based
on intensive research and preparation. When his team was
faced with a challenge, Garfield, the acknowledged leader,
would divide the question into its various categories and ap-
portion the research among his teammates. Garfield supervised the whole project, analyzing the problem, correlating
the information, and plotting the tactics. An example of his
generalship can be seen in his advice to leave an opening for
the opponent: "Give him a chance to get at you where he
may think you weak; and then, to meet his attack, throw in
your reserves and repulse him."[13]

His debating fame helped Garfield become a force in the
Philogian Society, one of the two major campus literary
societies, and in the spring of 1855 he was elected its president, despite the organized opposition of the fraternities. Thus,
by the end of his first year at Williams, Garfield had become a campus politician, caught up in "this interminable
rush, this whirl of excitement."[14] In each of the campus activities in which he took part his friends invariably chose him
to be their leader. He never lost an election at Williams, a
record he was to maintain throughout his entire political career.
He was elected editor of the *Williams Quarterly*, a pioneer
college publication of exceptional quality. He contributed
extensively to the journal. Much to his embarrassment, one of
these student efforts, "Old Autumn, thou art here," was resur-
rected during the presidential campaign of 1880, giving him,
he joked, his first serious doubts as to the outcome of the
election.[15]

Garfield's religious interests at Williams drew him to the

37

Mills Theological Society. Overlooking his Campbellite beliefs, his Calvinist friends elected him president of the society. In his religious activities at Williams Garfield had to walk carefully. Mark Hopkins's brand of Calvinism was far less sectarian than that of most New Englanders, but many of Garfield's fellow students who were preparing for the ministry, or for missionary posts abroad, held more zealous views. Back home Garfield was an evangelist for his faith, but at Williams he refused to be drawn into religious arguments which might antagonize his friends' sensibilities. He was remembered for his rectitude, yet all testified to his lack of "cant." John J. Ingalls, the future senator from Kansas, insisted that "there was nothing of gloomy bigotry or monastic asceticism about his religion. He never held himself aloof from the society of intelligent and vivacious sinners, while enjoying the fellowship and communion of the saints." An illustration of Garfield's style of piety, as well as his hold on his fellow students, occurred one summer day at the top of Mount Greylock. There the students had assembled for the annual Mountain Day frolic. They finished the climb at sunset, and in high spirits prepared to celebrate. They turned to Garfield to lead them in their festivities, but he soberly drew a battered Bible from his pocket. "Boys," he said, "I am accustomed to read a chapter with my absent mother every night: shall I read aloud?" No one snickered; all bowed their heads in prayer. The gesture could easily have backfired, but Garfield carried it off.[16]

From one phase of collegiate activity Garfield held aloof. He took no part in the fraternity movement which was then transforming college life. To many religiously inclined students of that era exclusive fraternities seemed incompatible with the ideal of Christian brotherhood. Garfield was a Christian; he could not be a Greek. Furthermore, the Disciples frowned upon secret societies. Therefore, Garfield joined a nonsecret society, the Equitable Fraternity, which was designed to combat the influence of the six secret fraternities on campus. He became the leader of the nonfraternity element, and championed their cause in debates. This activity inspired one of his major student literary efforts—a long satiric poem,

"Sam," which mocked the Know Nothing Party and, by implication, the local fraternities.[17]

By the end of 1855, Garfield had ample reason to be satisfied with his collegiate career. His earlier fears had proved groundless and, as he admitted to a friend, "my standing and influence here are all that I could wish, notwithstanding the prejudice against Western men, still I can make no complaint of the respect shown me by the New Englanders."[18] It was high time he settled down to the serious business of college.

Apparently Garfield did not realize that in his extracurricular activities he *had* been partaking of the serious, or at least the more intellectual, side of Williams life. The academic level of Williams, although considerably higher than the Eclectic, was not outstanding by Eastern standards. As one faculty member later candidly confessed, "The general instruction given in college at that time was poor. . . ." A more sophisticated student than Garfield bluntly catalogued the school's deficiencies: "Culture, in its ordinary sense there is none; men leave the college frequently with as little grace as they entered; of acquaintance with general literature there is scarcely anything; thorough scholarship in the classics is quite unknown. . . ."[19] None of this particularly bothered Mark Hopkins. He was more interested in developing the moral character of his boys than in stuffing their minds. Exacting standards of scholarship could scarcely be expected from Hopkins, a professor of philosophy who could ridicule Kant as "nonsense," and write a refutation of David Hume, without having bothered to read either philosopher. Finding a more scholarly colleague buried in the library, Hopkins chided him: "You read books: *I don't read any books; in fact I never did read any books.*" The extracurricular activities at Williams were designed to fill the intellectual needs that Hopkins and his curriculum failed to satisfy.[20]

But even within the curriculum, unenterprising though it may have been, an eager student could still learn something. At Williams Garfield was introduced to the natural sciences, which fascinated him, with the exception of chemistry, which he detested. His German studies made him an enthusiast for "that sweet tongue, the language of the heart, the repository

of such sweet soul-striking thoughts," and for a moment he
toyed with the fanciful notion of attending Göttingen.[21] Garfield also studied Political Economy with Arthur Latham
Perry, later to be famous for his free-trade views. They had
no effect whatsoever on Garfield at the time. He was far too
absorbed with other matters to pay much attention to what
must have seemed a prosaic, useless study.

Although he boasted that he had never "stumbled" in a
recitation, Garfield's academic record at Williams was not
outstanding. Students and teachers alike regarded him as a
good, but not brilliant student, who stood well in the upper
half of his class, but never seriously challenged his better-
trained colleagues. Mark Hopkins admitted that Garfield was
without "pretence of genius," but that seems to be precisely
what endeared Garfield to him. Hopkins distrusted genius.
He was much more pleased with a steady, hard-working, well-
mannered student like Garfield, who "gave himself to study
with a zest and delight wholly unknown to those who find in
it a routine."[22] This was the sort of student for which the
Williams program had been devised, and Garfield fit the
pattern so well that he probably received more benefit from
it than did his more brilliant classmates. At any rate, he himself was satisfied that his course during his first year had
been "crowned with greater success than I anticipated."[23]

At the end of his first year he returned home for the summer.
With the air of a conquering hero he proudly displayed to
friends and family his new knowledge and his freshly grown
crop of whiskers. It should have been pleasant to be feted and
to renew old friendships, but no sooner had Garfield returned
to Ohio than "a most dark and gloomy cloud" settled over his
spirits, plunging him into melancholy despair.[24]

The problem was his fiancee, Lucretia Rudolph. Almost
from the very moment they had decided to marry, Garfield
had been troubled with second thoughts. Leery of matrimony
ever since his mother's unhappy remarriage, Garfield seemed
appalled by the step to which he had committed himself. He
professed to fear that Lucretia's apparent coldness unsuited
her for his ardent nature, and he even suspected that she was
toying with his affections. A friend, echoing his mood, offered
cold comfort:

40

although she is not what you would like in every particular, so is every other lady in this world . . . our whole life is made of a choice of evils . . . if you think that she means to hover around a while holding you at her own disposal, and perhaps decline at last . . . cut her at once.[25]

When Garfield returned home all his fears seemed realized. Instead of the impassioned reunion he had anticipated, his meeting with Crete was painfully strained. The unhappy Garfield, convinced that Lucretia's temperament was incompatible with his own, floundered in confusion. "Oh this strange wild heart of mine!" he moaned, "Can I ever know its motions and guide it aright?"[26]

Lucretia was equally disturbed. During his absence she had treasured his "blessed letters," despite the increasingly long gaps between "those little messages of love . . . from his dear hand." To the privacy of her diary she confessed her fear that she might love James even more than God. But when they met face to face his abrupt changes of mood and his apparent indifference bewildered her. How could she cope with his enigmatic nature which "at times almost overwhelms with affection and then . . . turns and in his own intellectual strength and greatness seems unapproachable."?[27]

She decided on a bold gamble to win back his affections. At their last meeting before James was to return east, she took her private diary out of her drawer and allowed him to read. It was a revelation. "Never before," he marveled, "did I see such depths of suffering and such entire devotion of heart. . . . From that journal I read depths of affection that I had never before known that she possessed."[28] Jubilantly Garfield returned to Williams with his confidence in Lucretia restored. "My soul once cried 'Rooms to let!!!' " he exulted, "but it is full to overflowing now. From foundation to top-stone its halls are choral with joy. My every thought goes winging westward, singing like a golden seraph, its song of rejoicing and love."[29]

Garfield was in love. But was he in love with a flesh-and-blood girl or a romanticized image of his own creation? He was infatuated with the Lucretia of the diary, and she, perhaps, with her James of the ardent letters. Both of them were trying to act the way they thought lovers were supposed to act.

41

Since they found these ideas in literature, only through literary efforts of their own could they live up to their expectations, illustrating La Rochefoucauld's observation that few people would ever fall in love if they had not first read about it.

Their fragile relationship was soon challenged. Garfield frequently visited the isolated Disciple communities near Williamstown. At one of these, Poestenkill, N.Y., he met a young Disciple named Rebecca N. Selleck. It was not long before Garfield and Sister Rebecca were corresponding regularly. Rebecca's gushing letters were filled with the unabashed sentimentality which so delighted Garfield's "wild, passionate heart," and he responded in the same style. Naively, he reported each step of his new friendship to Lucretia, insisting that he liked Rebecca only because she reminded him so much of her. Soon Rebecca had joined Lucretia, Almeda Booth, and Garfield's mother in the ever-widening circle of women who read a chapter of the Bible along with him each night.[30]

Crowded though his social life may have been, it could not divert Garfield from his college tasks. The work of the senior year was under the direct supervision of President Hopkins. Every Williams student looked forward to this experience. President Hopkins's course on Evidences of Christianity was designed to be the climax and capstone of the student's collegiate career. It attempted to integrate anatomy, psychology, zoology, logic, and metaphysics into one grand system which would justify God's ways to man. The popularity of the course was due to President Hopkins's method rather than to the subject matter. For most of their academic lives his students had been sitting in classrooms passively repeating their recitations before bored drillmasters. Now, in Mark Hopkins's class, for the first time they found themselves confronted by a dynamic teacher who encouraged them to participate in classroom discussion, and even argue with his authority. The "Prex" wanted his boys to think for themselves, and express their own ideas in their own way, although he was careful not to let them carry the process so far as to arrive at independent conclusions. "What do *you* think about it?" he would ask a youth who up to that moment had never considered that his opinions could possibly interest anyone. Stimulated by the

42

challenge, and encouraged by Hopkins's genial personality, the flattered student felt compelled to examine the furniture of his mind and, if necessary, rearrange it.[31]

The always articulate Garfield, never reticent about expressing his ideas, became one of President Hopkins's favorite students. "He was," Hopkins fondly remembered, "prompt, frank, manly, social in his tendencies, combining active exercise with habits of study, and thus did for himself what it is the object of a college to make every young man to do—he made himself a *man*." Garfield returned the admiration, and his respect for "our powerful and beloved president" was unbounded. He would have agreed, without hesitation, with the enthusiastic student who wrote home, "The Prex. is the greatest teacher entirely that was ever suffered to appear on this earth."[32]

Contact with Mark Hopkins's warm personality prompted Garfield to reexamine his earlier contempt for the "cold and comfortless" creed of Calvinism. Indeed, many of his old Disciple-based assumptions underwent rethinking in the light of his new experiences. This, after all, was why he had come to New England—because he felt the necessity of "breaking the shell of local notions and getting mentally free."[33] Inevitably, some of his articles of faith eroded under the pressure of new ideas. As a good Disciple, Garfield had once inclined towards pacifism. But in his study of German literature he encountered the works of the "Poet Warrior," Theodor Koerner, and was carried away by his martial enthusiasm. In a long article on Koerner in the *Williams Quarterly* Garfield maintained that

> Koerner's whole life gives a withering rebuke to that puling sentimentalism of modern days which, in the safe closet, will pray for freedom; but holds up its hands in pious horror when the sword is unsheathed to purchase that precious boon amid the carnage of the battlefield.[34]

In a student debate on the question, "Is War Justifiable?" Garfield upheld the affirmative.

At Williams, contact with New England ideas caused Garfield to abandon his earlier indifference to politics and slavery.

At this time all of New England was agitated by the Kansas question, and Garfield was caught up in the excitement. After hearing a speech on "Bleeding Kansas" he set down in his journal a new resolve:

> I have been instructed tonight on the political condition of our country. . . . At such hours as this I feel like throwing the whole current of my life into the work of opposing this giant Evil. I don't know but the religion of Christ demands some such action.[35]

He was not an abolitionist. He favored the gradual elimination of slavery at some time in the distant future, and approved the moderation of those Republicans who wanted only to limit slavery in the territories.

New England ideas may have liberalized Garfield's political beliefs somewhat, but the hard core of his religious faith remained intact. Indeed, in his revulsion against Massachusetts puritanism, or perhaps simply out of homesickness, Garfield's Disciple zeal grew more fervent. "I have had a fine chance to see the workings . . . of New England Orthodoxy," he told a friend back home, "and I am more convinced than ever of the fact that the reformation pleaded by Bro. A. Campbell is the brightest light of the age."[36] Curiously, his objections to puritanism were not based on the common view that it was too dour and cold a faith. On the contrary, to Garfield, raised in the austere and equalitarian Disciple creed, the rites of New England Calvinism seemed almost indecently pretentious. Compelled "to sit in the Gallery of the old frescoed 'Church' . . . and listen to the roar of their pealing organ and the exquisite and artificial strains of their aristocratic choir," his thoughts turned to the simple devotions of home. "I had much rather," he insisted, "hear the whole congregation at the red schoolhouse sing 'How firm a foundation &c' in their energetic and lively manner."[37] While at Williams Garfield continued to preach, scouring New England for Disciple meeting houses. "It seems so good to get among our brethren," he said after attending a service in Vermont. "Oh! how I long to be among them permanently! We have the truth and our cause must triumph."[38]

In matters of faith Garfield remained a loyal Disciple, but

44

on a more personal, practical level he was beginning to feel serious doubts. When he had studied at Hiram his friends had assumed that he would enter the ministry, and at Williams he had naturally gravitated into the company of future clergyman. Now, as graduation loomed nearer, and with it the prospect of marriage, Garfield began to question his vocation. During the spring of 1856 he thrashed out the matter with his fiancee. Speaking more bluntly than usual, he admitted that "the distracted and disorganized state of the Brotherhood rather repels me from them and renders the ministry an unpromising field."[39] There was a more delicate aspect to be considered: "It is always disagreeable to talk of money in connection with the Gospel, and yet I must, and will here say that I do not intend to abandon my earthly support to the tender mercies of our Brotherhood." By the middle of June his mind was made up, and he concluded, "I think I shall not become a preacher now, if I ever do."[40]

His education had prepared Garfield to become either a preacher or a teacher. Rejecting the one career, he examined the possibilities of the other. From the region around Troy and Poestenkill, N.Y. came a tempting offer of about $1,500 a year to head the local high school. True to his resolve to "court neither office or a wife," he lost the job to a more aggressive candidate, much to the disgust of a friend who advised him to "learn to kiss the Blarney Stone" if he wanted to succeed.[41]

From Hiram came a steady stream of letters urging him to return to the Eclectic. President Amos Sutton Hayden, who had been advancing money to defray his college expenses, insisted that it was Garfield's "duty" to return to the school that had nurtured him. But aside from questions of salary, it was President Hayden himself who constituted Garfield's chief objection to returning to Hiram. "I have said, and still say (in all love to Bro. H[ayden])," he declared "if he is to *remain the Principal permanently* I will not go there."[42] When he had taught at Hiram, Garfield had often chafed under Hayden's lax administration, and he refused to go back "unless there are some more marks of energy and force than I have seen manifested there. . . ."[43] President Hayden, however, who had never wanted the job in the first place, was in trouble with the trustees, and rumors poured in to Garfield that he would soon be retired.

Garfield's friends boomed him as Hayden's successor. Garfield denied that he aimed for the place, insisting: "I have by no means aspired to it; nor do I want it. Were *I a third person* I would counsel the trustees not to give it into the hands of so young a person as I am. I would not be willing to take it *now*, if ever. . . ."[44] But to his close friends Garfield was more coy. As for the Presidency, he told them, "I do not expect any such thing, and shall make no moves to bring it about, though perhaps I might echo the sentiments of Sam Houston, 'If the Presidency is thrust upon me, I shall do as I please about accepting.' "[45]

The rumors proved premature, and Hayden retained his uneasy position. Nevertheless, Garfield decided to accept his offer to return to Hiram as a teacher for $600.00 a year. He really had no place else to go, but he was not happy over the step. He deeply resented the "patronizing" attitude of Hayden and others who seemed to think that "the Eclectic made me what I am, and that I am bound as a dutiful child to return to her," but return he did, despite all misgivings.[46]

On August 7, 1856 Garfield graduated from Williams College. Lucretia Rudolph and other Ohio friends came to Massachusetts to see the commencement exercises. Rebecca Selleck was in the audience also. They were not disappointed. Garfield graduated with honors, and in the ceremony delivered the Metaphysical Oration, an address on the conflict between Matter and Spirit. It was a fitting theme, for it symbolized the unrest in his own soul, where the charms of matter were contending with the duties of the spirit for supremacy.

The next week Garfield and Lucretia returned to Ohio. Still ringing in their ears was Mark Hopkins's final charge to the graduating class:

> Go to your posts; take unto you the whole armor of God; watch the signals and follow the footsteps of your Leader. . . . You may fall upon the field before the final peal of victory, but be ye faithful unto death, and ye shall receive a crown of life.[47]

It was a call for heroism—but Garfield was only going back to Hiram.

CHAPTER FOUR

THE DECISION *MUST* COME

Soon after he rejoined the faculty of the Western Reserve Eclectic Institute, Garfield realized that all was not well with the little Disciple school. President Hayden's loose supervision and frequent absences had left the school virtually leaderless, and it seethed with petty intrigue and "undercurrents of maneuvering that never see the light." "Had I known before all I now know," Garfield ruefully reflected, "I would not have come here at all." He was determined to stay at Hiram no longer than the year for which he had contracted unless conditions improved. To his mother, who asked if he were happy, he grimly replied, "I cannot say I am the happiest one in the world." To his fiancee, he unloosed a torrent of self-pity, whimpering, "I turn away from the past with a tearful eye, and I dread to look forward to the great unknown and I stand writhing under the direct piercing eyes of the terrible *now*. . . . I don't know how I can live through the week."[1]

Even for the moody Garfield, such intense despair was unusual. Dissatisfaction over school affairs, acute though it may have been, could hardly have evoked such utter dejection. What really disturbed Garfield was not the inefficiency he found at Hiram, but the fact that he was there at all. Two years earlier he had left his old school with the confident expectation of making a new life for himself in the East. His success at Williams College had exceeded his hopes, yet here he was at Hiram again, doing just what he had been doing two years before. Williams was to have been a turning point in his life but, stubbornly, his life refused to turn. "Why did we go away to Old Williams and see the world just as it is," asked Charles Wilber, "and then come back to our own so dissatisfied and rebellious?"[2]

This dissatisfaction soured all that Garfield had once enjoyed—home, family, school, even church. He knew only one way to make his life tolerable—to plunge himself into "a whirlwind of work," and forget his cares. To Garfield, hard work was more than a duty, it was almost a religion. As he once told a class: "Gentlemen, I can express my creed of life in one word: *I believe in work!* I BELIEVE IN WORK." Now he found solace in an exhausting round of labor, the way other men might find it in drink. His teaching load was heavy, at least six classes a day and often more, but he found even more activities to keep himself busy.[3]

A political campaign was then under way, and Garfield, a fledgling Republican, volunteered his services, lavishing upon Free Soil and Frémont the eloquence once reserved for the gospel's sake. Not that the gospel was forsaken. Although he had no regular congregation, he was a fully ordained minister whose eloquence was much in demand at various Disciple churches. Soon after the close of the political campaign he mounted the pulpit again. In early 1857 Ohio was swept by what was to prove the last of that series of Great Awakenings which had periodically electrified the nation ever since the mid-eighteenth century. At a protracted camp meeting Garfield spoke every day for two weeks, immersing nearly forty converts. Garfield was a successful evangelist even though his speeches were free from the sulfurous reek of hell-fire. He stressed ethics rather than salvation; God's love rather than His wrath. The stricter brethren complained that he lacked "unction," but younger Disciples flocked to hear him speak.[4]

By the end of the spring term, affairs at the Eclectic reached a crisis. For all his admirable Christian qualities, President Hayden had proven to be a lax disciplinarian and a weak administrator. "He was marked by smoothness of language and plausibility of explanation," a student later recalled, "but he was not marked by the vigor of will that was necessary to the thorough control of such a large body of young people."

Unable to tolerate his bumbling ways any longer, the disgruntled faculty resigned in a body in order to force his removal.[5]

After President Hayden had been compelled to devote himself to "other important duties in the Kingdom of God," many expected that his place would be filled by Norman Dunshee, the oldest and most distinguished member of the faculty. For years Dunshee had been exercising many of the duties of the presidency, and he had been the chief instigator of the campaign to unseat President Hayden. Instead, the trustees, perhaps wary of his capacity for intrigue, bypassed Dunshee and reached down into the faculty to give the post to Garfield. Technically, Garfield was appointed "chairman" of the faculty, rather than president, but he was generally recognized as the de facto president, and the actual title followed within the year.[6]

His promotion could hardly have taken Garfield by surprise, for he had been considering just such a possibility for over a year. He protested, however, that he had accepted the position only at the "urging" of the trustees. "I had never by word or action," he solemnly averred, "manifested the least desire to gain the Presidency. . . ."[7] Dunshee and his friends were not mollified by Garfield's explanation. They suspected treachery and retaliated angrily, spreading dark rumors and innuendoes. For a time the new chairman felt that "all the enginery of wire-working and slander seem to be in full play," as old accusations, dating as far back as the Hubbell affair, were raised against him.[8]

Much of this criticism was inspired by the bitterness of the disappointed Hayden and Dunshee factions, but some of it reflected a real concern over Garfield's youth and lack of experience. Hiram Disciples, like other groups of the Brotherhood, were split between the old founders and a younger generation out of tune with their aspirations. Garfield, the representative of young Hiram, was a natural target for the resentment many pioneer Disciples felt at seeing their movement wrested from their hands and bent into new directions.

Always acutely sensitive to criticism, Garfield interpreted the clamor as the persecution of enemies, and he wildly imagined that "they" were "looking on with vulture eyes and longing for me to fail." Determined to "stop the mouths of the barking hounds around me," he threw himself into his new job with desperate energy. Although his salary was not increased, he was expected to continue to teach all his old classes as well as perform the new duties of the presidency, plus all of the work necessary to restore the faction-ridden school to order. On top of all this, he kept up his preaching and lecturing activities. Little wonder that at the end of a day he complained, "my head throbs wearily and my tired heart and body are calling for rest. . . ."[9]

Under Garfield's direction the Eclectic embarked on a new, liberal policy. Less emphasis was placed on theology, while secular subjects received greater prominence. Religion was certainly not abandoned, but it no longer dominated the school to the extent it once had. This new spirit was displayed in the chapel talks the president was required to give the students each morning. President Hayden had always devoted these to Biblical expositions and moral homilies. Garfield ranged further afield, touching on a host of subjects President Hayden would have considered frivolous and unedifying.

The chapel talks symbolized Garfield's new conception of the Eclectic. His goal was to transform the school from a narrowly denominational academy into the educational center of the region. Explaining his plans to Harmon Austin, a sympathetic trustee, he argued that Disciples would come to Hiram without any special inducement. He intended to devote extra efforts to attract local students of other denominations. Garfield's reasoning was sound. Education was respected on the Reserve, yet many local farm boys who might want to attend a college near home avoided the Eclectic because of its Campbellite reputation. Under Garfield's administration, however, even a staunch Methodist could enroll at Hiram with a clear conscience, confident that the *odium theologicum* was now pretty well shaken off the institution."

The new students found themselves at a school whose appearance as well as character was in the process of change. For the first time Hiram Hill began to look like a campus. One spring day the president led his boys on an expedition to the nearby woods, from which each one returned, like Malcolm's army, with a sapling in his hands. Each tree was then named after some lady and tenderly planted in the bleak Eclectic yard. The old sagging chestnut rails were ripped down, and a "neat and substantial" yellow board fence was erected to enclose the grounds.[10]

A few fresh innovations even found their way into the curriculum. Garfield was growing increasingly dissatisfied with the traditional college program which had nurtured his own intellectual development and he was beginning to suspect that the time students devoted to Greek and Latin might be better spent on such "practical" matters as history, science, government, modern languages and physical education. Within a few years he would conclude that the American system of education was doomed to "absolute failure" unless it could train its students "to go into the practical business of life, and transact it like sensible men!"[11] In 1858, however, neither Garfield nor Hiram was ready for wholesale educational reform. He contented himself with minor changes. He instituted teacher training workshops, with lectures and seminars on pedagogy and school administration and, on his own initiative, prepared a series of lectures on American history, at that time an almost unheard of novelty for American higher education. But on the whole, the curriculum jogged comfortably along in its well-worn, familiar path. Elocution, grammar, and arithmetic remained, as before, the pillars of the Eclectic program. In an average term each attracted between one hundred and one hundred and fifty of the approximately two hundred and fifty students enrolled in the school. Algebra and natural science were not far behind in popularity, and other subjects, ranging from Latin and Greek to German and surveying, satisfied the wants of the more venturesome students.[12]

To handle this program Garfield relied on a staff of five full-time instructors (including himself), and two specialists. The rock of the faculty was steady, versatile Almeda Booth, who worked harder than anyone else, and whose salary was, of course, far less than that of the male teachers. The highest-paid teacher was Norman Dunshee, whose six hundred dollar salary equaled Garfield's own. Dunshee's closest ally on the faculty was Harvey Everest who had recently been hounded out of Bethany College for his outspoken abolitionist views. He owed his position at Hiram to Dunshee, and the two usually stood together against Garfield in policy disputes. The youngest member of the faculty, James Harrison Rhodes, was Garfield's closest friend and confidant. His specialty was elocution, which he taught by a bizarre "Gymnastic" method, designed to develop lung power and rhetorical ability simultaneously. Rhodes soon left the Eclectic, to follow in Garfield's footsteps at Williams College. Rounding out the staff were Hannah Morton, who introduced Hiram ladies to the graceful accomplishments of music, and Platt Spencer, who taught the elements of his famous Spencerian script.

None of the faculty could afford to specialize in only one field. An Eclectic teacher was assumed to be capable of teaching any subject, even though his formal training in that field might be weak or nonexistent. If enough students demanded a course, a teacher would be drafted for it. Garfield was officially listed in the catalogue as "Principal and Teacher of Ancient Languages," but he also taught mathematics, history, philosophy, English literature, rhetoric, geology and various other subjects whenever the need arose. Perhaps he was spreading himself a bit thin, but no one objected. His favorite class was English analysis, and it was his most popular. His 5:00 A.M. geology class overcame the handicap of its hour, and was regarded as especially stimulating.[13]

Garfield modeled his teaching technique after that of Mark Hopkins but he went much further than his mentor along the path that future generations would label "progressive education." He had nothing but contempt for traditional rote learning "which keeps a little child sitting in silence, in a vain attempt to hold its mind to the words of a printed page, for six hours a day. Herod was merciful, for he finished his slaughter of the innocents in a day; but this practice kills by the savagery of slow torture." He found it remarkable "that any child's love of knowledge survives the outrages of the schoolhouse."[14] As a college teacher he was more interested in encouraging his students to independent thought and in sharpening their powers of observation than in imparting information. "He gave more attention to the boy than to the book," recalled a colleague. A boy who discovered an encouraging note from the president tucked away in his hat band after a recitation would never forget the gesture. Students fondly remembered his kindness, his enthusiasm, his immense vitality, and his readiness to praise, long after they had forgotten his lessons. The young principal who could at one moment inspire them with their first glimpse of the world of culture and learning, and the next join them in their sports, was literally worshiped by his hero-starved boys fresh from the farm. Burke Aaron Hinsdale, an early student and a life-long friend, testified to the power Garfield wielded over the affections of his students:

> To him the phlegmatic would stir, the cold warm, the icy melt. When he put his great brotherly arm around a discouraged or fainting boy—poor, homesick, or blind to the way before him,— the boy very likely shed tears; but somehow the mists began to clear away from his vision, and his heart grew strong.[15]

Under Garfield's leadership the Eclectic prospered. Enrollment rose to a new peak, and financially the school managed to keep its head above water, even though the traditional niggardliness of its supporters was intensified during the hard times following the depression of 1857. But Garfield was not satisfied. He had originally intended to take charge of the Eclectic for only one year, but as that year stretched out to two and three, he grew more and more restless: "When I am sitting," he complained, "I long to be walking and when I am walking I long to be sitting."[16]

Garfield felt cramped in the narrow confines of the classroom. He longed for a larger stage in which to display his powers—powers which he felt were wasted in a provincial academy. "There is a spirit in me" he declared,

> that can rise up to the level of the occasion when it comes—and yet more—can ride upon the waves and balance itself upon the rocking elements. Napoleon felt as he was going over the Bridge of Lodi that he had in him the power to lead, and I have had it told me by my inner consciousness.[17]

Young Bonaparte, chained to a blackboard, chafed with unrest. "My heart will never be satisfied to spend my life in teaching," he confided to a friend. "Indeed, I never expect to be satisfied in this life; but yet I think there are other fields in which a man can do more."[18] But when he came to the hard question of what other field he should choose, he floundered in irresolution, strangely unable, he complained, to flex "the muscle of my will." In his uncertainty over the future direction of his life, Garfield grew irritable and despondent. Such agony could not be endured indefinitely. "The decision," he resolved, "*must* come . . . before long." In the meantime, he pleaded to his fiancee, "all who love me can aid me by support and forebearance."[19]

His fiancee certainly had need of forbearance. Their embarrassingly prolonged engagement had now drifted along for over four years, and marriage seemed as remote as ever. To Garfield, the subject of marriage, "with all its necessities and hateful finalities," was a painful one. Most happy when surrounded by a coterie of sympathetic, admiring friends, Garfield feared that "the narrow exclusiveness of marriage" would shrivel his social circle. He often denounced the hypocrisies and limitation of modern marriage. His friends, however, began to suspect that his aversion to marriage was not so much due to dislike for the institution as to a growing estrangement with his fiancee. Charles Wilber openly scolded him for his "unpardonable neglect and coldness" towards Lucretia.[20] He blamed this on Rebecca Selleck: "Since James' acquaintance with Rebecca he has changed in his attentions and manner toward Lucretia. Rebecca is not the cause of it—but she is the occasion. He is the cause: It took place in college. I saw it. . . ."[21]

Garfield vigorously denied this charge, insisting "if I ever marry, I expect to marry Lucretia Rudolph." But he continued to correspond with Rebecca, and seized on every opportunity to return east to visit her. A letter from Rebecca was cherished as evidence that she was still "the same full ardent soul that she has ever been since our acquaintance raised her pulse one beat higher in a minute." After reading it he moaned, "What a strange power is in the human heart. Oh my God to what end didst thou create such an infinite power of loving and yearning. . . . Whither Oh whither will this soul of mine drive me? . . ."[22] Actually, as he well realized, he had no choice. To desert Lucretia after such a well-publicized courtship would confirm the charge of loose morals which had clung to his name ever since the Hubbell fiasco. Furthermore, Lucretia's father, Zeb Rudolph, a pioneer Hiram Disciple who had helped build the Eclectic with his own hands, was one of the school's most prominent trustees.

In April of 1858, after much soul-searching, Garfield and Lucretia resolved to "try life in union" before the year was out. "I will not at this time," he told his diary, "go down into the depths of all my thoughts on this sorrowful theme." He left the details to Lucretia, telling her curtly, "I don't want much parade about our marriage. Arrange that as you think best." Still he hesitated, and it required a long heartfelt talk in Zeb Rudolph's east woods in late September before the decision was finally sealed.[23] On November 11 they were married. The wedding was a quiet, solemn ceremony held at the bride's home. Strangely, they were married by a Presbyterian Minister, Henry Hitchcock, rather than by a Disciple. There was no honeymoon.[24]

A few weeks after his marriage, Garfield threw himself into a fresh project which he enthusiastically hailed as "by far the most momentous occasion of my life." In late November a wandering freethinker named Denton turned up on the Reserve. Denton believed that life and matter had originated through "spontaneous generation and progressive development" without the assistance of God. He was eager to debate this proposition, and Garfield, the most skillful debater in the region, accepted his challenge. Garfield realized that he was in for a difficult time. Denton was not a Treat who could be put off with a childish diversion on Greek verbs. He was an accomplished debater who had argued this subject forty times before; "a rapid, elegant, fiery speaker, quick as a lightning flash to seize a thought . . . a bold, dare-devil kind of man."[25]

To meet the test Garfield studied for weeks, cramming himself with astronomy, geology, physiology, ethnology, etymology, phrenology, and related sciences. "I have never so fully resolved to try anything as this," he said. He was not deceived by Denton's pretense to scientific objectivity. Before him, he recognized, stood the enemy—a man who intended "to invalidate the claims of the Bible and remove God from immediate control of the universe."[26] "Science" had nothing to do with the question. As a matter of fact, Garfield had the better of the scientific arguments. Denton's evolutionary views were not supported, as yet, by any firm scientific evidence. *Origin of Species* was still a year in the future, and the earlier research which had paved the way for Darwin's work was unknown on the Reserve. Denton had been led to his conclusions through his atheism, much as Garfield had reached his through his belief. Both positions were equally dogmatic, and equally unsubstantiated. If anything, Garfield was the more openminded and "liberal" of the two.

The debate was held in the village of Chagrin Falls, before crowds ranging from seven hundred to a thousand. It began on December 27 and continued, with two sessions a day, until New Years Eve. Denton opened the contest with "a gallant charge . . . full of chivalric and self-confident daring," in which he attempted to sustain the nebular hypothesis. Garfield countered his arguments at every point, and after five sessions Denton abandoned this line of battle, and switched to an outright attack on the Bible itself. For five days and nights Garfield wrestled with the heathen, with each contestant delivering over twenty speeches. "For the last two days and evenings it was a fierce hand to hand fight," but finally Garfield "felt the iron of his strength bend in my grasp."[27]

By all accounts (or at least those that reached Garfield) Denton had been demolished. The spiritualists in the region were disconsolate; "Bro. Hamlin says he has not seen them so down in the mouth for years." By this stroke Garfield had made himself a well-known figure in the region, a man looked up to by the godly as their champion. He followed up his success with a series of lectures on "Geology and Religion," determined to "carry the war into Carthage and pursue that miserable atheism to its hole." Some of the Disciple brethren, however, regarded him as little better than an apostate because he had admitted in the course of the debate that the world was millions of years old.[28]

In truth, Garfield's religious views had altered because of

the debate. His intensive cram course in science had convinced him that religion must be harmonized with the evidence of the natural sciences. Science, he now thought, was of greater importance than literary studies; greater because "it is the literature of God written on the stars—the trees—the rocks—and more important because [of] its marked utilitarian character."[29] This was a new Garfield speaking. A few years earlier he would not have ranked mere "utility" so high. In line with his new interests he increased the role of science in the Eclectic curriculum, introducing a geology class, and organizing a Natural History Society.

The praise he won from the Denton debate was all the more welcome to Garfield because of the criticism he was encountering over school affairs. Not everyone was pleased with his administration of the Eclectic. The more conservative brethren resented his innovations and attacked his every move. "Croakers are as thick as the frogs in Egypt," Garfield told a friend. They concentrated their criticism on Garfield's character rather than his policies, greeting his every act, so Garfield thought, with a muttered comment: "For ambitious purposes"—"sinister motives" . . . "General manners bad" —"morals doubtful." He could not pay an innocent visit to Almeda's room without raising the eyebrows of the "dastard race of rotten hearted, evil eyed fools" in the village. Another scandal which rocked the school arose over Garfield's fondness for chess. The local bluenoses protested his endorsement of a vain amusement and forced him to cancel plans for a chess league with neighboring colleges.[30]

Behind the agitation, Garfield suspected, stood Norman Dunshee, who had never forgiven him for taking the job he felt had rightly been his. So assiduously did Dunshee spread his grievances that even Amos Sutton Hayden, once Garfield's warm friend, began to believe "what I have often heard others say, that Mr. G——— is not a really honest man."[31] Dunshee and Everest even brought up their charges at a teachers meeting, formally accusing Garfield of having plotted to take over the school. Garfield answered them with patience and restraint, but the bitterness continued to fester. They and their allies seized on every opportunity to embarrass him. When, for example, Garfield bought a small keg of ale (purely for medicinal purposes), the town was thrown into an uproar.[32]

The ale controversy was small beer, but Garfield's enemies soon latched onto a more promising issue. Antislavery sentiment was then particularly intense on the Reserve. Disciples, traditionally indifferent to political matters, were of two minds on the matter, but most of the local brethren had come to detest slavery as an intolerable sin. Garfield was as hot for the cause as any man. On one occasion he sheltered a fugitive slave on his way to Canada, and on another, hearing that a federal posse had arrested two runaway Negroes harbored by an Eclectic student, he quickly assembled a group of vigilantes to free them, grimly determined that "no slave shall ever be returned to slavery from Hiram Hill." The "slaves" turned out to be college pranksters in blackface, and the abashed Garfield had to march his troops down the hill empty-handed.[33]

Sympathetic though Garfield was to the cause, he drew the line at involving the school in politics. When two friends of Dunshee planned to hold an abolition rally in the Hiram meeting house, Garfield refused permission. "While I stay here," he vowed, "the school shall never be given over to an overheated and brainless faction." In the resulting controversy Garfield found himself "between two fires. . . . One party of my friends blame me as being too cool on the slavery question; another for being too hot."[34]

In May of 1859, the trustees abruptly fired Norman Dunshee and offered his job to J. Harrison Rhodes. Before the meeting Garfield had huddled privately with Harmon Austin, his closest friend on the Board of Trustees, but nonetheless Garfield professed surprise at Austin's action. "The move was made by the Trustees without plotting or connivance," he assured Rhodes. "I not only did not directly counsel it but did not expect it." Rhodes must have been somewhat puzzled by this disclaimer, for only a month earlier Garfield had urged him to return to Hiram. "If you should do this," Garfield added, "I think the Trustees would dispense with Norman soon and your salary would be a fair one."[35]

Dunshee refused to be consoled by Garfield's protestations of innocence. He accused Garfield and the Board of foul play and all manner of underhanded dealings. He insinuated that his dismissal was politically inspired, and he held himself up as a martyr to the antislavery cause. This won him some sympathy among "the hot element in town" who reviled Garfield "as the prince of slaveholders and plotters." But the trustees remained "wonderfully firm," and Garfield rode out the storm. Austin assumed full responsibility. "Things have come to a strange pass," he said, "if the Trustees of a public school have not a right to select such teachers as in their opinion the interests of the school demand."[36]

With Dunshee's removal, Garfield's authority at the Eclectic was at last secure, but academic life, with all its petty bickering, had now become so intolerable to him that he began to cast about for another profession. The problem of his career had been plaguing him for years, but he could not bring himself to make a final decision. "My life has been beset with glorious visions," he explained, "and perhaps their existence had held me back from making any selection of a course of life which must inevitably exclude many of them."[37] The law had always attracted him, but for a long time his religious scruples had stood in the way. "Though I do not regard the Legal Profession [as] incompatible with Christianity," he had argued in 1854, "still I think it would be much more difficult to cultivate and preserve that purity of heart and devotedness to the cause of Christ when partak[ing] of those ambitious aspirations that accompany the Gentlemen of the Bar."[38] By 1859, however, his religious zeal had sufficiently mellowed to permit him to study law privately.

There was still another career open to him, the intriguing possibilities of which he carefully weighed. Garfield was now a prominent local figure. His preaching and lecturing activities, capped by the Denton debate, had made his name known to a large public in his corner of the Western Reserve. Why not enter politics? He was young, commanding, well-known, respected, and soundly Republican—eminently available in every respect. He outlined his plan to Rhodes: "If I do not take the law the next best course seems to me to [be] an Educational and political one—the latter (polit.) to be reached through the former (Educ.)." He could use his college position as a stepping-stone to higher station. "We have a reputation and influence of not inconsiderable power as a capital to start on, and I think that judicious management would go very far toward giving us the lead of the chief movements in our immediate territory and ultimately to a larger area." He brushed aside his earlier religious qualms. "Shall I run for State senator or representative . . . this fall? I know there would be a theological storm but I don't care for that."[39]

As he expected, a flurry of disapproving cackles greeted this suggestion. "Your best friends in Christ all shake their heads when you are named in connection with law or politics," warned an Eclectic associate.[40] Harmon Austin, the Warren banker and flagstone merchant who had taken Garfield under his wing, begged him to forgo politics and devote himself to the ministry: "I cannot but feel that it is a *burning shame* for one possessing such *rare abilities* to bless our race, both for this life and the next, that you should for one moment indulge the idea of leaving a field of labor for which you are so admirably fitted." From the Honorable O. P. Brown of Ravenna, who fancied himself a local kingmaker, came an objection of a more practical sort. He advised Garfield to contain his ambitions for another two years, when he would be in a far stronger position with both the electorate and the party organization. For the coming election, he told him, leading local Republicans had already pledged their support for the State senatorship to Cyrus Prentiss, whose nomination seemed assured.[41]

In August, with his future still uncertain, Garfield journeyed back to Williamstown to receive an honorary Master's degree from Mark Hopkins. When he returned to Ohio, a somber-faced delegation of Republicans met him at the station. Cyrus Prentiss, they told him, had suddenly died, and the senatorial nomination was now wide open. The convention was due to meet in only two weeks. Would Garfield allow his name to be entered?[42]

Garfield was willing, but only if the nomination could be his "without wading through the mire [into] which politi-

60

cians usually plunge." He refused to campaign, or make any promises, but his friends had no such inhibitions. Frantically they canvassed the district, lining up support. Delegates for the district nominating convention had to be chosen at the party caucuses which convened in each township. Garfield's friends were busy at these meetings, pleading his cause and insuring the election of well-disposed delegates. "As the darkey said, 'things is working,'" reported one agent with considerable satisfaction. Time was short, and when the nominating convention met on August 23, the issue was still in doubt. Garfield was conceded to have the edge, but three other active candidates were in the field. On the eve of the convention Garfield was confident but wary. "James—*Keep your balance*," his diary admonished, and he manufactured consoling excuses in case of defeat.[43]

On August 23, 1859, fifty-five Republicans, representing the townships of the 26th Ohio Senatorial District, assembled at Franklin, Ohio. They were divided almost equally between Garfield's home county of Portage and the neighboring county of Summit. Apparently by prearrangement, Portage County was entitled to pick that year's senatorial candidate. The Portage delegates caucused separately for four ballots. Fourteen votes were needed, and on the very first ballot Garfield was only two votes short of victory. His chief rival, William Wadsworth, a Ravenna banker, trailed with seven, and the remaining votes were split evenly between the two weaker candidates. On the third ballot both Wadsworth and Garfield picked up one vote, and on the next the two dark horses collapsed, leaving Garfield with fifteen votes and the support of the Portage delegation. The delegates then returned to the convention hall and formally presented Garfield's name. Without further deliberation the Summit delegation agreed to the choice, and Garfield was nominated by acclamation. The nominee was called for, he responded with "some very appropriate remarks," and the convention adjourned, its work done. Garfield was somber at his moment of triumph. "I am aware," he realized, "that I launch out upon a fickle current and am about [to undertake] a work as precarious as men follow."[44]

Returning to Hiram, Garfield set school affairs in order, so

that the Eclectic would run smoothly while he was busy at
Columbus with his legislative duties. The election was still a
month and a half away, but he confidently assumed that he
would win. A Republican nomination in Garfield's district was
tantamount to election. Few sections of the nation were so
strongly attached to the principles of the young Republican
party. At the very moment that Garfield was running for office,
other citizens of the 26th District were forging pikes and
gathering arms for an expedition to Harper's Ferry that would
put their antislavery convictions to the test of action. John
Brown was one of Garfield's constituents, and most of his
neighbors shared his views. Of them, a Southern editor fumed,
"a more hypocritical, canting, whining, totally depraved and
utterly irredeemable set of rascals have never walked the face
of the earth."[45]

The Reserve returned the sentiment. Hatred of slavery was
there the sole touchstone of political reliability. Garfield was
running for a purely local office, and although there were many
pressing problems facing the depression-ridden state, the
slavery issue dominated his campaign to the exclusion of other
topics. It would be misleading to say that the slavery question
was debated during the canvass; it was simply assumed as a
political fact of life. Arguments on both sides were already
worn so thin by repetition that it scarcely seemed worth while
to bring them up again.

The candidate of the Democracy, Alvah Udall, also of
Hiram, maintained a discreet silence throughout the campaign. He realized that his only hope of victory lay in the slim
chance that the politically inexperienced Garfield might stumble. Udall could not win the election, but Garfield, conceivably, could lose it. The Democrats circulated whispered rumors
that Garfield actually "was a stronger Dem. than any they had
in their party." Garfield was told that the opposition was saying
"you have come out in favor of slavery and state that it is a
divine institution according to the Bible." The extreme wing of
Garfield's own party, assisted by his personal enemies, echoed
this accusation, objecting to the fact that "all of our radical
Abolition friends are compelled to vote for a man whose prejudices are as much against the negro as Alexander Campbell."[46]

The source of these attacks was a Republican splinter faction in Aurora. Earlier they had met in a rump convention and decided to withhold support from those candidates of the regular slate whose views on slavery were too tame. They concentrated their fire on Garfield, sending him a brief, impertinent questionnaire. The key question involved a recent controversial judicial decision arising out of the Oberlin-Wellington rescue case. In that imbroglio a fugitive slave had been snatched from the hands of federal marshals by an incensed abolitionist mob and hustled to safety. Some of the rescuers, prominent, respected men, had been imprisoned for violating the Fugitive Slave Act. The spectacle of these men being jailed like common criminals for conscience's sake aroused Ohio Republicans to a new pitch against slavery. The special object of their wrath was Judge Swan, the only Republican member of the Ohio Supreme Court, who had joined with his Democratic colleagues to sustain the obnoxious verdict. The Aurora committee demanded that Garfield commit himself on the matter, asking "Was the decision of the Sup. Court as held by Judge Swan . . . Republican or anti-Republican?"

The question was artfully contrived to place Garfield in a dilemma. No matter how repugnant it might be, Judge Swan's decision was clearly legal. If Garfield repudiated it he would seem a "higher law" fanatic; if he supported it, a luke-warm Republican. He could not ignore the question, but if he answered it he would be put in the awkward position of allowing a self-appointed fringe group to catechize him on party regularity. Garfield fell back upon the classic refuge of beleaguered politicians—a ringing defense of legislative integrity and independence. To his inquisitors he declared, "I have not pledged, nor shall I now pledge myself to any men or measures, but shall, if elected to the Senate, hold myself free to adopt any course of State Legislation which my own judgement, aided by the advice of constituents, may dictate. . . ." A more prudent man might have stopped there, but Garfield went on to answer the question at hand. "If Judge Swan was to follow the precedents of the Federal and State courts," he said, "he could not have decided differently. But his decision was in conflict with the Republican doctrine of States Rights."[47]

This ambiguous reply, combining "the adroitness of the

63

canal boy and the erudition of the L.L.D." failed to satisfy the Aurora committee, and the attacks on Garfield continued. In an otherwise remarkably placid election the opposition to Garfield was conspicuous for its intensity. The *Portage County Democrat* noted that "Mr. Garfield seems to have been singled out for more especial, bitter, malignant attacks than anyone else."[48] Not only was he anti-Negro and pro-Southern, he was insincere, treacherous and hypocritical. He was no more a resident of his district than a "tin-trunk peddler or an itinerant doctor," and furthermore, he had won the nomination through the grossest fraud.[49]

The violence of these attacks was actually a tribute to Garfield's political effectiveness. He campaigned hard and well, impressing seasoned observers as a coming man. His platform ability drew the most praise. "Mr. Garfield is a really fluent speaker," declared a political reporter. "Fluent he is, but every word carries its thought. No public figure within our acquaintance uses fewer empty figures of speech, or utters more weighty thoughts in apt and expressive words." His opponents, of course, belittled his talent. A Garfield speech reminded them "of the lady who borrowed a dictionary, and on returning it was asked how she liked it, replied she thought the words very beautiful but that she didn't think much of the story."[50]

Garfield's major campaign address was delivered at Akron. Salmon P. Chase, the outgoing Governor, was the main speaker, and when he had finished Garfield expressed the hope that "our worthy Governor" would soon be "in an official point of view, greater than a Governor." Hearty cheers from the crowd seconded this suggestion, and Chase, whose own thoughts were tending in that direction, could not help being pleased. Garfield's speech on that occasion betrayed his evangelical training. Expounding on Martin Luther's principle of private judgment, he applied that lesson to the current political situation, illustrating the affinity between Protestantism and Republicanism. This speech and others led the *Portage County Democrat* to predict that as Garfield said Chase would be greater than Governor, "so we would say of Mr. Garfield; we believe he will yet be greater than a State Senator."[51]

All of Garfield's campaign speeches (and he delivered over thirty) were devoted to the slavery issue. Addressing a meeting of working men he contrasted free labor and slave; praising the Republicans as the champions of free labor, and warning that the Democrats, with their contempt for the "mudsills of society," intended to make slavery the rule in the North as well as in the South.[52] He never mentioned his opponent. Indeed, from the tenor of his speeches an uninformed observer might have concluded that Garfield was not running against Alvah Udall, but against Simon Legree.

Apparently this was what the voters wanted to hear, for on election day, October 11, 1859, Garfield won his expected victory, and won it with surprising ease. The vicious attacks made upon his character affected the outcome not at all. Garfield carried his district 5,176 to 3,746, a plurality of 1,430 votes, one hundred and thirty more than the district gave to the head of the ticket, gubernatorial candidate William Dennison. Strangely, Garfield's strength was greatest in those areas where he was least known. His plurality in Summit County was almost double that of his home county of Portage, and he carried Hiram township by only four votes.[53]

Garfield, as might be expected, was pleased with the happy outcome of his political debut. What pleased him most of all was the manner by which victory had been won: "I never solicited the place, nor did I make any bargain to secure it. I shall endeavor to do my duty, and if I never rise any higher, I hope to have the consolation that my manhood is unsullied by the past." His pious friends shared the hope, but they feared the outcome of the path Garfield had now begun to travel. Isaac Errett, then gaining renown as the leading Disciple of Garfield's generation, took his friend aside and beseeched him to consider the consequences of his step. "Is political honor the highest honor?" he asked, reminding Garfield that "the truth, which he so well understood, and the Lord, whom he so devotedly loved, had superior claims upon him, which no earthly temptation must lead him to compromise."[54]

Garfield listened respectfully, but remained unmoved. He scarcely seemed to realize that his life had reached a turning point. Ever since his conversion, less than ten years before,

65

his soul had maintained an uneasy balance between personal ambition and Christian humility, but as the passage of time eroded his faith, the allure of worldly success could no longer be contained. With this decision to enter the sinful world of politics he turned his back on the influences which had hitherto shaped his life. There were some who muttered, "I always thought he'd go to the Devil, and if he goes to the *Capital, I am sure he will!*"[55] but Garfield himself felt no such apprehension. He was cheerfully resolved to make the best of both worlds, even if they were incompatible.

CHAPTER FIVE

A RISING MAN

When James A. Garfield, the freshman senator from Ohio's 26th District, arrived at Columbus in the waning hours of 1859, he found William Bascom, chairman of the state Central Republican Committee, waiting at the depot. Bascom escorted Garfield to his own home, which was to be Garfield's Columbus residence for the duration of the session. The house was only two blocks from the Capitol, and as soon as he was settled Garfield strolled down to the State House. There he met many of his Senatorial colleagues and discreetly took their measure. "They are not as gods," he dryly remarked.

His next stop was the Governor's Mansion, where he paid a courtesy call on Salmon P. Chase, the outgoing governor. Chase, who was then soliciting legislative support to send him to the United States Senate, greeted Garfield warmly. He read him portions of his farewell address and asked for suggestions, which the flattered Garfield readily offered. Garfield left the interview marveling at his own coolness, but somewhat disenchanted with Chase.[1]

Garfield was much more impressed with Jacob Dolson Cox, the new Senator from the district adjacent to Garfield's. Cox was also boarding at the Bascom's and the two young Senators shared the same room and bed. These two bedfellows made strange politicians. Both had reached political office by way of an educational career rather than through the more conventional routes of law or business. Cox was the more versatile and accomplished of the two. Three years older than Garfield, he had passed his childhood in circumstances only slightly less pinched. After some drifting, he had enrolled at Oberlin, where he had capped a successful college career by marrying President Finney's daughter. At the time of his election to the Ohio Senate he was superintendent of schools of Warren, Ohio, and was also beginning to attract attention for his legal skill. His interests were wide. He was a talented writer, and an able shorthand reporter. French literature was his passion, and he had translated French novels and military manuals into English. In his later life, in addition to his political and business interests, he would become something of an expert on European cathedrals, as well as the most prominent amateur microscopist in the nation.[2]

Cox and Garfield took to one another from the start. They overlooked a potential rivalry which could easily have created friction between them. Both men were from the same congressional district, and, as Garfield readily admitted, "both he and myself are occasionally visited with that impulse which men call ambition." It was not impossible that someday their ambitions might bring them into conflict, but this did not prevent them from becoming fast friends.

Basically very much alike, Cox and Garfield seemed, on the surface, an unlikely pair. The dapper Cox presented a striking contrast to his rumpled, massive, bear-like friend. They differed in temperament as well as appearance. The expansive Garfield thought Cox "very much of a man," but he added, "I could wish that he were a little more demonstrative." For his part Cox, whose cool aloofness masked a fundamentally shy nature, admired, even though he could not emulate, Garfield's "vigorous, impulsive nature" for its "animal spirits" and ready humor. Garfield "was demonstrative and active in all his ways," Cox later recalled. "Big and strong, he was apt to show his liking for a friend when walking with him by grasping him with a hug that would almost make his ribs crack, and his hearty roar over a bit of fun . . . would be emphasized by a grip like a vise upon your arm. . . ." Together with James Monroe, an Oberlin professor, they formed an intellectual senatorial triumvirate which would make a name in the coming Senate session for unyielding radicalism on the slavery question.[3]

The session began slowly. Three weeks after it had been gaveled to order, Garfield explained why so little had yet been accomplished: "Men are still shy of each other, are taking each other's measure." He predicted, however, that "there will be grappling by and by."[4] Garfield had originally proposed to hold himself aloof from the parliamentary grappling until he found his bearings. "I do not intend to say a great deal this winter," he told a friend. But the loquacious Garfield was incapable of holding to a vow of silence. His ready tongue soon drew him into debate. On the very first full day of the session he offered some suggestions on a procedural question, and in succeeding days he displayed no hesitation over voicing his opinion on various issues. A Cincinnati reporter noted his activity and predicted "Mr. Garfield will prove one of the twenty-four pounders of the Senate."[5]

Garfield's first major oratorical salvo was touched off in defense of a subject close to his heart—education. When Richard Harrison, the spokesman for the conservative wing of the Republican Party, introduced an economy measure which would curtail public school libraries, Garfield responded with a ringing defense of books. After defending the desirability and constitutionality of schools in general and school libraries in particular, he attacked the proposed bill as a false economy. "Sir," he exclaimed,

> I am not behind the gentlemen in my desire for retrenchment, but I would not strike the first blow at our cherished school system. The Governor has lately appointed a committee to select a site for a new penitentiary, for our present one is filled to overflowing with convicts. Further our Educational System and you strike a blow at ignorance and crime which will greatly reduce our jail and prison expenses. . . .

In his peroration Garfield was moved to verse. "Let us sir, in our work of retrenchment strike down all extravagances, but aim not a blow at our school system.

> 'Woodman spare that tree,
> Touch not a single bough—
> In youth it sheltered me
> And I'll protect it now.' "[6]

Despite his eloquent objections, the bill passed. Garfield was not particularly disheartened by this failure. His speech had been well received and had won him the favorable notice he craved. Privately, he even admitted that the bill he had opposed was probably a wise one. "In regard to the Library Tax," he told a friend, "I think as you do that in many places the books do little good . . . I think it is quite a safe place, personally considered, to be *on the negative and in the minority*."[7]

Once he had gotten the taste of speaking, nothing could stop Garfield. He had a word for almost every measure that came before the Senate, from the proper method of assessing real estate to the compensation of School Examiners. On January 19, a climax of sorts was reached when Garfield addressed himself to a bill designed to tax dogs for the protection of sheep. He discussed at length the constitutionality of a dog tax. Is it a poll tax? he wondered. Are dogs really property? He referred to Blackstone and cited an impressive number of previous statutes and precedents. The bill was finally sent to committee with an amendment exempting ladies' poodles.[8]

This was all very well in its way, but Garfield's constituents were growing impatient. He had campaigned for their votes not as a friend of books and dogs, but as a champion of freedom against slavery. Slavery was not exactly an issue which fell under the jurisdiction of the Ohio Senate, but Garfield's constituents demanded that *something* be done about it, and Garfield had to oblige. The session was scarcely a week old before Garfield found an opportunity to demonstrate his radicalism to the voters back home. Embarrassed by John Brown's raid on Harper's Ferry, conservative Ohio Republicans, led by Richard Harrison, introduced a bill designed to quiet the fears of Virginia by promising that no further raids would be launched from Ohio. Garfield had not approved of John Brown's expedition but he had admired Brown's "honesty of purpose and sincerity of heart," and had been deeply moved by the heroism with which he had faced death. "Brave man, Old Hero, Farewell!" his diary had grieved. "Your death shall be the dawn of a better day." Naturally, Garfield resented Harrison's "Sedative Bill" as an affront to Brown's memory and an insult to the people of Ohio. In a major speech he blasted the measure for implying that Ohioans were in fact plotting against their sister states. If it had not been for Garfield's outburst the bill might have been quietly shelved, but he insisted that a full-dress debate be held. The debate was postponed and the bill was sent to committee to give tempers on both sides a chance to cool.[9]

Garfield's radical stance was assumed primarily for the benefit of his constituents. He was not, by nature, a firebrand. If the occasion required, he could be gentle and conciliatory towards the South. The impulse of the moment, rather than any deep conviction, seems to have determined his stand. On January 21, for example, carried away by the spirit of debate, he found himself acting as a spokesman for the peacemakers. Governor Dennison had just received a message that the legislatures of Kentucky and Tennessee planned to visit Cincinnati. This excursion was designed to promote the newly opened Louisville and Nashville Railroad, but some Ohioans saw in the junket an opportunity to demonstrate Ohio's good will towards her Southern sisters. A resolution was introduced in the Senate authorizing the Governor to invite the Southern legislatures to Ohio, and five thousand dollars was asked to provide a suitably hospitable reception. Harrison and other economy-minded Republicans objected, and a heated debate ensued.[10]

Garfield followed the debate intently. After half an hour "one of those critical periods came when all is confused," and Garfield stepped into the breach with an impassioned speech favoring the expedition. The crowded lobby hung on his words, and when he was done his colleagues clustered around his desk to congratulate him. Garfield's speech had carried the resolution, and he was accordingly appointed chairman of a committee to tender the invitation in person. All in all, Garfield told a friend, this debate was

the most exciting time we have yet had and I have taken a position [which] will do me either a good deal of good or a good deal of harm. . . . The meeting of three legislatures will be an event which never before happened. How the country will regard it, I cannot tell. . . . In moments like these we must de-

71

cide in two minutes and our names stand on the record forever.
I [would] rather act wrong than to dodge as some do.[11]

The next day Garfield set out for Louisville on his mission
of peace, well aware of the delicate position in which he had
placed himself. "The fire-eaters of Tennessee will be there,"
he reflected, "and yet every word I say will be read in Ohio."
He decided to confine his remarks to a few safe, well-chosen
phrases extolling the Union. At Louisville, Garfield and his
party were feted by "the Chivalry of the South" with a ban-
quet the likes of which he had never seen.[12] Garfield delivered his invitation with a fervid union-saving speech. "Brethren," he exhorted,

> we have heard too long of the North and the South. Their angry
> words have too long vexed the hearts of our fellow-citizens.
> But there is a third voice to be heard ere long. I hope and be-
> lieve the day is not far distant when the Great West shall speak
> and her voice shall be heard from sea to sea. In that voice shall
> mingle no tone of doubt or uncertainty—no note of disunion
> shall be heard in that utterance.[13]

The Southern legislatures then wended their way to Ohio,
greeted at every stop by booming cannon, brass bands, bon-
fires, many toasts, and many speeches. The expedition turned
into an orgy of good will. It was a gigantic social success,
and the Louisville and Nashville Railroad certainly reaped
even more publicity than it had expected, but the practical
effects of the junket were doubtful. Despite the plethora of
union-saving speeches, the Union was not, in fact, saved.
In his next visit to Kentucky, two years later, Garfield, no
longer the peacemaker, would appear at the head of an Ohio
army.

Even at the time many expressed misgivings over the legislative visit. The *Portage County Democrat* grumbled: "The
frolic will be a big one, and costly one to the people of Ohio."
Other papers caustically referred to the peace mission as "The
Great Drunk." Indeed, the whole Ohio Republican administration was beginning to come under newspaper fire. Lyman W.
Hall, a local editor, advised Garfield that the voters were
growing restless: "I already begin [to] tremble for the popularity of this Legislature. Too much time is spent on compar-

ative trifles. The repeal of the Library law; the tedious, time-consuming 'dog' discussion . . . the Cincinnati excursion," as well as other follies, he warned, could easily "overthrow us as a party in the state. . . . Do not . . . speak too often on trivial matters. . . . Try to prevent useless debate and a needless consumption of time."[14]

Except for the personal admonition, Garfield was inclined to agree with Hall, especially on the ineptness of the "weak backed" Republican leadership. Garfield was particularly disappointed in Governor Dennison. Dennison, a banker and railroad magnate whose previous political experience had been limited to a single term in the Ohio Senate, was not proving to be an inspirational leader. Ohioans, accustomed to flamboyant frontier-style politicians of the Thomas Corwin school, found Dennison, with his genteel Eastern airs, too aristocratic and intellectualized for their taste. In the popular mind he was stamped as "a man wholly frittered away in polish," an impression which his unfortunate inaugural address only served to reinforce. Common folk, as well as purists like Garfield, shuddered at his use of "succeedaneum," and other Latinized barbarisms, and after his inauguration speech, the "Succeedaneum Governor" never fully enjoyed the confidence of the people.[15]

Nor was Garfield satisfied with the performance of the legislature. Elected on a pledge to pare expenses, his colleagues seemed to Garfield obsessed with "a crazy crusade in favor of retrenchment." As he saw all of his pet schemes rejected one by one, Garfield bitterly complained, "We have a miserably penurious legislature and nothing of a liberal-minded policy can be expected from it."[16] The rejection of his most cherished plan proved especially galling. Ever since the Denton debate, Garfield had been an enthusiastic amateur geologist. In pursuit of this hobby, he now proposed a geological survey in order to determine the extent of Ohio's mineral wealth. As chairman of a committee to consider the project, he labored long and hard, writing to more experienced states for advice. In spite of his efforts, his bill, an ambitious plan requiring the services of at least six scientists for four years, met with stony indifference.[17]

The failure of this, his major legislative effort of the session, did not strike Garfield as a serious setback to his political career. To him, politics was mainly the business of making speeches, a belief he was to abandon only gradually during the coming years. To sway a crowd, to crush an opponent, to deliver an apposite sally—these, rather than the quiet drudgery of framing legislation, comprised his conception of political activity in the early days of his career. By this standard he was a success. "Garfield wants only experience to become a leader," a political observer declared, "he impresses everyone favorably and, as he ripens in Senatorial experience, his influence, even now weighty, will be more sensibly felt and acknowledged."[18] Garfield was even becoming something of a celebrity, and the public prints began to take notice of his doings. A Cleveland reporter described him at length:

> In his personal appearance, Senator Garfield is robust and healthy; about six feet high, light hair and whiskers, which latter are inclined to be curly. His head is unusually large; his forehead is very prominent. . . . His voice is very pleasant—he has a quiet, undemonstrative style of speaking, and clothes his ideas in such clear and unambiguous language that they are at all times readily comprehended. As a lecturer, he excels. . . . Senator Garfield's gestures, when speaking in public, are few in number, and made altogether with the right hand.[19]

Garfield's rhetorical skills were not restricted to politics. Even though his attachment to the church had slackened of late, he still continued to preach from time to time. Sometimes his sermons were delivered under unusual circumstances, as when he discoursed on "faithfulness" to the inmates of the Ohio penitentiary. A newspaperman who conveniently happened to be present reported that Garfield

> addressed his peculiar audience with a pathos and power which affected many of them to tears. While holding up the mirror of their early homes, and reminding them of the innocence of their childhood, the pure aspirations of their youth, the fond hopes of their mothers, the speaker suddenly faltered, his voice grew tremulous, and he seemed as if suffocating with grief.

74

The pathos of the occasion was somewhat dispelled when, at the end of his remarks, Garfield was greeted heartily by an old friend, now a prisoner.[20]

The legislature adjourned in the spring. Garfield took leave of Columbus well satisfied with his performance. Even crusty Lyman Hall, often a severe critic, told Garfield, "You will leave the Legislature with reputation, fully enjoying the respect and confidence of your constituents." Cox agreed, assuring his roommate that "we did quite as well as we had any reason to anticipate."[21]

Home once more, Garfield busied himself for a time with school and family matters. The school had run smoothly during his absence; his family life had not. During his stay at Columbus, Garfield had discouraged his wife from joining him, claiming that the press of business would prevent him from devoting as much time to her as he would like. Lucretia was not deceived. Her husband's coolness towards her was unmistakable. In truth, Garfield had not taken to married life. Bluntly he informed his wife that he considered their marriage "a great mistake."[22] Before their marriage, she had once overheard Almeda Booth tell a friend that Garfield was "one of that class of men who did not want a wife for society." Now that they were married Lucretia realized the truth of that remark. Pathetically she pleaded for understanding:

> If you are so constituted that the society of others is more desirable than a wife's or if the strange untoward circumstances of your life in its relations to me have driven you for sympathy to others . . . then you are not to blame. . . . But you must not, O, No, you *must not* blame me if I feel it. . . . I try to hide it. I crush back the tears just as long as I can for I know they make you unhappy.[23]

Unhappy he was. To Garfield, these were "the dark years," spent in a "sadness almost bordering on despair." His soul, he moaned, dwelt in the "darkness and shadow of death," and he "died daily." His friends, who so admired his show of jovial good humor, were unaware that Garfield was actually on the brink of emotional collapse.[24]

On July 3, 1860 a daughter was born into the Garfield

75

household. She was christened Eliza after Garfield's mother, but no one ever called her anything but "Trot," a nickname her literary father appropriated from *David Copperfield*. Not even Trot could keep her restless father home for long. The very day after she was born Garfield was off to Ravenna to deliver a Fourth of July address.

In his speech, Garfield scoffed at the threats of secession then rumbling out from the disgruntled South. "Has Maine, as a state, any quarrel with Alabama?" he asked, and immediately answered,

> No! . . . . Is there any one of all these states that would break the bond of the Union, and deprive itself of all the blessings which it affords? . . . And if there were, would not the thirty two remaining sisters throw their arms of affection around the erring one and bring her gently back again to the sacred circle of home?

He assured his audience that secession was impossible. "Who can divide the mighty Mississippi, and bid its waters flow back to their mountain streams, or who roll back the restless tide of commerce that sweeps down its valley?"

Years before, in the first bloom of his religious enthusiasm, Garfield had often deplored the patriotic cant of the glorious Fourth. Now he was no longer quite so pious, but that earlier attitude found an echo in his Ravenna speech. In contrast to the spread-eagle oratory traditionally deemed appropriate for the day, Garfield boldy criticized Americans for their faults. Pointing to the individualism that Americans cherished, he told his surprised listeners that

> The results of this intense individualism are not unmixed with evil . . . it has made us a conceited, dogmatic and sensitively irascible people. The most absurd and ridiculous extremes of opinion readily find followers; and every sect or creed which has blessed or cursed the world has its representatives among us.[25]

This Ravenna address was only the first of a long series of speeches Garfield was called upon to deliver during the campaign season of 1860. Ever since the State Republican Convention in mid-June, he had been deluged with requests to speak. Garfield had gone to that convention at the request of Jacob Cox, who wanted to be nominated for state Attorney General. Unable to attend the convention in person, Cox had asked Garfield to be his "alter ego." As John Sherman would discover, at another convention twenty years later, Garfield was ideally equipped to play John Alden for his friends. Garfield failed to help his friend Cox's cause, but his speeches at the convention did enhance his own reputation. The *Cincinnati Commercial* expressed the opinion of many delegates when it said, "The young Senator from Portage . . . stepped at once from comparative obscurity into genuine popularity as a political speaker, on that occasion, and from this time to the end of the campaign his party will demand his services on the stump." "Your praise is on every one's mouth," reported William Bascom, who was following his star boarder's career with special interest. "Now dont be alarmed at this sudden popularity," he cautioned. "I dont deal in flattery, but really that speech, short and unpremeditated as it was, has appeared to me as one of the happiest and best delivered efforts I have heard for years."[26]

The next few months sped by in a "whirlpool of excitement and work" as the demand for his eloquence outran even Garfield's capacity. He spoke for Lincoln at over forty meetings and was compelled to turn down at least that many more invitations. Everywhere he went he attracted favorable notice. The Republican papers were jubilant. "Mr. Garfield needs only the experience of Carl Schurz," boasted one, "to be in Ohio what that champion is in Wisconsin—*the leading orator of freedom.*"[27] Even the Democratic papers grudgingly conceded that "he presented the doctrines of his party in a straightforward manner, and aside from some ingenious reasoning in support of them made a very good speech."[28]

Bascom was delighted at the success of his protege. "You have made a *first rate* start," he congratulated. "No man in my recollection has sprung so suddenly into favor as an orator as yourself." "A rising man," concluded the *Ohio State Journal*, and the *Western Reserve Chronicle* echoed the praise in the same words—"A rising man." Bascom dangled the possibility of Congress before Garfield's dazzled eyes, and Cox hinted that he would not stand in the way.[29]

The campaign of 1860 was the most exciting that Northern

Ohio had seen in years. Garfield's major meeting was held at Ravenna on September 11. Beginning early in the morning, a steady stream of wagons clogged the dusty roads leading to Ravenna. Within the town a festival atmosphere prevailed. Bands played campaign songs and orators held forth to cheering crowds at every corner. Processions from neighboring villages poured into town, each wagon draped with appropriate banners, mottoes, and badges. A delegation of workingmen from Freedom, Ohio lumbered through the streets proudly proclaiming themselves "The mudsills of society," and "the greasy mechanics of the North." On their wagons could be seen living tableaus of workers engaged in their occupations, and in the last wagon there was a representation of young Abe Lincoln splitting rails in honest toil. The Streetsboro parade featured thirty-three young ladies dressed in white, one for each state of the Union, and the Edinburg delegation was led by a phalanx of forty mounted riders, each carrying a flag.

By midafternoon an estimated twenty thousand people had gathered in Ravenna. With wild enthusiasm they heard the main speaker of the day, Cassius Marcellus Clay, an antislavery Kentucky printer whose press had been destroyed by a Southern mob, describe the evils of slavery. Garfield was scheduled to follow, but a sudden downpour drove the crowd to shelter. The meeting was continued later in the evening inside the packed town hall, where Garfield delivered his postponed speech. The crowd then surged into the streets to watch a band of Republican Wide Awakes parade by torchlight through the mud. Children squealed with delight as the marchers shot off Roman candles. A salute from Captain Cotter's artillery company signaled the end of the day's festivities and the tired Republicans slowly headed their teams homeward.[30]

Few meetings were this exciting, but Garfield, an indefatigable campaigner, devoted as much effort to a small rally as to a large one. One evening he arrived at a country schoolhouse to deliver a speech only to find that no one had remembered to post advance notice. Undaunted, Garfield held the meeting as scheduled, delivering "one of his most eloquent and convincing speeches" before an audience of only nine men, five of whom were Democrats. "He was not loud," one of that small band remembered. "He made no attempt at wonderful oratorical flourishes. But he made each man there feel that he was being talked to especially; that the argument was prepared for his benefit." Three of the Democrats were so impressed that they converted to Garfield's cause.[31]

A few weeks later, election day revealed that Garfield's labors had not been in vain. Lincoln and Hamlin were elected, and the Republican ticket swept Garfield's district 6,672 to 3,998. "God be Praised!!" Garfield rejoiced.[32]

Further south, the news of Lincoln's victory evoked a much grimmer reaction. Within six weeks South Carolina had read itself out of the Union and other states seemed likely to follow her lead. Garfield had always dismissed Southern threats of secession as bluster, but now, confronted by "the terrible reality of our country's condition," he trembled for the future. By January, he was resigned to the fact that nothing "this side of a miracle of God" could avert civil war. With almost religious fervor the one-time pacifist even welcomed the possibility of war, for he saw in it "the doom of slavery." "To make the concessions demanded by the South would be hypocritical and sinful," he declared. "I am inclined to believe that the sin of slavery is one of which it may be said that 'without the shedding of blood there is no remission.' All that is left for us . . . is to arm and prepare to defend ourselves and the Federal Government."[33]

Garfield's constituents back in Hiram did not share his fear. To them the crisis seemed remote and unreal. A friend of Garfield's marveled at their lack of concern:

> it seems to me that the masses are quite indifferent to the civil crisis that is coming upon the country. Do not the people read and think concerning it very much as they do of any other important town news? Very few have followed the matter out to its consequences—few have thought of themselves thrust through with a bayonet—or of their sons upon the battle field.[34]

Hiram was too preoccupied with "oil fever" (even Garfield had taken a flyer on an oil well) to pay much heed to Southern threats. Columbus, however, was seized by a "strong war-like sentiment." Legislators could be seen drilling on the Capitol grounds, and Garfield and Cox were being coached in the use of the light infantry musket.[35]

By the first of February all of the Gulf States had ratified ordinances of secession, and delegates were on their way to Montgomery, Alabama to form a Southern Confederacy. In Washington the expiring Buchanan administration had lost control of events. The President, betrayed by his friends and repudiated by his country, said his prayers and hoped that the explosion would wait until he was safely out of office. President-elect Lincoln refused to take the lead, and contented himself, in public at least, with oracular statements of good will, while Congress busied itself with futile schemes of compromise.

The people of the North, lacking any clear voice of national leadership, looked to their state capitals for direction. Columbus, however, was as confused as Washington. Republican legislators, aghast at the demon they had helped conjure up, wrung their hands in despair and hoped for the best. Gone now was the fiery defiance so recently proclaimed on the hustings. Republican leaders now trembled lest they offend the South. Groping for a compromise, they refused to prepare for war in the fear that such moves would be interpreted by the South as "coercion."

Garfield stood firm in the midst of this timidity. Convinced of the righteousness of his stand, he resisted all peaceful gestures made by a coalition of Democrats and "emasculated Republicans" which was led by his old foe, Richard Harrison. "I have endeavored to be—and have been conservative," Garfield insisted,

> but I believe I have now done about all that justice requires and now I am resolved to fight these fellows to the bitter end.
> . . . I fear some of our decisive, bold measures will be lost in the House by the nervousness of our timid men. In regard to the aspect of national affairs, I am really growing more cheerful and hopeful as the clouds thicken.[36]

He deplored all efforts at compromise, such as the peace conference then meeting in Washington. When Ohio was invited to send delegates to this convention, Garfield denounced the entire scheme as "wrong and cowardly," and assailed those who would deal with armed rebels and traitors. Nonetheless, the Ohio Peace Commissioners were sent, with the blessings of the entire Senate except for Garfield, Cox, and one other irreconcilable.[37]

Garfield wanted Ohio to arm rather than negotiate. He was appalled at the decayed condition of Ohio's defenses. Her active militia had dwindled to less than twelve hundred men, and only six thousand muskets were available in the state armory. He supported a bill to increase Ohio's armed forces. To the objections of his timid colleagues Garfield replied,

> It is said that it [the militia] will irritate our Southern brethren and precipitate revolution and disunion. If the Senator will look at the policy of other states, he will find that military preparation is not so unheard of a thing as to be a source of irritation. Other states may be arming to the teeth, but if Ohio cleans her rusty muskets it will offend our brethren of the South. . . . I am weary of this nervous weakness.[38]

The *Ohio State Journal*, Senator Chase's organ, congratulated Garfield for this "suggestive and pointed speech," which exposed the "miserable cheat of the senseless gabble about 'coercion' pouring so incessantly from the mouths of sympathizers with treason."[39]

Conservative Republicans did not take this attack lying down. Harrison dredged up Garfield's old speech to the Kentucky legislature and read it "with fine declamatory effect," contrasting Garfield's former conciliatory sentiments with his present fiery attitude. The Senators and the gallery roared with laughter at Garfield's expense. Garfield, "looking a little flush, yet confident," slowly rose to reply, nervously buttoning and unbuttoning his coat. He thanked Harrison for reading his speech with such "peculiar and effective emphasis." He still stood by the sentiments of the speech, he insisted, but he reminded the house that other Senators could also be accused of inconsistency. Warming to his subject he cited Harrison's own speeches to show that he too had changed his stand. The tables were turned and Harrison, thoroughly squelched, retreated before the laughter of the House. Even the conservatives conceded that "Mr. Garfield took the laurels," and Garfield crowed about his "glorious victory over Harrison and his fogies."[40]

Absorbed though he was in the nation's crisis, Garfield could still find time to further his own career. Ever since he had entered the legislature Garfield had felt handicapped by his lack of legal training. For some time he had been reading law in his spare moments, and early in 1859 he had entered his name as a student with the Cleveland firm of Williamson and Riddle. His association with this firm was perfunctory, consisting of only a five minute chat with Albert Gallatin Riddle who advised him to read Blackstone. Garfield continued his studies in his room at Hiram without further outside assistance. By early 1861 he felt ready to apply for admission to the bar. Cox assured him that a man of his influence could be certified without an examination. "Your position in the Senate and the *formal* fulfillment of your two years of reading will be amply sufficient to ensure the admission," he guaranteed. Legislators, he insisted, were considered qualified "by courtesy" no matter what their scholarly attainments. "So be at rest on that point, and dont overtax yourself to read. . . ." Garfield, however, preferred a proper examination. For his board the State Supreme Court appointed Thomas Key, a Democratic Senator and Richard Harrison, Garfield's chief Republican antagonist. Neither was inclined to let Garfield off lightly, but after a "thorough and searching examination" they reported that his mastery of the law was "unusual and phenomenal." Garfield was now a lawyer but, for the time being, he had no intention of practicing.[41]

On February 17, another self-taught Western lawyer, Abraham Lincoln, passed through Columbus on his way to Washington. Garfield was not overly impressed by his party's new leader. Despite Lincoln's freshly grown whiskers, Garfield thought him "distressed homely." From his elevated college-based vantage point, Garfield looked down upon Lincoln with a touch of condescension. "He clearly shows his want of culture—and the marks of western life,"[42] he loftily observed. Mrs. Lincoln, a "stocky, sallow, pug-nosed plain lady," betrayed even more marks of the "primitiveness of western life."

Yet, with all his reservations, Garfield caught a glimpse of something in Lincoln's character that inspired confidence. "Through all his awkward homeliness," he noted, "there is a look of transparent, genuine goodness which at once reaches your heart, and makes you trust and love him."[43]

> There is no touch of affectation in him—he is frank—direct—and thoroughly honest. His remarkable good sense—simple and condensed style of expression—and evident marks of indomitable will—give me great hopes for the country. . . . After the long dreary period of Buchanan's weakness and cowardly imbecility the people will hail a strong and vigorous leader.[44]

As far as Garfield was concerned, these early hopes for Lincoln turned out to be much too generous. In the next few years his opinion of the President would harden into cold contempt. But for the time being, he was willing to withold judgment and hope for the best.

When Lincoln finally arrived in Washington to assume his new office, one of his first acts was to appoint Ohio's Senator Chase to his cabinet as Secretary of the Treasury. This left an empty seat in the United States Senate for the Ohio Legislature to fill. Garfield backed Governor Dennison for the post. He had gotten over his early dislike of the Governor, and now regarded him as "one of the wisest, most honest, capable and faithful Governors Ohio ever had." "I think no member of the legislature is on more intimate terms with them than I," he boasted. "They are quite free from the pomp and stiffness which is usually met with in such cases. Personally I like Gov. D. much better than Gov. Chase." He was a frequent guest at the governor's home, and on occasion he even accompanied the governor and his lady to worship at the Episcopalian church. Though he deplored the formality and lack of "real devotion" he saw there, he was impressed by the pomp and beauty of the service, so different from the humble ritual he knew at home.[45]

Garfield and Cox threw all their energies into Dennison's cause. They were kept so busy buttonholing legislators that for three successive nights they scarcely slept. Garfield dashed off to Cleveland to line up support for Dennison in the Western Reserve. There he argued the necessity of defeating John Sherman at all costs. His chief talking point was that if Sherman should be successful he might become a rival to Senator Ben Wade, the Reserve's favorite son, while Dennison, from the southern part of the state, would not.

Two years before, Garfield had been an obscure schoolteacher. Now he was trying to make a United States Senator. It was a heady experience, even though his efforts were not successful. The legislature was bitterly divided. After forty-nine ballots the field had narrowed to Sherman, Dennison, and Robert Schenck. Sherman denied that he was in any way eager for the honor, but he left Washington for a quick trip to Columbus to supervise his campaign in person. His presence tilted the balance, and the legislature appointed him to fill out Chase's term. Garfield attributed Dennison's defeat to the general distrust of Lieutenant-Governor Kirk, who would have succeeded as governor if Dennison had been elevated to the Senate. He did not realize that the deciding factor in the election had been the behind-the-scenes support of Sherman's campaign by the financial resources of banker Jay Cooke and family. In spite of defeat, Garfield was proud "that our advocacy of Gov. Dennison was acknowledged on all hands to have been *honorable* as well as *able*." Perhaps that had been their trouble.[46]

As the session drew near its scheduled close, Garfield, harried and overworked, looked forward to the end of his labors. Restless when at home, he felt equally "sad and unhappy" at Columbus. The "rising man" was not enjoying his success. His old malady, irresolution, still plagued him. "Never," he confessed, "did I feel so sadly, and almost despairingly over my future life as I do at times this winter." He was even tempted to resign. But what then? Law? The law seemed too full of "weary details" to suit his taste. Politics? His political experiences had filled his heart with distrust for his fellow man, and left him yearning only for a "happy secluded home with a small, choice circle of friends around me, and the great world shut out." But he knew that once he retired to such a peaceful life his restless nature would soon cry out for activity.[47]

In the past few years Garfield had sampled four professions: the pulpit, teaching, politics and law, and he had yet to find his true vocation. He feared that such vacillation was "a mark of an inferior mind." "Do you suppose that *real strong men* have such waverings?" he asked his wife.[48]

Garfield's personal problems were soon dwarfed by the tragedy of his nation. On April 12 he was sitting in the Senate chamber while the ordinary business of the session was droning on around him. Suddenly Senator Schleigh burst into the chamber frantically waving a telegram. "Mr. President," he shouted, "the telegraph announces that the secessionists are bombarding Fort Sumter!" For a moment all was hushed. Then from the galleries a woman's shrill voice rent the silence. "Glory to God!" she shrieked, "Glory to God!" The Civil War had begun.[49]

CHAPTER SIX

COLONEL GARFIELD

When Cox and Garfield returned to their room, still stunned by the news from South Carolina, they slumped wearily in their chairs and sat for a long while in silence. "The situation hung upon us like a nightmare," Cox later recalled, ". . . and we half hoped to wake from it as from a dream."[1] For months they had been living under the threat of war. In their own bookish way they had tried to prepare themselves for the coming struggle. They had read biographies of Wellington and Napoleon, and littered their desks with military handbooks. Now they felt something close to relief. The waiting was over. The worst had happened, and it could be met with action.[2]

Garfield had no doubt as to where his duty lay, but he feared that his friend was too frail to follow him into the army. "I am big and strong," he told Cox, "and if my relations to the church and college can be broken, I shall have no excuse for not enlisting; but you are slender and will break down." Within ten days, however, Cox was wearing the uniform of a brigadier general of Ohio Volunteers, while Garfield was to tarry behind as a civilian for months to come.[3]

His delay in entering the army was not due to lack of enthusiasm. From the very outbreak of the war he had hailed it as a holy crusade. "I hope we will never stop short of complete subjugation," he thundered. "Better lose a million men in battle than allow the government to be overthrown. The war will soon assume the shape of Slavery and Freedom. The world will so understand it, and I believe the final outcome will redound to the good of humanity."[4] Nor was his hesitation due to modesty. Even though he was innocent of military knowledge, Garfield never doubted his fitness to command. Years before, a phrenologist had felt that he possessed the bumps of a general, and Garfield saw no reason to question this prophecy. Like most Americans, he had a low opinion of the military mind. "Pluck," he insisted, was far more important than "military science."[5]

Consequently, when Garfield offered his services to Governor Dennison, "in any capacity he may see fit to appoint me," he was confident that Dennison would not undervalue his offer. Garfield felt that he was entitled to be a colonel at the very least, and even a brigadier general's star did not seem out of the question. He scorned the suggestion that he enlist as a private as "buncombe . . . an unmanly piece of demagogism." "I looked the field over," he explained, "and thought if I went into the army I ought to have at least as high a position as a staff officer. . . . The Governor would have given me one still higher if he had one in his gift."[6]

For the time being, though, Garfield had to defer his military career. Governor Dennison needed support in the legislature more than he needed another enthusiastic amateur soldier. During the early months of the war the burden of defending the Union fell almost entirely on the states. Ohio was pitifully unprepared for the exertions it was now called upon to make. Its militia had become a joke, its defenses a scandal. No one in the state administration was experienced in military matters, and costly blunders were inevitable. Under the President's first call for troops, Ohio was assigned a quota of thirteen regiments. So enthusiastic was her initial patriotic impulse, and so inept her military administration, that twenty-three regiments had volunteered and been accepted before the state knew what to do with them. There were no uniforms for the soldiers to wear and no muskets to put in their hands. There was not even a camp to receive them, and so the first volunteers were boarded at hotels, while the state picked up the tab.

Money was the most urgent need. Dennison asked the legislature for the unprecedented sum of one million dollars. Party lines seemed forgotten as the legislature hastily closed ranks to support his request. One note of partisan rancor spoiled the harmony in the senate. Judge Thomas M. Key, a leading Cincinnati Democrat, voted for the bill under protest, because he felt it "in his soul to be an unwarranted declaration of war against seven sister states." He accused the Republicans of plotting to divide the Union by driving the border states into the arms of the South, and he warned that Lincoln intended to establish a "military despotism" on the ruins of the old Union. Garfield felt duty bound to refute these slurs on his party. He had hoped, he said, that the Senator would not "in this hour of the Nation's peril, open the books of party," but since he had, Garfield reminded him with considerable relish that it had been a Democratic cabinet "that embraced traitors among its most distinguished members, and sent them forth from its most secret sessions to betray their knowledge to their country's ruin!"[7]

Garfield's reply to Key was applauded by the Republican press, but in many ways it was an unfortunate speech, for it dragged what could have been an elevated debate down to the level of partisan name-calling. Garfield, of course, did not see it in that light. He was against treason, and in his eyes, the line between a traitor and a Democrat was often hazy. Fearing that certain Ohio Democrats, particularly Clement Vallandingham, might sabotage the state's war effort, Garfield had earlier introduced a bill to punish treason against the state of Ohio—"to provide that when her soldiers go forth to maintain the Union, there shall be no treacherous fire in the rear." As originally drafted by Garfield early in February, the bill had omitted the customary safeguards which prevented anyone from being convicted of treason except on the testimony of two witnesses to the same overt act. Consequently, under Garfield's bill a man could be jailed for treason against Ohio, while at the same time be acquitted of treason against the United States, an oversight which had to be remedied by an amendment from his old rival Richard Harrison. The Democratic press had made sport of Garfield's treason bill when it was first introduced, but after Sumter the subject no longer seemed so amusing, and the bill quickly passed, supported by Republicans and Democrats alike.[8]

Despite the support that so many Democrats were giving to the war effort, Garfield could never bring himself to trust them completely. He suspected that any Democrat was a potential Vallandingham. Consequently, he was leery of the Union Party movement. Any such coalition of Republicans and War Democrats, he warned, would be a "disaster."

> The result will be that Democratic counties will have Democratic members in the Legislature, and strongly Republican counties will have union Democrats, and the General Assembly will be Democratic. . . . Our men are taking the bait and will be caught unless some strong measures can be taken to avert the calamity. The Democratic leaders here are aided by a bevy of fossil Republicans who hope to ride into power on the wave of the war.[9]

He was particularly incensed at the efforts being made to replace Governor Dennison with David Tod, a former Douglas supporter. Garfield, who thought Tod was "an ass," tried to stem the Unionist tide, telling all who would listen that "to elect a Democrat at this crisis would be unwise [;] to elect Mr. Tod would be a fatal blunder." His pleas were disregarded, and Tod was nominated later that summer on a fusion ticket.[10]

Garfield had but little time to devote to politics in the crowded spring and summer months of 1861. Immediately after the legislature adjourned he hurried home to rouse his neighbors to the war effort. He and Senator John Sherman made a whirlwind circuit of the district, addressing patriotic meetings in every corner of the Reserve. "Garfield goes forth, like an apostle of Liberty, a preacher of righteousness, proclaiming the Gospel which demands equal obedience to God and resistance to tyrants."[11]

For once, however, mere talk did not satisfy Garfield. He longed to be in the thick of action. In late April, he helped raise troops for the Seventh Regiment of Ohio Volunteer Infantry, and he confidently expected to become colonel in return for his services. In the early days of the war many volunteer regiments, in an excess of democratic zeal, were allowed to elect their own officers. Garfield's friends in the Seventh

89

Regiment presented him before the men as a candidate. Others, notably Erastus B. Tyler of Ravenna, were also in the running. The election was to take place around the first of May in Camp Taylor, near Cleveland. Garfield's supporters nervously urged him to come to camp to present his case in person. "There is no *doubt* of your Election," wrote one, "but your *presence* would make a sure thing of it. Come if *possible.*"[12]

Unfortunately for his cause, Garfield was unable to campaign, for at that moment he was in Illinois on a secret mission for the Governor. Dennison had learned that Illinois possessed a surplus of muskets, and he had dispatched Garfield to procure them for Ohio. While there, Garfield was also to negotiate with the governors of Illinois and Indiana to place their troops under the command of Ohio's Major General George B. McClellan. Garfield carried off both projects, and returned to Ohio with five thousand muskets and a plan to consolidate all Western troops under McClellan's direction.[13]

While Garfield was away in Illinois, Erastus Tyler was busily campaigning in his flashy Ohio militia uniform, which so impressed the recruits that it virtually assured his election as commander of the Seventh Ohio. "You've been sold!" cried Garfield's friends, and Garfield, who had somehow gotten the impression that Tyler would support him for colonel, was outraged at his "treachery." Tyler, he fumed, had triumphed only "by bargains-and-brandy," and he vowed revenge. Actually, Tyler had a legitimate claim to the position. He had raised more troops for the regiment than Garfield had, and his military experience was more impressive than his rival's. As for the charges of foul play, they may have been true, but if so, they would have been out of character. Tyler was a teetotaler who during his subsequent military career would campaign to stamp out drinking among his soldiers. He was hardly the sort of man who would buy an election with booze. Perhaps Garfield's real grievance against Tyler was that he was a Democrat. He was also a popular figure in the district, and Lyman Hall warned Garfield that if he contested the election he might seriously damage his own political prospects.[14]

Garfield withdrew with as good grace as he could muster and looked around for another command. The Nineteenth Ohio beckoned, but Garfield was no more successful here than before. After two such setbacks Garfield felt persecuted. He suspected that his failures were caused by "a set of unscrupulous men, who want me out of the way."[15] His enemies gleefully made political capital out of his discomfiture. The opposition press gloated:

> when a man, without military education, experience or training, refuses to join the ranks, but endeavors to leap from the walks of a private citizen to the position of a military chieftain, it is transparent that *self*, and not country, prompts his actions. In our opinion, Hon. James A. Garfield is of this class. Ever since the commencement of the present troubles, he has been hovering around military encampments, (always cautious, however, to keep clear of the ranks) literally begging for a commission, but failing to get it, his patriotism has oozed out and for the last two weeks, he appears to have subsided.[16]

During June and July, while Cox and other Ohio soldiers were fighting to secure northwestern Virginia for the Union, Garfield sulked at home. In mid-June Governor Dennison offered him a commission as lieutenant colonel in the 24th Ohio Infanty. Originally Dennison had rashly promised to make him a full colonel. Now he backed down and offered only a subordinate post. William Bascom, the Governor's private secretary, tried to soothe Garfield's ruffled feelings. "Of course, you understand it is solely on the point that you have no special military education or experience," he explained, assuring Garfield that the Governor "is fully satisfied as to your military *genius* and capacity. . . . But the trouble is, the people, the rest of mankind do not know this, and will not justify the [appointment] to the Chief Command." Garfield struggled with his pride for a few days, but finally he declined the commission on the grounds that "the condition of my personal affairs, and my relations to those with whom I am in business connection," compelled him to remain at Hiram, at least for the time being.[17]

Actually, as he privately admitted, his refusal had nothing to do with his obligation to the school. He dreaded to return to the

Eclectic, and was well aware that under wartime conditions his salary ,there would be much less than an officer's pay. To his friends he offered a different explanation from the one he had given the Governor. If there were a scarcity of volunteers, he insisted, he would have accepted the commission, but since so many qualified soldiers were available he had decided to hold back for awhile, and volunteer later if the need should arise for more troops. It is doubtful whether his friends were convinced by all this. Probably not even Garfield himself believed it. But his refusal to serve was not, as his enemies insinuated, due to wounded vanity or excessive ambition. For all his success, Garfield was still as unsure of himself as he had been when a schoolboy, still prone to the same deep fits of depression and doubt. His disappointments with the 7th and 19th Regiments had triggered one of his recurring emotional crises and he could not assume any new responsibilities until he pulled himself together again.[18]

He frittered July away, reading the Federalist Papers, dipping into de Tocqueville, tidying up school affairs, and delivering a scattered speech here and there. Late in the month he journeyed to Michigan to visit friends and family. When he returned to Ohio he found a letter from Governor Dennison waiting on his desk. New regiments were being organized. Would Garfield accept a lieutenant colonelcy? This time there was no hesitation. Garfield immediately wired back his acceptance. In mid-August he was sworn in as Lieutenant Colonel[19] of the 42nd Ohio Volunteer Infantry, and a few weeks later Governor Dennison relented and appointed him full colonel of the regiment.

Garfield *was* the 42nd Regiment. Except for him the regiment existed only on paper. He had no officers to instruct, no troops to command, no horses, no uniforms—only a commission. He had to create his entire command from the ground up. To find his soldiers Garfield turned first to those he knew best— his students at Hiram. Since Sumter the Eclectic had rapidly disintegrated. The students had only one eye for their lessons, as with the other they eagerly scanned the exciting news from Virginia. Hiram Hill became a drill field. The boys practiced the rudiments of infantry maneuvers under the supervision of a doddering veteran of the War of 1812 who limped across the campus barking orders in a quavering voice. Some, unable to restrain their enthusiasm, volunteered at once, but most held back from joining the army. They wanted to enlist as a unit so they could fight together, preferably under the command of their principal. Garfield's commission was the signal for which they had been waiting, and when he came before them in his new uniform to urge them to sign up, they needed little persuasion. Within an hour after he spoke at the village church sixty boys stepped forward, and the rest of the company was filled within the week. The Hiram boys were mustered in as Company A, taking the traditionally honorable position on the right of the regimental line. They left behind a school drained of students. In J. H. Rhodes's history class, for example, only girls (and one lone male Democrat) remained.[20]

The Hiram boys were shipped down to Camp Chase, on the outskirts of Columbus. They were soon joined by six more companies, and drill began in earnest. Not all of these companies had been recruited by Garfield. By September he had the help of two officers, Lieutenant Colonel Lionel A. Sheldon and Major Don Pardee, both of whom were destined eventually to command the 42nd Ohio. Sheldon, an Elyria lawyer, was well known in Lorain County. Before entering Garfield's regiment he had been a brigadier general of militia, which gave him a slight familiarity with military affairs. During the war he would win a reputation as a relentless drillmaster and a tireless administrator. Major Pardee boasted an even more impressive background. He had studied for a time at Annapolis, and so had some acquaintance with the rudiments of military science. Garfield was so impressed with Pardee that he had been unwilling to take command of the regiment unless Pardee were assigned to his staff. No longer quite so confident in the sufficiency of "pluck" alone, Garfield wanted Pardee at his side to instruct him in military matters.[21]

Both Sheldon and Pardee raised companies in their districts, but despite their efforts the regiment did not reach its full strength until November. Until then Garfield had to scour the countryside for recruits. His recruiting methods were modeled on the revivalist techniques he had learned on the pulpit, the only difference being that at the end of his sermon he would ask his listeners to stand up for the Union rather than for Jesus. Naturally, he used Disciple churches for his platform whenever he could. Some of the brethren, however, still clung to their pacifist principles and refused to open their churches to a warrior. In Ashland County, for example, Garfield encountered "a style of over-pious men and churches . . . who are too godly to be human." He had to hold his meetings on the platform of the town hall, where he castigated "the Christianity of Ashland and all people who were afraid to 'do good on the Sabbath Day.' " Eight recruits, including a Methodist minister, came forward to enlist after this appeal.[22]

These recruiting trips were snatched whenever Garfield could spare a few days from his duties at camp. Camp Chase, a hastily thrown together collection of whitewashed barracks, swarming with flies and mired in mud, was as little prepared for war as Garfield himself. His first night in camp, Garfield could find no bed except for a pile of straw. The next day, bone-stiff and weary, he began his military lessons. Before his regiment showed up at camp, Garfield had to learn how to command them. "It is a little odd for me to become a pupil again," he mused, but he quickly adjusted, and found himself, much to his surprise, "busy and cheerful in the work of tearing down the old fabric of my proposed life, and removing the rubbish for the erection of a new structure."[23]

He had much to learn. Before he could turn his green recruits into soldiers he had to become a soldier himself. Applying the studious habits of a lifetime, he conned his strange new curriculum with all the persistence and ingenuity he had once devoted to Latin verbs. He whittled a set of wooden blocks to represent companies, battalions, officers and men, and each night he would march his blocks across his desk in response to the proper command until he had mastered the elements of infantry tactics and drill. Camp Chase had no officers' training school; Garfield had to learn his job as best he could. The daily routine of camp life could be an education in itself for an officer who kept his eyes open. His very first day in camp Garfield was appointed officer of the day. He supervised sentry duty, issued passes, reprimanded disorderly soldiers, censoréd mail, guarded rebel prisoners ("a hard looking set— of the species of the great unwashed"), and in countless little ways began to learn the great truth that war is mostly drudgery.[24]

By the time his troops reached camp, Garfield was ready for them. The Hiram boys of Company A were the first to arrive. Most of them had never been this far from home before, and in the high good spirits of college boys off on a lark, they looked upon the war as a great adventure. They had spent the previous night at Columbus. The legislature was not in session and the Hiram boys were bivouacked in the State House. After supper, too excited to sleep, they took over the empty legislative chamber, chose up sides, elected a "chief justice," and launched into a hilarious mock debate on "The Right of Secession." Their fun was short-lived. Once they settled in camp it was hardtack and sow belly from then on. The beds were hard, and they had to be vacated by six o'clock reveille. Some grumbled at the "aimless barbarism" of this early hour, but the farm boys enjoyed the unaccustomed luxury of sleeping so late.[25]

Garfield had only a few weeks to whip these boys into shape. No time was wasted. For six to eight hours each day his tired, sweaty troops marched and countermarched across the sunbaked fields of Camp Chase, practicing company and squad drill, regimental evolutions, tactical maneuvers, and bayonet exercises until ready to drop with fatigue. The officers were not spared. Always a schoolmaster at heart, Garfield organized an officers' school and drilled them with his little wooden blocks. In the evening the colonel and his staff would repair to the rifle range for target practice, where Garfield, the veteran of innumerable squirrel shoots as a boy in Orange, invariably came off the best shot.[26]

During the first few weeks of their training the unmilitary bearing of the boys of the 42nd was accentuated by their dress. No uniforms or supplies had yet been issued, and they had to drill in the checked blouses and faded trousers they had worn to camp. They even had to sleep in these clothes since there were no blankets for their cots. Garfield filled out form after form, but the supplies never arrived. Finally, despairing of action through regular channels, he took matters into his own hands and went to Columbus, where, after having "dragooned and chased down nearly every state officer," he was finally able to obtain the proper requisitions. After two sleepless nights he reached Cincinnati to fill his requisitions, only to find empty warehouses and uncooperative, harried quartermasters. Garfield himself had to make the rounds of the contractors, one by one, to beg or bully them into issuing his long-overdue supplies. "I was never so tired in my life," he groaned, but by the beginning of October his men looked more like soldiers, even though their fatigue caps turned yellow after the first rain and shrank so much that they perched ludicrously on the tops of their heads. When the snows set in, the men shivered through sentry duty without overcoats until they were issued late in November. By the end of November, after some companies had been drilling since September, rifles finally arrived. The troops, who had hoped to be armed with new Harper's Ferry or Enfield rifles with showy sabre bayonets, were crestfallen when they saw their accurate but cumbersome Belgian rifles with prosaic lance bayonets. Even so, they were grateful to have been spared the obsolete smooth bore muskets that were issued to some unlucky recruits.[27]

Thus armed, uniformed, and equipped (mainly through the exertions of its colonel), the 42nd Ohio finally presented a smart military appearance. But, as Garfield fully realized, a gun and a uniform do not by themselves turn a boy into a soldier. Intangibles of discipline and spirit had to be instilled as well. The boys of the 42nd, raw as they were, were excellent military material. They were a well-educated, homogeneous, self-reliant group, with enough faith in their cause to volunteer to defend it. Given good leadership they could excel. The 42nd was fortunate in its officers. Sheldon knew every man in the regiment by name, a rare accomplishment in the Union army. Pardee became the terror of the regiment, imposing strict discipline on the high-spirited boys. When a drunken company rioted and threatened to shoot a corporal and his guard, it was Pardee who cooly disarmed them and marched their leaders to the guardhouse.[28]

Garfield, too, displayed unexpected qualities of military

leadership. His civilian experience turned out to be highly appropriate for his present tasks. Managing a thousand boys was, after all, very much the same whether they were in school or in uniform. One difference that saddened Garfield was the aloofness required to preserve military discipline. Friendly by nature, it pained him to have to assume the role of "the scourge of many rather than the co-operant friend and leader." Overwhelmed by the loneliness of command, he turned to his horses for affection, caressing their flanks and whispering in their ears three or four times a day.[29]

Aside from his horses, his closest friend at camp was J. H. Jones, a Disciple preacher who served as the regimental chaplain. Before leaving for the army both Garfield and Jones, oppressed by the uncertainty of their future, had sworn a pact of mutual friendship and assistance. They were joined in this covenant by Isaac Errett and Dr. and Mrs. J. P. Robison. The five friends called their little society the Quintinkle, a group which although later expanded, was to remain one of Garfield's closest circles throughout his life.[30]

After three months of Camp Chase, the long hours of drill and discipline began to transform the boys of the 42nd into soldiers. They were proud of their regiment—and proud of their colonel. Garfield's friend J. H. Rhodes found himself on a train one day seated next to a group of boys from Garfield's regiment. Pretending ignorance, he disparaged Garfield in order to sound them out. "You would have been delighted to have heard the expressions in your favor by these men . . ." he reported to Garfield.

> I said he [Garfield] was a man of no military education. . . .
> They vehemently insisted he had the best drilled regiment in
> the camp. I said he must be quite unpopular among his men.
> They replied his men loved him more and more each day and
> would die for him. . . . They said he was a strong man. I said
> he was more fat than anything else. They told me how without
> calling for help he took hold of several big cavalry men. One
> counted his deeds as a boat driver.

On the whole, concluded Rhodes, "I found by these men that a strong clannish feeling was growing among them which will serve a good purpose in the hour of danger."[31]

97

That hour was near at hand. The 42nd had been marking time at camp until its ranks could be filled. By the end of November, after repeated recruiting forays by Garfield and his officers, the regiment finally reached its full strength of ten companies. Garfield, bored and weary from filling out all the forms required to activate his regiment, looked forward to action. His only fear was that the 42nd might be assigned the inglorious duty of guarding the "slaughter yards and pork packers" of Cincinnati. He need not have worried. On the 14th of December he received orders to proceed at once with his regiment to Kentucky.[32]

The next day the men packed their knapsacks with three days' rations, and marched four miles down the pike to Columbus. They were in good spirits, happy to leave the now detested Camp Chase. A private of Company K vividly remembered how "when we marched out on that clear cold December morning to the step of martial music, every heart was buoyant and hopeful and fully resolved to battle manfully for the Old Flag."

This early in the war, troops on their way to battle were still enough of a novelty to inspire enthusiasm. In Columbus flags fluttered from every window, and curious crowds gathered at the railroad depot to watch as the regiment was reviewed by Governor Dennison. After "an earnest and patriotic address," he presented the regiment with a stand of battle flags, admonishing them never to let these colors trail in the dust. Colonel Garfield accepted the flags and assured the governor that they would be carried "through many a sanguine field to victory." The men gave the governor three cheers, and marched smartly into the train.

As they traveled south, patriotic citizens at every station thrust baskets of fruit and other delicacies into their hands. At one stop, a private recalled, "one very pretty girl assured me that she would rather kiss a soldier than eat her dinner. I did not take the hint, but I took a cup of coffee from her hands instead." Garfield's soldiers were, after all, still only boys. Soon they would be called upon to be men.[33]

CHAPTER SEVEN

THE HERO OF THE SANDY VALLEY

In the days when Indians roamed at will through the mountains of Kentucky they instinctively dreaded this "dark and bloody ground." Later the white man came, first a cautious trickle through the passes, then a torrent of settlers with axes, rifles, and families. They cleared the forest, shot the game, and settled their families in cabins and cities. The Indians went away, and left Kentucky to civilization. But in 1861 Kentucky promised once again to be a dark and bloody land. As the nation split asunder, Kentucky held its breath while hostile armies gathered on its borders.

Alarmed Kentuckians, hoping to deflect the conflict from their soil, declared the state "neutral." It was a fatuous attempt. Neither North nor South could afford to surrender Kentucky's strategic position. Well aware that "to lose Kentucky is nearly the same as to lose the whole game," President Lincoln quietly mobilized Union sentiment in the state at the same time he was solemnly promising to respect its "neutrality." In September the Confederates, suspecting that they had been outfoxed, occupied Columbus in western Kentucky. Her soil invaded, her neutrality violated, Kentucky called upon the North to expel the aggressors.[1]

Kentucky was saved for the Union; but would it remain saved? Confederate columns under the skillful direction of Albert Sidney Johnston were massed on her borders, and Confederate agitators were busy raising troops even in those areas nominally under Union control. Union commanders followed one another in rapid succession with scant success. Even William Tecumseh Sherman failed to provide the effective leadership needed, and had to be relieved from command.

He was replaced in November by Don Carlos Buell. General Buell soon realized that his command was little better than an undisciplined rabble. He found his officers slovenly and ignorant of war, his men poorly equipped and poorly trained. Whatever may have been his later shortcomings as a fighting leader, Buell was the sort of martinet Kentucky then needed. From his command post at Louisville came a steady stream of orders: officers must wear uniforms when on duty; reveille and taps must be sounded at the proper hours; troops must refrain from looting—all these elementary but essential procedures of military life had to be firmly impressed upon his raw soldiers. What was to become the Army of the Cumberland began to take shape under Buell's hand. Bolder men would lead it to victory, but Buell forged the instrument they would use.[2]

Buell's strategic objective was Nashville, but before he could safely move into Tennessee he had to secure his left flank. Two Confederate columns were pushing through the mountains into southeastern Kentucky to threaten that flank. One, under Felix Zollicoffer, had already marched through Cumberland Gap and was menacing the interior. Buell sent his most able lieutenant, George H. Thomas, to block Zollicoffer's advance. The other threat was less serious, but it could not be ignored. Humphrey Marshall, with a force rumored to exceed 7,000 men, had entered eastern Kentucky through Pound Gap and was making his way down the Sandy Valley.

Few less likely battlegrounds could be imagined, for few regions had so little worth fighting over. This was a land that had scarcely changed since the days of Daniel Boone: a land where dulcimers still twanged out Tudor ballads in their original purity; a land where mountaineers scratched a bare living wherever they could find enough level ground to pitch a cabin; a land of quick violence where a word could lead to bloodshed and where feuds smouldered for generations with the intensity of Corsican vendettas; a land cut off from the rest of the nation, with no railroads and scarcely any roads at all. Because of the difficulties of terrain and supply, eastern

100

Kentucky had little strategic value for either side. In the hands of the Confederacy, however, rebel raiding parties hidden in its valleys could threaten Buell's supply lines and delay his proposed advance into Tennessee.

Despite its isolation the valley had already seen scattered fighting. Both sides had been anxious to secure its only natural resource—manpower. Confederate recruiters had raised over six hundred men before being driven out by General William ("Bull") Nelson in November.[3] Later that month Nelson had been recalled, leaving behind only a small garrison under Colonel Labe T. Moore. When Humphrey Marshall crossed the mountains in early December, Moore's force fled for safety, leaving the valley undefended. Buell could not allow Marshall to entrench himself on his flank. Without delay he ordered fresh troops to the Sandy Valley. These troops were the boys of the 42nd Ohio.

After their enthusiastic send-off at Columbus, Ohio, the boys of the 42nd had been shipped by rail to Cincinnati. There men, mules, and supplies were stuffed into crowded steamers bound up the Ohio River for Catlettsburg at the mouth of the Sandy River, the point where Ohio, Kentucky, and West Virginia meet.

Garfield left the regiment in the hands of Lieutenant Colonel Lionel Sheldon while he sped from Cincinnati to Louisville to confer with Buell.[4] His first interview left Garfield favorably impressed. "He is a direct martial spirited man, and has an air of decision and business which I like." The general wasted no time on small talk or preliminaries. Brusquely he told Garfield that he had decided to put him in charge of a brigade to deal with the invasion of eastern Kentucky. Buell airily confessed he knew little about the country or the extent of the danger; he left the details of the campaign entirely to Garfield, who was to report back to Buell the next day with a plan of operations.[5]

Garfield returned to his hotel room almost overwhelmed by the responsibility which Buell had so casually thrust upon him. He had never seen a battle, "never heard a hostile gun." He was not a soldier, only a country schoolmaster who dabbled in politics, and now he found himself with an inde-

101

pendent command in a strange wild country, bearing sole responsibility for the success or failure of an important campaign against an unknown enemy. All that night he paced the floor alone, turning plans over in his mind. The more he studied a map of the region, the more appalled he became. His command embraced six thousand square miles of wilderness untapped by railroads or telegraph lines. The land was too desolate to support an army even in the best of seasons, much less in winter.[6]

Supplies would hold the key to the entire campaign. And here, as the one-time canal boy realized, was where he held the advantage. So long as he held close to the river he could float supplies up from the Ohio by water, while Marshall would have to haul every item painfully over the mountains from Virginia. Marshall's advance, therefore, would be slow. Garfield could meet him in the valley, block his advance with part of his brigade, and send another part around the mountains to trap him and cut off his retreat. Garfield spent the rest of the night working out the details of his campaign. The next morning he reported back to Buell. The general listened impassively, without comment or question. Garfield anxiously watched his face, but Buell did not betray his opinion by so much as a raised eyebrow. The plan must have pleased him, for Garfield's orders the next day were nothing more than an elaboration of his own ideas.[7]

Now the 18th Brigade, Colonel Garfield commanding, had only to be set in motion. The 42nd Ohio would join with what remained of Colonel Moore's 14th Kentucky and proceed up the valley until they met the rebels and blocked their advance. Meanwhile, the 40th Ohio, then at Paris, Kentucky, under the command of Colonel Jonathan Cranor, was to march east from Paris overland to the upper Sandy Valley where, with luck, it would sneak behind the rebel rear at just the proper time and place, and crush them in a nutcracker movement. To round out the brigade, Garfield was assigned four squadrons of cavalry, mostly Kentuckian, while the 16th Ohio Infantry was held at Lexington as a reserve. Much to his dismay, Garfield was given no artillery. Buell insisted that artillery in that rough country would only prove a hindrance, but Garfield, unconvinced, continued to pester him for field guns at every opportunity.[8]

The rapidity with which things were happening left Garfield breathless. He hardly knew what to make of his new job. He regretted being separated from his boys of the 42nd for even a short time. He would have preferred to remain as their colonel in a subordinate position in the main column, but Buell consoled him with the thought that an independent command offered greater opportunity for distinction. Neither Buell nor Garfield mentioned what must have crossed both their minds: that the opportunities for conspicious failure were equally great.

Garfield did not have much time to brood over the matter. The situation in the Sandy Valley was deteriorating rapidly. According to rumor, Marshall had already reached Prestonburg, and Colonel Moore's 14th Kentucky had retreated to Catlettsburg. Garfield hastily assembled his staff, ordered supplies, engaged Union sympathizers familiar with the region to act as scouts, and hopped on board the steamer *Bay City* for Catlettsburg. Before he left Louisville, Buell gave him some parting advice and washed his hands of responsibility. "Colonel," he said, "you will be at so great a distance from me and communication will be so slow and uncertain, that I shall commit all matters of detail, and much of the fate of the campaign, to your discretion." Garfield was on his own.[9]

While Garfield was busy in Louisville, his regiment was invading Kentucky. After an acutely uncomfortable voyage, the 42nd Ohio had steamed into Catlettsburg on the 19th of December. The 14th Kentucky, dressed in splendid sky-blue uniforms, lined the shore and greeted its arrival with cheers of welcome. The Ohio boys, glad to be on land once more, disembarked and unloaded their baggage from the steamer. For the rest of the day Catlettsburg was a busy, bustling place: mules were coaxed ashore, wagons loaded, tent stakes pounded into the hard ground, and by sunset a sea of white tents covered the area, and coffee pots were bubbling over camp fires. It was all new and exciting. The boys of the 42nd had never slept in tents before and they relished the experience of camping in a hostile country. No enemy was nearby, but sentries were posted, and, as a private fondly recalled, "we began to assume the airs of Veteran soldiers, if Veterans have airs peculiar to them."[10]

The next day the brigade set out for Louisa, some twenty miles up the Big Sandy. The line of march, so neat and simple on the map, was furrowed by ridges, hills, and valleys. Roads were a mapmaker's fiction; only bridle paths ran through this country. The 150 mules brought from Ohio were not yet broken to the harness, and until they were (with language which must have disturbed Chaplain Jones) the baggage wagons had to be pushed painfully up each hill. Superfluous baggage was dumped by the road side: a spoor of discarded mess chests marked the path of the 42nd Ohio through Kentucky. Then it began to rain—a cold, pelting rain, almost sleet. The men hunched under their coats and slogged through the mud. There were no bridges, and swollen streams coursed through every ridge and gulley. One perversely twisted creek had to be crossed twenty-six times in five miles. It took two full days to reach Louisa, and the march was long remembered as "a thirty mile wade."[11]

Garfield caught up with his sodden troops at Louisa in time to administer a moral lesson. His tired, hungry men had been unable to resist the temptation of foraging in Louisa's unguarded pastures. Amid the squawks of terrified chickens, "poultry, pigs and fences . . . passed away like a dream." Suddenly the drums sounded the long roll, and the regiment, sensing trouble, ran to assemble at attention. They formed a hollow square in front of their colonel, who looked down on them from his horse with obvious anger.

> Men of the Forty-Second [he said], I thought when I left our old Buckeye State at the head of this fine-looking body of soldiers, that I was the proud commander of a Regiment of gentlemen, but your actions this evening, were I not better acquainted with each and all of you, would bitterly dispel that illusion. Soldiers, we came to Kentucky to help her sons free her sacred soil from the feet of the rebel horde. . . . Show these Kentuckians, who are your comrades under one flag, that you did not come to rob and steal . . . and hereafter I shall believe that I command a regiment of soldiers, not a regiment of thieves.

104

The Sandy Valley Campaign. The map is from *The Selfish and the Strong*, by Richard Schuster, published in 1958 by Random House, Inc., through whose courtesy it is reprinted.

The chastened soldiers slunk away, leaving behind a mound of cabbages, hams, and corn meal. "In our simplicity," one of Garfield's light-fingered men recalled, "we then thought it wrong to confiscate rebel property, but as time moved on and our faces became bronzed, so also did our conscientious scruples, and we totally forgot the moral teachings of Colonel Garfield."[12]

The next day the rain turned to snow. After spending a sleepless night huddled around the camp fires for warmth, the brigade prepared to move further south. Wagon wheels spun helplessly on the ice, and the baggage had to be loaded onto flatboats and poled up the river. Sticking close to the river so as not to be cut off from its supply line, Garfield's brigade pushed step by weary step to the source of George's Creek, a branch of the Big Sandy. There they established a base, called Camp Pardee, and waited for their stores to catch up with them. "It is the worst country to get around in I ever saw," Garfield complained. "There is not room enough to form a regiment in line, for want of level ground."[13]

Meanwhile, as the 18th Brigade was toiling up the valley, Humphrey Marshall was slowly advancing from the south to meet Garfield and his "damn Union Psalm singers."[14] Marshall's expedition had fared badly from the first. Although he was an experienced soldier with a West Point education and a distinguished Mexican War record, General Marshall was a poor choice for this assignment. His mission required speed and daring, but Marshall's three-hundred-pound bulk and his cautious temperament rendered success unlikely. Petulant with his superiors, indulgent with his men, Marshall inspired affection but not respect. Under his lax guidance, discipline inevitably sagged: one disgruntled aide volunteered to eat the first man Marshall should shoot for a crime.

Marshall had been selected for his political connections rather than his military prowess, and from the start he had allowed political considerations to interfere with his main task. He had been ordered to Kentucky as early as November 1, so as to reinforce the Confederate garrison then retreating before Bull Nelson. But Marshall, who felt slighted by the command arrangements, particularly the precedence given to General George Crittenden, a political rival, halted his brigade in Virginia while he shot off angry letters to his high-placed friends. Eventually the matter was settled to his satisfaction, and on December 11 he finally crossed the mountains into Kentucky. But by this time the troops he was supposed to rescue had already been routed while he was busy squabbling with Crittenden. Unperturbed, Marshall continued his advance. His command consisted of about 3,000 men from Virginia and Kentucky units. The brigade was deficient in cavalry, with only one battalion of 400 mounted men, but it did have an asset which Garfield coveted—an artillery battery of four pieces.[15]

A cold, wet winter had set in by the time Marshall was ready to move. He had come to liberate Kentucky's sacred soil; instead, he was in danger of being swallowed by Kentucky mud. His artillery, sunk axle-deep in quagmire, slowed the entire advance. It took three full days to drag the guns six miles. The weather took its toll on the soldiers. They were a scraggly band of liberators. Many marched barefoot, few had blankets, and almost none wore overcoats. Even to friendly observers they seemed "ragged, greasy, and dirty . . . more like the bipeds of pandemonium than beings of this earth." Trying to live off the land in a region that could barely support its own inhabitants, Marshall's hungry men turned into an army of beggars. A charitable group of Shakers was appalled to see these soldiers fight one another over a loaf of bread. "They surrounded our wells like the locusts of Egypt," the Shakers complained, ". . . and they thronged our kitchen doors and windows, begging for bread like hungry wolves."[16]

Exposed to the elements, weakened by hunger, many of Marshall's soldiers succumbed to such unmilitary maladies as the measles, and even Marshall himself suffered the indignity of mumps. Out of the 3,000 men who had set forth from Virginia, less than 2,000 were fit for combat. Marshall, whose heart, according to an aide, was "tender as a woman's," suffered along with his men. He often gave up his tent to the sick, and made his bed on the ground under a wagon.

"I sometimes wonder," Marshall asked himself, "why I undergo all this exposure and Hardship?"[17] It was a good question, and one which must have puzzled the Confederate high command as well. Marshall's expedition had almost no military justification. He could not use the valley as a base from which to launch raids behind Buell's lines, for he lacked sufficient cavalry. In his reports to headquarters he outlined grandiose plans for dashing into Kentucky, destroying railroads, and wreaking general havoc, but these plans depended on a large mounted force which, he lamely suggested, would have to be raised "in some way." At other times Marshall spoke as if he regarded his campaign as nothing more than a recruiting expedition. He apparently believed that once he set foot upon his native soil, the supporters of his cause would flock to his standard. He was disappointed. Confederate recruiters had already skimmed the cream of Southern sympathizers from the valley. Those left behind were mostly indifferent to the struggle. Even if Marshall did find a large body of eager volunteers, how would he arm them? Many of his own soldiers were without weapons. He had a few good Belgian rifles, but most of his men carried nothing more deadly than shotguns or squirrel rifles. General Robert E. Lee sympathized with Marshall's plight, but he too had no rifles to spare. The best he could do was to offer to supply Marshall with pikes.[18]

By early January, Marshall had inched his way to Paintsville, only eighteen miles from Garfield's camp on George's Creek. Advance scouts from both sides met, traded shots and scurried back to their commanders with the news that a large enemy force was approaching. Marshall frantically dug in, fortifying the approach to Paintsville to meet the expected assault. His position was difficult. He could, conceivably, dash forward, surprise Garfield, and smash his way through his lines, but this was risky. And even if it should succeed, what could Marshall do then, except continue his aimless advance, with each step carrying him further from his base of supplies and closer to that of the enemy? He could sit in Paintsville and wait for the enemy to attack him, but supplies and morale were too low to survive a lengthy siege. To retire without a fight would be shameful, so Marshall decided to hold the line at Paintsville for the time being and hope for the best. If dis-

108

lodged, he vowed he would strike for the interior of Kentucky "and rouse the country as I go, or fall in the effort." At all costs he had to avoid the humiliation of a retreat from his native state, "for I know that if I am driven over the mountains again," he told his commander, "our cause in Kentucky is lost."[19]

Garfield, too, was in a quandary. From the reports of his scouts and spies he had pieced together a reasonably accurate picture of the forces moving against him. He knew that Marshall had between 2,000 and 2,500 men entrenched behind the Paintsville fortifications, and an additional three or four hundred cavalry at a separate camp on Jenny's Creek. He also knew that his own force was woefully weak in comparison. His only reliable soldiers were the thousand well-equipped but green recruits of the 42nd Ohio, and about five hundred poorly-armed Kentuckians in Colonel Moore's regiment. Most of the Kentucky units in his brigade were "little better than a well disposed, Union-loving mob," while his "demoralized, discouraged" Kentucky cavalry, untrained and unarmed, was worthless for any task more demanding than scout duty. The 40th Ohio under Colonel Cranor, which was supposedly hurrying with reinforcements, was lost somewhere in the Kentucky mountains. Garfield had heard no word from Cranor from the time he had left Louisville until January 1, when a weary scout staggered into camp with the news that Cranor was still about a week's march away.

According to a popular military maxim of the day, which Garfield must have known, an attacking force was supposed to outnumber the defenders by about three to two. By this rule of thumb Garfield needed three or four thousand men rather than the 1,500 he could muster. Furthermore, he keenly regretted his lack of artillery and was convinced that without it he could not dislodge Marshall.[20]

Had Garfield been looking for excuses to justify inactivity, he could certainly have found enough to satisfy even Buell. Instead, Garfield, a strong believer in "vigorous and well directed audacity," was eager for action. At a council of war, his staff recommended caution, but Garfield refused to listen to the "timid croaking of a lot of officers who were not willing to risk anything for the sake of success." He overruled their advice and prepared to advance on Marshall's works. Enraptured with the prospect of capturing an enemy army, he brushed aside all objections. "I cannot tell you how deeply alive to the scheme in hand are all the impulses and energies of my nature," he wrote his wife. "I begin to see the obstacles melt away before me, and the old feeling of succeeding in what I undertake gradually taking quiet possession of me."[21]

Too impatient to wait for the 40th Ohio to catch up with him, he ordered Cranor to cut south in the direction of Prestonburg. This would bring Cranor's regiment into the valley about ten miles south of Marshall's camp at Paintsville. Garfield was still obsessed with his original plan of surrounding and trapping Marshall's force. However Napoleonic this scheme may have seemed in his eyes, it was actually the height of recklessness. Cranor's regiment united with his own would have given his brigade a rough equality with the enemy. Instead, Garfield chose to divide his force in the face of a foe superior in numbers to each of his columns. To make matters worse, he had made no provision for cooperation between Cranor and himself. Indeed, he was not even sure of Cranor's location nor of the condition of his regiment. Rather than trapping Marshall, the most likely result of this maneuver would be the destruction of Garfield's own army should Marshall be so unobliging as to attack each of Garfield's isolated wings before the trap could be closed. When Garfield looked back on his campaign in the years after the war, he shuddered at his folly. "It was a very rash and imprudent affair on my part," he admitted. "If I had been an officer of more experience, I probably should not have made the attack. As it was, having gone into the army with the notion that fighting was our business I didn't know any better."[22]

In the comedy of errors that constituted the eastern Kentucky campaign, Garfield held the advantage. He may have had a weakness for overly elaborate plans and combinations, but Marshall had no plan at all. It has been said that God judges the sins of the warm-blooded and the sins of the cold-blooded on a different scale. Garfield was a warm-blooded commander, impetuous and overly optimistic, but not afraid to take a chance, and resourceful enough to exploit good fortune when it came his way. Marshall, huddled behind his trenches, allowed his opponent to seize the initiative at every turn. Marshall's works were thrown up at the foot of a hill on the main road three miles south of Paintsville. Three roads led into Paintsville. Uncertain which approach Garfield would take, Marshall posted pickets on each road about a half mile above the town. Within the town he stationed a regiment of infantry and an artillery battery, ready to rush to the defense of whichever route should be threatened.

By the 4th of January, Garfield had reached the outskirts of Paintsville. Cranor's location was still a mystery, but a timely cavalry reinforcement had brought the 18th Brigade to something close to full strength. This cavalry squadron actually belonged to Garfield's old political crony, Jacob Dolson Cox, now a major general in charge of operations in the neighboring Kanawha Valley. Cox, a good neighbor, lent some of his cavalry, commanded by Colonel William M. Bolles, to his friend for a few days.

The temporary nature of these reinforcements gave urgency to Garfield's moves; he could not afford a long siege but had to dislodge Marshall while he still had the loan of this squadron of cavalry. But which road should he take? Garfield decided on deception. On the morning of January 5 he divided his forces into three small detachments and sent them down each of the roads, placing cavalry in front to mask their size. The first group rode down the river road on the left. When they encountered the Confederate pickets, they made a show of noise and activity. As expected, the pickets reported their movements to the regiment in town, which came charging up the road to their defense. About an hour later Garfield's second detachment made a similar demonstration against the pickets on the hill road at the right. Marshall's reserve regiment quickly wheeled about to march to *their* aid. When they reached the left flank they heard of the attack on the center. Marshall's forces, weary from scurrying from threat to nonexistent threat, were now convinced that a large army was moving against them on all three roads. They fled to the security of their entrenchments in wild panic, leaving Paintsville deserted.

Behind his earthworks Marshall nervously peered up the

road for signs of the approaching enemy. While he was waiting, messengers brought reports of Cranr's force closing in on his position from the east. This vague rumor, magnified by his overactive imagination, was all that was needed to set Marshall packing. Prudent by nature, he easily convinced himself that his position was now untenable. Leaving his cavalry behind to disguise his intentions, he packed his wagons, burned what he could not carry, and retreated up the valley.[23]

This was the decisive moment of the campaign. From this point on Marshall could only keep retreating, with no logical place to stop this side of Virginia. Garfield's only task would be to prod him along more quickly. It was fortunate for Garfield that Cranor did not obey his order to block Marshall's line of retreat, for if Marshall had been trapped he would have been compelled to stand and fight. Instead, Garfield gained his objective without firing a shot. The bloodless victory at Paintsville was the true turning point. The more spectacular action that followed was all anticlimax.

Unaware that the enemy had flown the "trap" he was setting, Garfield picked his way cautiously through the empty streets of Paintsville. He dispatched his borrowed cavalry up Jenny's Creek to ferret out the rebel cavalry encamped there, while with the rest of his men he edged toward Marshall's fortification. Night had already fallen on the evening of January 7 when Garfield finally entered the deserted fort. He was struck by the signs of Marshall's hasty exit—"their camp fires were still smoldering, and the scattered remnants of their stores lay in sad confusion. The frozen tracks of thousands of feet were plain under the light of the new moon."

He had barely begun to savor the pleasure of sitting at Marshall's captured desk when an urgent message came from Colonel Bolles that he had contacted the enemy cavalry at Jenny's Creek. Garfield sent word to Bolles to hold off his attack until he could bring help. He assembled a detachment of four hundred men, ferried them across the Big Sandy on flatboats, and then struck out across the hill for Jenny's Creek. The plan was his old favorite—the flanking movenent. While Colonel Bolles occupied the enemy's attention, Garfield would sweep from behind and attack their rear. Even under ideal conditions this type of maneuver (to which Garfield seemed addicted) required delicate timing; at night, through unfamiliar country, its success was doubly uncertain.[24]

Garfield's men marched for thirteen miles, "wading streams of floating ice, climbing rocky steeps, and struggling through the half-frozen mud," until ready to collapse. Jenny's Creek, swollen by the recent snows, had to be bridged at two separate points. Garfield stood deep in the mud himself, directing the construction. They reached the junction point at midnight, only to find the enemy was gone. Instead of waiting for Garfield to arrive, Colonel Bolles had attacked the rebel cavalry on his own, killing six, wounding several more, and so scattering them that they were of no further use to Marshall.[25]

Garfield's march had been a wild goose chase, and his half-exhausted soldiers had to turn around and trudge the thirteen miles back to camp. As they marched, they grumbled about their officers, "mounted on good horses," who rode in comfort. Some of the men, unable to take another step, lay down behind fences, and would have frozen to death had they not been prodded awake and forced to move on. As they neared camp, a volley of bullets from the hills drove them scurrying for cover. This was the 42nd Ohio's baptism of fire, but the circumstances were far from heroic, since the barrage was from their own advance pickets who had mistaken them for the enemy.

Returning to camp, they found that Colonel Cranor and the 40th Ohio had arrived during their absence. Wisely disregarding Garfield's order to move towards Prestonburg across the enemy's line of retreat, Cranor had gone to Paintsville instead, where he could join the rest of the brigade. His arrival was timely, for it coincided with the departure of Colonel Bolles's borrowed cavalry.

Worn out by their long march across Kentucky, Cranor's men needed rest before they could be of much use, but the impatient Garfield could not wait. As he saw Marshall slip from his grasp, he yearned to pursue: "I felt as though we had . . . out-generalled the enemy, but I was unwilling he should get away without a trial of our strength." He assembled all of his men who were fit to march, about 1,100 in all, stuffed their haversacks with three days' rations, and at noon on January 9th

113

moved up the river road. "I fear we shall not be able to catch the enemy in a 'stern chase,' " he said, unconciously lapsing into the jargon of his canal days, "but we shall try."[26] Resorting once again to his pet flanking maneuver, he dispatched his cavalry to follow the fleeing enemy, while Garfield at the head of his footsoldiers planned to take a roundabout path to cut off their retreat.

The pursuit was hampered by a cold, sleety rain, and by the steady harassment of Marshall's rear guard. Felled trees blocked their path, and as they climbed over these obstructions hidden snipers fired pot shots and then melted back into the hills. These wild volleys did no damage, but Garfield, now alert to danger, picked his way "inch by inch" up the valley to the mouth of Abbot's Creek. As the tempo of skirmishing increased, Garfield realized that he was approaching the main body of Marshall's forces, and that a battle was imminent. He sent a courier back to Colonel Sheldon at Paintsville with an urgent plea to bring reinforcements. Shortly after dusk he led his men to the top of a high hill overlooking Abbot's Creek, where they bedded down for the night. The enemy was too near to permit the luxury of camp fires. Wrapped in their greatcoats, Garfield's men shivered through the night as an icy rain beat down upon them.[27]

That same night in Marshall's camp, the dispirited, retreating rebels decided they had had their fill of Kentucky. A round robin signed by Marshall's company captains urged him to quit the state for winter quarters in Virginia or Tennessee. They had no heart for the approaching battle; their hopes were set on home, not victory.[28]

At three o'clock on the morning of January 10th Garfield roused his men. After scraping the ice from their sleet-stiffened clothes, they ate a cheerless breakfast and within an hour were on the move once more. To Garfield, that morning presented "a very dreary prospect. The deepest, worst mud I ever saw was under foot, and a dense, cold fog hung around us as the boys filed slowly down the hillside." From the reports of local inhabitants, Garfield had gathered the impression that Marshall's main force was encamped some miles up Abbot's Creek. He therefore pushed on to Middle Creek, the next river upstream from Abbot's, hoping to entrench himself in a strong position across Marshall's line of march. As he moved up Middle Creek, signs of rebel activity became more prominent: shots were exchanged with mounting frequency, and a prisoner fell into his hands. Near midday Garfield reached the Left Fork of Middle Creek. As he rounded the point of a hill he saw before him a level plain filled with rebel cavalry who charged towards him and then fell back on the protection of a nearby ridge. Behind that ridge Garfield could see the glint of muskets. Instead of cutting off Marshall's retreat as planned, he had stumbled upon the main body of the enemy.[29]

Garfield drew his column to a halt and surveyed his position. Middle Creek ran through a deep, twisting valley, which occasionally broadened into an open stretch of level ground. The hill that Garfield's advance guard had just rounded commanded one end of such a plain. Half a mile across the valley rose a steep, crescent-shaped ridge, somewhere behind which Marshall's forces lay deployed. It was a strong defensive position, with the advantages of terrain and concealment in Marshall's favor. Garfield sent two companies up the slope of the ridge on his side of the valley to clear it of any rebels who might be stationed there. While they were climbing up the hill, Garfield in the valley below fretted with impatience. Too keyed up to stand passively by, he ordered the rest of his troops into battalion drill, "for the sake of bravado and audacity," as under the eyes of the puzzled Confederates they wheeled and marched as if on parade. By marching his men round and round the base of the hill Garfield also hoped to give the watching Confederates an exaggerated impression of his forces. Apparently the deception succeeded, for Marshall, never one to minimize difficulties, was convinced that Garfield commanded at least 5,000 men.[30]

Assured by his scouts that the hill was unoccupied, Garfield transferred his command post to the top, on a peak ominously named Grave Yard Point. His next step was to determine the precise location of the enemy, but Garfield's cavalry, which should have been available for reconnaissance, was still off somewhere chasing Marshall down the wrong valley. Garfield had to make do with what he had. He ordered his personal mounted escort, less than a dozen men in all, to ride across the plain in the hope of drawing the enemy's fire. As expected, Marshall's green troops nervously blazed away long before the riders came within range, revealing their position.[31]

The enemy's salvo had scarcely ceased reverberating before Garfield launched two Kentucky infantry companies under Captain Frederick A. Williams across the valley to dislodge the rebels. Holding cartridge boxes and rifles above their heads, they waded the icy, waist-deep creek, and dashed towards the opposing ridge. This was the opportunity for which Marshall's artillery captain had been waiting. For a month he had nursed his precious guns, hauling them over mountains, tugging them through mud, and delaying the advance of the entire brigade. Now, all his work could be justified. He zeroed in on the charging federals, waiting until they reached point-blank range before pulling the lanyard. With a high-pitched scream a twelve-pound shell lobbed high in the air, headed unerringly for Williams's advance guard—and plopped harmlessly into the mud. Marshall's shells were all duds, and although his cannon boomed noisily away throughout the rest of the afternoon, they inflicted no damage other than splattering a few federals with mud.

When Garfield's men had crossed the valley, they came to the base of an almost perpendicular ridge. Grabbing hold of projecting limbs and roots, they scurried up the hillside as best they could. The hill was too thickly wooded to permit elaborate tactical maneuvers. Each man climbed and fought at his own speed, firing and reloading as he advanced. From the safety of a large clump of rocks at the top of the ridge, the rebels let loose volley after volley at the exposed Union line, but the steep downhill angle of fire, combined with the natural tendency of green troops to aim high, caused most of their bullets to whiz wildly over their enemies' heads. Their fire inflicted a fearful toll on tree branches and low-flying birds, but it left Garfield's men virtually unscathed. Eventually they worked their way to the top of the hill, close enough to exchange curses as well as shots. Every now and then a group of rebels would detach themselves from their sheltering boulders and dash down the hillside. The Union troops would then fall back for a while, and then climb up once more.

116

This was the pattern of the day's fighting: a succession of uncoordinated charges and withdrawls, with a great deal of shooting and very little bloodshed—"a regular 'bushwhacking' battle." Garfield handled his troops with little imagination or enterprise, flinging them against the rebel line in driblets, never committing more than two or three hundred at any one time. He confined his attacks to Marshall's well-entrenched right flank; the Confederate left wing had no occasion to fire a shot during the entire day's action. Marshall, for his part, fought a completely passive battle, content, by and large, merely to maintain his original position. At various times during the afternoon a well-directed charge could have sent Garfield's disorganized men reeling down the valley, but Marshall did not really want a victory. He was satisfied to continue his retreat in peace.[32]

By the bloody standard of later battles, Middle Creek was a tame affair, but to the participants, few of whom had seen combat before, it was a dangerous and exciting afternoon. From his vantage spot on Grave Yard Point, overlooking the smoke-filled valley, Garfield had no doubt that he was witnessing "one of the most terrific fights which had been recorded in the war." By late afternoon Garfield feared that the battle was approaching its climax. As he vividly reconstructed the situation: "My reserve was now reduced to a mere handfull, and the agony of the moment was terrible. The whole hill was enclosed in such a volume of smoke as rolls from the mouth of a volcano. Thousands of gun flashes leaped like lightning from the clouds. Every minute the fight grew hotter. In my agony of anxiety I prayed to God for the reinforcement to appear." He was just on the point of leading his men in person on a final desperate charge when he looked behind him "and saw the Hiram banner sweep round the hill."

It was Colonel Sheldon, at the head of seven hundred reinforcements from Paintsville. Since receiving Garfield's message earlier that morning, they had been marching at a frenzied pace, their urgency stimulated by the distant sound of gunfire. When they finally hove into sight, they were greeted with a wild cheer from their embattled comrades, who took new heart at their appearance and charged once more up the hill, forcing the rebels back to the rocky summit. The sun was

117

setting when Sheldon's reinforcements began to pick their way across the muddy valley, and by the time they reached the foot of the hill it was too dark to fight. Fearing that his men might fire on one another in the dark, Garfield recalled his troops, leaving Marshall still ensconced upon his ridge. On this inconclusive note the battle of Middle Creek came to an end. "We had many hard fights for two years after," a veteran later told his grandchildren, "but Middle Creek was cold and cheerless, and a sharp fight."[33]

That night Garfield's men slept on their arms on Grave Yard Point, confident that the fighting would be renewed in the morning. In the middle of the night the sentries were startled by a brilliant flash from across the valley. It was Marshall burning his stores to lighten the load of his soldiers, who were then stealthily evacuating the scene of the battle. In the morning Garfield's cavalry, "ingloriously" absent during the fighting, finally arrived. Garfield sent them after the retreating enemy, but after a desultory pursuit they drifted back to camp empty-handed. Garfield knew that his supplies were too low to permit the brigade to follow Marshall in force, and since he certainly did not intend to remain on Grave Yard Point forever, he ordered his troops to fall back to replenish their stores and lick their wounds.

These wounds were remarkably light considering how sharp the fighting had been. Only twenty-one men had been wounded, three of them mortally.[34] The rebel dead, scattered over the field, were buried by Garfield's men where they fell. From the excited, boastful reports of his soldiers Garfield estimated that the Confederates had suffered 125 killed and at least that many wounded. He even implied that he had seen twenty-seven, or sixty, or eighty-five of these dead himself. Marshall, who was certainly in a better position to know, calculated his losses at no more than eleven killed and fifteen wounded. When he came to estimate Garfield's casualties, however, Marshall too displayed considerable imaginative flair, claiming to have killed 250 and wounded 300 more. "We saw his dead borne in numbers from the field," he insisted.[35]

It was not bluster alone that led Garfield to exaggerate the carnage at Middle Creek. This was his first battle and it left him shaken. "It was a terrible sight," he told his family, " . . . to walk over the battle field and see the horrible faces of the dead rebels stretched on the hill in all shapes and positions." Years later, he told William Dean Howells that "at the sight of these dead men whom other men had killed, something went out of him, the habit of his lifetime, that never came back again; the sense of the sacredness of life and the impossibility of destroying it."[36]

Yet, at other times Garfield seemed to regard the war as a glorious adventure, a grand test of manliness and virtue. "We have all frequently heard of the horrors of war," he told a Cleveland audience, "but we have not so often thought of the horrors of peace. Bad as war may be, greater evils sometimes emerge from a long peace. The nation's life becomes stagnant. . . ." He conceded that war had its horrors. "But," he added, "there is one advantage of this war that is evident. . . . The young men of the present day never saw or read of a time as grand as this. They never had such opportunities of doing great and noble actions."

Was Garfield's war hell or heroism? Another soldier, Captain Oliver Wendell Holmes, perhaps spoke for Garfield when he said, "the generation that carried on the war has been set aside by its experience . . . in our youth our hearts were touched with fire. It was given to us to learn at the outset that life is a profound and passionate thing." Holmes believed that the sufferings of war had made its participants better men. But suffering need not always be ennobling: it can teach the cheapness of human life as well as its value. Garfield was neither brutalized nor ennobled by his wartime acquaintance with violence and death, but he was changed. Along with his entire generation, Garfield had lost his innocence. His world—the sheltered, benevolent, providential world of prewar America— was shattered, and try as he might, it could never be reassembled.[37]

After tidying up the battlefield, the 18th Brigade withdrew to Prestonburg. Finding that that "mud-cursed village" had already been picked bare by Marshall, Garfield had to fall back all the way to Paintsville. Marshall interpreted (or professed to interpret) Garfield's return to Paintsville as an ad-

119

mission that the federals had been "signally and unmistakably whipped." Garfield's "footsore" but proud soldiers, however, never doubted that the victory had been theirs. "Soldiers of the Eighteenth Brigade!" their Colonel grandiloquently proclaimed, "I am proud of you. You have marched in the face of a foe of double your numbers. . . . With no experience but the consciousness of your own manhood, you have driven him from his stronghold, leaving scores of his bloody dead unburied. I greet you as brave men. Our common country will not forget you. I have recalled you from the pursuit that you may regain vigor for still greater exertions. . . . Officers and soldiers, your duty has been nobly done."[38]

Back in Ohio these sentiments were heartily applauded. Morale was low on the home front. "You scarce meet a man that dont look and talk gloomily," Garfield's friend J. H. Rhodes observed. To victory-starved Northerners the news from Middle Creek was a welcome relief from the constant humiliation of defeat and inactivity. Fathers and friends of the boys of the 42nd Ohio took Garfield to their hearts. "The feeling of the public for you has deepened remarkably," Rhodes reported. "I cannot begin to tell you how strongly you are fixed in their affections. . . . I have heard the most extravagant expectations of your future." Even Governor Tod let it be known that he had forgiven Garfield for opposing his nomination, and was ready to help further his career. From General Buell came an official commendation for "perseverance, fortitude and gallantry," and a movement was afoot, inspired by his friends in the Ohio Senate, to promote Garfield to general.[39]

To satisfy a public avid for details of its new hero, the press invented graphic accounts of Garfield shucking off his coat in the heat of battle and charging in his shirt sleeves while shouting, "Go in boys! Give em Hail Columbia!" Newspapers all over the North hailed "the bold lion in the path of Humphrey Marshall" for having led "the quickest and most thorough move since the breaking out of the Great Rebellion." Colonel Garfield, "the Kentucky hero, who so signally routed the Falstaffian Humphrey Marshall," was a ten-day wonder until news of Thomas's more spectacular victory over Zollicoffer at Mill Springs gave the public a new hero to admire.[40]

On the Confederate side of the lines, the "Falstaffian" General Marshall vigorously insisted that he, not Garfield, was the true victor of Middle Creek. "Let a few facts decide that question," he argued. "He came to attack and did attack, and he was in force far superior to mine. He did not move me from a single position I chose to occupy. At the close of the day each man of mine was just where he had been posted in the morning." If Garfield had won, he asked, why did he not pursue? Instead, he had fallen back to his base at Paintsville, "whence he came in mass to drive me out of the state. He returned without accomplishing his mission."[41]

There was some force to these arguments. Neither side, in truth, had come out of Middle Creek with much glory. But no amount of explanation could disguise the fact that Garfield was now well established in Kentucky while Marshall was leaving the state. Garfield may or may not have won the battle; he certainly won the campaign. Marshall insisted that hunger, "an enemy greater than the Lincolnites," was the only reason for his withdrawl, but he missed the point. Supplies were as important to military success as victory in battle. Garfield handled his supply problem with imagination and skill; Marshall trusted to luck. A truly enterprising commander would have solved his supply shortage (as some Confederate generals were to do) by attacking the federals and seizing their stores.[42]

Instead, Marshall was content to manufacture excuses and slink away. His only problem now was in which direction to retreat. His proper course should have been to head towards central Kentucky and join with the other Confederate column. By drawing Garfield away from his river supply line, Marshall could neutralize his opponent's main advantage. Originally this had been Marshall's intention, and he had grandly sworn to die in the attempt if need be. By mid-January, however, the situation in Kentucky had changed. With the defeat and death of Zollicoffer at Mill Springs, the Confederate invasion of Kentucky had collapsed, leaving Marshall with no place to go but back to Virginia. Besides, he was now thoroughly sick of Kentucky. Disease, hunger, and desertions had inspired him with "a personal hatred for the country," and he longed to return once more "to the haunts of cultivated men." Later that month, when he was ordered to fall back to Virginia through Pound Gap, he hastened to comply. Except for a small garrison left to guard the gap, eastern Kentucky was now free of Confederates.[43]

With Marshall's abrupt departure, Garfield found himself responsible for the administration of eastern Kentucky. Civil authority had collapsed, leaving Garfield and his soldiers as the only force in the valley capable of maintaining order. Although the territory under his command had never formally seceded from the Union, it had given aid and support to the Confederacy and needed to be brought back to loyalty. The phrase was not yet current, but Garfield was actually engaged in reconstruction.

This early in the war there was no settled official policy on the matter; Garfield had to feel his way. He had few precedents to guide him. In Missouri, General John C. Frémont had faced similar problems, but he had come to grief over the slavery issue. Fortunately for Garfield his problem was not complicated by the Negro question. There were no slaves in this remote corner of the South, but there were difficulties enough from the white population.

Garfield's Ohio soldiers were appalled by the squalor and ignorance they found in the valley. In isolated cabins they encountered families that had never seen a church, never heard of railroads, and who stared in open-mouthed amazement at a common jackknife. Such people had not the slightest understanding of the issues of the war that had intruded into their valley. Some had supported the South only because Confederate recruiters had told them the Yankees were coming to murder them all, but "who or what the Yankees were, they had no idea." Others, as was fitting in a region whose most famous families were the Hatfields and McCoys, had seized upon the confusions of wartime to settle their own private feuds, turning the valley, Garfield said, "into a home of fiends and . . . this war into a black hole in which to murder any man that any soldier from envy, lust or revenge, hated."

How could such a region—isolated, backward, lawless, ignorant, sullenly resentful of all authority, including that of the federal government—be brought back into a loyal relationship

122

with the Union? In later years this problem would be thrashed out on a larger scale and two basic lines of policy would emerge: the radical position advocating stringent punishment of treason, and the moderate approach favored by Lincoln. Later on, when he sat in Congress, Garfield was to become a spokesman for the radicals, but in 1862, faced with the actual problems of administration, he adopted a moderate policy. This policy was far more lenient than that of the Kentucky legislature itself. By state law all Kentuckians who fought for the Confederacy could be fined, imprisoned and deprived of citizenship, while teachers, jurors, preachers and all public officials were compelled to swear that they had never aided the rebellion.[44]

Whatever merit these measures may have had in the rest of the state, their value, Garfield realized, was dubious in the Sandy Valley, a region of such low political sophistication that parts of it had not yet even heard the news of Lincoln's election. Most of the valley's citizens left politics to their local courthouse politicians. These were the men whose opinions mattered, and without their support reconstruction was impossible. Although many of them had been tainted with rebel sympathies, Garfield did not punish or proscribe them. Instead, he merely ordered them to take an oath to defend the government, and placed them on bond for their future loyalty, confident that as realists they would now use their influence to support federal authority.

While pursuing this mild policy of reconciliation, Garfield showed no mercy to anyone, no matter what his politics, who disturbed the peace of the valley. To demonstrate his determination he even hanged one of his own Kentucky soldiers who had shot a rebel prisoner in cold blood.[45] Garfield realized that the valley needed peace and good order more than anything else. "While all force and rebellion against the government must be promptly put down," he argued, "it must also be remembered that the people in this valley are to live together as fellow citizens and neighbors after the war is over."

He announced his reconstruction policy in a "Proclamation" couched in the full-blown rhetoric that Southerners appreciated. "Fellow citizens," he declared,

123

> I have come among you to restore the honor of the Union and to bring back the old banner which you all once loved, but which by the machinations of evil men and by mutual misunderstandings has been dishonored among you. . . . To those who have taken no part in this war, who are in no way aiding or abetting the enemies of the Union—even to those who hold sentiments averse to the Union, but yet give no aid and comfort to its enemies—I offer the full protection of the Government, both in their persons and property.

He called upon all who had taken up arms against the government to return to their homes, promising them full amnesty.[46]

In the later years of the war, after Garfield had learned to hate the enemy, this sort of leniency would infuriate him when practiced by others, but at the time it served his purpose well. When they heard of the proclamation, Marshall's Kentucky soldiers, "men of no brains who had been scared into the rebel army and whose lives," according to Garfield, "are not worth to the country what the bullet would cost to kill them," quietly slipped away from Marshall's camp and returned shamefaced to their families.[47]

Within a remarkably short time Garfield had restored order to the valley. Except for scattered guerrilla activity in the distant reaches of his command there was scarcely a sign to indicate that only a few months earlier many had feared that this same region might throw in with the Confederacy. In part, this represented a personal triumph for Garfield. To the folks in the valley Garfield was almost as big a hero as he seemed in the newspapers back in Ohio. "I believe I have never made a more favorable impression of myself than I have upon . . . the citizens of this valley," Garfield confided to his wife, with a touch of pride. "They have the most extravagant notions of my doings here and hereafter."[48]

Had these Kentuckians known of Garfield's true intentions towards the South they might not have been so friendly. In his official pronouncements Garfield never mentioned the delicate subject of slavery, but the problem was never far from his thoughts. For public consumption he spoke of the war as an effort to restore the Union, but at heart he was still as strong an antislavery man as he had been back on the Reserve. Indeed, all his old evangelical fervor was now focused on the hope of emancipation. He realized, however, that the times were not yet ripe for an antislavery crusade. "Let the war be conducted *for the union*," he privately urged, "till the whole nation shall be enthused, inspired, transfigured with the glory of that high purpose." Let the war be sanctified by the blood of martyrs, let the full patriotism of the North be roused and marshalled, and then, and only then would the people realize that the preservation of the Union required the destruction of slavery. "That this war will result fatally to slavery I have no doubt. This assurance is to me one of the brightest promises of the future. But," he added, "I am equally clear that a declaration of emancipation by the administration would be a most fatal mistake." In God's own good time the logic of events would bring about the inevitable end of slavery.

Garfield viewed the war in an almost mystical light, as a great force rushing with inexorable purpose to an end which mere human agency could scarcely foresee, much less direct. "Gen. McClellan is weakly and wickedly conservative . . . and the President nearly as bad," he charged. "But out of the very weakness and timidity of our leaders I draw the hope that thus God has willed it—that He is the commander-in-chief of our armies, and there is no central iron will making ends for the war and effectively thwarting the Divine purpose. If McClellan will discipline and mobilize the people into armies, and let them meet the enemy, God will take care of the grand consequences."[49]

The war might be a holy crusade, but it could also be grand fun. Even in the midst of his solemn speculations concerning God's will, Garfield could be diverted by an opportunity—rare in the life of any man—to enact a favorite childhood daydream. After a week of violent rainstorms the Big Sandy River, the lifeline of Garfield's brigade, had risen so high that navigation was blocked. When Garfield saw his supplies dwindle to the point where his men were compelled to go on half-rations, he resolved to take matters into his own hands. Riding back to Catlettsburg he found that no riverboat captain could be induced to risk the swollen current. All persuasion failing, Garfield expropriated a rickety steamer, the *Sandy Valley*, and

125

forced the captain to weigh anchor. Not even the threat of Garfield's pistols could induce the captain to take the responsibility for such a lunatic voyage, so Garfield himself had to take the wheel. This was the moment of glory he had dreamed of so many years before as he had trudged along the canal towpath, and he made the most of it.

It was a rough trip. The river was clogged with floating debris, and the trees which usually lined its banks were nearly submerged. One careless twist of the rudder and these hidden trees could rake the bottom clean off the boat. The overburdened steamer paddled slowly upstream, making only two or three knots an hour against the current. Garfield manned the bridge around the clock, despite the captain's distraught protest that navigation was impossible in the dark. At one point the rushing current picked up the boat and whirled it over a hundred yards downstream before control could be regained. At another spot the *Sandy Valley* ran aground. Garfield ordered the crew to row to shore and stretch a cable from the banks. The terrified crew jumped into a small boat, made fast a line from the banks, and pulled the steamer loose. The *Sandy Valley* at last puffed into Paintsville, with the triumphant Garfield at the helm, just in time to feed the hungry soldiers. "So you see," he proudly told his wife, "I have turned sailor at last."[50]

In February, the 18th Brigade transferred its headquarters to Piketon (now Pikeville), fifty miles further up the Big Sandy. Garfield, who now had reason to distrust this capricious river on which so much depended, cached his stores on high ground, ten feet above the highest known flood level. For a while his precautions seemed needless, as the unpredictable river steadily dropped so low that Garfield feared it might dry up altogether. Then, without warning, the weather turned. During the night of February 22, after a succession of torrential rains, the Sandy overflowed its banks and inundated the town. With water lapping at their tent flaps, the frightened soldiers grabbed what they could carry and scrambled for high ground. Garfield tried to salvage his precious supplies but, as he confessed, "I was conquered for the first time." The surging river rose twelve feet in an hour, and over sixty feet during the night. When morning came Garfield's men looked out over a lake which covered what had been the town of Piketon. Two steamboats were moored in the main street, while floating trees and log cabins careened by.[51]

The waters receded as quickly as they had risen, but Garfield expected further trouble. "I tremble for the sickness and suffering which must follow. Four battles would not be so disastrous to us," he predicted.[52] Just as he feared, disease crept into camp in the wake of the flood. By the middle of March sickness had depleted the brigade to skeleton strength. It was a rare company that could muster as many as forty men fit for duty. Surgeon Joel F. Pomerene's medicine chest was worse than useless, and the men (with reason) feared the hospital more than disease. Garfield, a firm believer in "the power of will to resist disease," tried to encourage his men back to health. When two of his old Hiram boys came to him in tears, begging to be sent home, Garfield threw his arms around them and told them that he had been wrestling with sickness himself, "as with a giant enemy," and they must do the same. Within a few weeks both boys were dead.

Before the epidemic had run its course, over fifty Ohio boys had found Kentucky graves. As he helplessly watched them sicken and die, Garfield was tormented by guilt. "I declare to you there are fathers and mothers in Ohio that I hardly know how I can endure to meet," he confessed to his wife. "A noble young man from Medina County died a few days ago. I enlisted him, but not till I had spent two hours in answering the objections of his father who urged that he was too young to stand the exposure. He was the only child. I cannot feel myself to blame in the matter, but I assure you I would rather fight a battle than to meet his father."

Until now it had been an easy war for Garfield, a trifle uncomfortable at times, but not, on the whole, unpleasant. Now, for the first time, he was face to face with the senseless misery of war. "This fighting with disease is infinitely more horrible than battle," he groaned. "This is the price of saving the Union. My God, what a costly sacrifice!" He now had a personal stake in the war, an implacable determination that those responsible for the death of his boys would not escape lightly. "If the severest vengeance of outraged and insulted law is not visited upon those cursed villians who have instigated and led this rebellion," he vowed, "it will be the most wicked crime that can be committed. The blood of hundreds of the 18th Brigade will, before summer, be crying from the ground to God for vengeance."[53]

At the height of the epidemic, by a touch of ironic timing, Garfield learned of his promotion to brigadier general. The commission, which was dated from his victory at Middle Creek, had been engineered by his Ohio political colleagues, with the assistance of Secretary of the Treasury Salmon P. Chase (who smugly took full credit for the promotion), but it was not entirely a political appointment. Garfield had been doing the work of a brigadier general for some time and had already proven that he could handle the post satisfactorily.

Garfield had not angled for the promotion personally. His old superstition against place-seeking was as strong as ever. This refusal to promote his own fortunes was not due to a lack of ambition, but to a dread of nemesis. Garfield put his trust in his destiny, and when good fortune struck he always tried to placate fate by disclaiming personal responsibility. In this instance he insisted, in a phrase that would run through his career like an incantation, "I have never by word or written sentence made any approach to forwarding the movement or inviting it. Had I done so I should feel that I was marring the plans of God, and should not succeed."[54]

The new stars on his shoulder were a cause for regret as well as pride. Always a sentimentalist, Garfield was pained by the thought that his promotion might tear him away from his boys of the 42nd. After all they had been through together since the days at Camp Chase, Garfield had developed a strong attachment to his regiment. "I cannot tell you," he confided to a friend, "how strange[ly] and painfully my whole being has been drawn out in love for that body of men. The very sound of the word Forty Second has a strange charm in it. It seems to me that I could never love any other like it." On the other hand, Garfield looked forward to the chance of exercising a wider command. Cooped up in "this God-forsaken valley," he half feared that the war was passing him by. Numerous signs seemed to indicate that the rebellion might soon be crushed, perhaps as early as June, and he did not want to sit out the remaining days of the war in an obscure theater of battle.[55]

Before he could leave the valley, however, he still had one job left to finish. Rebel marauders were terrorizing the lower reaches of the valley. Reports of atrocities had filtered back to Garfield's headquarters: tales of men shot down at their doorsteps by masked riders, of Union sympathizers hanged in the sight of their horrified families, of cattle maimings and barn burnings. Garfield dispatched an expedition of forty men after these rebel guerrillas, but the rebels knew this country better than they did, and when Garfield's men blundered their way through the mountains they were neatly bushwacked, and had to limp back to camp. Despite his overwhelming superiority in arms and men, Garfield was helpless before this handful of raiders. He could not dissipate his force in futile hunts down every valley; he had to destroy the enemy at its source. The only effective way to stop the guerrillas was to smash the rebel garrison at Pound Gap which gave them arms and encouragement.

Pound Gap, the last remaining Confederate toehold in eastern Kentucky, was manned by a bedraggled contingent of fewer than three hundred men. The Gap was located on the border of Kentucky and Virginia, in the middle of some of the wildest country in the entire region. To approach the gap from the Kentucky side required a hard climb across rugged mountains and through tangled thickets. These natural barriers had been augmented by the Confederates, who had been busy for weeks tearing down bridges and blockading the roads with fallen trees.

On March 14th, Garfield rode out from Piketon at the head of a picked force of six hundred infantry and one hundred cavalry. In order to preserve the advantage of surprise, they followed a roundabout trail, cutting across obscure bridle paths, and wading through the beds of gushing creeks. By the morning of the fifteenth, Garfield's band was assembled at the foot of the mountain leading to the gap. Hesitant to risk his force in a frontal attack on the Confederate breastworks, Garfield divided his troops. The plan was his old standby—the flank

129

movement. The cavalry would take the main road to the rebels' works and distract their attention, while the six hundred infantrymen would sidle around the mountain, climb an unguarded path and surprise the enemy from the rear, cutting off their retreat and capturing the entire garrison. This maneuver, so bold yet so simple, never failed to appeal to Garfield, despite the fact that it never managed to work out as planned, nor would it in this instance.

A light rain was falling when Garfield's men began their climb. As they climbed higher, it turned to sleet, and then to a heavy snowfall. On to the summit pushed Garfield's six hundred, in an eerie silence as the snow muffled their footsteps and a thick white fog shrouded their movements. Before the column reached the peak, the sound of gunfire told them that the cavalry had already begun its attack. The trap had been sprung prematurely. It was not the cavalry's fault but Garfield's, for he had missed the right path in the storm. Abandoning all thought of surprise, his infantry ran at full speed towards the Confederate camp, but the rebels were forewarned. They fled in haste, with only a feeble show of resistance, leaving behind everything that could not be scooped up on the run. As Garfield's men rounded the gap they saw only the fleeing backs of the enemy. They had time for a few hurried vollies but, as one of Garfield's disappointed warriors complained, "it was like shooting birds on the wing." For the first, and possibly the only, time in the war Garfield himself fired upon the enemy. "I fired one shot among them," he told his wife, "and the boys say I killed one but I think and hope not."[56]

Most of the rebel garrison scampered to the safety of Virginia. Garfield sent his cavalry in pursuit, but after a six-mile chase through wild country, they returned to the gap, confident that the dispersed garrison would keep on running for the rest of the day. Garfield's unscathed soldiers sat down in the Confederate mess hall to finish the dinner the rebels had left behind. It was a poor meal but, under the circumstances, delicious. That night they slept in the enemies' beds, and in the morning they loaded themselves with bacon, blankets, and other loot and returned to Piketon after burning all the buildings and destroying what they could not carry. "In most respects," Garfield concluded, "it is the completest thing we have accomplished, but it lacks blood to give it much place among the movements of the time." It was also, though he did not realize it, Garfield's last independent command, the last time he would lead his own troops in battle.[57]

By the time the fleeing rebel garrison reached Marshall's Virginia headquarters to spread their version of the raid, it had begun to assume the proportions of a major onslaught. Marshall, as usual, flew into a panic. Although he tried to minimize the loss of the Gap as an affair "of no earthly consequence," he was convinced that it was the signal for a full-scale invasion of Virginia. In nervous haste he called out the militia, urged the declaration of martial law, and renewed his pleas for at least 10,000 reinforcements to meet Garfield's "7,500 men," which force he imagined was even then on the march against him.[58]

Garfield, of course, had no such plans. He was finished with eastern Kentucky, and wanted nothing so much as a change of scenery. His future, however, was the subject of a tug-of-war within the Union command. A dashing, successful brigadier general was very much in demand, particularly if he had political connections. General Frémont, always on the lookout for a like-minded associate, put in a bid for Garfield, while Secretary Stanton gently hinted to Buell that Garfield's talents should be put to better work than patrolling a useless valley. Buell replied that he was preparing an extensive move against Cumberland Gap, and that he was considering placing Garfield in charge of the operation. It would have been a choice assignment, involving full command of ten infantry regiments, five companies of cavalry, and an enviable chance to win fresh glory, but Buell unaccountably changed his mind only two days later, and merely sent Garfield instructions to return to Louisville with the 42nd Ohio to receive further orders.

Near the end of March, the 42nd Ohio, veterans now, marched out of Piketon, happy to leave the valley they had entered only four months before, Their faces broadened into wide grins and they gaily cheered as the regimental band, echoing their thoughts, struck up a familiar gospel song, "Oh, Aint I glad to Get Out of the Wilderness."[59]

CHAPTER EIGHT

AT THE FRONT

All winter an endless rain had dripped from the dreary slate-gray sky, but with spring, warmth and life slowly returned to Kentucky. To Union soldiers the spring of 1862 was doubly welcome, for it signaled the beginning of fresh activity. Winter camps were struck, and marching men clogged the roads leading south. Hopes ran high, and not without cause, for Kentucky had been the only bright spot of the war for the Union thus far. The winter had begun with Kentucky on the verge of secession; it ended with Confederate troops in full retreat from all parts of the state.

Garfield had contributed, in a small way, to this result, but his victories were soon overshadowed by more substantial gains. While Garfield had been chasing the last tattered remnants of Humphrey Marshall's forces from eastern Kentucky, other Union commanders were also driving the enemy before them. The victories of Thomas at Mill Springs, and Grant at Forts Henry and Donelson, had cleared the way to Nashville and beyond. With their line of defense shattered, the Confederates were compelled to evacuate central Tennessee while their commander, Albert Sidney Johnston, hastily concentrated all his available forces at Corinth, Mississippi.

Only twenty miles further north, near a bluff called Pittsburg Landing, Grant was collecting a large Union army, which awaited only the arrival of reinforcements from Buell to begin its march on Corinth. The stage was set for the great battle for the West, a battle which many hoped would end the rebellion.

The impending battle was the reason for Garfield's recall
from the Sandy Valley. When he reached Louisville, he found
that Buell had already gone ahead with the main body of the
army, leaving behind orders that Garfield should join him as
soon as possible on the road to Pittsburg Landing. Much to
Garfield's dismay the orders were for him alone: his boys of
the 42nd Ohio were needed elsewhere. This sudden separation
seemed to Garfield "the severest trial I have suffered since the
war began." He left for the front quickly and silently, unable to
bring himself to say good-bye to his old regiment. At three
o'clock on the morning of April 4th, he caught up with Buell
outside of Nashville and an hour later he was introduced to
his new command, the 20th Brigade of the Army of the Ohio.[1]

Compared to these raw soldiers fresh out of training camp,
Garfield was a grizzled veteran. There were four regiments in
the 20th brigade, none of which had yet seen action. So far,
their military experience had been confined to mending roads
and bridges. The nucleus of the brigade consisted of two Ohio
regiments, the 64th and 65th, the so-called "Sherman Brigade," which had been recruited from the Mansfield region
by Senator John Sherman. Attached to these were the 13th
Michigan and 51st Indiana volunteers. The brigade had been
under the command of Colonel Charles G. Harker, a young
West Point trained officer, who could scarcely conceal his irritation at being superseded on the eve of battle by a political
general.[2]

Garfield, too, was far from happy with his new assignment.
By nature he was deeply suspicious of any change, even a promotion, and now he was filled with foreboding. "The thought
. . . of taking command of nearly 4000 men who had never
been tried in battle, who were strangers to me . . . ," he said,
"made the future a gloomy one." Later that evening, when the
regimental bands from his new Ohio units gathered before his
tent for a welcoming serenade, Garfield still refused to be consoled: "no matter what other regiments may be to me I mourn
like a bereaved lover for my dear old 42nd."[3]

At the very moment that the regimental bands were serenad-
ing their new commander, many miles away near Pittsburg
Landing Confederate troops were quietly infiltrating the

woods near the Union camp. While Grant was marking time, waiting for Buell, Albert Sidney Johnston had seized the initiative. He knew that his 40,000 men could not withstand the combined forces of Grant and Buell. Rather than wait in Corinth for the inevitable siege, he decided to launch a bold surprise attack while he still held something close to numerical equality with the enemy. Union commanders were completely unaware of Johnston's plan. Their minds were so set on their own offensive that they had neglected to take even the most elementary precautions. The unsuspecting Grant had pitched his headquarters at Savannah, ten miles downstream, out of touch with the main body of his army, and the soldiers on the field were encamped on open, exposed ground, since hiding behind trenches was scorned as unmanly.

At dawn on the morning of April 6th, near a church called Shiloh, the full weight of the Confederate army suddenly fell upon a sector of the thinly guarded Union camp. Some regiments were overwhelmed before they could get up from breakfast. Others simply disintegrated, but enough remained· to improvise a gallant defense which slowed, if it did not stop, the Southern charge. By late afternoon the Confederates were within sight of the Tennessee River, and Grant's army was in danger of annihilation. But confusion in the Confederate battle plan, the untimely death of Johnston, and the stubborn rearguard defense of Illinois's General Benjamin Prentiss all conspired to stop the Confederates short of their goal. By nightfall the exhausted armies had ground to an inconclusive halt. The next day's action would be decisive, and the outcome hung on whether Northern reinforcements would arrive in time.

On the morning the battle began, Buell's army was still stretched out for miles along the roads of west Tennessee. Garfield's brigade was camped at Turkey Creek, about halfway along the line of march, and some thirty-five miles from Savannah. Roused at four a.m., his men grumbled around the morning campfires. From the clammy predawn darkness they could tell that it would be another gray, wet day. They had been marching for a week already, their first strenuous activity since leaving camp, and many were so stiff as to be almost crippled. By midmorning they had settled into the mindless routine of men on the march, one step automatically following the other, when far from the west came a continuous rumble like distant thunder. The more experienced soldiers identified the sound as artillery, and as the word passed down the line, the men quickened their pace. A few hours later their suspicions were confirmed when a frantic courier, his horse lathered with foam, galloped through the ranks and handed a dispatch to General Wood, the division commander. Instantly, the line was ordered to halt and lighten for the march. Superfluous baggage —blankets, overcoats, and knapsacks—was tossed on the side of the road, and each man filled his canteen with fresh water, his haversack with hardtack and bacon, and stuffed twenty extra Minie balls in his pockets. Leaving behind a small guard to collect the discarded supplies, the brigade moved out at quickstep toward the sound of gunfire.

Relieved of their heavy load and stirred by the prospect of danger, Garfield's brigade pushed on briskly, all thought of weariness, for the moment, gone. Gone too were the easy jests which usually lightened the monotony of march. All faces were grim as the untested, frightened boys reassured themselves and each other with mighty boasts of bravery. "We appeared to be chiefly distressed by the fear that it would be over before we could get there . . .," one of the men later recalled. "I doubt if the world has ever seen more heroic battalions than were ours—at least at that distance from the field."

Nightfall brought no respite. After a hasty supper the brigade stumbled forward over stump-strewn, rut-ruptured roads, "through darkness so absolute that no one could see his nearest neighbor." Shortly before midnight a violent lightning storm broke overhead. "The road was flooded. There were holes into which men sank to their knees in water and mud. The flashes of lightning disclosed to view for an instant a mass of struggling men, drenched and drenched again, floundering in the mire and falling over rocks and stumps which impeded the way." Artillery caissons stuck fast in the mire and the terrified horses refused to budge them loose. After futile attempts to pull the guns and wagons free, they were left behind as hopeless. The only consolation the men found during the whole long, wet night was that the officers were compelled to dismount and trudge along beside them.

When morning finally came, they halted for a breakfast of

soggy hardtack. By this time they were too tired, too wet, to be afraid of the battle. "As nearly as I can recall our state of mind that wretched morning—and my recollection is sufficiently vivid —," Sergeant Hinman later recounted, "we were considerably in doubt whether the Union was worth saving or not." In the middle of breakfast the sound of guns, nearer now, began anew, and the men gulped down their coffee and took up the march again. Along the road they passed lines of grim-faced, anxious Southern civilians silently glaring at the men hurrying to kill their sons and neighbors. At ten o'clock they reached Savannah. The little riverfront town had been pressed into service as a headquarters, depot, and hospital for the Union army, and it seethed with frantic activity: officers rode pell-mell through the crowded streets, surgeons operated on kitchen tables, and wounded and dying men lay groaning on front lawns. Pushing their way through a mob of stragglers, Garfield's brigade reached the waterfront and boarded a steamboat (whose decks were slippery with the blood of the wounded) to take them to the battlefield.[4]

Garfield was the first of the brigade to jump ashore at Pittsburg Landing, with Colonel Harker but a step behind. The men scampered off the boat and stood in amazement, their senses numbed by the sights, sounds, and smells of the greatest battle that had ever been fought on the Western hemisphere. They had no time to gape, for as soon as they were assembled on shore a staff officer ordered them on the double-quick to the front, five miles away.

Earlier that morning, with the arrival of reinforcements from Lew Wallace and Buell, the battle had finally turned in favor of the North. The beaten Confederates, their bolt shot, were pulling back towards Corinth. As Garfield's brigade ran to meet them, across fields which had been fought over bloodily for two days, they passed piles of blue and gray-clad corpses lying side by side in tangled heaps. "Hundreds of stretcher bearers were carrying the wounded from the field, and ambulances were hurrying to and fro. . . . The dead lay thickly about, and among them were the desperately wounded, screaming and moaning with pain. . . ."[5]

Garfield rode at the head of his troops, occasionally dashing forward and recklessly exposing himself to fire. A stray shell narrowly missed him and turned an unlucky officer only a few feet away into "a quivery mass of bleeding flesh."[6] Soon the brigade came close to the front. Spent bullets whizzed all about them, injuring some, but not seriously. Garfield ordered a halt while his men inspected and loaded their weapons. As they ran to join the battle they heard a tremendous cheer rise from the Union lines, and when they reached the front they saw that the last rebels were running away. The Battle of Shiloh was over, and it had been won without them.

The brigade pursued the enemy for a few miles, but before it could make contact, it was ordered back to guard the battlefield. After having been caught napping once, Union commanders were obsessed with the fear of another surprise attack. Beauregard and his army were streaming back to Corinth with all the fight out of them, but the Northerners were taking no chances. Combat units were sent to the rear for rest, and the "fresh" soldiers of the 20th Brigade were detailed for sentry duty. This meant another wet, sleepless night, even more exhausting than the preceding one, for it lacked the stimulus of excitement. Guns primed, the weary men peered into the blackness for signs of the enemy, while officers conferred in hushed whispers, and orderlies stood alert for orders. No fires were permitted, and the drenched men began to regret the blankets and overcoats they had so blithely tossed by the Tennessee roadside. Two Northern boys hovered over a badly wounded rebel, impatiently waiting for him to die so that they could take his blanket. Off to one side, Garfield and Harker sat on a log, huddled together under one dripping blanket, waiting for the night to end.

It was not until midnight the next night, after sixty-eight continuous hours of duty, that the 20th Brigade was finally allowed to rest, and it was not until April 16 that their baggage, including tents and fresh clothes, finally caught up with them. By this time the "siege" of Corinth had begun. General Henry Halleck, commander of all Union armies in the West, personally took charge, assembling over 100,000 men to dislodge Beauregard's considerably smaller force. His bulging forehead and ready supply of military maxims had earned Halleck the nickname "Old Brains," but at Corinth his caution outran his wisdom. Halleck was determined not to repeat Grant's neglect of fortifications, so for two months his vast army crept towards the enemy, throwing up earthworks each step of the way—virtually tunneling its way to Corinth.

To Garfield's brigade, the prolonged march to Corinth proved a greater disaster than battle. Sleeping for weeks on end in wet, filthy uniforms, on a campsite that was actually a burial ground for thousands of decaying corpses, many of the men under Garfield's command succumbed to "camp fever." The rest endured, as best they could, the endless monotony of picket duty, drill, and maneuver. When he wrote home, Garfield tried to make light of his discomforts, assuring his worried mother, "I have become so accustomed to living in a tent that I would hardly know how to get along in a . . . house. You would be amused to see my furniture. My bed consists of crutches driven into the ground, and small poles laid across. A few leaves spread over them, and one blanket over and another over makes me very comfortable."[7]

But to his friends, Garfield bitterly unburdened his indignation at seeing this magnificent army go to waste. This indignation rose even higher with the absurd conclusion of the Corinth campaign. For weeks Halleck's mammoth army had inched its way towards the Confederate stronghold, carefully preparing all the proper textbook parallels and investments until it was finally positioned perfectly. Garfield's men were nerving themselves for the expected battle, when into their lines early on the morning of May 30 sauntered an old Negro gaily shouting, "Dey's all gone, boss, shuah! Ole Burygard and his army done lef las night. . . . You-uns can jess walk right into de town if yer wants to!" Beauregard had read the textbooks too, and he had no intention of allowing himself to be trapped. He nimbly evacuated his entire army while the fatuous Halleck was blindly perfecting his dispositions, leaving the frustrated Union Army with nothing to show for two months' labor but the possession of an abandoned town.[8]

Garfield was disgusted with this "disgrace upon Generalship," and he fumed even more when he read in Halleck's dispatches that Corinth was claimed as a glorious Union victory. "I am nearly disheartened at the way in which the war is conducted here . . . ." he sadly declared. "There seems to be neither Generalship nor patriotism at the heads of the armies."[9] For this state of affairs Garfield, like so many other citizen-soldiers, blamed West Point. "If the Republic goes down in blood and ruins," he solemnly warned, "let its obituary be written thus: 'Died of West Point.' " His explanation was simple—officers trained at West Point did not want to win the war if victory meant the end of slavery. After all, he reasoned, "a command in the army is a sort of tyranny and in a narrow and ignoble mind engenders a despotic spirit which makes him sympathize with slavery and slave holders." West Point villainy was compounded of equal parts of incompetence and treason. His commanding officer, General Wood, seemed to Garfield a typical West Point product: "a very narrow, impetuous, proslavery man in whose prudence, and patriotism and brains I have but very little confidence; and a shamefully rough, blasphemous man, quite destitute of fine or manly feelings." But Wood was only part of a concerted plot, "amounting almost to a conspiracy among leading officers—especially those of the Regular Army—to taboo the whole question of anti-slavery and throw as much discredit upon it as upon treason."[10]

Here was the heart of Garfield's quarrel with the regular army—the Negro Question, or in the inelegant language of the day, "What to do with Sambo." Garfield knew what to do. As the representative of the Western Reserve, the inheritor of decades of antislavery fervor, he naturally looked upon the war as the culmination of that crusade. Many of the older officers, however, hated Negroes, abolitionists, and rebels with equal passion. To them the war as not an antislavery crusade at all and Garfield suspected they were more anxious "to keep the 'Peculiar Institution' from harm than anything else."[11] If this was treason, as Garfield seemed to think, it was widespread. It was shared by a large segment, possibly a majority, of Northern opinion, and it even had official sanction. At this stage of the struggle, the official war aims of the North remained merely the restoration of the Union, without interference in the "established institutions of the States," i.e., slavery. A resolution to this effect had been approved by a nearly unanimous Congress a year before, and the same resolution had just been adopted as the platform of the Ohio Union party.

Garfield, of course, disagreed. As he saw the war drag on, as he felt the deep hostility of the Southerners he met, as he witnessed the bumbling efforts of seemingly half-hearted Union commanders, he found himself "coming nearer and nearer to downright Abolitionism." If slavery was the war's cause, then only the end of slavery could hasten the war's end. He swore a solemn oath: "Before God I here record my conviction that the spirit of Slavery is the soul of the rebellion and the incarnate devil which must be cast out before we can trust in any peace as lasting and secure." The Lord, Garfield knew, moved in mysterious ways, and even in these dark days he saw His hand at work. "It may be a part of God's plan," he reflected, "to lengthen out this war till our whole army has been sufficiently outraged by the haughty tyranny of pro-slavery officers and the spirit of slavery and slaveholders with whom they come in contact that they can bring back into civil life a healthy and vigorous sentiment that shall make itself felt at the ballot box and in social life for the glory of humanity and the honor of the country."[12]

This reference to the ballot box was not haphazard. Garfield's thoughts were beginning to turn back to politics. With each mail came letters from home imploring him to run for Congress. The indefatigable Harmon Austin, always ready to promote Garfield's interests, was "feeling about quietly," and had uncovered considerable favorable sentiment.

The time was ripe. Recently the political balance of the 19th district had been upset by redistricting. The strength of the incumbent, John Hutchins, had been reduced by the addition of two new counties in which he had little popularity, but no one was quite sure of the political complexion of the new district. Even without the uncertainties brought on by redistricting, Hutchins faced a hard fight, especially with the radicals who had never forgiven him for unseating their idol, Josh Giddings, four years earlier.

A number of hopeful Republicans dreamed of fishing in these muddied political waters, but only Garfield enjoyed more than local prominence. J. H. Rhodes was so confident of his friend's success that he urged Garfield to resign his commission in order to campaign personally, assuring him that if he were only on the scene his nomination and election "would almost be a spontaneity."[13]

Garfield was tempted. "I would, of course, rather be in Congress than in the army, if there is to be no more active service," he admitted, "for I have no taste for the dull monotony of Camp life." Nor was he eager to continue in the army if that meant taking "any place which West Point management will be likely to assign me." If, as he believed, "the war in the west is substantially ended, and its future operations are to consist of holding garrisons here and there, and keeping down guerrillas," then he could honorably retire from a military career that would be "doing the country little good and myself but little credit."[14]

On the other hand, he had promised Almeda Booth not to use the military as a stepping-stone to political preferment. Would there not be a risk that his constituents might resent his leaving the army for personal gain while their own sons were still fighting? "I believe I entered the service with patriotic motives, . . ." he insisted. "I cannot for a moment think of taking any course which may even by inference throw a shadow of suspicion upon those motives, as being for political and demagogical purposes."[15] Nor did he relish the prospect of being "hauled over the coals of political persecution again." Furthermore, he added, "it would be almost a mockery for me to lay any plans for a life over which I have so little control and on the continuance of which I have no pledges." No, he concluded, "I will take no steps whatever in the matter. . . ." And yet (the thought could not be repressed): "Should the people, of their own motion, without any suggestions from me, choose to nominate me for Congress, I should esteem it a mark of high favor." He left the entire matter to the discretion of his friends. This was all his friends needed to hear. They expected Garfield to wrestle with his conscience (and probably expected him to win). They had nursed him through the same agony many times in the past, and they knew what it meant. It meant that Garfield was will-

141

ing, but that he preferred (because of his peculiar superstition) to avoid taking responsibility.[16]

His friends gladly assumed the responsibility that Garfield shunned, and almost immediately a Garfield-for-Congress movement was set in motion. Letters and editorials appeared in local papers praising Garfield for his humble origins and his brilliant military career. *"Through all his record is clean,"* testified one enthusiastic supporter. "It is the record of a man who has left at every step *complete satisfaction, . . ."* and he went on to depict the candidate as a tireless superman: "Endowed with great strength, an iron constitution and sleepless energy, he toils on without weariness, and when he sleeps it seems more from habit of boyhood than from necessity."

In every corner of the district Rhodes, Austin, State Senator John Q. Smith, along with many other of Garfield's political champions, were busy hatching plans and lining up support. After sounding out various local notables, including most editors, Rhodes was confident that they could win without Garfield's lifting a finger. "From all I can see it seems to me *now* that your nomination and election are a dead certainty." Garfield received the news with studied equanimity. Whatever the outcome, he replied, "Be assured I am not anxious in the matter, and shall lose no sleep, nor have one Diarreah less or more. . . ."[17]

In the meantime, of course, there was still a war to be fought, not that Garfield was doing much fighting at the moment. Just before the canny Beauregard had pulled out of Corinth, he had ordered his rear guard to tear down all the mileposts and road signs. The gesture was ingenious, but hardly necessary since Halleck was already too thoroughly muddled for signposts to straighten him out. "Strangely enough," Garfield marveled ten days after the occupation of Corinth, "we do not yet know where the rebel army have gone." Instead of finding out and pursuing in force, Halleck scattered his great army in all directions, dissipating its strength on secondary objectives. Wood's Division, including the 20th Brigade, was sent east in the general direction of Chattanooga, repairing roads and bridges along the way. In a leisurely, almost idyllic fashion, they strolled across northern Mississippi and Alabama, through Iuka, Tuscumbia, Decatur, and other Southern towns without once stumbling across any sign of the rebel army.[18]

Garfield, who regarded war as something to fight and be done with, could not enjoy this excursion while the nation was undergoing what he regarded as its greatest hour of trial since Washington had shivered through the winter at Valley Forge. He yearned to see an "overwhelming blow, struck home *bloodily and soon. . . ."* Instead, as he noted with exasperation: "We have rebuilt over a hundred miles of Rail Road and are now lying still with no apparent aim or future purpose."[19] He whiled away the time with the usual aimless diversions of camp life: playing games, swapping stories, preaching sermons and fiddling with his uniform. His wide-rimmed, high-crowned field hat was particularly bothersome because, as a friend pointed out, Garfield's head was so large "that a hat, round all the way up gave the impression of a hat walking away with a man." He solved the problem by breaking down the top of the crown into a deep, M-shaped wedge, inaugurating a fashion that would sweep the Union army. Such imitation was flattering, but this was not the sort of fame Garfield had sought when he entered the army. Instead, confined to "the inglorious quiet of a Brigade camp," he feared that his military talents might rust and his reputation tarnish. The public he knew, was fickle and could easily forget the hero of the Sandy Valley. "I have been so thoroughly dead militarily since I came to the Tennessee," he complained to his wife, "that I hardly see how I can be sufficiently remembered to make my return a matter of comment."[20]

He managed, however, to put his inactivity to some good use by ferreting out Union sympathizers and enlisting them into the army. Hearing rumors of a band of Unionists hiding in the caves of the Sand Mountains, he sent Colonel Abel D. Streight of his command to investigate. In three days, nearly four hundred loyal mountaineers came down from the hills to join the old flag: "The only regiment of white men," Garfield later claimed, "raised in any of the [Southern] states. . . ." Apart from this one encouraging note, however, Garfield

143

found nothing but hostility as he marched through the heart of the Confederacy. "In one thing, I fear we have been mistaken," he concluded. "We have believed in a suppressed Union sentiment in the South. It is my opinion formed against my will that there is not enough strong union (unconditional) feeling south of Ky. to plant the seeds of public faith in."[21]

The more he saw of the South, the more Garfield was convinced that the eradication of slavery and the destruction of the planter class were necessary before the Union could be restored. As he marched past rich plantations heavy with grain, "which the planters boast openly is intended to feed the Southern Army," he burned to make these proud Southerners pay for the war they had started. He wanted to carry the war to Southern civilians, but his commanders, bound by the traditional rules of warfare they had learned at West Point, refrained. In the later years of the war, after bitter passions had been aroused, the fine distinctions between soldiers and civilians would be forgotten, and many Union commanders, especially Sherman and Sheridan, would wage the total war that Garfield advocated. In 1862, however, it was still possible to retain some notions of chivalry. Garfield regarded this chivalry as nothing more than coddling the enemy, and he suspected treason lay behind it. "My heart sinks down very low when I see the mode in which the war is conducted," he said. "Until the rebels are made to feel that rebellion is a crime which the government will punish there is no hope of destroying it. I declare it as my deliberate conviction that it [is] better in this country, occupied by our troops, for a citizen to be a rebel, than to be a Union man. Everything they have is protected with the most scrupulous care, especially their property in human flesh."[22]

Negroes, sensing the Jubilee, flocked to the Union camp, forming pathetic bands of stragglers, sometimes helping with information and labor, but more often impeding the army's movement. Garfield was deeply touched by the plight of these sad spoils of war. "Just now I was surprised by a burst of music about ten feet to the rear of my tent," he wrote his wife. "It is a little band of slave minstrels who have come up from the village to visit our colored people, and to serenade

me. The rude music is really charming. . . . Poor fellows!
How can they sing songs? They told [us] if the army would
protect them, they would follow us to the end of the world.
But they get no countenance from an American army. We
seem to be as much their enemies as their masters."[23]

This "contraband" posed a problem for Union commanders. Legally, they were still the property of their masters,
and some punctilious Union generals insisted that they be returned to bondage. When Garfield was directed to surrender
a fugitive slave hiding in his camp, he exploded in anger and
openly defied his commander, telling him that if the general
wanted to hunt down slaves, he would have to do it himself.
"We do not even inquire whether a black man is a rebel in
arms, or not," Garfield indignantly told the folks back home,
"if he is black, be he friend or foe, he is to be kept at a distance. It seems to me hardly possible that God will let us succeed while such enormities are practiced."[24]

Another Union soldier, Colonel John Basil Turchin, shared
Garfield's indignation and found more concrete measures to
give it vent. Turchin, a Russian-born and trained cavalry
officer, was accused of sacking (in Cossack fashion) the town
of Athens, Alabama, in retaliation for the murder of one of his
soldiers. Garfield was assigned to Turchin's court martial. At
first he was outraged by the atrocity, but after talking to
Turchin he changed his mind. In his heavy Russian accent,
Turchin justified his actions. "I have tried to teach rebels that
treachery to the union was a terrible crime," he explained.
"My superior officers do not agree with my plans. They want
the rebellion treated tenderly and gently. They may cashier
me, but I shall appeal to the American people and implore
them to wage this war in such a manner as will make humanity better for it." Hearing these, his very thoughts, Garfield
could not help but sympathize. His early revulsion at Turchin's brutality gave way to admiration, and throughout the
long trial Garfield stubbornly defended the Russian. His sympathy, however, was not enough, for Turchin was drummed
out of the service over Garfield's objections.[25]

Even before the trial Garfield had been complaining of poor
health. As the trial dragged on, for almost forty days, his health

further deteriorated. Cooped up in a stuffy court room without air or exercise, smitten with diarrhea, his skin yellowed from jaundice, he broke down completely. He lost forty-three pounds in less than a month, and for the last ten days of the trial he had to be carried to court in a litter. As soon as the trial was over, Garfield was relieved of command and shipped home for sick leave. In early August, he reached Hiram, carried by his aide, Captain D. G. Swaim. Closer to death than he had ever been in battle, with his yellowed skin hanging in loose folds from his body, General Garfield came home to convalesce. It was almost a year to the day since he had entered the army.[26]

To escape the press of well-meaning friends, Garfield and his wife retreated to a secluded farmhouse at nearby Howland Springs. In that rustic hideaway, nursed by his wife, Garfield slowly recovered his strength. This was the first privacy they had known since their marriage, and for the first time a warm, intimate affection was kindled between them. The grim shadows of those black years of estrangement miraculously lifted, and now, almost four years after their wedding day, Garfield and his wife finally had their honeymoon. "It is indeed," he marveled, "a 'baptism into a new life' which our souls have received and which, after so many years of hoping and despairing has at last appeared in the fulness of its glory."[27]

While Garfield and his wife were fondly repairing the neglects of the past, only a few miles away, at Garrettsville, the 19th District Republican nominating convention was deciding his political future. Garfield did not bother to attend. "If the people of the District want me," he aloofly declared, "I take it that it is their business to tell me so, and not mine to coax them to have me."[28] He boasted that he had "not lifted a finger, nor made a move in my own behalf," but his friends had been busy indeed.

To steer Garfield's candidacy through the shoals of Reserve politics took all the skill and ingenuity they could muster. It required finesse to salve the pride of dozens of local party leaders, to engineer friendly combinations and head off unfriendly ones, and to keep the name of Garfield alive through newspaper and word-of-mouth publicity. Garfield's managers were equal to the task. They waged an aggressive campaign, boldly storming Hutchins's stronghold, Trumbull County, and capturing twenty-four of that county's forty delegates. Even in Hutchins's home township they packed the nominating caucus with their friends and elected Garfield-instructed delegates.[29]

Despite their careful preliminary spadework, the issue was still in doubt when the nominating convention met on September 2. Contrary to the confident predictions of Garfield's friends that the nomination would fall effortlessly into his hands, the balloting was tense and hard fought. Seventy-five votes were needed for the nomination. On the first ballot Garfield and Hutchins were neck-and-neck, with 46 and 45 votes respectively. Three other hopefuls divided the remainder of the votes between them. As the balloting progressed, their supporters slowly drifted to the front-runners and they dropped out of contention, but there was no dramatic break to either major candidate. By the seventh ballot, Garfield had climbed to within one vote of success, but Hutchins still pressed hard at his heels with 71. With the eighth ballot it was all over, and Garfield was the Republican choice to represent the 19th District in the next Congress. "It was the spontaneous act of the people," the candidate asserted, rather ungratefully overlooking the months of effort that had been necessary to secure the result.[30]

The nomination was well received throughout the district, and the candidate was commended to the voters as a man "of pure and spotless private reputation, presenting in all the adornments of a high-toned morality, one of the most attractive samples of a Christian gentleman." Congratulations poured in from all corners of the state and even distant newspapers took notice of his success. Election day was still over a month away, but these congratulations were not premature. It was inconceivable that the 19th Ohio would return anyone other than a Republican, and Garfield's election was considered as certain as anything in politics could be.

After the hard-fought nomination, the election campaign itself was an anticlimax. The public, diverted by the war news,

147

was apathetic, and some nervous observers feared that this unnatural calm was a Democratic trick designed to lull Republicans into overconfidence. Republicans in other parts of Ohio had good cause to worry, for, despite fusion with War Democrats, the Union ticket was soundly trounced in the October election, carrying only five of Ohio's nineteen Congressional seats. The 19th District, however, ran true to form, sending Garfield to Congress by an overwhelming margin—13,288 to only 6,763 for his opponent, D. B. Woods.[31]

By election time Garfield was already in Washington, but not for political reasons. Shortly after the nomination he had felt strong enough to return to active duty. His Congress would not convene until December of 1863, which meant that he still had more than a year of military life ahead of him, should the war last that long. He was impatient to return to action after his unaccustomed rest. "Every day seems twice its usual length while I am away from the field," he said.[32] Early in September, he was ordered to Washington to confer with the War Department about his next assignment. Leaving his family and his campaign to take care of themselves, he buckled on his sword and left for the capital.

CHAPTER NINE

AT THE CAPITAL

In the second year of civil war the city of Washington wore a shabby, unfinished look. Scarcely any of the public buildings and monuments that dotted its vast distances were yet completed. At one end of what would later be the Mall the truncated Washington Monument stabbed at the sky like a broken finger, and at the other end the uncompleted Capitol stood covered with cranes and pulleys, symbolizing (in a metaphor which seemed to occur to practically everyone) the unfinished union itself. It was a dirty city. The imperially named Tiber Creek oozed from Capitol Hill to the Potomac covered with a thick green scum. After a rain the wide avenues became seas of mud, causing the fastidious to walk blocks out of their way to find a clean spot to cross the street. Thousands of squalid, tumble-down Negro shanties gave the nation's capital the air of a "third rate Southern city," graphically reminding many visitors that here, only a few years before, slaves had been openly bought and sold.

Above all else, Washington was a city at war. Soldiers were everywhere. In the fall of 1862 over a quarter million were encamped in the area. They marched through the city's streets on their way to the front, and many bivouacked on the floor of the Capitol Rotunda or the steps of the Treasury Building. After battle they limped back to fill the District's twenty-one military hospitals. Officers were so thick on Pennsylvania Avenue that, so the story ran, a boy who threw a stone at a dog hit three brigadier generals instead.[1]

To this city came Garfield, one more unemployed brigadier general looking for an assignment. He had no reason to expect a long delay. His credentials were solid, if not spectacular, and in a war that had thus far been a graveyard for military reputations, his at least had the rare virtue of being unmarred by failure. Furthermore, he was a rising young Republican politician with an assured seat in Congress—a circumstance that certainly could not hurt his military prospects. He spent his first day in Washington closeted with Secretary of War Edwin M. Stanton. Interviews with the energetic, excitable little tyrant of the War Department could be nerve-racking, but towards a potential political ally like Garfield, Stanton was all charm and cordiality. They spent most of the afternoon denouncing West Point and all its works, and though the Secretary grandly promised to give Garfield any position within his power to bestow, he warned that it would be difficult to find a place in the army where he could be free from West Point harassment. The best Stanton could offer on short notice was command of western Virginia, but Garfield, true to his time-honored superstition, refused to commit himself. He would go if ordered, but he would not take responsibility for the choice.[2]

Actually, Garfield's hesitation was based on more than his peculiar superstition. He had his eye on a more tempting assignment. This was Cumberland Gap, which had, in fact, already been offered him during the summer when he had been too sick to accept. The chief attraction of Cumberland Gap, from Garfield's viewpoint, was that it offered him an opportunity to be reunited with his beloved 42nd Ohio. There were, however, complications in the way, principally that the region already had a commander, Brigadier General George Washington Morgan. Morgan was ill, however, and furthermore, the general, an Ohio Democrat, objected so violently to the use of Negro troops that his resignation was a distinct possibility. Garfield, an Ohio Radical, would make an ideal replacement for both geographic and political reasons. But for the time being, until Morgan could be dealt with gracefully, Garfield's prospects for that assignment were dim.

In the meantime, he was free to shop around. He looked the

150

field over, but the hand of West Point was everywhere. He scouted the non-West Point generals, but they all seemed out of favor and out of work. He toyed with the idea of joining General Franz Sigel's German brigade, but on second thought rejected Sigel's "Dutchmen" on political and personal grounds. He then offered his services to the Massachusetts politician-turned-soldier, Nathaniel Banks, whom he ranked, for some curious reason, as "one of our finest generals," but Banks was not very encouraging. "In short," Garfield sadly concluded, "it is quite impossible to see any way to usefulness or distinction that does not go down before West Point first."[3]

Fortunately, Garfield found an ally in his war against the regular army in the person of Salmon Portland Chase, Secretary of the Treasury. Chase too was indignant that the army was so overstocked with Democratic generals while good Republicans like Garfield went unrewarded. He took up Garfield's cause, virtually adopting the younger man as his protege. Their association was more than political. Chase saw in Garfield a younger version of himself: a self-made man whose career seemed to parallel his own. He was flattered by the obvious admiration of the young general, and they soon became close friends.

Genuine friendship was rare in Chase's life. A man of ponderous dignity and massive self-esteem, Chase was propelled by an egotism so vast as to be almost comic. "Chase is a good man," Ben Wade tartly observed, "but his theology is unsound. He thinks there is a fourth person in the Trinity." Inevitably, Chase grew dissatisfied with his subordinate place in the administration and continually plotted with heavy-handed intrigue to become president himself. Convinced that he alone could supply the strong leadership the nation needed, he was contemptuous of Lincoln's weak temporizing.

Soon Garfield was echoing the Secretary's every opinion. Chase and Stanton, he declared, were the only true men in the cabinet, and at times he had his doubts about Stanton. Towards Chase, however, his admiration never wavered. Not only did he regard him as "by far the strongest man in the administration," but (what to Garfield was even more impor-

151

tant) he wholeheartedly approved of his "moral and religious sense of the duties of the government in relation to the war."[4]

Chase and Garfield hit it off splendidly from the start. They had much in common: both admired Chase, despised copperheads, and looked down on Lincoln. They spent many pleasant hours in cozy chats, as Garfield told Chase horror stories about the pro-Southern, proslavery West Point officers he had known, and Chase regaled Garfield with fresh evidence of Lincoln's incompetence. One day, on the way to the Insane Asylum for a visit with Chase's favorite general, "Fighting Joe" Hooker, who was confined with a wounded foot, Chase treated Garfield to an inside view of the administration. McClellan, he predicted, could never become a soldier —"has no dash, no boldness in him and is the curse of our army." How disgraceful, Chase growled, that Lincoln lacked the "spunk" to dismiss him. "If I had been the President," he insisted, "I would have arrested McClellan for his conduct at 2nd Bull Run, . . . ordered him tried and, if he had been convicted of what I believe him to be guilty of, I would have had him shot."[5]

He then gave the attentive Garfield an analysis of the War Department. Spreading his first and second fingers to form a V, he pointed to the end of his forefinger. "Here is Stanton," he said, "full of earnestness, has immense powers of propulsion—but impatient of opposition, lacks steady constancy of action, and when his plans are thwarted . . . feels a kind [of] reckless desperation which keeps him from making the best out of a situation." Pointing to his second finger, he continued: "There is Halleck with an immense brain, knows perfectly all the details of his business . . . but as cold as a stone, has no more heart in the work than a shoemaker has over the boot he is pegging." Here is the President, he said, tapping his knuckle at the juncture of the fingers, "with a great true honest heart—wanting to do his duty but don't quite know how. . . ."

"If we had the President's heart, Halleck's head, and Stanton's propulsive energy united in one man," Chase concluded, "it would make a splendid Secretary of War—or President. As it is they are forces at the three ends of a triangle and nearly neutralize each other." With becoming modesty, Chase refrained from suggesting whom he had in mind as a replacement.[6]

When, shortly after this conversation, the Emancipation Proclamation was issued, Lincoln's stock rose somewhat higher in Garfield's estimation. "The President's heart is right," he conceded. "God grant he may have the strength to stand up to his convictions and carry them out to the full."[7] Yet, in spite of his grudging admiration for Lincoln's proclamation, his contempt for Lincoln the man lingered. "Strange," he mused, "that a second rate Illinois lawyer should be the instrument through which one of the sublimest works of any age is accomplished." In later years, however, after the Great Emancipator had been canonized by the Republic Party, Garfield would eulogize Lincoln as the "most remarkable character in modern history." From earliest boyhood, he asserted, Lincoln's "soul ceased not to loathe slavery, until in the wonderful development of his life, he was enabled to speak the word that broke four millions of fetters."[8] This high praise was clearly an afterthought on Garfield's part. While Lincoln was alive, Garfield openly wondered "if the history of government shows anything to equal the stupidity and weakness of our War Administration of 1862. Mr. Chase," he insisted, "is the only strong earnest man in the cabinet."[9]

Chase was so taken with his young friend's good sense that he impulsively declared, "Garfield, I would rather have you for Sec. of War than any man I know."[10] He insisted that Garfield leave his lonely hotel room and move into the Chase household. In the privacy of his home, Garfield discovered to his surprise, Chase unbent. His grim austerity vanished, and he exhibited a curiously "playful and childlike spirit." He revealed a passion for chess that matched Garfield's own, and he often compelled his guest to play a half-dozen games a night, sometimes keeping visitors waiting until the match was done.

At the Secretary's home Garfield was also thrown into the company of Chase's favorite daughter, the dazzling Kate, Washington's reigning beauty. He squired her around the town, and on one occasion escorted her to the camp of General

Carl Schurz for dinner, after which they joined Schurz, Sigel, and the rest of those "noble fellows," around the piano for a sentimental evening of lieder. Lest his wife draw the wrong conclusion from his association with Kate Chase, Garfield hastened to assure her that Kate "has a good form but not a pretty face, its beauty being marred by a nose slightly inclined to pug." Lucretia need not have worried. Kate Chase was after bigger game than an obscure brigadier general. Her father's career was her only passion, and to further it she was even then angling for the hand of Rhode Island's millionaire hero, William Sprague.[11]

Life with Chase was not, however, all chess games and dinner parties. There was work to be done as well. Chase was, after all, Secretary of the Treasury, the man responsible for the nation's finances during their most critical period. Before his appointment to the Cabinet Chase had never studied economics, had never even read a book on the subject. His ideas of finance, he boasted, were entirely intuitive. Even Chase realized that intuitive notions, no matter how inspired, were inadequate to deal with the problems he faced. Not only did he have to pay for an expensive war, but he had to reorganize the national banking system, devise new taxes, reshape the tariff, float loans at home and abroad, and issue the first truly national currency the country had ever known. At the same time he had to maintain price stability, preserve confidence in the dollar, and above all, keep the troops paid. A failure by Chase on the financial front could have been a greater disaster to the Union than defeat in battle.

While his policies were taking form, Chase turned for advice to financial experts of all varieties: professors, practical businessmen, dogmatists and cranks. Almost every night he would invite a set of eminent economists to his home, and across the dinner table they would thresh out the problems facing the Treasury Department. The Chase dining room housed an informal seminar. On a typical night Henry Carey, the Philadelphia protectionist, might argue with Amasa Walker, the Boston sound-money advocate, while Garfield eagerly absorbed every word. At college, economics had bored him, but now, as he watched state policy being made before his eyes, he was enthralled. This was the beginning of what would become a lifelong passion. Garfield had found his calling at last.[12]

He read all he could find on finance, voraciously gulping down the works of Macaulay, Webster, Calhoun, Benton and others. Most of his financial education, however, came not from books, but from the talk around the Chase dinner table. Before long he felt bold enough to enter the conversation. During a discussion of the currency question he advanced the argument that since Congress had the responsibility to regulate currency, Congress, and only Congress, must have the power to make currency; otherwise, he insisted, "there can be no national regulation of the amount of issue." As matters stood, however, Congress had, in Garfield's opinion, "most unwisely allowed states and corporations and even individuals to make currency. Thus we have a thousand different parties tinkering at the currency." He urged that the national government "sweep away all currency but its own." This proposal would do more than eliminate the traditional state bank notes; it would also greatly expand the power of the federal government at the expense of the states—an economic counterpart to the political centralization being brought about by the war. "It was considered a very novel proposition," Garfield claimed, but he was gratified to see his suggestion incorporated into the Secretary's annual report.[13]

From the Chase table-talk Garfield imbibed the financial principles which he would defend throughout his entire career —principally the belief in "honest money," which he would later elevate into a dogma. Chase's financial instincts were deeply conservative. Money, in his view, meant gold and silver, and he abhorred the very thought of an irredeemable paper currency, "than which," he ponderously warned, "no more certainly fatal expedient for impoverishing the masses and discrediting the government of any country can well be devised." Yet, in spite of himself, Chase was compelled by the necessities of war to suspend specie payment and issue the very sort of paper money he despised. He agonized over this dilemma, and Garfield, his confidant, shared his fears. "Nothing impressed me so strongly," Garfield recalled in later

155

years, "than the great reluctance with which he consented to any departure from the standard of value recognized by the Constitution. . . . I recollect that he said, that specie payment being suspended, the next best thing to specie was a bond whose interest was payable in gold and the principal finally redeemable in gold. . . . It is worthy of remark," Garfield noted, "that during all that period I heard no expression of desire or even a purpose to tolerate a long continued suspension of specie payment. Every effort was made so as to guard the paper issues, that they should be speedily redeemed and the old standard restored."[14]

For this goal Garfield would crusade all his life, devoting to it the energy and moral fervor he had once given to the Gospel. In a sense, Garfield remained a preacher all his life. Whether it was souls, or the Union, or the principle of honest money that he was saving, he invariably viewed his current crusade in terms of moral imperatives, and in each of his crusades his inspiration came from the influence of a respected elder. What Alexander Campbell and Mark Hopkins were to his boyhood, Chase was to his adult life: teacher, friend, and father.

The Chase hospitality was pleasant, but it was not for this that Garfield had come to Washington. As the weeks dragged on without an assignment from the War Department, the restless Garfield fretted with impatience "at being kept here in suspense, like Coleridge's Ancient Mariner—'As idle as a painted ship; Upon a painted ocean.' " While he was sitting quietly and ingloriously in Washington, the war was going badly for the Union. In the East, a Northern army had been defeated at Bull Run for the second time in two years and for a while the capital itself had been threatened until Lee's army was turned back at Antietam Creek. In the West, the gains of the spring offensive had been undone. Tennessee was lost, Kentucky was tottering, and Garfield's old brigade had retreated back to Louisville, the city it had left in April with such high hopes. "It seems almost criminal for anyone to be still when there is so much to be done," cried Garfield in frustration.[15]

All the while, the War Department, with fiendish ingenuity, kept dangling assignments before his eyes, only to snatch them away. A week after his first interview with Stanton, which had tantalized Garfield with the prospect of Cumberland Gap, the War Department changed its plans and considered him for commander of a projected Florida campaign instead. No sooner had the dutiful Garfield begun to study the geography of Florida when a new possibility arose —South Carolina.

It occurred to Chase—whose inventive mind often wandered far afield from his Treasury duties—that a successful expedition against Charleston, South Carolina, might be mounted with the unemployed brigades of Garfield and General Ormsby M. Mitchell. Garfield was not entirely pleased with the prospect of serving under Mitchell, for he suspected that the scholarly former astronomer was not sufficiently radical, but like a good soldier, Garfield was prepared to forgo his political objection and do his duty. Besides, he realized that if they should succeed in capturing Charleston, "the cradle of secession," there would be glory enough for two.

Chase convinced Stanton of the merits of the plan, and together they pushed for the expedition at cabinet meetings. Their enthusiasm was momentarily dampened by the objections of Secretary of the Navy Gideon Welles, who was unable to spare the necessary iron-clads, but undaunted, the two radical ministers pressed for an alternate invasion by land which would not require naval support. The President, Chase reported, "seemed much pleased" with their plan, but insisted on obtaining Halleck's approval. "I left the Cabinet with more hope than I have felt for months," Chase declared, but when the orders for the campaign were issued, they were for Mitchell alone. Garfield remained in Washington, while Ormsby Mitchell was sent to Carolina, where he would soon die of a fever.[16]

Almost immediately after the Carolina disappointment the Florida venture was revived and Garfield busied himself with it once more. This project was the brainchild of Eli Thayer, a Massachusetts Republican whose prewar New England Emigrant Aid Company had helped fill "Bleeding Kansas" with antislavery men. A fanatic on the subject of emigration,

157

Thayer had long advocated populating the South with true Northern men as the surest way of ending slavery. The war seemed a heaven-sent opportunity to carry out his plan, and he haunted the lobbies of Washington lining up support. By the fall of 1862 the Administration was willing to give Thayer's plan a try. According to Garfield, they were convinced "that there is not a sufficiently strong loyal element in the South to build up States that will be true to the union. Slavery has left such a blight upon them that a new and more loyal population must be sent there to possess the land and help make free institutions."[17] Garfield's task as commander would be more political than military. He would secure a beachhead on the Florida coast and organize the district so as to pave the way for twenty thousand Northern men and European immigrants who would settle on land confiscated from the rebels. These colonists could then draft an anti-slavery constitution, apply for recognition from Congress as the true government of Florida, and be admitted into the Union as a safely Republican state.

From a political point of view the Florida scheme looked promising. But there was a further aspect which gave the project even greater allure in certain quarters—cotton. Early in the war the Confederacy had foolishly destroyed its cotton reserves in the vain hope of forcing textile-hungry England to intervene for Southern independence. By the time Southerners realized the magnitude of their blunder a tight naval blockade prevented them from exporting their cotton. Undeterred, a brisk, if clandestine, trade in cotton sprang up across the Union lines. As Northern armies penetrated deeper into the Cotton Kingdom, they were followed (and sometimes even preceded) by cotton merchants. There were fortunes to be made, and temptation often overrode patriotism. To a shocking extent the Confederate economy, and hence the Confederate army, was supported by this cotton trade with the North.

The Florida plan could, in theory, end this scandal and put the cotton market on a more legitimate basis. When they were not voting, the Northern settlers (with the aid of freed Negroes) would be busily growing cotton which could then be sold to England aboveboard, without any of the profits drifting into the pockets of Northern speculators or Southern planters. (The plan was not quite foolproof. Unless superhuman vigilance and incorruptibility were exercised, Southern cotton could slip through the Union lines. How anyone could then tell patriotic Union cotton from the rebel variety was a question which seemed to occur to no one. Instead of ending the illicit trade, the venture could easily have turned Florida into a mecca for speculation.)

The possibilities of the Florida scheme intrigued many leading financiers, particularly Secretary Chase's favorite banker, Jay Cooke. Cooke himself had some reservations, but his associates, especially his irrepressible brother, Henry, were enthusiastic. Jay Cooke had often scolded Henry and his friends for their many shady ventures, including some in contraband cotton, but Henry, unchastened, insisted that his cotton dealings with the enemy, if understood correctly, would be praised as acts of purest patriotism. When the Florida project was broached, Henry Cooke hastened to sound out Garfield, whom he had known slightly in Columbus. He assured his brother that "a warm and intimate friend of mine, General Garfield, is to be assigned to a new department embracing southern South Carolina and Florida and he will cooperate with us in getting out cotton. Garfield is a glorious fellow and will do anything that is proper for us." Henry Cooke was probably exaggerating to impress his brother, since it was very likely that Garfield's conception of "anything that is proper" was considerably less expansive than Cooke's.[18]

Garfield, in fact, scarcely seemed to comprehend all the ramifications of the Florida project. He viewed it only as a welcome chance to see action again after so many months of enforced idleness, an idleness that was all the more unbearable because it brought on once more those black fits of depression to which his moody nature periodically succumbed. Each day of delay stretched his already taut nerves closer to the snapping point. "My heart cries out, How long, O Lord, How Long!" he groaned. Rather than continue to mark time waiting for a suitable assignment, he declared himself ready to take command of a brigade, a regiment, or even a company. "I am thoroughly ashamed to be seen on the streets in uniform," he said, and he seriously considered resigning his commission and issuing an angry public letter expalining his reasons. "Still," he reflected, "my work is always to be assigned '*very soon*,' but I, like every other general of positive opinions, am kept in idleness. I shall wait a few days more."[19]

Loneliness, shame, personal frustration, and disappointment over Republican setbacks in the recent elections all combined to plunge Garfield into an "exceedingly blue" mood—"a kind of feeling of desperation which would make me welcome fever within and rebels without. . . ." He projected his despair upon all that he observed. "Everywhere there is a settled gloom on nearly every face," he said:

> A great nation groaning in an agony of suspense and anxiety to have something done. A people that have poured out with a most lavish hand, their life and treasure to save their government, a people that have trusted their executive head with a constancy and faith which in these degenerate days is really sublime—are now beginning to feel that their confidence has been betrayed, their treasure squandered and the lives of their children sacrificed in unavailing slaughter.[20]

In mid-October, while his spirits were at this low ebb, Garfield was required to travel to New York with Eli Thayer to confer with leading capitalists about the Florida project. Since he was in the neighborhood, he paid a call on Rebecca Selleck, his sweetheart of college days. The visit, with its melancholy reminder of happier times, only served to deepen his present gloom. When he returned to New York, he was in even greater need of solace, and he found for a time a measure of comfort in the arms of a Mrs. Calhoun.[21]

A few months later Lucretia somehow learned that her husband had been burned by "the fire of . . . lawless passion." In bitter sorrow she wrote, "*James, I should not blame my own heart if it lost all faith in you.* I hope it may not . . . but I shall not be forever telling you I love you *when there is evidently no more desire for it on your part than present manifestations indicate.*" Stung by the charge, Garfield replied that if she really felt that way, "I should consider it wrong for us to continue any other than a business correspondence." He appealed to the new happiness they had discovered at Howland Springs and (as far as his pride would allow) begged for forgiveness. Lucretia forgave. By January, Garfield and his wife happily proclaimed a "truce to sadness," and the crisis was past.[22]

His other problems, unfortunately, could not be resolved as readily as his domestic difficulties. When he returned from New York he found that the government had unaccountably cooled on the Florida campaign, leaving him as far from an assignment as ever. In the meantime, in order to keep him busy, the War Department had placed Garfield on a court of inquiry to examine the charges against the disgraced general, Irvin McDowell. How fitting, Garfield sardonically observed, to "let the dead bury their dead," but even so, he greeted the trial as a welcome relief from the monotony of idleness.[23]

In one respect, however, the McDowell hearing was a grave embarrassment to Garfield. He had already met the unlucky general and was convinced of his innocence. Early in October McDowell had sought out Garfield and laid his defense before him so that a fellow Ohioan might understand his case. Garfield was won over by McDowell's somewhat pedantic charm, and the two men became such close lifelong friends that Garfield even named a son in McDowell's honor. "He is frank, open, manly, severe, and sincere, . . . " he told his wife. "That he is a true, brave man I have no doubt. *I like Gen. Irvin McDowell.*" He promised to do all he could in the general's cause and sent home for safekeeping a lengthy memorandum which he hoped might serve as the basis for a defense. When he found himself placed on McDowell's board, he told his wife to lock this manuscript in a cupboard to prevent evidence of his bias from falling into unfriendly hands, but his sympathies were too deeply engaged to permit him to desert a friend, especially one whose situation seemed to parallel his own.[24]

To a degree, Garfield's sympathy for McDowell's misfortunes was just a reflection of his own self-pity, a self-pity which was aggravated by the collapse of the Florida venture.

161

With no prospect of useful service in sight, Garfield toyed once more with the thought of resignation but decided to give the President one more chance. "I feel what you say about the effect on my reputation to lie here so long," he explained to his wife, "but my resignation would do no good. If I supposed this curse of idleness were intended as a slight to me I would of course resign at once. But when I see it is the same thing with every Republican General in the army, I think it is our duty to bear a little longer and see if the President wont conclude that having failed to buy up his enemies by kindness, he had better not drive away all his friends by neglect."[25]

Two days after this despairing letter was penned the light finally broke through—Garfield was at last assigned to duty. Ormsby Mitchell was dead, General David Hunter was ordered to take charge of the Charleston campaign, and Garfield was appointed his second in command, with at least a division under him. "For 24 hours I felt more joyful than I have at any time since I left the Sandy Valley," he said but then word reached Washington of a yellow fever epidemic on the Carolina coast. The expedition was cancelled, and Garfield's hopes were dashed once more. But at the very moment that Garfield's spirit was cast down by this latest disappointment, news reached him that gave fresh hope—General McClellan, his evil genius, had been removed from command. "God be praised, . . ." Garfield rejoiced. "The day is dawning. I cannot leave the army now."[26]

Garfield now settled down for a long war. Chase's prolonged hospitality had become embarrassing, so Garfield seized upon the arrival of his staff to move to their bachelor quarters in a Pennsylvania Avenue boarding house. There he sat, as the weeks slipped by, "still doomed to drag out my days here in Washington." The War Department insisted that an assignment of some sort was in the offing, and to insure that Garfield would be available when it came, they transferred him from the McDowell hearing, which promised to be a long one, to the Fitz-John Porter trial, which they optimistically hoped could wind up its business more quickly.

Garfield left the McDowell case purely for administrative reasons, not because of his bias. Indeed, he was quite as biased

162

(although in the opposite direction) in the Porter case as in the McDowell. Although he had no great personal animus against Porter, it was not really Porter who was on trial. Everyone knew that the trial was aimed at McClellan. "Porter," said John Hay, "was the most magnificent soldier in the Army of the Potomac, ruined by his devotion to McClellan." The unhappy Porter was to be the sacrificial goat for the sins of his chief.[27]

Garfield's hatred of McClellan amounted to an obsession. "Little Mac" was the epitome of all the Democratic, West Point, proslavery generals who had thwarted his military career and kept him idle in Washington. Chase had once suggested that McClellan deserved to be shot for his conduct at Antietam, and Garfield, as usual, agreed with Chase. They were convinced that the General sat at the center of "a very insidious and determined scheme" to overthrow the government "by a kind of French *Coup d'etat*." Much to their disgust the President laughed at their fears. "These things . . . would forbode a thunder gust if there were any lightning in him," they complained. "But doubtless he will respond with an anecdote and let these raskals fillip his nose or pluck his beard at pleasure."[28]

As fresh "evidence" of McClellan's treason mounted, Garfield grew more and more alarmed. He was particularly disturbed by a remark attributed to a McClellan aide, Major Key, the brother of Judge Thomas Key, the Democratic legislator with whom Garfield had crossed swords in the debate over Ohio's military preparations. Major Key was overheard to explain McClellan's slowness at Antietam by saying, "It is not the plan to whip the rebels. They are to be kept in the field till both sections of the country are exhausted, and the armies and the Democracy will compromise the matter." "From all I can see," Garfield concluded, "I am almost convinced that McC[lellan] is not misrepresented in that statement."[29]

It was widely believed by Republican officers, especially friends of McDowell and Pope, that Porter's fatal tardiness at Second Bull Run had been inspired by similar treason, as well as by personal pique. It was rumored that at the critical moment of the battle Porter had advised McClellan to withold reinforcements, since, as he was supposed to have said, "we have Pope where we can ruin him." These suspicions were reinforced by Porter's arrogant manner which had led him to such indiscretions as denouncing Stanton as an "ass," the abolitionists as "our enemies in rear," and Pope as a fool. At Pope's instigation official charges were brought against Porter, and in November of 1862 a court martial was ordered. The court was composed entirely of generals of volunteers; no West Pointers were allowed who might have sympathy with their old classmate. It was not a friendly court, and Garfield could well have been considered a hanging judge.[30]

The Porter case became the cause célèbre of its day, inflaming passions which would not be quenched for generations—"An American Dreyfus Affair," one Porter partisan later termed it. The testimony was so tangled, the charges and countercharges so complex that years of patient investigation have not yet unraveled all of its intricacies. To the members of the court, however, there was no doubt whatsoever of Porter's guilt. The only question in their minds was the proper sentence. The first impulse of the court, a witness later recalled, was to order Porter shot, but at the suggestion of General Benjamin Prentiss, Porter was merely drummed out of the army and prohibited from ever again holding federal office.[31]

Porter fought for vindication for the rest of his life, eventually winning over many who had originally condemned him. Garfield however, remained convinced of Porter's guilt. "No public act with which I have been connected was ever more clear to me than the righteousness of the finding of that court," he later insisted. Porter never forgave Garfield for his "treachery," and until his dying day he believed that Garfield had engineered his disgrace for purely political reasons.[32] However, General Prentiss, the only member of the court whose integrity not even Porter's most loyal defenders dared challenge, vigorously denied that the court had carried out a radical vendetta. "You will remember," Prentiss later reminded Garfield, "how careful all were to investigate full and fairly, and I know . . . that some of the members had no idea that the charges against Porter could be sustained. . . . I am constrained to believe," Prentiss concluded, "that under the circumstances our verdict was extremely light."[33]

164

The Porter trial moved with glacier-like deliberation. It required over two weeks merely to organize the court, and not even the recent innovation of shorthand reporting could speed the endless flow of testimony. Garfield, who was trapped in Washington at least until the trial was over, grew more and more morose as the case dragged on. Although he was fascinated by the revelations uncovered by the testimony, his patience was almost at an end. He vowed to have a showdown with the War Department as soon as the work of the court was done. "They must give me something to do," he raged, "or they must take my commission. I will not endure it." From the depths of his despair he moaned that he "would infinitely rather die on the Rappahannock" than stay much longer in Washington.[34] Clutching at straws, he was almost ready to believe that his prolonged idleness was a plot on the part of his political enemies to dim his reputation in order to keep him from being elected to the U. S. Senate.[35]

Turning by instinct to his tested remedy for depression, he busied himself with work to help the time pass more quickly. Always a schoolmaster, even when in uniform, Garfield found relaxation in intellectual activity. He dashed off an article on the currency question which was well received by economists, and then plunged exuberantly into a study of his latest hero, Frederick the Great. A thoroughgoing pacifiist only ten years before, Garfield had now quite characteristically swung to the opposite extreme, taking for his model the archetype of Prussian militarism. He now believed that the pacifism he had once endorsed had nearly been the cause of the nation's undoing. "In our present war," the one-time Campbellite preacher argued, "the Republic is paying a fearful price for its neglect of military organization and its failure to preserve the military spirit among its people. . . . No nation ever so recklessly neglected the art of war, nor came so near to ruin in consequence of that neglect."[36] To remedy that neglect and to reawaken the nation's slumbering martial spirit, he undertook to edit the works of Frederick for publication.

Garfield never completed his study of Frederick: the real war intruded into his scholarly battles. Around the beginning of 1863 fresh stirrings in the War Department gave signs that Garfield's long Washington vigil was about to come to an end.

Parson Brownlow, the vindictive Tennessee preacher-politician was in town, loudly demanding that a radical general be sent to liberate the Unionists of East Tennessee. Stanton hinted to Chase that Garfield would be the man. Garfield was hopeful, but wary. "I have not much expectation that the War Department will hold one mind for a week," he said numbly.[37] A week later the War Department did, in fact, change its mind and vetoed the choice of Garfield, possibly (so Garfield thought) on the advice of Halleck. By this time Garfield was so desperate that he was ready to violate his deepest scruples. Hearing rumors of fresh activity in South Carolina he swallowed his pride and actually wrote a letter asking for the job. He did not, of course, forget himself so far as to mail it, but even so his hopes were again disappointed.

By the middle of January, after four months in Washington, Garfield's hopes were still revolving from South Carolina to Florida to East Tennessee and back to South Carolina, with no certain prospects anywhere. His book on Frederick needed only a few more days of polishing to be ready for the printer when suddenly there came a summons from an unexpected quarter: William S. Rosecrans, commander of the Army of the Cumberland, needed a general. Garfield snapped at the opportunity. Without waiting to say goodbye to Chase he hopped aboard the first train west, leaving his unfinished manuscript forgotten on his desk, as he headed once more for the front.[38]

CHAPTER TEN

BOBBING AROUND

A squad of cavalry accompanied General James A. Garfield as he made his way through Tennessee to his new post. The general rode (at some cost to his dignity) inside an army ambulance, which bounced and teetered down the Nashville Pike. Seven hours later, after narrowly escaping a band of rebel raiders, ambulance and escort pulled into Murfreesboro, Tennessee, base of the Army of the Cumberland, and headquarters for its commander, General William Starke Rosecrans.

Both the commanding general and his army were at the focus of national attention. Less than a month before Garfield's arrival they had collided with a large Confederate force under Braxton Bragg at Stone's River, outside Murfreesboro. The ensuing battle was an indecisive bloodletting, but when the fighting was done, and the two armies had glowered at each other for a day, it had been Bragg's nerve which gave way first. He retreated, leaving Rosecrans holding the field and the victory.

Stone's River (or Murfreesboro, as it was known in the South) was a dubious victory at best, but whatever glory it shed belonged by common consent to Rosecrans personally. Critics could argue that the battle should not have been fought at all, but none could deny that once it had begun, Rosecrans's leadership had been magnificent. Possessed by that exaltation which sometimes transforms men in battle, Rosecrans was everywhere on that frozen field, encouraging, rallying, indomitable: his very presence an inspiration. "Stone's

River under Rosecrans, and Cedar Creek under Sheridan," declared Whitelaw Reid, "are the sole examples in the war of defeats converted into victories by the reenforcement of a single man."

Stone's River was singularly well timed. In December of 1862, Northern morale was reeling under a series of defeats. In the East the disaster at Fredericksburg had dashed hope for Hooker's Virginia campaign, and in the West both Grant and Sherman had been humiliated outside of Vicksburg. In this black hour Stone's River, for all its flaws, stood out like a beacon. Without it, Lincoln himself averred, "the nation could scarcely have lived over." "God bless you and all with you!" he said to Rosecrans, and the nation echoed his prayer.[1]

The general was well cast for the role of hero. For a people that prided itself on being peace-loving, Americans were re-markably susceptible to military glory. This was an age still dominated by the Napoleonic myth, and it demanded that its military heroes be men of genius, larger than life. Rosecrans, far more than the unpretentious Grant, looked and acted like a great man. Though not overly tall, Rosecrans was broad shouldered and erect with a trim military bearing. He made a splendid figure on horseback, though his short, bow legs rendered him less impressive on foot. Despite his somewhat hooked nose, his narrow sensitive face which terminated in a neat, well-trimmed beard was generally deemed handsome. Behind that beard, there constantly played a curious, haunting smile, compounded "half of pleasure, half of some exquisite nervous feeling, which might be intense pain."

His most striking personal characteristic was an abundance of nervous energy. Voluble, inventive, excitable, charming and irritable by turns, Rosecrans was always in motion: "nervous and active in his movement, from the dictation of a dispatch to the rearing and chewing of his inseparable companion, his cigar." His restless energy and teeming mental fertility struck many as authentic evidence of genius. "He thinks of every-thing, Sir," an awed subordinate was reported as saying. "I reckon he never sleeps." But others (with the advantage of hindsight) were less impressed. "His mind scattered; there was no system in the use of his busy days and restless nights," declared Charles A. Dana, who was later to play such a sinister role in Rosecrans's career; while another observer put it more succinctly—"it seems as if a screw was loose in him somewhere."[2]

Into the hands of this curious, contradictory personality, Garfield had placed his military future. With mingled feelings of apprehension and curiosity he climbed out of his cramped ambulance and reported to his new commander. The two men chatted about the Sandy Valley campaign, but they did not get down to serious business. Rosecrans promised to see him again in the morning, and as Garfield was about to leave, he dropped the encouraging hint that two or three divisions were "fishing" for a commander. Tired from his long journey, Garfield went straight to bed. Along about midnight he was awakened by the general, who came to his room and talked for an hour "till his darkey came and took him by the shoulder and led him away to bed."[3]

This was the first of a long series of sleepless nights for Garfield. At the end of a busy day, Rosecrans was usually too keyed up to sleep. He needed to unwind, to let his nervous energy run down, and after midnight he turned to conversation with an almost compulsive appetite. His interests ranged from religion to literature, politics and war, and he had decided opinions on each topic. In Garfield he found the perfect foil—"the best-read man in my army," he said—and he was reluctant to let such a prize go to waste. When Garfield went to the general's quarters his second night in Murfreesboro to discuss his assignment, Rosecrans would not let him leave. He insisted that Garfield sleep in his room, and kept him up until three o'clock while they discussed religion, a subject particularly close to Rosecrans's heart. "He is the intensest religionist I ever saw," Garfield marveled.[4]

Rosecrans insisted on telling Garfield his entire spiritual history. In his youth, he said, he had felt the need of "an authorized supernatural teacher." He investigated the Greek Orthodox, the Episcopalians, and the Roman Catholics, but only in the latter church could he find the discipline and assurance he craved. Garfield, who had been brought up to regard Popery with horror, listened with fascinated repulsion and well-bred

169

curiosity. This was the first respectable Catholic he had ever met close up, and he plied Rosecrans with questions. How, for example, he asked, could Rosecrans reconcile his fierce swearing with his religion? Rosecrans replied: "I do still curse and damn when I am indignant, but I never blaspheme the name of God"—a distinction which Garfield regarded as Jesuitical. With fastidious distaste, Garfield watched his general go through the rituals of his faith, noting that before retiring Rosecrans ostentationsly took out his rosary, "a dirty-looking string of friars beads," and knelt in prayer beside his bed. "I don't know but he thought he could proselyte me," Garfield suspected. But within a few months Garfield had so shed his boyhood prejudices that he found himself attending mass with his commander. He assured his worried mother that he had no intention of converting, but he added, "I have no doubt the Catholics have been greatly slandered."[5]

These midnight sessions continued night after night, often until four o'clock in the morning. "I have been engaged in the most fearful dissipation in regard to sleep," Garfield wearily complained. One night in desperation he rented quarters on the other side of town, but no sooner had he slipped into bed when an aide knocked on his door and hauled him back to Rosecrans's company.

Were it not for the late hours, Garfield would have thoroughly enjoyed his association with Rosecrans. He genuinely liked the general's conversation and grew to admire him as "a man of very decided and muscular thoughts," who shared with Garfield's current idol, Frederick the Great, "the rare . . . quality of having his mind made up on every important question." Although he did not rank Rosecrans as a great man or a profound thinker, he respected his "sharp, clear sense, ready, decisive judgment, and bold reliant action." In any event, an opportunity to become so intimate with one's commanding general was well worth a few hours of lost sleep.[6]

Rosecrans, too, profited from the friendship. Garfield had come to Murfreesboro armed with letters of introduction from Stanton and Chase. A man with such high-placed friends was well worth cultivating. The cultivation paid off. Within a few weeks Garfield was writing to Chase about his commander in glowing terms. "I think I have seen the interior of Gen. Rosecrans' nature as fully as I ever did that of any man I ever knew," he reported, "and I am glad to tell you that I believe in him—that he is sound to the bone on the great questions of the war, and the way it should be conducted [i.e., the use of Negro troops]. . . . If the country and the government will stand by him," he pleaded, "I feel sure that he will justify their highest expectations."[7]

Even though there may have been an element of opportunism on both sides of this friendship, the association between Garfield and Rosecrans was, Garfield later insisted, "not a mere official or even social acquaintance, but a meeting and mingling of spirits"—a true comradeship. Yet the very intimacy of their association was becoming an embarrassment to Garfield. Rosecrans enjoyed his company so much that he was reluctant to assign him to active duty. Almost a month passed in this manner without further mention of the divisions Rosecrans had alluded to on their first interview. Was it for this that Garfield had joined the army—to become the paid companion of an insomniac?

As he brooded over his inactivity, Garfield felt his old melancholy descend upon him once more. "The continual dreary rain, the broken and devastated country with its impassable roads, and the dreary battalions that go dripping and soiled to their daily monotony of mingled labor and idleness all act with depressing force upon one's spirits," he sighed. What with one thing and another, Garfield had been kept from active duty for over six months now, and the whole frustrating sequence of events, he said, "has tried my powers of endurance, and my natural restlessness more than it was ever tried before. I have gone through all the cycles of restlessness and chafing impatience until I think I have learned to endure with a considerable degree of patience if not with meekness what is laid upon me."[8]

One evening in the middle of February Rosecrans suddenly turned to Garfield and said: "I am almost alone in regard to counsel and assistance in my plans, and I want a power concentrated here that can reach out through the entire army and give it unity and strength." Would Garfield, he asked, be willing

171

to take the post of chief of staff and become that power? If not, he added, Garfield could command a division in the field. The flustered Garfield evaded a reply until he could think the matter through.

As usual, when compelled to make a choice regarding his career, Garfield wallowed in an agony of indecision. Although he had had his heart set on a field command he was, he admitted, sorely tempted by Rosecrans's offer. "Considered personally," he reflected, "Gen. Rosecrans could not pay me a higher compliment, nor in any way express more confidence in me. Furthermore, if by Chief of his Staff he does not mean merely a chief clerk, but an adviser, a kind of *alter ego*, I have no doubt, while the confidence remains, I could do more service there than in any other [position] in this army." His study of Frederick the Great had led Garfield to admire the Prussian staff system in which the chief of staff was second in importance only to the commanding general himself. But in the American army, where the chief of staff was often a lowly major or lieutenant colonel, the staff corps was in no way comparable to the Prussian. "Could I in this case make it so?" he wondered. What would his friends think? What would the army think? More to the point, what would his constituents think? "Would I be considered as having taken a step up or down?" He had his own career to consider and he uncharacteristically tried to analyze his problem with a cold-blooded, commercial eye. "By taking that position," he calculated, "I should make a large investment in Gen. Rosecrans and will it be wise to risk so much stock in that market?"[9]

To make his decision even harder, he also had to consider the possible effect his remaining in the army might have upon his congressional career. When he had been nominated, he had insisted that he "would rather be in the field than in the Congress." He was not scheduled to take his seat until December, "and should we be so unfortunate as not to have broken the back of the rebellion by that time," he said, "I should prefer to resign the seat and keep the saddle."[10] Now, to complicate matters further, it appeared that he might have to make that decision sooner than anticipated. John Hutchins, Garfield's defeated but still resourceful opponent, was claiming that

172

unless Garfield resigned his commission by March 4, he would be ineligible to take his seat. This argument seened to have some legal basis, so to quell his fears, Garfield obtained advisory opinions from Chase, Ben Wade, and Attorney General Bates that supported his right to remain in the army until December. Their opinions were reassuring but not completely satisfactory, and Garfield was left "in quite an uncertain and uncomfortable state." "In that election," he glumly said, "I fear I have drawn an elephant."[11]

Near the end of February, Rosecrans handed Garfield an order assigning him to duty as chief of his staff. Grateful to have the decision made for him, Garfield accepted at once. "The long agony is over," he breathed in relief, but the very next moment he suspected that because of "the perverseness of human nature I shall no doubt often regret that I am not in command of a division. . . ." His friends fed his suspicion, warning that he might lose all chance for distinction if he should hide himself behind a desk. (In Rosecrans's army, however, chief of staff was more than a desk job. One of Garfield's predecessors, the scholarly, ascetic Julius Garesché, had had his head blown off by a cannonball at Stone's River.) Garfield conceded that, as chief of staff, "I may not make as much reputation as I could in another place." Nevertheless, he was willing to forgo glory for the opportunity to "exercise more influence on the army, and more fully impress my views and policy on its administration."[12]

With the painful decision safely behind him, Garfield cheerfully settled into the routine of his new post. Army headquarters occupied the old Keeble residence, a spacious, if slightly down-at-the-heels, Southern mansion hastily vacated by its secessionist owner. Inside, within rooms of shabby gentility, arose a constant hum of activity. Work at headquarters followed the rhythm of Rosecrans's day. Customarily he rose at eight. After prayers and breakfast, the morning was devoted to reports and meetings, often followed by a tour of inspection through the camp. This inspection tour was a splendid pageant. The general, preceded by flag-bearers, surrounded by his staff and flanked by a cavalry escort, galloped through camp to the cheers of his enthusiastic soldiers. Dinner, the second and

173

last meal of the day was at four, and from then to midnight, when Rosecrans was at his best, the important work of the army was conducted.

Rosecrans drove his staff hard. He expected from others the same tireless energy that propelled him. Few could keep up with the pace. Young aides, groggy with fatigue, often slumped at their desks until their commander, suspending his dictation in midsentence, would pinch their ears and send them off to bed. Despite the hectic pace, Rosecrans was popular with his staff. Fraternal, solicitous, often attentive and thoughtful with inferiors (habits which he should have cultivated when dealing with superiors), he was held in genuine affection. He was not, however, an easy man to work for. Occasionally his nervous irritability exploded in anger, and when it did he was blind to reason, deaf to explanation, as he rained upon the humiliated offender a torrent of profane (but not blasphemous) abuse. But, by and large, it was a happy, bustling staff. Neatly dressed clerks and orderlies went about their business with quiet, purposeful efficiency. Drunkenness and bickering, though not unknown, were less in evidence than at many other army headquarters. As might be expected from Rosecrans's habits, the Sabbath day was observed with respect.

Headquarters was Garfield's domain, and he presided over all this activity from an anteroom, where he sat perched regally on a high stool in front of an unpainted pine desk. Visitors to camp were impressed by the chief of staff. To Henry Villard, of the New York *Tribune*, he presented "a far more commanding and attractive appearance" than Rosecrans himself. "Very nearly, if not fully, six feet high, well formed, of erect carriage, with a big head of sandy hair, a strong-featured, broad and frank countenance, set in a full beard and lighted up by large blue eyes and a most pleasing smile," Garfield seemed to Villard the very picture of "a distinguished personage."[13]

Another passing journalist described Garfield to his readers as

> a tall deep-chested, sinewy built man, with regular, massive features, a full, clear blue eye, slightly dashed with gray, and a high, broad forehead, rising into a ridge over the eyes as if it had been thrown up by a plough. . . . A rusty slouched hat large

174

enough to have fitted Daniel Webster, lay on the desk before him, but a glance at that was not needed to convince me that his head held more than the common share of brains.

The reporter was particularly charmed by Garfield's "open, expressive face," and democratic demeanor, which seemed to indicate that the young general was a true "man of the people." Should he live, the reporter ventured to predict, "he will make his name long remembered in our history."[14]

This admiration, though widespread, was not universal. To Colonel (later General) John Beatty, who affected the blunt, soldierly virtues, Garfield's uniform, with its gleaming double row of buttons, seemed ostentatious, and he read in Garfield's very handshake the message, "Vote right, vote early." Many officers resented Garfield's influence. General Stanley, the testy, irascible cavalryman, sputtered in rage at Garfield's "meddling." Stanley never forgave him for foisting upon the cavalry unwanted officers, most especially Garfield's Russian friend, John B. Turchin, who, according to Stanley, could not even ride a horse and was appointed "simply to please the foreigner and the radical." "Rosecrans was in many respects a man of genius and disposed to do right," Stanley conceded, "but he was easily influenced, and Garfield's blarney and deceitful tongue captured Rosecrans."[15]

Military jealousy, possibly the most highly developed form of human envy, was only to be expected in view of Garfield's rapid rise to prominence in the Army of the Cumberland. Rosecrans ignored the criticism. In Garfield he had found, for once, an aide whose capacity for work matched his own, and he entrusted to him many duties and responsibilities beyond his official position.

The chief of staff was supposed to serve as the transmission belt between the general and his army. He handled all the routine business that kept the army running smoothly, issued orders in the general's name, collected information and summarized it for the general's attention. But because of Garfield's intimacy with his commander (he was the only one privileged to call him "Rosy" to his face), his actual influence was much greater than his official position might warrant. "Rosecrans shares all his counsels with me," said Garfield proudly,

175

"and places a large share of the responsibility of the management of this army upon me, even more than I sometimes wish he did."[16]

With Rosecrans's encouragement, Garfield had his hand in every aspect of army organization, from the creation of an intelligence corps unsurpassed in the Union army to plans for injecting some "of the old Prussian and French fire" into troop morale. Bubbling over with plans and projects, Garfield helped pull the Army of the Cumberland into shape during its long stay at Murfreesboro. To a large extent, therefore, Garfield had succeeded in his goal of elevating the authority of the chief of staff beyond that of a mere clerk.

In at least one instance Rosecrans did not, unfortunately, heed Garfield's advice. The two wing commanders of the army, Alexander McCook and Thomas L. Crittenden, lacked the ability of George H. Thomas, who commanded the center. Garfield had had his doubts about McCook ever since he had ordered a fugitive slave hunted out of Garfield's camp during the Corinth campaign. He had even sounder military reasons for distrusting him. Although personally brave, in battle misfortune followed McCook like a specter. To Beatty, McCook was "a chucklehead . . . deficient in the upper story," and he marveled "that he should be permitted to retain command of the corps for a single hour." Garfield begged Rosecrans to replace McCook and Crittenden with Buell and McDowell, two generals who had failed in independent commands but who would make excellent subordinates. Along with "Pap" Thomas, these men would have given Rosecrans, thought Whitelaw Reid, "the best officered army in the service of the nation." Rosecrans agreed in principle, but Crittenden was a good storyteller and McCook had a pleasant lyric tenor, and both were so loyal to him that he "hated to injure two such good fellows." He ignored Garfield's advice and retained the two officers, with consequences that would ultimately prove disastrous.[17]

Generally, however, Rosecrans leaned heavily upon Garfield for advice, especially for problems of a political nature. During their daily rides together and in their long evening chats, they discussed all the problems facing their army. Perhaps the most perplexing, certainly the most tragic, of these problems involved the swarms of Negroes, both men and women, who had flocked to the safety and security of the Union camp. "Old Rosey's down in Tennessee," they sang, "Bobbing around, Bobbing around. And setten all the darkies free, As he goes bobbin 'round."

Able-bodied Negroes could be put to work digging fortifications and driving wagons, but the thousands of women and children abandoned by their masters, who presented, Garfield thought, "one of the saddest pictures I ever witnessed," threatened to become "a burden which this army cannot safely assume." The army was not geared to conduct large-scale charity, yet what to do with these homeless, helpless Negroes was a question which Garfield and Rosecrans spent many earnest hours in studying, without reaching any humane, yet practical solution.[18]

Garfield used his influence with Rosecrans to press at every opportunity for his favorite measure of arming Negroes and enlisting them to fight for the Union. Like Chase, he wanted them employed in something more useful than "pick and shovel brigades." He did not recoil from the prospect of Negro troops even if their presence should (as some feared) inspire a slave insurrection. Such a result would be bloody, Garfield conceded, "but it is not in my heart to lay a feather's weight in the way of our Black Americans if they choose to strike for what was always their own." Rosecrans seemed to be swayed by his radical arguments, and when Garfield reported his success to Chase, the secretary was jubilant. His confidence in Garfield was unbounded: "My trust in you is as complete as that of the good deacon in his minister. I can sleep if it is you who preaches."[19]

Garfield's reports gladdened the hearts of Chase and his radical friends who were beginning to number Rosecrans as one of their own, and who were planning a bright political future for him. A procession of curious journalists and politicians made the pilgrimage to Murfreesboro to examine the general with their own eyes and assess his political prospects.

In the middle of May one of these visitors rode into camp on a curious mission. James R. Gilmore of the New York *Tribune*,

177

better known for a series of stirring books for boys published under the nom de plume of Edmund Kirke, had been sent by editor Horace Greeley for the ostensible purpose of writing a series of articles for his paper. Actually, Greeley had charged Gilmore with nothing less than to sound out Rosecrans to determine whether he was the man who could save the Union.

According to Gilmore's memory (which was not his most reliable faculty), Greeley was convinced that if Lincoln stayed in office the republic was doomed. In Greeley's judgement (which was certainly not *his* most reliable faculty), only a military dictator could save the country, and Rosecrans was his choice. A successful general, a certified genius, a Catholic popular with the Irish, a former Democrat respected by the radicals, Rosecrans was available on all counts—if he were willing to run. Greeley claimed to have the support of an impressive array of Republican leaders, including Thaddeus Stevens, Ben Wade, Henry Winter Davis, and others, all of whom were supposedly waiting only for the result of Gilmore's mission. "I will give you my word," Greeley solemnly told Gilmore before he left for Murfreesboro, "that if you find Rosecrans is the man that is needed, I will go personally to Lincoln and force him to resign. Hamlin will give Rosecrans command of the armies, and there'll be a chance of saving the country."

After a few days of discreet snooping at Murfreesboro, Gilmore was ready to broach the plan to Rosecrans. But before he committed himself fully, he turned to Garfield for advice on how best to approach Rosecrans. The two had become close friends. Gilmore had nursed Garfield through a bout of fever, and Garfield had returned the favor by telling Gilmore the story of his life. When Gilmore confided to him the nature of his mission, Garfield, who suddenly saw his investment in Rosecrans stock about to pay an unexpected dividend, gave it his enthusiastic approval. No better man for the presidency than Rosecrans could be found anywhere, he told Gilmore, and urged him to put the question to Rosecrans frankly and openly.

Rosecrans, however, refused the bait. Suspicious of Greeley's promises and wary of his flattery, he refused to lend himself to such a dubious game. He told Gilmore to thank his backers for their kind opinion of him, "but my good friend," he added, "it cannot be. My place is here." If the Union were to be saved from Lincoln, it would have to be by someone other than Rose-crans. Gilmore returned to New York, but the trip was not a total loss, for he carried away from his talks with Garfield enough material to make several more novels.[20]

That spring was a crowded tourist season at Murfreesboro. Shortly after Gilmore left camp, another prominent guest passed by. Clement Vallandingham, the Ohio Copperhead leader, had recently been arrested for criticizing the war. Be-cause of the dubious constitutionality of the arrest, Lincoln had commuted Vallandingham's sentence from imprisonment to deportation to the Confederacy. He crossed the Union lines at Murfreesboro, and it fell upon Garfield to issue the pass that let him through. Garfield had no sympathy for Vallanding-ham's plight. He regarded the Bill of Rights as suspended for the duration of the rebellion. When, for example, he learned that some Hiram students had been heard to disparage the war, he suggested that the "young traitors" be expelled from school. "They entirely mistake and misapprehend the char-acter of the times if they suppose that the same license can now be used as in the days of peace," he indignantly wrote to acting-president Hinsdale back in Hiram, and he offered to escort the boys personally into the Confederacy as he had done with Val-landingham.[21]

The constant activity at Murfreesboro guaranteed that being chief of staff for a great army would keep Garfield's days (and nights) full. Yet, with all the varied demands that Rose-crans made on his attention, Garfield never lost sight of the reason he had taken that position rather than command of a division. More than anything else, being chief of staff meant to Garfield an opportunity to carry out his own strategic con-cepts unhampered by West Point opposition. Ever since he had left the Sandy Valley, he had resented his West Point com-manders. During his long, bitter feud with the regular army he had accused them of incompetence, and even treason. These were serious charges, but they seemed to Garfield the only way he could account for the otherwise incomprehensible be-havior of the West Pointers.

There was, however, a simpler explanation. At West Point

179

young officers were trained in the strategic doctrines of Baron Jomini, whose classic textbooks on the art of war had shaped the strategic concepts of a generation of plebes. To Jomini and his many translators and popularizers, including Halleck, war was a fine art which was best left in the hands of professional soldiers. Their ideal was eighteenth-century warfare, conducted with a minimum of bloodshed by well-disciplined soldiers fighting for limited, clearly-defined aims, the most important of which were the occupation of the enemy's territory and the capture of his capital city. Enthralled by the prospect of turning war into a science, Jomini and his school disregarded all the untidy and unscientific factors, such as politics and ideology, which could upset their neat diagrams. Recoiling in horror from the excesses of the French Revolution, they deplored total wars, or wars waged for the subjugation of entire peoples.

These principles might have been sound for European wars of the eighteenth century, but the American Civil War was a different case entirely. It was preeminently a political war, fought between peoples, not soldiers. Garfield, no soldier, but very much a politician, was actually better equipped to understand the true nature of this war than were many professional soldiers. Convinced that no military solution was possible without the abolition of slavery and the thorough reconstruction of Southern society, he rejected Jomini's principles and advocated a total war fought to the finish. "It may be a philosophical question whether 11,000,000 of people *can be subdued*," he conceded, but he insisted "this is the thing to be done before there can be union and peace."[22]

If Southern submission were at all possible, Garfield contended, it would have to be accomplished by bloodshed; by destroying their armies and breaking their will to resist, so as to impose a political solution they would not accept otherwise. Garfield had not read Clausewitz, but he instinctively regarded war as a continuation of politics by other means. Consequently, he advocated an offensive strategy—"striking, striking and striking again, till we break them." "One thing is settled in my mind," he declared,

> direct blows at the rebel army—bloody fighting—is all that can end the rebellion. In European wars if you capture the chief

city of a nation, you have substantially captured the nation. The army that holds London, Paris, Vienna, or Berlin, holds England, France, Austria, or Prussia. Not so in this war. The rebels have no city, the capture of which will overthrow their power. If we take Richmond, the rebel government can be put on wheels and trundled away into the interior . . . in two days.

"Hence," he concluded, in flat contradiction to conventional military doctrine, "our real objective point is not any place or district, but the rebel army wherever we find it. We must crush and pulverize them, and then all places and territories fall into our hands as a consequence."[23]

With such aggressive views, Garfield could not help being unhappy over the protracted idleness of the Army of the Cumberland at Murfreesboro. After Stone's River, Bragg had retreated to Tullahoma, some thirty-five miles to the south. Rosecrans, whose army had been as exhausted by victory as the Confederates had been by defeat, was in no position to pursue until his supplies were replenished.

In the first flush of enthusiasm after Stone's River, Stanton had gratefully assured Rosecrans: "There is nothing you can ask within my power to grant to yourself or your heroic command that will not be cheerfully given." He soon had cause to regret his rash generosity. Rosecrans's demands were endless: food, medicine, revolvers, horses, above all, horses. A constant stream of requests, excuses, and recriminations clogged the wires to Washington, until an irritated Halleck was heard to grumble that Rosecrans's telegraph bills were becoming an excessive item in the army budget. Stanton became so annoyed by Rosecrans's repeated demands that he lost all patience with the nagging general. "I will be damned if I'll give Rosecrans another man," he exploded. Rosecrans replied that the War Department's neglect constituted "a profound, grievous, cruel, and ungenerous official and personal wrong," and from then on it was open warfare between them.

As the months passed by without Rosecrans stirring from Murfreesboro, Union gratitude for Stone's River began to sour into exasperation. "I would not push you to any rashness," Lincoln gently prodded, "but I am very anxious that you do your utmost, short of rashness." Lincoln's irony passed unnoticed; no one else seemed to be worried about rashness from Rosecrans. On the contrary, Halleck was eventually moved to telegraph bluntly: "I deem it my duty to repeat to you the great dissatisfaction felt here at your inactivity." And even the quartermaster-general, not usually considered one of the more aggressive departments of the army, chimed in with some gratuitous advice: "The rebels will never be conquered by sitting in their front."[24]

To Garfield, chafing for action, impatient for the great battle that would smash the rebellion and let him go home, this long delay while Rosecrans perfected his interminable preparations was maddening. "It is very trying to the patience," he grumbled, "to stand here like a wrestler tripping and making feints at his adversary, and watching his movements, keeping the muscles strained all the while, yet never grappling and making a decisive end to the delay and struggle." Contrary to his commander's opinion, Garfield was convinced, as early as March, that the Army of the Cumberland was ready to move. "This is a splendid army," he boasted, "—not so much in its numbers as in its character. Nearly every man is a veteran, and has been tested in battle. It is in a fine state of health and discipline, and it will make a terrible fight when it next meets the enemy." Yet, as weeks continued to be wasted in inactivity, with Rosecrans piling up (and consuming) mountains of supplies, Garfield's impatience mounted. Impatient though he was, Garfield could still appreciate the reasons for Rosecrans's apparent timidity, even though he could not agree with them. The chief of these was Bragg's superiority in cavalry. Rebel cavalrymen roamed boldly behind Rosecrans's lines, forcing him to detach an excessive number of troops to guard his tenuous supply lines.[25]

It occurred to Garfield that two could play at this game of cutting supply lines. Why could the Army of the Cumberland not launch a cavalry raid behind Bragg's lines, smash his bridges, rip up his railroad tracks, burn his wagons, and destroy the wealth of the Confederacy that fed his army? Then, while Bragg was off balance, cut off from supplies and reenforcements, the Army of the Cumberland could move on Tullahoma with excellent chance of success. The raiders themselves would be expendable. After they had wrought the utmost damage, if worse came to worst, they would have to surrender, but "the loss of the whole force," Garfield estimated, "would be trifling in comparison with the advantage to us."

Since the raid was his responsibility, Garfield felt it only proper that he should lead it himself. "I have set my heart on this expedition more than on any one thing since I have been here," he told Chase. But Rosecrans refused to let Garfield risk himself on so dangerous a mission. Instead, the assignment went to Colonel Abel D. Streight of Indiana, who had served under Garfield after Corinth.

After weeks of careful planning, the raid was launched in late April. Bad luck dogged Streight's steps from the start. His supplies proved inadequate, especially the mules he had intended to use as mounts. Heavy rains slowed his movements, but the crowning misfortune came within a few days after Streight had cut loose behind the rebel lines. By an unhappy coincidence, Nathan Bedford Forrest, prince of Confederate cavalrymen, happened to be in Streight's path. For three days, Streight tried to shake his pursuers, in a running battle that covered one hundred and twenty miles, but to no avail. His supplies gave out, and his men were so exhausted that they even fell asleep "while lying in battle under severe skirmish fire." Streight surrendered, and his entire command was lost before it could even begin to inflict the damage for which it had been sent.

Lincoln was sorely disappointed at the failure of Garfield's "pet expedition," and General Stanley was furious at the "contemptible fizzle" of Garfield's "fool's plan." He blasted the raid as "the most senseless thing I saw done during the war to waste men and material," and he placed the blame squarely on Garfield, who "had no military ability, nor could he learn anything."[26]

This was hardly fair. The raid had come very near succeeding, and with a little luck it could have rendered Bragg's entire position untenable. The flaws were in the execution, not the conception. Garfield's role in the planning demonstrated a sound strategic sense coupled with boldness and flexibility: qualities that struck Henry Villard as remarkable, "for one whose experience as a commander had been limited to petty warfare, at the head of a small brigade . . . in Kentucky."

With the failure of the Streight raid, Rosecrans stepped up his demands on the War Department for supplies. His telegrams to Washington became even more petulant and acrimonious. Garfield tried to soften the tone of these dispatches, but to no avail. Rosecrans was convinced that he was being deliberately persecuted, and he made no secret of his feelings. He poured out his accusations to anyone within earshot. A passing journalist was appalled at Rosecrans's indiscretion: "he criticized General Halleck and Secretary Stanton with such freedom—with such total disregard of official propriety—not once, but repeatedly, that it really embarrassed me to listen to him. . . . He dwelt upon the disregard of some of his wishes by these superiors as a public wrong, and denounced as criminal their efforts to force him into the offensive before he was ready."[27]

As Garfield brooded over Rosecrans's reluctance to act, he was filled with "a sense of disappointment and mortification almost akin to shame." "I have been so distressed at the long delay of this army to move, . . ." he apologized to his wife, "that I could hardly write to anyone, more than to utter my disgust." In his opinion, the Army of the Cumberland had reached a peak of fighting efficiency by the early weeks of May. When at the same time his spies reported that Bragg had weakened his army in order to send reinforcements to Vicksburg, Garfield was sure that the hour to strike was at hand. "I pleaded for an advance," he said, "but not till June began did General Rosecrans begin seriously to meditate an immediate movement." In utter dismay Garfield watched the golden moment slip by. "I have no words to tell you," he wrote Secretary Chase, "with how restive and unsatisfied a spirit I waited and pleaded for striking a sturdy blow."[28]

To prod his reluctant chief, Garfield drafted plans for an offensive, plans which by early June seemed to have won Rosecrans's approval. Orders for the march were issued, and all the preparations set in motion for a grand offensive. "I have made my personal preparations, said my goodbyes to absent friends by letter, commended the cause, and myself to God and nerved myself up for the shock," Garfield announced. But on the eve of the movement, much to Garfield's dismay, "there seemed to fall down upon the leading officers of this army, as suddenly as a bolt from the blue, a most determined and decided opinion that there ought to be no immediate or early advance. Officers who . . . were restless and impatient for a forward movement, became suddenly conservative and cautious and think masterly inactivity the chiefest of virtues." The offensive was canceled, and Garfield told his disappointed friends back home, "I have given up all hope of either fighting or dying *at present.*"[29]

Before calling off the offensive, Rosecrans had taken the precaution of polling his leading generals. Not surprisingly, they voted for delay, perhaps sensing the answer that was expected of them. Garfield chose to believe that Rosecrans was eager to advance but had been overruled by his officers. "I know the General desires to move," he loyally insisted, "but it is hard to go with so many unwilling men in high places." But if Rosecrans really wanted to fight, why would he ask his friends to hold him back? Rosecrans, who knew all the military maxims, scarcely needed Halleck's cutting reminder: "Councils of war never fight."[30]

Garfield did not participate in the council's deliberations, but he was asked to prepare a report summarizing its arguments. On his own initiative, he expanded this report from the expected bare synopsis into an examination and refutation of the council's decision.

The most serious argument put forth by the council against the advance was that with Hooker's army beaten on the Potomac, and Grant's tied up in front of Vicksburg, "it is bad policy to risk our only reserve army to the chances of a general engagement. A failure here," the generals warned, "would have most disastrous effects on our lines of communication, and on politics in the loyal states." Therefore, they urged that the Army of the Cumberland stay its hand until Grant was safely done with Vicksburg, on the assumption that the best service they could render was to continue to keep Bragg immobile, and prevent him from reinforcing that beleaguered city. Of fourteen generals polled, ten believed that an advance on

Bragg's front, no matter what its outcome, would only make it easier for him to detach reinforcements against Grant.

Eleven out of thirteen generals expressed the fear that an advance would not result in a great or successful battle. "We should be compelled to fight the enemy on his own ground, or follow him in a fruitless stern chase," they argued; "Or if we attempted to outflank him and turn his position, we should expose our lines of communication, and run the risk of being pushed back into a rough country well-known to the enemy and little to ourselves." They pointed out that Middle Tennessee was dangerous terrain. "In case the enemy should fall back without accepting battle he could make our advance very slow, and with a comparatively small force posted in the gaps of the mountains could hold us back while he crossed the Tennessee River, where he would be measurely secure and free to send re-enforcements to Johnston."

In view of these hazards, Rosecrans's generals were inclined to be cautious. As Garfield summarized their arguments he found that although their premises varied, their conclusion was virtually unanimous in favor of delay:

> One officer thinks it probable that the enemy has been strengthened rather than weakened and that *he* (the enemy) would have a reasonable prospect of victory in a general battle.

> One officer believes the result of a general battle would be doubtful, a victory barren, and a defeat most disastrous.

> Three officers believe that an advance would bring on a general engagement. Three others believe it would not.

> Two officers express the opinion that the chances in a general battle are nearly equal.

> One officer expresses the belief that our army has reached its maximum strength and efficiency and that inactivity will seriously impair its effectiveness.

> Two officers say that an increase in our cavalry by about six thousand men would materially change the aspect of our affairs and give us a decided advantage.

This chorus of despair was grounded in part on the fear that Bragg's forces outnumbered those of the Army of the Cumber-

186

land. Garfield disagreed. For months his intelligence corps had been busy collecting information. From this data Garfield calculated that even in the improbable event "that Bragg would abandon all his rear posts, and entirely neglect his communications and could bring his last man into battle," he could still muster no more than 41,680 men[31] to meet the 65,137 effectives of the Army of the Cumberland. Since as a rule more soldiers are needed to attack a position than to defend it, this advantage in numbers was not so great as it might appear from a hasty comparison. Garfield, however, could not understand why the Army of the Cumberland, "which in January last defeated Bragg's superior numbers, can not overwhelm his present greatly inferior forces."

According to Garfield's calculations, Bragg's army was weaker because of his recent detachments to Vicksburg than it had ever been or was ever likely to be again. The Army of the Cumberland, on the other hand, was at its peak strength and, as Garfield pointedly reminded Rosecrans, in view of Washington's unsympathetic attitude, "we have no right to expect re-enforcements for several months, if at all." Garfield, therefore, was for striking at once, while they still retained their advantage. He brushed aside the argument that they should wait to see the fate of Grant at Vicksburg before committing themselves. "Whatever be the result at Vicksburg," he argued, "the determination of its fate will give large re-enforcements to Bragg. If Grant is successful, his army will require many weeks to recover from the shock and strain of his late campaign, while Johnston will send back to Bragg a force sufficient to insure the safety of Tennessee. If Grant fails, the same result will follow, so far as Bragg's army is concerned." In either case there was no valid excuse for delay.

Garfield then examined, one by one, the possible results of his proposed advance. These were three: defeat; victory in battle; and the retreat of Bragg without a battle. The possibility of defeat had to be faced. "No man can predict with certainty the result of any battle. . . . Such results," he reminded his pious commander, "are in the hands of God." Garfield was willing to run that risk, confident that God generally favored the strongest battalions.

But Garfield was hopeful that if Bragg could be maneuvered into an all-out battle, the chances of victory were excellent, and the consequences, Garfield thought, "would be in the highest degree disastrous to the rebellion." As Garfield had argued, over and over again: "Our true objective point is the Rebel army, whose last reserves are substantially in the field, and an effective blow will crush the shell, and soon be followed by the collapse of the Rebel government."

The advance could result in neither victory nor defeat, if Bragg fell back without giving battle. The other officers had argued that this situation would be most undesirable, since Bragg could thereby lure the Army of the Cumberland deeper into the wilds of Tennessee, where its superior numbers would be neutralized by rugged terrain and lengthened supply lines. From a purely tactical point of view their fears had considerable substance, but Garfield's superior grasp of the economic and psychological factors of warfare led him to conclude that such a retreat would be disastrous for Bragg. "Besides the loss of *materiel* of war and the abandonment of the rich and abundant harvest now nearly ripe in Central Tennessee," he retorted,

> he would lose heavily by desertion. It is well known that a widespread dissatisfaction exists among his Kentucky and Tennessee troops. They are already deserting in large numbers. A retreat would greatly increase both the desire and the opportunity for desertion and would very materially reduce his physical and moral strength. While it would lengthen our communications, it would give us possession of McMinnville, and enable us to threaten Chattanooga and East Tennessee; and it would not be unreasonable to expect an early occupation of the former place.

On the other hand, what would be the consequences of *not* advancing? A politician like Garfield always had one eye on the coming elections. He realized what the professional soldier, who scorned "mere politics," often tended to forget—that the ultimate decision depended as much on the steadfast will of the voter back home as it did on the soldier in the field. The Administration needed a military victory to sustain public confidence, and it needed it before, not after, the elections. In this

188

case, the much-derided "political general" displayed a broader vision than the West Point military specialists when he argued that "the turbulent aspect of politics in the loyal States renders a decisive blow against the enemy at this time of the highest importance to the success of the Government at the polls, and in the enforcement of the Conscription Act."

Garfield reminded his chief, perhaps unnecessarily, that "the Government and the War Department believe that this army ought to move upon the enemy. The army desires it, and the country is anxiously hoping for it." There was an implied threat behind these words, and it took genuine courage for Garfield to utter them. If Rosecrans continued to disappoint the government, Garfield not so subtly suggested, the government might very well replace him with a more aggressive commander.

Garfield immediately softened this threat with praise for Rosecrans's previous course of action. "You have, in my judgment," he said, "wisely delayed a general movement hitherto, till your army could be massed, and your cavalry could be mounted." Now, however, the time for delay was past, and the time for action had arrived. "Your mobile force can now be concentrated in twenty-four hours, and your cavalry, if not equal in numerical strength to that of the enemy, is greatly superior in efficiency and morale. For these reasons," Garfield concluded, "I believe an immediate advance of all our available forces is advisable, and, under the providence of God will be successful."[32]

With this report Garfield performed what may very well have been his greatest service to the Union cause during his entire two years in uniform. Faced with Garfield's arguments, which undercut all his excuses, Rosecrans had no choice but to advance.

In later years General Stanley scoffed at the claims made for Garfield's share in promoting the advance, contemptuously dismissing them as "a little cheap glory." As far as Garfield was concerned, Stanley snorted, "as he had no command, and had no right to vote, and as he was not consulted I cannot see the propriety of his claim. At any rate the council fully sustained Rosecrans and when he was ready to march he was cheerfully supported by every commander in the army."

Stanley's memory was as short as his temper. At the time, Garfield was given full blame for the advance. On the morning the Tullahoma campaign finally got underway, Crittenden stomped up to Garfield with an angry message: "It is understood, sir, by the general officers of the army, that this movement is your work. I wish you to understand that it is a rash and fatal move, for which you will be held responsible." He turned and stalked off without waiting for an answer. Ready or not, the Army of the Cumberland was on the move.[33]

CHAPTER ELEVEN

TO THE RIVER OF DEATH

On the twenty-fourth of June 1863, the Army of the Cumberland struck camp and began its long-delayed advance into Tennessee. Garfield had been pressing for just such a move for months, but when it finally got underway, he was uneasy. Instead of moving at once, as Garfield had urged in his report of June 12, Rosecrans had lingered at Murfreesboro for twelve days—"days which seemed months to me," Garfield said.[1]

The task facing the Army of the Cumberland was a formidable one. Advance rebel pickets were posted only five miles south of the Union lines at Murfreesboro, and behind the pickets Confederate general Braxton Bragg had constructed an elaborate defense in depth. Between Murfreesboro and the Tennessee River the Confederates had thrown up seven lines of defense, adroitly taking advantage of rivers, mountains, and other strong natural barriers. Only three gaps cut through these mountains, and each of them was guarded by a strong rebel detachment, capable of holding the pass until reinforced by the main army.

The tactical problem was remarkably like the one Garfield had faced outside Paintsville during his Sandy Valley campaign, although on a much larger scale. Rosecrans's solution to this problem bore a striking resemblance to Garfield's earlier strategy, a similarity so close as to raise a suspicion that Garfield might have planned the campaign himself. Rosecrans implied as much when, in his official report on the Tullahoma campaign, he singled out Garfield, "ever active, prudent and sagacious," for special praise. "I feel much indebted to him for both counsel and assistance in the administration of this army," he testified. "He possesses the energy and instinct of a great commander." Garfield remained discreetly silent on the matter. He believed that the commander, who was responsible for the ultimate decision and who stood to be blamed for any failure, should also reap the credit for success. As chief of staff, Garfield aspired only to become Rosecrans's alter ego. "I believe my army life has been as free from self-seeking and pride as any part of my whole life," he said, as he somewhat incongruously boasted of his humility. "I am doing a work here for which I shall never get a tithe of the credit that others will. Let it pass. I am glad to help save the republic."[2]

Whoever was responsible for the Tullahoma campaign (and the plans undoubtedly passed through many hands, including Garfield's), the conception was bold, vigorous, and ingenious. Each of the three passes was threatened in rapid succession (just like the deceptive moves on the three roads leading to Paintsville), but the main force was concentrated on Manchester Gap, the most difficult to approach, and hence the most lightly defended. At the same time, Wilder's cavalry brigade was sent behind the lines to destroy Bragg's communications. It was a dangerous plan, for it entailed splitting the army into segments which, for a perilous time, could not be coordinated with each other. Had Bragg maintained his poise and divined Rosecrans's intentions, he could have easily siezed the initiative and destroyed the Army of the Cumberland piecemeal. But like Humphrey Marshall at Paintsville, Bragg lost his nerve. Seeing three armies of uncertain size moving toward him, he decided to retreat and concentrate his scattered forces at Tullahoma for a defensive battle. No sooner had he reached this decision than, on June 29, word reached his headquarters of Wilder's raid behind his lines. Bragg's leading general, Leonidas K. Polk, demanded that he give up Tullahoma and fall back across the Tennessee towards Chattanooga, lest they be trapped in Tullahoma like Pemberton in Vicksburg.

Up to this point Garfield had been gratified at the progress of the campaign. "Our operations thus far have been success-

192

ful beyond the expectation of every one outside Hd Qrs," he declared with justifiable pride. ". . . I am delighted to see how fully my judgment has been vindicated." Bragg had clearly been bewildered by Rosecrans's deception. He had first concentrated at Shelbyville, allowing an advance Union division to sieze Manchester Gap by the 27th with scarcely any fighting. Garfield was right behind the troops, moving headquarters virtually to the front lines.[3]

Now all that remained to be done for complete success was to march on Tullahoma, which was then only lightly garrisoned. The portion of the Union army at Manchester Gap was actually closer to Tullahoma than Bragg's main force, which was stranded at Shelbyville. If they could reach Tullahoma before Bragg, the rebels would be trapped. With the enemy sitting on his line of retreat, Bragg would have to choose between fighting a battle on unfavorable ground, or else falling back in disorder to the hills of Alabama, where his army would be helpless to prevent the fall of Chattanooga, the gateway to the lower South. Everything hinged on getting to Tullahoma first. "The success of our whole movement depends upon throwing our force upon that place at the earliest possible time," Garfield pleaded, scenting victory.

Rosecrans's army, however, was in no condition to concentrate rapidly. His scattered men, mules, and wagons were too worn out from their forced marching to take advantage of the opportunity before them. Excess baggage further hampered their movements. In a near frenzy of frustration, Garfield furiously ordered these baggage trains lightened. "Officers and soldiers who are ready to die in the field," he exclaimed, "do not hesitate to disgrace themselves and imperil the army by luxuries unworthy of a soldier." To make matters worse, the whole campaign was waged during one of the most intense, prolonged rainstorms Garfield had ever seen, transforming the roads into nearly impassable bogs. The storm had begun on the very day that Rosecrans had moved out of Murfreesboro. Garfield found a measure of melancholy satisfaction in the reflection that the campaign might have succeeded completely had Rosecrans taken his advice and started the advance while the weather was still clear: "I shall never cease to regret the sad delay which lost us so great an opportunity to inflict a mortal blow upon the centre of the Rebellion," Garfield told Chase.[4]

As it turned out, Bragg was able to transfer his army from Shelbyville to Tullahoma by rail just ahead of the Army of the Cumberland. From there, taking Polk's advice, he retreated across the Tennessee River to Chattanooga. Like all of Garfield's carefully prepared traps in the Sandy Valley campaign, this one too failed to spring properly. Middle Tennessee was in the Union's hands once more, at the cost of less than a thousand casualties, but Bragg's army, the main object of Garfield's strategy, although demoralized, was still intact. Garfield had foreseen this possibility when he had first conceived the Tullahoma campaign. It was not the ideal result for which he had hoped—for that he needed a battle—but it was a substantial victory nonetheless and amply vindicated Garfield's judgment in arguing for the advance against the opposition of virtually the entire army.

On the third of July, the Army of the Cumberland marched into Tullahoma, just a few steps behind the fleeing Bragg. Had this taken place a few weeks earlier, the news might have been received by the victory-starved North with thanksgiving, and Rosecrans's reputation would have been secure but the public mind was so preoccupied with the more spectacular news from Gettysburg and Vicksburg on that same day that it scarcely noticed the less bloody victory in Tennessee. In discerning quarters, however, Rosecrans's achievement was appreciated. Whitelaw Reid hailed it as "a campaign perfect in its conception, excellent in its general execution." Even Halleck conceded that the campaign was "admirable," and another general pronounced it "not only the greatest operation in our war, but a great thing when compared to any war."[5]

Garfield did not join in the congratulations over the Tullahoma campaign. He looked upon it as only half a victory, and he could not rest content until the true objective—Bragg's army —had been crushed. With his customary eagerness he begged Rosecrans to follow up his success with a vigorous pursuit. "There are the strongest possible reasons for using every moment now before the rebels can recover from their late disaster," he pleaded. Rosecrans ignored his advice. After his burst of energy in the Tullahoma campaign, he lapsed once more into his customary caution. One of his favorite maxims dealt with "the importance of minor preparations," such as linchpins, to the success of military movements. After Tullahoma Rosecrans halted his army while he accumulated a fresh stock of linch-pins, as well as other supplies. His ill-tempered correspondence with the War Department was resumed, and the unhappy Gar-field suspected that the long story of procrastination which had followed Stone's River was about to be reenacted. "I can't tell you how disgusted I am with our slow movements," he con-fided to a friend. Although his personal affection for Rose-crans remained undiminished, Garfield was beginning to lose confidence in his commander's military judgment.[6]

Had he confined his misgivings to the circle of his friends and family, Garfield might have saved himself considerable embarrassment in later years. Instead, he also expressed his dissatisfaction to Secretary Chase. In a long letter, dated July 27, and marked "confidential," he poured out his pent-up grievance to the Secretary. "I have refrained hitherto," he explained, "lest I do injustice to a good man, and say to you things which were better left unsaid." But the time had come when Garfield could no longer keep his silence. "I cannot conceal from you the fact, that I have been greatly dissatisfied with the slow progress that we have made in the department since the battle of Stone River."

Garfield conceded that Rosecrans had not wasted all of this time, yet ever since early May, Garfield said, he "could not but feel that there was not that live and earnest determination to fling the great weight of this army into the scale and make its power felt in crushing the shell of the Rebellion." He told Chase of his efforts to induce Rosecrans to embark on the Tul-lahoma campaign, and of his disappointment over the failure to follow up that success with vigor. "I have . . . urged, with all the earnestness I possess, a rapid advance, while Bragg's army was shattered and under cover, and before [Confederate gen-eral Joseph E.] Johnston and he could effect a junction. Thus far the General has been singularly disinclined to grasp the situation with a strong hand, and make the advantage his own." If this inactivity continued much longer, Garfield de-

195

clared bitterly, he would ask to be relieved of his post, "and sent somewhere where I can be a part of a working army. . . . Pleasant as are my relations here, I would rather command a battalion that would follow and follow, and strike and strike, than to hang back while such golden moments are passing."

Garfield assured Chase that his unhappiness with Rosecrans was not due to any personal animosity. Quite the contrary, "I love every bone in his body," he insisted, "and next to my desire to see the Rebellion blasted is my anxiety to see him blessed. But even the breadth of my love is not sufficient to cover this almost fatal delay." Despite his affection, Garfield placed the blame for this delay squarely on Rosecrans. The general was blaming his failure to move on the neglect of the War Department to furnish him adequate supplies, but Garfield undercut this excuse by telling Chase (who could be counted on to pass the word to Stanton): "If the War Department has not always been just, it has certainly been indulgent to this army. But I feel that the time has now come when it should allow no plea to keep this army back from the most vigorous activity."[7]

This from a subordinate at a time when his chief was pleading with Washington for more supplies could hardly be considered proper military etiquette. Indeed, there were those who applied even harsher words to Garfield's conduct. In later years, after both Chase and Garfield were safely dead and unable to reply, Charles A. Dana "exposed" this letter, implying that it had been responsible for Rosecrans's dismissal from command. Rosecrans was outraged at this revelation of "blackest treachery" on the part of a trusted aide. "I had no idea," he said, "that I was harboring a person capable of such falseness and double-dealing or there would have been a court martial at once." Others shared Rosecrans's indignation. General Stanley, for one, could scarcely contain his anger when he thought of Garfield "sitting complacently cheerily at Rosecrans' table, whilst writing daily letters to cut his throat."[8]

Yet, what did Garfield's "treachery" consist of? Rosecrans knew of Garfield's views, which were scarcely kept hidden. He also knew that Garfield was in the habit of writing to Chase about army affairs. He had known of their close association when he had first brought Garfield into his official family, and had never objected to Garfield's earlier glowing reports of his doings to Chase. Quite the contrary, this friendship with Chase may have influenced Rosecrans to appoint Garfield in the first place. Was it disloyal for Garfield to go over his commander's head? That depended on where Garfield's first loyalty lay—to his chief or to his country. If Garfield truly believed that Rosecrans's inactivity was needlessly prolonging the war, how could he have kept silent? Perhaps he should have first resigned from Rosecrans's staff, but this would only have brought the disagreement out into the open. Besides, Garfield intended to enter Congress in a few months, which scarcely gave him enough time to settle into a new spot in the army. Had Chase allowed Garfield's accusations to fall into the hands of Rosecrans's enemies, there could have been some valid cause for condemning Garfield's course. But Chase kept the letter confidential, as Garfield had requested, and it was not made public until years after his death. Garfield's letter may have been indiscreet and unmilitary, but he was not a military man, and was not bound by military ethics. The military code may require closing up ranks against the civilian world, but Garfield, always a civilian at heart, did not regard civilian authority as alien or hostile. In short, Garfield believed that he was performing a painful, but necessary, duty.

Actually, Garfield's letter to Chase could not have done Rosecrans any damage, for official Washington had already reached the same conclusion. On July 24, Halleck had bluntly demanded that Rosecrans move on East Tennessee "immediately," before Joseph Johnston could join forces with Bragg. "There is great disappointment felt here at the slowness of your advance," Halleck chided. "Unless you can move more rapidly, your whole campaign will prove a failure. . . ." In a confidential aside, Halleck warned that, "the patience of the authorities here has been completely exhausted, and if I had not repeatedly promised to urge you forward, and begged for delay, you would have been removed from the command."[9]

Prodded by Garfield and the War Department, Rosecrans finally set his army in motion by mid-August, almost a month later than Garfield had thought he should. His hesitation had been prompted in part by apprehension over the difficult terrain which lay between him and Chattanooga. In this country stood some of the steepest, most inaccessible ridges in the entire South: a series of jagged slopes and narrow clefts dominated by Lookout Mountain, whose long, sinuous spine ran a twisting course through much of northern Alabama and the entire northwest corner of Georgia, terminating only at the suburbs of Chattanooga itself. Lookout was only one of a series of mountains, including Raccoon Mountain, Missionary Ridge, and Pigeon Mountain, which stood between Rosecrans and Bragg. According to the military textbooks, this was the most difficult of all terrains in which to wage aggressive war, and Rosecrans thought he had good cause to be cautious.

On the other side of those mountains, however, Braxton Bragg was equally nervous. Standing on the summit of a ridge, he gazed at the magnificent prospect before him and turned in irritation to General Daniel H. Hill. "It is said to be easy to defend a mountainous country," he snapped, "but mountains hide your foe from you, while they are full of gaps through which he can pounce upon you at any time. A mountain is like the wall of a house filled with rat-holes. The rat lies hidden at his hole, ready to pop out when no one is watching." Sweeping his arm across the valley below, he asked rhetorically, "Who can tell what lies hidden behind that wall?"[10]

Hidden behind that wall, just as Bragg feared, was the Army of the Cumberland, moving swiftly and silently along a wide front, ready to pour through every rat hole. Rosecrans now thought that he had taken Bragg's measure, and he had sized up his antagonist as a man who could be counted on to jump at shadows. Rather than force him out of Chattanooga by a risky battle or a lengthly siege, Rosecrans decided to outmaneuver Bragg, just as he had done in the Tullahoma campaign.

Dividing his army into fragments, he sent Wilder's unit north of Chattanooga to shell the town and divert Bragg's attention. Wilder's threat was pure bluff. With only a small detachment he managed to create the illusion of a large force. Each night his men would lay out a long string of campfires to warm imaginary regiments. During the day they pounded on barrels. When the sound was wafted to Chattanooga, it sounded as if a fleet of boats were being built for an attack across the Tennessee River. As a final touch, his men industriously sawed boards into pieces and threw the scraps in the river, so that the Confederates downstream might see them float by and conclude that the Federals were building pontoon bridges. While Bragg's attention was riveted on Wilder's nonexistent threat to his north, Rosecrans threw the main body of his army across the Tennessee at various points to the south and west of Chattanooga, using Lookout Mountain to screen his movements.

This campaign was to be the climax of Garfield's military career, but he almost missed it. When the Chattanooga campaign began, Garfield was lying in sickbed with a recurrence of the fever that had laid him low the preceding year. "Oh, how puny I have become," he groaned. He was almost tempted to return to Ohio on sick leave. John Beatty, who visited his tent, freely admitted that if he were as sick as Garfield seemed to be, he would unhesitatingly pull "the sick dodge," riding all the way to Ohio and swimming the rivers, if necessary, in order to see his home once again. But Garfield felt bound by duty. "You came near having me at home, . . ." he told his wife, "and nothing but my will, and the great work before this army in which the Gen. says he don't know how to spare me, kept you and the *little coger* from seeing me." After pleading so long for an advance, Garfield could not bear to leave his post once the move had begun. "It is not vanity," he candidly asserted, "for me to say that no man in this army can fill my place during this movement. It would take him several months to learn the character and condition of affairs as I know them and to hold that influence with the commanding General that I do."[11]

Loyal Captain Swaim had Garfield's cot hauled to the banks of the Tennessee, near the proposed crossing, and Garfield forced himself to sit up and regain his strength. He was determined to allow nothing to keep him from being in on the kill, even if he had to watch it from an ambulance. That was not necessary. By August 29, when the bridge was ready, Garfield was able to pull himself into the saddle and ride to the banks overlooking the Tennessee to watch the crossing. The river at this point was five hundred feet wide, and uncommonly beautiful. To Beatty, who rode alongside Garfield, the peaceful, bucolic setting seemed inappropriate for all this military bustle. "The island below, the heavily wooded banks, the bluffs and mountains," he observed, "present a scene that would delight the soul of an artist." The crossing was more like a picnic outing than a military expedition. "A hundred boys were frolicking in the water near the pontoons, tumbling into the stream in all sorts of ways, kicking up their heels, ducking and splashing each other, and having a glorious time generally."[12]

The ruse was a complete success. Not a shot was fired to mar the crossing. Once safely across the river, the Army of the Cumberland debouched behind the mountains, swiftly pouring through the gaps south of Chattanooga. When Bragg woke up to what was happening, it was almost too late. He pulled out of Chattanooga before he was trapped inside, allowing this nearly impregnable citadel, and with it all of East Tennessee, to fall effortlessly into the hands of the Union. It seemed to be the story of Tullahoma all over again, with Bragg outmaneuvered and retreating before Rosecrans's superior generalship. Rosecrans was convinced that Bragg was retreating in confusion to Rome, Georgia. Anxious to intercept Bragg's fleeing army, Rosecrans, reckless for once, flagged his scattered columns on, rushing them down all the roads leading to Rome, rather than concentrating them in Chattanooga for an orderly advance in strength. Victory was in the air, and Garfield's thoughts began to turn to Congress, now that peace seemed so near.

But to more experienced officers, something seemed terribly wrong. General Hazen sensed that Bragg's force was not behaving the way a retreating army should. Where were the stragglers and deserters, he wondered? Where was the pillage and looting that always accompanied a demoralized army? Bragg, in fact, was not demoralized, nor was he in flight towards Rome. After abandoning Chattanooga on September 8, he had withdrawn behind the mountains, ready to pounce upon the unsuspecting Army of the Cumberland. The mountains hid both armies from each other, and neither was aware of the position of the enemy. For the first half of September, Rosecrans's scattered columns poured blithely through the mountain passes of Georgia, unaware of the trap which lay ahead. As Confederate General Daniel Hill later wryly commented: "Surely in the annals of warfare there is no parallel to the coolness and nonchalance with which General Crittenden marched and counter-marched for a week with a delightful unconsciousness that he was in the presence of a force of superior strength."[13]

Meanwhile, at his headquarters in Chattanooga, a glimmer of suspicion was beginning to disturb Rosecrans's tranquility. He confided his fears to Charles A. Dana, Second Assistant Secretary of War, who had just arrived at Chattanooga on a special mission from Secretary Stanton.

Dana was probably the last man in the army Rosecrans should have trusted at that moment. Although his official duties were vague, his real purpose in camp was to spy on Rosecrans for the War Department. Dana was not an impartial observer. A loyal friend of Grant's, Dana would unhesitatingly undermine any general who might rival his hero. Archibald Gracie was astounded that "any general of a great army or any man of self-respect could have tolerated as did Rosecrans, the presence in his camp of such an official, whom he knew to be there to spy on him and to criticize his every action." Dana's "sole duty," Gracie claimed, was "custodian of all the gossip of the army that could be collected . . ." Most of Rosecrans's officers shunned Dana, that "loathsome pimp," as General Gordon Granger inelegantly labeled him, but Rosecrans, whose judgment of enemies was as inept as his judgment of friends, took him into his confidence and treated him to his customary indiscreet harangue on how Stanton, Halleck, and other enemies in Washington were deliberately starving his army.

After he calmed down, Rosecrans explained his situation to Dana. His army, he said, was spread out over a fifty-mile front, and so widely dispersed that his three main corps, those of Thomas, Crittenden, and McCook, could not possibly come to each other's aid if one were attacked. In view of Bragg's suspicious behavior, Rosecrans was ordering his corps commanders to pull back in order to concentrate east of Lookout Mountain. Although cautious, Rosecrans was not yet unduly concerned.

He still thought that he had Bragg on the run, and he interpreted the signs of resistance as nothing more than an attempt to delay his pursuit.[14]

He clung to this delusion for a few days longer, but as signs continued to mount, he was compelled to face unpleasant reality. "A battle is imminent," Garfield declared on September 13. "I believe the enemy now intends to fight us." The overconfidence of the past weeks was replaced by a sobering conviction that Bragg, far from being defeated, actually held the advantage. "He has a large force, and the advantage in position," Garfield calculated. "Unless we can outmaneuver him, we shall be in a perilous situation. But we will try." Rosecrans's imprudently scattered divisions were hastily called together, and telegrams went out to clergymen all over the nation to pray for victory.

While this frantic concentration was being carried out, Bragg obligingly stayed his hand. Apparently as bewildered by Rosecrans's moves as Rosecrans was by his, he let slip the opportunity to deliver a counterstroke while his enemy was off balance. By the 16th of September, Garfield was beginning to breathe easy once more. The danger, however, was still acute. Rumors, which proved to be true, had reached headquarters that Bragg was being reinforced by a number of divisions from Lee's army in Virginia, but Garfield still felt confident of success. "Thank God that the forces are concentrating on both sides for a final struggle," he said. "It will I believe be the finishing great blow."

By September 19 the two armies were face to face. The Army of the Cumberland had crossed over Missionary Ridge into McLemore's Cove, which lay between that ridge and Pigeon Mountain. Bragg was concentrated behind Pigeon Mountain. Only a narrow, wooded valley separated the two armies. This valley was of crucial importance, for it held the key to Rossville, which, in turn, commanded the road to Chattanooga. If Bragg could turn Rosecrans's left flank, and come between him and Rossville, Chattanooga would fall, Rosecrans would be isolated, and not only would the work of the summer be undone, but the Army of the Cumberland might well be wiped out. Both armies, therefore, desperately needed control of this

valley, which was named for the stream which ran through it—
Chickamauga Creek, a Cherokee word which (according to a
dubious tradition) meant "River of Death."[15]

At nine o'clock on the morning of September 19, the roar of
gunfire reached Garfield's headquarters at Crawfish Spring,
Georgia. From the confused reports that began to pour in, it
appeared that the bitterest fighting was on the left, where
Thomas was guarding the vital road to Chattanooga. At one
o'clock Rosecrans shifted his command post nearer to the
scene of action, taking over a cabin belonging to the Widow
Glenn. Garfield spread out his maps and dispatches on her
kitchen table, while the widow herself, with frightened children
clinging to her skirt, hovered nervously by. Every now and
then, Garfield would look up from his work to give the children a reassuring pat on the head. Then he would return to his
desk to take up again the direction of the bloodiest battle yet
fought in the West.

Actually, at this stage of the battle there was very little to
direct. More than any other fight of the war, Chickamauga
was a "soldiers' battle." The overgrown thickets, dense woods,
and tangled underbrush that grew along the River of Death
made it impossible to supervise the rapidly shifting battle
front. The men fought desperately in small clumps, wherever
they ran across the enemy. They were on their own, often unaware of what was happening only a few hundred yards to
either side. Rosecrans was at his best when he could personally
oversee all the action, as at Stone's River. Like many generals
of the Civil War, he found it difficult to command troops he
could not see. At Stone's River his presence had turned a lost
battle into victory, but the broken terrain of Chickamauga would
make it difficult to reenact that miracle.

The battle raged throughout the day—a series of blind, uncoordinated, bloody skirmishes. With the approach of night the
firing died down, and the weary soldiers slept on their arms,
ready to resume the battle with the dawn. Neither side had any
great advantage to show for the day's fighting, but the tactical
victory, such as it was, seemed to belong to Rosecrans. "The
result of the battle," Dana hopefully reported that night to
Washington, "is that the enemy is defeated in [his] attempt to

turn and crush our left flank and regain possession of Chattanooga. His attempt was furious and obstinate, his repulse was
bloody, and maintained till the end. If he does not retreat Rosecrans will renew the fight at daylight."[16]

While the soldiers slept, the Union generals were assembling at the Widow Glenn's for a council of war. Old "Pap"
Thomas, whose corps had seen the heaviest fighting, had not
slept for two nights. He settled into an armchair and dozed
through the entire meeting. Every time someone asked him a
question, he would nod and mumble, "I would strengthen the
left." "Where are we going to take it from?" Rosecrans kept
asking him. But Thomas, asleep again, gave no reply.

His drowsy advice was sound, and by midnight Rosecrans
had determined to reinforce the left by closing in McCook's
corps, so as to protect the all-important Rossville Road. The
orders for the next day's dispositions were read, coffee was
served, and McCook was called upon to end the meeting on a
cheerful note by singing "The Hebrew Maiden." The council
of war broke up, and Garfield and the rest of the staff tried to
get some sleep for the hard day ahead. The night was bitter
cold, and the wind whistled through the cracks in the cabin's
walls and floor.[17]

That same night, while Garfield was tossing uneasily on the
cold cabin floor, the rebels, only a few miles away, were making their preparations. Reinforcements from Lee's army had
been arriving by rail all day. Direct rail connections with Virginia had been broken, and these troops had had to take a
roundabout route. Some advance units had managed to
arrive in time to take part in the fighting on the 19th, and
others were streaming in even after the battle had begun. With
the addition of these two fresh, battle-tested divisions the Confederates would be able to field, for the first time in any
major battle of the war, an army significantly stronger than
their enemy's.

James Longstreet, Lee's second-in-command, reached Georgia on the afternoon of the 19th. No one from Bragg's staff
was there to greet him, and he had to find his way to headquarters by the sound of gunfire. In his search he wandered
into the federal lines and barely escaped capture, but by

204

midnight he had located Bragg, and by early morning he was at his post, commanding the left, directly opposite Rosecrans's right wing, which had been weakened during the night to strengthen Thomas on the Union left.

A clammy fog hung over the battlefield on the morning of September 20. By a freak of light, the atmosphere was suffused with a dull red glow—an eerie and ominous portent that would long be remembered as "the bloody dawn" of Chickamauga. Rosecrans was up before the sun to hear mass. He emerged silent and withdrawn, clenching an unlit cigar between his teeth, with an abstracted, moody air about him. He was clearly tired, and for once he seemed drained of his usual store of nervous vitality. In the presence of his soldiers he made a show of confidence and high spirits, but when he thought he was unobserved, the evidences of strain were unmistakable. A newspaper reporter who knew him well saw the mask drop for an unguarded moment and was frightened by his haggard appearance. "Rosecrans is usually brisk, nervous, powerful of presence," he said, "and to see him silent and absorbed in what looked like gloomy contemplation, filled me with indefinable dread."[18]

At dawn Rosecrans mounted his ungainly gray horse, collected his staff, and rode silently down the line to inspect his troops. He was not satisfied with their arrangement, and he fussed over their location all morning, shifting them back and forth to the general confusion of his subordinates. The battle was resumed at about nine o'clock, concentrated, as on the day before, mostly on the left, but with increasing activity on the right.

Shortly after ten-thirty, a staff officer galloped up to headquarters and reported that Brannan's division seemed to be out of its proper place in line, leaving a gap between Wood and Reynolds. Jumping to the conclusion that he had already sent Brannan to Thomas earlier that morning, Rosecrans dashed off an order to General Thomas J. Wood to close up the gap.

The order was written down by Major Frank Bond, not by Garfield. Garfield wrote most of the orders Rosecrans issued that day,[19] but although he was standing nearby, he did not, for reasons never explained, write this fatal order to Wood.

205

Garfield prided himself on the clarity and precision of his prose. As chief of staff, he had cultivated a direct, vigorous style for his dispatches. For the sake of clarity, he was always careful to explain the reasons behind orders, as well as to provide a discretionary escape-clause to take care of changing circumstances. The prose style of Rosecrans, on the other hand, tended to be ambiguous, running from windy oratory to laconic obscurity. As General Gordon Granger once complained, "Frequently I have great trouble in making out your exact meaning, owing to the haste or imperfect manner in which dispatches are written or copied."

The order to Wood was terse and peremptory: "The general commanding directs that you close upon Reynolds as fast as possible and support him." When the messenger hesitated for a moment, not fully understanding the order's intent, Garfield called out that its purpose was to enable Wood to fill the gap left by the withdrawal of Brannan. The order, with its supplementary verbal explanation was carried to Wood, who was at that time only six hundred yards from Rosecrans's command post. When he read the order, Wood was dumbfounded. As anyone could plainly see, Brannan was right where he belonged, between Wood and Reynolds. In that case, the messenger replied, there is no order, and he rode back to Rosecrans to explain the mix-up.[20]

This was not the end of the matter, however. Wood, whom Garfield had once described as a very narrow and impetuous man, lacking both prudence and brains, was still smarting from a squabble he had had with Rosecrans only a few days before. On that occasion Wood had, on his own discretion, disregarded an order which he had thought unwise. When Rosecrans had learned of the disobedience, he had given Wood a humiliating dressing-down. Rosecrans had a fearful temper and a sulphurous tongue. The contents of his reprimand to Wood were not reported, but probably the gist of it (interlaced with profanity) was that Rosecrans would do any thinking that needed to be done in the Army of the Cumberland. Wood submitted a fifty-page rejoinder on the impropriety of "blind obedience to orders," but he had not yet received a satisfactory reply from his chief, and the humiliation still rankled.[21]

Now, as he looked more closely at the order handed him on the battlefield, he saw that technically it left him no discretion. Whether through spite, or an untimely conversion to the virtues of blind obedience, he decided to ignore the verbal qualifications and execute the written order to the letter. Had he wanted clarification he could easily have checked with Rosecrans, who was only a five-minute walk from his position, but just as in a similar situation at Balaclava, when somebody blundered, the two men were not on speaking terms. Smugly reasoning that "however unfortunate the mistake, . . . the responsibility . . . rests on General Rosecrans who gave the order . . . and not on the subordinate who executed it," Wood directed his division to "close upon Reynolds," as commanded. Since Brannan's division was in the way, Wood had to take his troops out of line and march them behind Brannan. By doing this, Wood created the very thing Rosecrans's order had intended to prevent—a gap in the line.

Directly opposite Wood's position, on the Confederate side of the lines, Longstreet had been preparing an attack for most of the morning. By unhappy coincidence he launched it at the precise moment when Wood was out of place. Longstreet's men poured out of the woods, screaming their wild rebel yell and sweeping over the token resistance that tried to stem them. The Union line was shattered, and astonished Federals looked up to see a horde of gray swarming over what had been, only moments before, rear headquarters. Charles Dana had earlier stretched out on the grass for a nap. Awakened by "the most infernal noise I ever heard," he sat up and saw Rosecrans crossing himself. "Hello," Dana said to himself, "if the general is crossing himself, we are in a desperate situation," and he hopped on his horse and galloped to safety. "I saw our lines break and melt away," he said, "like leaves before the wind. Then the headquarters around me disappeared." Garfield was in the very center of the rout. He and other officers tried to restore order, but it was no use, "for men were as deaf to reason in their mad panic as would be a drove of stampeded cattle." Both Garfield and Rosecrans were swept completely off the battlefield by the human tide.[22]

When they realized that nothing could be done to check the

collapse of the right wing, Garfield and Rosecrans turned down the Dry Valley Road to the safety of Rossville and Chattanooga. Making their way through the debris of defeat, they struggled past overturned wagons, abandoned artillery, terrified horses, and the panic-crazed stragglers swarming to the rear. Rosecrans was oblivious to the tumult. He sat slumped in his saddle, lost in despair, drained of both energy and will. Never again would he be "old Rosy," so confident and assured. He was now a broken man, and across his face would flit forever a haunted look—"the shadow of Chickamauga."[23]

From all that Garfield and Rosecrans could see, the disaster had been complete. Yet as they rode north, they could still hear sounds of battle coming from Thomas's position on the left. To Garfield, the steady, disciplined volleys seemed to indicate that Thomas's men were still holding their ground. If so, the battle was not yet lost. He begged Rosecrans to go to Thomas, or at least halt for a time at Rossville until they had definite information. Rosecrans, however, insisted that the gunfire they heard was only scattered firing, such as would come from a shattered army. Convinced that the field was already lost, his only thought was to reach Chattanooga and prepare its defenses. Garfield disagreed, and he asked for permission to try to contact Thomas on his own, to determine for himself the condition of the army. Rosecrans finally gave his assent, "listlessly and mechanically," and then bade Garfield an emotional farewell, as if he never expected to see him alive again. The two men parted, and the dazed general took up his mournful retreat to Chattanooga. Rosecrans had made a fatal mistake. However well justified his action might have seemed at the time, he had given the impression of running away from the battlefield at the very time his presence was most needed. For the rest of his life he would have to explain, with tiresome insistence, why he had left the field of battle. But it was too late for explanations; his career had been destroyed.[24]

As Rosecrans was trudging sadly northward, Garfield was riding across Missionary Ridge into legend. Garfield himself never described his ride except in conversation with friends, but in later years it would be embroidered by imaginative biographers into a heroic epic. As they told the story of "that world-famous ride," Garfield and his small escort galloped up and down the Dry Valley Road, past the gantlet of rebel troops, trying to find a way to reach Thomas. Longstreet's men seemed everywhere, and for all Garfield could tell, Thomas might be completely surrounded or even wiped out. "It was a race between the rebel column and the noble steed on which Garfield rode." Despairing of finding a clear road, they cut across open country: "Over ravines and fences, through an almost impenetrable undergrowth, sometimes through a marsh, and then over broken rocks, the smoking steed plunged without a quiver." Passing by a Confederate pest-house "the great-hearted chief-of-staff" tossed his purse to the unfortunate men and rode on. "Crashing, tearing, plunging, rearing through the forest dashed the steed. Poet's song could not be long to celebrate that daring deed." In a cotton field they suddenly ran into a rebel ambush. With rifle-balls whizzing about their ears, they scattered for safety. One by one, the escort dropped by the way, until only Garfield was left to reach Thomas and discover that the Union still held the field. As a final touch to the epic, "the horse which had borne Garfield on his memorable ride, dropped dead at his feet," when he reached safety.[25]

Whatever did happen on that famous ride, its practical results were negligible. Thomas was perfectly capable of holding firm without Garfield's assistance. Garfield had really undertaken the ride for his private satisfaction. By leaving Rosecrans he had disassociated himself from the taint of defeat. There was nothing he could do for Thomas; he just wanted to be there. The experience was for him, he said, "a glorious moment." He alone, of the entire army, had witnessed both the defeat of the morning and the triumph of the afternoon.

Garfield reached Thomas shortly before three forty-five, just in time to take part in the heaviest fighting. He spent the rest of the day at Thomas's side in a fever of exaltation. At one point he and Thomas almost rode into the enemy lines before an alert soldier pulled them back to safety. Garfield fully realized that he was watching one of the great moments of the war. Outnumbered, almost surrounded, Thomas held his ground for five hours against repeated Confederate charges. Displaying a calm determination and steady will that contrasted sharply with Rosecrans's nervous impetuosity, Thomas saved the demoralized Union army and prevented Longstreet from recapturing Chattanooga, earning forever the title "Rock of Chickamauga." Garfield's admiration for Thomas from that day on amounted almost to hero-worship. He thought him the strongest general of the war: "His character was as grand and simple as a colossal pillar of unchiseled granite." Had Thomas only lived longer, Garfield later claimed, he would have been President of the United States.[26]

The last Confederate attack was beaten off shortly before sunset. Ammunition was so low that the charging rebels had to be shoved back by naked bayonets. "Longstreet's Virginians have got their bellies full," Garfield crowed, and he begged Rosecrans to return to Rossville and take up the battle again the next day. Flushed with excitement from the glorious day's stand, Garfield was probably overoptimistic. General Beatty, whose judgment was probably sounder, thought that the army was "simply a mob," and he feared that if the fighting should be resumed, it would be "blotted out." Garfield himself admitted that he was "half dead with fatigue," and the rest of the army was probably in no better condition. On Rosecrans's orders Thomas withdrew to Rossville. Garfield returned to Chattanooga to tell the story of the gallant stand to Crittenden, McCook, and the other generals who had left the field. Shortly afterwards the rest of the army, including Thomas, joined them, as the entire Army of the Cumberland concentrated in Chattanooga.

Rosecrans tried to put the best face on the situation with a congratulatory proclamation to his army: "You have made a grand and successful campaign," he told them. "When the day closed you held the field, from which you withdrew in the face of overpowering numbers, to occupy the point for which you set out—Chattanooga."[27] True enough, the army still held Chattanooga, but they were imprisoned in their own fortress. Cut off on three sides, with its back to the river, the Army of the Cumberland, so lately the pursuer, found itself trapped, and in grave danger of starvation, if not annihilation. As he looked out upon the line of rebel campfires that ringed the city, General Beatty felt something close to despair:

> The two armies are lying face to face. The Federal and Confederate sentinels walk their beats in sight of each other. The quarters of the rebel generals may be seen from our camp with the naked eye. The long lines of campfires almost encompass us.[28]

Garfield expected the battle to be resumed shortly, and, as he wrote his wife on the twenty-third of September, he clearly expected the worst. "If calamity befalls us you may be sure we shall sell ourselves as dearly as possible," he declared, striking what he thought to be the proper heroic tone. "The country will triumph if we do not. Kiss little Trot for me, a hundred times. . . . Whatever betide, I hope you will never have cause to blush on my account."[29] That same day he sent a desperate telegram to Chase in Washington:—WE CAN STAND HERE TEN DAYS, IF HELP WILL THEN ARRIVE. IF WE HOLD THIS POINT WE SHALL SAVE THE CAMPAIGN, EVEN IF WE LOSE THIS ARMY.

This telegram set in motion an extraordinary chain of events which ultimately saved the Army of the Cumberland. It reached Washington shortly before midnight, and a messenger was immediately sent to fetch Chase from his bed. He hastily dressed and dashed over to the War Department, filled with the dread suspicion that the news could only be the loss of Chattanooga and the destruction of the army. "More bad news?" he asked Stanton. "No," the War Secretary replied; "what there is [is] favorable," and he handed Garfield's telegram to Chase. Within a short time, Lincoln, Seward, and Halleck arrived, and they discussed the situation long into the night. Stanton suggested that 30,000 men be detached from the eastern front and rushed to Chattanooga by rail. He boasted that it could be done within five days, but Lincoln was skeptical. The President was willing to bet that the troops could not even reach Washington in five days, much less Chattanooga.

Stanton rose to the challenge. Calling together the nation's leading railroad men, he bullied and inspired them to supreme effort. Orders were issued, all available rolling stock was requisitioned, the tracks were cleared, and locomotives sped west at full throttle. Only seven days later, over 20,000 soldiers, with horses, ammunition and equipment pulled into Chattanooga, in the greatest logistic feat of the war.[30]

The Army of the Cumberland was reinforced, but it was not yet out of danger. Until the "Cracker Line" for supplies could be reopened, it faced actual starvation. Until then Rosecrans had to stand firm. Lincoln sent a message to stiffen his resolve: "If he can only maintain this position," the President asked Halleck to assure Rosecrans, ". . . this rebellion can only eke out a short and feeble existence, as an animal sometimes may with a thorn in its vitals."

"Bragg is a good dog," Rosecrans had conceded in an expansive mood after his victory at Stone's River, "but Hold Fast's a better." Hold Fast was now the order of the day as the Army of the Cumberland dug in until help could arrive. "Bruised and torn by a two day's unequal contest, its flags are still up and its men still unwhipped. It has taken its position here, and here, by God's help," Beatty grimly vowed, "it will remain." Morale was high. Even though Confederate cannon shelled the helpless city from the heights of Lookout Mountain (which Rosecrans had unwisely abandoned without a struggle, overruling Garfield's anguished protest that it could and should be held), there was no panic. One shell whizzed right through the open flap of a pup tent, narrowly missing two Ohio boys inside. One turned to the other and said, "There you damn fool, you see what you get by leaving your door open."[31]

The cool determination of the enlisted men was not shared by the bickering generals. Cooped up inside the city, tempers flared as they turned upon one another. The aftertaste of defeat soured army relations. Leading officers sought scapegoats for the disaster, and they settled upon Crittenden and McCook for their "desertion" of the battle field, threatening to resign in a body unless the offending generals were dismissed. This put Rosecrans in an awkward position, for his behavior at the battle could be interpreted in the same light.

Garfield found himself in a painful dilemma. Although he was bound to his commander by ties of loyalty and friendship, he could no longer serve under him. His faith in Rosecrans's military judgment had been lost forever somewhere along the Dry Valley Road. Acutely uncomfortable amid the intrigue

212

that swirled around army headquarters, Garfield was thankful
when orders came commanding him to report to Washington.
Certain officers, jealous of his influence with his chief, were
just as happy to see him go. "Garfield, though smart, is by no
means a strong man," commented one, "and with less confidence and assurance of his own superiority would be a much
safer and more valuable chief advisor. I do not believe, though
he was a useful man, his absence will prove a serious loss."
Rosecrans, however, who needed every defender he could muster, regretted his departure and gave him a handsome commendation to carry off with him. When Garfield was about
to leave, Thomas called him aside and said, "You know the
injustice of all these attacks on Rosecrans. Make it your business to set these matters right."[32]

It was too late for Garfield, or anyone else, to set matters
right for Rosecrans. The President and Stanton had already decided that a change in command was necessary, and only their
fear of the effect of such a move on the fall election in Ohio had
delayed their action. Rosecrans's position hung by a thread.
Symbolically, the day after Garfield and Steedman left Chattanooga, the long pontoon bridge across the Tennessee
snapped, and with it went the army's last link with the north.

Garfield's first stop was Louisville, where he was scheduled
to confer with Stanton. Shortly before he arrived in Kentucky,
Garfield picked up a newspaper and read that Grant had been
named commander of all union forces in the West, Thomas had
been placed in charge of the Army of the Cumberland, and
Rosecrans was about to be shunted off to chase guerrillas in
Missouri. Garfield sent his old commander assurance of sympathy. "The action of the War Dep't fell upon me like the
sound of a fire bell," he wrote in tones of shocked surprise. "I
am sure that it will be the verdict of the people that the War
Dep't has made a great mistake and have done you a great
wrong."

Rosecrans blamed his humiliation on Stanton's spite. "I
was removed by Stanton because he hates me," Rosecrans
charged. "I am Mordecai whom the little Haman wants to
hang on a gallows 'sixty cubits high.' " This was not quite
the whole story. Stanton certainly welcomed the removal of a

213

general who had given him so much trouble, but the final decision was not made by him, but by Grant. Given the choice between Rosecrans and Thomas, Grant unhesitatingly chose the latter rather than Rosecrans, whom he regarded as unreliable and insubordinate.[33]

For years, however, rumors were whispered about to the effect that Garfield had played some part in the dismissal of Rosecrans. These rumors were brought into the open by Charles A. Dana, who had long carried on a vendetta with Garfield in the sensation-filled pages of his *New York Sun*. On November 26, 1879, Dana published an expose, revealing that a letter from Garfield to Chase had persuaded the government to relieve Rosecrans. Dana's accusation, if true, Rosecrans told Garfield, "sets you in the light of a double dealer and traitor to your chief." Although he assured Garfield that he did not for a moment believe Dana, Rosecrans asked for a specific denial, just to set the record straight. Garfield righteously repudiated the charge: "I can only say . . . that any charge, whether it comes from Dana, or any other liar, to the effect that I was in any sense untrue to you or unfaithful to our friendship, has no particle of truth in it," and he challenged "all the rascals in the world" to publish their evidence.[34]

Rosecrans professed himself satisfied, but the matter refused to die. Two years later, with Garfield fresh in his tomb, Dana resumed the attack. He published Garfield's letter to Chase of July 27, 1863 (which was, of course, written well before Chickamauga), and implied that in this, and other letters to Chase, Garfield had stabbed the trusting Rosecrans in the back. Dana was not inhibited by the fact that he had not seen these other letters (for the very good reason that they had never existed), and he raised a fresh torrent of accusations against the dead President. This time Rosecrans believed the charges, and a shocked nation, scarcely recovered from months of unparalleled mourning, was so stung by this evidence of duplicity in its hero that Garfield's reputation began to dim.[35]

Despite the confidence with which he made his charges, Dana's evidence was flimsy, based primarily on inference and hearsay. His informants were none too reliable: James R. Gilmore, a notorious romancer; Jacob Schuckers, the eccentric

214

biographer of Chase (whose testimony, upon closer examination, actually undercut Dana's charge rather than supported it); and Montgomery Blair, Postmaster General in Lincoln's cabinet.

According to Blair's recollection, Lincoln once told him that he had fired Rosecrans on the basis of damning testimony from Garfield. "On that point," Blair insisted to Dana, "I can not be mistaken. I was astonished at Garfield's treachery at the time as the whole world is now." Blair's explanation for Garfield's betrayal was that Garfield had hoped to become commander of the Army of the Cumberland himself, once Rosecrans was out of the way.

> Garfield although a base fellow was not a fool to volunteer such treachery, except for a great personal object. His betrayal of Rosecrans, like his betrayal of [John] Sherman at Chicago [at the Republican convention of 1880] was to further an intrigue, to procure for himself the place from which Rosecrans was removed in one case and to which Sherman aspired in the other.[36]

It took Blair almost twenty years to get around to making his charges against Garfield. By that time he was an old man whose memory had been blurred by decades of partisan bitterness. His recollection of the chronology of events was jumbled, and he contradicted himself. In a letter to Rosecrans of 1880, he implied that Garfield had *talked* to Lincoln before the dismissal, a manifest impossibility. In 1882 he still stuck to his earlier story, but he hedged it with so many qualifications and inferential suppositions as to cast grave doubts upon his reliability.

When Blair had first met Garfield, in the fall of 1863, at the very time when, according to his later memory, he was "astonished at his duplicity," he showed neither resentment nor suspicion. According to Albert Gallatin Riddle, Blair's first impression was one of unqualified admiration. "Garfield," he was heard to say, "is a great man." Within less than a year, however, the two men had become bitter political enemies. A Blair never forgave nor forgot: an enemy was to be pursued to the grave, and beyond, if possible.[37]

215

Dana's informants, therefore, were unreliable. Yet, when Dana made his charges against Garfield, he knew something they did not. He knew, from first-hand evidence, that a trusted associate of Rosecrans *had* written secret reports to Washington, reports which undercut Rosecrans and led to his dismissal. But these reports (and this is what gives the whole episode such a fantastic character) were written by *Dana himself.*

From the day he had attached himself to the Army of the Cumberland, Dana had openly boasted that, if he had his way, "Rosy's head should fall into the basket." His reports to Stanton were intended to sharpen the axe. After Chickamauga these reports grew more urgent. He blamed Rosecrans for the disaster and suggested that some Western officer with great prestige, "like Grant, for instance," be appointed in his stead. If Grant should not be available, Dana recommended Thomas: "there is no other man whose appointment would be so welcome in this army." He implied, without stating so directly, that Garfield and other officers approved of the move. Dana poured a steady stream of gossip and vituperation along the telegraph lines, all designed to undermine Rosecrans. "Our dazed and mazy commander cannot perceive the catastrophe that is close upon us, . . ." he scornfully reported. "I never saw anything which seemed so lamentable and hopeless." And a few days later: "the practical incapacity of the general commanding is astonishing, and it often seems difficult to believe him of sound mind. His imbecility appears to be contagious. . . ."

The final shot was a telegram to Stanton, warning that Rosecrans was planning to evacuate Chattanooga. This was an out-and-out lie, but it had its effect. Rosecrans was removed that very day. Thomas was perfectly aware who had engineered Rosecrans's dismissal and his own promotion. When he read the orders, he turned to Dana, and said in mock-resignation, "Mr. Dana, you have got me this time." Thomas never joined the accusations against Garfield; he knew where the real responsibility lay.[38]

If the charges against Garfield were so flimsy, why were they so widely accepted? The fact was that they were not completely without foundation. Although Garfield was probably telling the truth when he insisted, "It is a lie out of whole cloth that I ever recommended the removal of Rosecrans," many people had somehow derived the impression that he had done just that. The manner in which this impression was created can be seen in the conflicting accounts of Garfield's interview with Stanton a few days after Rosecrans had been removed. Stanton had been waiting at Louisville for Garfield to report. Having already made up his mind, he was interested only in information which would support his position. Armed with Dana's damning dispatches, he grilled Garfield mercilessly. Stanton was one of the great courtroom lawyers of his generation, perfectly capable of extracting whatever he wanted from a witness. After the meeting he triumphantly wired Washington that Garfield's testimony amply confirmed the worst reports about Rosecrans's conduct at Chickamauga.[39]

Garfield, however, blandly assured Rosecrans that, "on the way from your army to Washington, I met Mr. Stanton at Louisville, and when he denounced you in vigorous language I rebuked him, and earnestly defended you against his assaults." Yet, General Anson Stager, who had also been there and had heard the whole interview, recalled that "Garfield in my presence denounced Rosecrans as incompetent, unworthy of his position, as having lost the confidence of the army," and that he approved of Rosecrans's removal.

Was someone lying? Not necessarily. Garfield knew two Rosecranses—the private man whom he respected as a friend; and the general, whose mistakes he could not, in honesty, overlook or defend. He was always careful to distinguish between the two. "He always mentions Rosecrans with kindness, even tenderness," Lincoln's private secretary observed of Garfield; yet at the same time he noticed that Garfield was sharply critical of Rosecrans's leadership at Chickamauga. It was this double vision, not duplicity, that gave rise to the charges against Garfield. Those who heard him criticize Rosecrans's generalship assumed that Garfield was also a false friend, and from there it was only a short step to assume that he was capable of betraying that friendship.[40]

This was not the first time that Garfield had been accused of hypocrisy, nor would it be the last. Something about his

217

character, perhaps a certain unctuousness, seemed to invite such a charge. Yet in this instance at least, his actions had not been dishonorable, only somewhat disingenuous.

Fortunately for Garfield's peace of mind, this controversy was still in the future as he traced his way north from Chattanooga in October of 1863. After he left Stanton at Louisville, he headed for Hiram. He had not been home since January, and now he made the acquaintance of the fruit of that earlier visit: a son, Harry Augustus Garfield. The reunion was brief, for Garfield was due in Washington.

He scarcely had time to take off his coat in Washington before he found himself caught up once more in the familiar whirl of politics. An election campaign was under way in Maryland, and Chase invited him to address a Union Party rally in Baltimore. Here in the same city that had stoned Union troops only two and a half years before, Garfield delivered an out-and-out abolition speech before fifteen or twenty thousand cheering Southerners. He stressed the incompatibility of slavery with the democratic ideal, warning that Southern leaders planned to set up a titled aristocracy based on slavery:

> a government such as the people of the Old World will not laugh at. They intend to have their Count Bragg and their My Lord Beauregard. You mudsills, who rejoice that God has given you strong hands and stout hearts—who were not born with silver spoons in your mouths—are to be mudsills a long time.

Garfield was astonished and delighted with his reception: "when I spoke to them the same words I would address to our people on the Reserve and heard their long applause, I felt as if the political millennium had dawned."[41]

The speech was such a success that party managers begged Garfield to take the stump in other parts of the state. At a meeting in a strongly antiabolition district on the Eastern Shore, someone heaved a rotten egg at him. Garfield stopped his speech and said to the heckler that he had recently fought rebels who defended their cause with more dangerous weapons and that he was perfectly willing to renew the fight then and there. The crowd, which had been hostile, was completely won over. They turned on a suspected egg-thrower, thrashed him soundly, "and wound up going into a regular emancipation jubilee."[42]

Shortly after the election Garfield was called back to Hiram on a tragic errand. On December 1, his first-born child, Eliza, "our blessed little Trot," had suddenly died. She was three and a half years old, and she had known her father for only eight months. Garfield was deeply shaken by her death, perhaps as much by guilt as by grief. For a time he felt as if he could no longer bear to live in Hiram, surrounded by memories, but his wife reconciled him. Garfield carried his sorrow for the rest of his life. "He was never quite the same after the death of Trot," his wife said in later years.[43]

After Trot had been laid to rest in the little cemetery on Hiram Hill, Garfield returned to Washington. His congress was scheduled to begin in a few days, but Garfield seriously considered giving up his seat: "if this terribly weary work, and desolation of heart continues, it seems as though I must go back into the wild life of the army." He had originally stood for Congress on the assumption that the war would be over by the time it convened. But the war still dragged on, and Garfield felt that his proper place was in the field. He was a major general now, with his commission dating from the battle of Chickamauga, and he could reasonably expect a desirable command.

He took his problem to the President. Lincoln told him that although the government "had more commanding generals around loose than they knew what to do with," there was a shortage of administration congressmen, particularly those with a practical knowledge of army affairs. Garfield bowed to Lincoln's suggestion and resigned his commission.

On December 5, 1863, still wearing his general's uniform, Garfield was introduced to his future colleagues in Congress. The next day, a soldier no more, he put aside the old uniform and took the Congressional seat he would occupy for the next seventeen years.[44]

219

PART TWO

CHAPTER TWELVE

PUSHING LINCOLN

The roar of one hundred cannon saluted the Goddess of Liberty as she was hoisted to the top of the Capitol dome—now crowned and completed just in time to greet Garfield as he began his congressional career. Beneath that dome, then the tallest structure on the continent, he would spend the next seventeen years of his life, passing daily up and down grandiose marble stairways and through corridors whose unswept tiled floors were littered with apple cores and stained with tobacco juice and whose extravagantly frescoed walls and ceilings drew gawks from tourists and contempt from artists.[1]

The south wing of the Capitol belonged to the House of Representatives. The Hall of the House was 139 feet long, 93 feet wide, and windowless, except for a skylight ceiling thirty feet above. It was not designed for comfort. Garfield later would describe it as a "skillfully contrived human slaughter-house." It was poorly-lit, poorly-ventilated, and overheated. "Any man sitting here, during the evening," Garfield vividly complained, "can feel his skull and brain going through the slow process of roasting."[2]

Nor was it designed for intimate debate. Its vast spaces and acoustical dead spots discouraged that sort of face-to-face discussion which was the glory of the House of Commons. In addition to the architectural hazards, members had to contend with the disorderly habits of their colleagues. Except on rare occasions, a steady hubbub of noise rose from the floor. Members were continually coming and going, exchanging greetings and small talk, while young pages zipped up and down the aisles with messages and papers. None but committee chairmen were entitled to private office space, so less fortunate congressmen had to use their desks as makeshift offices. There, while debate droned on about them, they conducted their correspondence and caught up with the newspapers.

Few men were able to cut through this confusion and capture the attention of this large, unruly House. Garfield could. "In no one of the Congresses that I have attended," he later boasted, "have there been over ten or twelve members who could be heard all over so easily as I could." To a reporter, who had often sat bored in the gallery, "while members of small calibre have risen, with their maiden speeches in their hands, and attempted to read, in the midst of indescribable confusion, their school-boy effusions to which nobody listened," the contrast with Garfield was striking. For when he takes the floor, the reporter noted, "*Garfield's* voice is heard. Every ear attends . . . his eloquent words move the heart, convince the reason, and tell the weak and wavering which way to go." No matter what his other attainments might be, Garfield's voice alone would mark him out for distinction in the new career he was about to enter.[3]

He had, of course, other assets, not the least of which was his military experience. That experience seemed singularly appropriate on the first day of the session, for the Thirty-eighth Congress opened in a warlike atmosphere. Garfield was advised to wear a pistol strapped under his new civilian suit, ready to use it, if need be, to forestall a threatened Democratic plot to capture the organization of the House by trickery. Fortunately, the precautions were needless. The session opened smoothly, without even the hint of a coup to mar the election of the affable Indiana Republican, Schuyler ("Smiler") Colfax, as Speaker of the House. Garfield took his oath to support and defend the constitution and then waited to draw his seat. After the threatened melodrama of the opening day, this madcap ritual was a refreshing touch of low comedy. As the clerk read off the numbers on marbles drawn from a box by a blindfolded page, grown congressmen scampered like schoolboys to the most desirable vacant seats before their colleagues could occupy them. Garfield grabbed a choice spot, second row center, and now, sworn and seated, he took his place among the lawmakers.[4]

They were a mixed group, with strong personalities and diverse goals. On the Democratic side of the aisle the opposition was demoralized. The empty seats of their Southern colleagues were a silent reminder of the follies of the party's former leadership. The Democrats found themselves in an awkward quandry: if they opposed the war, as Vallandingham had done, they risked the label of treason; if they supported it, as most did, they faced the loss of their identity. The dilemma led one of the best of their leaders, S. S. Cox (nicknamed "Sunset" after a youthful rhetorical extravagance) to retreat into humor and irrelevance.

The majority Republican (or Union) party was held together by support for the war and by little else. Years of opposition in an era of weak presidents had bred into the party's congressional wing a factious spirit that Lincoln was unable to subdue. The party's strongest leaders were all more radical than the President on the questions of war and peace. The most conspicuous of these radicals was Pennsylvania's Thaddeus Stevens, chairman of the powerful Ways and Means Committee, whose whiplash sarcasm could terrorize an opponent. Equally radical, though less prominent in the public eye, was Robert C. Schenck, of the Military Affairs Committee, who had resigned from the army to unseat Vallandingham the previous year. A bluff, vigorous speaker, Schenck was unexcelled in the compact style of debate required under the five-minute rule when the House was in Committee of the Whole. Henry Winter Davis of Maryland was perhaps the most radical and the most brilliant of them all. In formal debate his small, wiry body quivered with intensity and his shrill, high-pitched voice took on an eloquence which Garfield described as "clear and cold, like starlight."[5]

There were also many lesser lights, in whose company Garfield was far from the least conspicuous. He was, for one thing, the youngest member of this Congress, and he won attention for his boyish exuberance. He liked to put his arm around a colleague and walk up and down the aisles in earnest conversation, much to the amusement of the galleries. To some, he

225

seemed faintly ridiculous. In his "short-skirted business coat almost brief enough to be witty," he looked more like a school-master "mending pens for the scholars" than a congressman. He loved to talk. On the floor he was seldom reticent about expressing his opinions, but it was off the floor, in the lobbies and back rooms, that his conversational talents really flowered. With youthful zest and eager affability, he regaled his fellow-congressmen with the story of his life and with incidents from his wartime experiences. "Some of the older and staider members smiled at his overflow and vehemence, and endless good nature," a friend later recalled, "but in their hearts they wished that they were young again, and had as clear a conscience as he had."[6]

They were not amused, however, by another expression of his boyish high spirits: his independent voting habits. "I made myself rather unpopular in the beginning by . . . a reckless defiance of opinion in the House," Garfield later realized. On January 6, only a month after he had entered Congress, Garfield defied the whole House. At issue was the question of whether bounties should be continued to be paid to encourage volunteer enlistments in the army. Only a few weeks before, he had spoken in favor of that system. Now he reversed his stand, arguing that to pay bounties to both volunteers and reenlistees would "swamp the finances of the Government." Garfield wanted to reserve bounties for reenlisting veterans and secure fresh soldiers through the draft. Loftily, he declared it beneath the dignity of the government "to use the conscription act as a scarecrow, and the bounty system as a bait to alternately scare and coax men into the army." Garfield stood on the high ground of principle, but his colleagues, who were well aware that the draft was the most politically sensitive issue facing the Congress, refused to join him. When the roll was called, he stood absolutely alone against an otherwise unanimous House.[7] Back home, most local newspapers commended his solitary stand as evidence of "his sagacity, his courage and his independence." "Fearless for the right, and true to his convictions, he is always to be trusted." But not all were so favorably impressed. A Cincinnati newspaperman, for one, observed that "A man threatened with a Major General's commission can afford to be more patriotic in the way of bounties than a private soldier."[8]

Secretary of the Treaury Chase took his young protegé aside and warned him not to overdo his independence. "Now Garfield," he patiently explained, "you have just started in public life. I was proud of your vote the other day. You were right, but I want you to bear in mind that it is a very risky thing to vote against your whole party. It is a good thing to do it sparingly, but you must not do it very often." Chase had a point. Garfield would not become an effective congressman until he could learn to be a better partisan. But Garfield, who as a schoolboy had gloried in "defending unpopular truth against popular error," could not follow Chase's advice. Eventually he would learn, but now he was enjoying himself too much to submit to the restrictions of party discipline. A few weeks later he again bucked the majority of his party by opposing a bill to revive the rank of Lieutenant General, dormant since Washington's day. His stand on this matter was not based on principle but upon a personal antipathy for Grant, the expected recipient of the honor, whom he still blamed for the ouster of Rosecrans. This time Garfield, though in the minority, at least had some company: he was joined by Thaddeus Stevens, among others.[9]

Garfield and Stevens did not always see eye-to-eye. In fact, Garfield seemed to go out of his way to quarrel publicly with Stevens. Early in the session he even came to the defense of the arch-Democrat, Fernando Wood. Ostentatiously disdaining partisanship, Garfield told the House that if a Democratic proposal appealed to his sense of justice he would regard it "just as important as if it had been offered by the gentleman from Pennsylvania." At times Garfield, the youngest congressman, seemed positively eager to pick a fight with Stevens, the oldest. In his major speech on Confiscation of Rebel Property he pointedly refuted Stevens's views on the status of the rebellious states. During the debates on the conscription bill he repeatedly needled the venerable Pennsylvania radical. Stevens had supported the system which allowed soldiers to volunteer as substitutes in whichever district would pay the highest bounty. With clumsy sarcasm, Garfield replied that it seemed "a little singular" that Stevens, "who is so strongly opposed to free trade in gold, is in favor of free trade in substitutes, in the bodies and lives of men." In May they clashed once more, this time over the issue of equalizing pay for white and Negro soldiers. Some Negro privates had been mustered in at ten dollars a month, as compared to thirteen dollars for white troops. This inequity had been corrected, but some radicals, especially Stevens, wanted to have the extra three dollars paid to the Negro soldiers retroactively. Garfield opposed the suggestion. In a transparent reference to Stevens's well-known identification with the cause of the Negro, Garfield piously declared himself unwilling "to pat the black man upon the back merely because he is black," concluding with an obvious (and unfair) slur at Stevens: "I am not desirous of making political capital by showing an excessive zeal for the black man."[10]

Months of Stevens-baiting gave Garfield a reckless contempt for his party's leader. "Old Thad," he gloated to a friend, "is stubborn and meddlesome and quite foolishly mad because he can't lead this House by the nose as has been his custom hitherto." Garfield was overconfident. In the next session Stevens would teach him a lesson. On February 27, 1865, they had a sharp exchange over a trivial issue. Stevens wanted to press for certain payments to House employees which had been denied by the Senate. Garfield impatiently objected to having what he regarded as a minor matter stand in the way of the important business of Congress, and he and Stevens threw harsh words at each other. Two days later, Stevens showed Garfield his teeth. When Garfield tried to tack $10,000 onto the appropriation bill in order to improve Ashtabula harbor, Stevens objected and forced the measure into the limbo of another committee. Garfield's constituents lost their harbor, but Garfield had gained a valuable lesson in the effective use of Congressional power.[11]

Despite his show of independence—sniping at Stevens on the one hand and sneering at Lincoln on the other—Garfield was not a maverick. He was a follower, but he did not look to Stevens for leadership and certainly not to Lincoln. Instead he enlisted in a small band of congressional super-radicals.

Gideon Welles, the acerbic Secretary of the Navy, dismissed Garfield and his friends as "a little clique of self-constituted and opinionated but not very wise radicals . . . who have really little influence and deserve none," but he underestimated their power. The leaders of this group were Henry Winter Davis and Robert Schenck. Garfield respected and admired Davis. Years afterwards he unhesitatingly ranked him as "the most brilliant member of the House I have ever known." To Schenck, however, he gave not only respect but genuine affection. Both from Ohio, both generals, both radicals, the two men were drawn together by many common bonds.[12]

Consequently, when Schenck, a widower, invited Garfield to board with him, Garfield welcomed the move. Life in his solitary rented rooms had been not only expensive but depressing. Still tormented by memories of his lost daughter, he was, he whimpered, "more alone than ever before in my life. . . . I find myself sitting alone, calling her by pet names, and asking her if she loves me." Life with Schenck was one way to banish such morbid thoughts. The peppery little general was not given to moody introspection. Brisk, impatient, emphatic, with small, darting eyes and a firm, outthrust chin, Schenk was the very model of the no-nonsense Yankee. An authority on draw poker, his definitive monograph on the subject would captivate Queen Victoria and spark a fad for the game that would sweep English drawing rooms.

Garfield and Schenck turned their rooms on C Street, near the corner of 4½ Street, into a "second army headquarters." There flocked all who had business with the army: men with ambition, men with grievances, generals, contractors, hangers-on, "inventors of new arms and projectiles, the devisers of schemes to end the war, and similar unappreciated geniuses." Business was conducted in the bluff, masculine atmosphere of an army barracks-room. A breakfast visitor found that even early in the morning "the door already had a crowd of common folk impatiently waiting its opening," and the overflow "crowded the stairs and were soon in close siege of the breakfast room door." When the noise disturbed the two generals at their mess, a second guard had to be posted, but to no avail. Finally Schenck bellowed to his valet, "Tell them by G—d that the animals are feeding, and dangerous," punctuating his command by banging his fist on the breakfast table, "which caused every article to leap an inch from the surface."[13]

With all the tumult in his new quarters, Garfield had very little time to brood. He filled his remaining hours with a frenzy of work, spending up to half the night on committee assignments until overcome by exhaustion. Ever since his schoolboy days, Garfield had used hard work as a drug. Now, lonely and tormented, he turned to it once more. "I try to be cheerful, and plunge into the whirlpool of work which opens before me," he told a friend, "but it seems to me I shall never cease to grieve over the little one that was to me so perfect, and so lovely."[14]

He had ample work before him. His committee, Military Affairs, headed by Schenck, was a choice but demanding assignment. In peacetime, Garfield noted, the committee was "rather a decoration than an influential committee." But with the war overshadowing all other business, Garfield's committee leaped into unaccustomed importance and through it Garfield himself, he later observed, gained "a prominence in the House in the beginning that I could not possibly have had in any other way."[15]

The first task Schenck handed him was to prepare a revised conscription bill, which Garfield was then to manage in its passage through the House. This assignment may have been an honor, but it was certainly no favor. The draft was possibly the most unpopular issue in the nation and no prudent congressman relished having his name associated with it. Garfield was not yet prudent and he came from such a safely Republican district that he could afford to take political risks. Furthermore, his army experience had convinced him that the prevailing method of raising troops was ineffective. To Garfield, fresh from the field of battle, the need for more soldiers was obvious. "The rebels have brought about all the force in the field they can," he argued, "and now, if our Government put the conscription law into vigorous operation we shall soon see the power of the rebellion broken."[16] Instead, the government preferred to rely on volunteers, using the draft only as a last resort.

Two features of this system (if such an administrative hodgepodge was entitled to be considered a system) especially aroused Garfield's ire: substitute brokers and commutation. To Garfield the folly of the "nefarious" traffic in substitutes was self-evident. "If any man can see any justice in allowing one township to take the enrolled men from another, and leave that other to bear its full burden beside," he exclaimed in bafflement, "he has been reared in a different school from what I have." Most congressmen, apparently, had attended that different school, especially those from the East, for they persistently refused to alter that happy arrangement, which allowed their own districts to avoid meeting their draft quotas.[17]

Garfield was even more disturbed by the commutation feature of the law which allowed a man to buy his way out of the army. Few congressmen shared his indignation. Garfield complained that they acted as if the right to pay $300 to escape the draft was "one of the inalienable rights guaranteed to us by the Constitution." He bluntly told his colleagues that they must either give up the war or give up the commutation, but his fellow-congressmen were paying more attention to the complaints of their war-weary constituents than to Garfield's scolding. Even Garfield found himself the target of angry constituents who protested, in a bitter round robin, that "Your whole action since you have been in Congress has seemed to warrent [sic] the opinion that you would force men into the army by draft instead of recieving [sic] a compensation." They threatened to withdraw their confidence (and their votes) unless Garfield changed his stand.[18]

Garfield could shrug off these threats, but other congressmen from more precarious districts could not. Even the Military Affairs committee itself mutinied and refused to present the bill ending commutation to the House. In June, Schenck and Garfield tried once more. This time the bill reached the floor but was voted down, two to one, with the opposition led by the young New Englander James G. Blaine, who had himself escaped the army by hiring a substitute.

"We were in desperate straits," Garfield recalled. "It was a very solemn moment." Lincoln himself came before a secret session of the committee and grimly told them that enlistments were expiring and that unless he was given the power to draft the war would be lost. The Republican members of the committee argued that to enact a strong draft law on the eve of an election would give the Democrats an issue with which they could carry the country. As Garfield recalled the scene, "Mr. Lincoln raised himself up to his full height and said, 'It is not necessary for me to be re-elected, but it is necessary for me to put down the Rebellion, and you give me that law I will put it down before my successor takes his seat.' "

Moved by Lincoln's appeal, Garfield and Schenck renewed their fight for the measure. "I stood in the breach then and made a large number of men furious whose reelection was pending," Garfield recalled. Time after time their bill was rejected, but Garfield and Schenck persisted. Finally, after a rousing speech by Garfield and some shrewd concessions by Schenck, the opposition was worn down. The Senate was just as obdurate, but ultimately Lincoln had his way and a strong draft, without commutation, was enacted thanks, in no small measure, to Garfield.[19]

Garfield's support for a strong conscription law was consistent with his newly-developing philosophy of government, a philosophy which magnified the authority of the national government and brushed aside states rights and constitutional restraints. "If a nation has a right to protect itself," he argued, ". . . it may take every dollar of every citizen, if so much should be necessary to support and maintain the government. And if the nation has the right to the citizen's money, has it not equally the right to his personal service?" The logic of wartime was turning Garfield into a nationalist. Radical convictions pervaded all of his major speeches and shaped his policy views. These views were reinforced by the example of Henry Winter Davis, who served as his political and ideological mentor, but Garfield had arrived at them independently and held them with tenacity. "I have never been anything else than radical on all these questions of Freedom and Slavery, rebellion and the war," he assured a friend who suspected him of weakening.[20]

As a certified radical, Garfield, of course, insisted upon a relentless prosecution of the war to total victory. He had only contempt for those who advocated a negotiated peace, those "gentle-hearted patriots who propose to put down the rebellion with soft words and paper resolutions." They reminded him, he told Congress in his first major speech, of the hero of a nursery rhyme:

There was an old man who said, How
Shall I flee from this horrible cow?
I will sit on the stile
And continue to smile,
Which may soften the heart of this cow.

"Not by smiles," he concluded, "but by thundering volleys, must this rebellion be met, and by such means alone."

The South must be beaten to its knees, and to insure its eternal submission, the twin props of Rebellion—slavery and landed estates—must be abolished. "This is an abolition war," Garfield boldly avowed. That slavery had to be abolished went without saying. The army, Garfield declared, demanded it. "They have been where they have seen its malevolence, its baleful effects upon the country and the Union, and they demand that it shall be swept away."[21]

But the abolition of slavery, Garfield insisted, was not a radical enough remedy to insure a lasting peace. He wanted to go further, to confiscate rebel estates and give the land to loyal men. "It is well known that the power of slavery rests in large plantations . . . and that the bulk of all the real estate *is* in the hands of the slaveowners who have plotted this great conspiracy. . . . Let these men go back to their lands and they will again control the South." (If this argument was not convincing enough, Garfield added a further rhetorical fillip by pointing out that if Southern estates were not confiscated, rebels would own the sacred battlefields and cemeteries of the war.)

After their slaves and plantations have been confiscated, what then should be the punishment for Confederate leaders? "If you would not inaugurate an extermination warfare to continue while you and I and our children and children's children live," Garfield inexorably continued, "set it down at once that the leaders of this rebellion must be executed or banished from

233

the republic." To those who thought Garfield's program too harsh, he replied that it had not only historical precedent in our treatment of the Tories after the Revolution, but it had divine sanction as well. "Let the republic drive from its soil the traitors that have conspired against its life, as God and his angels drove Satan and his host from Heaven. He was not too merciful to be just. . . ."

Garfield was prescribing bitter medicine for the conquered South: abolition, confiscation and exile. He implacably dismissed those who shrank from the logic of his conclusions and advocated a peace of reconciliation. "Let no weak sentiments of misplaced sympathy deter us from inaugurating a measure which will cleanse our nation and make it the fit home for freedom and a glorious manhood." With equal impatience he brushed aside constitutional objections. He argued that the rebellious states were still in the Union, still bound by the obligations of the Constitution, "but by their own act of rebellion they have cut themselves off from all rights and privileges under the constitution." That being the case, no appeal to constitutional rights could be made by those who had so willfully cut themselves off from its benefits. But even if the Constitution should stand in the way of his policy, Garfield declared in a later speech, this would not deter him. "The nation," he insisted, "is greater than the work of its own hands. The preservation of its life is of greater moment than the preservation of any parchment, however replete with human wisdom."[22]

The logic of these views led Garfield to advocate equal rights for the Negro. For some time he had been haunted by a mystical conviction that the nation's wartime suffering was divine punishment for the sin of slavery and the injustice done to the Negro. "For what else," he asked his wife, "are we so fearfully scourged and defeated?" In February, 1865, he introduced a resolution to end the practice that required Washington Negroes to carry passes, and he further asked Congress to determine "what legislation is necessary to secure equal justice to all loyal persons, without regard to color, at the national capital."[23]

Garfield's radicalism spilled over into some aspects of his economic thought as well. Intellectually, he was still commit-

234

ted enough to laissez-faire to utter such pieces of conventional wisdom as: "I would not interfere with the laws of trade; they are as immutable as the laws of nature." But on the emotional level, he could not prevent his radicalism from infecting his economic faith. It was only a short step from advocating the confiscation of property in the South to supporting the regulation of corporations in the North. "Here," he observed, "corporations are more than kings. It is the doctrine of our common law . . . that corporations have neither consciences nor souls; that they cannot commit crimes; that they cannot be punished; and that they are immortal." Garfield disputed the sanctity of corporate property. Early in 1864, the Camden & Amboy Railroad of New Jersey had complained to the War Department that a combination of rival roads was carrying troops across the state, in violation of the monopoly of through traffic which it had been granted by its state charter. Garfield was so outraged at this "barefaced" monopolistic pretension that he vigorously sponsored a measure for federal regulation of railroads, a measure which he later proudly claimed as the first step towards the regulation of interstate commerce.[24]

In attacking the Camden & Amboy, Garfield gladly "struck a blow at those baleful monopolies which," he said, using the time-honored rhetoric of radicalism, "had been so long preying upon the body of American industry." But more than that, he saw a link between this state-chartered corporate monopoly and state secession. Both were the enemy, for both were attempts by states to thwart that nationalism to which he was now so devoted. His radicalism and his nationalism conjoined to inspire him to denounce the hated concept of states rights. "Nothing more false was ever uttered in the halls of legislation than that any Sate of this Union is sovereign," he thundered. Can New Jersey declare war? he asked. Make peace? Coin money? Sign treaties? No. Only the Union is sovereign. "I am proud," he concluded, "of all the citizens of New Jersey who are fighting in our army. They are not fighting for New Jersey, nor for the Camden & Amboy monopoly, but for the Union. . . ."[25]

Garfield's radicalism and his glibness in debate combined to produce his first major congressional sensation, which was extravagantly hailed as "perhaps the most complete and per-

235

fect piece of invective . . . ever heard in the American Congress." On April 8, Alexander Long, a hitherto unnoticed Ohio Democrat, delivered an out-and-out copperhead speech advocating an immediate end to the war and recognition of the Confederacy. As Garfield listened, horror-struck, he decided that "such atrocious utterances should be answered and denounced and as no one else appeared to be ready to do it, I did." No sooner had Long finished speaking than Garfield sprang from his seat with a polished, impassioned speech already crystallized in his mind. He began dramatically, asking the sergeant-at-arms to plant a white flag between himself and Long, as he was accustomed to speak with rebels only under a flag of truce. He complimented Long on his courage and implied that Long was speaking openly what other Democrats were afraid to avow. He continued in this vein for some time; learned, sarcastic, eloquent and dramatic, before an enthralled House. "I think in some respects it was the best effort of my life," he proudly told his wife. Had he stopped there the speech would have been an outstanding success, but he went too far. To lend verisimilitude to his charge of treason against the opposition party, he accused two Indiana Democrats, by name, of treasonable correspondence with the enemy, and claimed to have intercepted the incriminating documents at Murfreesboro. It turned out that Garfield had been taken in by a forgery, but despite overwhelming evidence he never apologized or retracted his charges. This blunder somewhat detracted from the effect of the speech but, despite its flaws, Garfield had produced, on the spur of the moment, a fine campaign document and had further established his radical credentials.[26]

As a bona-fide radical of the radicals, Garfield was as opposed to the moderate policies of President Lincoln as he was to those of the Democrats. Familiarity with Lincoln had only bred further contempt for that "second-rate Illinois lawyer." Jacob Dolson Cox, fresh from the battlefield where "Hurrah for Lincoln!" was the soldiers' favorite war cry, was shocked and fascinated by the venomous attacks on the President that enlivened the table-talk of Garfield, Schenck and Davis. While Garfield laughed and prodded his friends on, Cox was treated to a "witty and scathing denunciation of Lincoln and all his works," in which "baboon" was the kindest term applied to the President during the entire evening.

Garfield's bitterness towards Lincoln was compounded of more than personal dislike. He interpreted the President's conservative caution as indicating a lack of commitment to the great ideals of the war. Lincoln had once complained that McClellan had "the slows." Garfield thought the same of Lincoln and was growing weary of trying to push the chief executive onto a more daring path. With the President's first term coming near its end, Garfield faced the prospect of Lincoln's reelection without enthusiasm. "I hope we may not be compelled to push him four years more," he said in despair.[27]

But what were the alternatives? There was a movement afoot, backed by Garfield's radical associates, to make Salmon P. Chase the next president. Garfield naturally sympathized with Chase's aspirations. The Treasury Secretary was not only Garfield's close personal friend (insofar as Chase had any friends), but he also gave allegiance to Garfield's most cherished radical ideals. Yet Garfield stayed on the fringes of the Chase movement, never committing himself to it publicly. His hesitation was prompted by the failure of his political scouts to discover any enthusiasm for Chase back home in the 19th District. Even Chase supporters regretfully observed that "the mention of his name . . . meets no cheering response among our people." If the Chase movement could gain support anywhere, one would think it would be here, in the most radical section of his own state. Yet Garfield's friend Rhodes, now a Cleveland newspaperman, warned Garfield, "if you have any regard for the popular voice . . . of Ohio you will not waste your powder over Secy. Chase." Rhodes had conducted an opinion poll on Cleveland's busy Superior Avenue and had failed to uncover a single Chase supporter. The general reaction to Chase was summarized by a Warren courthouse politician who described him as "cold, heartless, selfish, a power in politics, but a pestilent power." "His name will be a great one in history," he predicted, "and his memory execrated by thousands who have thought themselves his friends."[28]

Garfield could see that the handwriting on the wall spelled Lincoln, though he regretfully concluded, "I think we could do better." He broke the news to Chase, advising him to give up an ambition which had "no hope of success, and could only distract the party." In a letter to a constituent, designed for publication, he reluctantly announced that he would support the President. It was not a gracious endorsement. Garfield made it clear that he was capitulating to a distasteful, but inevitable, situation. "It seems clear to me that the people desire the reelection of Mr. Lincoln. I believe any movement in any other direction will not only be a failure, but will tend to disturb and embarass the unity of the friends of the Union." In honesty, he had to admit that "the Administration is not all I could wish," but he added that it would be a "national calamity" for radicals to desert Lincoln and throw him into the arms of the Blairs and other conservatives.[29]

Garfield's distrust of Postmaster General Montgomery Blair and his politically aggressive family ran deep and strong. With their political bases in Maryland and Missouri, the Blair family were the chief advocates of a pro-border-state policy which inevitably clashed with the radical aspirations of Chase and his circle. Garfield had tangled with the family as early as November over their opposition to Davis and Schenck in the Maryland elections. The feud was continued on the floor of Congress where Frank Blair, Montgomery's younger brother, accused Chase of treason and corruption, and demanded that Congress investigate the conduct of the Treasury Department. Garfield was able to stifle or divert these demands despite Blair's indignant cry of "whitewash." On April 23, a stormy climax was reached when Blair delivered a long, bitter phillipic, charging Chase with responsibility for "the most gigantic robberies of modern time, exceeding the famous operations of Clive in India." This was Frank Blair's last word on the subject. Leaving the Capitol, he went straight to the White House where he received a major general's stars and a command in the field from the President, a reward which seemed to give Lincoln's blessing to the whole affair.[30]

Garfield was appointed chairman of a committee to investigate Blair's charges. To no one's surprise, he discovered that they were groundless. "Chase is coming out splendidly," he rejoiced. He could not say the same of the President, whom he regarded as the true instigator of the business. Lincoln denied responsibility for the attacks on Chase but Garfield was not deceived. "The President is bound hand and foot by the Blairs and they are dragging him and the country down the chasm," he complained. His attitude towards the President, never cordial, was now soured almost beyond repair. How, he asked, could the "infatuated" President expect further support from friends of "the innocent and outraged" Secretary of the Treasury after they had been so grossly insulted?[31]

Garfield was now convinced that the President could not be reelected and he half felt that Lincoln deserved to lose because of his "painful lack of bold and vigorous administration." "I don't know a dozen men in Congress who believe it can be otherwise," he reported, "and they are sitting down in stupid despair awaiting the catastrophe." He now regretted his earlier endorsement, but with the Baltimore convention only a few weeks away, it was too late to organize effective opposition to Lincoln's renomination. True, some radicals were trying to drum up support for a third party headed by John C. Frémont, but Garfield had not "the slightest notion" of deserting his party for a "humbug" like Frémont. Instead, he resigned himself, with helpless impotence, to Lincoln's inevitable nomination and equally inevitable defeat. "I have no candidate for the Presidency," he told his friends, "and only speak as a sad and sorrowful spectator of events."[32]

It was as a spectator rather than a delegate that Garfield attended the Republican Convention at Baltimore early in June. He was not, however, so constituted that he could remain a bystander for long. He was soon intriguing to obtain the vice-presidential nomination for his old commander, William S. Rosecrans. Despite the strained circumstances of their parting, Garfield had remained a loyal defender of his old chief. He had scarcely arrived in Washington before he, along with Ohio Senator Ben Wade, was interceding with Lincoln to give Rosecrans a command. In Congress, he had repeatedly defended Rosecrans's record against its detractors, including Stevens. Rosecrans was effusively grateful for Garfield's "manly defense," but the moody general was not long satisfied. Unlike the rest of the world, Rosecrans had not yet recovered from the delusion that he was a great man and he expected appropriate fealty from his followers. Within a few weeks, Garfield learned that Rosecrans was again questioning the sincerity of his friendship.[33]

Garfield was certainly not blind to Rosecrans's erratic temperment, his vanity, his constant need of reassurance. Under the circumstances, his efforts in his behalf at Baltimore bear a touch of irresponsibility. It seems to have been a spur-of-the-moment effort, without advance preparation or consultation; an expression of Garfield's boredom with the convention and his desire to play the role of kingmaker. He dashed off a telegram to Rosecrans asking permission to enter his name in the vice-presidential contest. Rosecrans sent back a verbose but indecisive reply, as ambiguous as the famous order at Chickamauga and with similar effect.[34] His friends at the convention retreated in confusion and the nomination went to Andrew Johnson, with whom Garfield had been in "intimate acquaintance" ever since Johnson had been War Governor of Tennessee. Johnson was a friend of Garfield's and presumably radical, so that Garfield was content. He was not as well pleased with the main work of the convention. "Of course we must all go for Lincoln if a Copperhead is the alternative," he told a friend, "but we have made a fearful mistake in nominating him."[35]

Garfield and his embittered radical friends returned from Baltimore to resume their congressional chores convinced that control of the Republican Party was further than ever from their reach. They were soon struck by another blow: Treasury Secretary Chase, their chief friend at Lincoln's court, was dismissed by the newly-confident president. The circumstances of Chase's retirement were characteristically petty, arising out of a patronage squabble that led to Chase's petulant resignation. He had resigned often enough before, but Lincoln had always soothed his ruffled feelings. Now that the President no longer needed radical support for his renomination the resignation was hastily (almost gleefully) accepted. Garfield had dreaded this eventuality with dire foreboding for some time. Two months earlier he had despaired that should Chase resign it "would be as great a calamity as the defeat of Grant. . . .

240

It hangs in the balance whether he will or not, and God only sees the result."[36] Now that it had come to pass, Garfield was more convinced than ever of Lincoln's unworthiness.

The radicals were able to muster one last effort before adjournment to push Lincoln. They passed the Wade-Davis Bill designed to insure that the program of reconstruction would be under congressional rather than executive control. Once more they were thwarted by Lincoln as the President killed the bill with a pocket veto. With Congress adjourned, the frustrated radicals were compelled to work off their fury in the public press. Henry Winter Davis dashed off an angry "manifesto" which, co-signed by Ben Wade, appeared in the New York *Tribune*. The radicals accused the President of "dictatorial usurpation" to benefit his own personal ambitions and warned Lincoln that "he must understand that our support is of a cause and not a man; that the authority of Congress is paramount and must be respected . . . and if he wishes our support he must confine himself to his executive duties . . . and leave political reorganization to Congress." The manifesto created a sensation. At first Garfield was believed to be its author. He denied that, but he supported its sentiments. Not too many months earlier Garfield had scorned the President for lack of boldness and vigor; now he condemned him as a power-hungry dictator. His dislike of the President was too great to be held within the confines of consistency.[37]

Until the appearance of this manifesto, Garfield's renomination had appeared to be a certainty. True, there had been some grumbling in his district over his advocacy of the draft. There were also some potentially damaging rumors circulating through the district to the effect that Garfield had become a drunkard in the army and was now leading a life of the grossest profligacy in Washington. Garfield was perplexed as to how these charges could be answered. He admitted privately that his life was not spotless: "I sometimes have played cards as an amusement with a friend and I have sometimes tasted wine," and in his youth he had occasionally used profanity, though never since his conversion. This was not too shameful a record, but the prospect of parading his virtues up and down the district was so distasteful that Garfield decided to ignore the accusa-

241

tions. This would become his invariable reaction to character assaults. Time after time in his career he would ignore personal attacks, or else reply so tardily and reluctantly as to give the impression that there must be something to them after all. But as he decided in this instance: "I long ago said to myself there were two courses before every man who hoped to do anything in the world. One was to turn aside and kick every dog that barks, which would cost a good deal of precious time. The other was to go on one's way and, if possible get out of the reach of both the dog and his bark."[38]

As Garfield expected, the barking died down, doing little damage to his reputation. The Wade-Davis Manifesto, however, was altogether more serious business. In Maryland, the reaction to it cost Henry Winter Davis his seat in Congress and in the 19th Ohio district it threatened to cost Garfield his renomination. Shortly before the district nominating convention Garfield got wind of "a little white squall" blowing up on his political horizon. He traced the trouble to former governor Tod "and a few of that breed of cattle [who] learned that I was not so devoted to Mr. Lincoln as to be blind to his faults." He was determined not to give an inch before the coming storm. "I know what they want and when they attempt to catechize me, and make me the slave of their bigoted whims, they will find one young man who will not give his freedom of opinion for a seat in Congress."[39]

By the time the convention assembled in Warren, Garfield had worked himself into the reckless, uncompromising mood of Luther at Worms. He sat on the platform, inwardly fuming, while the convention chairman asked him to explain his connection with the obnoxious manifesto. Disdaining even token compromise, he answered the charges with a defiant twenty-minute speech. No, he said, he did not write the manifesto. Yes, he believed in it. "Abraham Lincoln was not my first choice. . . . I hold it to be my privilege under the Constitution and as a man to criticize any acts of the President of the United States. . . . *If I go to Congress I must go as a free man.* I cannot go otherwise and when you are unwilling to grant me my freedom of opinion to the highest degree I have no longer any desire to represent you." With that he stalked out of the convention hall.

He was scarcely out the door when he heard a tremendous roar behind him. He took it to be the angry jeers of the delegates, but he was mistaken. Immediately after Garfield left the stunned hall, an Ashtabula delegate moved the renomination of such a courageous and independent congressman. Taken by surprise, the convention emotionally agreed. The sound Garfield heard was his nomination by acclamation. Prearranged? Possibly. Garfield's managers were not as reckless as he was. They were aware of his intentions and were certainly capable of taking precautions to neutralize their candidate's impetuousness. In any event, whether through a spontaneous gesture or a carefully planned scenario, Garfield had passed a major test. He was not only renominated, but on his own terms without having to concede a speck of his independence. He was now clearly the political master of the 19th District. Governor Tod, in admiration and disgust, said that "a district that would allow a young fellow like Garfield to tweak its nose and cuff its ears in that manner deserved to have him saddled on it for the rest of his life."[40]

With the nomination behind him, Garfield packed his bag for the campaign trail. He traveled light: no tooth brush nor night shirt; only a dilapidated bag stuffed with two shirts ("one very dirty"), two collars, and his ever-present rectal ointment, "for," he mused, "are we not commanded to prepare for our latter end." Like a "shabby genteel vagabond" he trooped from one Ohio town to another, spreading the gospel of the Republican Party. His reputation had preceded him, and curious crowds flocked to gawk as if, he complained, he were a hippopotamus. At meeting after meeting he had "to invent some sort of reply to the oft repeated 'I have read a great deal about Jineral Garfield and watched his course for a long time.' "[41]

Garfield's labors were not wasted on his own candidacy. In the 19th Ohio a Republican did not need to campaign; nomination was usually enough. Nor could he bring himself to campaign for Lincoln. The President was scarcely mentioned in Garfield's stump speeches. Instead, he blasted the Democrats from one end of the state to the other. Such an attack was a labor of love on Garfield's part. The Democrats had nominated his old enemy, George B. McClellan, for president on a platform drafted by another foe, Clement Vallandingham, which flatly declared: "The war is a failure." McClellan had repudiated the platform, but Garfield could not resist the opportunity to fasten the "cowardly peace party" label on the opposition even though he was well aware of the support War Democrats had given the Union. The Democrats tell you the war is a failure, he harangued a Cincinnati crowd. "Why is the war a failure to them? It is only a failure *because if it succeeds they fail.* . . . What do you say to a party whose success depends upon the destruction of their country?" He carried the warfare into the very heart of Copperhead country, in the southern part of the state where Vallandingham was "esteemed a saint," goading the Democrats in his audience to riot by accusing them of treason and taunting them with cowardice when they refused to be provoked. Electioneering had its lighter side. In Ashtabula he announced: "We have taken Atlanta . . . we are about to capture Richmond." What else, he rhetorically asked, remains for us to take? "Let's take a drink," suggested a voice from the crowd and the meeting broke up.[42]

These military victories undermined the Democratic charge that the war was a failure and insured Republican success at the polls. Garfield, of course, won reelection by an awesomely lopsided margin, trouncing his hapless Democratic opponent by a margin of almost three to one. Loyal Geauga County gave Garfield a sweep of over twenty to one.[43]

After the campaign Garfield returned home to Hiram for an unaccustomed rest. As he was sitting in his front parlor one evening, his wife slipped a piece of paper into his hand. On it were some figures she had jotted down which summarized their life together. They had been married four and three-quarters years and, according to Lucretia's computations, they had lived together for only twenty weeks. Garfield got the point. When he returned to Washington for the second session he moved out of Schenck's bachelor quarters and rented rooms for his family. From then on, his wife would always live with him while he was in Washington.[44]

Despite his more congenial domestic arrangements, the second session of the Thirty-eighth Congress proved to be an anticlimax for Garfield. His major speech of the session was a routine effort on behalf of the thirteenth amendment, distin-

guished chiefly by the number of learned classical and historical allusions he managed to cram into it. With the end of the
war clearly in sight, his work on the Military Affairs committee
had now lost much of its urgency and glamour. To prepare for
the coming problems of peacetime, he began to bone up on
financial questions, a subject he had neglected since his intimacy with Chase two years earlier. He was now, he complained, studying with as much diligence as he had ever done
in his life.[45]

Garfield was bored, tired, and not a little disappointed with
the direction his life was taking. To his cousin and childhood
friend, Henry Boynton, he unburdened himself: "Henry, this
public life is a weary, wearing one, that leaves one but little
for that quiet reflection which is so necessary to keep up a
growth and vigor of Christian character." Even though his ambitions had been realized, his lot still seemed a "peculiarly
hard" one. "It is a fearful price to pay for a little publicity,"
he sighed.[46]

This self-pity reflected Garfield's discontent with the
progress of his political career. At first glance, it would seem
as if that career was progressing splendidly. Despite his youth
and inexperience he had, within a single session, placed himself
near the top rank of congressional leadership. As Albert Gallatin Riddle told him, with pride for a native son, "you are now
recognized in Congress as in the field one of the most valuable
as well as promising men of these times." A Cleveland journalist was even more extravagant, comparing Garfield to Webster and Clay, and hailing him as "strong, clear, earnest, a true
Christian hero and statesman . . . one of the grandest types
of manhood that you will find in the House of Representatives." This was praise enough to satisfy most men, but Garfield's sights were set higher, perhaps too high. As one observer
noted, "if he has not attained the rank to which his advocates
laid claim, it proves not so much his lack of ability as their
excess of enthusiasm."[47]

The fact was that Garfield was not as popular with his
colleagues as he was with the galleries or the journalists. Burke
Hinsdale suspected that his rapid rise had bred jealousy, but
there were other causes. His pedantic schoolmaster demeanor

was a constant irritation to the more down-to-earth politicians. Sunset Cox could never resist poking fun at "the learned gentleman from Ohio," as he liked to call Garfield. The style of oratory that could sway a revival meeting or dazzle a classroom often fell flat on the ears of congressmen. Garfield began to realize this after his first session. "Diffuseness," he admitted, "is the almost universal fault of American speakers." He vowed "to cultivate a more condensed style" of speaking, but it was hard to unlearn years of rhetorical excess. It was even harder to learn when to keep silent. His remarkable facility in debate had first impressed his colleagues but, according to Whitelaw Reid, "by and by the House wearied a little of his polished periods, and began to think him too fond of talking." Too many congressmen were inclined to second Rutherford B. Hayes's early judgment of Garfield as a "smooth, ready, pleasant man, not very strong." James G. Blaine, for one, was frankly disappointed by his first view of Garfield in action. "He is a big good natured man that doesn't appear to be oppressed with genius," Blaine concluded.[48]

Garfield not only irritated his colleagues, but he also began to neglect his constituents. When Edwin Cowles, the cranky but influential editor of the *Cleveland Leader*, visited Washington he was so incensed at the lack of attention he got from Garfield that he ordered his reporters never again to mention the name of the offending congressman in his paper. After a similar episode in which Garfield was "too busy" to attend to the wants of a constituent, Harmon Austin admonished him for his habit of "holding yourself at a distance from those who would like to be and would otherwise be your friends and admirers."[49] Cowles was eventually jollied out of his pique and Garfield was persuaded to devote less time to lofty affairs of state and pay more attention to relocating the West Farmington post office and other such bread-and-butter local issues. But his heart really was not in this sort of thing.[50]

In truth, Garfield was not yet a successful congressman, despite appearances to the contrary, nor would he be until he could earn the respect of his colleagues and the affection of his constituents. Eventually he would learn, but until then, for Garfield, the House would not be a home.

Disappointed with politics, Garfield began to search for a more congenial career, sifting through his talents and experiences to find a basis on which to build a fresh life. First of all, there was the army. Stanton had promised to keep a spot open should Garfield ever tire of civilian life. Unofficially, he offered Garfield command of the Department of California, which included the entire southwest territory. The Pacific frontier fascinated Garfield and Stanton's offer was a tempting one. He toyed with the idea briefly but nothing came of it.[51]

He could always go back to teaching school. His friend Isaac Errett told him of plans for a new Disciple college at New Castle, Pennsylvania, to be endowed by the Phillips brothers, two wealthy and devout oilmen, to the tune of half a million dollars. This would be a much more substantial venture than the usual run of struggling denominational colleges. Garfield was asked to head the college. He did not discourage the proposal, but on close inspection it turned out that the promised endowment was "temporarily" tied up in land and the project never did materialize.[52]

Then there was the law. Garfield was technically a lawyer, even though he had never practiced. Flimsy though his credentials might appear, they were sufficient for Jeremiah Sullivan Black, considered by many the outstanding lawyer in the nation. Black wanted Garfield to become his partner, dangling the prospect of "large mutual advantages" should Garfield accept. Garfield was to be the firm's California representative and would move to the west coast at the end of his congressional term. In early April he and Black signed partnership papers, but the California project, on which Garfield apparently set so much store, was abandoned.[53]

That left politics. William Bascom, Garfield's Columbus landlord of legislative days, was strongly urging Garfield to trade his House seat for the governor's chair. He assured Garfield that he was the most "available" candidate the party could find. "You would go in like a top," he promised. And after that? When Garfield's gubernatorial term was due to expire, Ben Wade's Senate seat would be free. Bascom expected that Wade "would by that time be laid on the shelf," and

247

Garfield could easily replace him. Bascom was carried away by the audacity of his plan. "I think I hear you say: Bascom is crazy," he exclaimed. Garfield said no such thing. If anything, he encouraged Bascom's kingmaking ambitions. There was, however, a serious obstacle. Ohio paid its governors even less than Garfield received as a congressman. Bascom realized that Garfield could not afford the luxury of the governorship. "The thing that troubles me," he admitted, "is that you have not yet had a chance to make your *pile*, and politics is a bad place for that."[54]

Garfield agreed. For the first time in his life he was worried about money. His financial growth had been painfully slow. At the time of his marriage he had managed to save $1200. After that, he recalled, "we lived very economically, carefully and frugally," accumulating $3000 by the outbreak of the war. In the army he had made more money than he had ever earned before and was able to add $2000 to his savings. As a major general he was paid at the rate of $5000 a year, but he had to give up that rank after only a few months for the safer but less rewarding life of a congressman. With two homes to maintain, one at Washington and the other at Hiram, Garfield helplessly watched his savings dwindle. "I am more persuaded every day," he told his wife, "that our first duty is to secure a competency, such as will place us above the narrow pinching of provident frugality, and leave us free from the apprehension of painful poverty."[55]

How could he grow rich and still remain in public life? He was pondering this question when Ralph Plumb, who had once served as assistant quartermaster on his staff, suggested a plan. While campaigning down the Sandy Valley, Plumb and Garfield had apparently been looking as hard for signs of oil as for signs of rebels. Garfield's interest in geology, originally cultivated in order to refute the evolutionists, was now put to a more practical use. "Oil, not cotton is king now," he exulted, ". . . and it is a beautiful thought that oil is found only in the free states and in the mountains of slave states where freedom loves to dwell."

Plumb proposed to form a company to tap the riches of the Sandy Valley. There were two obstacles to be overcome: they had no capital and they had no assurance that oil was actually present. Plumb unfolded an elaborate plan to solve these difficulties. First a small "inner ring" of five men, including Garfield, would be formed. An agent would purchase likely-looking land cheaply from the natives, without disclosing his real purpose. To maintain the deception the agent would disguise himself as a Quaker, "complete to say thee and thou," and pretend to be looking for sheep pasture.

Plumb expected that the land would cost only pennies an acre, but it would be deeded to the inner ring at the price of $100 per acre. Meanwhile, Garfield would be busy organizing a company of wealthy subscribers who could raise large sums of capital and join forces with the inner ring. This company would buy the land from its new owners at the full rate, unaware that the secret "inner ring" was the true owner of the land. In effect, the members of the inner ring were planning to buy their own land at a grossly inflated rate with the company's money and then pocket the difference. Plumb hoped to pyramid $4000 into $100,000 in this manner. What passed as an oil-drilling venture was in reality a real-estate scheme, and the members of the inner ring stood to profit whether oil was discovered or not. Plumb saw no ethical objections to this arrangement. "To the pioneers belongs legitimately the benefit accruing of finding and bringing forward these lands," he argued, and besides "with good luck in getting oil," everyone might ultimately prosper.

Garfield was convinced and he lent his name and influence to a project that had some of the trappings of an out-and-out swindle. He made trips to Detroit and elsewhere selling parcels of the "oil lands," raising enough money to recover the inner ring's original investment. Plumb was encouraged. "Another sale," he estimated, "will enable us to make a very handsome affair out of this project. "But alas for Plumb's ingenuity. No more sales were forthcoming, no oil was ever discovered, and the inner ring was left holding a large tract of worthless Kentucky property that ultimately had to be sold for taxes. Garfield's first venture into high finance was a failure.[56]

His next effort was slightly more successful and considerably more respectable. It involved the sale of stock in Pennsylvania oil land (with real oil) held by the Phillips brothers. The work was not to his taste. He could not quite rid himself of the feeling that "the pursuit of wealth is not the noblest thing in the world." But poverty overrode his genteel qualms and he plunged into the grubby enterprise "like a slave working in the mines for his freedom," giving to business such single-minded attention that he scarcely noticed the collapse of the Confederacy and the end of the rebellion.

A business trip took him to New York City on April 14, Good Friday, the night on which the President whom he had held in such contempt was assassinated. The next morning, when he heard the news he was stunned. "I am sick at heart," he said, "and feel it to be almost like sacrilege to talk of money or business now."[57] The city seethed with rumors and frightened crowds gathered in the streets for news and reassurance. They were in an ugly mood. According to "a distinguished public man, who was an eyewitness of the exciting scene," fifty thousand people were crammed in the Wall Street area ready to lynch suspected Southern sympathizers. The mob had just about decided to wreak its vengeance on the office of the Copperhead newspaper *The World* when a figure appeared on the balcony of the customhouse holding a small flag in his hand. "Fellow citizens!" he cried. "Clouds and darkness are round about Him! His pavilion is dark waters and thick clouds of the skies! Justice and judgment are the establishment of His throne! Mercy and truth shall go before His face! Fellow citizens! God reigns, and the Government at Washington still lives!"

According to the eye witness: "The effect was tremendous." The crowd was miraculously hushed, turning its thoughts at once from violence to a contemplation of God's eternal yet inscrutable will. It was the greatest triumph of eloquence the "public man" had ever seen, and he turned to a neighbor to ask who the orator was. "The answer came in a low whisper. 'It is General Garfield of Ohio!' "[58]

This incident grew into an enduring aspect of the Garfield mythology. Under the heading "Garfield Stills the Mob," it became an obligatory chapter of his campaign and memorial biographies and one of the best-known incidents of his career.

Yet Garfield himself never mentioned it nor was there any verbal tradition in his family concerning it. Garfield's son, Harry, devoted a great deal of effort to authenticate the legend, without success. His correspondents scoured the New York newspapers for contemporary accounts but could find none that recorded the exciting scene witnessed by the "distinguished public man." Both the *Tribune* and the *Herald* covered the Wall Street meeting and gave what purported to be verbatim accounts of a speech delivered by Garfield. Although both versions contain echoes of the famous speech, neither version matches the eloquence or the brevity of the speech of the legend, nor is there any indication that Garfield's words pacified an angry mob although, according to the *Herald*, a lynch mob *was* calmed shortly before the meeting by Moses Grinnell.

Yet the unnamed "public man" was not the only one to remember the incident. Chauncey Depew recalled it vividly, and a Mr. McElway of the *Brooklyn Eagle*, who witnessed the speech, assured Harry Garfield in 1905 that his father had, in fact, stilled the mob and that the memory of that event was one of the most thrilling of his life. The value of this sort of ex post facto "eye-witness" testimony can be measured by the recollection of another such eye-witness, Charles Townsend Harris who, according to his autobiography, was working on Wall Street during the Gold Panic of 1869. Just as a mob of crazed brokers was about to run amuck, Garfield suddenly appeared at the Exchange. "God reigns," he shouted, "and the Government at Washington still lives!" He then announced that the government would place ten million dollars of gold on the market and the mob was miraculously stilled. Alas for myth-making! Garfield was not even in New York at the time of the Gold Panic.[59]

CHAPTER THIRTEEN

TRYING TO BE A RADICAL . . .

Once the pressures and passions of wartime were lifted, Garfield's commitment to radicalism began to cool. The role had never really been a congenial one for a man of his reflective, essentially passive personality. "I am a poor hater," he admitted with a twinge of regret. Henry Winter Davis, a splendid hater, was now out of public life and would be dead within the year, depriving Garfield of his chief radical inspiration. Yet even as Garfield's zeal slowly waned, his admiration for radical activism persisted. Years later, he would still cling to the conviction that "Nobody but radicals have ever accomplished anything in a great crisis."[1] Torn between his convictions and his temperament, he tried, as usual, to find some middle path. As he told his friend Burke Hinsdale, "I am trying to do two things, viz. be a radical and not be a fool—which, if I am to judge by the exhibitions around me, is a matter of no small difficulty."[2]

During the long recess of Congress—from April to December —he tried to evade this dilemma with a brief holiday from political life. He looked forward to a relaxing stage-coach journey across the continent with Schuyler Colfax but reluctantly had to abandon his hopes of seeing California in order to devote his full energies to the sale of oil lands for the Phillips brothers. The project was "almost as great as a military campaign" in its scope and Garfield hoped that the outcome would insure his family's financial security, which was becoming increasingly critical in view of the expected arrival of another child in October. But if Garfield expected to get rich from this project, he was disappointed. A modest fee, some oil stock and a few parcels of Western land, totaling about six thousand dollars in all, were the rewards of his summer's labor.[3]

Even during the summer, the call of politics could not be ignored, especially after the nomination of Garfield's close friend Jacob Dolson Cox for governor of Ohio. Garfield, of course, felt compelled to help his friend's cause, but serious policy differences rose to embarrass him. In the years since they had roomed together in Columbus, Garfield and Cox had gone different ways. Cox had spent the entire war in the army and had missed that education in radicalism that Garfield had acquired in Congress. Negro suffrage was the sticking point. Garfield advocated it as the only way to secure the fruits of the war. Privately he had misgivings. "It goes against the grain of my feelings to favor negro suffrage," he admitted to a friend, "for I never could get in love with [the] creatures. . . ."[4] But in public, he suppressed his qualms.

Addressing a Fourth of July crowd in Ravenna, he reminded his audience of the terrible sacrifices that had been made in order to secure freedom for the Negro, sacrifices which had been shared by over two hundred thousand Negro soldiers. But what, he asked, is freedom? "Is it the bare privilege of not being chained . . . ? If this is all, then freedom is a bitter mockery, a cruel delusion, and it may well be questioned whether slavery were not better." If government is indeed based on the consent of the governed, then there can be no "pariahs" in American political life. True, the Negro is ignorant, he admitted, but so is the immigrant. An educational test might be necessary, he conceded, "but let it apply to all alike. Let us not commit ourselves to the absurd and senseless dogma that the color of the skin shall be the basis of suffrage, the talisman of liberty." To do less for the Negro would render the victors guilty of "the unutterable meanness . . . of committing his destiny to the tender mercies of those pardoned rebels who have been so reluctantly compelled to take their feet from his neck and their hands from his throat."[5] Garfield advocated impartial, rather than universal suffrage, but failing that he was willing to allow "the blackest negro that ever lived" the vote rather than see him helpless before his former master.

253

He rested his case on a "golden sentence" of John Stuart Mill's: "The ballot is given to men, not so much that they may govern others as that they may not themselves be misgoverned."[6]

These radical sentiments were well received in the Western Reserve but not in the rest of the state, which, whatever might be its feelings about Negroes' voting in the South, was determined not to allow them to do the same in Ohio. Cox, who had to run on a statewide ticket, was aware of these prejudices and, to a degree, he shared them. Fancying himself a hard-headed realist, he was scornful of the "humbug about humanity and justice" he found in the rhetoric of the radicals. Cox not only opposed Negro equality for Ohio but thought it unworkable in the South. Assuming the innate inferiority of the black man, he advocated the separation of the races with the creation of segregated Southern communities where the freedmen would not have to face the demoralizing competition of the superior race. Cox rashly proclaimed his segregationist principles in an open letter to a group of Negro students at Oberlin College. Though pained by the indiscretion, Garfield realized "we must stand by Cox and the platform and not let the party split." He tried to salvage something from the situation by persuading Cox to soften the implication of his Oberlin Letter. Together they worked out a face-saving formula and the issue was successfully swept under the rug before major damage could be done.[7]

Thanks to Garfield's diplomacy, party unity was preserved and Cox was elected, but their dispute, which could divide even such good friends, was an ominous harbinger of discord within the ranks of the Union Party over the unsettled questions of Reconstruction. Cox based his stand on the assumption that "for practical political purposes, loyal whites in the unrestored states are simply *nil.*" The number of sincere Unionists in the South, he argued, was too insignificant to deal with, let alone put in positions of power. "What a farce then, what a very unrepublican farce to think of their governing that country!" The only alternatives that he could see were either to rely on former rebels or else on freed slaves. Cox dismissed the latter alternative as unworkable since he assumed that "the white brain and will are certain to continue the ruling powers

254

there." That left him with no other policy than to urge the immediate and unconditional restoration of the defeated Southern states to full participation in national life. To do otherwise, he solemnly warned, would cause the Union Party to be "broken to pieces" and insure the victory of a reinvigorated Democratic Party.[8]

Garfield, on the other hand, was less inclined to forgive "the sublime impudence of those villains" who had made the rebellion and now blithely expected to be restored to civic life as if nothing had happened. "So long as I have a voice in public affairs," he vowed, "it shall not be silent till every leading traitor is completely shut out [of] all participation in the management of the Republic." This was a harsh policy but not, he insisted, a vindictive one. "There is not in my heart the least feeling of personal vengeance towards those who are now in our power," he claimed. Indeed, he admired the gallantry of Confederate soldiers—"traitors though they are, I am proud of their splendid courage when I remember that they are Americans." To demonstrate his lack of malice, he interceded with President Johnson to free Alexander Stephens, the imprisoned vice-president of the Confederacy.[9]

Despite his professed lack of personal animus, Garfield was dead set against readmitting any of the rebel states to Congress until, as he put it, using the language of revivalism, they "show works meet for repentance." But during the summer, President Johnson had taken advantage of the long Congressional recess to organize Southern governments. These new governments contained a disturbingly large number of former rebels whose actions, such as the creation of onerous Black Codes to regulate the lives of the freedmen, gave few signs of that repentance Garfield was looking for. Now these same men were presenting themselves for admission to Congress, apparently with the blessings of the President. It was one thing to help Alexander Stephens out of jail, but to seat him as Senator from Georgia seemed to strain the bonds of charity. Garfield feared that the process of reconciliation was proceeding with unseemly haste and suggested "that it would at least be decent to wait until the grass is green on the graves of our murdered patriots" before the rebels were welcomed back into the gov-

255

ernment they had sought to overthrow.[10] Only a few months
earlier these sentiments would have been enthusiastically endorsed by Andrew Johnson himself. As war governor of Tennessee he had earned the reputation of an implacable foe of
the rebellion. His accession to the presidency had been welcomed with relief by some radicals who saw in Johnson a more
pliable executive than Lincoln. Instead, his course as President
had been marked by a steady drift away from the radical position.

Andrew Johnson had once been a Democrat. Was it possible, Republicans asked themselves with increasing concern,
that he still was? If so, then his strategy would require the
reconstruction of the elements of the old Democratic coalition:
the Northern cities plus the South. Before the war that coalition had represented the majority of the nation. Reconstituted,
with a vigorous president at its head, it could be the majority once
again. To secure this result, however, the Southern wing of the
Democracy would have to be restored to political activity as
quickly as possible. No one could tell whether this was Johnson's intention or not, but his insistence upon the speedy
readmission to Congress of Southern representatives, his
wholesale pardoning of former Confederates and his apparent
encouragement of white supremacy in the conquered states
seemed ominous signs to nervous Republican leaders. Garfield was not yet ready to draw any such hasty conclusion. He
excused President Johnson's apparent flirtation with former
rebels as an "experiment" and hoped for the best, while in the
meantime he relied on that "blessed clause" in the Constitution that gave to Congress, not the President, the power to
judge the qualifications of its members.[11]

In this apprehensive frame of mind he returned to Washington in December. He rented an apartment for his family, including his new son, James Rudolph, and began to reconnoiter
the political situation. He was satisfied with the ability and
"robust spirit" he detected in his Congressional colleagues
but feared the rashness of "some foolish men among -us,"
specifically Thaddeus Stevens, who seemed "bristling up"
for a fight with the President. Garfield himself had no relish
for such a fight. The radical passions of recent years had

almost burned themselves out, leaving his moderate instincts once more in control of his political behavior. He abandoned the role of firebrand for that of peacemaker, advising his friends in Congress to assume that the President was friendly: "treat him kindly, without suspicion . . . leaving him to make the break with the party if any is made."[12]

He was confident, however, that the President would prove reasonable. This confidence was not mere wishful thinking, but was based on "full and free" conversations between Garfield and Johnson. The President had renewed their old friendship and was wooing Garfield ardently, hoping to use him as a mediator with the congressional radicals. Garfield was flattered by all this presidential attention, but he found that the path of the peacemaker had led him into "one of the strange fixes which have always beset my life," as he was now torn between the fear of betraying his radical friends or disappointing the President's confidence.[13]

He walked this tightrope for a few months longer, growing increasingly uncomfortable. On February 1, 1866, he delivered a major speech on the "Restoration of the Southern States" that was designed to find some common ground on which both Congress and President could stand. The debate over the readmission of the Southern states had degenerated into a stale repetition of what Lincoln had once labelled "mere pernicious abstractions," such as, for example: were the Southern states still (and always) in the Union, as the President claimed, or had they committed "suicide" by rebellion, as some radicals maintained? Garfield tried to cut through these abstractions and thus "resist two opposite currents of opinion and action which are sweeping our party to ruin as rapidly as wind and tide can carry us."[14] To resolve the vexing metaphysical status of the recently rebellious states, Garfield raised once again an argument he had brought up over two years earlier, an argument which when later adopted by Samuel Shellabarger would be called the "forfeited rights" theory. "Alabama let go of the Union," Garfield insisted, "but the Union did not let go of Alabama. . . . She must be held forever in her orbit of obedience and duty." This argument was designed to counter that of Thaddeus Stevens and his followers whose position, Garfield thought, threatened to destroy the Republican Party by its ideological rigidity.[15]

Stevens did not let this challenge pass unnoticed. Remembering Garfield's religious background, he posed a theological question. "Some of the angels undertook to dethrone the Almighty, but they could not do it. And they were turned out of heaven because they were unable to break its laws. Are these devilish angels in or out of heaven?" Replying in the same vein, Garfield reminded Stevens that those "devilish angels" did not secede from paradise. "It was the Almighty who opened the shining gates of heaven and hurled them down to eternal ruin." Similarly, if the rebellious states are no longer in the Union it could only be because the sovereign people have expelled them. Since, on the contrary, the people had fought to keep these states in the Union, Garfield rejected Stevens's logic. This did not mean that he accepted the President's contention that the Southern states had to be readmitted without further conditions. "The burden of proof rests on each of them to show whether it is fit again to enter the Federal circle in full communion of privilege, . . ." he argued. "They must give us proof, strong as holy writ, that they have washed their hands and are worthy again to be trusted." He suggested that the most convincing proof of repentance would be to grant Negroes the right to vote.[16]

The speech was well received but it failed in its intended purpose of averting a collision between the President and Congress. It was probably too late for oratory. Within two weeks Garfield began to suspect that "we are losing if we have not already lost the President. He is fast falling into the hands of our enemies," and the very next day he wondered whether Johnson was not "gone to ruin without hope." These misgivings were confirmed within the week when the President vetoed a bill designed to extend the life of the Freedman's Bureau, the only effective agency capable of protecting the rights of the former slaves. With this veto the President had, in Garfield's eyes, declared war on Congress. Garfield now abandoned his dreams of peacemaking and reenlisted in the radical camp, driven there by Johnson himself. "He has left the true men of the country no choice but to fight him,"

Garfield announced grimly, "and fight it is." The decisive battle, Garfield forecast, would be for control of the next Congress. If the "unholy alliance of the President with rebels and copperheads" could capture that Congress then they could reverse by legislation what the nation had won on the battlefield. "Then woe to liberty, and the public debt," Garfield warned with a shudder.[17]

The President's actions did nothing to relieve these fears. On Washington's Birthday he publicly branded leading radicals as traitors and soon afterwards he vetoed yet another Freedmen's Bureau Act as well as a Civil Rights bill which had the support of moderate as well as radical Republicans. By April, Garfield was half-convinced that the President was either "crazy or drunk with opium." By May, he was actively campaigning against the President. In a speech at Hagerstown, Maryland, he labelled the Democrats the party of secession and rebellion and linked President Johnson to their cause. "If he has gone over to the Democratic party, it is not the fault of the Union party." Hinting at impeachment, he warned Johnson of the consequences of his betrayal. "The American people are greater than any one man in this land— greater than any President or Congress."

The break was complete. Within less than six months Garfield had moved from a well-wisher and confidant of the President's to an avowed enemy. His constituents supported this political shift with enthusiasm. William C. Howells, editor of the *Ashtabula Sentinel*, reported "there is scarcely a man in the range of my acquaintance who hesitates to express the most radical views," and he passed along the comforting news that Garfield need not fear that a Johnson supporter would attempt to challenge his renomination to Congress: "I don't believe any man not sentenced to Newbury Asylum, will try it."[18]

Once it became obvious that the split with Johnson could no longer be healed, Garfield began to pay less attention to Southern affairs. He followed the lead of congressional radicals, but seldom participated in debate. From time to time, he would deliver speeches on the subject, but these were in the nature of obligatory performances designed for the hometown

259

newspapers. Otherwise, he seemed to have found little satisfaction in a situation where the battle-lines were so firmly
drawn as to eliminate that middle ground on which he felt
most truly at home. To be an "extreme man," Garfield often
thought, must be comfortable, but as for himself, he was often
incapacitated by objectivity. "It is painful to see too many
sides of a subject," he confessed.[19]

Increasingly, his energies in Congress were absorbed by his
first love—finance. In the days when he had boarded with
Secretary of the Treasury Chase, he had vowed to make
finance his life work. Now the opportunity had come with his
appointment to the influential Committee on Ways and
Means. This was a rare honor for such an inexperienced congressman and Garfield was proud that he had won it without
breaking his superstition against seeking office. Indeed, the
appointment took him by surprise. Chase, now Chief Justice,
and Hugh McCulloch, the Treasury Secretary who regarded
Garfield as the best-read congressman on financial matters,
had both suggested the appointment and Speaker Colfax, who
was much taken with Garfield, was pleased to oblige. "I
could not have a more creditable or desirable place," said Garfield with satisfaction. The committee was not as all-powerful as it once had been. In order to relieve its overburdened chairman, Congress had recently given some of its functions to two
newly-created committees: Appropriations, and Banking and
Currency. Though shorn of some of its duties, it was still
considered the most desirable assignment in the House, responsible, as Garfield noted with undisguised relish, for "those
great dry questions of detail about tariff, taxation, currency and
the public debt."[20]

Some might regard these topics as "dry," but not Garfield.
To him, statistical tables were full of hidden romance, and economics, which many dismissed as the "dismal science," was
capable of arousing his most intense passions. His economic
thought was shaped by his own intensive studies but it also
owed much to the influence of Chase and to a half-remembered
course on Political Economy at Williams College taught by
Arthur Latham Perry, whose best-selling textbook would
inculcate into a whole generation of college students the pre-

cepts of laissez-faire. Garfield endorsed all of the conventional maxims of economic orthodoxy but he brought to them an intellectual excitement and a moral fervor which elevated these commonplaces into a creed. He was not merely convinced of their truth, he was converted to them, with much the same righteous fervor which had once possessed him after that earlier conversion when, years before, he had been immersed under the cold waters of the Chagrin River.

In his very first major financial speech he set the tone he would maintain for the rest of his career. The speech dealt with the resumption of specie payment, a subject he would make peculiarly his own. During the war, the government had been compelled to abandon specie payments and issue nearly half a billion dollars worth of paper money "greenbacks" to serve as legal tender. Though the war was over, these notes continued to circulate, contributing not only to inflation but to business uncertainty because of the fluctuation of the exchange rate between greenbacks and gold. Garfield was appalled at this violation of the most sacred rules of fiscal orthodoxy. "We must bring value back to the solid standard of gold," he pleaded time and again.[21]

Specie resumption became more than a policy to Garfield: it was a panacea that "would settle more difficult and dangerous questions than any one such act has done in history." He conceded that the program of currency contraction that this entailed was likely to cause some "temporary stringency" in the nation's economy, but he had nothing but contempt for those "lotus eaters" who were unwilling to pay that price in order to attain "solid values" once more. "A man's hand is hopelessly shattered," Garfield said, "it must be amputated or he dies; but the moment the surgeon's knife touches the skin he blubbers like a boy, and cries, "Don't cut it! take away the knife! the natural laws of circulation will amputate it by and by.' " To Garfield, the inflationists were just as cowardly and shortsighted. He foresaw a depression worse than that of 1837 if his advice should be ignored and warned that "any party which commits itself to paper money will go down amid the general disaster, covered with the curses of a ruined people."[22]

What could induce a man whose instincts generally led him

to prefer moderation to commit himself to the hard-money cause with a single-mindedness bordering on monomania? It would be futile to attempt to account for Garfield's position on the basis of economic or class interest. He owned a few government bonds but no other sort of property that might prosper under deflation. In fact, his investments were of the sort that required inflation to become profitable: western lands, oil stock and other such speculations. Garfield was actually voting against his own interests, a fact which dismayed his financial advisers, the Phillips brothers. After a dinner with these Pennsylvania oilmen, Burke Hinsdale reported that during the whole meal they kept repeating the common cry of most businessmen: "Greenbacks, greenbacks or the country is ruined!" and were quite irritated at Garfield for his stubborn refusal to help.

Nor can Garfield's hard-money views be explained as a response to political pressure. In fact, his stand placed him in an embarrassing political situation. He found himself an ally of Johnson's Secretary of the Treasury, Hugh McCulloch, who was trying to contract the currency by withdrawing greenbacks from circulation, while many of the radical leaders of Garfield's own party, most vocally Thaddeus Stevens, championed inflation and the greenbacks. Garfield did not allow party loyalty to prevent him from accusing Stevens of lacking both nerve and patriotism on the currency issue.[23]

Garfield and Stevens had clashed before, but their disputes had always remained within the framework of radical principles. Now, however, it seemed that Garfield's laissez-faire commitment was beginning to undermine some aspects of that radical nationalism he had espoused during the war. "The chief duty of government," he would eventually decide, "is to keep the peace and stand out of the sunshine of the people." Applied consistently, this maxim would seem incompatible with his Southern policy, which required vigorous federal intervention, but Garfield hesitated to draw such a conclusion. Instead, he tried to compartmentalize his philosophy: "a radical in most things [I] desire to be thoroughly conservative on questions of finance."[24]

Any weakening of his radicalism was bound to be greeted

with suspicion by his constituents in the 19th District, "the famed Gibraltar of Radical Republicanism," as it was proudly called. In fact, local political advisors were warning Garfield that his hard-money position was hurting him at home and suggested that in the future he not allow "conscientious convictions to put yourself . . . in sympathy with Administration measures" and against his fellow Republicans. Garfield ignored the advice. "Whatever be the effects of such a doctrine upon me at home politically," he stubbornly insisted, "I must adhere to it."[25]

This was his favorite role—the lonely champion of unpopular truth against mass delusion, standing steadfast "against a rabble of men who hasten to make weather cocks of themselves." It bothered him not at all that for a time he was virtually the only Ohioan, in fact almost the only Western congressman, to oppose inflation. It only strengthened his determination to educate his colleagues and constituents. He liked to think of himself as trying an "experiment" in politics, "to see whether a man can think and speak his convictions." "If it fails," he said fatalistically, "the world is wide and we are free."[26]

Since neither his financial nor his political interests were furthered by Garfield's economic philosophy, its roots must be found elsewhere. His attachment to the hard-money doctrine was, in fact, based on abstract intellectual and moral principles. Garfield was proud of his status as an intellectual in politics. He was one of the very few congressmen who could find his way around the Library of Congress. Spofford, the librarian, said that Garfield used its books more than any other legislator. He always liked to keep some scholarly project on hand for relaxation: a translation of Horace, perhaps, or Goethe, or else a directed program of reading on history or religion. Even in the midst of the most stormy political controversy, he tried to devote some part of his energies to the life of the mind. In his correspondence with his friend Burke Hinsdale during 1865 and 1866, for example, one finds interspersed with comments on current events serious discussions of classical poetry, the doctrine of Neo-Platonism in the Byzantine Empire, the historiographic theories of Buckle and Froude, and other such weighty topics, all testifying to a nostalgia for the scholarly life he had put aside. As he confessed to an educator friend, "Not a week passes in which I do not long to be out of the dust and smoke and emptiness of political life; and engaged again in study and teaching." Failing that, the next best course was to apply the techniques of scholarship to political life. "I could not stay in politics unless I found some philosophy," he often told a friend, who noted further that Garfield "was never satisfied until he could reduce facts to order."[27]

To such a mind, the impact of classical economics, with its symmetry, its precision and scope, must have had the force of a revelation. Here at last was a true science of society. "I believe a man's first thoughts on Currency, like his first notions of Astronomy are almost always erroneous," Garfield said in a revealing comparison. Furthermore, the sound money doctrine was intellectually respectable. It was held by just the sort of men Garfield envied and admired: English scholars, Eastern financiers and intellectuals such as Edward Atkinson, David A. Wells, Amasa Walker, Francis Lieber and John Murray Forbes—men whose companionship and respect Garfield craved since they represented that life of intellectual gentility he had dreamed of at Hiram and briefly glimpsed at Williams.[28]

To Garfield the hard-money doctrine was more than true; it was virtuous as well. Even though he had left the pulpit he still tended to think in terms of moral imperatives. In this sense, the issuance of greenbacks was a fiscal sin that had to be atoned for through economic suffering. Greenbacks were not merely impolitic, they were immoral: "the printed lies of the government." It was axiomatic in Protestant theology that one sin begets another in the slippery slide to damnation, and thus the original sin of greenbacks had corrupted the nation. It had bred inflation, which was sinful since it encouraged that "conjurers art, by which sixty cents shall discharge a debt of one hundred cents." It had bred speculation, which unleashed the sin of avarice. When a speculating Cleveland banker shot himself after his embezzlement was uncovered, Garfield knew where to place the blame for the tragedy: "The great criminal is irredeemable paper money—which is every day opening hell on our people." A return to "honest money," on the other hand, could cleanse and redeem the Republic. To Garfield, sound currency was more than a political issue, it was more than an intellectual theory; it had an element of the apocalyptic about it.[29]

By the same logic Garfield should have been an adamant free-trader, for that theory was as orthodox and respectable a part of laissez-faire doctrine as sound money. Yet on the tariff his stand was ambiguous. In part, this was because the tariff issue lacked the clearcut moral certainty of the money question, but, to a greater degree, his wobbling was due to the pressure of political realities. He had no doubt that "as a mere doctrine of abstract theory the doctrine of Free Trade was the true doctrine," and he looked forward to the day when all tariff barriers would be lifted.[30]

These sentiments were balm to the tariff reformers who began to number Garfield as one of their own. But if his votes on the tariff debates of 1866 and 1867 are any indication, they had misread their man. Years later, Garfield's opponent for president in 1880 would be laughed at for maintaining that the tariff was a local issue. This was regarded as a demonstration of economic ignorance, but the fact was that Garfield had proved the truth of that maxim by his own behavior. His tariff stand was dictated more by considerations of local 19th congressional district *Realpolitik* than by any abstract doctrinal considerations. Like most of his fellow-congressmen, he advocated free trade in general but insisted upon protection for the products of his district.

Without any other information one could get a fair idea of the economic interests of Garfield's district simply by examining his tariff votes. It comes as no surprise to discover that the district contained nineteen iron furnaces, mostly in industrialized Trumbull and Mahoning counties, for Garfield vigorously opposed reducing the tariff on iron rails. In doing so, he did not hesitate to raise the bogey of cheap foreign labor in rhetoric that might have made even the most ardent protectionist blush, as when he replied to an opponent by saying: "He wants to know where this cry for protection will end. . . . I will answer the gentleman. It will be, if that unfortunate day ever comes, when American labor is only equal to the pauper labor of Great Britain in its wages. . . ." On the other hand, when it came to coal, which his iron manufacturers needed as a raw material, he quite forgot that he was a champion of the American workingman against foreign pauper labor and voted to keep the duties low. Likewise, he discovered a need for the protection of American flax at about the same time that farmers in northern Ohio began to produce linseed oil. The Ohio Wool Growers Association, an aggressive lobby with headquarters in Youngstown, continually pressed Garfield to support their interest. Garfield was so obliging, both in committee and on the floor, that over a decade later the lobby was still grateful for his "very efficient aid," which they claimed "saved the sheep husbandry of the U.S. from destruction."[31]

The iron men of Trumbull and Mahoning were not as easily satisfied. They continued to suspect their congressman of harboring free trade sentiments. To mollify them, Garfield indulged in some uncharacteristic flights of protectionist eloquence, waving the American flag as the high tariff banner. To a Democratic congressman who had advocated buying foreign goods if they were the cheapest, Garfield retorted, "Is he not also in favor of living where he can live cheapest, and therefore of leaving the United States and moving to Canada, or if he wants to live still cheaper, to the Fejee Islands where he can pluck bread fruit from the trees and wear primeval fig-leaves, at little expense, and thus avoid the troubles of tariffs and woolens? It occurs to me, Mr. Chairman, that it is worth something to live in a country like this." Coming from someone who aspired to be in the vanguard of financial reform and who was privately convinced that "no man . . . can study [the tariff] thoroughly without finding himself drifting more and more towards a liberal policy," this sort of speech somehow rang false. Nor did it succeed in pacifying his opponents.[32]

Taking refuge in ambiguity, he hit upon a formula with such a splendid ring that he could not resist repeating it on every appropriate occasion: "I am for a protection which leads to ultimate free trade. I am for that free trade which can be achieved only through protection."[33] This was ingenious, but Garfield found that by trying to be all things to all men on the tariff he managed only to alienate everyone. "I was . . .

denounced by the extreme protectionists as a free trader; and denounced by the free traders as a sort of protectionist," he recalled. Revealing an incredible misunderstanding of his own career, he later claimed that his tariff stand was "the only position in my life that has been a middle between two extremes. I have usually been at one pole or the other; there I stood on the equator. . . . and I esteem it one of the greatest of my achievements in statesmanship to have held that equipoise."[34]

There was a certain amount of irony in the picture of Garfield sitting on the Ways and Means Committee and guiding the financial destiny of the nation while his own personal finances were so precarious. In Congress he cooly dealt in the hundreds of millions of dollars but at home he had trouble paying the bills. The contrast was not lost on his friend J. H. Rhodes, who chided Garfield for not getting rich on the inside information and influence available to a man in his position. "You talk of the wolf howling at your door," Rhodes said. "Were I in your boots I'd soon put an end to his howling. I wouldn't fleece the government, but if I could not make a fortune with your chances, with your knowledge of movements in Congress and intimacy with McCulloch, then I'd hang my harp on the willows. . . . Let me be in your place and in six months I would *honestly* make enough money for all the sons and daughters it may be your good fortune to have."[35]

In a few years, Garfield's reputation would be blackened when it appeared to some that he had done what Rhodes and others expected him to do—make money from his official position. But in 1866, Garfield turned down two "opportunities" to convert his influence into cash. The cruder of the two offers came from Pennsylvania oilmen. Early in the year they had sent a delegation to Washington to lobby for the repeal of a tax on petroleum. They found the Pennsylvania congressmen "entirely indifferent" to their pleas, but when the Phillips brothers introduced them to Garfield they realized they had found the perfect agent. He diligently advocated their case before key congressmen, pushed their bill through the Ways and Means Committee and shepherded its passage through the House. In gratitude for his "cordial interest" in their welfare,

267

the oil men "without his knowledge" naively subscribed $2,750 as a token of their appreciation. In embarrassment, Garfield wrote the Phillips brothers that he "would rather suffer from the severest want than to seem to anyone to take advantage of my position here." With utmost delicacy he added, "I know my dear brother you will appreciate my gratitude for all your kindness and also why I think you had better let the . . . matter drop."[36] Even so, rumors that Garfield had accepted a $10,000 bribe circulated through the district. Garfield defended his honor vigorously. "I wish I were not a poor man . . . but poor as I am there is not wealth enough in this world to buy me or my vote for any purpose," he proclaimed with indignation. "The man does not live who will dare to look me in the face and say that he ever made or heard made a dishonorable or corrupt proposition to me."[37]

Yet despite his protests, there was something indelicate about Garfield's activities on behalf of the Pennsylvania oilmen, although it was not the bribe, so crudely offered and so gently rebuffed. Garfield himself owned oil stock. The 29th rule of the House prohibited congressmen from voting on questions in which they had a personal financial interest. The rule was so universally disregarded that little blame could be attached to Garfield for ignoring it in this instance were it not for his display of righteousness a few years later. During a vote affecting the Union Pacific Railroad, he would insist that the Clerk read the 29th rule, thereby implying that his fellow-congressmen were guilty of conflict of interest. The rebuke would have come with better grace from someone who had not violated the rule himself.[38]

Garfield's second temptation came from his irrepressible friend, Ralph Plumb. After his disappointing Kentucky oil venture, Plumb had settled on an isolated Illinois trading-post called Scrabble as the place to make his fortune. Scrabble was sitting on top of a rich but neglected coal field and Plumb was determined to tap that wealth. He enlisted Dr. Worthy S. Streator, a prominent Cleveland railroad promoter who was an intimate friend of Garfield's through his membership in the Quintinckle Club, to be the president of the new Vermillion Coal Company. Scrabble was rebaptized as Streator, Illinois and mining operations were begun.

Both Plumb and Streator wanted their friend Garfield to get in on the ground floor of what promised to be a very good thing, and in February Plumb "cordially invited" both Garfield and Schenck to come in. Ten thousand dollars worth of stock was set aside for each of them and, as Plumb expansively said, "you are at liberty to consult your own convenience about the time of paying it." In return, Plumb had one small request. Unless a railroad ran by the mines, the coal could not reach the market. It would cost at least $80,000 to build a spur to the Illinois Central, but if the projected American Central could be induced "to bend their lines" to Streator, Plumb's problem would be solved cheaply. He hoped that Garfield and Schenck would suggest this possibility to the road's managers· and he hinted that "if by your influence the Am. Central supplies our necessity the company will feel very kindly towards you both I am sure."[39]

The message seemed clear enough: Garfield and Schenck were expected to sell their influence for $10,000 worth of free stock apiece. Schenck's role was obvious. He was president of the board of directors of the American Central. Garfield's mission was less clear. Apparently he was to serve as an intermediary with Schenck and look after the company's interests generally. Early in April, just as the first assessment on the stock was due, Garfield suffered a financial setback when the Ocean Oil Company, in which he had invested heavily, went under. Plumb gallantly offered to hold the Vermillion stock on the company's books in Garfield's name without any payment, at the same time reminding his friend, "all we need is a Rail Road." But Schenck was unable or unwilling to persuade the American Central managers to go along with Plumb's plans and the Vermillion Company had to make other arrangements with the Fox River line. Schenck stayed with the company, paying for the stock in the conventional manner, and probably did quite well by it, for the company prospered and Plumb grew rich and respectable, ultimately serving two terms in Congress. Garfield, however, was unable to meet the payments and had to give up his stock. Plumb advised Dr. Streator, in a phrase prophetic of the Crédit Mobilier scandal, to place the stock "where its influence will do us the most good," and Garfield resigned himself to another lost financial opportunity.[40]

269

Some of the sting was taken from this disappointment by the enticing prospects that opened before him with the start of a new career. Garfield had, at long last, become a practicing lawyer, and in the most spectacular fashion imaginable. He began his legal career at the top. His very first argument in any courtroom was before the United States Supreme Court in the most celebrated case of the decade, *Ex parte Milligan*. Such a debut was unprecedented in the history of the American bar, and Garfield would remain inordinately proud of having bypassed the regular channels of his profession. "The regular channels," he explained, "are to study in a lawyer's office, sweep the office for a year or two, then to pettifog in a justice court, and slowly and gradually, after being sub to everybody, when the older heads begin to die, the man begins to feel his way as a lawyer, and after he has been fifteen or twenty years in practice, if he ever gets a case into the Supreme Court, and gets admitted there, it is considered a red letter day in his history when he does it. I made my study of the law as complete as anybody I know of, but did it in my own room at Hiram. . . ."[41]

The agent responsible for this remarkable transformation of Garfield into a lawyer was Jeremiah Sullivan Black, one of Garfield's closest, yet most unlikely, friends. Twenty years older than Garfield, Black was then at the height of his fame as one of the nation's most flamboyant constitutional lawyers after having served as Attorney General and Secretary of State in the Buchanan cabinet. Politically, their friendship was a *mesalliance*. Black was a Democrat through and through, a supporter of McClellan, an advisor to Andy Johnson, and such an unremitting, unrepentant partisan that he was only half joking when he explained that the only thing keeping him from becoming a Republican was that "I believe in a hell!"[42]

Religion brought them together. Black was a Disciple. He had sent his son Chauncey to Hiram from whence, thanks to Garfield, he was soon expelled. It was not the most promising beginning for a friendship, but when Garfield next ran across young Black, late in 1862 in Washington, they were able to laugh about the incident and Chauncey introduced Garfield to his father.[43] The two men hit it off splendidly from the very

270

beginning. This was one more example of how the Campbellite connection worked to further Garfield's career. His education, his constituency, his devoted campaign workers, the Phillips brothers, and now Jere Black were all attached to Garfield through the Disciple brotherhood, an association he exploited, wittingly or not, all his life. Garfield and Black had more than religion in common. Both loved Horace and Shakespeare and both were hearty, vigorous, self-made men. Black assumed a paternal role, filling a void in Garfield's own life, but he also had a practical eye open for promising young men. In 1865 he had brought Garfield into his law firm as a limited partner, but found no use for him until March of 1866, when he suddenly asked him to help argue the Milligan case, less than a week before it was scheduled to be heard.

Lambdin P. Milligan and his friends were Indiana copperheads who had been accused of conspiring to aid the Confederacy by seizing federal arsenals, releasing rebel prisoners and creating general havoc behind the Union lines. Hustled before a military court, they had been promptly tried under martial law, convicted and sentenced to be hanged. In its haste, the military tribunal had ignored the civil courts as slow and unreliable, even though those courts were open for business in Indiana at the time. The war ended before the execution could take place and President Johnson commuted their sentences to life imprisonment. From their cells, the prisoners appealed their conviction. The appeal was not based on the facts but on the technical question of jurisdiction. Black, who saw an opportunity to strike a blow against military courts and the Republican Party at the same time, was happy to take their case. But how did Garfield, a soldier and an impeccable Republican, become involved?

As Garfield later told the story, Judge Black had approached him out of the blue. Black had been favorably impressed with Garfield's wartime speeches in which he had "resisted some attempts to extend the power of Military Commissions so as to try civilians who were interfering with the war—such fellows as Vallandingham." Black explained the case to Garfield, who agreed that an injustice had been done and who offered to help Black correct it. Whereupon, as Garfield

271

recalled, the following dialogue ensued: "Said he, 'Young man, you know it is a perilous thing for a young Republican in Congress to say that, and I don't want you to injure yourself.' Said I, 'It don't make any difference. I believe in English liberty and English law.' "[44]

This story is unlikely on two counts. First of all, Garfield had not been particularly devoted to the cause of civil rights and free speech in wartime. His 1865 congressional attack on arbitrary arrests had been directed against the summary imprisonment of *army officers*, not civilians. He had no sympathy with civilian dissent, as was revealed by his explosion of fury upon discovering that some Hiram students had expressed sympathy for the South. Were he still in charge of the school, he raged, he would not only have them expelled, but would ask the military to arrest them at once and ship them off to the Confederacy. "They entirely mistake and misapprehend the character of the times if they suppose that the same license can now be used as in the days of peace."[45]

Nor does Garfield's recollection of being approached so gratuitously by Black seem convincing. He already was Black's law partner and had been for over a year, although their association was not generally known. Black needed someone on his team with military experience to counter Ben Butler on the government's side. But most importantly, in a case with such political overtones, he needed a respectable Republican, especially one with radical credentials who was also a friend of the Chief Justice. What more logical choice than his junior partner?

His young colleague's lack of experience did not deter Black, but Garfield was overwhelmed by the challenge. It reminded him of the time General Buell had assigned him his first military campaign. For four days and nights he worked, with scarcely any sleep, reviewing his half-forgotten legal training. His plea before the court lasted two hours and dealt with the historical and legal precedents applicable to the case. In contrast to the eloquence of Black, who relied more on Shakespeare than on Blackstone, Garfield's speech was learned and relatively matter-of-fact in its style, but its effect, he diffidently boasted, was judged "not altogether a failure."[46]

272

When the decision was announced, in Milligan's favor, it unleashed a political storm among radical Republicans, who realized that it might set a precedent that could cripple military Reconstruction in the South. The Supreme Court was assailed as it had not been since the Dred Scott case. Congressional radicals spoke of impeaching the justices but contented themselves with legislation designed to hobble the Court and restrict its future jurisdiction over similar cases. Garfield discreetly refrained from opposing these restrictions, wisely calculating that he had already displayed enough heroism on this issue.[47]

Garfield might be charged with betraying his party, but no one could accuse him of selling out. He never made a cent out of the Milligan case, even though his clients included some· of the wealthiest men in Indiana. From time to time, whenever he was strapped for cash, he would dun Milligan and his friends for payment, but his appeals were ignored.[48] The experience, however, was more valuable than any fee. Garfield had won an overnight reputation as a constitutional lawyer which, if properly managed, could nourish a lucrative career.

Intrigued by the possibilities of a legal career and discouraged by his recent financial reverses, Garfield began to doubt his political vocation. "I sometimes think it would be better for me to quit public life, and try to get some property," he suggested to a friend. While playing chess with the Chief Justice, he harped on the same theme. Chase reported to his daughter that Garfield "talks of quitting Congress and devoting himself to law. His renomination is contested and he seems half to wish for defeat." Chase knew Garfield too well to be alarmed and cynically assured his daughter, "you may believe however that the other half of his will is much the biggest." Chase was shrewd. Every two years, with calendar-like regularity, Garfield would talk of quitting politics, yet each time he would allow himself to be persuaded to run for Congress for one more term.

This year it took very little persuasion. He knew that the next congress would chart the course of Reconstruction and he had no intention of sitting it out.[49] Historians would later call 1866 "the critical year," and they would scrutinize the congressional elections for their bearing on Reconstruction. Yet in Garfield's campaign for the nomination (which insured election in his district) the Southern question was virtually ignored. This silence indicated unanimity, not apathy. Republicans in the 19th Ohio were united behind radical Reconstruction. This did not, as Garfield discovered, prevent them from finding other issues to use against their congressman.

The opposition to Garfield was much better organized than it had been two years earlier. Some suspected that it was stoked by Garfield's foes from outside the district. Former Governor Tod was a prime target of these suspicions, as was Ben Wade, whose kinsman, Darius Cadwell, was a leading contestant for Garfield's seat. Garfield himself thought he saw the hand of Senator John Sherman. Recently Garfield had labored hard, but unsuccessfully, for his friend Schenck, "so bold and true," to wrest the Senate seat from the "bloodless" Sherman whom they both held in such contempt. In retaliation, Sherman followers, so Garfield claimed, bluntly threatened "to break me down" in the coming election.[50]

A host of local lawyers had their eye on Garfield's seat, but the most formidable opponents were Cadwell and John Hutchins. Four years earlier Hutchins had been defeated by Garfield and now he was anxious for vindication, skillfully courting the voters with all the time-honored arts. "He is a remarkable wire-puller and politician," Rhodes marveled. "It is amazing to see how he greets cordially men, women and children." Some of his tactics were less innocent. He tried to play on the religious prejudices of the district, "rallying Methodists, Presbyterians and Baptists to the overthrow of Campbellism." Some of Garfield's friends even hinted that Hutchins was "going so far as to make free use of money in the canvass."[51]

All of Garfield's opponents tried to exploit the grievances that had accumulated over the past four years, "burrowing in the townships and coming above the surface now and then in the newspapers" every time they found a responsive chord. The three most promising issues were the draft, the Milligan case and the tariff.

For well over a year Cadwell had assiduously fanned popular discontent over "Garfield's law," as the unpopular draft legislation had come to be called. Even though the war was over, that law still rankled and in some parts of the district its memory was strong enough to create "the most violent and telling opposition" Garfield faced. There was little Garfield could do to counter this issue except patiently explain his stand and hope that with the passage of time the storm would subside.[52] Garfield's role in the Milligan case was even harder to explain. Radicals in the district could not understand why their congressman would "defend rebels." That decision was so unpopular throughout the North that, as Garfield noted with disgust, "the papers are calling for the abolition of the [Supreme] Court." His own district was not immune, and even some of Garfield's former supporters were heard to exclaim: "I want no man in Congress that will apologize for traitors."[53]

The tariff issue hurt Garfield the most, especially in the iron regions of Trumbull and Mahoning counties. His scouts reported that in Youngstown and "up and down the valley the Hutchins men have been hard at work and have damaged you greatly by their 'free trade' report." Heeding their pleas to "put yourself right" on the tariff, Garfield delivered what could be construed as protectionist speeches in Congress, but the iron men remained unconvinced. He did succeed, however, in blunting some of the opposition in Mahoning County by sponsoring a bill to authorize a railroad from Youngstown to Pittsburgh.[54]

Although he was willing to appease the opposition, even at the cost of blurring his own tariff principles, Garfield could not bring himself to indulge in the sort of political management Hutchins and others practiced. "If a plain honest course of hard work will not secure the approval of the people—" he righteously declared, "I prefer to be beaten." Nor could he bring himself to appear before the public as "a beggar for office." The thought of "going from township to township saying to the people 'Behold me! I am your man. Don't choose that man. I am worthier! Take me!' " was repugnant to his sensibilities. "This may be squeamishness," he admitted, "—but it is a genuine and very deep-seated feeling with me."[55]

Fortunately for his career, Garfield had friends who were less squeamish. Preeminent among them was Harmon Austin.

For almost a decade the Ravenna flagstone merchant and banker had, with rare dedication, made Garfield's cause his own. As Rhodes observed, "He has the most natural way of taking a man under his wing." Garfield needed just this sort of local alter ego, a man who relished the fine points of political infighting, yet who had no political ambitions of his own; who was shrewd enough to read the district's pulse and frank enough to speak plainly. Austin's well-meant bluntness sometimes led Garfield to complain that "His desire to manage people and their affairs is very marked, and though I like him very much indeed and accept his admonitions in the same spirit in which they are given (that of the most faithful friendship), I cant say they are entirely reasonable or pleasant." But he was well aware that Austin was indispensable and was grateful for his devotion. During a political campaign Austin would let his flagstone business run itself while he worked night and day, "in my own quiet way," to safeguard his friend's interest. Politics, to Austin, was not a matter of principle, or issues, or glory, or even patronage. It was a sport, to be pursued for excitement. "I have such a horror of being whipped that I cannot let it alone," he admitted in a revealing confession.[56]

After scouting the ground thoroughly, Austin predicted that despite all their noise Garfield's opponents would fade before the convention. His confidence was justified. Cadwell pulled out by the end of June and Hutchins was so badly beaten in the township primary meetings that he would not even allow his name to go before the Convention. "Honesty *is* the best policy, even in running for Congress," rejoiced a happy Garfield supporter. By the time the district convention met in mid-August, Garfield was the only candidate left in the field and was nominated by acclamation for his third term in Congress.[57]

In the ensuing campaign he took the stump against President Johnson and his alliterative allies: "the unwashed, unanointed, unforgiven, unrepentant, unhung Rebels of the South [and] . . . the dishonored, depraved, defeated remnants of Northern Democracy." The President, he warned, has joined the Democratic Party, and who, he asked, are the Democrats? John Wilkes Booth was a Democrat.

276

Every Rebel guerrilla and jayhawker, every man who ran to Canada to avoid the draft, every bounty-jumper, every deserter, every cowardly sneak that ran from danger and disgraced his flag, every man who loves slavery and hates liberty, every man who helped massacre loyal negroes at Fort Pillow, or loyal whites at New Orleans, every Knight of the Golden Circle, every incendiary who helped burn Northern steam boats and Northern hotels, and every villain, of whatever name or crime, who loves power more than justice, slavery more than freedom, is a Democrat and an indorser of Andrew Johnson.[58]

He took this message on the road, traveling 7,500 miles and delivering 65 speeches. It must have been well received, for he won his expected reelection by a margin of 5 to 2, slightly down from 1864 but still an impressive display of his hold on the district.[59] More important, the Republicans were everywhere victorious, winning over two-thirds of the next congress, enough to enact their program without fear of further presidential vetoes.

Despite these personal and party triumphs, Garfield returned to Washington in a mood of depression that not even the birth of his daughter Mary (affectionately nicknamed Mollie) could dispel. Even though he had easily beaten back his recent opposition, the revelation of the intensity of popular feeling had left him shaken. "There is passion enough in this country to run a steam engine in every village," he realized, and he was aware that if he persisted in his unpopular tariff and currency views, that passion could be directed against him. But he could not change. "My own course is chosen," he said resignedly, "and it is quite probable it will throw me out of public life." He was further discouraged by the behavior of his Republican colleagues, who seemed to think that they must do "some absurdly extravagant thing to prove their radicalism." In particular, he was disturbed by the "insane scheme" to impeach President Johnson. Although he thought impeachment might prove "a blessing" in many respects, he could not believe that it would succeed, while the attempt, he feared, would prove "ruinous both to the party and the general peace of the country."[60]

277

The *Anti-Slavery Standard* interpreted Garfield's caution as a betrayal of radical principles and darkly implied that he had sold out the cause in return for patronage favors from the President. In reality, his Southern policy had hardened considerably in recent months. He had once been willing to admit the Southern states back into the congress and close the books on Reconstruction as soon as they ratified the Fourteenth Amendment. Although certainly not satisfied with that measure, which in his view "did not come up to the full height of the great occasion," he conceded that Congress was "morally bound" to admit the Southern states if they should accept it. Instead, with President Johnson's encouragement, the amendment was rejected by all the Confederate states but Tennessee. One by one, Garfield said, "the sinful ten has . . . with contempt and scorn, flung back into our teeth the magnanimous offer of a generous nation."[61]

Until this rebuff, Garfield had regarded Reconstruction as mild and benevolent. Congress, he argued, clearly had possessed the legal right to hang every rebel and confiscate every Southern dollar if it so chose. Instead, it had been as "magnanimous" and "merciful" as God Himself when He "offered forgiveness to the fallen sons of men." Yet the Southerners had perversely interpreted forebearance as weakness, and Garfield was forced to conclude that since this mild policy had proved "a complete and disastrous failure," the time had come "when we must lay the heavy hand of military authority upon these Rebel communities, and hold them in its grasp till their madness is past." He granted that military rule would be a harsh remedy, yet "bayonets have done us good service before." And if, out of all the travail, there would come a new South with equality for men of all races, the result would justify the effort. Viewed in this light, Southern intransigence could be considered providential and Garfield discerned that "the hand of God has been visible in this work, leading us by degrees out of the blindness of our prejudices to see that the fortunes of the Republic and the safety of the party of liberty are inseparably bound up with the rights of the black man."[62]

This was music to the ears of Ohio Radicals who had had enough of the moderation of Governor Cox. A formidable

Garfield-for-Governor boom was launched, which won the support of over forty Ohio newspapers. Garfield's close advisers, however, warned against the movement, hoping that after another term in Congress he might be in line for a Senate seat. He did not need to be persuaded. The financial objections that had led him to refuse Bascom's proposal two years earlier were even stronger now that his congressional salary had been raised to $5,000. Furthermore, he was sick from overwork— "dizzy, stupid sick"—and needed a rest to ward off complete collapse. Under the circumstances, a political campaign was out of the question. He spiked the gubernatorial boom and urged (without enthusiasm) the retention of Cox. Instead, the party gave the nomination to Garfield's junior congressional colleague, Rutherford B. Hayes, and with it Hayes laid the foundation for his future political career.[63]

Garfield had had his fill of politics for awhile. Public life had given him no respite for over five years. His preoccupation with finance had grown to an obsession which devoured his days and nights. "I have thought of but little else, read of but little else, talked of but little else for the last four months," he complained.[64] Overwork exacted its inevitable toll: he could no longer sleep nights and feared that his health was crumbling. The doctor prescribed rest, and Garfield's thoughts turned longingly towards Europe. He had made a little money over the winter as agent for the sale of coal fields and with it he booked passage on *The City of London* for the ocean voyage he had dreamed of ever since he had been a sea-struck boy.

There was one unpleasant errand to perform before he could leave. Mrs. Calhoun, the New York widow with whom he had had a brief love affair, still held Garfield's indiscreet letters. Repentant now, Garfield feared that these papers "might some day and in some way be troublesome." While in New York awaiting embarkation, he determined to get hold of the papers to avert future blackmail. Back home, Lucretia wrung her hands at the thought of her husband once again entering her rival's "preserve." Perhaps, she nervously suggested, "it would be better to let the fire of such lawless passion burn itself out unfed and unnoticed." Despite Lucretia's forebodings, the interview went smoothly and Garfield was able to retrieve the

279

papers. Mrs. Calhoun soon married an indulgent New York lawyer who could support her literary aspirations and the case, Lucretia fervently hoped, was closed.[65]

They set sail on July 13 for a seventeen-week grand tour. Until the very last minute, Garfield was not sure his wife could tear herself away from the children, but she showed up just before embarkation to join him in what would prove to be their only vacation together. Carrying two large leather satchels and armed with a French dictionary, these two innocents abroad set forth to see the world. The crossing was moderately rough and Garfield was boyishly proud of escaping sea-sickness. As he watched the waves, he could "almost feel the old passion for the sea arise in my heart again. Were I not what I am," he reflected, "I should have been a sailor."[66]

In England he cased the House of Commons with a professional eye. "The speaking is much more conversational and businesslike than in Congress, but there is a curious and painful hesitation in almost every speaker." The historic debate on the Reform Bill was in progress and he paid close attention to the chief actors: John Stuart Mill, attentive with his chin resting on the palm of his hand; Disraeli, impassive, his face a mask; and Gladstone, "the most un-English speaker I have yet heard and the best."[67]

The Elgin Marbles failed to live up to his expectations as did Westminster Abbey, while the British Museum gave him corns. Undeterred, he doggedly limped across London for two weeks, leaving for a pilgrimage to Stratford-on-Avon where he experienced "a hushed and reverent feeling . . . which I never felt before."[68] After a literary tour of Scotland and the North Country, they crossed over to Europe, zipped through the Low Countries, then up the Rhine, admiring the cathedrals along the way, and on to Switzerland for a view of the glaciers, then across the Alps to see at last that fabled Italy he had dreamed of as a student. In Florence and Milan he indefatigably tramped through every church and gallery and he stood in Venice on the Bridge of Sighs with copies of Ruskin and Byron in either hand. Not even the threat of a revolution could keep him from Rome—"the home and centre of so many years of study and thought!"

280

This was the emotional high-point of the trip, as he wandered for five happy days through the familiar landmarks of classical antiquity. Like Gibbon a century before him, his feelings were mixed. "For two hours," he said, "I could do but little else than sit in silence and try to repress the conflict of emotions that arose between my love of classic Rome and my indignation at the infinite impertinence with which every symbol of its greatness . . . has been converted into papal symbols." But love of Rome triumphed over contempt for Catholicism and after taking in all the monuments he returned to his hotel "to sit and dream and be unutterably sad."[69]

After almost two weeks in Paris, which they inspected from the sewers up, Garfield and his wife were happy to be back in England, "a land that has a Sunday and a conscience," and even happier to book passage for home. As land drew in sight and the trip drew to its close, Garfield nostalgically catalogued his memories as he reluctantly prepared himself "to enter the world again."[70]

CHAPTER FOURTEEN

. . . AND NOT A FOOL

The Garfields are back from their travels, Robert Schenck reported to his daughter, still the same "right good, kind true people," who offer their guests "plain comfortable country like entertainment" without frills or sophistication. "Mrs. Garfield," he observed snobbishly, "has not brought home any particular style from Europe." She did, however, return with bric-a-brac for her home, while her husband brought back renewed strength and energy which he hoped to devote to the cause of honest money. He quite agreed with his friend Hinsdale that "The men who rise to the demands of the time on the money matters will be the men who will make a name for the future," and he planned to make his mark as chairman of the Ways and Means Committee.[1]

His ambition might seem excessive for someone with only four years of congressional experience, but Garfield apparently believed that his two years of intensive financial study entitled him to be chairman of the most powerful committee of the House. To him, his claim seemed so obvious that he refused even to discuss the matter with Speaker Colfax, trusting that the prize would come unsolicited, as a reward for merit. He was bound to be disappointed. Colfax put Schenck at the head of Ways and Means and gave Garfield command of the Military Affairs Committee; an important place, Garfield conceded, "but out of the chosen line of my studies."

Stunned by Colfax's "cowardice," Garfield professed himself "greatly wronged" by the decision. In his bitterness, he forgot for the moment that Schenck was his good friend and declared him unfit for the post: "he has not given much thought to finance, and so far as he has formed opinions they are in the main wrong." He brushed aside as "pretense" the Speaker's quite reasonable explanation that the Ways and Means chairman should reflect the sentiment of the House on fiscal policy. Garfield, with his emphatic hard-money notions, definitely did not reflect that sentiment.

Had he considered the matter coolly, he would have realized that he had no right to complain. Colfax had always treated him generously, assigning him to major committees from the first. James G. Blaine and William B. Allison, two promising young men who had entered Congress at the same time as Garfield, had not yet been given charge of any committee, while Garfield now headed an important one. Though rebuffed, Garfield did not surrender. "I do not intend to be thrown out of financial work," he declared, and he and some like-minded congressmen were talking of forming "a sort of voluntary outside committee" to defend the hard-money position.[2]

There were some compensations. The Military Affairs committee rooms had just been redecorated with new chairs, rich carpets and plush draperies, so that Garfield was able to conduct his deliberations in an atmosphere of elegance. The committee's work, unfortunately, was not as glamorous as its surroundings, but someone had to clean up the loose ends of the late war. The work was necessary, but hardly stimulating: pensions; the disposal of surplus army property, ranging from abandoned campsites to unneeded cannon; and other such routine demobilization matters. The committee's main task was to find a way to put the armed forces back on a peacetime footing. That mighty army which for two triumphant days had passed in review down Pennsylvania Avenue, had now melted away, leaving behind an organizational debris. There were too many surgeons, too many regimental bands, too many generals for a peacetime army. Garfield tackled the problem in his usual painstaking manner. His committee commenced a systematic review of the entire military establishment with a view towards efficient reorganization and reduction.

Their report would not be ready until near the end of the

Congress, but in the meantime there was one reduction Garfield was impatient to make—Major General Winfield Scott Hancock. General Hancock, a hero of Gettysburg, had replaced Sheridan as military commander of Louisiana and Texas. Unlike his predecessor, who had been heard to mutter, "If I owned Texas and hell, I'd rent out Texas and live in hell," Hancock took pains to conciliate the native white population. President Johnson singled him out for special commendation in his annual message, but Garfield heard a different story from his friend and successor as Colonel of the 42nd Regiment, Lionel Sheldon, now a self-proclaimed "Carpetbagger" in New Orleans. According to Sheldon, "Hancock played the very devil [in Louisiana] . . . picked out every scoundrel he could find and lent his name to every scheme of the rebels. I consider him the most infamous man in America." Garfield did not need Sheldon's advice. He was already sufficiently indignant over Hancock's "insubordinate" course in defying Congress by supporting Louisiana's civil authority in order "to obstruct the work of Reconstruction." The general, Garfield charged, "has been made a party to the political madness which has so long marked the conduct of the President," and he accused him of harboring presidential ambitions of his own. The accusation was prophetic, but premature. Hancock would run for the presidency, but not until 1880, when his opponent would be Garfield himself. For the present, Garfield planned to clip Hancock's wings by introducing a bill to reduce the number of major generals by one. The pretext was economy but the object, as everyone knew, was Hancock, the least senior officer of that rank. Garfield did not expect to carry the measure; he intended only to show Hancock "how completely he was in our hands."[3]

Actually, the threat was aimed higher than Hancock. It was directed at the President himself, whose "facile instrument" the general was. Garfield shrank from striking a direct blow at the President even though he had an opportunity. Some of his radical colleagues, hot for a showdown, had prepared a bill of impeachment against the President. After much soul searching, Garfield decided to vote against impeachment, "not because I did not believe his [Johnson's] conduct deserved the severest condemnation, but because I did not believe the attempt was likely to be successful." An unsuccessful attempt at impeachment, he feared, could only damage the Republican Party and comfort its enemies.[4]

Much as he disliked Johnson, Garfield was compelled to admit that the impeachers had not made a strong case. He threw his influence against impeachment and convinced enough of his colleagues so that it was decisively defeated. "It may—and probably will cost me my political life," he glumly assumed. His district was not likely to approve any act that could be construed as a defense of the hated President, but beyond that, there was an additional complication. If Johnson should be removed, Wade, president pro tempore of the Senate, was by law the next in line of succession to fill the presidential office. If, however, impeachment should fail, Wade had no political future. Ohio voters had recently turned against radicalism, defeating a proposal for Negro suffrage and electing a Democratic legislature. This left Wade a senatorial "lame duck." In his frustration, Wade might turn against Garfield, which could, Garfield feared, "open the way for a campaign in the 19th District in which he will have all the popular passion added to his own, against me." It was not inconceivable that Wade might even challenge Garfield for his congressional seat.[5]

Both Hinsdale and Austin, however, reported the cheering news that "all the best minds in the district . . . are opposed to impeachment," which meant that, for the moment at least, Garfield's political flanks were secure. It was at this point that he counterattacked with the Hancock bill, to show the district that his heart was still radical and to show the President "that our refusal to impeach . . . did not arise either from want of courage—nor from any purpose to abandon our work of reconstruction." He kept the impeachment door ajar, warning the President not to push Congress beyond the limits of forebearance.[6]

These limits, Garfield felt, were exceeded by the President's defiance of the Tenure of Office Act, which prohibited the removal of cabinet officers without the consent of the Senate. Garfield had voted for that act, had even attempted to make it more severe. He had even advanced the curious theory that the act was unnecessary since the Constitution already vested the power of removal in the Senate rather than the President. Otherwise, he argued, Congress would lose its independence and become "the mere recorder" of presidential edicts. He felt so strongly about this that he solemnly vowed: "never by my vote shall Congress give up the constitutional power, and allow to any one man, be he an angel from heaven, the absolute and sole control of appointments to and removals from office in this country."[7]

Less than a decade later, he would have reason to regret his uncompromising stand. By 1877 he had come to regard Senatorial control of appointments as a "power most corrupting and dangerous," which fostered the "invasion of the executive functions by members of Congress." "This evil," he finally realized, "has been greatly aggravated by the passage of the Tenure of Office Act. . . ." As President, Garfield would, in a very real sense, give his life to determine whether (as he put it, in a curious echo of his earlier stand), "the President is the registering clerk of the Senate or the Executive of the Nation."[8]

But in 1868 he was too filled with anti-Johnson bitterness to harbor such misgivings. When the President attempted to remove Secretary of War Stanton, in defiance of the Tenure of Office Act, Garfield was convinced of Johnson's dictatorial intention "to trample under foot the authority of the Constitution." Fresh articles of impeachment were drawn and this time Garfield supported them. "The recklessness of Johnson left us no choice," he explained, "and I hope we may now have done with him, by putting him out of the way."[9]

He was not able to vote for impeachment because he was called away from the Capitol to try his second law suit. The case involved the will of his boyhood idol, Alexander Campbell, founder of the Disciples of Christ. Campbell's children had challenged the will on the grounds that their father had been mentally incompetent. Garfield derived great satisfaction from vindicating Campbell's reputation as well as from the $3,040 fee he pocketed—the first tangible rewards of his legal career.[10]

He returned to Washington to find that preparations for the

286

great political show trial were already underway. "We have Andy in the grip of the law at last," Garfield gloated. His constituents supported his stand. Not a single correspondent during these months opposed the impeachment trial; all hoped, some quite violently, that Johnson would be convicted, though few went so far as the 109 citizens of Cleveland who petitioned that the office of president be abolished. Garfield expressed confidence that Johnson's conviction "appears to be as certain of success as any future thing in human affairs," but privately he admitted that he was worried about the outcome.[11] In strictest confidence, he told James H. Rhodes that "Many of our friends are greatly depressed and consider the result very doubtful." He knew of conservative Republican Senators who were thinking along these lines:

> Conviction means a transfer to the Presidency of Mr. Wade a man of violent passions, extreme opinion & narrow view; a man who has never studied or thought thoroughly or carefully on any subject except slavery—a grossly profane, coarse nature, who is surrounded by the worst and most violent elements in the Rep. party . . . that already the worst class of political cormorants from Ohio and elsewhere are thronging the lobbies and filling the hotels in high hope of plunder when Wade is sworn in. . . .

Garfield disclaimed these sentiments, but he recognized their force. "I shall not be greatly surprised if he is acquitted," he concluded, "nor if that sad event happens, will it be wholly without compensating results."[12]

In retrospect, the trial of Andrew Johnson seems like one of the most dramatic chapters of American political history, but at the time it was greeted, on the Western Reserve at least, with remarkable calm. To Garfield, who was a spectator, the trial was a colossal bore: "we have been wading knee deep in words, words, words, for a whole week," he complained, "and are but little more than half across the turbid stream."[13] He suspected "that if the choice were given to some of our fiercest impeachers to speak and lose their case—or to keep silent and win it—they would instantly decide to read a six hour speech to an unwilling audience."[14]

> Then think of the speaking itself! Stevens, reeling in the shadow of death, struggling to read what could not be heard twenty feet

287

off, Williams sitting up nights to add a few dozen pages to the manuscript which he spends two days reading; and Nelson using nearly two days in the worst type of Tennessee stump speech. We do not yet know whether Stanbery will be able to snatch his speech from the jaws of dyspepsia and fling it into the Senate. . . . and then it is not improbable that the fires of debate will be lighted in Senatorial breasts and burn with unquenchable ardor. . . . Speech may be silver; silence is surely golden.[15]

He half expected that the trial would fail to convict Johnson, but when that "great wrong was consummated" he was stunned. He blamed the outcome on Chief Justice Chase, the presiding officer of the trial, who, Garfield claimed, used his influence to convince wavering Senators to vote for acquittal. Chase had been his friend but they were friends no more. "It is the hardest thing I ever have to do, to withdraw confidence and love from a man to whom I have given them," Garfield said, but Chase's "outrageous" conduct gave him no choice. Garfield had never been blind to his former friend's ambition, but now he felt that ambition had carried Chase beyond the bounds of decency. "I have no doubt he is trying to break the Republican party and make himself President by the aid of the Democracy," he angrily charged. "It is treachery for personal ends and deserves the contempt of all good men."[16]

At the same time that Garfield was breaking off personal relations with Chase he was advocating the financial doctrines which Chase had taught him. True to his vow, Garfield had continued to speak his mind on finance, even though the platform of the Ways and Means Committee had been denied him. In February, he had introduced a pair of bills designed to provide for the gradual return to specie payment and the legalization of gold contracts. Buried in committee, they would one day rise again to become the fiscal policy of the nation. His major financial effort was embodied in a two-hour speech on "The Currency," which he delivered at what must have been the worst possible moment—on May 15, just when the House was absorbed by the trial of the President. "Notwithstanding the excitement and anxiety with which the shadow of impeachment filled every member, I had the undivided attention of the best minds in the House," Garfield noted with gratification.[17]

It was an extremely able speech and, granted the premises, a convincing refutation of the paper money delusion. What was even more striking was the style. Gone were the Latin tag lines, the classical allusions and the flowery eloquence that used to embellish Garfield's rhetoric. Instead, he relied on history, logic and experience, spiced with homely illustrations to make his point clearly and economically. He spoke as a teacher rather than as an orator. "The age of oratory has passed," Garfield would later announce. "The newspaper, the pamphlet, and the book have abolished it. Only plain speaking— argument and fact that may be printed—are of any great value now." It was this sort of plain speaking, which Garfield so admired in Lincoln's prose, that would henceforth be his model. In later years, Garfield would be eulogized as the greatest debater of his day. This was misleading. He lacked the killer instinct of the truly great debater who glories in personal combat, "but in the ability to deal with large subjects, after deliberation, with broad and comprehensive strength, he was not excelled by any contemporary."[18]

The currency speech won the acclaim of the House. Schenck told Garfield it was the best effort of his career and Colfax praised it in terms that led Garfield to think he was sorry to have dropped him from the Ways and Means committee. David A. Wells was enthusiastic and E. L. Godkin, editor of the influential reform journal, *The Nation*, told Edward Atkinson: "I quite agree with you about Garfield. We must back that class of men up. They will be the salvation of the country."[19] The speech crossed the Atlantic and came to the attention of the officers of the Cobden Club, a British organization designed to promote the cause of liberal economic reforms. They were so impressed with the appearance of a new American disciple that they elected Garfield to the Club. In future years this honor would prove a political handicap for Garfield. He would constantly have to explain that the Cobden Club was not, as his opponents charged, a free-trade society nor was it an agency of any conspiracy of British bankers and Wall Street speculators, despite the presence of many

Rothschilds on its membership list. In fact, the society was purely honorary, with such disparate members as "Sunset" Cox, Emerson, William Lloyd Garrison, Henry Ward Beecher and Garibaldi.[20]

Judge Ebenezer Hoar was so taken with the speech that he dashed off a note of appreciation. "And just as I had done reading it [the speech]," he told Garfield with dismay, "I saw in a newspaper a disgusting rumor that from some silly or selfish notion of 'rotation in office' it is doubtful whether you will be nominated for re-election!" In fact, as Garfield assured Hoar, his nomination was more certain than in any previous contest. His friends could uncover few serious objections to Garfield in the district, although there were some muted grumblings about his association with Jere Black and his European trip, as well as a general complaint of "want of interest in the affairs of your district." This last charge, Garfield was assured, "is one gotten up for convenience to embrace every thing and mean nothing."[21]

What opposition there was centered in Warren where Garfield's "enemies" were reported "insane in their bitterness" over his supposed free-trade views. This opposition was fanned by Darius Cadwell. Cadwell claimed that Garfield's friends had promised him two years earlier that Garfield would step aside for him at the next election. He reminded the ambitious young men in the district of the dangerous precedent set by Joshua Giddings who had represented the 19th in Congress for 21 years, and he hinted that Garfield hoped to match that record. It was not impossible that Cadwell was playing the role of stalking-horse for Ben Wade. To forestall that threat, as well as to refute the charges of undue ambition, Garfield went to Wade and offered to withdraw in his favor. He congratulated himself on his generosity. "I do not know of many men situated as I am who would have made the offer." But Wade, as Garfield had probably anticipated, declined the offer on the grounds that he expected a good place in the forthcoming Grant administration.[22]

As the nominating convention drew near, Garfield's opponents grew desperate over the lack of issues. They launched a last-ditch campaign of personal abuse that left the bewildered candidate feeling as though he were "a first class convict just from the penitentiary," rather than a candidate for high public office. "They say that you are a horemaster," a friend reported, "went to England to get cured of a bad disease, that you are in market for any kind of bid that any one sees fit to make. . . . They say that you are a free trade man." "I was not aware . . . what an immoral and unprincipled man I was supporting," another friend dryly observed, while J. H. Rhodes burst out in mock indignation: "You gambler you rake You are immensely wealthy out of jobs and frauds and the devil only knows what else."[23]

Despite these wild charges, Garfield was easily renominated. He based his letter of acceptance on his financial doctrines, which might have seemed a deliberate provocation in view of the soft-money platform of the Ohio Republican Party and the widespread inflationist "delusions" of his own constituency.[24] But on this point Garfield refused to bend, for it involved his conception of the duty of a congressman. "It is a fixed opinion of mine," he explained, "that a representative bears to his constituents a relation similar to that of a lawyer to his clients. He is to watch and defend their interest, but to use his own judgement in reference to the particular method of doing so. . . . If the Dist. wish me to vote for inflation, or any form of repudiation, I should be bound to follow my own convictions and trust to the vindication or condemnation of my course at the next election."[25]

Fortunately for Garfield, the Democrats in 1868 had appropriated the inflationist position. The national Republican convention had, in turn, come out firmly for hard money, thus casting a patina of party regularity over Garfield's position. This was sufficient to persuade most of Garfield's constituents, but not his opponents in Trumbull County. On July 4, they printed a petition asking Milton Sutliff, a local lawyer, to take the field as an independent candidate against Garfield. "Our chief objections to Mr. Garfield," they remonstrated, "are his financial views, which we believe represent the interests of capital rather than the honest yeomanry of the 19th Cong. Dist., and which if carried out would result in a dangerous monied aristocracy. . . . His failure to represent the manufacturing and producing interests of this District, by a persistent free trade theory . . . evinces to us that he represents Wall Street, New York, and capitalists generally, better than he does the people of the 19th Cong. Dist."

From the tone of the petition one might suspect that the "honest yeomen" behind the movement were the iron manu-facturers of Trumbull County aided by a few lawyers. Some of Garfield's nervous scouts, however, reported that thousands of dissidents in all parts of the district were flocking to sign the petition. But when Garfield investigated the movement for himself, he found it nothing more than "a crazy effort of a few sore-headed men in Warren and Youngstown."[26]

He campaigned with his accustomed vigor, speaking sixty-six times and was, he told his wife, "greatly surprised at the generous enthusiasm with which I am met by the people of the district." His hold on the district was as secure as ever. The independent movement played itself out as "a roaring farce," and Garfield doubted whether even a hundred voters would scratch his name from the ticket. "If any man take the 19th Dist out of my hand," he recklessly boasted, "I dont know his name."[27] The confidence was justified. Grant won the pres-idency and Garfield won his usual smashing victory with a two-to-one majority, slightly behind the national ticket but nonetheless an impressive vote of confidence. As one disgrun-tled opponent suggested, if anyone in the 19th District has ambitions for Congress, "they better go home and educate their *grandchildren* for that position or else remove to some other district!"[28]

Garfield had clearly won the hearts of his constituents. Had he also won the approval of his colleagues? Was he yet an ef-fective congressman? In some respects, yes. Certainly his ready eloquence made him a useful figure on the floor of Con-gress, as he demonstrated on the anniversary of Lincoln's death. The leadership of the House had made no preparation for a memorial and were caught by surprise when President Johnson ordered all government offices closed in commemo-ration. Colfax burst into Garfield's office at fifteen minutes before twelve and told him to prepare "a happy, touching and elo-quent" tribute for delivery at noon. Garfield was not chosen because of his attachment to the late President, but because Colfax knew that no one else could summon up comparable eloquence on such short notice. He was not disappointed. At the appointed hour, Garfield rose and delivered what Albert Gallatin Riddle, no mean stylist himself, hailed as "one of the most felicitious things of the kind in our Congressional history."[29]

A talent of that magnitude could hardly remain unappreciated and Garfield found himself in great demand as a speaker. "He spoke so readily," observed Whitelaw Reid, "that members were constantly asking his services in behalf of favorite measures; and in the impulsive eagerness of a young man and a young member he often consented." Mark Hopkins feared that his prize pupil was putting himself "in danger of losing influence from speaking on too many subjects and too often." Garfield himself realized that he possessed "a fatal facility" with words and vowed to "atone" for "the mistake I made in speaking too much in the early years of my congressional life." But some damage had already been done and it would take years for him to live down his reputation for glibness.[30]

Nor could he expect to gain the comradeship of his fellow-congressmen while certain traces of unctuous sanctity from his ministerial days still clung to him. One day, clad in the armor of self-righteousness, he announced that he had been credited with more mileage payments than he was entitled. Other congressmen, he charged, had also received too much and he demanded that an investigation be made.[31] The demand was ignored but Garfield's public show of virtue could hardly have endeared him to his colleagues. Nor did his personality win universal admiration. Garfield would be assailed on the floor of the House as a snob and a meddler, "whose nose is generally in everybody else's business." Sunset Cox, later a friend, would accuse Garfield of superciliousness. "The gentleman from Ohio has a way of sneering at everybody," Cox complained.[32]

The true measure of a legislator's effectiveness, however, is not popularity, but the ability to legislate. Yet even by that standard, Garfield was not yet a success. His legislative record

293

in the 39th and 40th Congresses added up to a series of disappointments.

The measure closest to Garfield's heart was his bill to establish a federal Department of Education. Not only had he been an educator himself, but his Western Reserve constituents were singularly devoted to the cause of education. As he proudly boasted: "this is no ordinary district. There is no district in the country equal to it in the diffusion of general intelligence."[33] With such a district behind him, Garfield could devote attention to his favorite cause without fear of grumbling from back home.

The bill to establish a national Bureau of Education began life as a Reconstruction measure. Late in 1865, Ignatius Donnelly, the eccentric Minnesota congressman, Baconian, and future Populist, introduced a resolution to set up a bureau "to enforce education, without regard to race or color" upon all states whose educational system failed to meet minimum standards. The suggestion was ignored by Congress but it did set educators to thinking, and early the next year the National Association of School Superintendants asked Congress to establish some sort of bureau. The request was passed along to a special committee chaired by Garfield; a bill was drafted along the lines suggested by the educators, and Garfield introduced it into the House.

This bill was quite different from Donnelly's original proposal. Consistent with his belief in limited government, Garfield opposed any form of national control over education. Nothing, he warned, could be more dangerous than federal authority over the nation's schoolrooms. "There is no midway ground between an abstract assertion of that right," he insisted, "and the assumption of power to dictate text-books, schoolhouses, teachers and every minutiae of the work of education."[34] Consequently, his bill was a much more modest proposal than Donnelly's had been. He envisioned a sub-cabinet level Department of Education which would serve as a central clearing-house of information, gather statistics and prepare reports, with no power to enforce its recommendations. With a Commissioner at $4,000 a year and a handful of clerks, the Department's annual budget would not exceed $15,000.

294

Even so, the bill faced strong opposition. Democrats professed to see in this innocuous measure the opening wedge for a federal takeover of the nation's schools and churches. Samuel Randall of Pennsylvania deplored the proposed Department as unprecedented, unconstitutional, unnecessary and expensive and moved to emasculate it by placing it in the Interior Department with only two clerks. The friends of education rallied to the bill's defense. Donnelly quoted Bacon, and Garfield delivered a moving plea on the noble object of the bill and its incalculably beneficial results. He reminded those who objected to the expense that Congress had authorized a Coast Survey Bureau. Shall we now, he asked, refuse to "explore the boundaries of that wonderful intellectual empire which encloses within its domain the fate of succeeding generations of this republic?" We have established a Light House Board. Can we refuse "to set up beacons for the coming generation . . . ?" We have surveyed the mineral resources of the continent. "Will you refuse the pitiful sum of $13,000 to collect and record the intellectual resources of this country, the elements that lie behind all material wealth and make it a blessing?"[35]

To Garfield's dismay, a majority of the House answered "Yes" to all these questions. The bill failed, but by only two votes, 59-61. It was not, however, laid upon the table and later that same day James G. Blaine, as he ruefully recalled, was "good natured enough, or weak enough" to yield the floor at Garfield's urging to Upson of Michigan, who moved for a reconsideration. A few days later, the bill was passed and it became law the next year.

Garfield single-handedly persuaded the House to reverse its first stand. Between the two votes he buttonholed his colleagues, pleading with all the fervor he could summon that they reverse their position. They did, more to humor him than out of conviction, and so, as Elihu Washburne later complained, the Department of Education was "by dint of his [Garfield's] persuasion and eloquence finally reconsidered and foisted upon the country."[36]

Congress may have been less than enthusiastic but educators were overjoyed. "May you live a thousand years, and your shadow and that of your wife never be less—but I dont believe you will ever do a work more beneficial and fruitful . . ." was the happy reaction of Henry Barnard, the famed New England educational authority. Barnard had special reason to be pleased. He expected to be the new Department's first Commissioner. It was a logical choice. After a lifetime spent in the service of educational reform, Barnard's name was generally bracketed with that of Horace Mann's in any list of prominent American educators. Essentially a publicist, Barnard perhaps lacked Mann's originality and deep compassion, but his sincerity and energy had made him a dynamic force in his profession, chiefly through the influence of his monumental *American Journal of Education*.[37]

Barnard had been pleading for some sort of federal educational bureau for almost thirty years, but when his opportunity came he proved strangely unable to grasp it firmly. A sense of political reality should have warned him that a Department that had secured no more than halfhearted approval from Congress would have to prove its worth quickly or else face extinction. Instead, as Garfield complained, Barnard "laid out a scheme so vast as to make it impossible to realize its object without tons of reports." When Congress asked the Department to reorganize education in the District of Columbia, Barnard proposed a scheme so intricate that even an admirer dismissed it as "hopelessly complex and unworkable."

There were some valid reasons for the Department's slow start. Because of defects in Garfield's draft of the enabling legislation, the Department lacked a headquarters, and Barnard found his office shunted from place to place without warning. He had to dip into his own pocket to furnish the office with books and supplies. In his first Annual Report, Barnard pleaded for extra clerks and funds. Instead, Congress seemed inclined to abolish the Department altogether. Hardheaded congressmen could not see that it had served any useful purpose, and Barnard was attacked for using the pages of his Report to promote his *Journal*. Thaddeus Stevens derided Barnard as a "worn-out man," and said that he regretted his vote to establish the Department "more than almost any vote that he ever gave." Garfield was not able to defend the agency as vigorously as he might have liked because Barnard had foolishly, and against his specific advice, reprinted one of his speeches in the Departmental Report, opening Garfield and the Department to the devestating charge of forming a "mutual admiration society."

Faced with the opposition of an economy-minded Congress, the Department managed to escape obliteration "by a hair's breadth." It was reduced to the rank of a Bureau in the Department of the Interior and, as a rebuke to Barnard, the Commissioner's salary was cut $1000 and his clerical staff decreased. Garfield blamed Barnard for the "miserable failure" of the Education Department. He sadly concluded that the Commissioner had been "utterly destitute of administrative ability. . . . It was a great misfortune that he should have been appointed." The Bureau clung to life, *sans* Barnard, and ultimately proved its worth, but Garfield could not help being disappointed by the lame conclusion of a project he had so enthusiastically inaugurated. The fault was not his, but he certainly reaped no credit from the outcome.[38]

Another pet scheme of Garfield's fared even worse. From somewhere (certainly not out of his own experience), he had picked up the notion that Indian affairs should be transferred from civilian to military control. It was more than a conviction; it became an obsession. In December of 1868 he brought out of committee a bill he had prepared which would transfer the Department of Indian Affairs from the Interior Department to the War Department. He defended this plan with unaccustomed vehemence and persistence. The army, he argued, with its military discipline and code of honor, could handle the Indians with more efficiency, economy and honesty than could the agents of the Indian Bureau, which he denounced as "so spotted with fraud, so tainted with corruption" as to be "a stench in the nostrils of all good men." In the course of the debate he revealed a lack of sympathy for Indians that amounted to contempt. Their unpronounceable names, their "roaming" habits, their crude clothing, all roused Garfield, normally a tolerant and gentle man, to derision and fury. It is a "mockery" he sputtered, "for the representatives of the great Government of the United States to sit down in a wigwam and make treaties with a lot of painted and half naked savages."

He introduced his bill on the second day of the session and

forced it through to passage in less than an hour, over the angry objections of some congressmen that an important measure was being railroaded without sufficient time for debate. Angriest of all was William Windom, chairman of the Committee on Indian Affairs, who resented someone else meddling in his committee's preserve. Garfield ignored the objections and bulled his measure through the House. The Senate refused to concur, but Garfield, angered at the failure of his plan, vowed to continue the struggle. "On my responsibility as a member of this House," he publicly pledged, "I shall now and henceforward vote in the negative on the final passage of every Indian bill for the appropriation of money until the channels of that expenditure be cleansed and the whole service purified." He reintroduced his bill on every possible occasion, sometimes trying to sneak it by the House as a rider to appropriation bills, but Windom was now alerted and succeeded in blocking what he caustically called Garfield's "monomania." Garfield's persistence, sneered Windom, had made him the laughingstock of Congress.[39]

After the failure of his bill, Garfield despaired for the future of the Indians. He considered the possibility of establishing an Indian state in the far west that would allow civilized Indians to vote and manage their own affairs, but he was not too hopeful that anything could be done to arrest "the passage of that sad race down to the oblivion to which a large part of them seem to be so certainly tending." It is possible, he prophesied, "that the race of red men . . . will, before many generations, be remembered only as a strange, weird, dream-like specter, which had once passed before the eyes of men, but had departed forever." Perhaps, he concluded, it was best to let the Indians slip down the road to extinction "as quietly and humanely as possible." On one occasion, he casually suggested that the Indians might be prodded a little faster down that road. Perhaps, he wondered, if the buffalo were exterminated, might not the Indian be compelled to abandon his savage ways? His horrified colleagues jumped on this plan "of civilizing the Indian by starving him to death" as "a disgrace to anybody who makes it," and Garfield, who was only speaking off the top of his head anyway, never mentioned it again. In fact,

298

his attitude towards the Indians began to mellow. By the mid-1870's the success of Grant's "peace policy" led Garfield to conclude that civilian Indian agents were capable of reform after all. He recanted his earlier hostility and supported the policy he had once condemned. His record on Indian matters did not show Garfield at his best. Not only did he have to admit that he had been wrong, but he had also shown himself to be a poor legislative tactician.[40]

Nor did he have better success with other major bills arising out of his own committee in the 40th Congress. In December, 1868, he introduced a bill to provide for a system of military education in the colleges, a forerunner of the ROTC. Although the plan was well thought out and would have been inexpensive to operate, it aroused no interest. After a desultory debate, the House laid it on the table and promptly forgot it. If Garfield had really expected the measure to pass he should have prepared his ground better. He certainly gained no prestige by throwing his committee's handiwork into an apathetic House and letting it sink.[41]

The most important work before the Military Affairs Committee in the 40th Congress was the preparation of a bill reducing the size of the army. An easy way to do this was suggested by Ben Butler, who proposed a simple fifty percent slash in personnel. Garfield rejected such a crude solution. He proposed to reduce the number of officers gradually, by leaving vacancies unfilled rather than by a wholesale mustering-out, which he regarded as both cruel and wasteful. He coupled this gradual plan of reduction with a sweeping reorganization of the army designed to achieve efficiency as well as economy. It offended Garfield's logical mind that the Ordnance department, which designed guns, had nothing to do with the Artillery, which fired them. He proposed to consolidate all departments with overlapping functions. He streamlined the entire army, from the general staff down to the marching bands, creating a modern military establishment which could readily be expanded in time of war.[42]

It was an impressive piece of legislation, but Garfield threw it away on the floor of the House by careless management. He introduced the bill into the House on July 10, 1868. Despite his lucid explanation it was opposed at every step by Butler and John Logan, "whose hatred of the regular Army," Garfield said, "amounts almost to insanity." Skillfully playing on fears of an "overgrown" army and appealing to the economizing mood of Congress, Butler and Logan offered amendment after amendment designed to gut Garfield's carefully calculated plan. Butler accused Garfield of plotting to protect the officer corps along with its sinecures. Logan dismissed the bill as "a humbug" and called Garfield a coward to his face. There was a certain irony in Garfield, the former foe of West Point, playing the role of the defender of the regular army, but he was too flustered to appreciate it. He simply could not cope with this sort of personal, demagogic attack and he lost control of his own bill. All of Butler's amendments passed. The House did not support Garfield once.

After his shattered bill had been "torn to atoms," Garfield managed to have it referred to his committee where he sat on it for the rest of the session, preferring no bill at all to one so disfigured by amendments. Garfield had shown that he could not yet manage the House when it was in an unruly mood. As an orator he was unsurpassed but he had not yet acquired what the British call a "House of Commons manner"; that intuitive feel for the mood of the House, that sense of timing and appreciation of the interplay of personalities which are the mark of the master legislator. A Schenck could not have written the army reduction bill but he might have been able to pass it.[43]

In the next session Garfield was given another chance to introduce his army reduction bill as an amendment to the army appropriation bill. But when the amendment was read it was found to contain his Indian transfer bill as well, much to the surprise of the House which thought it had already disposed of that question. Windom loudly objected, and in the ensuing confusion Butler was able to present *his* army reduction measure as a substitute. Garfield almost lost his right to the floor and had to withdraw the section dealing with Indian affairs. He had fumbled badly. Once again he had misread the mood of the House.[44]

Ten days later the measure came to a final showdown. Butler's substitute emerged triumphant out of the parliamentary

300

tangle by the margin of one vote. The Senate, however, saved the day. Its measure was similar to Garfield's plan, and on the last day of the Congress a conference committee decided in favor of the Senate version. A sensible army reduction bill was thus finally passed, though it lacked some of Garfield's cherished administrative reforms. Garfield could take little satisfaction from this outcome. The bill had passed in spite of his management, not because of it.[45]

His demonstrated inability to control Congress would seem to disqualify Garfield from the Ways and Means Committee, whose chairman tended to be the de facto floor leader of the House. But Garfield's hopes would not die. These hopes seemed more creditable with the prospect of a new Speaker now that Schuyler Colfax was about to be sworn in as Vice President in the new Grant administration. In the days before the application of the seniority rule became customary, committee posts were assigned at the discretion of the Speaker of the House. The contest for Speaker had narrowed down to Henry Dawes of Massachusetts and James G. Blaine. Blaine and Garfield were on good terms and Blaine anxiously solicited his friend's support, hinting broadly of favors to come. "I am sure," he reminded Garfield, "that it will be of advantage to you to have some one in the chair *on whose friendship you can rely—and I trust you can rely on mine.*"

There was nothing secret about Garfield's expectation. Everyone knew he wanted to be chairman of a financial committee, preferably Ways and Means. He did not push himself for the post. Such vulgarity was beneath him. "I suppose I am morbidly sensitive about any reference to my own achievements . . . ," he had once admitted. "I so much despise a man who blows his own horn, that I go to the other extreme of not demanding what is justly my due." He trusted that Blaine would understand.[46]

When a week had passed after the opening of the 41st Congress with committee assignments still unannounced, Garfield began to fear that his trust had been misplaced. Blaine was acting very strangely. With a becoming air of statesmanlike integrity, he loftily denied having made any bargains for the Speakership. "I can say with absolute truth," he insisted, "that I never *solicited* a vote, and especially that I never agreed to give or withdraw any position in the House for the sake of securing any man's support." Dawes was astonished at this assertion. "Half the House are liars or he is mistaken," he said.[47]

Garfield sought reassurance. On three occasions he called on the new Speaker, but his card was always sent back with word that Blaine was not in. Just as he had been turned away for the third time, to his astonishment Schuyler Colfax walked by and breezed right into Blaine's office. Garfield suspected that Blaine was avoiding him. He dashed off an angry note. "After the frank and cordial understanding we had about the Speakership . . . ," he said, "this disavowal of my right to see you has filled me with sorrow and amazement." He was now worried that Blaine not only might renege on their understanding but could even go so far as to remove him from his present chairmanship. He warned the Speaker "that while my tastes lead me to financial rather than military legislation, yet I shall regard a displacement of myself from a chairmanship of a standing committee of the House as a personal and official degredation to which you have no right to subject me. . . ."[48]

Blaine effusively assured Garfield that no slight was intended. "Your letter pains me," he replied soothingly, "for it implies that you think it possible for me to show you a discourtesy. . . . You are one of the very few that I really desire to see." But when he got down to business it was clear that Garfield's fears were justified. "Now about your committees," Blaine hastily explained.

> You told me long ago that your greatest desire was to be on one of the leading financial committees and you remember that our conclusion upon the whole that the one most desirable was that of Appropriations. I accordingly assign you to a membership of that Comtee. I make you chairman of the Census Committee. (You are the only man on either Ways & Means or Appropriations that has a chairmanship big or little) and as a mark of my special personal regard and interest as a compliment I place you on the Committee of Rules.[49]

No amount of smooth explanation or expression of "special personal regard" could disguise the fact that Blaine had dealt his friend a crooked hand. To be stripped of the chairmanship of a major standing committee was a gross insult, and Garfield, for once, shed his diffidence. Whatever he told Blaine, it must have been effective, for when the committees were announced four days later, Garfield was chairman of the Committee on Banking and Currency. It was not the Ways and Means chairmanship for which he had so long yearned, but it was finance and, for the time being, it would have to do.

CHAPTER FIFTEEN

RULING ELDER

By 1869, Garfield's place in Congress seemed so secure that he could now consider making Washington his permanent home. For five years he had been dragging his growing family from one set of furnished rooms to another, at a cost, so he estimated, of $6,000 for rent alone. Had he invested that same amount in a house, he now realized, he would have had something solid to show for the expense. He carefully canvassed the city for a suitable homesite. Capitol Hill was the most convenient location but the area was too "infested with negroes" to suit his taste. He settled instead for a more distant lot on the corner of 13th and I, with a fine view of Franklin Square across the street. There he contracted for a plain three-story brick house.

While their new house was rising, Garfield's family stayed behind in Hiram, where Lucretia awaited the birth of her next child, Irvin McDowell Garfield, named for the general "as a protest against the unjust treatment that that noble man has received from the public." The expectant father, lonesome for his family, visited the construction site every day. Sentimentally, he told his wife that "as I watch the spadefuls of earth going out to make way for us and our little ones," it almost seemed as if "my love and prayers for their happiness were in the very mortar that held its walls."[1]

In his less sentimental moments, Garfield admitted that building a house was a "very unwise" move. For one thing, he could not afford it. The lot alone cost $3,250 and the construction another $8,600. A thousand dollars for furniture plus extra expenses for landscaping, plumbing and gasfitting pushed the total cost over $13,000. Garfield did not have that sort of money to spare. By disposing of some Western lands, collecting old debts and scraping together legal fees and savings, he could raise about $6,000. For the remainder, he was indebted to an old friend of army days, Major David G. Swaim, who came to the rescue with a $6,500 loan which was paid back at irregular intervals over the years.

This was only one of many favors that Swaim performed for his friend. From his post at Fort Leavenworth came a steady stream of gifts: cigars, jewelry, investment tips and even buffalo meat for the Garfield breakfast table. In return, the grateful congressman watched over the progress of his friend's career. Soon after the completion of his Washington house, Garfield lobbied to secure Swaim a promotion, and in 1880, on Garfield's recommendation, President Hayes would appoint Swaim to the choice post of Judge Advocate General.[2]

This would be a welcome appointment for all concerned, as it enabled Swaim to live in Washington and keep his friend company. Garfield liked to have Swaim around. The little officer, who looked so much like General McClellan, was certainly not an intellectual giant, but Garfield could relax by playing cards and billiards with him and by listening to his stories. Some of Garfield's friends suspected that Swaim was exploiting the association, but in the harassed moments of his presidency Garfield pleaded that Swaim "looks so contented sitting there smoking his cigar that it soothes me to have him around."[3] The suspicions seemed confirmed when, after Garfield's death, Swaim would be court-martialed and suspended from duty. Some of Garfield's friends were so outraged that Swaim, the custodian of the President's last words, could betray the memory of their lost leader that they refused to have anything further to do with him. Yet the fault, if any, was Garfield's, who was incapable of resisting any plea made in the name of friendship. It was this sort of indiscriminate amiability that would be responsible for Garfield's subsequent reputation as a poor judge of men.

Yet in the summer of 1869, Swaim made himself invaluable,

not only by financing his friend's house but by his daily supervision of its construction while Garfield was preoccupied with
public duties. During those hot months, while other congressmen were comfortably at home, Garfield was held in Washington by a congressional subcommittee on the census, of
which he was chairman. Despite the heat, this was the sort of
work Garfield relished. He had, as an opponent perceptively
jibed, "gone mad on the subject of statistics." Convinced that
"This is the age of statistics," Garfield became a fanatic on the
subject. He shared his enthusiasm with the members of the
American Social Science Association in an address to their
annual meeting. From a politician, the scholarly audience had
glumly anticipated a routine, superficial speech, containing
nothing more substantial than "a few solid facts . . . gar-
nished by a very frothy syllabub of 'buncombe' and patriotic
oratory." Instead, they were treated to a learned analysis of the
evolution and application of statistical science. His main theme
was the forthcoming census, but in the course of the speech
Garfield also dealt with the impact of statistics upon the writing of history, shrewdly anticipating the later developments of
social history and historical quantification.

Inevitably, his passion for figures found legislative outlets,
leading one congressman to complain that the gentleman from
Ohio "would have the Congress and the officers of all the
Departments of the Government constantly running up and
down the country gathering statistics." As the census was the
chief statistical instrument of the government, Garfield's
attention was naturally drawn to it. It was, he realized, a
highly imperfect instrument. The census act of 1850, which was
still on the books, had grave defects. Among other things, it
still required an enumeration of slaves, which was now happily
an anachronism. Garfield felt that the time had come to bring
the census up to the level of modern statistical science, and
because of his interest he was placed in charge of a subcommittee to overhaul the entire census-taking apparatus.[4]

The committee assembled over the recess in a mercifully
cool basement room of the Capitol and began its "Herculean
task." Armed with its findings as embodied in a report of over
two hundred pages, Garfield introduced a modernized census

306

bill at the opening of the next session. His proposed reforms were of two sorts: changes in the census-taking machinery and changes in the schedule of inquiries. In the first category, he proposed to relieve the U. S. marshalls of responsibility for census-taking, partly because their police function might create "unease and suspicion" in the minds of the populace, but primarily because the marshalls were not trained for statistical work. In their place he would substitute a corps of nonpolitical enumerators chosen solely for their ability. The schedule was to be revamped from top to bottom in order to uncover all manner of demographic, industrial, agricultural, educational and miscellaneous statistical data that Garfield deemed indispensable.

The result was a model of thoughtful, comprehensive legislation, justifying Garfield's prodigious labors. At least one census expert, however, criticized it as too comprehensive, arguing that Garfield had confused the legislative and administrative functions. Rather than allowing the measure to become bogged down in the minutiae of questionnaire-making, he suggested that Garfield's strategy should have been the preparation of a simple bill establishing the general machinery and leaving the details to the Superintendant of the Census. In addition to saving Garfield a great deal of work, such a bill would have aroused less opposition in Congress. As it happened, however, the bill did pass the House after an intense eight-day struggle, giving Garfield the most satisfactory legislative victory of his congressional career thus far. He had, at last, shown that he could manage the House.

The Senate, however, was another story. There, without Garfield's guiding hand, the bill was summarily rejected after a desultory debate. Some senators objected to the complexity of the schedules but the main attack was led by Roscoe Conkling, the elegant New York spoilsman, who resented having the census-takers removed from political patronage. As far as 1870 was concerned, Garfield had labored in vain. Ten years later, however, the next census was taken under a law identical to the one he had earlier proposed. The manager of that bill, "Sunset" Cox, although a Democrat, was a gentleman and handsomely acknowledged his debt to Garfield.[5]

307

Notwithstanding its disappointing outcome, Garfield enjoyed his work on the census because, as he put it in a curious phrase for a professional politician, it was not "distorted by partisan politics." The bill's reception in the Senate, however, should have demonstrated that nothing in Washington could stay completely free from partisanship. The course taken by the new administration seemed to point up the same moral. President Grant had not been elected as a political leader but as a national hero pledged to bring peace to a divided land. Yet Grant found it difficult to remain above political passions in the new role in which he was cast. To more than one American, "Grant the general, as first beheld in military dress, appeared . . . quite a different person from Grant the President, rigged out at a ball in white tie and black suit. . . ." As his military aura faded, so did Grant's hold on the affections of his countrymen.[6]

Garfield did not share in this disillusionment, for he had never held any illusions about Grant that could be shattered. During the war, Garfield had been a friend of Rosecrans, and had been exposed to his contempt for "that maker of false reports and unjust little puppy Grant," as Rosy called the hated rival who had displaced him. Garfield had somewhat more respect for Grant than that, but he had been decidedly unenthusiastic at the prospect of his nomination for president. Garfield had accepted it as inevitable, however, for he could see no other available leader.

The Republican Party after the Civil War, according to Garfield's analysis, was stronger than its leadership. The old antislavery leaders had developed, in their long years of powerlessness before the war, "a peculiar kind of talent, very efficient in its object—[but] it was of the *destructive* not the *constructive* kind." When the party came into power it needed builders, not destroyers, but the habits of opposition were too ingrained to be discarded. This, to Garfield, accounted for the "sad fact that hardly one man among the old leaders of our Anti-Slavery Party continued to be a leader when they came into power. Hardly one of them has risen above the dead level of mediocrity since that time." The party was forced to mark time between generations. The older men were "unfitted by habit and character of mind" to be leaders, while the younger men were "unfitted by their youth and inexperience." This left a void which only Grant could fill. Garfield could understand this, but he was still not happy about it and during the campaign of 1868 he gave his standard-bearer a cool endorsement. In turn, Grant was equally cool to Garfield and his friends, whom he bluntly dismissed as a bunch of "d——— literary fellows."[7]

Grant had scarcely moved into the White House before Garfield began to find fault with the new administration. Like many others, Garfield was appalled at the caliber of Grant's appointments, but Garfield had an additional reason of his own to be soured on the new President: they had already. clashed over patronage. It was customary for a president to consult the wishes of pro-administration congressmen before appointing postmasters in their districts. Congressmen (as opposed to Senators) had few enough privileges, and this was one they jealously guarded. Garfield normally regarded post office squabbles as vexing nuisances. Of all his difficulties, he said, "nothing has been more trying than Post Office fights when once the blood gets up." Nuisance or no, Garfield knew his rights and he knew they had been grossly violated when, in the administration's first weeks, his recommendation for the Ravenna Post Office was ignored. Instead, Grant nominated an old friend of his father's for the place. Garfield tried to defeat the nomination but the President was reluctant to humiliate his father, whom Garfield angrily called "a weak vain old man." After high-level negotiations between the President and the congressman, with Senator John Sherman as intermediary, Garfield grudgingly gave way. Grant learned a lesson from the episode and kept his father from further meddling, but Garfield's self-esteem had been wounded and he would carry the grudge to his grave.[8]

Despite this bad beginning, Garfield was not yet prepared to write off the Grant Administration. "The wheels of the new government creak and the whole machinery moves heavily," he said, "but I still have hope that the native good sense of General Grant will lead him out of his difficulties." He was heartened by two cheering harbingers. The first was the appointment of his good friend, Jacob Dolson Cox, to the cabinet as Secretary of the Interior. The other was Grant's commit-ment to the resumption of specie payment. To Garfield's great delight, the President stressed this theme in his first annual message to Congress. "It is recognized on all hands as my plan," Garfield gloated, "and has done me much good per-sonally."[9]

No president who opposed inflation could be all bad. This was Garfield's pet cause. He was afflicted with what one oppo-nent diagnosed as "inflation on the brain." In the 41st Con-gress he intended to use his position as chairman of the Com-mittee on Banking and Currency to oppose all inflationist schemes. His strategy was apparent in the opening days of the session when a bill was introduced to permit the issuing of additional currency. The author wanted to refer his measure to Ways and Means but Garfield insisted that it belonged un-der his jurisdiction. He got his way and then proceded to sit on the bill for the rest of the session.[10]

Garfield was framing even more ambitious plans to use his committee to strike further blows for honest money when he was temporarily sidetracked into an investigation of the seamy side of the Grant era. On September 24, 1869 ("Black Friday" as it would henceforth be called with a shudder), Wall Street had been shaken by panic when an attempt to corner the gold market had collapsed, leaving behind a wake of dazed brokers, ruined speculators and shattered reputations. The engineers of this disastrous plot were the notorious Erie Railroad pirates, Jim Fisk and Jay Gould. They made a striking pair: the flam-boyant Fisk who dressed like a riverboat gambler and guzzled champagne; the morose Gould who dressed like a preacher and sipped milk. Fisk kept a harem and Gould kept the sabbath, but despite their differences the two partners shared a common zest for the intricacies of high finance. They were able to recruit a third partner for their gold-corner enterprise in Gen-eral Abel Corbin. Corbin's only asset lay in his supposed influ-ence with his recently acquired brother-in-law, President Grant. Through him, the conspirators were able to gain access to the unsuspecting President, whose companionship they con-spicuously flouted, lending credence to their whispered boasts that the President was in on the scheme.

After the corner had collapsed (almost dragging the entire economy down with it), Congress authorized the Committee on Banking and Currency to investigate the episode. As chairman, Garfield took command of an investigation that would introduce him to "the dens of the Gold Room" on Wall Street and might even lead, he suspected, "into the parlors of the President." Aided by the sub rosa advice of Charles A. Dana and Henry Adams, Garfield plunged into the investigation, astounded at "the abysses of wickedness which are opening before us. . . ."[11]

The committee began its hearings in a crowded, smelly basement room in the capitol, squeezed between the restaurant and the men's room, with glass partitions unable to keep out the odors that wafted from either side. More wholesome quarters were soon found, but some feared the committee itself might raise a political stench. "Thus far the President stands untouched," Garfield reported with relief, though he was disturbed that Grant could accept the hospitality of such rascals as Fisk and Gould. He was not certain that the President's family would emerge from the probe as clean as the President, but he was determined to pursue the investigation without regard for political consequences. "I intend to hew to the line and let the chips fly as they may," he boldly declared. Yet, when the President (using Jacob Cox as an intermediary) asked him not to call Mrs. Corbin to the witness stand, Garfield chivalrously acceded. The Democrats on the committee protested this failure to summon a key witness and they hinted at a whitewash, but the President, Garfield observed with satisfaction, "expresses himself under a good many obligations to me" for the way in which the investigation was handled.[12]

In his report Garfield cleared the President and his family (except for General Corbin) from wrongdoing. He placed the blame on Gould who, aided by the "singular depravity" of Fisk, was "the guilty plotter of all these criminal proceedings." Gould was too good a businessman to take these harsh words personally. Within a few years he would cheerfully grant Garfield's request for free passes over his railroad as if nothing unpleasant had ever passed between them.

In fact, Garfield did not pin the ultimate blame for the Gold

Panic on Gould. As he saw it, the true villian was his old enemy, the greenback. It was the existence of this fluctuating paper currency which had made speculation on the rise and fall of gold possible and perhaps inevitable. "I do not endorse the doctrine of total depravity," he had once declared in another context, "nor will I assert that man is corrupt whenever he has a fair opportunity to escape detection, but it is true that opportunity is the door through which corruption always enters. . . ." The greenback had furnished the opportunity for corruption; Gould had merely taken advantage of that opportunity. It followed, therefore, that the true remedy lay not in punishing Gould but in eliminating the greenback by a rapid return to specie payment and a restoration of solid values free of the corrupting temptation of inflation.[13]

He would pursue this theme further in the committee's major work of the session: the preparation of a new banking law. The National Bank system, a legacy of the Civil War, had come under increasingly severe attack from the inflationists who blamed it for keeping the nation's money supply too stringent. Many of them would prefer to see the National Bank Notes, which were based on government bonds on deposit in banks, supplemented or even replaced by massive infusions of additional greenbacks, which were based on nothing. To Garfield, the champion of sound money, this was a heresy that could not go unchallenged. He prepared a bill with the ostensible purpose of reforming the banking system; but its real purpose was to quash the greenback agitation. He argued that there was already ample currency in the nation but it was poorly distributed owing to the heavy concentration of banking facilities in the Northeast. His bill authorized the creation of additional banknote currency and the simultaneous withdrawal of an equal amount of greenbacks. This new currency would be furnished to such additional banks as might be organized in the currency-starved West and South.[14]

The measure was so complex that not even the banking specialists in Congress could agree whether it would be inflationary or deflationary. Business sentiment was equally divided. Edward Atkinson told Garfield that "The hopes of every conservative business man in America are in it and with you

312

. . . ," but a Wall Street newspaper was indignant at Garfield's temerity. "The member from the Nineteenth District," it patronizingly advised, ". . . should bear in mind that he is comparatively a young man, and a novice in financial matters, that while he was devoting his time and study to the pulpit and then to military science, there are other men both in and out of Congress who were giving their whole attention to our finances. . . ."[15]

In its passage through the House the banking bill was subjected to a tangled series of ups and downs. Garfield defended it in three major speeches and countless brief remarks, demonstrating a thorough grasp of banking and an appreciation, rare in his day, of the importance of checks and bank credit to the money supply. Despite his efforts, the bill seemed doomed when, on June 8, the House in effect refused to bring it to a vote. The next day, however, Garfield was able to bring it back to life by tacking it onto a Senate measure. His tactics, however, almost backfired. He had neglected to consult the Democrats on the committee because, so Garfield claimed, the measure had been quickly considered during a ten-minute recess when they were not available. When the bill was read and was obviously too elaborate to have been concocted in only ten minutes, the Democrats were outraged at the trick they suspected Garfield of plotting. They threw up such a cloud of parliamentary obstacles that the bill had to be postponed.[16]

It was this sort of inept duplicity that helped account for Garfield's poor standing among his colleagues. He was not, however, a trickster by nature. On the contrary, his instincts were generally so straightforward and frank that when he attempted sharp practices he usually fumbled, unable to carry them off with the audacious flair of a Butler or Blaine. As his parliamentary confidence grew more secure, he would abandon these half-hearted efforts to be "slick" and would follow his better instincts, ultimately taking his place as an authentic leader of Congress.

But in 1870 he was still viewed by his colleagues with suspicion. When the banking bill returned from the conference committee, congressmen were surprised to discover that its inflationary features had been dropped. They accused Garfield, the manager of the conference from the House side, of failing to represent the position of the lower house with sufficient vigor and sincerity. "The chairman [Garfield] tells us that he tried for two hours to persuade the Senate portion of the committee to concur in the views of the House," said one angry inflationist. But in view of Garfield's well-known antagonism to anything that smacked of inflation, it was doubtful "whether his arguments had the force and effect . . . of some one who believed in what he was doing." Garfield's report was rejected by a lopsided margin. A new conference committee was named and Garfield was denied a hand in the final shaping of his own bill with what amounted to a vote of no confidence.

The new conference committee had only slightly better success. The Senate usually prevailed in stubborn conferences, and this was no exception. Garfield noted with satisfaction that the final bill, as signed by Grant, was "almost exactly in the shape that it left my hands," except for some minor inflationary concessions to the soft money forces. The overall effect, he crowed, "is regarded on all hands as having settled the greenback question in this country. Henceforth the democrats can have no opportunity for breaking up the National Banks System and substituting greenback currency." This had been his intention from the beginning. Garfield was more interested in contracting the currency than in expanding banking. There was no rush to organize new banks under this law and it took three years to absorb the new currency it authorized. In the meantime the inflationists were neatly thwarted since their claim that the nation was starving for more money rang hollow so long as this currency lay unused.[17]

Garfield was delighted with the successful outcome of the trap he had set for the inflationists. For a time his preoccupation with banking was so intense that he even made this unlikely topic a favorite theme for his stump speeches back home. Even skeptics were surprised to find that his "faculty of presenting dry statistics in a remarkably attractive, clear and forcible manner" could captivate a political audience accustomed to more exciting fare. Not all of his constituents were equally enthralled. The local iron men were indignant that their congressman should choose to spend so much time on matters unrelated to their own pressing needs. "The immense manufacturing interests of the Mahoning Valley," they complained, "can not, nor should not be, jeopardized by a Representative who is more taken up with making speeches on banking and the currency than with the material interests of his own constituents." Convinced that their congressman's "back bone needs stiffening on the tariff question," they threatened to throw their support in the coming district nominating convention to someone who could give greater enthusiasm to the cause of pig iron.[18]

"Why is there such a *distrust* of you on this subject," asked Harmon Austin. "Are you not understood?" Perhaps not. Misunderstanding was one of the hazards of the ambiguity Garfield had cultivated on this issue. Garfield, however, understood the iron men perfectly. "The fact is," he told Austin, "many of these men want a representative that they can carry around in their pantaloons pocket." He refused to be swayed by their pressure. "I intend . . . to vote precisely as I please," he adamantly insisted. "If they do not want me to represent them they need not have me." Nor would he be bullied—"I intend they shall find I do not scare a cent." The spectacle of other congressmen buckling under the pressure of local tariff interests distressed him. "It is a terrible thing," he reflected, "for men to live in the fear of their constituents to the extent which many members do. I would rather be defeated every day in the year than suffer such fear."[19]

To clarify any possible misunderstanding, Garfield delivered a long speech explaining his tariff position. In it, he attempted to strike a balance between the claims of free trade and those of protection but he was unable to disguise his true sympathies. What was intended to be an even-handed discussion somehow turned into a low-tariff apology. Recovering a measure of prudence, he made an exception for pig iron. "I refuse to be the advocate of any special interest . . . ," he declared, "But . . . I shall not submit to a considerable reduction of a few leading articles in which my constituents are deeply interested, when many others of a sim-

315

ilar nature are left untouched. . . ." This meant, as "Sunset" Cox cruelly explained, that Garfield "is willing to rob for his constituents as gentlemen all around us are willing to rob for theirs." Cox, an avowed free-trader, was not impressed by Garfield's low-tariff professions. "Such gentlemen as the gentleman from Ohio," he charged, "are responsible for our present onerous and unjust tariff. They are such liberal debaters for free trade, but they put the knife into it whenever they have an opportunity to vote it into practical legislation!"[20]

The protectionists, on the other hand, were equally enraged by Garfield's speech. In New York, Horace Greeley, editor of the influential *Tribune*, threatened to make Garfield regret his stand. Closer to home, the embittered iron men resolved to make every effort to replace Garfield with "a gentleman who is at *heart* true to the *protective tariff* interests of the country."[21] There was the usual talk of inducing Ben Wade to take the field, but the old radical spurned their overtures and no other likely candidate could be uncovered on short notice. The iron men blundered by circulating seven thousand copies of Garfield's tariff speech throughout the district. To their dismay, most of the farmers of the 19th District found it a very sensible document and Garfield's popularity rose. As the convention drew near, the frustrated iron men prepared to "sullenly acquiesce in the inevitable." "We here don't like Garfield very well," they grumbled, "and have been trying to beat him, but cannot. . . . [Consequently] we will all here be Garfield men, as it is no use to make boys play of the matter."[22]

The tariff was the only substantive issue raised against Garfield in 1870. There was also, of course, the customary whispering campaign. "It is singular how a certain class of people revive and create slanders against me every two years," Garfield marveled. "I am treated as a very respectable and moral man for about one and three quarters years and then comes two or three months, just previous to the nomination, in which I am everything that is bad." This time the attacks centered on his new home in Washington. The Cleveland *Plain Dealer* revealed that it was a $40,000 mansion and estimated its owner's worth at half a million dollars, all corruptly accumulated. Even the unexaggerated facts sounded bad enough. On the Western Reserve, where a substantial home could be had for about $2,000 (the value of Garfield's Hiram home), a $13,000 house seemed unwonted luxury for a representative of the people.[23] To counter these rumors, Garfield wrote out detailed statements of his financial condition for the eyes of "a few friends," who were authorized to use the information as they thought best.[24] "It is most humiliating to be compelled to parade one's debts and private affairs," he complained, but it was effective, for within a few months he was relieved to hear that "The slanders about your wealth have gone where the woodbine twineth." On the eve of the nominating convention the same scout reported that the opposition had collapsed for want of a suitable candidate. "Be of good cheer," he counseled. "You *are going to win*."[25]

And win he did. The convention was so packed with Garfield supporters that the opposition was demoralized. After Garfield's name was presented to the delegates, W. C. Howells immediately moved to close nominations, "not waiting for some cunning fellow to try something new." A motion for secret balloting was shouted down and Garfield was nominated by acclamation. "Vene, Vede, Vincit," Howells crowed in bad Latin but good spirits. The candidate was gratified by the honor but was well aware that the apparent unanimity of the convention had not dampened the smouldering resentment of the industrialists. One angry coal mine owner threatened to throw the vote of his 150 workers against Garfield. "Of course it will not do any good as you will be elected but it will cause you to run behind your ticket." Other iron men talked of bolting the party, and there were rumors that a $50,000 war chest was being raised to help them unseat Garfield.[26]

Garfield stood firm. In his campaign speeches he advocated a moderate tariff and publicly rebuked the protectionists. He refused, however, to let himself be drawn into an extended debate on the tariff. As he saw it, the chief issues were the blessings of the National Banking system and the progress of Reconstruction. The previous year Garfield's stump speeches had been filled with the crudest sort of bloody-

317

shirt waving. Then he had invoked the dependable horrors of Andersonville prison as a campaign issue. "The man who starved your boy and the one who shot him in his agony, was a Democrat, and to-day, if he lives, would vote the Democratic ticket. My God! dare you vote with him and call yourself the father of the boy?" Continuing in this vein, he had asked his old comrades-in-arms to take their rifle from the wall and ask how it would vote. "It will tell you that every shot from its muzzle went right against the rebellion and for the Union. Vote with your trusty gun, my boy," he advised, "and you cant vote wrong."[27]

In 1870, however, his campaign oratory struck a more elevated tone. The Democrats were assailed in calm, measured terms as "a party of negations . . . almost wholly destitute of both sweetness and light, those heaven-born qualities which a great writer has described as the two angels of civilization." He preferred to discuss the accomplishments of the Republicans rather than the villainy of the opposition. His tone seemed almost too pedantic to be effective on the stump, but it must have struck a responsive chord, for at the campaign's close the chairman of the party's state executive committee thanked him effusively, adding that "it is but stating the truth that you did us more hard work, and effective service than any speaker in this campaign."

Despite the expected off-year election slump, the Republican Party did well, in Ohio at least, and Garfield himself, of course, was easily reelected. "After all the noise of the Iron men," he was pleased to see that only a handful of voters had scratched his name from the ticket.[28] Nonetheless, there were signs that indicated his grip on the district might be slipping. This was the first time that his vote had failed to double that of his opponent and, also for the first time, he came within a hairsbreadth of losing a county (Mahoning). Perhaps the opposition of the iron interests had been more effective than Garfield and his friends cared to admit.[29]

There was one unexpected Ohio casualty in the 1870 election: Robert C. Schenck went down to defeat in his Dayton district. He took it badly. From now on, he told Garfield, he planned to work "with much satisfaction for one Schenck—

318

a particular friend of mine—not for the great stupid, exacting thankless public!" Bitterly, he blamed his defeat on the failure of his friends to come to his aid. "I *did* feel hurt," he admitted, "when it was known that I must have a close hard fight . . . [and] I could get no help of speech from the State Central Committee or any outside friend. I fought it all single handed."[30] Garfield may have blushed when he read his friend's angry recriminations. He had been asked by the state committee to help out in Schenck's district but had declined on the grounds that since Schenck was in no danger his efforts could be better spent in more doubtful districts.

Garfield could find a ray of comfort in his friend's misfortune when he considered that the Ways and Means committee was now without a chairman. Schenck would go on to the Court of St. James and to eventual disgrace when he was caught selling Englishmen shares in the fraudulent Emma Mines. Garfield would spend the next year in an intensive campaign to fill the vacated committee post Schenck left behind. This time he was confident of success. The appointment, he predicted, was "about as certain as any future event could be." Blaine had already, so Garfield claimed, "come as near saying this to me as he ought to. . . ." Low tariff men (or Revenue Reformers, as they were beginning to call themselves) had even more specific pledges from the Speaker, promising in writing that Garfield, their spokesman, would be in a position to work for tariff reform in the next congress.[31]

With the coveted Ways and Means chairmanship almost within his grasp, Garfield was "really annoyed" at the persistent efforts of Ohio Republicans to nominate him for governor. Governor Hayes himself urged Garfield to be his successor but Garfield was unwilling "to make the sacrifice." For one thing, he explained, "it would almost ruin me pecuniarily to be a candidate. . . . Governor Hayes has lived as economically as any Governor of Ohio ought to live, and it has not cost him less than $6,000 a year. At the end of my term (should I be elected) I would be almost broken up financially." More to the point, as he confided to a friend, "My tastes do not lead me in that direction. . . ." With real power in his grasp, why step down to an underpaid, ornamental office? "Any Justice of the Peace in Cleveland has more to do than the Governor of Ohio," Garfield observed, and he ignored the barrage of pleas made in the name of "duty" or party loyalty that he divert his career from Congress to the Governor's Mansion.[32]

His plans, however, depended on Blaine. "I cannot believe that Blaine will be perfidious in the matter," Garfield assured himself. Yet in view of the Speaker's devious behavior two years earlier, perhaps there was some cause for concern. Some revenue reformers were beginning to be wary of Blaine's good faith. David A. Wells, who suspected that Blaine "dont care for any thing but personal advancement," had picked up disturbing rumors to the effect that Blaine "would deceive us and you and appoint Dawes" to the chairmanship.[33] As the months streched out, without any further announcement, Garfield began to fear that Blaine was beginning to wilt under pressure from the high-tariff advocates. A breakfast *tête-à-tête* with the Speaker failed to dispel these doubts. "The impression is gaining ground that he is tricky," Garfield reported. Heeding Swaim's warning that "Time will give B. a chance to worm from under you," Garfield asked his friends to apply some counterpressure on his behalf, but the high-tariff forces had the bigger guns. Horace Greeley, who had not forgiven Garfield for his tariff speech of 1870, was making a bitter, personal effort to thwart him, and Blaine, who was already eyeing the White House, could ill afford to offend the most influential editor in the nation.[34]

The objections to Garfield's appointment were not without force. Even his advocates had to concede that he was "unhappily less popular with the House than he is before the country, and is imputed to have less of that especial ability to carry measures through its confusion and over its conflicts than is almost necessary for a man in that place [Ways and Means]. . . ." But to the revenue reformers, the appointment of Garfield was more than a personal issue; it had become a touchstone of the good faith of the Republican Party.[35]

Many of these men were already weighing the possibility of organizing a party of their own. As a first step, they threatened to bolt the Republican caucus and join with the Democrats to dump Blaine and elect a reform-minded Speaker of

the House should the Ways and Means Committee be organized contrary to their wishes. Blaine was worried enough to
arrange a series of clandestine hotel-room conferences with
reform spokesmen. The threatened revolt was bought off by
a deal to give them the committee in return for support on the
Speakership.[36] The reformers rejoiced in their "victory" and
concluded that there was hope for the Republican Party after
all. But later on, when they had a chance to examine Blaine's
promises free from the spell of his personality, they detected a
disturbing note of ambiguity. Blaine had given no specific
pledge regarding Garfield, and this, to the reformers, had been
the crux of the bargain. A betrayal of Garfield, Edward Atkinson bluntly warned Blaine, would be the signal for a massive
defection which could destroy the present party organization.
But once he was securely fixed in the Speaker's chair, Blaine
remained unmoved by all such attempts "to put on the
screws" and force him to a decision.[37]

By November, Cox hopelessly concluded that "Blaine is
wholly given to intrigue. His writing to all the new members
[of Congress] for their views . . . is only a way of freeing
himself from the responsibility. . . ." Garfield still refused to
believe that Blaine could go back on his word. Even when a
reformer visited his study with evidence to the contrary, Garfield insisted that the Speaker's promises were too explicit
to be broken. Pacing his room, he growled, "If Mr. Blaine
does not appoint me chairman of the ways and means committee, he is the basest of men." Dawes felt the same way.
Hearing rumors that he might be made head of the Ways and
Means Committee, Dawes incredulously wrote Blaine: "I
cannot believe that you will put me on the Com. of Ways and
Means against my wishes. . . . I have earned the right to
decline a service so against my wishes—against my habits of
thought, and so outside of all my experience in Congress that
I shall surely fail."[38]

Not until the opening of the second session, early in December of 1871, was what Garfield called "The long agony of com-
mittee-making" finally ended. His fears, and those of his
friends, were realized when Dawes was named to head Ways
and Means and Garfield was put in charge of the Appropria-

tions Committee. "Blaine has played us false as we expected," cried a disgruntled reform spokesman. "Well, he can take the consequences." Garfield took his disappointment in better grace. Philosophically, he admitted that Dawes had, in some respects, a better claim to the post. If he felt any bitterness towards Blaine, it was only momentary, for he quickly resumed cordial relations with the Speaker who had now betrayed him two times in a row.[39]

Had the situation been reversed, Blaine could not have displayed the same equanimity. To Blaine, politics was made up entirely of personal encounters. Friends were to be rewarded; enemies were to be destroyed; affronts were to be revenged. In 1866, he and Roscoe Conkling had exchanged harsh words on the floor of Congress. They had not spoken to each other since, though thrown into almost daily contact, and both would spend the remainder of their lives plotting how best to humiliate the other. Garfield was not capable of this sort of behavior. In spite of his wistful resolve to try to be a "better hater," he could not carry it off. Once, for example, when he tired of the hypocrisy of a newspaper acquaintance who acted friendly in person but was hostile in print, he swore never to speak to the man again. Yet, when he next saw the offending journalist, his cold frown instinctively melted and he shouted happily, "You old rascal, how are you?"[40]

Some interpreted this amiability as weakness of character, and others saw it as evidence of a greatness of spirit that was rare among the primadonnas of the political stage. But there was also an element of fatalism in Garfield's nature that accounted for his apparent passiveness. He was convinced that he was destiny's child, marked out for some special providence. Secure in this faith, he placed his career in the hands of his destiny, preferring to drift with the tide of fortune rather than take the initiative and oppose it. Consequently, he was able to view the progress of his career with a sense of detachment that could be misinterpreted as indifference and which led some to underrate him as an amiable backslapper, vacillating and unsure of himself. There was some truth to this analysis. Garfield was painfully lacking in self-confidence, yet deep down, he managed to cultivate an inner poise which

322

allowed him to shrug off setbacks as part of some hidden but beneficent scheme.

He easily reconciled himself to the loss of the Ways and Means committee by interpreting his failure as a backhanded tribute to his integrity. "In Church and in state," he observed, "it seems to be the rule that men of no opinion, or those who conceal their opinions, succeed best." As for himself, "I would rather believe something and suffer for it, than to slide along into success without opinions." There was yet another consideration to soothe his disappointment. Blaine, devious to the end, had prepared two committee slates, each, so Garfield had heard, "marked by the same peculiarity. One made Mr. Dawes the Chairman, with a Committee that overruled the Chairman's opinion. The other made me a Chairman, with a Committee overruling mine. Rather than be at the head of a Committee which I could not lead, I greatly prefer to be where I am. . . ." As it turned out, Dawes was unable to control his committee, which prepared a bill he could not support. This humiliation, at least, was spared Garfield, but he still regretted his assignment to Appropriations—"my tastes and studies all lead me in another direction. I have a passion for figures when they have a scientific significance, but the mere figures of the ledger are not so interesting."[41]

Interesting or not, he buckled down to do his duty by his new committee. He did not underrate its importance. Government, he observed, "is a vast Colossus, whose every motion depends upon the expenditure of money." His new post could be considered a "cashier's desk," before which all the domestic operations of the government lined up to demand payment. The scope of this committee that sat at the center of the web of government was resented by some congressmen who called it "a little petty despotism," but all acknowledged its power. In his first week at his new post, Garfield tried to enlarge that power even further. When a bill to pay the expenses of the Geneva Commission was routinely routed to the Foreign Affairs Committee, he raised a point of order. Since the bill carried an appropriation, he argued, it should go to his committee first. The Speaker slapped down this transparent power grab by reading the rules of the House which specifically exempted expenses incurred under treaty obligations from the jurisdiction of the Appropriations Committee. Garfield should have known better. A little homework would have saved him embarrassment, but a knowledge of the rules would never be one of his strong points as a congressman.[42]

Even without the enlarged jurisdiction for which he had unsuccessfully grasped, Garfield found ample work to keep him busy in his new duties. The Appropriations Committee had charge of twelve major bills[43] which encompassed every governmental expense from the brass spitoons in the Treasury Building on up. Each bill had to be guided, clause by clause, through the House three separate times: first during its initial consideration; secondly, after it returned, loaded with amendments, from the Senate; and finally, after the conference committee had ironed out the differences between the two Houses. It was hard, demanding work, which dragged on from opening day until "the wee sma' hours of the last night of the session." Garfield lightened this burden somewhat by sharing it with the other members of the committee. Rather than treating them as subordinates, which had been the practice, he entrusted to each the command of a major bill, charging them to "go to all the dapartments, heads of bureaus, and down to the hidden, unknown men, who did know" to gather information on the needs of the government. Flattered by the trust and responsibility given them, the committee members forged themselves into a nonpartisan band of brothers, each an expert in his own area, yet ready to come to the aid of a colleague.[44]

The chairman bore the brunt of the labor, working up to fifteen hours a day for months on end. Guiding a major appropriation bill was "like launching a man of war," and the effort, Garfield complained, left him "about as near used up as I ever was in my life." On some days he had to speak more than forty times. This made him a familiar figure on the floor of the House, "But mere vulgar prominence has no great charms for me," he said. "I greatly prefer a work that has a scientific side to it."[45] Consequently, he attempted to devise some "scientific" principles which could guide his work. A mind such as his, which was "never satisfied until he could reduce facts to order," could not accept the traditional view

324

of appropriations as a mere bookkeeping chore: he had to find "the laws by which expenditures increase and decrease." The answer came to him through "an immense induction of reading" and he announced his discovery in his maiden speech as Appropriations chairman, a speech which, he later proudly claimed, "whatever I may say about it myself, others said that it was the first interesting speech that was ever made on that subject."[46]

Two opposing forces, Garfield declared, determined the level of government expenditures: "first, the normal increase of ordinary expenses, dependent upon increase of population and extension of settled territory; and second the decrease caused by the payment of war obligations." The time will come, he predicted, when "the normal increase, being a constant element, will finally overcome the decrease caused by the payment of war debt, and a point will be reached from which the annual expenditure will again increase." In short, he expected that the annual cost of running the government would continue to go down from its wartime high until, at some time in the future, it started to rise once more. When could that time be expected? A study of British and American precedents convinced him that it would take a period of time roughly twice as long as the duration of the war before a new peace level of expenditures could be attained. The Civil War had lasted over four years. Therefore, he predicted that by 1875 or 1876 the decrease of expenditures would cease and appropriations would begin to rise once more. Garfield was inordinately proud of this discovery, especially since his prediction turned out to be off by only one year.[47]

That such a crude rule of thumb could parade as a general law testified to the primitive level of understanding that prevailed on the subject. By later standards, Garfield's efforts may seem unsophisticated, but he was one of the very few at that time to think about appropriations in a general way rather than as the piecemeal budget making that Congress usually engaged in. In the absence of an official budget even the best informed congressmen could be confused about such elementary matters as how much it actually cost to run the government, or whether there was a deficit or a surplus. How could Congress exercise its constitutional power of the purse when it had no staff to gather information, no concepts to organize data, and precious few facts on which to legislate? The executive branch offered little help. It had no centralized budget bureau; each department prepared its own estimates and lobbied in Congress for appropriations without regard for the needs of the other departments.[48]

Little wonder that Congress had, over the years, abdicated its control of the budget and, except during periodic economy drives, had generally let the departments drift along their independent paths without tight legislative control. After the Civil War, however, when Congress assumed its role as the dominant branch of the government, this degree of executive independence seemed anomalous. Garfield took steps to correct it. He endeavored to replace permanent, indefinite appropriations with annual, specific ones. Vague, lump sum appropriations gave way to detailed, itemized estimates that allowed the heads of executive departments less discretion. The scandalous arrangement by which the departments could evade congressional control by diverting funds from one purpose to another, or by drawing upon unexpended funds from prior years was tightened under Garfield's management, as was the abuse of deficit appropriations. These budgetary reforms were designed, Garfield explained, "to bring all the expenditures, as far as possible, directly under the eye of Congress." This goal was not attained, but that it could even be approached was a tribute to Garfield's tenacious energy. Here, as elsewhere in his career, his capacity for intense, sustained work led to success. During his tenure as Chairman, the Appropriations Committee reached its high point of responsible congressional control over the executive budget. Even Henry Dawes, who had led the committee himself, admitted that "the country is more indebted to that committee since the gentleman from Ohio has been its chairman than to anyone I have ever known in this House, for systematizing and curtailing expenditure."[49]

A tribute from Dawes was welcome, for he was one of the few men who could appreciate the intricacies of the job. Most observers judged the performance of the committee by a simpler standard—economy. "Now, fight the thieves, plunderers

326

and grabbers to the death," exhorted Joseph Medill. "Cut off supernumeraries, dead-heads, sinecures. . . . Eliminate offices. Chop off expenses." Considerable political capital could be accumulated by following such advice, as witness the career of Elihu Washburne after he had won the nickname, "Watchdog of the Treasury." Garfield, however, rejected the theory "that we should make our expenditures come within our revenue—that we should 'cut our garment according to our cloth.' " Instead, he took the less popular position that "Our national expenditures should be measured by the real necessities and the proper needs of the government. We should cut our garment so as to fit the person to be clothed. If he be a giant, we must provide cloth sufficient for a fitting garment."[50]

This was a commendably responsible stand, but it placed Garfield in the awesome and thankless role of arbiter of just what "the real necessities" of the government were. In one typical month he had to inspect the Columbia Hospital to determine how much its maintenance should cost; weigh the claims of arctic heroes and Southern planters; decide on the necessity for a subsidy to the Pacific Steamship Company, a federal office building for Saint Louis and a statue honoring General Herkimer. He had to study the fine points of lighthouses, schools for the deaf and dumb, telegraph lines and fish culture.[51] He did his work diligently, but it is questionable whether it should have been done at all, whether any man or committee should have been saddled with such responsibility.

In the process, however, Garfield acquired an unsurpassed knowledge of the inner workings of the government. As he said to a friend: "No wheel, no shaft, no rivet in our governmental machinery performs its function without money. If I find out where every dollar goes and how it is used, I shall understand the apparatus thoroughly, and know if there are any useless or defective parts." Armed with this comprehensive knowledge, Garfield would enter the presidency with a greater technical command of the fine points of government than any of his predecessors.

Contrary to his original expectations, Garfield enjoyed his four years at the helm of the Appropriations Committee more than any other phase of his congressional career. His earlier

327

ambitions for Ways and Means were quite forgotten. "I am surprised to find what a change . . . has wrought in the topics which interest me," he noted. "Three years ago I was alive to all questions of taxation and cared little for appropriations." Now he sat through tariff debates with bored indifference but was "wide awake to any question of appropriations." He liked his committee post, in part, because of the inside knowledge it gave him and also because the work was free from "mere partisan politics." Most of all, he could not help enjoying the feeling of power his position gave him.[52]

With power came responsibility and with responsibility came a new sense of ease. During his tenure as Appropriations chairman, Garfield would gain a mastery of parliamentary techniques and, what was more important, the respect and trust of his fellow-congressmen. He would outgrow the fumbling ineptness of his apprentice years and emerge as one of the acknowledged leaders of his party in Congress. If, as George Frisbie Hoar maintained, the House of Representatives was "a sort of presbytery,"[53] Garfield had, at last, become one of the ruling elders.

CHAPTER SIXTEEN

STANDING BY THE OLD SHIP

Even as Garfield was emerging as a leader of the Republican Party, his enthusiasm for that party had begun to cool and his faith in its future was growing dim. This discontent festered through President Grant's first term. Even before Grant's inauguration Garfield had feared that the Party might destroy itself. Three years later, that possibility no longer seemed so frightening; indeed, he almost welcomed it. The two great political parties, he predicted, "must die from exactly opposite causes. The Democratic Party, because every substantive idea it has advocated for the last twelve years is now utterly and hopelessly dead. The Republican Party, because every substantive idea it has advanced has been completely realized. The career of one is likely to end by failure, the other by having finished its work."

These sentiments would carry Garfield to the brink of deserting his old party. To the brink, but not beyond; for despite his conviction that "the informing life" had departed from both parties, Garfield would reject the role of party maverick, even though many of his friends were jumping the political fences. He would resist the temptation of the Liberal Republican movement and remain, safe but insecure, in the bosom of party regularity.[1]

One source of his discontent was purely personal. The people who had taken charge of the Republican Party were not his sort of people. "The war," he observed, "has brought to the surface of National politics many men who are neither fitted in character, nor ability, to be leaders of public thought or representative of the true men of the country." He exempted Grant from this category. Although Garfield did not particularly like the President, he did not hold him in contempt, as did so many of his friends. He was simply baffled. The silent hero in the White House was an enigma to Garfield, but he continued to hope for the best from the President despite frequent disappointments. He could not be so forbearing about the President's friends and advisers. Such congressmen as John Logan and Ben Butler, "the cunning gentleman from Massachusetts," and such senators as Roscoe Conkling, Simon Cameron, Oliver Morton and Zach Chandler "are not likely to confer any permanent honor on anything they touch," Garfield noted with disdain. Yet, much to his disgust, these very men had attached themselves to Grant, "close as an undershirt," and were setting the tone for his administration.

The prominence of these spoilsmen dismayed Garfield, who still cherished the belief that a political party should be based on some great moral principle (a luxury that only a representative from such a safe district could long afford). But now, "having settled triumphantly, the great articles of faith, on which the Union Party was founded, namely: putting down the Rebellion, destroying slavery and restoring the Union," the party, he felt, had to find new issues if it were to retain its vitality.[2]

For a time, he toyed with the idea of striking out along the fresh lines of economic radicalism. Now that slavery was dead, he predicted that "the next great fight in this country will be against corporations." Still smarting from his inconclusive wartime clash with the Camden and Amboy Railroad, Garfield was tempted to resume the fight against monopoly. "I believe it is high time," he declared, "to require of these great corporations . . . to tell us what they are doing with the national wealth which is in their hands." If present trends were to continue, he forecast, "it will not be long before the greatest of our States may be less powerful than some of the corporations it has created."[3]

Consequently, he tended to view with suspicion all proposals to grant government aid to corporations. He protested a bill to subsidize Great Lakes shipping, even though his district included Lake Erie ports. For a time, in the early 1870s, he even advocated that the government take over the telegraph lines and operate them as an adjunct to the postal service, but on second thought rejected the idea as impractical. His main fire, however, was directed at the railroads, especially those that demanded land grants from the government. Garfield regarded that practice as a "public scandal." He was appalled at the brazen manner with which the railroads pressed their claims in congress, and stoutly, but unsuccessfully, resisted an attempt by one line to gobble up a chunk of the Capitol grounds.

Garfield was not as radical as he sounded. He was not really hostile to corporations, only to those which threatened to become monopolies. Consistent with his laissez-faire conviction that unfettered competition was the path to economic bliss, he opposed both monopoly and government interference with equal vigor. In his vision of Utopia, "the golden age of politics will come when on all industrial questions the Government only acts as the Keeper of the Peace." For this reason he also opposed labor unions and the movement to limit the work day of government employees to eight hours, which, he sputtered, was nothing more than "an unwarrantable interference with the rights of the laborers."[4]

These were promising new issues, but Garfield soon realized that he had made a false start. His reformer friends, such as David Wells, Edward Atkinson and Henry Adams, aided by such sympathetic editors as Sam Bowles and E. L. Godkin, had already mapped out a comprehensive program of their own which was even more appealing to Garfield than his tentative assault on monopolies. These reformers welcomed Garfield to their circle. They were the men who had supported his campaign to head the Ways and Means Committee, and they regarded him as their natural ally. Godkin paid him the highest possible compliment by asking him to succeed Henry Adams as *The Nation's* Washington correspondent. Garfield, in turn, adopted the reformers' program as his own. Its main features were: sound money, low tariffs, amnesty for the South and, above all, civil service reform. These issues, Garfield hoped, would give the Republican Party an honorable alternative to Grantism.

The currency and tariff features of this reform program had

long been associated with Garfield's name. Ever since his entry into Congress he had championed both revenue reform and a return to specie payments. A conciliatory Southern policy, on the other hand, seemed to represent something of a change of heart for Garfield. Actually, however, he had been gradually moving in this direction for the past few years. Once a fierce radical, Garfield had mellowed as his wartime hatreds receded into memory. As early as 1868 he had advocated a liberal amnesty policy to remove the political disabilities imposed upon Southerners. Rejecting the contention that the former rebels were not yet sufficiently penitent, he insisted that "it belongs not to us but to the Searcher of all hearts to decide whether a man sincerely loves the Union." If a Southerner should, "for whatever reason, work with us in seeking to restore this Union," Garfield saw no reason to probe his motive. He disclaimed any personal bitterness against the men he had so recently fought. Quite the contrary, he admired their bravery and persistence, which he hoped could now be harnessed to the common cause of the nation. "The country needs not only territorial reconstruction but a reconstruction of good feeling," he argued, even if this meant stretching out the hand of friendship to the former foe. Garfield did his part by resolving to eliminate the epithet "rebel" from his political vocabulary as a gesture of reconciliation.[5]

By 1870 Garfield's Southern policy had moved closer to the stand he had once rejected when it had been advocated by Jacob Dolson Cox in 1865. In those days, Garfield, still a radical, had insisted on a rigid supervision of the South in order to protect the Negro and preserve the fruits of the war. But with the passage of the Fifteenth Amendment in 1870, which he hailed as "the triumphant conclusion" of the slavery controversy, Garfield felt that the Negro now had ample legal protection. "It is not the theory of [our] government that any able bodied citizen shall be carried," he argued, "but that none shall be impeded in the fair and equal race of life." The right to vote, he declared, "confers upon the African Race the care of its own destiny. It places their fortune in their own hands." From now on, as far as Garfield was concerned, the Negro was on his own.[6]

With this obstacle to sectional reconciliation out of the way, Garfield was now more receptive to the suggestion of Cox that the proper Southern policy should aim towards "making a union with enough of the thinking and influential *native* [i.e., white] Southerners to give the Republican party a *status* among them different from that of the party of the negroes." Following, for a time, this path of conciliation, Garfield voted to readmit Georgia to Congress, "as a question of right, and not merely of party politics," despite the opposition of the radical segment of his party. For the same reason, he stood against the Grant administration and opposed legislation aimed at the Ku Klux Klan. "I have never suffered more perplexity of mind, on any matter of legislation," he declared. He was torn between his indignation at the outrages performed by these hooded terrorists and his newly-discovered concern for states rights.[7]

Ever since his involvement in the Milligan case, Garfield's wartime nationalism had been giving ground to his new-found respect for local autonomy. Influenced more than he realized by that old Democrat Jere Black, he now adopted a legalistic reverence for the Constitution that contrasted sharply with his former impatience when that piece of "parchment" had once stood in his way. Now, as he listened to the proposals to put down the Klan, he feared that Congress was "working on the very verge of the Constitution and many of our members are breaking over the lines." He was particularly distressed by the proposals which authorized the president to suspend *habeas corpus* and declare martial law. This seemed to undermine all he had accomplished by the Milligan case. Consequently, he delivered a long speech attacking the bill. "I took no small risk in throwing myself boldly onto opposition of the Bill, on a question about which there was so much feeling," he said. "The speech which I made may not be a popular one, but in some respects it is the most important I have ever made." Thanks to his opposition, many of the objectionable features were dropped from the bill.

Garfield was proud of his independence in the face of "party terrorism," but was amazed to find that "after having done this to my own peril, I am now receiving letters charging me with 'lack of backbone.' " He congratulated himself for having stood so firmly behind a principle, but there was more than principle involved. Ever since the end of the war, the radicals had excluded the bulk of white Southerners from full participation in politics. This exclusion could not last forever. Sooner or later the disabilities would have to be lifted. In what political direction would the South then move? Would it return to the Democratic Party or could it, perhaps, be wooed into a new organization? If there were to be a massive reorganization of parties, as Garfield's reformer friends hoped, then any new party would have to find allies in the South. By snapping the last ties with his former radicalism, Garfield had brought himself another step closer to participating in that reorganization.[8]

So too with his espousal of civil service reform; to the reform Republicans, the excesses of the spoils system under Grant had become a national disgrace. The elimination of this scandal assumed an importance in their program which led it to rival and ultimately surpass revenue reform as a panacea. In Garfield they found an experienced soldier for their crusade. "I have," he proudly declared, ". . . supported it strongly from the beginning."[9] By 1870 he was regarded by such reformers as Henry Adams as one of the measure's most reliable champions in the lower house. Yet, in a sense, they were deceived. Garfield's view of reform was not theirs. Adams and his friends hoped that a reform of the civil service could return the government to the hands of that "better element" which had been excluded from power ever since the days of Andrew Jackson. Garfield had more practical grounds for supporting it. "I should favor the Civil Service," he admitted, "if for no other reason [than] of getting partially rid of the enormous pressure for office." A congressman, as he had discovered early in his career, was the target for a horde of place seekers, "who infest every public place, and who meet you at every corner, and thrust their papers in your face as a highwayman would his pistol." Finding government jobs for all these eager applicants was, he groaned, "the most intolerable burden I have to bear," and it was little wonder that he welcomed any plan which might lighten that load. His predecessor, John

Hutchins, had selected cadets for the military academies by competitive examination rather than as political favors and Garfield was happy to continue a practice which spared him so much trouble.[10]

To his regret, post office appointments could not be settled so easily. This was potentially the most troublesome patronage problem a congressman could face. The salary was small but there were always more candidates than positions. To a country storekeeper, for example, a post office could generate enough traffic to mean the difference between success and bankruptcy. Most congressmen dispensed post offices to loyal party workers in order to build up local machines. Garfield's district was already so secure that he could afford to take a more lofty stand. "I do not see on what ground of public policy or justice I have any right to dictate who shall be P.M. at Conneaut . . . ," he declared. Instead, he left the responsibility for choice up to "the people themselves." By "people" Garfield meant Republicans. It was his practice in post office disputes to find the will of the local Republican voters and abide by their decision. This was not civil service reform as the reformers envisaged it. Instead of building an elite corps of nonpartisan government officials, Garfield was content to let the local party dictate appointments rather than the political boss. This might not bring about the political millennium the reformers dreamed of, but Garfield was satisfied just to be "relieved from the disagreeable necessity of choosing between a half dozen good people."[11]

When a proposal for competitive civil service exams was introduced in Congress, Garfield was cool to the idea. Still, he was willing to give it a try rather than "let the wild dance go on in the old way." He warned his colleagues that "the old mad whirl of office brokerage, of coining the entire patronage of the United States into mere political lucre," constituted an evil "so deep, so wide, so high, that some brave Congress must meet it, must grapple with it, must overcome it, if we propose to continue a worthy and noble nation." Garfield had no solution but he did have two suggestions. First, it was necessary "to correct the habit of regarding mere political service as the chief qualification for office." This did not mean that political considerations should be ignored, only that they not be all-important. Next, and most significant, the appointing power had to be placed firmly and uncontestably in the hands of the President. "I am satisfied that no plan of competitive examination or advisory board can cure the evil until the Executive is left free and untrammelled in the exercise of his constitutional powers, and is held to a strict responsibility for the result of his action," he insisted. Although a congressman himself, Garfield blamed the corruption of the patronage on the habit of congressional interference with appointments. Congressmen could, he conceded, give the president advice if asked, but for a legislator to claim the right to dictate appointments subverted the Constitution and blurred the responsibility that the president rightly bore.[12]

In later years, some civil service reformers would condemn Garfield as a traitor to their cause. Yet Garfield's position would remain consistent throughout his career. During his presidency, when he aroused the ire of the reformers, he was upholding the same principles he had proclaimed when he had been their ally. But *their* program for the civil service was fixed so strongly in their minds that they assumed that anyone who advocated reform automatically endorsed their specific proposals. Garfield was no "shady" backslider as Henry Adams would assume. Adams, who was always gratified to find hypocrisy in others, had simply never taken the trouble to understand what Garfield's views really were.[13]

In the early 1870's, however, the reformers were grateful for whatever support they could get. In Garfield they had found a prominent congressman whose views on civil service, Southern affairs, currency, the tariff and other issues agreed so well with their own that they hoped to enlist him in their struggle against Grant. Garfield himself, however, showed little inclination to give them more than sympathy. An open break with his old party was too serious a step to be taken lightly. Yet each successive move of the Grant administration drew him closer and closer to the opposition.

Late in 1870, just before the elections, Garfield was stunned by the abrupt departure of his friend Jacob Cox from the Cabinet. As Cox explained it to Garfield, he had been forced out as a martyr to civil service reform. Some of his regulations for the Interior Department, particularly his refusal to allow clerks time off to go home to vote, had aroused the wrath of the spoilsmen. In September, "the pack opened in full cry" after the reform Secretary. Zach Chandler could be seen prowling the Department offices boasting that Cox was to be dumped. In October, after the President had overruled his directives, Cox submitted his resignation which, if stripped of its diplomatic language said, in effect, "My commitment to civil service reform seems to be a load you do not choose to carry."[14] Garfield was "grieved and pained" by these revelations of the President's "criminal blunder" in dismissing Cox and replacing him with Columbus Delano, "a facile man who is ready to fall among thieves as soon as he can find a nest of them to fall into." The whole affair, he concluded inelegantly, "is a clear case of surrender on the part of the President to the political vermin which infest the government and keep it in a state of perpetual lousiness."

Cox appreciated his friend's sympathy but he also needed his advice. Should he publish his side of the story now or wait until after the elections? A loyal party man would have counseled delay; Garfield told him to publish. An "unmistakable rebuke" at the polls, Garfield hoped, might bring the deluded President to his senses. The party did lose ground in the 1870 congressional elections, and many suspected that popular sentiment for civil service reform had something to do with that result. The President apparently agreed, for his next annual message contained a gesture in the direction of reform. Cox thought it pure sham but advised Garfield "to force this lip service into real action, if possible," by treating the President's conversion to clean government as sincere and inducing him to live up to his professions.[15]

This would be Garfield's strategy for the next two years. Time after time, he would rise up in Congress to defend Grant's proclaimed civil service policy, "which is rudely denounced by those who assume to be his special champions." But Ben Butler and other friends of the President mocked his efforts while the ever more blatant signs of official corruption made it increasingly difficult to portray Grant as a reformer.

337

Garfield's efforts were "whistled down the wind" by Congress and he was forced to give up the game of squaring the President's professions with his practice.[16]

Garfield should have shown more sympathy for Grant. Even he found it difficult to be consistent when it came to civil service reform. Of all the abuses in the civil service, the one that aroused his fiercest indignation was the practice by which government workers were forced to kick back a percentage of their wages as political contributions. The money extorted in this manner, Garfield claimed, "in many cases never gets beyond the pockets of the shysters, the hangers-on, and the mere camp-followers of the party," and he called for an end to the "shameful practice." Yet he was not at all embarrassed when, less than four months later, the expenses of circulating one of his speeches as a campaign document was met by an assessment upon the wages of those government workers who owed their jobs to him. The speech dealt, among other things, with the need for civil service reform.[17]

If Garfield retained any lingering hopes for the Grant administration, they were laid to rest by the President's persistent efforts to annex Santo Domingo. This scheme, which the President pursued with a tenacity bordering on obsession, split the Republican Party in two, with Charles Sumner, head of the Senate Foreign Relations Committee, leading the opposition. Garfield's sympathies were with Sumner, though he was somewhat put off by the Senator's arrogance of manner. Garfield expected that the West Indies would ultimately belong to the United States but he was not happy at that prospect. Racial and religious prejudice convinced him that these tropical regions, with their enervating climate and their Latin population, "Strangely degenerated by their mixture with native races," could never be assimilated into our civilization. Consequently, he advocated an end to further American expansion, with the possible exception of Canada.

When Congress refused to be stampeded into approving Grant's annexation scheme, Garfield was gratified to report that Santo Domingo and, by implication, the President had suffered "a very black eye." But when the President struck back by engineering the removal of Sumner from his committee post, Garfield was aghast at this act of "stupendous folly." And when the fruits of this "foolish and wicked removal" were revealed by the subsequent Republican setback in New Hampshire, he was convinced that Grant was leading the party to disaster. "If the recent events do not open the eyes of the President to the dangerous path he has been travelling recently," he glumly predicted, "it will not be long before our defeat will be assured."[18]

The President paid no heed to these danger signals, and the Party, Garfield mournfully observed, drifted rudderless. At times the situation seemed almost comic. "The President left for Long Beach at 8 o'clock yesterday," Garfield maliciously noted one summer morning, "leaving a great many Congressmen with fingers in their mouths, waiting to complete business at the Executive Mansion. The President has done much to show with how little personal attention the Government can be run. Perhaps this is the drift of modern thought. It is said that Queen Victoria's retirement from public affairs has proved to England how unnecessary a sovereign is to the wants of a people. We can say as the Methodist shouter did in Bedford, 'The same thing over here.' "[19] But Garfield could not dismiss the "ugly signs of disintegration in our party" with frivolity. "Public affairs," he complained, "are growing about as bad as the devil could wish if he were arranging them his own way." For this sad state of affairs he blamed the President's inept leadership. "His power is waning very rapidly," he declared, "and many of the best men here think that his re-election is impossible. It is feared, however, that his nomination is inevitable."[20]

Not all Republicans were prepared to acquiesce in another four years of Grant. In March of 1871, Jacob Dolson Cox told his friend that in Cincinnati, "We are forming a little organization of Revenue Reform and Civil Service Reform Republicans here, which will I think have some influence upon the politics of the State bye and bye." From this modest beginning would soon emerge the Liberal Republican Party, which would directly challenge the rule of Grant. Garfield respected the strength of the new movement. "The political elements are full of nitre just now," he observed. "If the opposition to Grant were to concentrate, he would stand a good chance to be beaten." Such a result would not displease Garfield. Indeed, he would regard it as "a great blessing to the party if we could select another man." But would he lend himself to such a movement? His intentions were put to the test early in 1872 when the Ohio legislature met to select a U.S. senator.[21]

The incumbent, John Sherman, was not one of Garfield's heroes. "I do not admire the statesmanship, or courage of the Senator," he confided. Sherman's ruthless brand of machine politics repelled him, but his worst sin in Garfield's eyes was his desertion of the sound money cause in an earlier hour of trial. Since then, Garfield contemptuously snorted, Sherman had "twice boxed the compass on the greenback and bond question, and each time has supposed he was catching the wind of popular favor."[22] When Garfield learned that a group of reform-minded Republicans were planning to challenge Sherman's reelection, his ears perked up in interest. He discreetly advised his friends in Columbus that "if the Senatorship is thus to be thrown open for honorable competition, I should be sorry to be wholly omitted from consideration in that direction."[23]

He made no secret of his ambition for the Senate. The only problem was one of timing: should he wait two more years to contest the seat now held by Democrat Allen Thurman or should he accept the support of the rebellious Republicans and challenge Sherman now? The first course was risky, for who could tell what the situation might be two years hence. On the other hand, if he were to accept the offer of the handful of caucus-bolters who promised to support his candidacy, he would face more immediate hazards. He could only be elected with the assistance of the Democrats and such a move would commit his fortunes to the Liberal Republican revolt and damage, perhaps irrevocably, his position in his own party unless, as seemed unlikely, the Liberals should succeed in capturing the regular party organization.

As usual, when faced with a decision concerning his career, Garfield chose to do nothing and allow his destiny to take care of itself. "Thus far in my life," he reminded himself, "I have asked for no office. I may sometime do so but will not begin now." He telegraphed his would-be supporters to use their own judgment, which they correctly interpreted as a refusal.

Once the decision had been made for him, Garfield felt a twinge of doubt. "It was, I confess, some temptation," he admitted. "For some reason a position, obtained in that way would have been an independent one." He could have saved his regrets, for he really had almost no chance of success. For one thing, he was not the bolters' only candidate. They had also approached Governor Rutherford B. Hayes with the same proposal, and had probably sounded out others as well. Hayes turned them down without any hesitation, even when they dragged him out of bed to urge him to reconsider. Furthermore, Sherman and his cronies had the legislature sewed up so tightly that no revolt could succeed. When some Democrats started to switch their vote to Cox, they were ruled out of order by the Lieutenant Governor, who gaveled Sherman into another Senate term.[24]

If the senatorial contest was a test of Garfield's intentions towards the new party, he had flunked it as far as the Liberal Republicans were concerned. Yet for the next few months, as he watched the new party movement gather momentum, Garfield wavered in hesitation. "The dissolution of parties is near at hand," he prophesied darkly. "A new birth is needed." He was sorely tempted to follow the example of Cox. "If I were free to follow my own judgment," he confessed, "I should say that every consideration of national good requires a new candidate for the presidency." But in the end, he could not bring himself to trust any reform movement that allied itself to the Democratic Party, "with all its ugly traditions of hatred to the war and its results." Distrust of Democrats outweighed his distaste for Grant. Although he knew of few Republicans who were anxious to see President Grant serve another term, most of them were resigned to his renomination. "Frankly," he admitted, "I am of that number . . ." On the eve of the Liberal Republican convention at Cincinnati, his mind was made up. "I expect to stand by the old ship and fight the battle this fall to protect the Republican Party, but I confess . . . that the case begins to look desperate." The prospect of having to campaign for a man like Grant depressed him. "I look

341

forward with positive dread to the work that will be required on the stump next fall to defend him from the criticisms which will certainly be made . . . ," he admitted candidly.[25]

Deeply discouraged by the tendencies of national affairs, Garfield sought whatever comfort he could find in work and family. His work, however, was becoming a numbing routine which tended to drain his spirits rather than replenish them. "The same old story," he sighed after one typical day. "Letters in the morning; committee at half-past ten. House at twelve. Went nearly through the estimates for the Post Office Department. After the morning hour took up the Legislative Appropriation Bill. Pushed it steadily until one quarter before five. Made good progress, Completed nearly thirty five pages of the bill. Had a brisk debate as usual on the Bureau of Education. Came out of the House with a severe headache."[26] Such headaches were becoming only too frequent, as was an alarming numbness in his arms and fingers which often kept him from sleeping. Weekends frequently found him "worked down almost to the point of exhaustion." He recognized the danger signals but could see no way of lightening the load that so oppressed him.[27]

That load was far heavier and much less glamorous than any of his constituents could imagine. "Whoever supposes that the duties and semi-duties of the average member of congress are limited to those of his representative character, pure and simple, needs light," explained Albert Gallatin Riddle. The official duties of a congressman, according to Riddle, included "his share of work on the committee, the discussions in the room, the study, writing of sub-reports of cases referred to him, and writing and considering final reports for the house; the presentation of memorials, attending in the house, answering official letters, seeing to the sending off of public documents, attending to the debates, and taking his share in the conduct of such bills as have been entrusted to his hands."[28] For all of this labor, plus the bottomless mound of correspondence on his desk, Garfield had no other help than one part-time shorthand secretary, the faithful and overworked clerk, George U. Rose.

Yet even all these official legislative chores, which the public imagined to be the whole duty of a congressman, were, in the view of Riddle, merely "the lighter and more grateful part of his work." An even larger share of his time was spent in running errands for constituents. Using the imaginative license permitted a novelist, Riddle caricatured a typical day in the "mosaic and monotonous life" of a congressman.

He rises as soon as he can wake and identify himself in the morning, unrefreshed from scant sleep, dresses as he may, finds a strange, uncouth man in his little parlor, whom he has found there before, and whom he recognizes as the man from Nova, with the greatest discovery of the age—about the dozenth time of its discovery and exposure, whom in a moment of forgetfulness, he promised to accompany to the patent office. He had forgotten that; but the grim, silent inventor of destiny has not; this he now adds to the other list for that morning. In the corridor outside— he has heard his footfall—is an amateur detective. . . . This man draws him to the remote corner and whispers, he has just begun to think he is almost on the track of one of the most gigantic frauds ever conspired against the bleeding treasury of an already ruined country. He brings letters of marque and reprisal from important political deadbeats, urging his immediate employment. He is ready to proceed to New York at once, all he requires is money and a letter of credit. . . . He is escaped from. At the bottom of the stairs is that widow with three children, whom he had promised to help return to Wisconsin. Just beyond her is the mother with her son, for whom he is to see Defrees, and get a place for him in the congressional printing office—he will be the ninth refusal which the kindly head of that beseiged asylum of unfortunates has been obliged to give him the present session. No matter, though he knows that the chances [are hopeless]. . . . the hopeful mother does not. She "knows he can secure the place if he will." It is worth adding one more pang to the poor mother that he demonstrate the truth of what he says, and he will take her bright-eyed boy, whom he likes, with him as a witness. Now he escapes to his belated breakfast . . . cold coffee, with toast that has become crusty. . . . He finds on his plate a note marked private, and puts it unopened into an inside pocket. . . . A card soon reaches him, and what is more serious the carder is not remote. The name, though, is all right, and the owner respects his breakfast. . . . He finds his friend in the parlor and dismisses him with a pleasant word. There in a corner is a timid, shrinking form waiting for him. She had been there twice to see him. She was just dismissed from the bureau of engraving and printing, for lack of funds to pay employees. She has a mother and two brothers all out of employment—all mothers and brothers at the capital always are. This is genuine. Innocent and timid, she came to him because they told her he had influence. . . . He gave her tender words of assurance and promised God and himself to save her. Then he went out to find a meek, long-haired, white-necktied, sandy, seedy individual, who introduced himself as the Rev. Green Cheese from Arkansas, a pastor of the church in which the representative some times finds rest. He was specially recommended to him as a zealous brother. He came to Washington to raise money to patch the roof and buy a lightning rod for his church. He received five dollars for his church and a flash for himself, and then the representative broke away.

The greatest discoverer since Newton shouldered up his changer of current history—a funny looking package, and attended by the boy for the printing office, they hurry down F street to the patent office—really the department of the interior—where he deposits the great revolution, for whom he afterward secured a pass on the Baltimore and Philadelphia railroad. From there he went into the post-office department, across F, to have a stopper put on the pay of a mail contractor, until he should pay arrears due a sub-contractor in Kansas. Then he hurried off to the congressional printing office, half a mile further, realized his expectations from Mr. Defrees, took a car back to the treasury department, had an interview with the superintendant of the printing bureau; ran into the controller's room, and thence to the secretary of the treasury, who showed him an error (caused by the inaccuracy of a treasury clerk), in his report—forthcoming—to be that day submitted to the appropriation committee for final action, and where he waited till the chief of a bureau could be sent for, make an excuse and furnish the missing link. Then he took a car down Pennsylvania avenue, into which he was followed by a capital tramp. When he reached the capitol he entered by his new way, to avoid those awaiting his approach by the usual, and found that now ambushed. He finally reached his committee, where on mature consideration, it was decided that the report must be re-cast, the tables gone over with, changes made, the bill re-written, and the whole ready at ten o'clock the

344

next forenoon. Then he escaped to the restaurant under the capitol, lunched, and up a private way into the lobby, in rear of the speaker's desk, and so reached his seat after the morning hour. The morning's mail encumbered his desk. He clapped his hands, a page came, tied it up with the traditional tow string of the house and constitution, with orders to send it to his boarding house. The debate on the legislative bill was pending. A gentleman on the speaker's right had the floor. Cards came to him; pages came with notes. He resisted, watching the debate which he was to close after the previous question. He had party consultations, finally had to obey a call from the ladies' gallery. There he learned he must go to a party that night. There was trouble in the home camp. Flabber Gaster was moody and discontented, had come to Washington. The set had decided to give him a reception. "Flabber be ———." There was no help for it. He listened and tried to catch what the gentleman was saying below. Several other eyes, in pairs, bored him literally and figuratively, but he got back and sat it out, and then set out for home. The bores of the house called to him, put their arms in his. He was stopped on the way home, met at his own door, and found parties awaiting him. He got a good dinner at six. . . . it was time to dress for the reception. At half-past twelve he sat down to re-cast and finish his report, which his secretary had cut up and got ready. The committee would be called to-morrow on the floor, where he was also to reply to the speeches of today. . . .[29]

Riddle's caricature was drawn uncomfortably close to life. Under the burden of this trivia, Garfield's health and spirits were being ground down. He was over forty now and the newspapers, as he noticed, no longer spoke of him as "a rising *young* man." Twinges of rheumatism signaled the approach of old age and the marks of overwork could be read in his physical appearance. Senator John J. Ingalls, who had not seen Garfield since their student days at Williams, was shocked by the change the years had wrought in his friend: "He had become stout, heavy, and dusky, with a perceptible droop of the head and shoulders, as if bent with burdens." His spirit, too, sagged under the weight it had to carry. Late one night, "so near dead with overwork" that he could not sleep, he moaned to his distraught wife: "I would be glad to die and get out of it."[30]

345

There were, however, less drastic ways to retire from politics. Late in 1871, an officer of Jay Cooke's Northern Pacific Railroad approached him. "Are you," he asked, "so wedded to public life and your noble constituency that it would be useless to submit business propositions to you?" If not, would Garfield consider accepting an appointment as Land Commissioner to supervise the vast landed interests of the company? He mentioned a salary of $8,000 a year plus "the opportunity of obtaining at a merely nominal cost, say $100,000 of the capital stock of the Company." The job, he explained, would be a permanent one: "Fifty million acres of land, stretching across the Continent are not sold in a day." Garfield would take charge of this empire, directing the sales of the land and supervising emigration companies in both Europe and America. The scope of the project could not fail to stir whatever unfulfilled Napoleonic dreams still lurked in Garfield's breast, and it further inducements were necessary, the company shrewdly appealed to his thwarted missionary urge, reminding him of the opportunity to "civilize and christianize one of the noblest sections of the Continent."

Harmon Austin was suspicious. "You are in great danger of getting involved with a set of sharks," he warned. The offer of $100,000 of stock disturbed him. "Why should you or any one have it thus," he asked, "—is it not a bad omen?" He reminded his protege that "corporations have no souls and that it is not love for you but *for themselves* that induces the offer." Besides, the impression was gaining ground "that the whole thing is a great swindle." This advice confirmed Garfield's initial misgivings, and so, even though Cooke upped the ante to $10,000 a year (requesting at the same time that Garfield approve an appropriation for Duluth harbor), the congressman declined the offer.[31] It was a wise decision. Cooke's ambitious project was on the verge of bankruptcy and would go under in 1873, dragging the entire nation into one of the most severe depressions in its history. Garfield's refusal, however, was not based on any premonition of impending disaster but on a reluctance to become a part of such a mammoth corporate enterprise. "If I leave public life," he concluded, "I much prefer to go into the law." Early in 1872, he began negotiations with the

346

Cleveland law firm of Burke and Estep. The negotiations hung fire for three years, and despite veiled warnings concerning Estep's "habits," Garfield was on the verge of concluding the partnership when Austin decisively quashed the project by bluntly informing his friend that his proposed partner was known as "an intemperate and licentious man."[32]

Even though each passing year left Garfield "heartily wishing to be rid of public life," there seemed to be no help for it. He deeply regretted this, not only for financial reasons but because he feared that the disruptions of political life might have an unsettling effect on his children. It occured to him one day in 1872 that with four children, and another due in November (Abram), he was the head of what could be considered a large family. As his family grew, so did his concern for their welfare. To an extent he could scarcely have imagined ten years earlier, the focus of his life had now shifted to home and family. As he reflected contentedly, "it is every year more sweet to lose myself in the sweet circle which has gathered around my hearthstone. . . . The triumph of love could not be more complete."[33]

At the center of this family circle stood his wife, "the best woman I have ever known." In abject but happy dependence, Lucretia's husband admitted that her well-being had become "the continent, the solid land on which I build all my happiness and hope. When you are sick, I am like the inhabitants of countries visited by earthquakes. They lose all faith in the eternal order and fixedness of things." Out of their early misunderstanding and coolness, out of "the long and anxious questionings that preceded and attended the adjustment of our lives to each other," had blossomed at last a genuine passion. "We no longer love because we ought to, but because we do," Garfield assured his wife. "The tyranny of our love is sweet. We waited long for his coming, but he has come to stay."[34]

Garfield had become so domesticated that he begrudged having to spend any of his leisure hours away from his fireside. The Garfields were stay-at-homes. Except for literary societies, such as the Burns Club, they took little part in the capital's frantic social life. They found the compulsive Washington ritual of New Years Day visits so tiresome that one year they

347

fled to New York just to escape it. When Garfield did dine out he usually left his wife at home: of the almost sixty dinner invitations he accepted from 1872 to 1874, only three included Lucretia.[35] Washington society was predominantly masculine. At times the table talk was not suitable for the ears of ladies, but more often the evening was spent in talking shop. Congressmen instinctively sought out each other's company and their dinners tended to be an extension of politics by other means. Partisanship, however, did not extend across the dinner table. "Some of the best men socially in the Congress are political adversaries," Garfield observed after a congenial evening with "Sunset" Cox and other Democrats. Journalists and lobbyists made the best hosts. He especially enjoyed the champagne suppers of "The King of the Lobby," "Uncle Sam" Ward, whom William Evarts gratefully dubbed "the help and hope of Washington." By the early 1870s, Garfield had become an accomplished diner-out and a graceful toastmaster. Still, he regretted that he was too busy to indulge in "the better social life" of Washington. Though he realized that much of it was "uncomfortable and meaningless," there was also, he admitted, "a stratum of really valuable society that I would love to cultivate."

Lucretia played almost no part in her husband's social world. Eight pregnancies in the fifteen years from 1860 to 1874 kept her tied to the house and gave her little time to cultivate the arts of a Washington hostess. From 1872 to 1874 she entertained only nine times, and the guests at these dinner parties were invariably family and friends, mostly from Ohio. To a man of the world, such as Robert Schenck, an evening with the Garfields and their friends could be torture. "Very good people I am sure they are;" he said of the company after one such evening, "but a plainer, stiffer set of village people I never met."[36]

Garfield felt at home in such unsophisticated company. "Indeed, to the very last it was apparent that Garfield was country-born," noted John Ingalls. "There was an indefinable something in his voice, his dress, his walk, his ways, redolent of woods and fields rather than drawing rooms. . . ." To Ingalls, this "splendid rusticity" in Garfield's nature was

348

responsible for his characteristic "cordial, effusive manner."
Some dismissed Garfield's uninhibited sentimental gusto as
"gush," but Ingalls recognized it as an "exuberant freedom
that had none of the restraint and effacement which commonly characterize the moods of the man who has mingled
much with men." Children found in Garfield a kindred spirit.
The son of Charles Henry treasured all his life the memory
of his father and General Garfield sitting on the lawn in front
of his Hiram house on a warm afternoon laughing so hard at
some joke that they "rolled over and over upon the ground and
stirred the very trees with their Olympian laughter." "To see
grown men act thus like joyful children," the boy later recalled,
". . . seemed queer to me. But I soon came to understand
something of that attractive boyish enthusiasm which General
Garfield, often manifesting, kindled also in those around
him."[37]

Unlike some veteran congressmen who lost touch with
their home folk after years of Washington service, Garfield
never outgrew the 19th District. Yet, after July of 1872 Washington was, technically, his only home. His Hiram house,
which he had bought during the war in the course of a hasty
stopover on his way to the front, was sold to Hinsdale. For the
next few years Garfield would be a guest in his own district,
living with his in-laws or renting summer cottages whenever
he came home. He would continue this nomadic life for the
next few years, unwilling to tie himself to a house while his
future was still uncertain. If he should leave politics to practice
law in Cleveland, as he still hoped, a house in the country
would only be an encumberance. But in the summer of 1872,
such hopes seemed premature and he prepared himself for
another political campaign, perhaps (if all went well) his last.

Originally, he had dreaded the thought of campaigning for
Grant's reelection. He was torn between his sympathies,
which lay with the Liberal Republican Party, and his loyalties,
which were commanded by the regular party organization. The
platform drafted by the Liberals at Cincinnati agreed so well
with his own political views that he could easily have campaigned for it. Some of his best friends had been responsible
for the new movement and Garfield had shared their high

349

hopes. "If we get an honest organization," Cox had told him before the convention, "we can control the future politics of the country. . . ." But after the convention, Cox could only moan in stunned disbelief: "Alas! . . . we have fallen among thieves." In an incredible turnabout, the party which had begun its life as a revenue reform movement chose as its standard bearer the nation's most vocal protective tariff advocate— Horace Greeley. "The movement was a revolution but the revolution has revolted," Garfield quipped. The fiasco of a convention that started so nobly and wound up with a candidate like Greeley reminded him of the fable of the beautiful woman who ended with the tail of a fish.[38]

The nomination of Greeley had at least one advantage—it reconciled Garfield to his party. Obviously, he could not support the man he blamed for blocking his path to the Ways and Means chairmanship the preceding year. Compared to a man of "crotchets and violent extremes of opinion" like Greeley, even Grant appeared "tolerable and respectable." "In my interior view of the case," Garfield concluded, "I would say Grant was not fit to be nominated and Greeley is not fit to be elected." Confronted with such a choice, he swallowed the lesser evil and backed Grant. The choice was made easier when the Democrats, with their disgraceful record of "rebelism and reactionary copperheadism," joined the Greeley movement. This coalition, he decided, was "so absurd and so wicked as to make our party relatively high toned and noble."[39]

If only the candidacy of Greeley "were as weak as it is ridiculous," Garfield fretted, "it might be laughed at and passed by, but unfortunately it has much strength." Reports from other parts of the country seemed to confirm his fears of impending political disaster. "I hope never again to be so anxious about the results of an election," he nervously admitted as the campaign drew to a close. "I hope we shall knock the socks off H.G. so that he will walk barefoot the rest of his political life."[40] His wish was granted. "The Philosopher," as Garfield sarcastically dubbed Greeley, went down to the most humiliating defeat any major political candidate had ever suffered. Yet the Republican Party's sweeping success left Garfield strangely depressed. "Next to defeat the saddest thing to me is victory," he reflected. This victory was almost too complete for comfort. "The Democrats," Garfield observed, "are stunned perhaps killed by their late defeat and and there seems to be no limits to the power of the dominant party. If to its great strength, it shall add, as I fear arrogance and recklessness, it will break in two before the next administration goes too far." Grant, of course, felt no such misgivings. In an expansive mood he told Garfield that the noise raised by the Liberal Republicans reminded him of the first time he had ever heard prairie wolves. From the tumult they raised, he estimated that there must be at least a hundred of them but when he drew closer he found only two lonely wolves barking at each other.[41]

Garfield's own reelection was even easier than Grant's. For the first time, there was not even a whisper of opposition to his nomination. One reason for this was that the old 19th District had been redrawn to his advantage. Mahoning County, with its troublesome iron men, was eliminated and replaced by Lake County. Aside from removing the chief center of the opposition, this had the further benefit of creating a homogeneous district. Freed from the necessity of trying to please a constituency "with pig iron at one end, and agriculture at the other," Garfield could now follow his own inclinations on the tariff question.

The nominating convention was cut-and-dried. As soon as it had assembled, Garfield was chosen by acclamation. In his acceptance speech he warned against Greeley but at the same time discreetly dissociated his own campaign from that of Grant's. His reelection was just as routine as his nomination. Without Mahoning to worry about, Garfield's sailing was even smoother than usual. He trounced his opponent, Milton Sutliff, a Warren lawyer who ran under the Liberal Republican banner, by a vote of 19,189 to 8,254.[42]

Garfield scarcely had any time to campaign. The day after his nomination he boarded a train for a trip to the West which would keep him far away from politics until the eve of the election. He had been planning such a trip for years but had never been able to find the time. In 1870, his friend Oakes Ames, a congressman from Massachusetts and a director of the Union Pacific Railroad, had given him passes over his line but they had lain unused. Early in 1872, when Garfield had wanted nothing more than some excuse to escape what promised to be an ugly campaign, he had wrangled an appointment as commissioner to negotiate with the Flathead Indians. Armed with this commission, he had a valid excuse to desert the campaign and see the West.

This was the first time he had been beyond the Mississippi and he enjoyed every minute of it. As his train rolled across the Kansas prairie, through an ocean of grass littered with mounds of bleached buffalo bones, he sat glued to the window. In Utah, one of the twelve apostles gave him a guided tour of Salt Lake City, and Brigham Young himself chatted briefly with the visiting congressman. At Ogden, Garfield and Swaim (who had been thoughtfully detailed as his companion) left the comfort of the train for a stagecoach. The Wild West was already becoming a legend and Garfield derived an almost adolescent pleasure from sitting up front with the drivers. He and Swaim enjoyed roughing it in the wilderness as they napped in the open air on a buffalo robe spread out on the ground with the sage brush for a pillow, at peace with the world. As they drove past the Rockies, Garfield enjoyed the rare pleasure of admiring a mountain named in his honor— Mt. Garfield, a splendid snow-covered peak on the continental divide.[43]

Two weeks out of Fort Leavenworth, Garfield arrived at Fort Owens, Montana, near the Flathead reservation. Since the Flatheads were unwilling to leave their valley for the new reservation the government had picked out for them Garfield was compelled to do what he had once condemned as a "mockery"—"sit down in a wigwam and make treaties with a lot of painted and half naked savages." The powwow was "somewhat tiresome," but Garfield amused himself by observing the peculiarities it revealed in the Indian mode of thought. After extensive negotiations, some of the Flatheads were finally persuaded to remove to their new quarters in the Jocko Valley. Garfield had many reasons to be pleased with the results of his first venture into diplomacy, not the least of which was the fact that the Indians' homes in their new reservation would be located far enough from the Catholic mission to "emancipate them from the undue influence of the Jesuits."[44]

His mission accomplished, Garfield retraced his steps and returned to civilization. At Fort Leavenworth he rejoined his family and caught up on a month's accumulation of mail and back newspapers. As he worked his way through the papers an item caught his eye. "I find my own name dragged into some story which I do not understand but I see only referred to in the newspapers," he noted with some bewilderment.[45] It was the first intimation of the Crédit Mobilier scandal. The train that Garfield unsuspectingly boarded for the East that evening would carry him into the worst political storm of his career.

CHAPTER SEVENTEEN

ANNO DIABOLI

The same railroad that carried Garfield home from the Indian Country was, indirectly, the source of the troubles he was about to face. Not too many years earlier, the prespect of such a transcontinental railroad had seemed an unattainable dream. Oakes Ames, a wealthy Massachusetts congressman who was intimately involved in the affairs of the Union Pacific, was not exaggerating the difficulties when he said that to undertake such a project—through wild and unexplored country, across three mountain ranges, with no supplies and provisions other than those that could be hauled across a thousand miles, and all the while beating off hostile Indians, "by whom locating engineers and conductors of construction trains were repeatedly killed and scalped at their work"—might well be regarded as "the freak of a madman."

And yet the railroad was built, thanks in no small measure to the efforts of Ames himself. Others may have surveyed the route, laid the tracks or fought off the Indians; Ames mobilized the capital. His instrument was a Pennsylvania-chartered construction company with a suspicious French-sounding title, The Crédit Mobilier of America. The directors of the Union Pacific, in order to limit their liability in what promised to be an extremely risky undertaking, made a contract with themselves (in their capacity as directors of the Crédit Mobilier) to build the road at what turned out to be an inflated price, thus in effect diverting the assets of the railroad into their own pockets. Despite its potential for fraud, this arrangement was neither novel nor particularly reprehensible. The device of the dummy construction company had been used to finance other railroads and, in view of the risks, it could be argued that the profits were not unreasonable.[1]

Yet the Union Pacific was not just another railroad. It was a vast national enterprise, so heavily supported by various federal subsidies as to be clothed with the public interest. Fraud in its construction would be no mere private scandal but could bring serious disgrace upon the government itself. Revelations which began to appear in the pages of the *New York Sun* in September of 1872 seemed to indicate vast fraud indeed. The *Sun* had gotten hold of the correspondence of Henry S. McComb, a disgruntled director of the Crédit Mobilier. In these letters to McComb, Ames indiscreetly boasted of having distributed Crédit Mobilier stock "where it will produce most good to us"—to various influential political figures. "We want more friends in Congress," Ames explained, "and if a man will look into the law (and it is difficult to get them to do it unless they have an interest to do so) he can not help being convinced that we should not be interfered with." Conspicuous on Ames's list of bribed congressmen stood the name of James A. Garfield.[2]

By the time his train reached Washington, Garfield had decided to head off the ugly rumors that were beginning to gather. He sought out a friendly reporter and issued a statement. Based wholly on his memory, without notes or advice, this hasty statement was bound to be incomplete. Yet even after allowance is made for these handicaps, there still remains a disturbing lack of candor in Garfield's initial explanation. He carefully avoided mentioning any connection with Oakes Ames, stressing instead that he had been asked to subscribe by George Francis Train, a journalist and promoter whose connection with Crédit Mobilier was peripheral at best. Garfield was extremely vague about the terms of this stock offer but he was emphatic in his insistence that "he never subscribed for a single share of the stock, that he never received or saw a share of it."[3]

A few days afterwards, too late to be of any use, Garfield received some urgent advice from his old friend Jere Black:

"say nothing without seeing me first." As McComb's lawyer, Black had a first hand acquaintance with the inner workings of the Crédit Mobilier, and as Garfield's friend, he was anxious to protect his reputation. Some years before the scandal had become common knowledge, Black had warned Garfield against Oakes Ames's scheme and now he tried to refresh his friend's memory. The facts, as Black remembered them, were considerably less innocuous than Garfield's bland denial of involvement might lead the public to believe. First of all, Black reminded Garfield:

> You regarded O.A. as a perfectly upright man—an example of solid integrity—had no suspicion that he had private interests to take care of as a member of Congress, much less that he was a ring-leader in any fraud.
>
> 2. He offered you some stock in Cred. Mob.—offered to sell it at par, and assured you that in his judgment it w'd be a good investment.
>
> 3. You declined at first to take it (tho you believed what he said about it) because you had not the money to pay for it; and then he offered and urged you to take it on credit, wh you did.
>
> 4. When you made the contract you were not informed, and did not believe, and had no reason to believe that the Cred. Mob. had any connection with the Un. Pac. RR Co. or with anything else upon w'h Congress c'd possibly be called upon to legislate.
>
> 5. At a subsequent time when you proposed to adjust y'r indebtedness for the stock, Mr. A. put you off by saying that the Co. was doing very well, was making dividends w'h he w'd credit on the price of the stock.
>
> 6. At a still later time, he showed you an acc't—in w'h you were charged with the price of the stock at par, and credited with the dividends rec'd by him for you. This left a balance in y'r favor, wh he then paid.
>
> 7. During all this time you were not informed and did not suspect that the Cred. Mob. was connected with the U.P. R.R. Co. or that either of those companies was committing any wrong against the U.S. or any body else.[4]

Furthermore, when Black did discover that his friend had become entangled in Ames's scheme (some time in the winter of 1869-70), he took Garfield aside and explained the whole tangled story. Garfield, so Black recalled, then returned the money to Ames and washed his hands of the whole affair.

Even if Black's recollection was correct, it did not thereby prove that Garfield was guilty of any wrongdoing in his dealings with Ames. Quite the contrary, for as Black assured his friend: "you were not the instrument of his corruption, but the victim of his deception."[5] This line of defence, how-ever, had unflattering implications, for it depicted Garfield as a gullible innocent, greedily snapping at Ames's poisoned bait. Furthermore, a defense along the lines Black suggested would concede the gravity of the charges and would, by implica-tion, rebuke those other Republicans who might also have been involved. Garfield could not bring himself to abandon his party associates on the verge of an election to save his own skin. Consequently, he decided to ignore Black's advice and instead try to brazen it out along the lines of his original denial in the hope that the storm might soon blow over. It was a decision which, as Hinsdale prophetically warned, would prove "one of the larger mistakes" of Garfield's career.[6]

The error was compounded by Garfield's testimony in the congressional investigation that followed. The investigating committee, headed by Luke Poland of Vermont, had been set up at Blaine's instigation. Arguing that "we have a choice only as to whether *we will investigate or be investigated,*" Blaine told Garfield "we shall be the biggest fools on earth if we fail to take the initiative." Blaine could afford such an inquiry— *his* name had been included on Ames's list by mistake—but Garfield had to proceed with care. He took the precaution of conferring with Ames, so as to coordinate their testimony before either could embarrass the other on the witness stand.[7]

On January 14 Garfield was called before the Poland Committee. He testified that in the closing weeks of 1868 Oakes Ames had offered to sell him ten shares of Crédit Mobilier stock for $1,000. Garfield admitted to having been interested but he had not been able to raise the money and, furthermore, was hesitant to invest until he knew more about the company. Ames had replied that he would hold the stock in Garfield's name until he made up his mind. There the matter rested for a year, until Garfield told Ames that he had decided not to take the stock after all. That was all there was to the transaction. With one exception, Garfield concluded, "Mr. Ames never gave, nor offered to give, me any stock or other valuable thing as a gift." That exception was a trifling matter—a loan of $300 which Garfield borrowed of Ames around the time the stock purchase was being considered.

Ames's testimony tended to support Garfield's version of events. He pointedly excluded Garfield from the list of congressmen who had bought the stock and confirmed that Garfield had never received any dividends or other money except for "some three or four hundred dollars" which Garfield called a loan. A disturbing vagueness seemed to creep into Ames's testimony from time to time. He refused to say whether he had regarded the money given to Garfield as a loan, and on the crucial question of whether Garfield had received any dividends his flustered string of evasions could hardly inspire confidence: "No sir; I think not. He says he did not. My own recollection is not very clear."[8]

A few weeks later, however, Ames suddenly underwent what Garfield dryly labelled as "a new accession of memory." He appeared again before the Poland Committee and repudiated his earlier testimony. Armed this time with memoranda and account books, he revealed that Garfield was indeed one of the congressmen who had snapped up the proferred stock. Garfield bitterly suspected that Ames was desperately trying "to drag down as many men with him as possible. . . . He seems to me as bad a man as can well be." Behind Ames's unexpected treachery, Garfield saw the cunning hand of Ben Butler. The two Massachusetts congressmen had been closeted together the night before Ames's testimony and Garfield thought that the ambitious, unscrupulous Butler might be using Ames as an instrument with which to destroy the established party leaders in the House.[9]

Whatever his motives, Ames's testimony was damaging. He now claimed that Garfield had not only taken ten shares of Crédit Mobilier stock but that he had not paid for them. Instead, the dividends had been allowed to accumulate until they covered the purchase price. These dividends were speedy and generous. Within a few months they had more than

358

doubled the original investment, allowing Garfield to own his ten shares free and clear and leaving besides a balance of $329 which Ames claimed to have paid over to him.

From a strictly legal point of view, Ames's testimony was worthless. He repeatedly contradicted himself on important points. At times he claimed to have paid the $329 in cash, at other times by check, and at other times he confessed that he could not remember. He did manage to produce a check of sorts as evidence. Yet this "evidence", a draft for $329 on the Sergeant-at-arms, could not be positively linked to Garfield and was, in fact, made out three days *after* the alleged payment supposedly took place. The account books were even worse. A confused jumble of notes jotted down in no particular order, often on loose scraps of paper, they could hardly be used to convict anyone—except Ames himself, on the charge of sloppy bookkeeping.[10]

Nonetheless, the Poland Committee chose to accept Ames's version of events rather than Garfield's. Garfield accused them of being "stampeded by the general spirit of panic that has prevailed," but Poland himself later explained that Garfield's refusal to testify in rebuttal had left the committee no other choice. Garfield himself claimed that his damning silence was due to an unwillingness to "bandy oaths" with a scoundrel like Ames. "If the people will believe the testimony of a man blackened all over with contradictions and fraud as against my statement I cannot help it," he maintained with quiet dignity, and he continued to hold his tongue until the public clamor began to abate. In this, he was following the cruel advice of Whitelaw Reid: "Shut your mouth and keep it shut." It was a wise course. When Schuyler Colfax tried to refute Ames's charges he only managed to ensnare himself and destroy his political career. Garfield's discretion spared him that fate but at the cost, so he feared, of having "the shadow of the cursed thing . . . cling to my name for many years."[11]

Actually, the report of the Poland Committee treated Garfield and the other accused congressmen rather gently. In effect, it condemned Ames for bribing congressmen but exonerated the congressmen of taking bribes. Ames was reminded of "the man in Massachusetts who committed adultery and the jury brought in a verdict that he was guilty as the devil, but that the woman was innocent as an angel." The House was inclined to be forgiving. Rather than expel Ames, as the Poland Committee had recommended, it merely censured him. (Congressman James S. Brooks of New York, a Democrat, was also censured to keep the party record balanced.) Attempts were also made to censure Garfield and the other recipients of the stock but Blaine repeatedly ruled them out of order and no action was taken. Garfield was spared official rebuke but he could not dispel the clouds of suspicion that darkened his reputation unless he broke his silence and issued a public defense.[12]

That defense, when it finally appeared, was not entirely satisfactory. Garfield wisely concentrated on poking holes in Ames's pitiful testimony. This was a sound tactic, for by itself Ames's testimony was too rambling, evasive and contradictory to prove anything. There would be absolutely no reason to give any credence to Ames at all if it were not for the embarrassing but unassailable coincidence that his version of events agreed in substance with the story told by Jere Black in his letter of September 29. Black had no reason to lie. Quite the contrary, he was trying to prepare a defense for his friend. Garfield chose to ignore Black's advice and even suppressed his letter. In view of this, his protestations of innocence and his outraged indignation at Ames's "shameless falsehoods" have a somewhat hollow ring.[13]

The whole truth in such a tangled controversy can probably never be wholly recovered but it should be possible to answer some of the questions raised by the affair. As a prelude, it would help to pinpoint the precise areas of disagreement between Ames and Garfield. These were surprisingly small. As Garfield himself conceded:

> [Ames] claims that I agreed to take the stock. I deny it. He claims that I received from him $329, and no more, as a balance of dividends on the stock. This I deny; and assert that I borrowed from him $300, and no more, and afterwards returned it; and that I never received anything from him on account of the stock.[14]

360

Did Garfield ever see the stock? No, but that proves nothing one way or the other since even if an agreement had been reached between them Ames would still have had to hold the certificates in trust for Garfield in order to fulfill the terms of the Crédit Mobilier contract.

Did Garfield agree to take the stock? This is a more complex question which can perhaps best be answered by Garfield's own revealing statement that he "never fully concluded to accept the offer. . . ." The line between accepting and *fully* accepting is a hazy one, capable of causing infinite misunderstanding. It was perfectly possible for Ames to think that Garfield had accepted his offer while at the same time Garfield might be harboring certain reservations. One might even conclude that although Ames sold the stock to Garfield, Garfield never bought it from Ames. Or, to put it less paradoxically, Garfield probably held an ill-defined, open-ended option to buy. Certainly, he did not act as if he owned the stock. He kept no written record of the transaction, and if he or Ames had died neither he nor his heirs could claim the stock. In June of 1869, he compiled a detailed list of his assets which made no mention of any Crédit Mobilier shares. Ames, too, seemed to have regarded this transaction as somewhat out of the ordinary. According to the Poland Committee, Garfield's dealings with Ames were the same as those of "Pig Iron" Kelley and both had apparently received a $329 dividend in June of 1868. Yet in September, Kelley was paid a further $750 dividend while Garfield got nothing. Either Ames was holding out on Garfield or else something happened between June and September to relieve Ames of any further obligation. Since it was admitted that Garfield did not turn the stock down until the following year, it seems likely that his claim to the shares was somewhat more tenuous than Kelley's.[15]

What about the so-called loan? Even Garfield's friends found this story hard to swallow, yet there is some evidence to support it. First of all, he did need money. The European trip had turned out to be more expensive than anticipated and Garfield had been compelled to draw several months of his congressional salary in advance. This left him embarrassed for cash upon his return and, to tide himself over, he arranged to sell a small holding of forty acres of Wisconsin land for ten dollars an acre. Payment from this sale was slow in coming but, until it did, he assured his agent, "I can make a temporary loan here." This was in April of 1868, right around the time that Ames was pressing Garfield to take the Crédit Mobilier dividend. If Garfield preferred to call the money a "loan," Ames would certainly not quibble. That the two transactions were linked in Garfield's mind is evidenced by the fact that he did not bother to repay this "loan" for over a year, and did so only when he had definitely concluded not to take the stock. The two stories were contradictory but not incompatible, and both men could well have been telling the truth as they believed it.[16]

Did Garfield lie? Not exactly. Did he tell the truth? Not completely. Was he corrupted? Not really. Even Garfield's enemies never claimed that his involvement in the Crédit Mobilier affair influenced his behavior. As a corruptor, Ames was a failure. How could he hope to get full value for his money if he neglected to tell his victims that the Crédit Mobilier was connected to the Union Pacific Railroad? Was Garfield corruptable? Probably. At least he was somewhat less able to resist temptation during the immediate postwar years than at any other period in his career. This was the time when he was flirting with Ralph Plumb's get-rich schemes, both of which had features similar to the Crédit Mobilier. The Kentucky oil project featured an inner ring that milked the assets of the company; the Illinois coal venture was designed to place stock "where its influence will do us the most good." Garfield did not recoil from either scheme.

Finally, was he innocent? This was the heart of Black's suggested defense—whether Garfield acted "with his eyes open." Black claimed Garfield did not and, therefore, "The case against him lacks the *scienter* which alone constitutes guilt." Yet, as Sam Bowles pointed out, a man in Garfield's position "had no more right to be ignorant in a matter of such grave importance as this, than the sentinel has to snore on his post." The Crédit Mobilier was not a very well kept secret. Tolerably accurate rumors appeared regularly in print throughout 1868 and 1869 and were even discussed openly on the floor of Congress. The most accurate expose was by Charles Francis Adams, whose brother Henry had ironically recommended Garfield as an authority on railroad corruption. If Garfield did not know about the Crédit Mobilier, he should have.[17]

Garfield's involvement in the scandal was, therefore, a complex and ambiguous one. The press and public, however, were in no mood to weigh subtleties with judicious detachment. Garfield was summarily judged to be guilty (of precisely what was never made clear) and was loudly condemned. Even the *New York Tribune,* which was edited by a personal friend, felt compelled to decry the "wickedness" of Garfield and Kelley who had "betrayed the trust of the people, deceived their constituents, and by evasions and falsehoods confessed the transactions to be disgraceful." Other papers were even harsher, but the cruelest blow came on the floor of Congress when, in response to Ben Butler's taunts, Garfield plaintively asked, "What personal quarrel does the gentleman desire to get up with me?" Butler brutally shot back, "I do not want any personal quarrel with you. *De mortuis nil nisi bonum,*" as the House rocked with malicious laughter. "Take it all in all," Garfield sighed, "it has been . . . a most uncomfortable Winter."[18]

There was worse to come. On February 24, the House was meeting in a late night session to consider the Legislative Appropriation Bill. This bill was Garfield's responsibility and if it were not passed before Congress expired on March 4, an extra session would be required. Garfield had the floor when Ben Butler introduced an amendment to increase the salaries of certain government officers. The President's salary would be raised to $50,000 and, of more immediate interest, each congressman's salary would be raised from $5,000 to $7,500, with the increase being retroactive to the beginning of the 42nd Congress, two years earlier.

Garfield smelled trouble. An increase of congressional salaries was bound to be less popular with the voters than with congressmen and, with the reputation of the 42nd Congress still reeling under the impact of the Crédit Mobilier revelations, it was prudent to avoid further complications. As chairman of the Appropriations Committee, Garfield was publicly committed to reducing expenses. The previous month he had stoutly resisted increasing the salaries of the clerks and pages who worked for the House. He could not now, in consistency, support a raise for congressmen themselves. Consequently, when Butler proposed his amendment, Garfield informed the House that "I not only regret that this proposition has been brought here and now, but I regret that it has been brought here at all." He resisted the Butler Amendment when it was introduced; he resisted it when it was reconsidered; he resisted it in conference committee and on the floor but, "after fighting to the extent of our power as a committee, overwhelmed in nineteen different votes taken upon the question, fighting it inch by inch as a captain would fight his ship in a naval battle, overpowered, boarded by those who took the other view, we were overborne . . . until at last the nefarious measure was passed."[19]

The measure found its most enthusiastic support among the "lame ducks" created by the recent Republican victory. To these were added the friends of President Grant who feared, as he confided to Garfield, that he would have to dip into his own savings unless his salary were increased. These forces were skillfully marshalled by Ben Butler, who pressed the bill with extraordinary persistence, gleefully laughing down the opposition. Garfield thought he detected a serious purpose behind Butler's clowning. During the Crédit Mobilier investigation he had spotted the hand of Butler behind the voice of Ames and it had convinced him that the squint-eyed demagogue was exploiting the scandal in order to discredit and then supplant the party leadership in the House. Perhaps the Salary Bill was an extension of this plot. By early February, Garfield suspected that "Ben Butler and the democrats are trying to force upon us an extra session, so as to continue the excitement and work as much injury as possible. . . ." If true, this placed Garfield in an awkward dilemma: given the mood of the House he could block the salary increase only by defeating the appropriation bill to which it was attached. This, however, would play straight into Butler's hands by forcing that extra session which was apparently the object of his plot.[20]

The dilemma was compounded when the bill was sent to conference committee. Garfield was appointed chairman from the House side, but both of the other conferees named by the Speaker were supporters of the salary increase: Butler and Randall, neither of whom were from the Appropriations Committee. Conference committees were always tense affairs. The hour was late, the stakes were high and nerves were stretched to the breaking point. One of Garfield's colleagues of other conferences could never forget those scenes "when we sat over the millions of public money, almost unqualified power in our hands, and with . . . temper[s] . . . so keyed that every touch jangled." This particular conference was even more tense than most. The Legislative Appropriation Bill ran to seventy printed pages and there were sixty-five separate points of difference between the two houses. The Salary Amendment, however, overshadowed all else. Garfield was outnumbered five to one on this issue but he fought a rear-guard action for six hours before he finally capitulated. First he urged the conference to reject the salary increase; then he moved to eliminate the retroactive feature; then he moved to make the increase retroactive for one year only, and on each point he was beaten down. Finally, he moved to deduct mileage payments from the salary increase and in this, at least, he succeeded, salvaging about $200,000 for the Treasury.[21]

This small victory could not disguise the fact that the salary increase was now firmly attached to the appropriation bill. "This will make great trouble," Garfield realized, "and I am in doubt what I ought to do. If I decline to sign the bill I abandon its management to Butler who knows but little of its details and would run the risk of an extra session. If I sign the report I shoulder a part of the responsibility of the increase of salaries." In the end, fear of the perils of an extra session outweighed all other considerations in his mind. Furthermore, he was tired. For almost a week he had averaged less than four hours of sleep a night and he had neither strength nor heart left to keep fighting for a clearly lost cause. He suppressed his misgivings and signed the conference report.

When the report came back to the House, a few hours before adjournment, he made one last halfhearted effort to disassociate himself from the salary increase but he finally voted for the appropriation bill, salary clause and all. He could have sustained his opposition to the last but he scorned such a futile gesture as "unworthy and cowardly." He was chairman of the Appropriations Committee. The bill was his responsibility; he could not disown it. "Every law is an act of compromise," he reflected, "and a man must always vote for some things he disapproves of, in order to carry a whole necessary measure."[22]

With the passage of this appropriation bill the 42nd Congress passed into history, unmourned and unregretted so far as Garfield was concerned. He looked forward now to a rest from the "carnival of calumny" he had endured all winter. Instead, to his amazement, he found that the increase of congressional salaries had touched a raw nerve of public opinion. The measure was immediately labelled "the salary grab" and Garfield was singled out as the chief villain. His stubborn resistance to Butler's amendment went unnoticed; the public saw only that he had signed the conference report and voted for the bill. "They blame me for that vote as if I had been for the increase all the time," he noted in bewilderment.

The storm over the salary grab eclipsed Crédit Mobilier. That scandal, which Garfield considered a far more serious blow to his reputation, was, with its intricate financial details and its tangled charges and countercharges, too confusing for the public mind to grasp. Five thousand dollars, on the other hand, was a sum that anyone could understand and the brazen manner of its appropriation seemed more offensive than the complex corporate fraud perpetrated by Oakes Ames and his friends. "The Crédit Mobilier hurt you some, but not much," a sympathetic friend reported. "We could have fixed that up all right, for the people were disposed to be just and lenient. But this salary vote on the heels of the other put things in bad shape." Even loyal Harmon Austin was despondent. The vote, he predicted, "will be the finishing stroke to your congressional career." Hinsdale confirmed that Garfield was "universally condemned" by friend and foe alike. "Good men in various places swing their fists and say they *never will* vote for you again." Former friends denounced him, local newspapers joined in the clamor and "Every ambitious and envious fellow in the district took up the cudgel and stirred up the people as much as he could." If the election were to be held today, Garfield was repeatedly warned, he would surely lose. "Ames and Colfax are received by their constituents with ovations," he bitterly observed. "My constituents are hunting for ropes to hang me with."[23]

This rapid plunge from public favor left Garfield stunned and bewildered. For a time he languished in a mood of black despair. His dreams were haunted by ominous visions of shattered idols and brooding thunderclouds and his letters were filled with self-pity. Public life, he dramatically exclaimed, "is the hollowest of all shams." Covering his disappointment with the comforting mantle of stoicism, he decided that "the Providence that presides over our lives, saw that I needed the discipline of trial and adversity. . . ." It was a hard lesson but he proposed "to make culture and sweetness" out of his troubles. "I shall try to meet manfully whatever comes to my lot," he resolved, but no amount of philosophy could reconcile him to the constant sniping of those "little carpers, who know nothing of the case, except that they think they smell a stink."[24]

Late in March, a Republican convention at Warren, made up of what Garfield called "the same cold, malignant set that have hated me for so many years," adopted a resolution condemning their congressman for his vote on the salary grab and demanding his immediate resignation. Similar resolutions were approved by conventions in other parts of the district. Before these troubles, Garfield had been half-tempted to retire from congress in order to devote his full attention to the law. Now that a storm had begun to rage, such an excape was out of the question. "If I were to consult my own personal preference in the matter, I would instantly resign," he told his friends but he could not allow himself to be driven out of public life in disgrace.[25]

His friends advised him to fight back. Austin reminded his protege that "there are times when a man must unsheathe the sword and *wade in*," but Garfield was too dispirited for such a struggle. "There does not seem to be in me as much fight as formerly . . . ," he sighed. "I can fight battles for others but to fight men for disliking me, for disapproving my course, hurts my pride and my self-love. . . ." Austin insisted that Garfield abandon, for once, his customary diffidence. Silence in the face of his detractors, Austin argued, "will be construed into weakness and perhaps guilt." Garfield was persuaded. "I am going to fight," he announced. With grim determination he declared, "I do not propose to be killed off without being consulted on the subject."[26]

His first move was to clear his flanks by rejecting the now infamous salary increase. All his friends had warned him, "If you *now take this back pay*, we cant help you. You must go by the board." Their advice was unnecessary. Garfield had already returned to the treasury the $4,548 to which he was entitled under the salary increase. He was the first, but by no means the last, of a long parade of congressmen whose sense of discretion would suggest the same act of self-denial. Having returned the money, he faced a small dilemma: should he publicize his gesture? Prudence said yes; pride said no. He took the problem to his friends who solved it for him by leaking the information to the press.

With this impediment out of the way, Garfield turned to the counterattack in earnest. His principle weapon in this early stage of combat was the pen. In addition to writing long explanatory letters to scores of influential constituents, he also composed a pamphlet on the Crédit Mobilier and an open letter "To the Republican Voters of the Nineteenth District" justifying his position on the salary grab. It was hard, unrewarding work. Although a glib speaker, Garfield was a slow, painstaking author. His total literary output in the four months since adjournment would, he estimated, fill a book of 300 pages, "and much of it," he complained, "has not been a kind of work that feeds the soul of the writer, and makes him love the work of pamphleteering." Distasteful though the labor was, it had the desired result. His *Review of the Crédit Mobilier* was hailed as "a clear, strong, manly, and èven masterly document," and he learned that his letter on the salary increase was everywhere "confirming the timid and doubting, and has made my enemies fighting mad." Newspaper comment was overwhelmingly favorable as was the reaction of the public. "I know of none who does not say my vindication is complete," Garfield rejoiced.[27]

As Garfield sized up the situation that spring, he thought that he had some grounds for confidence. His analysis was characteristically expressed in terms of personalities rather than classes, interest groups or other more sophisticated categories. Garfield tended to view politics in terms of people and in these terms he saw the hard core of opposition as composed of two groups: "The old set of malcontents, who hated me whether or no;" and "The narrow, mean men, who see a dollar more plainly than any other fact of life." These were lost beyond recapture. More encouraging was the response of "The hasty, passionate men, who see only the surface, and think if a man gets a bloody nose he is mangled to death." These men, Garfield was pleased to report, "were sadly sure that I was dead, and seem joyfully surprised to find that I still live and breathe, weigh two hundred pounds, and sleep o'nights, and are beginning to say knowingly, 'He's plucky, I tell you, he'll come out top yet.' These will come back and stay—till the next storm."[28]

To further convince the wavering, he delivered a speech on the railroad problem that was designed to demonstrate that he had not sold his soul to the Union Pacific. "Since the dawn of history," he said, "the great thoroughfares have belonged to the people. . . . But now the most perfect, and far the most important roads known to mankind are owned and managed as private property, by a comparatively small number of private citizens." Are our institutions, he asked, strong enough to harness the force of the steam engine? He quoted with approval a British authority who said: "We have tried the *laissez faire* policy, and it has failed. . . . We have simply to make our choice between two alternatives—either to let the state manage the railways, or to let the railways manage the state."[29]

By August, Garfield's counterattack seemed to have succeeded. "So far as my own district is concerned," he optimistically concluded, "the tide has not only turned but I am confident that I could be renominated and reelected this

369

month if the case arose." This confidence was premature. His enemies had not yet surrendered. In Trumbull County they attempted to impose an anti-Garfield pledge on all office seekers. Their move was beaten down by Harmon Austin who packed the convention with Campbellites, but it was an ominous indication that Garfield's troubles were far from over. The behavior of the party during the state elections that fall was even more disturbing. Garfield was treated as a political leper. His correspondence with the state committee went unanswered and his offers to speak for the ticket were spurned. "It is a suicidal policy on their part," Garfield fumed. "They cannot win democratic votes by that means." When the Republicans did lose the state he considered it a judgment upon the "short sighted selfishness" of those party leaders who had hoped to "ride into power by ignoring their comrades." Had his services not been rejected, he claimed, the state could have been saved. Others read the election returns quite differently. Ezra Taylor, a Warren politician who had once borrowed money from Garfield, now called him the "Jonah" of the party and insisted that he "must be thrown overboard in order to save it." He spoke for many who blamed Crédit Mobilier and the salary grab for the party's reverses.[30]

As 1873 drew to a close, Garfield's counterattack shifted from the home front to the capital. He had heard rumors that Blaine intended to deprive the so-called Crédit Mobilier congressmen of their choice committee chairmanships as a demonstration of his own probity. In view of Blaine's slippery past behavior and his consuming ambition for the presidency, such rumors had to be taken seriously. Garfield's friends urged him to stand up to the Speaker and demand his rights. "I don't like Garfield's deprecatory tone and position," complained Sam Bowles. "He and his friends have as much to give Blaine as Blaine has to them, and he ought to stand erect and ask no favors." This was not Garfield's way. He refused to discuss the matter with Blaine and professed indifference as to the outcome. Except for "the unpleasantness of being ignored," he airily maintained, he might even prefer the opportunity "to wield a freelance in the House without the embarrassment of running a Committee."[31] But the more he reflected on Blaine's inconstancy, the angrier he grew. If, as

Garfield now suspected, Blaine intended to shunt him off to a minor committee, he would dig in his heels and refuse to take anything except his old place. "I will make a sharp issue between that and nothing and let him take the responsibility." Blaine, however, did "the manly thing" after all and restored Garfield to command of the Appropriations Committee. He was also appointed to the Rules Committee.[32]

When the 43rd Congress assembled, its first order of business was the repeal of the salary grab. Twenty-five congressmen vied with each other to claim credit for repeal of the obnoxious measure but Garfield disdainfully held himself aloof from this "unseemly scramble." He did speak in favor of repeal and, of course, voted for it but not without a certain wistful regret. He really could have used the money. "The reduction of my salary has cut into my resources so deeply that I find myself pinched to get along with even ordinary expenses," he complained. Advised by his doctor to take up horseback riding for exercise, Garfield looked for an animal to buy. He found one "noble fellow" but the asking price of $350 was so beyond his means that he was reduced to renting a saddle horse by the month instead.[33]

The new Congress was confronted by both a foreign and a domestic crisis. The foreign crisis grew out of the capture by Spain of the Virginius, a ship flying the American flag that was caught running guns to revolutionaries in Cuba. When the Spaniards executed the crew, a brief war fever blazed in the United States. It died down as soon as the facts became known, but before it did some of Garfield's advisers suggested that he beat the war drums in order to distract public attention from his recent scandals. To Garfield, such a course was unthinkable. "My whole feelings shrink from so detestable an outcome to this terrible business," he said and he advocated a reliance on diplomacy and international arbitration as an honorable alternative to war. He deplored the lighthearted warmongering of the press. "The same newspapers that have been denouncing what they called our overgrown navy and war departments are now howling for war," he noted. "There is much in this as in other phases of public affairs to disgust one with public opinion."[34]

The domestic crisis was a more serious matter. "The great

financial panic which has swept and is still sweeping over the country will be the most difficult to handle," Garfield predicted. He feared that there would be "a babel of opinion and remedies laid before the public" and shuddered at the prospect of financial heresy triumphant in Congress. Garfield regarded the depression as a harsh but salutary lesson for a nation that had strayed from fundamental economic truths. In the palmy days after the war, he said, "We went ballooning, and in those days of unparalleled inflation . . . we found that all business was easy. Externally, at least there was an appearance of prosperity. But such prosperity," he gravely declared, "must always be paid for. The return to solid values is always hard. . . . Distress, panic, and hard times have marked our pathway in returning to solid values."[35]

Given this view of the depression, it followed that the proper remedy consisted of patience and self-denial. Congress could not cure the situation but, by its meddling, could only make it worse. "The laws of trade, the laws of credit, the laws of God," Garfield magisterially intoned, ". . . are superior to all legislation." Minor measures of relief were permissible. At the suggestion of Benjamin Bristow, Garfield urged the President to call for a modification of the bankruptcy laws. More far-reaching remedies, however, were to be fought like sin (which in a very real sense, they were). Near the end of 1874, the President was under considerable pressure to undertake an ambitious program of public works to provide jobs for the unemployed. Garfield was aghast at the thought of such a "foolish notion." As he saw it, "it is no part of the functions of the National government to find employment for the people, and if we were to appropriate a hundred millions for this purpose, we should only be taxing 40 millions of people to keep a few thousand employed. By no such artificial and reckless methods," he emphatically insisted, "can industry and prosperity be restored." In company with Bristow, who was now Secretary of the Treasury, he succeeded in persuading President Grant to reject this "fatal policy."[36]

Of all the nostrums proposed to cure the depression, the most popular was inflation. Garfield's war with this heresy was a never-ending one: each time he struck it down, up it would spring again. "The Senate," Garfield lamented, "seems to have lost its balance altogether and the inflationists have full sway there." The House was even worse. "We might as well address the patients in the Lunatic Asylum on finance, as to hope to change the tone of the House at present," he sadly declared. His was a lonely battle. Other western congressmen had surrendered to the public clamor for more money and Garfield, too, was advised not to antagonize the voters further on this issue. "I will not vote against the truth of the miltiplication table," he replied with dignity. His efforts were useless. Congress was "borne down by the inflation tide," and the bill was sent to the President for his signature.[37]

In reality, the inflationary effects of this bill would have been negligible, perhaps even nonexistent, but Garfield was too distraught to scrutinize the bill's fine print. "My soul," he declared dramatically, "is sick and indignant at the course of events on the currency." His spirits were as depressed as the nation's economy. "I now look back to the peace and quiet of other years with a sadness that hardly becomes a man of forty-two years," he observed in his annual New Years Eve stock taking. As he reviewed 1873, it seemed as if A.D. had stood for *Anno Diaboli*. "It has been a year of ferment; a year of trouble; a year of lessons; and a year that I part with without tears."[38] The future appeared equally bleak. "I can do but little to direct my life. The very pressure of my surroundings determines my pathway."

The trials of the past year had left their mark upon his health. Irvin McDowell was so alarmed at Garfield's haggard appearance that he bluntly warned his friend that he was heading for a breakdown. Garfield did not need to be told. His doctor had diagnosed his malady as "neuralgic dyspepsia" and had prescribed a diet of raw beef, bread and milk but, despite this regimen, Garfield still complained that "my dyspepsia haunts me like a ghost." The real trouble was overwork, for which there was no cure in sight. Too keyed-up to relax and too busy to be sick, he found relief in the works of Jane Austen. After discovering *Mansfield Park*, he went on to devour the rest of her novels. In the works of the Hampshire spinster, he found a restful corrective to the fiction of his own era. "The novel of today," he clucked, "is highly spiced with sensation, and I suspect it results from the general tendency to fast living, increased nervousness, and the general spirit of rush which seems to pervade life and thought in our times."[39]

If Jane Austen supplied balm for Garfield's woes, President Grant provided an unexpected tonic. Garfield's esteem for the enigmatic President had begun to rise when he noticed the careful study Grant was giving to financial matters. When Grant intimated that he was unhappy with the inflation bill, Garfield's drooping spirits began to soar. "If the President would interpose his veto," he allowed himself to hope, "millions of men would bless him and his memory." Until the last minute, Grant was undecided. He tried to find reasons to approve the bill but, as he told Garfield, the more he studied it the more convinced he became of its dangerous character. When the President finally decided to veto, Garfield began to see Grant in a new and favorable light. "I feel like forgiving him for a multitude of blunders in view of this veto," he magnanimously declared.[40]

As Garfield saw it, the government had to choose between three policies to meet the financial crisis: first, it could borrow money (which would be inflationary); second, it could raise taxes; and, finally, it could reduce expenditures. The first alternative had happily been defeated; the second was unlikely in an election year. The third was up to Garfield. As chairman of the Appropriations Committee, it was his responsibility to cultivate "that self-denial which shall reduce, *reduce*, REDUCE expenditures. . . ." It was not easy to scale down the expenses "of so vast and complicated a machine" as the government without damaging its efficiency, but Garfield estimated that his committee had been able to lop some twenty-five million dollars from the budget. He and Dawes were so proud of their work of retrenchment that they could not refrain from boasting a bit on the floor of Congress. In reply, "Sunset" Cox sarcastically suggested that "a vote of thanks ought to be passed for the gentlemen on the other side because of the wonderful amount of their goodness and sanctity." Speaking for the opposition, he poetically disputed Garfield's economy claims:

374

"Though the mills of the gods grind slowly,
Yet they grind exceedingly small,"
But the mills of your committees
Do not grind at all.

His skepticism was not shared by the public. Even a Democratic newspaper congratulated Garfield for keeping down the public expenses and urged that he be reelected.[41]

Garfield's own constituents, however, were unimpressed. They were more interested in Ashtabula harbor than they were in retrenchment, and continually embarrassed him by demanding a harbor appropriation just when he was trying to make a name for himself as an economizer. "Really," Garfield snapped in irritation, "it is very difficult to be a national man and still be supported by local influences." Nonetheless, he put first things first and set out to appease the folks back home. He knew that in the approaching campaign he faced the fight of his life. It promised to be an uphill struggle. Such reliable weathercocks as Ezra Taylor were spreading the word that Garfield was "a dead duck," and other political vultures were hovering by, waiting for the congressman to stumble.[42]

The prospect of waging an ugly, personal campaign left Garfield depressed, but Harmon Austin was exhilarated. In previous campaigns he had been frustrated by the ease with which his candidate won reelection. Now, for the first time, he could indulge his facility for political generalship to the hilt. He was clearly having the time of his life. He began to plot strategy as early as January. With undisguised eagerness, he pleaded that if only he "could command such forces as I want I could win the battle with ease." Garfield gave him *carte blanche* and promised somehow to raise the necessary money.

The first necessity, Austin told Garfield, was organization. He unfolded an elaborate plan by which "one brave and fearless Major General" in each county would be commissioned to look after Garfield's interests. To oversee their work, he recommended that Garfield hire a full-time secret agent who could answer newspaper attacks and wander through the district to spy out the opposition. In Dr. Lewis Pinkerton, a retired Disciple minister with considerable "power of ridicule," Austin found just the man for this delicate assignment, and soon after Pinkerton had commenced his missionary duties, anonymous but effective letters began appearing in various local newspapers.[43]

Federal appointees who owed their jobs to Garfield could be counted on to work for his reelection. Austin detailed Charles E. Henry to make sure that these men did their duty. A graduate of the Eclectic and a veteran of the 42nd regiment, "Captain" Henry was bound to Garfield by the strongest ties of personal loyalty. In his capacity as special investigator for the Post Office, he had access to all parts of the district and could speak with authority. An example of his effectiveness can be seen in the way in which he intimidated a wavering postmaster at Andover who was rumored to be "noisy, unprincipled, and disposed to mischief." Henry discovered that this post office was in violation of several department regulations and brusquely threatened to close it down. Abruptly switching the subject, he asked how General Garfield stood with the voters of Andover. The point was not lost, for when Henry was about to leave town he found a contrite postmaster waiting at the station. He "looked anxious," Henry reported, "and said he would look out and see Genl Garfield was all right in that town if I would see him straight in the P.O."[44]

Henry made a useful troubleshooter in a campaign dogged by trouble. When Garfield's managers were perplexed by conflicting reports on the attitude of the Grangers, Henry volunteered to infiltrate the Granger lodges. Within a few weeks, Garfield was assured that the Grangers would be friendly, and a few months later he was startled to receive an invitation to join the Grange himself. He declined, but his feelings were mixed. The Grangers, he suspected, represented "communism in disguise," yet he could not help but sympathize with their goals, especially in regard to railroad regulation.[45]

While his friends at home were busy perfecting the local organization, Garfield was doing his part at the capital. He saw to it that Ashtabula got its harbor appropriation, and he began to use the patronage in a more cold-blooded manner than ever before. Ben Wade, always a potential threat, was placated by the appointment of his son to a federal job, and a lukewarm editor was also given a government position in order to win his support for the coming campaign. This editor, William Ritezel of Warren, had been an enthusiastic Garfield man until the uproar over the salary grab had compelled him to "pitch into" his former friend. Now he was dropping hints to Austin that he could be persuaded to return to the fold. His price was cheap enough. All he wanted was a trip to California at government expense. This could be arranged but, as Garfield sternly reminded the editor, "I intend to stand by my friends, and give them the preference. I do not care to help my enemies any more than justice demands, and if Mr. Ritezel is going to play into the hands of my enemies, as it has sometimes appeared he would, I have no special desire to help him." This seemed fair enough, and soon the pages of the *Western Reserve Chronicle* were filled with Garfield's praises.

By mid-April all this careful attention to detail appeared to have paid off. Garfield's path to the nomination seemed clear. Even Harmon Austin who, as Henry perceptively noted, was always "exceedingly cautious and nervous and inclined to magnify a foe," had begun to relax. Then, suddenly, everything was once more thrown in doubt as Garfield's name was linked to yet another scandal bearing an ominous French-sounding title—DeGolyer pavement.[46]

Early in the 1870s, the city of Washington had finally been able to lift itself out of the mud. The District government, for too long a neglected stepchild of Congress, had at last been reorganized and given a measure of home rule. The first task before the new Board of Public Works and its strong man, Alexander ("Boss") Shepherd, was to pave the dirt roads that had been the capital's disgrace. Among the horde of paving contractors who competed for a share of this profitable privilege was the DeGolyer McClelland Company of Chicago, manufacturers of a patented "ironized" wooden paving block. The company was armed with impressive testimonials to the quality of its product, but in case these failed to convince it was also prepared to pay up to $90,000 in "fees" to strategically located individuals in order to smooth the way for what would ultimately amount to a $700,000 contract. In 1874, it was revealed that five thousand dollars of this money had found its way into the pocket of James A. Garfield.

Garfield defended the transaction as perfectly proper. As he told the story, the DeGolyer company had employed congressman Richard Parsons of Cleveland as attorney to present its case before the Board of Public Works. Before the business was completely settled, Parsons had been called out of town. He asked Garfield to help finish up the case. Garfield agreed and, as soon as Congress had adjourned, he prepared a brief, the company won its contract, Parsons received a $16,000 fee and paid $5,000 of it over to Garfield as his share. That was all there was to it, an innocent professional courtesy rendered by one lawyer to another.[47]

Certain "wicked" newspapers, however, saw the matter in a different light. They accused Garfield of selling his influence. "Of course Mr. Garfield's argument was successful," charged one. "How could it be otherwise? He was chairman of the Committee on Appropriations. Every cent of money voted to the district had to come through him. Shepherd could not afford to refuse him anything that he asked, and Mr. Garfield knew it when he asked and received for his services a fee which would have been grossly extravagant but for his official position." Abandoning his customary reticence, Garfield rushed to defend his beleaguered reputation. "It is time that we ascertain whether a member of Congress has any rights," he angrily declared. "The fact of my being a member of Congress does not disable me from the legitimate practice of law and this was as legitimate as any other practice."[48]

Legitimate or not, the DeGolyer transaction was certainly out of the ordinary and it raised doubts that even Garfield's vigorous defense could not quite dispel. For one thing, his claim that he worked on the case "as faithfully as anything I ever worked at," is not supported by the surviving evidence in the Garfield Papers. His file for the DeGolyer case is remarkably thin, containing only two printed pamphlets, with no notes or other indication of work in Garfield's hand. In contrast, the collection contains full notes and briefs for all his other legal cases. Either the DeGolyer notes were removed from his files or else Garfield simply did not put much effort into the case. Furthermore, Garfield's denial of any conflict of interest seems in retrospect to be unduly legalistic. It was true that the District of Columbia was self-governing and that the pavements were to be financed out of local taxes rather than federal appropriations, but that did not mean that the Appropriations Committee had no favors to bestow upon the District government. Quite the contrary, Boss Shepherd had deliberately overspent his budget in the hope that Congress would ultimately bail him out.[49]

Shepherd could hardly fail to appreciate Garfield's strategic position. On May 20, 1872, as the House was considering the Civil Appropriation Bill, it came to an item of $192,620.13 to refund the Board of Public Works for road and sidewalk improvements made adjacent to government property. The Democrats instantly objected. Sam Randall asked, "why should we run our hands so deeply into the public Treasury and donate . . . nearly two hundred thousand dollars to the Board of Public Works of this District, a board which has shown itself to be recklessly extravagant in its operations?" Garfield, the bill's floor manager, conceded that the government was not legally bound to pay the District, but he urged passage of the bill as a matter of "equity." This incident only underlined the "capricious, fitful, and uncertain" behavior of Congress toward the District in which Congress often acted a role which Garfield likened to that of "a whimsical step-mother." In such an uncertain situation, it would seem only prudent for Shepherd to insure the continuing good will of the powerful Appropriations Committee chairman. Even so, there were limits beyond which Shepherd would not go to placate Garfield. In the spring of 1873, David Swaim urged Garfield to use his influence with the Board of Public Works to secure a plush paving contract for a friend. Garfield dutifully badgered Shepherd about the matter, but in the end he was forced to admit failure. This demonstrated that, despite the newspaper innuendoes, Shepherd could afford to refuse Garfield. On the other hand, it also demonstrated that Garfield was not averse to trading on his official position.[50]

In later years, as further details of the DeGolyer matter began to trickle out, Garfield's role began to appear even more suspicious. A congressional committee in 1877 uncovered, among other items, a letter from George R. Chittenden, an agent of the paving firm, dated May 30, 1872, in which he boasted to his superiors that "The influence of Gen. Garfield has been secured by yesterday's, lastnight's, and today's labors. He holds the purse strings of the United States, is chairman of the Committee on Appropriations, and the strongest man in Congress and with our friends. . . . The connection is complete. I can hardly realize that we have Gen. Garfield with us. It is a rare success and very gratifying, as all the appropriations for the District must come through him." When this letter was revealed, Garfield shrugged it off as inadmissable hearsay. A lobbyist like Chittenden could be expected to exaggerate his influence in order to convince his employers that he was earning his pay.

Corroboration of a sort for Chittenden's claim, however, came to light in 1880, in the last days of Garfield's presidential campaign. According to the sworn affadavit of one Albert B. Kirtland, he had served as an intermediary between Chittenden and Boss Shepherd during the spring of 1872. Kirtland reported that Shepherd was worried about an appropriation bill then pending in Congress but he guaranteed "that if the influence of General Garfield could be secured for the passage of the appropriation . . . there would [be] no question about Governor Shepherd awarding the contract to anybody that General Garfield might request." Kirtland accordingly arranged for Garfield and Parsons to drive out to Shepherd's country home on Sunday, June 2. After the conference, as Shepherd escorted his guests to their carriage, he was supposedly overheard to say: "Gentlemen, pass that appropriation bill and your friend shall have the contract."

Kirtland's renewal of memory, eight years after the event, just in time to be published in a hostile newspaper on the eve of an election, would not ordinarily inspire confidence. Yet at every point where it can be compared with Garfield's

380

diary or private papers, Kirtland's story rings true. The crucial point involves Garfield's first association with the case. In his public defense, Garfield had insisted, with unequivocal precision, that the first time he heard anything about it was on June 8, when Parsons asked for his help. He then told Parsons that he would consider the matter, "but I can't do it until after Congress adjourns." The point, apparently, was that since Congress was not in session there could be no impropriety in taking the DeGolyer case. Unfortunately for Garfield's credibility, his diary entry for June 2 records that after church he "drove out to A. R. Shepherd's." This could have been an innocent social call, but the coincidence with Kirtland's testimony is too striking to be dismissed. This and other circumstantial corroborations tend to undermine Garfield's defense and to raise the suspicion that his DeGolyer involvement was not as innocent as he maintained.[51]

Of all the scandals that followed Garfield into the campaign of 1874, DeGolyer was potentially the most damaging, though it aroused the least public indignation. The salary grab uproar was based on a popular misunderstanding that could be corrected with patient explanation. The Crédit Mobilier affair was so tangled and ambiguous that the moral issues were hopelessly blurred. But in the DeGolyer affair Garfield had allowed himself to become trapped in a clear case of influence peddling. Despite his efforts to rationalize his behavior, it seems inescapable that it was not his legal services which he had sold for five thousand dollars but a small piece of his honor. Had the full accusation been revealed in 1874, rather than dribbling out little by little over the years, it could have destroyed Garfield's career then and there. Instead, the DeGolyer business was merely one more burden for Garfield to carry into an already overburdened campaign.

Despite all the handicaps, that campaign was far from hopeless. The inability of the opposition to unite behind a single banner gave Garfield a decided advantage. His enemies frittered away their opportunity by raising up candidates in each county, none of whom could bring more than a local following into the nominating convention. That convention was scheduled for August 13, but the real decision would be made a week earlier at the local primary meetings, which would choose the convention delegates. It was to these "ante-convention" meetings that all the efforts of Garfield's friends were now directed. If they could find "a few good men in each town" to control these meetings all would be well.

The prospects of success seemed so encouraging that by June Garfield thought that the campaign could run without his help. The Phillips brothers had offered to send him to Europe to sell oil lands and he was greatly tempted to accept. His friends, who had been laboring in his behalf for over a year, were horrified at the suggestion that the candidate himself might desert the field at this critical hour. Hinsdale sharply reminded his friend of the debt he owed to all those who had relieved him of so much of the dirty and disagreeable work of politics over the years. Furthermore, according to another adviser, the oil project looked like "a magnificent swindle," which, in the present condition of his reputation, it might be unwise to be associated with. Garfield reluctantly bowed to their wishes and cancelled his European tour. Instead of spending the summer basking in old world culture and making a little money in the process, he had to remain in Ohio "to be nibbled and kicked at by a little-souled set of men."[52]

He really had no choice; his efforts were needed on the home front. Ashtabula County was wavering, Lake was uncertain, and in Trumbull the opposition was said to be collecting ten thousand dollars to finance an anti-Garfield newspaper. Even formerly loyal Geauga County proved capable of treachery. Rumors had reached Garfield that Delos W. Canfield, a power in Chardon, might be unreliable but in view of their long and friendly association such a betrayal seemed most unlikely. Garfield had appointed Canfield's son, Ira, to West Point and had made every effort to revoke the wartime disgrace of another member of the Canfield clan. On July 27, Garfield dined with Canfield and received assurance of friendly support. Two days later, he learned that Canfield was openly seeking the congressional nomination for himself. "He has shown himself not the highest type of friend," Garfield frowned with commendable restraint.

This unexpected defection on the eve of the primaries, he feared, now left Geauga the least certain county in the district.[53]

His fears were groundless. Austin's machine was running too smoothly to be derailed at this late date. On August 8, Republicans in every township of the 19th District caucused to select delegates to the district convention. The turnout was large, enthusiastic—and overwhelmingly pro-Garfield. The results, Hinsdale jubilantly reported, "exceeded expectation and almost belief. The enemy are not only routed but overwhelmed." From all indications, it appeared that Garfield had captured over two-thirds of the delegates and only in Trumbull County had there been a significant contest. In Geauga County, poor Canfield had not been able to carry any delegates outside of his home township. Garfield was inevitably reminded of Grant's story about the prairie wolves.

In this, "the greatest political victory of my life," Garfield had taken a giant step toward the vindication he so anxiously sought. Yet he knew to whom the triumph really belonged. To Harmon Austin went a note expressing "the very deep and almost painful sense of gratitude" he felt for "the great wisdom and ability" with which the campaign had been conducted. "For more than a year," Garfield acknowledged, "you have carried me in your heart and thought almost hourly, as few men have ever carried a friend."[54]

By convention time the opposition had collapsed and Garfield's nomination went uncontested. Thirty-four blank ballots, however, gave ominous indication that his enemies were planning to continue the struggle outside the regular party organization. Within a few weeks, "A small squad of sore-headed anti-Garfield" Republicans assembled in a splinter convention to name an independent candidate. They chose H. R. Hurlburt, a venerable Methodist elder whose plea, "Stand by me brethren!" was expected to carry considerable weight with his co-religionists. Had the Democrats joined forces with these bolters, a formidable opposition might have been created. Instead, they went their own way, nominating Dr. Daniel B. Woods, a party regular who had run against Garfield in his first campaign twelve years before. Splitting the anti-

383

Garfield vote two ways was a concession of defeat but at least it insured that Garfield would be embarrassed by running behind the rest of the Republican ticket.

Garfield buckled down to endure what promised to be "the most disagreeable campaign of my life." It lived up to his expectations. He was continually forced on the defensive, compelled to answer a host of charges dating back to the Civil War. Crédit Mobilier and DeGolyer, of course, came in for their share of attention and his entire career was dredged for more mud to sling at him. The conscription bill, his opposition to Lincoln, the Cobden Club, the Milligan case and a host of other offenses were all raised to demonstrate his unfitness. He was blamed for the depression, which, it was claimed, was a direct consequence of his tariff and fiscal policies. He was even attacked for being so often attacked. "It is always suspicious," one especially bitter newspaper charged, "when a man . . . is compelled to explain and defend at every turn. It is not characteristic of honest men." The *New York Sun,* whose editor, Charles A. Dana, had long nursed a personal grudge against Garfield, printed a four-page special edition devoted entirely to vilifying his record. Nearly a ton of these papers was imported into the district to be avidly circulated by the opposition. Curiously enough, in all this torrent of abuse the most damaging charge against Garfield remained the salary grab. That, apparently, was one offense the transplanted Yankees of the Western Reserve could never forgive.[55]

To compensate for this abuse, Garfield could take comfort from the sympathetic testimonials he received from public men. Even a Democratic congressman, William E. Niblack of Indiana, hoped that Garfield would be reelected. "Although we belong to different political organizations," Niblack generously said, "I have always found you so fair minded and clever that I have found it difficult to class you as a political opponent." Tributes from Democrats were always cherished by Garfield. "The flowers that bloom over the garden wall of party politics," he liked to say, "are the sweetest and most fragrant that bloom. . . ." For this reason, he especially appreciated the kind words of Democratic senator Allen

384

Thurman absolving him from guilt in the Crédit Mobilier affair. Ohio's other senator, Republican John Sherman, was also induced to set aside their long-standing differences and pay a "very handsome" tribute to Garfield's character at a meeting in Warren. Support of a more tangible kind came from William E. Chandler, recent Secretary of the Republican National Committee, whose personal interest in Garfield's career prompted him to contribute a thousand dollars to underwrite campaign expenses, with the promise of more if needed.[56]

This help was welcome, but the main burden of the campaign rested on the shoulders of the candidate himself. Unlike other years when he could virtually ignore his own district, this time Garfield had to show himself at every crossroads village in the Western Reserve. "I have had a hard two days work since I left you," he wrote his wife from Jefferson.

> A cold ride of eleven miles from Baconsburg, a two hours speech at Gustavus. Yesterday morning in the rain, an ugly wagon ride of 17 miles—a speech at Andover—and then a colder wagon ride of 16 miles to this place, and a speech of two hours among enemies, in reply to an ugly two hours attack made here the night before by Judge Tuttle of Painesville and a cold cheerless night at the hotel. This brings me to morning, and near to the train time to go to Conneaut to speak again among enemies. . . . This is politics as I find it this fall.[57]

It was wearisome, discouraging work. At every stop, Garfield had to defend his record and convince all who would listen that he was an honest man. His opponents challenged him to debate, but he refused: "Let my enemies draw their own crowds. I draw mine." They dogged his footsteps, throwing embarrassing questions at him from the floor until he "finally opened up" on his chief tormentor, Judge Tuttle, with "a furious attack." "I doubt if he knew, when I left him, whether he was hash or jelly," Garfield gloated.[58]

By election day, Garfield was tired but confident of a majority of at least six thousand votes over his Democratic opponent. Despite the large turnout the election passed quietly, "as it always does on the Western Reserve." The candidate relaxed by reading Goethe's biography "and letting the calm of his great life fall into my own," as he awaited

385

the returns. Before the night was out he could rejoice at his victory which he accepted quite simply as "the triumph of truth over error."[59] As expected, his margin over Woods surpassed six thousand, but Hurlburt received a total of 3,427 which caused Garfield to run about 2,800 behind the rest of the ticket.[60] Had his opponents been able to unite and had Mahoning County not been removed from the district, the outcome might have been quite different, but even so it was a commendable performance for a man who had been reading his political obituary for over a year.

The result was especially gratifying in view of the "cyclone" that struck the Republican Party that fall. Two years earlier, the Democrats had seemed on the road to extinction; now they were everywhere triumphant. In Ohio alone they captured six more congressional seats and in Congress itself the vast Republican majority melted away under the impact of Grantism and hard times. "The people have gone crazy," Garfield sadly declared[61] as he prepared himself for the strange experience of being part of the minority for the first time in his congressional career.

If all went well, he might not have to endure that experience for long. His recent trials had left him "dreadfully disgusted with public life," and he warned that "The indiscriminate assault upon public men which has so characterized the last two years will soon drive out of public life all high-minded and sensitive men." He had himself in mind. Having won the vindication he had so urgently sought, he was now ready to turn his back on an ungrateful public and enter upon a legal career in Cleveland. He had talked of this before and nothing had come of it, but there were indications that this time he was serious. The day after the election he went shopping for a lot on Cleveland's Euclid Avenue, near a neighborhood with the enticing (and, it was hoped, prophetic) nickname, "Millionaires' Row."[62]

CHAPTER EIGHTEEN

IN THE BEAR GARDEN

Despite his welcome vindication at the polls, Garfield remained disillusioned with public life. The trials through which he had passed had left their scars. "I find that I have lost much of that exuberance of feeling—that cheerful spirit which I think abounded in me before," he sadly reflected. "I am habitually graver, and less genial than I was before the storm struck me." His youth was slipping away. Birthdays had once seemed to be milestones but now, he grimly joked, they began to look more like tombstones.[1]

So too, his faith in democratic institutions was shaken by his recent ordeal. His own experience now led him to conclude that one "should not overestimate the intelligence of the average American citizen." Once a follower of John Stuart Mill, Garfield was now willing to consider the possibility that there might be more truth in Thomas Carlyle's authoritarian philosophy "than we Republicans are willing to admit." Democracy at times seemed no longer a cherished ideal, but merely the lesser evil. "Perhaps the mass of the people may not be fitted to control and manage a government," he conceded, "but if they have no voice in it, they may be more dangerous to society than if they take part in its management." He scornfully rejected the doctrine that the voice of the people is the voice of God, but he clung to the faith that American social mobility and, above all, universal education could make this perilous experiment in democracy work.[2]

As he brooded over the ingratitude of his constituents, Garfield admitted that it "requires some effort to retain one's respect for the people," and as he contemplated American society he found much to dismay him. The spectacle of municipal misgovernment convinced him that, for the cities at least, universal suffrage was a failure. There had to be something wrong with a system that gave to an immigrant or a pauper the same vote that it gave to a millionaire. To remedy urban corruption, Garfield proposed that voting be limited to men of property. "In all other business corporations the member votes in proportion to the amount of his stock. Why should not a municipal corporation be treated partially at least on the same plan?" he asked.[3] He was equally critical of the workings of the jury system, a conviction that was strengthened by the adultery trial of Henry Ward Beecher. As Garfield watched Beecher in the witness stand, delicately sniffing at a bunch of violets, his heart went out to that "great, sentimental, big-hearted booby" and he was outraged that such a "kingly intellect" should have to submit to a jury of his intellectual inferiors.[4]

The masses, Garfield felt, were all too ready to condemn men in public life. For this he blamed sensation-seeking newspapers. How could big-city newspaper editors possibly understand the real aspirations of the American people, he wondered. "Rising from Champagne suppers and entering their offices to run over the telegraph dispatches from Washington," they blithely "pronounce upon the virtues or vice, the wisdom or folly of public men at the first glance." Notwithstanding the attempts of cheap journalists to portray politics as reeking with corruption, Garfield was convinced that "the standard of public and private morals is higher in the United States at the present time than ever before . . . and that the average moral tone of Congress is higher today than at any previous period in our history."[5]

He could not give the same high marks to the Grant administration, especially in view of the way Southern affairs continued to be "so terribly botched" by the President and his friends. Louisiana was particularly troublesome. The course of events in "that wretched state" had convinced Garfield of the failure of Reconstruction, and led him to despair for the future of self-government in a state where elections were

388

regularly marked by fraud on one side and intimidation on the other and where rival governments fought it out in the streets and on the floor of the state house itself. Louisiana politics, he observed, had degenerated into a struggle between "a reckless set of scamps . . . and the armed negro-hating band of murderers."[6] If forced to choose, Garfield would side with the scamps, but his patience wore thin as it became increasingly obvious that they were kept in office only by the support of federal bayonets. His patience snapped altogether early in 1875 when federal troops invaded the state house and expelled enough Democrats to enable the Republicans to organize the Louisiana legislature. This, Garfield cried in dismay, was "the darkest day for the Republican party . . . I have ever seen since the war." Such a "rash and indefensible act," he predicted, would be the signal for "a general howl of indignation throughout the country" which could only give further comfort to the already resurgent Democrats. Bleakly, he concluded that "all the Gods had conspired to destroy the Republican Party," and he contemplated making an open break with the President who had proved to be such a "millstone around the neck of our party."[7]

The worst part of the whole wretched Louisiana muddle, Garfield feared, was that it would very likely inspire a reaction in the North that could undo the work of Reconstruction and lead to the abandonment of the Negro. He tried to counter this tendency by pleading for further civil rights legislation. "God taught us early in this fight that the fate of our own race was indissolubly linked with that of the black man . . . ," he reminded his colleagues. "Justice to them has always been safety for us." There was little response. The truth was, as Garfield realized, that the public was bored with the Negro and tired of hearing about Southern outrages. He feared that the Republican Party had squandered too much of its moral capital. "The most extreme passions abound in the two parties, and I cannot forsee the end," he said dejectedly.[8]

Fortunately for Garfield's peace of mind, he could take comfort in two welcome, though flawed, successes: one domestic; the other political. The day after Christmas, as he and

389

his wife were sitting quietly at home, reading Shakespeare aloud, they came to a passage from *King John*:

> "But on my liege; for very little pains
> Will bring this labor to a happy end."

At that propitious moment, Lucretia felt her first labor pain and a few hours later she was delivered of a baby boy. Little Mollie burst into tears when she learned she would not have a sister but her father, who had wanted another daughter, consoled himself with a pun: "We receive not, when we ask amiss." A month and a half later the new baby was still without a name. His parents had prepared only girls' names and besides, as Garfield wearily admitted, "the sixth is a little harder to name than the first or second." Eventually they settled on Edward, nicknamed Neddie, and even Mollie reconciled herself to life in a household of boys.[9]

Garfield greeted the appearance of a long-awaited legislative brainchild with the same mixed emotions he had felt at the birth of Neddie. The resumption of specie payments had long been his most cherished legislative goal. At times he had despaired of its ultimate passage and as recently as the preceding spring it had seemed as though the House would be irreparably swept away by the inflationist tide. When the 43rd Congress assembled in December for its "lame duck" session, Garfield had wistfully hoped that the Republican Party might use "these last precious weeks of its power" to strike one final, gallant blow for honest money, but he admitted that such a course seemed unlikely. To his surprise, a bill providing for specie resumption did emerge from John Sherman's Senate Finance Committee. Garfield had nothing to do with the bill's preparation and, indeed, he was not even sure that he completely approved of it. A compromise measure, the bill contained a number of disturbing concessions to soft-money sentiment. Furthermore, it put off specie resumption until January 1, 1879, which would give the inflationists ample time to wriggle out of the commitment unless constant vigilance were exerted. "The bill is a weak and insufficient measure," Garfield complained, but he voted for it anyway. "It is an instance where we are compelled to accept a part when we cannot get the whole."[10]

As the 43rd Congress wound up its work, Garfield drew satisfaction from the record speed with which his appropriation bills sailed through the House. It was his last opportunity to exercise the skills he had acquired in four years' experience as head of the Appropriations Committee. The next Congress would be controlled by the Democrats who would retain their majority throughout the remainder of Garfield's congressional career. Never again would he be given command of a committee; from now on he would have to make his mark as a leader of the opposition.

Relieved of committee responsibility, Garfield was at last free to take up that long-deferred California trip that had been interrupted in 1865. Jay Gould, who had apparently forgiven the harsh accusations Garfield had made during the Gold Panic investigation six years earlier, graciously placed a private car at his disposal. Lucretia was forced to stay behind to look after the family, but Garfield had them follow his progress on a map and turned each letter into a little history and geography lesson for the children. Always the pedagogue, he set them puzzles to solve: "When I went to bed it was just 12 o'clock at night by Toledo time, but it was 12:28 by my watch, which is Washington time. Now please take a piece of paper out of the lower drawer of my desk, and cipher out how many degrees west of Washington I am."[11]

The Pacific coast lived up to his expectations, but the Yosemite Valley proved to be the most overpowering experience of the trip. The old rhetoric of his Hiram schooldays came gushing back as "In the midst of this immensity," he felt "the infinite littleness of man, when in the presence of God's mighty architecture." He rode down from the mountaintop "slowly and in awed and hushed silence. . . ."[12] And, he might have added, in extreme discomfort, for the cross-country ride had brought on a recurrance of his hemorrhoid affliction—"My thorn in the flesh," as he delicately called it.

The infirmity persisted, even after his return to Washington. Home remedies proved useless and Garfield was so alarmed at losing eighteen pounds in three weeks that he decided to call in a surgeon. When the operation was underway, it was discovered that Garfield had underestimated his malady.

Instead of hemorrhoids, he had actually been suffering from a rectal ulcer, "as large as a quarter of a dollar," which may have contributed to his chronic "dyspepsia." For the rest of the hot Washington summer, Garfield lay bed-ridden at home, alternately staring at the clouds and reading "charming, silly old Bozzy's Journal to the Hebrides" while Lucretia traced Boswell's path on a map of Scotland.[13]

As he tossed in his sickbed, Garfield longed to take the field once more against the "fanatical demagogues" of the opposition. His opportunity would come with the opening of the 44th Congress—the first Democratic-controlled House since 1859. Garfield was dropped from the Appropriations Committee, "on the ground that my thorough knowledge of the matter would be an embarrassment to the Chairman," and was assigned to Ways and Means and to the Pacific Railroad committees instead. After their long absence from power, the Democrats were hard put to find enough experienced parliamentarians to manage the business of the House. The committee chairmen, Garfield scoffed, were the weakest in forty years. By Garfield's count, 21 of the 34 most important chairmen were from the old slave states, many of them former Confederates only recently restored to political activity. "This is the old Southern rule returning again with a vengeance," he grumbled. Yet this conspicuous predominance of former rebels gave the Republicans a golden opportunity to "raise the old war spirit of our people. That," he shrewdly calculated, "is our main hope."[14]

A friend had once suggested that Garfield might prove ineffective in his new role as member of the opposition; that he was too high-minded to grapple in the "bear-garden" of partisanship. He overestimated Garfield's delicacy. Within a few weeks of the opening of the 44th Congress, Garfield (following the lead of Blaine) had seized the initiative from the bewildered Democrats and sent them reeling onto the defensive. The occasion was a Democratic proposal to grant amnesty to that small band of former rebels who were still barred from public life. Blaine at once leaped to the attack by moving to exclude Jefferson Davis, not because he had been president of the Confederacy but on the novel grounds

392

that Davis had been personally responsible for the horrors of Andersonville prison. His speech created the expected sensation and the Southerners were goaded into unwise replies. Blaine overdid it, as he tended to overdo things, and "lost his temper and some reputation," but Garfield saw in the "insolent and wicked" reply of Ben Hill of Georgia an opening by which the debate could be salvaged. The next day he obtained the floor to deliver a reply to Hill. The atmosphere was electric. "For ten years I have not seen so much passion and excitement in the House," he reported. "When I rose to speak the galleries were crowded to the utmost and hundreds went away who could not get in."[15]

His speech struck a somewhat more elevated tone than had Blaine's, but the intent was the same: to indict Jefferson Davis as a war criminal for the atrocities at Andersonville. In conclusion, he pleaded, "for the sake of three hundred thousand heroic men who, maimed and bruised, drag out their weary lives, many of them carrying in their hearts horrible memories of what they suffered in the prison pen,—do not ask us to restore the right to hold power to that man who was the cause of their suffering,—that man still unshriven, unforgiven, undefended." The impact of the speech, with its dramatic waving of telegrams and its startling revelations, was, if anything, more sensational than Blaine's. President Grant personally thanked Garfield on behalf of a presumably grateful nation, and the Republican National Committee printed literally millions of copies for use in the coming campaign. They had reason to be pleased. Garfield and Blaine had succeeded in turning public attention for the moment away from the current difficulties of the Republican Party and back to the old, dependable issues of the Civil War.[16]

With the battered Grant administration staggering from scandal to scandal, any such diversion was welcome. The most sensational of these scandals broke shortly after the amnesty debate and, in an oblique way, it involved Garfield. Early in 1872, his old comrade, General Hazen, then serving in the West, had informed Garfield of serious corruption at Fort Sill. The post trader there, he claimed, had bought the right to monopolize trade on the base and was charging the soldiers exorbitant prices. His information seemed to implicate the Secretary of War, William W. Belknap, in the whole shady business. Garfield was outraged at these revelations and showed Hazen's letter to John Coburn, chairman of the Military Affairs Committee. The two congressmen proposed to launch an investigation into the affair which, Garfield promised, would "drive a six horse team through the whole establishment." It turned out to be somewhat less thorough than that. Had they probed deeply, they would have discovered that the post traders had obtained their commissions through the most blatant bribery and that they had retained them by sending regular cash payments to the Secretary of War and his wife. Yet somehow in the course of the investigation, Secretary Belknap's complicity was overlooked. The only result was an innocuous directive from the War Department reforming the post tradership system—a reform which was loudly praised and then quietly ignored. Garfield publicly declared that the abuses had been corrected and a few months later went out of his way to extol Belknap on the floor of Congress. Despite what Hazen and others had told him, he could still say, with apparent sincerity: "I know of no Secretary of War during all of my public life who in reference to the extablishment of barracks and posts has shown so much thorough economy as the present Secretary of War."[17]

Cleared by Coburn and Garfield, Belknap was free to continue the corrupt arrangement at Fort Sill until 1876, when he was finally exposed. Garfield reacted to the expose with as much shocked surprise as if it were something new, even though most of these revelations had been available to him four years earlier. The House, stunned as it had not been since the death of Lincoln, immediately drew up articles of impeachment, but the Secretary of War artfully evaded punishment by resigning before he could be impeached. Fearful of a public outcry that might implicate them, Coburn and Garfield hastily cleared their skirts by writing each other letters (designed for publication) in which they solemnly denied having had any prior inkling of Belknap's guilt. This was a clumsy evasion and betrayed panic. Had their denials been challenged, it would have created the impression that the congressmen had something to hide when, in fact, they had sinned only through omission. Fortunately for Garfield's already bruised reputation, his explanation was generally accepted at face value and he was spared what could have been a major embarrassment.[18]

In contrast to Garfield's unseemly panic, President Grant displayed remarkable coolness when confronted with the disgrace of his favorite minister. He told Garfield that the first he learned of the affair was when Belknap burst into his breakfast "nearly suffocated with excitement" and blurted out an incoherent story. After accepting the distraught Secretary's resignation, Grant had walked nonchalantly to an artist's studio to pose for his portrait. "His imperturbability is amazing," Garfield marveled. "I am in doubt whether to call it greatness or stupidity."[19]

Somewhere between 1872 and 1876, Garfield had evidently misplaced his sense of moral indignation, at least so far as Belknap's tawdry corruption was concerned. Then he had been outraged; now he seemed mainly concerned with the effect the scandal might have on the fortunes of the Republican Party during this critical presidential year. He was relieved to discover, during a trip to New Hampshire, that the Belknap affair would not cost more than a few hundred votes in that state. Yet he realized that the party faced serious trouble in the coming months unless it could cast off the burden of Grantism, of which the Belknap affair was only a symbol.

The first step was to "throw off the third term nightmare," and scotch the alarming rumors that Grant might run again. The next step was to find a respectable candidate free from the taint of the present administration. Garfield was willing to support either of two men: Benjamin Bristow or James G. Blaine. Bristow was the candidate of the reformers. As Secretary of the Treasury, he had uncovered the frauds of the St. Louis Whiskey Ring, a public service for which Grant never forgave him. To Garfield, Bristow's hard-money convictions and crusading zeal were so appealing that he put the Treasury Secretary at the top of his list of presidential hopefuls, even ahead of Blaine. "Bristow is a higher type of man," Garfield explained, "and I should feel that his election would need no apology." Blaine, in contrast, was certainly not "the highest type of a reformer," as Garfield admitted with wry understatement.[20]

Garfield held few illusions about Blaine. "He is by no means my ideal of statesmanship," he bluntly confessed. He freely acknowledged that Blaine was an intriguer, that he was overly ambitious and that he was untrustworthy (as his own experience amply demonstrated). Yet in spite of all this, Garfield was bewitched by Blaine's famous "magnetic" personality and would remain under its spell for the rest of his life. The attraction was not hard to understand. Garfield's emotional life had been stunted by the curse of intellectual objectivity. His capacity for detachment and self-doubt at times paralyzed his will and rendered him incapable of any emotion stronger than sentimentality. Blaine, on the other hand, lived at a high pitch of emotional intensity, verging on hysteria, which was kept in check only by his massive self-assurance. Unlike Garfield, he never doubted, never hesitated, never wavered—especially when his own interests were at stake. "When I want a thing," he admitted, "I want it dreadfully." Garfield was overwhelmed by Blaine's unfailing vitality. In contrast, his own placid existence seemed but a pallid half-life, devoid of genuine deep feeling. Once, when speaking of his admiration for the historian Macaulay, Garfield admitted: "I am strongly drawn to the brave bold scholar, who loved so strongly and hated so royally. I am a poor hater." With the elimination of the word "scholar", this confession could stand as an explanation of Garfield's attachment to Blaine.[21]

Although the Speaker consistently disappointed his friend in the assignment of committee posts, Garfield continued to serve Blaine loyally. Once, when their mutual friend, Eugene Hale, was tempted to accept a place in Grant's cabinet, Garfield sent Hale a vaguely threatening warning that had all the earmarks of Blaine's style. Would not a cabinet seat, he asked Hale, compromise your relations with "our dear Blaine, from whose future we both expect so much?" Hale took the hint and turned down Grant's offer. Blaine was so confident of Garfield's dependability that he even asked him to perform such disreputable errands as blackmailing Roscoe Conkling to call off a Senate investigation into Blaine's financial dealings. Consequently, it was hardly surprising that Garfield should ultimately choose to wheel in line behind Blaine's banner despite his lingering suspicion that Bristow might be the better man. "I wish Blaine were less of a politician," Garfield concluded, "but I believe he would make a good President."[22]

The presidential sweepstakes of 1876 was run on an exceptionally crowded track. On the Republican side, in addition to Blaine and Bristow, both Roscoe Conkling and Oliver P. Morton were contending for the mantle of President Grant. To Garfield, who thought that eight years of Grantism had been more than enough, the prospect of either of these presidential cronies winning the nomination was so repugnant that he vowed to desert the party rather than support them. Far less disturbing were the reports of the growing strength of Governor Rutherford B. Hayes of Ohio. Though he had never been particularly close to Hayes, Garfield did respect him, especially after the governor had endorsed the sound-money position. There were more practical grounds for supporting the candidacy of the bland Ohioan. Some political observers suspected that he might prove stronger at the polls than many better-known but more controversial party leaders. "It is alleged by those in favor of Hayes," they claimed, "that no story will stick to him to his injury, that he was born lucky on that score and is just the kind of man to run because no nickname or slang phrase can be pinned to him."[23]

Garfield encouraged the governor's hopes. "I am greatly gratified at the way you are bearing yourself during these preliminary months of platform and president making," he wrote. "I have believed from the beginning that . . . we should give you the solid vote of the Ohio delegation and await the break which must come as the weaker candidates drop out." Hayes was deeply moved by Garfield's words of support but failed to realize how ambiguous they were. To Garfield, Hayes was one of those "weaker candidates," whom he expected to fall by the wayside. As he told a friend, "I do not find that the mention of his name excites much enthusiasm

397

outside of Ohio. He would make an eminently respectable President, and I should be glad on many accounts to see him elected. Still, he certainly would not be the strongest man we could choose." Garfield hoped to use Hayes as a stalking-horse to hold the Ohio delegation together until it could swing its strength at the proper moment to Blaine. To further this plan, he encouraged Blain supporters to go to the convention pledged to the governor but ready to switch whenever Hayes's strength should fade.[24]

The strategy had been devised by Blaine himself. Like everything he planned, it was clever, but Garfield, who did not share Blaine's faith in the "machinery of politics," was skeptical of all such preconvention tactics. His observations had taught him that "few men in our history have ever obtained the Presidency by planning to obtain it. In most cases it is got by the result, partly of accident, and partly of the popular sentiment seizing hold of a man who has not done much about it himself." Garfield's own career would demonstrate the truth of this lesson but Blaine never grasped it. The unabashed zeal with which he pursued his goal not only created widespread distrust but it also exposed him to the counterplotting of his rivals.[25]

Early that spring, as delegates were being chosen for the forthcoming Republican convention, the newspapers were filled with rumors that Blaine had improperly used his position as Speaker of the House to promote the interests of the Little Rock & Fort Smith Railroad and thereby enrich himself. Blaine loudly claimed that these attacks were directed by southerners in retaliation for his role in the recent amnesty debates, but Garfield learned that it was not Democrats but rival Republicans who were behind these charges. One April afternoon, he was summoned by Blaine to a committee room. There he found Blaine closeted with a man named Timoney, who proceeded to unfold a tangled tale of intrigue. According to Timoney, whose information had an authentic ring, the attacks on Blaine were part of a plot engineered by his archfoe Roscoe Conkling, with the aid of his cronies, Alonzo Cornell of New York, Senator Stephen W. Dorsey of Arkansas and George C. Gorham, Secretary of the

Senate. It was they who had supplied the press with incriminating stories concerning Blaine's railroad dealings, cleverly
timing the revelations so as to inflict maximum damage to his
presidential prospects. Garfield was deeply distressed by
Timoney's disclosures, not so much for what they suggested
about Blaine—for he dismissed that out of hand—but for the
further evidence they supplied of the "shameful way our public
men are assaulted."[26]

Blaine was also distressed, but for more pressing reasons.
If Timoney's story were true, this was one more score for
Blaine to settle with Conkling, but no matter what the source,
these accusations had to be dealt with quickly or else Blaine's
chances for the presidency would be hopelessly lost. He leaped
to the counterattack, vigorously denying all wrongdoing. His
task, however, was complicated when a disgruntled clerk
named Mulligan appeared in Washington bearing a packet
of letters which, he hinted, contained proof of Blaine's corrupt
railroad dealings. Blaine managed to snatch the letters away
from Mulligan, but he was caught, as Garfield realized, in
a dilemma: "If he publishes the letters they will probably
afford materials for a campaign scandal. If he refuses people
will say there is something very criminal in them." He was
inclined to believe that Blaine ought to keep the letters to
himself "and lose the presidency rather than surrender a
private right." But Blaine was gifted with a touch of reckless
audacity that Garfield lacked. The next day he boldly read
selected portions of the letters to a spellbound House, ending
by turning the tables on his accusers by demonstrating that
they had suppressed evidence favorable to him. This
"evidence" was inconclusive and had, in any event, been
manufactured by Blaine himself, but the electrified audience
was unaware of these details. Congressmen cheered themselves hoarse, and Blaine was mobbed by well-wishers. Garfield, too, was swept off his feet by the excitement. "I have
never witnessed so dramatic a scene since I have been in the
House," he gasped. "It may give Blaine the nomination."[27]

Cynics might scoff at Blaine's theatrics but Garfield was
convinced. Sympathetic almost by reflex to anyone whose
character was under attack,[28] he rejoiced at Blaine's trium-

phant vindication. Only the presidency was now needed to make his friend's victory over slander complete and that, Garfield believed, was well within Blaine's grasp, "unless they lie him to death." The Sunday before the Republican convention was scheduled to meet in Cincinnati, that figure of speech suddenly assumed a frightening reality when Blaine dramatically collapsed at the door of the Congregational Church on his way to worship. Carried unconscious to his home, he lay in a near-coma for days, unable to move or speak or answer any further questions about his railroad affairs.

Garfield was so distressed by Blaine's tragic plight that he could hardly sleep. If Blaine should die, he said bitterly, "it will be the work of political assassination, as really as though he had been stabbed to death." He tried to make himself useful, solicitously manning the telegraph line that linked the ailing candidate's bedside to the Cincinnati convention. The reports that clicked over the wires indicated that Blaine's illness was creating a tidal wave of sympathy among the delegates, but it was also giving rise to an understandable apprehension about the state of his health. On the morning before the convention was due to open, Blaine still lay unconscious, though Garfield suspected that he understood much of what was said around him. A conference was scheduled for that morning to decide whether or not to withdraw Blaine's candidacy. Shortly before it met, Blaine stirred himself, sat up and "took the matter into his own hands by writing a connected and beautiful dispatch." "The cloud has lifted," Garfield rejoiced, "and he is himself again."[29]

It was not quite enough. After leading for six ballots, Blaine was stopped just short of victory when the convention turned with a rush to Hayes. Garfield swallowed his disappointment. He immediately pledged his support to the party's nominee and bombarded him with good advice. He urged Hayes to wage his campaign on the issues of civil service reform and resumption of specie payments. When he read the nominee's letter of acceptance, "a very clear and sensible document," Garfield was flattered to find that his suggestions had been incorporated. As the campaign progressed, however, and it became apparent that the Republican party was facing the most desperate challenge of its career, Hayes began to advocate more emotional issues, such as the danger of handing over the government to the rebels and the public schools to the Catholics.

Hayes repeatedly pressed the Catholic issue on Garfield, urging that it be raised in every speech. Garfield was not blind to the Catholic menace. A loyal Mason, he had earlier led an unsuccessful struggle against granting federal funds to the Little Sisters of the Poor of Washington, and was well aware that "the batteries that are levelled at our school system are planted on the Vatican." Still, he could not get as worked up over the religious question as could Blaine, who had a Catholic background to live down, or as Hayes, who had successfully exploited the issue in the past. Garfield preferred to concentrate his fire on the Democrats rather than on their papal cohorts.[30]

That the Democratic Party was unfit to govern seemed a self-evident proposition to Garfield. Its followers were clearly drawn from the most disreputable elements of society. The sheriff of Portage County assured him that of the fifteen prisoners in county jail, fourteen were Democrats, confirming Garfield's suspicion that a large segment of the criminal class belonged to that party. Their elected representatives were scarcely any better. "This Democratic House is the most inefficient and discordant body I have ever been a member of," Garfield complained. "It was a good thing for the country that they got into power just enough to show their character." In case the country had not noticed the shameful behavior of the Democrats in Congress, Garfield developed this theme on every possible occasion, reminding whoever would listen that "the Democratic party has been and is now submissive to the despots of the South, that they are wrong and the Republican party right every time."[31]

The major elaboration of this simple, yet heartening, message was cast in the form of a reply to a speech by Mississippi congressman Lucius Quintus Cincinnatus Lamar. Lamar, whom Garfield admired as "by far the ablest Democrat in the House," delivered in the closing days of the

401

session a polished defense of the Democratic party that was designed to set the tone for the approaching campaign. The speech was the result of months of thought on Lamar's part; Garfield was expected to deliver an equally brilliant reply by the next morning. He sat at his desk at home, oppressed with "the despondent feeling that when I do get to the floor I shall not succeed." Despite his doubts, he rose the next morning to deliver what he later judged to be "one of the best speeches I ever made." Although its theme was a familiar one—the Democrats are not yet fit to be trusted—in its polished delivery and impressive research, the speech betrayed none of its hasty preparation. The effort left him exhausted. When he came home, his clothes were still drenched with sweat, and his overtaxed constitution bore witness that he had passed his physical prime.[32]

His weariness was soon forgotten in the face of the torrent of "absurdly extravagant" praise the speech evoked. "My friends talk like crazy men about it," he reported. Luke Poland compared it to Webster's classic reply to Hayne. "It ought to make your name immortal," he said to the man he had recently censured. Garfield was bombarded with hundreds of requests for copies and the Republican National Committee struck off an edition of four hundred thousand to meet the demand. The enthusiasm was not quite universal. Burke Hinsdale, who had hoped for a high-level campaign, was dismayed to see his friend wave the tattered "bloody shirt" once more. He notified Garfield that "if the presidential campaign is to be conducted on that key, I don't see how I can have much interest in it." Hayes, on the other hand, was delighted. Garfield's speech was thoroughly in line with the strategy the candidate had suggested to Blaine. "Our strongest ground," he argued, "is the dread of a Solid South, rebel rule, etc. . . . It leads people away from 'hard times' which is our deadliest foe."[33]

Indeed, unless heroic countermeasures were taken, it seemed as if hard times might overtake the Republican Party itself. Garfield could scarcely bring himself to believe "that the providence which has preserved our nation thus far would permit such a calamity as the ascendency of the rebel party," but such a possibility seemed frighteningly real. To help avert it, he decided to defer once more his long-deferred retirement from politics in order to campaign for the party ticket. He promised himself that this would be his last campaign. If he waited much longer it would be too late to start a new career as a lawyer and he could find himself trapped for the rest of his life in his present dreary "tread-mill round of burdensome duties." There was another possibility to be considered. With the recent elevation of Blaine to the Senate, the Speakership lay vacant and Garfield was assured that the prize could be his if the Republicans captured the House. Consequently, even though he admitted that he was "not at all happy in the prospect of continuing in Congress," and even though he had all but concluded a partnership with a Cleveland law firm, he decided to stand again for Congress and authorized Harmon Austin to pass the word quietly to his friends.[34]

This decision heartened his friends but dismayed the many local politicians who had been eyeing Garfield's congressional seat for so long. One editor reminded his readers that "We have other ambitious, honorable and right able men, whose patriotic hearts are burning, whose eloquent tongues are quivering, and whose zealous souls are yearning to be offered up as a sacrifice upon the Congressional altar. Life is short," he pleaded. "Give the boys a chance." One of these long-frustrated aspirants, Stephen A. Northway, entered the race in response to a petition signed by 140 of his townsmen who declared that "the time has come *when the office ought to seek the man.*" "As a commentary on this doctrine," Garfield dryly observed, "Northway is riding through the district to give the office a chance to find him." Northway's quest was unsuccessful and he soon dropped out of contention, as did all others who harbored thoughts of challenging Garfield's nomination. "The enemy see that they are beaten and they are now flocking to our side in droves," Harmon Austin reported gleefully. No civil service reformer, Austin used his political machine to promote his friend's career. "It is quite well understood here," he explained to Garfield, "that your friends control the offices of this county and all the office seekers are very polite. I tell you *it is a comfort*," said Austin, to see old enemies "get down on their knees for the little offices that they now see your friends control."[35]

With such support, Garfield's unanimous nomination was no surprise. What was surprising was the enthusiasm it evoked from so many former opponents. After the convention, as he doctored his hand, made lame from the grasp of so many well-wishers, he cynically reflected that the change in public sentiment, "though personally gratifying to me, does not enhance my respect for the popular steadiness of judgement." The opposition, however, had not vanished. It had simply given up hope of capturing the Republican organization and was now concentrating its efforts on a fusion movement with the Democrats. An anti-Garfield convention immediately assembled in Painesville to denounce their congressman for his "systematic corruption, perjury and bribery." "You was charged of every crime committed in this country and Europe this last two centuries," a spy informed Garfield. The convention nominated General John S. Casement, not as a Democrat or a Republican, but as a Reformer. Garfield was not worried by this development. "Let my enemies separate themselves so that all good men may know them and remember them," he calmly responded. Casement's campaign aroused little support. Had the opposition been able to unite two years earlier, it might have posed a formidable threat, but it was now too late. The charges against Garfield had grown stale with repetition and Democrats could not be expected to summon much enthusiasm for a Reform candidate whose platform was almost indistinguishable from that of his Republican adversary. Even the local Grangers threw their support to Garfield.[36]

Garfield spent most of the campaign outside the district working for the national ticket. In Hayes he had found, for the first time since he had entered politics, a presidential candidate "whose stuff and spirit one can wholly approve of." The Democratic candidate, Samuel Tilden, was reputed to be a reformer and a gentleman, but Garfield was not deceived. He knew that Tilden's followers were rebels and riff-raff and he quivered with "alarm and apprehension" at the thought of their victory. To prevent such an "irretrievable calamity" he spoke in every state the party thought his voice would carry votes, leaving his own campaign to run itself.[37] Despite his neglect, the old 19th responded loyally, giving him over sixty percent of the vote. Casement drew over 11,000 votes; more than any of Garfield's previous challengers had ever received, but this was due to the exceptionally large voter turnout in this exciting presidential year. Garfield himself received almost as many votes as had been cast for all three candidates two years earlier.[38]

The triumph was short-lived. A few days after his victory, as he was delivering a campaign speech in New Jersey, Garfield was handed a telegram summoning him home. His son Neddie was dangerously ill. An attack of whooping cough had apparently "left his brain in a state of exhaustion." When his father reached his bedside, Neddie was unconscious. He lay there for four days, gasping his tiny life away. The doctor confirmed that there was nothing to be done but wait for the end, and that evening the family ate their dinner "in the sadness of choking hearts." The next morning, Harry and Jim saw their mother pacing the halls, wringing her hands and sobbing. Composing herself, she sent them off to school "with a very gentle caress." When they were walking home for lunch with Charlie Plunkett, they saw a wreath of white crepe hanging on the door and Charlie gulped, "Guess he's dead." When they got home, as Harry remembered, "Jim and I were afraid to go into [Neddie's] room at first, but Papa finally persuaded us to go in with him. The great strong man was so sorrowful, and yet so loving that we almost felt that death must be something less terrible than we supposed." Garfield tried to console his children by teaching them "the better and more cheerful view of death," but privately he admitted that "the hurt stays in spite of all our philosophy." With tender sorrow he watched his last-born child laid to rest on Hiram Hill next to his first-born.[39]

The day after the funeral, Garfield was met by a blaring brass band and escorted through town in a torch-light parade to deliver a stump speech for Hayes before a wildly cheering crowd. "It was hard to push away the thoughts of darling

405

Neddy," he reflected, "—but it seemed to be a duty." The perils of the presidential campaign demanded that he suppress his private grief for the public good. He tried to convince himself that "the good sense and patriotism of the country" would never permit "the destiny of the nation to pass into the control of the rebels," but all the signs indicated that the election would be dangerously close. In New York, gamblers were offering two-to-one odds on Tilden. Garfield interpreted their confidence as further proof that the Democrats intended to steal the election. "I did not intend ever again to become so deeply interested in any campaign," he nervously admitted but, despite his intentions, election day found him filled with deep forebodings.[40]

CHAPTER NINETEEN

RETRIEVING THE IRRETRIEVABLE
CALAMITY

On election eve of 1876, as Garfield watched the returns
come in, it seemed as if his worst fears were about to be
realized. The Democrats had clearly captured the House of
Representatives and he saw his hopes for the Speakership
"gone down in the general wreck" of his party's fortunes.
It appeared that the presidency was lost as well. Surveying
the wreckage, Garfield concluded that "we are defeated by
the combined power of rebellion, Catholicism and whiskey"
—an analysis which anticipated in substance the Reverend
Dr. Burchard's famous "Rum, Romanism and Rebellion"
remark, though it lacked that minister's alliterative flair.[1]
While Garfield gloomily pondered his party's defeat, others
managed to discern a flicker of hope. Alert Republican managers quickly challenged the returns from the three Southern
states still under carpetbag control: Florida, South Carolina
and Louisiana. These states had first been announced for
Tilden, but if they could somehow be salvaged for the Republican ticket, Hayes could claim 185 electoral votes, one more
than necessary for victory.

The votes of these three disputed Southern states immediately became the focus of national concern. Political
managers of both parties crowded the trains heading south,
anxious to be on the scene to insure a favorable count for
their side. Much to his surprise, Garfield found himself among
their number. The day after the election, President Grant

asked him to go to Louisiana, "to see that the canvass of the vote is a fair one." At first Garfield had been inclined to refuse the request, but after the President assured him that the other "visiting statesmen" were all to be Republicans of impeccable integrity, he decided to accept. Garfield realized that this assignment placed him in a delicate position. Neither he nor the President had any legal authority to intervene in what was purely a local affair and he feared that he could act only in "a personal and irresponsible way, with the danger that I might be considered an intermeddler." There was the further danger that whatever he did in Louisiana might involve him in a partisan controversy "which would call down upon me all the passion of this passionate hour." To avoid this hazard, he made a promise to himself to avoid partisanship and to behave in Louisiana only as a neutral observer. "The day of choice is past," he sternly proclaimed. "We have only one duty, to ascertain who is elected and see that he is so declared."[2]

Undoubtedly he meant well, but this was not the sort of promise Garfield was able to keep. The stakes were too high and passion ran too deep. Despite his good intentions, Garfield could not help favoring the Republican side of any controversy. Soon after his arrival in Louisiana, even before he had a chance to examine the evidence, he had already made up his mind that Hayes was entitled to the state. This opinion was confirmed by his hosts in New Orleans, Lionel Sheldon and Don Pardee, two old comrades of army days who had gone south after the War to seek their fortunes and to dabble in local Republican politics. Neither could be considered an impartial observer (Sheldon was, in fact, a Hayes elector) and both men, as they bitterly told their distinguished house guest, would be forced to flee the state should the Democrats ever gain power.[3]

Under these circumstances, it was asking too much of Garfield that he hold to his pledge of neutrality. With injudicious haste, he decided that "the honest voice" of the people of Louisiana had spoken "clearly and decidedly" for Hayes. Yet he realized that to make this conclusion "so plain and clear as to satisfy an incredulous and suspicious public opinion" would prove a difficult task. At first glance, it seemed to be an impossible one. Unlike Florida and South Carolina, where the Democratic margins were paper-thin, in Louisiana the Republicans had to overcome a deficit of more than seven thousand votes. This posed a formidable challenge, but Republican managers were hopeful that with sufficient ingenuity they could rise to the occasion. The most promising approach seemed to be through the Louisiana system which gave to a state returning board the power to approve as well as count all ballots. This board was safely Republican and could be expected to do its duty.

Garfield was one of ten "distinguished Northern visitors" (five from each party) invited to witness the Board's work. The count began on a bitter cold day. Roses and orange groves were in bloom, but to Garfield, huddled close to a stove and wearing his overcoat, the treacherous weather seemed to symbolize the people of Louisiana, "who smile in the morning and murder at night." As he listened to the tangled tale of fraud and violence unfold, he was confirmed in his long-standing distaste for Louisiana politics. "I have been in what seemed a different world from ours," he reflected, "—a world in which the modes of thought and action are, in many respects, un-American and un-Republican." The testimony reinforced his contempt for "the Latin races"—a people that so clearly lacked "the genius for self government."[4]

As the investigators probed into the election, the conclusion seemed inescapable that Tilden had won a majority of the ballots that had actually been cast. But did that represent the true voice of the state? Garfield and other Republicans thought not. They argued that the Democrats had, by "the most malignant cunning," so intimidated and "bulldozed" the Negroes as to prevent Republicans from casting their votes. Before the election, Democrats had organized "rifle clubs" which had paraded fully-armed before the terrorized Negroes, breaking up Republican meetings and threatening violence to any Negro who dared to vote. Those who refused to buckle under this pressure were whipped and, in some cases, murdered to discourage the others. "I know of nothing in modern history so destructive of popular government, and so shocking to humanity as the conduct of the Rebel Democracy . . . in Louisiana," Garfield said. "They acted upon a preconcerted plan and intended to do just enough violence and murder to accomplish their purpose and no more."[5]

Abandoning their passive role of observers, the outraged Republican "visiting statesmen" widened the scope of their investigation. (Garfield and Sherman were accused of carrying their investigations even further, into one of the fancier New Orleans brothels, a charge they convincingly denied.[6]) John Sherman, the leader of the group, assigned each of his colleagues a "bulldozed" parish to examine. Garfield was responsible for West Feliciana Parish, a district that, on the face of the returns, had gone Democratic by a 471 vote majority. In past elections, however, this parish had consistently given the Republicans a safe margin of from eight to twelve hundred votes. "These facts," Garfield argued, "carry upon their face the strongest presumption that a sudden and unusual disturbance of the political elements has changed the ordinary relations of parties in the parish." He attributed this change to the work of the Democratic "rifle clubs" or "committees of safety" which, according to the evidence before him, had intimidated potential Negro voters. In preparing his report, Garfield did more than merely analyze the evidence at hand. He personally sought out the witnesses, interviewed them, polished their testimony and, very likely, coached them for future appearances.[7]

Fortified by such support from the "visiting statesmen," the Returning Board threw out thousands of Democratic ballots in the bulldozed parishes. West Feliciana was redeemed from its Democratic majority and given a Republican margin of 386 votes, while enough votes were garnered from other parishes to enable the official vote of the state to be awarded to Hayes. Irate Democrats, seeing the presidency slip from their grasp, screamed "Fraud!" They charged that the Returning Board was illegally constituted and blatantly corrupt, that the evidence of intimidation had been manufactured and that the witnesses were openly for sale to the highest bidder. Garfield was unmoved. "Which ever way the vote of the state may be counted," he calmly concluded, "the other side will complain; but if good men find any fault with Louisiana for rejecting the vote of the intimidated parishes I shall be greatly surprised."[8]

With his Louisiana mission safely accomplished, Garfield returned to Washington, after a brief stopover at Columbus to reassure Governor Hayes. His train carried him across a nation which seemed to be trembling on the edge of civil war. Both Democrats and Republicans were vowing to fight rather than surrender the White House. Some Democrats had adopted the grisly slogan, "Tilden or blood," a threat punctuated by the bullet which crashed through Governor Hayes's front window one evening. Garfield's Republican constituents were no less determined. One, a Union veteran, offered to reassemble his old cavalry regiment to ride on Washington, while another thundered: "we whipped them once and by the eternal we can again."[9]

For his part, Garfield was "tired of the namby-pamby way in which many of our Republicans treat public questions," and was resolved to speak out "more frankly and boldly" than ever before in what promised to be "the most violent and passionate debate" of his congressional career. He was not alarmed by all this talk of war. For one thing, he was convinced that the Democrats lacked the nerve to carry out their threats. For another, he could sniff a scent of compromise stirring in the air. He had scarcely arrived at Washington when L. Q. C. Lamar, the leading spokesman for conservative Southern Democrats, invited him to stop by for a chat. From their conversation Garfield deduced that "Wise management may break the strength of the Southern Democracy," a suspicion that was strengthened during the following days by the stream of Southerners who went out of their way to drop conciliatory hints in his direction. If these Southerners could be induced to desert their Northern Democratic colleagues and stand by Hayes, it might be possible to settle the election crisis without bloodshed.[10]

Garfield explained his strategy in a report to Governor Hayes. Be not alarmed at the violent threats of Tilden supporters, he advised, for behind the scenes "two forces are at work— the Democratic business men of the country are more anxious for quiet than for Tilden, and the leading Southern Democrats in Congress, especially those who are old Whigs, are saying that they have seen war enough and do not care to follow the lead of their Northern associates who as Ben Hill says were 'invincible in peace and invisible in war.' " Garfield suggested that "it would be a great help if, in some discrete way, those Southern men who are dissatisfied with Tilden and his more violent followers could know that the South was going to be treated with kind consideration by you." Just what sort of assurance these Southerners wanted, he complained, was not quite clear, but he had already been approached by some who hinted that "in matters of internal improvements they had been much better treated by the Republicans than they were likely to be by the Democrats."

If these men could indeed be attached to the Republican cause, then a dazzling opportunity presented itself: The Republican Party could gain a respectable, conservative white following in the South and no longer be burdened by disreputable carpetbag governments or tied to the cause of the Negro (whose constitutional rights, Garfield hoped, would be as well protected by one party as by another). Instead, men could seek out their party associates "on the great commercial and industrial questions rather than on questions of race and color."[11] The old issues left over from the Civil War could, at last, be laid to rest and a new political organization would emerge uniting business-minded, conservative and nationalistic men of all sections behind the banner of the Republican Party. He asked Hayes for advice, but the tight-lipped governor, who never committed himself to paper if he could avoid it, laconically replied: "Your views are so nearly the same as mine that I need not say a word." This was encouragement enough, and Garfield and others opened negotiations with leading Southerners.

The first step was to drive a wedge between Northern and Southern Democrats over the question of internal improvements. Northern Democrats, such as Indiana's "Objector" Holman had built their reputations as tight-fisted guardians of the nation's treasury and implacable foes of federal subsidies. Their Southern colleagues, on the other hand,

412

hungered for government aid to help rebuild their backward, war-disrupted economy. On December 19, Garfield cleverly exploited this potential division in Democratic ranks during a debate over an appropriation for the harbor at Galveston, Texas. Garfield supported the measure, shrewdly contrasting his generous, open-handed policy with the crabbed, penny-pinching program of the Northern Democrats who opposed it. Having established his liberality, the next day he made the demonstration even clearer at a meeting of the Pacific Railroad committee. Lamar, the chairman, was determined to push through approval of the projected Texas and Pacific Railroad. Garfield single-handedly tied the committee into procedural knots and prevented any action on the measure. The message was clear—the Republican Party could give and the Republican Party could take away. Those Southern leaders who hoped for government aid to build up their section would be well advised to look to the Republican Party.[12]

This Texas and Pacific Railroad proposal illustrated the dilemmas of compromise. Garfield was instinctively opposed to the project. He had been burned too badly over Crédit Mobilier to associate his name with another such scheme. Earlier in the year, the railroad's sponsors had inspired a petition campaign in the 19th District to convince him that his constituents supported it. Garfield was unimpressed. "I would not favor it at this time," he declared, "if every man in the District desired its passage." At the same time, however, he had hinted to Lamar that he might be persuaded to change his mind in return for Southern support of specie resumption. Nothing came of this suggestion, but Lamar was now alert to the possibility that Garfield's support could be had if the price were right. Now, in the midst of the election crisis, the Texas and Pacific gained new currency as one of the counters in the delicate compromise negotiations. It was rumored that the line's president, Thomas Scott, controlled enough Southern congressmen to swing the election to whichever party made the highest bid. Garfield himself suspected that a timely subsidy to Scott might turn Texas into a Republican state and hasten that realignment of parties he had envisioned in his report to Governor Hayes.

413

Next to Hayes himself, no one stood to gain more from such a realignment than did Garfield. With the elevation of Dawes and Blaine to the Senate, he was now the leading House Republican, in line to be Speaker if his party could gain control of the House. That was not as unlikely a possibility as it might seem. Even though the Democrats had a majority in the next Congress, their margin was thin enough to be endangered by any defections. Already, nine Southern congressmen were secretly pledged to bolt the Democratic caucus and cast their votes for Garfield. Their price—the appointment of David M. Key of Tennessee as Postmaster General—seemed reasonable enough and Hayes was hopeful that he could win these wavering Southerners to his cause.[13]

Garfield was much less confident. Although he thought the plan worth exploring, he was suspicious of Southern good faith. "I am not sure that these men can be trusted," he said warily. Even with the prospect of the Speakership dangling before him, he could not bring himself to endorse the Texas & Pacific Railroad. In January, when Lamar's bill was reported out of committee, Garfield's name was found attached to the minority report that harshly condemned the proposal as unwarranted, expensive and potentially fraudulent.[14] This was a blow (though not necessarily a fatal one) to the plan for winning Southern cooperation, but at this stage of the electoral crisis, Republicans had other things to worry about. While they had been busy wooing Southerners, the Democrats had pulled themselves together and had launched a raid on the Republican flanks.

In the early stages of the crisis, the Democrats had been demoralized. They were, Garfield gloated, "without a policy or a leader. . . . full of passion and want to do something desperate but hardly know how to get at it." The Republicans seemed to hold all the high cards: the army, the courts and the recognized governments in the three disputed states. The Tilden forces had, of course, submitted their own returns from these states but Garfield was convinced that these could be disregarded when the electoral votes were counted. Yet he was uncomfortably aware that the Constitution was ambiguous on just how these disputed votes were supposed to be counted.

414

Eight years earlier, anticipating just such a "great calamity" as now threatened he had asked Congress to clarify the vagueness of the Constitution on this point. Nothing had come of his suggestion, however, and Garfield now argued that the only proper constitutional precedure was to give the president of the Senate full power to count the electoral votes while the rest of Congress merely looked on. Democrats disagreed; not surprisingly, considering that the president of the Senate, Thomas W. Ferry, was a Republican. They argued that the authority resided in Congress as a body, and not merely in the hands of the presiding officer. Garfield advised Hayes that the Party should ignore the Democrats' claim and stick by its guns. "A little bluster, a new burst of newspaper wrath, and all would be over," he predicted.[15]

Instead, some Republicans in Congress broke Party ranks to support a Democratic-inspired plan to bypass Congress and create a special Electoral Commission. Some of these defectors were what Garfield characterized as "fair minded asses," the sort who seemed to think "that the truth is always halfway between God and the Devil, and that not to split the difference would be partisanship." More serious was the defection of the Stalwart wing of the party, those followers of President Grant who were led in the Senate by Roscoe Conkling. Some were carpetbaggers who were understandably alarmed by Hayes's friendly overtures to Southern Democrats. Conkling's motives were harder to explain. Some suspected that he was being blackmailed, but others thought the New York Senator's massive ego was piqued at the prospect of losing control of the party. This was Garfield's first acquaintance with Conkling's peculiar "rule or ruin" mentality; a foretaste of that struggle which, four years later, would end in both men's destruction.[16]

The proposed compromise bill nullified many of the advantages with which the Republicans had entered the crisis. The special Electoral Commission was to be composed of fifteen members: five each from the House, the Senate and the Supreme Court. Seven were expected to be Republicans, seven more were to be Democrats and the fifth Justice (to be chosen by the other Supreme Court commissioners) would presumably hold the deciding vote. "Better go back to

415

the days of the Roman augurs," Garfield said in disgust, ". . . and inspect the entrails of a calf and the flight of birds" than settle affairs of state by such a method. "I have no words strong enough to describe my indignation at . . . the surrender which the Senate has made of our position," he sputtered. It seemed to him "not only a surrender of a certainty for an uncertainty but . . . a cowardly mortgaging of the safety of the future to secure an escape from a present danger." He reminded the House that "the safeguards of liberty are only in danger in times of public passion, and in such times it becomes all thoughtful men to . . . make no precedents which may come back in calmer times to plague their inventors." If the bill should pass, he warned, there might never be an uncontested presidential election held in the United States again. For this reason he vowed to fight it "from beginning to end, and wash my hands of all responsibility for its result."[17]

He fought the Electoral Commission bill until his voice gave out and then continued to whisper his objections. His arguments were pitched on the high ground of constitutional principle, but his real fear was that the proposed Commission would be stacked in favor of Tilden. It was universally assumed that the crucial fifth Justice on the Commission would be David Davis, a quondam Liberal Republican whose heart, Garfield suspected, was secretly Democratic. The bill passed, but a startling and unexpected development gave the Hayes forces new hope. As Garfield piously explained it: "the Lord came in . . . just at the proper moment and removed from the bench just the one man that the Democrats had relied on for the casting vote." The Lord, Garfield knew, moves in mysterious ways His wonders to perform, and in this case His unlikely agency was the Illinois legislature, which had opportunely elected Davis to the United States Senate as a Democrat, thus discrediting his standing as an Independent. The Commission had to settle for Justice Bradley, also nominally impartial but in whose hands, Garfield hoped, the cause of Hayes would be safe.[18]

After his vigorous opposition to the Electoral Commission, Garfield was somewhat embarrassed at finding himself

416

elected as one of the Commissioners, though not so embarrassed as to follow the advice of some Democrats that he disqualify himself. "If they expect to find a man who has no opinions on the subject," he snorted, "they will certainly have to go outside of either house of congress."[19]

On the morning of January 31, the Commission on which so much depended assembled in the old Supreme Court room. Each member took an oath, kissed the Bible and found his seat around a long rectangular table. They deliberated until after dark, by the flickering light of candles, as there were no gas jets in the historic old chamber. Some nights, when the meeting ran especially late, an escort would see Garfield safely home to prevent his assassination by some desperate Democrat. Garfield scoffed at such fears but admitted that he had not been under greater tension since Chickamauga. "You can hardly imagine," he told a friend, "the strength of passion which seethes and hisses in this city. . . ." Most of it was focused on that little candle-lit room where the Electoral Commission gathered. For more than two weeks the arguments passed back and forth across the long table as the tension mounted. When Justice Bradley began to give his opinion on a key question, the nervous strain was so "painful" that Garfield could hear the watches of the commissioners ticking away in their pockets and when, after twenty minutes, Bradley finally gave some clue as to the drift of his decision, "there was a long breath of relief—up or down—but actual relief to all from the long suspense."[20]

The decision, of course, favored Hayes. The Electoral Commission divided along strictly partisan lines, 8 to 7, on every key vote. This did not yet settle the matter, however, for the Democrats, infuriated by the betrayal of the Commission they themselves had devised, continued the struggle in the House of Representatives. They launched a filibuster that threatened to postpone the count until after March 4, leaving the nation without any president at all. With time running out, Republicans resumed their negotiations with Southern Democrats. They realized that conservative Democrats (both North and South) had little taste for anarchy and sensed that a deal could be arranged.

Louisiana, that "wretched state" where the electoral crisis had in a sense begun, proved to be the key to its resolution. In return for abandoning the filibuster, Democrats wanted assurances that Hayes would abandon the carpetbag government of Louisiana. Garfield could not understand how his party could, in logic, admit that the Democrats had carried Louisiana without thereby undermining Hayes's title to the presidency, but to other Republicans the hour was too late to indulge in abstract logic.

On the evening of February 26, Garfield was invited to a conference at Wormley's Hotel. There, in the traditional smoke-filled room, certain Ohio politicians who were close to Governor Hayes were meeting with Southern Democrats. The cozy nature of the gathering led Garfield to conclude that a deal had already been arranged. Much to the irritation of his colleagues, he made a brief statement arguing that no one present could afford "to do anything that would be or appear to be a political bargain." Those Democrats who resist the filibuster, he loftily declared, "are doing so on the ground of high public duty and honor; and any bargain would make their motives far lower." Having thus cleared his skirts, he left the meeting early, though he managed to stay long enough to learn everything that was worth learning (and to leave the impression that he would not oppose whatever deal might be arranged.[21])

Shortly after this meeting, Democratic support for the filibuster weakened. Furthermore, Samuel Randall, the Speaker of the House, had decided that it had gone on long enough. On the last day of February the count drew to a close in the most stormy session Garfield had seen since he had entered the House. Wild-eyed Democrats stormed the Speaker's chair, shouting and shaking their fists while George M. Beebe of New York hopped up and down on top of his desk, screaming incoherently. Randall was shaken but resolute and, with the aid of Garfield who was managing Republican floor strategy, he finally brought the count to a conclusion. At fifteen minutes after four o'clock on the morning of March 1, Rutherford B. Hayes was declared President of the United States and the electoral crisis was over.[22]

With the passion of the crisis finally spent, Garfield could even make his peace with "the little man on horseback at the other end of the Avenue"—Ulysses S. Grant. At the beginning of the crisis it had dawned on Garfield that, despite all his evident weaknesses, Grant might possess some elements of true greatness. "His power of staying, his imperturbability, has been of incalculable value to the nation, and will be prized more and more as his career recedes." Now, as Grant made ready to move out of public life, Garfield realized that "No American has carried greater fame out of the White House than this silent man who leaves it today." The valedictory was premature; Garfield and Grant would cross swords again in the coming years.[23]

CHAPTER TWENTY

PARTY PACIFICATOR

Now that the ordeal of president-making was safely past, Garfield could expect to fill a prominent place in the new administration he had done so much to install. Though never intimate, he and the new President had much in common. Ties of gratitude as well as friendship ought to have bound the two Ohioans closely together. Instead, their relationship would be marked by at least two years of suspicion and misunderstanding.

The first indication that all might not be well came soon after the inauguration. The appointment of John Sherman as Secretary of the Treasury left a vacant seat in the United States Senate. According to Columbus insiders, Garfield was the favorite among a crowded field of aspirants to fill Sherman's unexpired term. Garfield was tempted; but was he tempted enough to fight for it? His deep-seated "infirmity of will" generally inhibited him from campaigning actively for any office. This lack of aggressiveness baffled his friends. One, Albert G. Riddle, diagnosed the malady as "lack of egoism." If there is a course open to Garfield, Riddle suggested, "which he can take without self-assertion, he will take it. . . . Setting oneself up above all others is not in his nature."[1]

Riddle underestimated the force of Garfield's ambition. In truth, he did want to be senator, as he would later want to be president, but his secret self-esteem (or sense of destiny) was too great to allow him to stoop for any prize. It would have to come to him as a gift, without strings or conditions, so that he could regard it as a tribute paid to merit, thrust upon him without any effort of his own. If he could not go to the Senate on his own terms, then the Senate would just have to wait for another opportunity. "I shall probably pursue my usual course of seeking nothing and letting events take care of themselves," he decided.[2]

The decision was simplified by the intervention of President Hayes. As an outgrowth of that understanding which had been attempted with Southern Democrats earlier in the year, there was still a faint chance that enough of them might yet be wooed from their party to enable the Republicans to capture the House of Representatives. In that event, the President wanted Garfield to hold himself available to be Speaker of the House. Consequently, he asked him to forgo the Senate, a decision which would (not quite incidentally) clear the way for Hayes's close friend, Stanley Matthews. Garfield was, he admitted, "a little nettled" at the request but, like a good soldier, he was willing to do his duty. If the President insisted, Garfield would "make the sacrifice." The President did insist, and so, on March 11, Garfield wired his supporters in Columbus to withdraw his name. One political observer drew the derisive moral: "A Senatorship in the Hand is better than Two Speakerships in the Bush," but Garfield had no regrets. "I cannot believe that, in the long run, a man will lose by self-sacrifice," he consoled himself.[3]

Three days after his renunciation, when it seemed for the moment that Matthews might not win, Garfield was flabbergasted when Hayes casually suggested that perhaps he should run for the Senate after all. Garfield ruefully told the President that it was too late. Later that year, Garfield's suspicion that he had been duped was confirmed. On November 24, Matthews revealed to him that he had not even considered running for the Senate until Hayes had suggested it. Matthews had then objected that the place belonged to Garfield, who would probably be nominated, but Hayes had assured him that everything could be "amicably arranged." "So after all," Garfield bitterly concluded, "the public view is the correct one that Hayes inaugurated his candidacy."[4]

Hayes's slick maneuvering on the senatorial question was a
bad beginning; worse would follow. In the politics of this era,
the best measure of influence was the power to distribute
patronage. Garfield soon found, to his dismay, that all
patronage doors were slammed in his face. For over a month
after the administration began, he vainly tried to obtain a
Treasury Department post for his old friend Horace Steele.
Instead, the job went to a friend of the congressman from
Cleveland. Garfield wrote Hayes a scolding letter but received
no satisfaction. Later in the year, he suggested that his
influential but eccentric supporter, Edwin Cowles, be named
commissioner to the Paris Exposition. Hayes personally
objected on the grounds that Cowles would bring ridicule upon
the Commission. Garfield "rather sharply" told the President
he was being unfair, but his wishes were again ignored. To
make matters worse, another friend of Garfield's, John Q.
Smith, who had been appointed Indian Commissioner by
President Grant, soon came under fire and was removed from
office at the instigation of Hayes's Interior Secretary, Carl
Schurz. Garfield took Smith to the White House and protested to the President himself that the dismissal had been
"outrageous and unjust," but Hayes refused to overrule his
cabinet minister. "He does not seem to be master of his own
administration," Garfield regretfully concluded. "I fear he
has less force and nerve than I had supposed."[5]

Smith was ultimately consoled with another office but,
after these repeated rebuffs, Garfield was convinced of the
President's ingratitude. When a constituent asked him to
exert his influence for a favor, Garfield sadly had to confess
his impotence: "it is almost hopeless to secure such appointments through Congressional influence, as the President
pays very little attention to the wishes of members, and in my
own case, has never made but one single appointment on
my application." Such appointive offices were the hard
currency of politics and it appeared to Garfield's friends that
he was being shortchanged. They were indignant that the
President should take such advantage of his "good nature
and generosity," and felt that he had been "snubbed and ill
treated" by the administration.[6]

Hayes was not wholly at fault. Part of the responsibility for their estrangement rested with Garfield. He was psychologically incapable of close friendship with any president. Even though he and Hayes had once been on good terms, as soon as the latter was inaugurated it seemed as if a veil dropped between them. "It must be that there is an innate reverence for authority in me," Garfield reasoned. "I remember how awful in my boyhood was the authority of a teacher." Furthermore, the two men were poles apart in temperament. Hayes's demeanor was somber, austere and forbidding to all but an inner circle of family and friends. To the rest of the world he presented a dour mask of icy correctness and frigid formality. "Among the curiosities of his mind," Garfield marveled, "is the fact that he sees no fun in Pickwick, Don Quixote and Gil Blas." Garfield, on the other hand, remained as open and effusive as a schoolboy. He always liked to throw his arm around a friend's shoulder and call him "Old Fellow!" Hayes would have responded to such crude familiarity with a disdainful shudder. Close personal friendship between the two was out of the question.[7]

The widening gulf between the two Ohio Republican leaders was due to more than mere personality differences. Garfield was becoming increasingly disturbed at the direction of Hayes's policies. His disquiet began with the appointment of the cabinet. Although he admired Secretary of State Evarts personally, he distrusted the influence his "dreamy doctrines" might have on the President. Garfield also considered the appointment of Carl Schurz "unfortunate and unwise" because of the Interior Secretary's conspicuous record of party disloyalty.[8] Nor had Garfield ever fully trusted the new Secretary of the Treasury, John Sherman. Years earlier he had dismissed him as "a man of fair abilities, much industry and considerable influence," whose success was due to the skill with which he had "studied the popular current and floated with the tide. . . ." Since then, Sherman had risen somewhat in his estimation but Garfield was still not satisfied with his appointment as head of the Treasury Department.[9] Nor did he approve of Hayes's experiment in putting an obscure former rebel, David M. Key, in the Cabinet as a gesture of sectional amity. The President, he said, "should either take none at all or the greatest. . . . I fear he is not quite up to this heroic method."[10] Thus, out of seven cabinet members, Garfield expressed misgivings over four—not exactly an endorsement of the President's judgment.

Garfield's chief policy disputes with the administration were over two issues for which he had once held the highest hopes: civil service reform and sectional reconciliation. His objections to Hayes's civil service policy were over means, not ends. As he told Jacob Dolson Cox: "You and I were among the earliest to urge Civil Service Reform. We cannot afford to see the movement made a failure by injudicious management." He particularly resented Hayes's practice of giving his old army cronies public offices while at the same time preaching against the spoils system. "If nobody is to be appointed because he is your friend or my friend," he complained to Cox, "then nobody should be appointed because he is any other man's friend. The President himself should exercise the same self-denial as other officials. . . ."[11]

To Garfield, some sort of civil service reform was needed if only to help stave off that flock of office seekers who lay in wait each day "like vultures for a wounded bison," but he felt that some of Hayes's proposals were silly and unwise. He particularly objected to the order that prohibited all federal workers from engaging in party politics. The postmaster at Hiram, Garfield protested, had as much right to attend local primary meetings as any other citizen. In general, he thought that there was "too much proclamation" in the President's method. Rather than a piecemeal reform of the system by executive decree, Garfield thought that a thoroughgoing reform through congressional legislation was the proper way to place the government service on a permanent and rational basis. As it was, he could find no system behind Hayes's policy. On the first anniversary of the new administration, he and Cox agreed that Hayes's civil service reforms had proved an utter failure. "The impression is deepening that he is not large enough for the place he holds," Garfield sadly concluded.[12]

Garfield's disenchantment with another of Hayes's policies

—sectional reconciliation—had a more personal basis, for he was its first casualty. His hopes of winning the speakership depended upon the success of that policy, yet, even though he had sacrificed the Senate for it, he had never really believed that it could succeed. On the surface, things seemed to be going smoothly enough to belie his suspicions. At least nine Southern congressmen stood pledged to vote for him in return for Hayes's appointment of Key to the cabinet. Thomas Scott, president of the Texas & Pacific Railroad was reported ready to throw his considerable influence behind Garfield if Hayes would favor his line and even South Carolina's governor, Wade Hampton, had told the President that he would aid in organizing a Republican House.[13]

Captivated by the prospect of enlisting former rebels into the party of Lincoln, President Hayes launched a major campaign to woo the South. Not only did he abandon the remaining carpetbag governments but, speaking before a Georgia audience, he announced that the federal government would no longer intervene in Southern affairs on behalf of the Negro. On a more practical level, he promised to consider federal subsidies for Southern projects and showered patronage upon his former foes. In the first months of his administration, over one-third of all Southern appointments went to Democrats. Blaine, who knew well the uses of patronage, also understood its limitations and was afraid that the gulf between North and South was "too deep to be bridged over by the proposed methods." Garfield, too, was skeptical but he urged Blaine and other restless Republicans to give the President's policy a fair trial.[14]

The practical test of Southern intentions would come when Congress assembled in October to elect a Speaker. The signs were not favorable. "If General Garfield . . . is counting upon the votes of Southern Democrats to elect him Speaker of the next House," a Southern newspaper ominously warned, "he is likely to come to grief. We should like to see the Southern Democrat base enough to betray, not only his own constituents, but manhood and common decency, by voting for that red-mouthed, false-hearted, narrow-minded, unprincipled jobber, hypocrite and persecutor of the South."[15]

Patronage was not enough, unity of economic interest was not enough, largesse from the federal pork-barrel was not enough to overcome the bitter legacy of the Civil War. When the House was organized, every Democrat, North and South, toed the party line and voted for Randall. A switch of nine votes would have made Garfield Speaker—exactly the number who had promised to bolt earlier that year. Even though the President had kept his part of the bargain, the Southerners deserted him at the first opportunity. With them went those grandiose visions of party reorganization which had so beguiled Garfield and Hayes the preceding winter.[16]

Along with his hopes for the Speakership, Garfield lost much of his enthusiasm for sectional reconciliation. "The policy of the President has turned out to be a give-away game . . . ," he complained. "He has . . . offered conciliation everywhere to the South while they have spent their time in whetting their knives for every Republican they could find." He blamed the trouble squarely upon the President's pronounced "weakness and vacillation" which was leading many Republicans to yearn for the good old days of Grant. In exasperation, Garfield "took occasion to speak very plainly to the President." He warned that his unrequited gestures to the South were splitting the Party, but Hayes would not listen. Instead, he complacently found comfort in the unanimous support given his administration by college presidents and Protestant journals. "It seems to be impossible for a President to see through the atmosphere of praise in which he lives," Garfield concluded.[17]

Although he had nothing against college presidents or Protestant ministers (he had, after all, been both himself), Garfield knew that the support of party professionals was much more important to the success of the beleaguered administration. Yet with fine impartiality, Hayes had managed to alienate all segments of his party. Virtually the only thing that James G. Blaine and Roscoe Conkling had in common was that neither of these proud chieftains was on speaking terms with the President. Garfield took upon himself the role of "pacificator of the party," but he continually found his efforts thwarted. "I am almost disheartened at the prospect of getting anything done by the President," he burst out in frustration. "Day by day the party is dropping away from him, and the present state of things cannot continue much longer without a total loss of his influence with the Republicans."[18]

As he listened to the widespread grumblings of Republican discontent, Garfield feared that Hayes's election might turn out to be "an almost fatal blow to his party." In fact, he himself was on the verge of a public break with the President he had done so much to elect. He was not alone. As minority leader of Congress, Garfield seemed to be presiding over a party that was tearing itself into pieces. "The tendency of a part of our party to assail Hayes and denounce him as a traitor and a man who was going to Johnsonize the party was very strong, and his defenders were comparatively few," he later recalled. Loyally he pleaded with his colleagues to stand by the President and, in order to forestall an open rupture, he deliberately avoided calling a Republican caucus for six months hoping, in the meantime, to find some issue which could unite the party.[19]

Yet the very first issue that Hayes pressed to a struggle served only to divide the party even further. With more courage than wisdom, he had decided that a campaign against inflation would be just the thing to reunite the party. In a depression year, however, the nature of money was no longer a mild, academic quesiton but a "midsummer madness" charged with emotion. "All other issues," Garfield reported in bafflement, "are swallowed up in the one absorbing question of what money is, and what it ought to be. The old questions . . . are as fresh and new . . . as the telephone." Hard times lent urgency to the inflationists' cause. All over the country businesses were collapsing, men were searching for work and the first serious labor violence the nation had known erupted in bitter railroad strikes. Garfield's prescription for labor unrest was to use the army to break strikes (though he did concede that the railroads had been "unjust and oppressive" to their workers). Otherwise, he advocated a textbook laissez-faire policy. He put his trust in the law of supply and demand —"higher than legislation and wiser than the wisdom of man."

427

Others, however, with less perfect faith in the inscrutable workings of economic providence, were angrily demanding that the government pump more money into the economy.[20]

The inflationists attacked on two fronts: greenbacks and silver. Garfield had hoped that the greenback mania had been cured by the passage of the Specie Resumption Act. Resumption, however, was not scheduled to begin until January 1, 1879, and in the meantime the paper-money advocates, abetted by their "lunatic" supporters in Congress, launched a last-ditch effort to retain cheap money. Garfield, of course, took up his favorite role of Horatius at the bridge, fighting to defend financial honor. His most vocal opponent in this struggle was not a Democrat but a fellow-Republican, William D. ("Pig Iron") Kelley of Pennsylvania. In mid-November of 1877, Garfield had delivered a long speech advocating specie resumption. Kelley took four months to prepare a rebuttal, boasting that it would "annihilate" his foe. Although Garfield was shocked at the bitter personal animosity it exhibited, he relished the opportunity to reply to Kelley's attack. He had only one day in which to prepare his response and when he arrived home, ready to work, his face beamed with anticipation. Harry stood by his father's desk until bed time, entranced as volume after volume was unerringly plucked off its shelf and rapidly consulted. Despite its hurried preparation, the one-hour speech was tightly organized and crammed with telling statistics and quotations. Kelley was so angry that he would not even listen. He sulked in the lobby, sending in messengers from time to time to "Find out what the damn fool is saying now."[21]

Angry though he was, Kelley's wrath could hardly compare with that of a Greenbacker from upstate New York who volunteered to hang Garfield for his "damnable traitors speeches." This was, however, the last gasp of the greenback. With specie resumption assured, Garfield noted, "all the greenback men who have been in favor of flooding the country with depreciated paper money have forsaken their paper idols and have turned to silver because it is cheaper."

The discovery of rich silver deposits in the West had increased production to the point where a silver dollar, if

428

only it could be minted, would be worth less than a gold dollar. Much to the inflationists' dismay, however, silver had been removed from the list of coins by the so-called "Crime of 1873." As the market price of silver kept dropping, they redoubled their efforts to reauthorize the coinage of these depreciated dollars. Garfield was appalled. "Since I have been in public life," he declared, "I have never known any proposition that contained so many of the essential elements of vast rascality, of colossal swindling as this."[22]

Despite this outraged rhetoric, Garfield had mixed emotions on the silver question. Previously a believer in the gold standard, he had recently embraced bimetallism and was willing to permit the minting of silver dollars, provided they remained equal in value with gold. He attributed his change of heart to reading a review of a book by a German economist which claimed that the world's gold supply was becoming exhausted. Burke Hinsdale could not understand how his friend could be "so suddenly converted" to bimetallism, especially by a book he had not read. He was not aware that Garfield's interest in silver was more than intellectual; that he had, in fact, recently invested thousands of dollars in Nevada silver mines and had, not coincidentally, begun to see some merit in the silverites' position at about the same time.[23]

Financial interest pulled Garfield one way on the silver question; an intellectual commitment to sound money pulled another. For a time he compromised with bimetallism, but in a showdown his intellectual convictions won out over self-interest. He had, after all, made his political reputation as an unswerving foe of inflation, and when Richard Bland introduced a silver-coinage bill in Congress, Garfield unhesitatingly fought it. Hayes unwisely tried to make opposition to the bill a test of party loyalty, but the inflationist sentiment was sectional, not partisan. Except for Garfield, every leading Republican congressman west of the Appalachians deserted the President.[24] Even though some of the sting was taken out of the measure in the Senate by the compromise Bland-Allison silver purchase bill, Hayes still vetoed it, only to be humiliated by seeing his veto decisively overridden without even the courtesy of a debate. Garfield found himself the only Ohioan, and virtually the only midwestern congressman of either party, who voted to sustain the President. Indeed, the veto was over-ridden by an even greater majority than had supported the original Bland bill, demonstrating how little influence Hayes exerted. "He has pursued a suicidal policy toward Congress," Garfield concluded, "and is almost without a friend."[25] The President was as unpopular with the people as he was with Congress, as Garfield realized when Hayes visited a veteran's reunion at Willoughby in the fall of 1878. There was no cheering when he stepped off the train, and the sullen coolness of the crowd towards the Chief Executive embarrassed Garfield.

Since Hayes's brief visit to the 19th District occurred shortly before a congressional election, Garfield could not resist the opportunity of saying a few words to the voters himself. It was not really necessary. This was his ninth congressional campaign and his automatic renomination was by now almost a habit. A Republican convention in the 19th Ohio, according to one political observer, had turned into "a stereotyped affair. The delegates come together, shake hands all around, find they are all of one mind, renominate General Garfield by acclamation, pass a few sound Republican resolutions, listen to a short speech from their Representative, shake hands again and go home." His hold on his constituency was so complete that Garfield scarcely bothered to campaign. "If the people of the 19th District want me for their Representative," he nonchalantly declared, "they will say so; if not I shall not ask them to choose me."[26]

Only two obstacles stood in the way of his reelection, and neither of them was serious enough to cause concern. The first was the appearance of a third party in the field: the Greenback Party led by Garfield's persistent old foe, Judge Tuttle. He could be easily ignored. On election day, scarcely eleven per cent of the voters responded to Tuttle's appeal. The other complication arose from a reshuffling of the district. In an attempt to gerrymander Garfield out of Congress, the Democratic legislature had taken his home county of Portage out of the 19th district and substituted Mahoning

430

County. Mahoning could spell trouble for the Republicans. Voters there were still bitter over an attempt to relocate the county seat, and the unemployed ironworkers tended to blame the Republicans for their economic woes. Matters were further complicated by the recent appearance of a new society, the Knights of Labor, said to be "Communistic in its purposes and secret in its acts."[27] Garfield did, in fact, fail to carry Mahoning but it scarcely mattered. The other counties in the district were so dependable that he outpolled the combined vote of his opponents by better than three to two.[28]

Garfield was able to outwit the Democratic gerrymander. No sooner had Portage been lopped off from his district, than he nimbly skipped to a new home in Lake County, remaining safely within the bounds of the 19th. Garfield had not really been a bonafide Ohio resident ever since his Hiram house had been sold to Hinsdale. For a while, his family had summered at various resorts, but by 1876 he had come to realize that this sort of rootless life was bad for the children. On the last day of October, shortly after the death of Neddie, he bought almost 120 acres of farmland in Mentor, Ohio, to which he soon added another forty acre parcel at a total cost of almost $17,500. A timely legal fee of $5,000 helped somewhat, but for the rest Garfield was obliged to take on a heavy mortgage.

It was not a bargain. Although the location was convenient, with a highway running past the front porch and railroad tracks cutting across a corner of the property, the farm suffered from gravelly soil and general neglect. The old Dickie place had been allowed to run down ever since the death of its former owner. The farm house, a simple one-and-a-half-story frame building, needed paint and thoroughgoing renovation. A fastidious visitor noted that "The shaky old barns stood amid heaps of rubbish . . . and in disagreeable proximity to the dwelling. The pig sty wafted its sweetness . . . to the windows of the parlor in the old family mansion."

Looking at the bright side of things, the new owner cheerily decided that "the general state of chaos opens before us a fine field for work and contrivance." The barns and pig pens were removed to more discreet locations, the swamp

431

was drained and the house expanded. A little cottage was built behind the main house to serve as a library, and Garfield, rediscovering long-unused skills, laid the floors himself. Even the boys pitched in as Garfield and the hired hands planted their first crop of oats, corn and barley. The bills sprouted faster than the crops. A pair of gray horses cost $425 and stables, fences, plumbing and all the unexpected expenses of property-owning led Garfield to wonder whether he had not taken on more than he could handle. He managed to convince himself that the expense was worthwhile for the children's sake, but the truth was that he enjoyed the farm even more than they did. He savored the new and delightful role of the rustic Squire of Mentor, learnedly discoursing on manure with his neighbors or allowing curious newspapermen to inspect his own system for precooking silage.[29]

Pitching hay and breeding cattle left little time for politics or anything else. Although Garfield begrudged "the passage of any day which does not bring intellectual growth," he suppressed his guilt with the hope that "the touch of the earth will give me renewed strength, as is related in the Greek fable." Allowing his mind to "lie fallow" seemed to prepare him for the congressional wars he faced when he returned to Washington in the fall.[30]

Those wars were less onerous than before. There was something to be said for being in the minority. Freed from the burdens of committee chairmanship, he could watch the Democrats prepare the bills while he relaxed with his family. He could sneak out to the ballpark to root for the Nationals or to the theater, where his tastes ran to Gilbert and Sullivan (in one year he saw *Pinafore* four times). More serious music, however, such as Handel's *Messiah*, left him bewildered. He could begin to take up his long-neglected law practice again or simply relax in his 3,000 volume library with his favorite poets: Horace, Burns and, above all, Tennyson. He could even find time to play games: croquet in the summer and cards and billiards all year round.

Life in the plain brick house at the corner of 13th and I had settled into a comfortable, though hectic routine. Shortly after daybreak, the boys would be up and about, careening noisily through all the rooms. After this "shirt-tail brigade" had been mustered in for an ample breakfast, Garfield would retire to his study, light a cigar and tackle the day's mail, a chore made doubly burdensome by his self-imposed rule of always answering every civil letter addressed to him. Faithful George Rose would drop by each morning on his way to his job at the Treasury Department and Garfield would dictate the day's crop of letters while the boys romped around the desk. Congress generally assembled at noon. Garfield carried his lunch, a sandwich of stale bread and raw beef, an unappetizing combination recommended by the doctor for dyspepsia. Dinner was at six, but the head of the house was usually late. The children would wait as long as they could but, as Harry remembered: "we would hardly be seated and Jim and I have hardly begun our strife as to which should take Papa's place, when we would hear the latch key rattle, and 'there's Papa' went around the table. His bright cheerful face always made our meal taste better and he seldom, even in the most depressing times, and when he was most tried, brought his trouble home to the table." As soon as he was seated, whether there was company present or not, the General (as his wife always called him) would invariably order: "Well boys, reports." As Harry and Jim stumbled through their day's lesson in the *Aeneid*, their father, who had not read Virgil for decades, would correct their slips from out of his awesome memory.[31]

It disturbed Garfield to see that his sons were not as studious as he had been. "They are bright, active, unusually full of animal spirits, and yet they hate books." Jim was a plodder, usually slow and careful but sometimes possessed by an uncontrollable temper. Hal was better natured but less thorough. Neither of them, their father complained, "seem to have that hunger and thirst for knowledge that I always felt when I was a child." He tried firmness, but the effects of a spanking seemed to wear off in a day. He tried religion, but even his minister friend Hinsdale blanched at the thought of enforcing three daily prayer sessions on such active boys. Garfield finally decided that the public school system, with its overemphasis on study, was the culprit, and he pulled the two older boys out of school, relying variously on tutors, private

433

academies or his own instruction. Lucretia insisted that the problem could best be solved by more paternal attention, which was why Garfield turned the dinner table into a nightly classroom.

After dinner came play time. While Garfield's mother (whose sweetly aged face belied a waspish cantankerousness) sat quietly knitting, her son and daughter-in-law might play "pussy wants a corner" with the children or perhaps Garfield might read from Greek mythology (which frightened the little ones to tears). Invariably, the evening's fun would be disturbed by callers. Up to fifteen visitors a night would stream into the front sitting room to beg a favor or ask advice of the man who was now the foremost Republican member of Congress.[32]

This ascendency was slow in coming, but Garfield had finally arrived at the peak of his influence. "Five or six years ago he was one of the most unpopular men in Congress," a candid reporter admitted, but little by little that unpopularity had worn off and he had attained the status of an institution. No matter how dull the debates in Congress might be, visitors to the capitol could count on seeing Garfield and Randall sitting "like faithful sentinels," patiently guiding the House. To these visitors, "Their names had become household words and their presence gave warmth to the great chamber."[33]

Garfield's leadership was not flawless. Though he shone in debate, he was considered "as helpless as a child" in plotting parliamentary tactics. Despite long service, his knowledge of the rules was surprisingly spotty, as was his mastery of constitutional law. (He thought that the Constitution prohibited the states from establishing a religion.[34]) It was fortunate for his reputation that he never achieved his ambition of becoming Speaker, for he lacked the strength of will needed to tame the often unruly House. Unlike Blaine, who could dominate Congress through sheer force of personality, Garfield had to rely on intellect and industry. He was not really a leader of men; he was a persuader, and now, as he approached what would be the last and most effective year of his congressional career, he would need all his powers of persuasion. His task was a formidable one—to bring his president and his party together.

The cause of party unity was not aided by the President's refusal to seek a second term. This noble (though superfluous) gesture had the effect of turning Hayes into a lame duck from the beginning of his term and let loose a free-for-all among his would-be successors. Blaine, as usual, was in the thick of contention, and it saddened Garfield to see how his friend's mind had been "warped" by presidential ambition.

A petty incident revealed to Garfield the extent of "the childishness and selfishness of Mr. Blaine" once the presidential fever had seized him. The *North American Review* had planned a symposium on Negro enfranchisement. Garfield was asked to contribute an article and Blaine was to write a summation to rebut the Democratic views. When Blaine read his friend's article, he complained that it made all the strong points and left him nothing fresh to say in his rebuttal. He sent the editor round to Garfield's house to ask that the article be withdrawn. Always inclined to be agreeable, Garfield was at first willing to oblige but on reflection decided that Blaine had no right to make such a request. "It is apparent to me," he concluded, "that Blaine cares more about the glory . . . than having the cause of negro enfranchisement defended." He told the editor that the article would have to stand as it was, "and they could reject it if they chose, either for being not good enough or too good and they must take the responsibility." The next day, a note came from Blaine saying that the editor had suggested that Garfield's article should be rewritten for appearance in a later issue. Garfield replied that the symposium "would squeeze the whole juice out of the subject and make an article in the next number dull and profitless." When he showed Blaine's letter to the editor, it came out that the suggestion was purely Blaine's and that the editor had opposed it for the same Reason Garfield had given. Confronted with this evidence of Blaine's petty duplicity, Garfield refused to budge. "I have already done too much complacent yielding to the demands of ambitious and aggressive friends and I think that Blaine will respect me more for refusing. . . ."[35]

Maintaining Blaine's respect meant a great deal to Garfield, even though after this incident he had to admit that he was not blind to his faults, "which it seems to me are growing rather than decreasing. He seems to have undoubted faith in management while I have but little. . . ." In his headlong pursuit of the White House, Blaine eagerly latched onto any popular issue. Early in 1879, he discovered the Yellow Peril and began to champion the movement to exclude Chinese immigrants. Although Garfield agreed that the wholesale importation of coolies ought to be stopped, he thought Blaine's bill "a great mistake," as well as a "palpable and flat violation" of international law and treaty obligations. When the bill passed the Congress, he advised the President to veto. Hayes took the advice and, with Garfield's management, the veto was sustained.[36]

It was a small victory, but at this stage in the Hayes administration a victory of any sort was welcome. Never particularly popular, even from its inception, it had now run out of steam. If the party were to avoid dissension and collapse, a fresh issue round which all Republicans could rally would have to be found. But the failure of Southern conciliation and the success of specie resumption had deprived Hayes of two of his most cherished issues, while a third, civil service reform, threatened to divide the party even further. To make matters worse, the Democrats controlled Congress and were in a position to block any administration program.

Garfield hoped to turn this last drawback into an advantage. He was convinced that the "fatal facility" of the Democrats for blundering would lead them into mismanaging their case in Congress. He was not disappointed. The Democrats were able to do what Hayes could not—unite the Republican Party. They appointed a special House committee under Clarkson Potter of New York to investigate the election of 1876. Potter's probe was clearly designed to discredit Hayes's title to the presidency and pave the way for a Democratic victory in 1880. This was a challenge that Republicans could not ignore and they closed ranks behind the President in self-protection (except for Conkling, who spitefully slipped incriminating secrets to Potter). Some feared that this "outrageous and revolutionary" investigation presaged a Democratic coup d'état. But Garfield was not alarmed. Confident that the Democrats were "manifestly lacking in parliamentary skill to manage their own case," he waited for them to fumble. Republican luck held good. Translation of the sensational "Cipher Dispatches" revealed that the Democrats in 1876 had been guilty of as much skulduggery as, or more than, their opponents, and the investigation turned out to be a stand-off.[37]

The Democrats were equally unlucky in their efforts to build a legislative record in Congress. This failure was not due so much to lack of parliamentary skill as to lack of policy. Democrats tended to be against things as a matter of principle—a useful stance, no doubt, for an opposition party but not for a party called upon to govern. Their two most cherished doctrines—localism and laissez-faire—were hardly the stuff of which progressive legislation could be made. The limitations of their platform were revealed by an outbreak of yellow fever. When Garfield introduced a resolution to investigate the epidemic, the Democrats objected to any federal supervision over local health regulations. "The Democrats are so fearful of interfering with States Rights," Garfield exclaimed, "that they are unwilling that the General Government should help protect them from Yellow Fever, unless they can degrade the nation in comparison with states."[38]

Hobbled by this sort of doctrinaire rigidity, the Democrats were bound to stumble. With an unerring instinct, they managed to hand the Republicans the one issue that could finally bring them together. They launched an attack on one of the last, lingering mementoes of Reconstruction: the law that authorized the use of federal troops to preserve order at polling places. Even though there were, as Blaine pointed out, fewer federal troops in the entire South than there were policemen in New York City, their presence assumed enormous symbolic importance. To Democrats, the use of soldiers to patrol elections was not only an odious infringement of state sovereignty but, more practically, an awkward deterrent to the wholesale disenfranchisement of the Negro then underway in the South. The issue had emotional impact in the North as well, for the Democrats were striking at the very foundations of the Republican heritage: the Army, the Negro, the Union, the fruits of the Civil War itself. Garfield

437

took up the challenge. "Gentlemen," he angrily charged, "you . . . virtually declare that the crimes of ballotbox stuffing, fraud at the polls, intimidation, and outrage of voters may go on without check or observation by national authorities; that to poison the very fountain-spring of the elective franchise shall be no crime against the nation; and that all the machinery for punishing it shall be destroyed."[39]

The Democratic attack was rendered even more offensive by the heavy-handed tactics they employed. Lacking the votes to override the President's inevitable veto, they tacked their measure onto the Army Appropriations Bill as a rider, leaving Hayes to make the unpalatable choice of either approving an obnoxious measure or else vetoing a forty-five million dollar appropriation bill and seeing the government grind to a halt for lack of funds. Garfield was inclined to compromise, but the Democrats adamantly forced Congress into an extra session rather than back down. Hayes was equally stubborn. He assured Garfield that he intended to veto any appropriation bill that had the repeal of the election laws attached to it. The stage was set for what Garfield would consider the most "effective and startling" speech of his career.[40]

According to one connoisseur of congressional oratory, "The high-principled orator, dignified in manner and unfailing in courtesy, who gives rhetorical finish to his sentences is deeply appreciated by the House; but the real leader is the original, daring debater, who seizes the opportune moment, and, without apparent preparation, hurls his forceful, compact sentences, loaded with destructive arguments, into the midst of his adversaries." The classic example of such leadership, this expert maintained, came on March 29, 1879 when "James A. Garfield, prodded by impudent questions and angered by satirical laughter, launched into a thirty minute speech" entitled "Revolution in Congress."[41] Normally, Garfield was the epitome of the "high-principled," stately orator. "His gestures are few and forcible," a reporter noted, "and there is a certain statesmanlike dignity about him. . . ." Eschewing emotion and vituperation, he spoke more as "a friend arguing with friends," than as a typical spellbinder. "When he puts home a point his brow knits and he stands looking intently

438

at his farthest hearer just as an artilleryman peers steadily through the cannon's smoke to see the effect of the last shot fired."[42] For the "Revolution in Congress" speech, however, Garfield shed his customary reserve: "rushing up and down the aisle, with pounding of books and desks, with clenching of fists and brandishing of arms, with posings and dashes toward the Democratic side, and bursts of defiance, ala Blaine," all of which, according to one spectator, "made up a highly entertaining spectacle and produced marked effect."[43]

The substance of the speech was as sensational as its manner of delivery. The Democrats, Garfield dramatically charged, are embarked on nothing less than "a revolution against the Constitution and government" which, if persisted in, could only result in "the total subversion of this government." The election law to which they object so strenuously, he reminded the House, was passed first in 1865 as a *Democratic* measure which even Sam Randall and Sunset Cox favored. And now

> after fourteen years have passed, and not one petition from one American citizen has come to us asking that this law be repealed, while not one memorial has found its way to our desks complaining of the law . . . the Democratic Representatives declare that, if they are not permitted to force upon the other house and upon the Executive, against their consent, the repeal of a law that Democrats made, this refusal will be considered a sufficient ground for starving this government to death. That is the proposition which we denounce as revolution.

Such behavior proved that the Democrats had learned nothing from the Civil War. Then they had said to the nation: "If you elect the man of your choice President of the United States, we will shoot your government to death." That was treason, but at least it was manly. Now, however, "by a method which the wildest secessionist scorned to adopt" they threaten to starve the government rather than fight it. The method may differ, he concluded, but it is the same revolutionary spirit.[44]

Republicans were galvanized. When Garfield tried to sit down he was so mobbed by well-wishers that the House had to suspend business until he fought his way into the cloakroom.

439

Their enthusiasm was understandable. Republicans had been on the defensive for too long. Now they could seize the initiative under the familiar issues of the Civil War. The dream of sectional reconciliation was laid to rest and the old "bloody shirt" taken out of mothballs to be waved as the banner of a unified, self-confident political party.

Praise for the speech poured in from all over the country. Even a Democratic journal admitted that "the like of it had not been heard in many, many years." In Boston, an Irishman was supposedly heard to jabber: "Have ye red Gineral Garfield's spache? . . . Faith, he's good enough for a President, if he has got that stouf in im," and a more literate Ohioan confirmed the prediction. "If the entire North is as completely electrified and aroused as . . . here in Cincinnati," he reported, "it would not be surprising if you would be called upon to accept the nomination in 1880." The speech was not a universal success. Garfield's high-minded friend Hinsdale deplored what he regarded as cheap sensationalism. "Here you are," he chided, "using language that, if used by a partisan candidate for a small office the evening before election . . . would not surprise me. . . . And yet you are the man who taught me to use my mind—to cultivate the judicial temper, and to speak the words of truth and soberness!" Friends of the President, on the other hand, complained that Garfield was not partisan enough. "Garfield made a good speech today," Congressman William McKinley told Hayes. "It was full of which his speeches generally lack, i.e. fire, earnestness and courage. Yet when he was through, he came around amongst us and said he was afraid he had been too radical. He was afraid that he had offended some one."[45]

Such wishy-washy behavior confirmed what had become an article of faith among the President's cronies: that, as one put it, "Garfield's old weakness, lack of moral pluck, attacks him too often for his own good." Another agreed that Garfield's "Lack of moral courage" flawed his character. "A man of great ability, with good impulses and an honorable ambition he [Garfield] too often surprises his friends and mars his own prospects by yielding in the very midst of a contest." It was hardly surprising that Hayes himself should eventually

440

pick up this theme and dismiss his successor as "not original, not firm—not a moral force."[46]

What did all this talk of moral cowardice really mean? It seemed to refer to Garfield's inability to push a dogma to its extreme bounds; to his willingness to admit that he might, on occasion, be wrong; to his distaste for the sort of personal conflict that a true partisan might relish. Hinsdale, who understood Garfield better than most men, attributed these alleged weaknesses to the fact that his friend was "as fair minded a man as I ever knew. . . . His distrust of his conclusions in all tentative stages of investigation, and his anxiety to see the subject from every point of view, led him to defer, sometimes absurdly, to other men. . . ." More comfortable when dealing with ideas than with men, Garfield often gave the impression of being spineless in debate. "They complain of you because you don't assault the Democrats," a friend advised. "Somehow I never could learn to do nagging," Garfield replied. To his diary, Garfield confessed his weakness. "I think there is danger I [am] getting too spiritless in regard to personalities," he acknowledged, "but the fact is I thoroughly despise all mere personal debate. I never feel that to slap a man in the face is any real gain to the truth."[47]

This special session of Congress, however, would see Garfield cast in an uncomfortable role. The appropriation struggle had developed into a naked test of power. Time after time, the Democrats would pass an appropriation bill with an objectionable rider attached to it and on each occasion the President would send back a ringing veto. Garfield managed the Republican case on the House floor with skill and tenacity. In a series of speeches and floor maneuvers, he succeeded in painting his opponents as unreconstructed rebels bent upon something akin to treason. Under this steady pressure, the Democrats wilted. With each successive veto their demands grew more and more modest until Garfield began to fear that they might be unduly humiliated. He implored Hayes to find some face-saving compromise that could spare the Democrats total embarrassment. The President scoffed at Garfield's chivalrous concern. "A square backing down is their best

441

way out," he firmly replied, "and for my part I will await that result with complacency."[48]

The President vetoed five appropriation bills within the space of three months and, with Garfield's help, each was sustained. His tactical ingenuity in managing the President's case showed how far Garfield had come since those apprentice days when he had lost control of the Army reorganization bill. When Conkling, along with other stalwart Republican senators who wanted to embarrass the President, tried to go his own way Garfield thwarted their efforts to call a joint caucus that might have swayed some House Republicans from his control. When some Southern Democrats showed signs of a willingness to compromise, he dropped well-timed hints of subsidies for Mississippi River navigation in exchange for their cooperation. At no time did he lose the tactical initiative. Even though they were in the majority, the hapless Democrats were kept continuously on the defensive. By the end of the session they had, as Garfield said with quiet pride, "completely abandoned the main ground which they at first took; and the most sensible among them do not hesitate to admit, privately, that it was wholly untenable." They had begun the session by threatening to withhold $45,000,000 of appropriations; they ended by withholding a token $600,000.[49]

Garfield was so delighted with the outcome that he even named his dog "Veto." He had good reason to be pleased. Along with the President, he had given a tired, riven party a fresh issue which, in his estimation, "has united the Republicans more than anything since 1868—and it bids fair to give us 1880." Garfield himself had emerged from the ordeal as a leading spokesman for an administration that had once snubbed and rejected him. He was especially proud of the confidence that Hayes now placed in his leadership. "I think I have never had so much intellectual and personal influence over him as now," Garfield boasted. "He is fully in line with his party." The patient work of party pacification had succeeded.[50]

Yet even as he was reaching the peak of his effectiveness as a leader of the House of Representatives, Garfield was aware that it was time to move on. The rough and tumble of the lower house had left its mark on his health. Although not yet fifty, he had reached that stage of life when a man begins to note, with clinical fascination, each of the signs that he is no longer young. A touch of rheumatism in the shoulders, flecks of gray in the hair, his first pair of reading glasses, all whispered the same warning: "I must begin to husband my fuel." The gentlemanly pace of the Senate made that chamber seem like a restful haven compared to his present life. And so, he decided, if a senatorship should come his way, he would take it, though not without "some sadness and regret."[51]

As the first step on the road to the Senate, Garfield was required to silence the biennial Garfield-for-Governor speculation. This place, which he had never wanted to fill, was continually urged upon him by his Ohio friends. To their pleas was added the advice of President Hayes, who twice hinted to Garfield that "the surest road to the Presidency" lay through the Governor's mansion at Columbus. Garfield appreciated the courtesy but he could not help recalling that the last time Hayes had been solicitous about his career it had cost him election to the Senate. He thanked the President for his compliment but at the same time he instructed his Ohio agents to quash the boom and work instead for his affable millionaire friend, Charles Foster of Fostoria.

The next step was to insure the election of a Republican legislature. With the return of prosperity, Republican prospects for carrying the state appeared rosier than they had been in years. Throughout the off-year campaign of 1879, Garfield and Foster criss-crossed the state, speaking wherever a crowd would assemble. At Caldwell, no less than seven brass bands and five thousand people were on hand to cheer an hour-and-a-half oration. That same night, as he was being driven through the little village of McConnelsville, Garfield was hauled out of his buggy to address a few dozen lonely Republicans in this Democratic corner of the state. Weary as he was, "The sight of a little schoolhouse, crowded full of eager people, who were surrounded by the worst type of copperheads, overcame me," and he delivered a forty-five minute speech.[52]

443

The only unpleasantness during the exhausting campaign was created by Blaine. The year before, Garfield had stumped Maine and had been assured that Blaine would return the favor. The testy Senator, however, was reported to be "a little out of humor" because his Ohio friend had not spent what he thought was enough time in Maine. Blaine was scheduled to be the main attraction at the Ashtabula County Fair. Instead, without giving any notice, he went off to Iowa, leaving Garfield to stumble through a two hour impromptu address before a restless crowd of 7,000. "I made the best of it," he reflected, but he could not help being indignant at this fresh evidence of Blaine's tendency to be "a little reckless of his promises, and a little selfish withal."[53]

Otherwise, the campaign was a vast success. By the end of September, Garfield was so hoarse that he could hardly speak in public, and Foster was afraid he would never again be able to fall asleep unless he had a brass band to play a lullaby before he went to bed. The result justified the effort. Foster was elected governor and the Democrats were decisively outnumbered in the next state legislature, insuring that whoever might be chosen to succeed Allen Thurman in the Senate would be a Republican.

Now all that remained was to make sure that these legislators voted for Garfield rather than for some other Republican. Alphonso Taft of Cincinnati, Stanley Matthews and old Governor Dennison, a ghost from the past who lacked the discretion to fade away, headed the small list of rivals. None of them were serious contenders but they stayed in the race hoping for some "fortunate accident" to befall Garfield, the acknowledged front runner. The only real threat came from a man who kept insisting that he was not a candidate—John Sherman. Sherman was not a popular figure in Ohio. Cold and formal in his manner, he lacked the art of arousing personal loyalty. "His whole political career," Garfield was reminded, "has been a commercial one. He has not got the hearts of the people and never had." Still, he was a respected and familiar name and, with the power and patronage of the Treasury Department at his disposal, he could not be dismissed lightly.[54]

444

Fortunately, Sherman seemed to have his eye on higher things than the Senate. He had spent his term as Treasury Secretary building a personal organization, and now, with the prestige of specie resumption behind him, he began to make his move for the presidential nomination. He knew that in order to capture the 1880 convention he would have to have his home-state delegation lined up solidly behind him. He could not, therefore, risk antagonizing any influential Ohio Republican. As early as March, Sherman had indicated to a mutual friend that he would not stand in Garfield's way, and in July he confirmed the promise to Garfield himself during the privacy of a carriage ride through the Maryland countryside.

As might be expected, Sherman's friendship carried a price tag. He wanted Garfield to issue a public endorsement of his presidential candidacy, preferably before the senatorial question was settled. For once, Garfield was cagey. Playing his cards closer to his vest than usual, he made no commitment other than a guarded indication that "my course towards Sherman's candidacy for the presidency would depend, in part, upon his conduct towards me in the pending contest." Garfield's friends suspected a trap. Harmon Austin warned that "what Sherman wants is to hold both the Senatorship and the Presidency in his hands and he wants to hold you where you will not be in his way for either." Another friend suggested that Sherman realized that his chances for the White House were slim, "and though he may continue to put up a dust cloud of presidential aspirations, it will be done only as a blind, for a dash at the Senate while your friends may be looking the other way and wiping their eyes."[55]

Some of his more nervous advisers urged Garfield to go to Columbus to take personal charge of the contest, but he refused to violate his scruples by appearing to seek office. "A man who is fit to be U. S. Senator," he argued, "ought to be so well known that his presence is unnecessary." Besides, he wanted to avoid raising the least suspicion of any deal or bargain which might taint his victory. Charles Henry agreed that "to oblige you to be there would be like compelling a virtuous woman to act the part of a street walker." He volunteered to go himself, to guard against "bushwacking." Gar-

445

field allowed Henry to set up campaign headquarters in a Columbus hotel, but he laid down strict orders: "no liquors of any kind, no offer of offices nor anything to any member for his support," though he did unbend and allow a supply of cigars to be kept on hand for visitors.[56]

From the encouraging tone of the reports that reached him, it appeared that the cigars might be an unnecessarily extravagant touch. Of the 90 Republican legislators, 43 were reported pledged to vote for Garfield as early as October, and by November, 52 could be counted as safely in the Garfield camp, more than enough to capture the nomination. The earlier suspicions of Sherman's intentions proved unfounded. True to his word, he gave Garfield generous support. He persuaded the usually hostile Murat Halstead to treat Garfield gently in the pages of the *Cincinnati Commercial*, and he sent one of his most trusted political henchmen to Columbus with express instructions to look out for Garfield's interests.

Garfield very likely could have won even with Sherman's opposition; with his help, the issue was never in doubt. As the day set for balloting drew near, the other candidates realized the hopelessness of their position and withdrew, one by one, from the unequal race. Old Governor Dennison was the first. Judge Taft proved more stubborn, but a Garfield lieutenant took aside his personable young son, William Howard (then only a few months out of college), and convinced him that his father had no chance. The remaining candidates arrived at the same conclusion, and then there was one. YOU HOLD FOUR ACES AND ASHTABULA, Henry jubilantly, if enigmatically, wired from his Columbus headquarters.[57]

The nominating caucus, which was held on January 6, was an anticlimax. According to the *Ohio State Journal*, it was "in every respect the most remarkable meeting of the kind ever held in the state." The Republican members assembled after supper with their minds obviously made up. Without even bothering to clear the hall of outsiders, they nominated, seconded and approved Garfield as the next United States Senator from Ohio, all in less than half an hour. Older legislative hands were heard to say, "that no such scene was

446

ever before witnessed in the State Capitol, that no Senator was ever before elected by acclamation for his first term, and that no Senatorial contest was ever before held without the candidate considering it expedient to be on hand to see how things were going. . . . It is a glorious result, and so unanimous that no one feels sore."[58]

The Senator-elect professed to be more gratified at the manner of his victory than by the victory itself. "I want the Senatorship with absolute freedom, or not at all," he had repeatedly insisted. He was especially proud to have gone through the contest "without promising one office or any other thing." This was not quite true. His friends had briskly traded off committee chairmanships and speakerships in exchange for support in the Senate race, and Garfield himself was now pledged to support Sherman's presidential hopes. Still, considering the cynical auctioneering which usually accompanied an Ohio senatorial contest, Garfield had every right to be proud of the way in which his campaign had been conducted. It had certainly been cheap enough. When Henry submitted his bill for campaign expenses, it totaled only $148.60, and he meticulously returned the dollar and forty cents change remaining from the money Garfield had advanced.[59]

Now that the prize was his and fairly won, Garfield could go to Columbus to claim it. He had not set foot inside the old Senate chamber since the war; now he returned in triumph. He thanked the legislators for the honor they had bestowed upon him but, in a characteristically generous gesture, he could not forebear paying tribute to the Democrat he had displaced: "Ohio has few larger minded, broader minded men in the record of our history than . . . Allen G. Thurman." Garfield had never forgotten those few kind words of defense Thurman had uttered during the storms of the Crédit Mobilier scandal, and now he repaid the debt in accordance with his favorite maxim: "the flowers that bloom over the garden walls of party politics are the sweetest and most fragrant that bloom in the garden of this world."[60]

The new Senator-elect was in an expansive, jovial mood. With the peak of his ambition finally attained, he seemed boyishly happy. When Charles Henry extended his hand in

447

congratulation, Garfield brushed it aside and gave him a bear-hug instead, lifting his friend off the floor and swinging him round in giddy circles. Yet behind this exuberance, Garfield felt a touch of that melancholy that often overcame him when he was faced with a change. "I go," he said, "into the unknown and to the untried. . . ." He could not possibly realize, at this point, just how far that untried path would soon carry him.[61]

PART THREE

CHAPTER TWENTY-ONE

THE PUT-UP JOB

On January 9, 1879, with the Republican National Convention still seventeen months in the future, Garfield received a prophetic message from Thomas Nichol in Chicago. "Jerry Rusk was here yesterday," Nichol reported, "and says we'll put up a job and make you President."

Despite the bantering tone, this was no idle fantasy. Both Rusk and Nichol were seasoned, professional politicians. Jeremiah M. Rusk was a recent congressman and Republican National Committeeman from Wisconsin. In his youth he had once won a wrestling match by throwing a husky Ohio canal boy over his shoulder. Grown up, their paths had crossed again, in the army and in Congress, and Rusk and Garfield had become good friends. Now one of the most popular and influential leaders of the Wisconsin Republican party, Rusk could prove a valuable friend indeed. Even this early he was planning to be a convention delegate in Garfield's interest and was openly discussing his friend's prospects with his fellow-delegates.[1]

Tom Nichol, for his part, preferred to work behind the scenes. An accomplished organizer and pamphleteer, he was currently in charge of something called the Honest Money League, a pressure group which, despite its devotion to sound dollars, had not, at the moment, enough of them to pay its bills. Behind his "dirty shirt and still dirtier paper collar" was a shrewd political mind that had accurately assessed the forthcoming presidential contest.[2]

That contest was complicated by President Hayes's refusal to seek a second term. There was, however, no shortage of aspirants to fill his post. The most prominent of these was Ulysses S. Grant. Fresh from a well-publicized round-the-world tour, Grant was beginning to emerge as a hero once more in the eyes of his short-memoried countrymen. Grant was the favorite candidate of the machine politicians, those self-styled "Stalwart" Republicans who saw the influence they had enjoyed during Grant's two presidential terms melt away under the mildly reformist administration of Hayes.

Leading the Stalwart pack was a powerful senatorial trium-virate composed of John Logan, Donald Cameron and Roscoe Conkling. "Black Jack" Logan of Illinois might have been a "scabby dog," as John Hay contemptuously sneered,[3] but his teeth were sharp, especially in his stronghold of southern Illinois, which he ran as a fief. His other base of support was among the many veterans of the Grand Army of the Republic who revered him as a hero, not so much for his military prowess as for his postwar battles on behalf of pensions. Don Cameron ruled Pennsylvania by family right. His father Simon had helped found the Republican party in the state. After a brief, inglorious service as Lincoln's Secretary of War he had retired to the Senate. His control of the state party was so complete that he could pass his senate seat on to his son after Don had served his stint as Secretary of War under Grant.

Preeminent among the Stalwarts, as was only fitting for the boss of the nation's largest state, was Roscoe Conkling of New York. "Lord Roscoe" presented a bewildering mixture of elegance and arrogance. Even an age as yet uninstructed by Freud could not help being fascinated by Conkling's dread of being touched, his predilection for lavender ink and canary waistcoats, his blond spitcurl, and his strutting, aggressive show of masculinity. Years earlier, James G. Blaine had likened that pompous strut to a turkey gobbler, and from that moment the two had turned from friendship to the bitterest of rivalries. Conkling had no use for friends he could not dominate. He ruled his henchmen by terror and by the unabashed use of patronage. Garfield had correctly appraised him as "a great fighter, inspired more by his hates than his loves," and that hatred was currently directed at President Hayes and his detested "snivel service" reform policy. Conkling was opposed to reform on general principles. "When Dr. Johnson defined patriotism as the last refuge of a scoundrel," he scoffed, "he was unconscious of the then undeveloped capabilites and uses of the word 'Reform.' " His feud with Hayes, however, had grounds more immediate than a dispute over political philosophy. Hayes had struck directly at Conkling's control of the New York Republican party by removing his crony, Chester Alan Arthur, from the strategic post of Collector of the Port of New York. Deprived of patronage, Conkling began to lose his grip on the state party organization. It was essential that the next president be more friendly, for another four years in the wilderness could destroy Conkling completely. He looked to Grant for salvation.[4]

The Grant bandwagon, however, was beginning to falter. Prodded by his homesick wife, the hero had been persuaded to return to America prematurely. On his arrival, he was greeted by an unprecedented outpouring of adulation, but after it had died down, rival candidates were able to catch their balance and regroup their forces. Grant's two chief rivals for the nomination were James G. Blaine and John Sherman. The most popular and dynamic figure in the party, Blaine was a perpetual candidate but this year his heart was not in the race. He went through the motions in order to help block a third term for Grant, but he seemed aware that a nomination achieved at the expense of a knock-down fight with Conkling would only split the party and insure its defeat.[5] John Sherman pinned his hopes on his record as Secretary of the Treasury. His feat in smoothly resuming specie payment had been one of the few outstanding achievements of the Hayes administration. "The Ohio Icicle," however, was respected rather than loved, and in Conkling's camp he was positively hated for his part in the removal of Arthur. Among the avowed dark horses were the reformers' darling, George Edmunds of Vermont, whose flinty reserve could be mistaken for integrity, and Elihu Washburne, once Grant's sponsor, but now cast in the role of rival.

In short, the situation, as Nichol divined, was ripe for a

compromise candidate, some undeclared dark horse who might be acceptable to all factions. Why not Garfield? Lionel Sheldon assured his friend that he was uniquely qualified to harmonize the party in 1880: "You have not created any antagonisms, and all the other men spoken of have their foes." Sparked by this sort of reasoning, a faint Garfield boom began to rumble in the early months of 1879. In January, the Cumberland, Maryland *Daily News* became the first newspaper to hoist the Garfield banner. It was soon followed by the Monongahela City *Republican*. These obscure stirrings understandably passed unnoticed, but before long bigger guns came into action. Stanley Matthews, who often served as Hayes's spokesman, speculated publicly that Garfield might be more popular in Ohio than Sherman, and Hayes himself even dropped some hints in that direction.[6]

Such talk was flattering, but Garfield was wary. "I long ago made a resolution that I would never permit myself to let the Presidential fever get any lodgement in my brain," he declared. "I think it is the one office in this nation that for his own peace no man ought to set his heart on." Besides, he had long since concluded that "few men in our history have ever obtained the Presidency by planning to obtain it." All things considered, it was probably best to follow his natural inclination and let events take their own course, but it certainly would not hurt, as a friend advised, to "cautiously, quietly, modestly, but persistently work the machinery necessary to bring you gradually to the foot-lights. Let it seem to be done by others."[7]

As if on cue, Wharton Barker appeared on the scene near the beginning of 1880. An aristocratic Philadelphia banker with no experience in practical politics, Barker had decided as early as the previous May that Garfield was "more worthy" of the presidency than any of the avowed candidates. His motives were mixed, but prominent among them was a craving for recognition which led him, in later years, to exaggerate his role as a kingmaker. "I made James A. Garfield President. . . . I was the man behind the scenes. . . . I planned everything," he boasted, unaware that the Wisconsin plotters had anticipated him by almost a full year. Garfield did not

454

disabuse Barker of this comforting illusion. He listened to his plans without committing himself one way or the other.[8]

There was a sound practical reason for Garfield's reticence. His recent election to the Senate had been smoothed by an accord with John Sherman. Now it was time for Garfield to make good his part of the bargain. On January 26, a few days after his interview with Barker, he sent a letter on the presidential question to R. A. Horr, a downstate Ohio politician who could be counted on to pass it along to influential newspapers. Read carefully, however, the letter was not the unequivocal endorsement Sherman had undoubtedly expected. "Your letter is not you at all," a critical friend observed. "It is the first time that I have ever seen in your position the finger of the diplomat and the politician." Garfield did not say that he preferred Sherman above all other candidates nor did he suggest that the Ohio delegation should stick with him to the end. Instead, he hedged:

I have no doubt that a decisive majority of our party in Ohio favors the nomination of John Sherman. He has earned this recognition at their hands by twenty five years of conspicuous party service. . . .

I am aware of the fact that some Republicans do not endorse all his opinions. But no man who *has* opinions can expect the universal concurrence of his party in all his views; and no man without opinions is worthy of the support of a great party.

I hope the Republicans of Ohio will make no attack on other candidates. They should fairly and generously recognize the merits of all. But I think they ought to present the name of Mr. Sherman to the national convention and give him their united and cordial support.

The statement, Garfield realized, was bound to dampen his own boom and "put to rest the loose talk in the papers, which is connecting my name with the Presidency just enough to embarrass me." He was now committed, publicly at least, to Sherman. Privately, however, he kept in touch with his Pennsylvania and Wisconsin friends.[9]

Rusk was disappointed, but not discouraged by Garfield's pro-Sherman stand. Putting on a brave front, he continued to assure his friends that "Garfield is the only man we can elect and he will be nominated." Nichol moved more deviously. He had somehow managed to work his way into the heart of the Sherman organization. Although some of Sherman's lieutenants were suspicious, Sherman himself had so much confidence in Nichol's "fidelity and ability" that he entrusted him with missions of delicacy and importance. This confidence was not entirely misplaced. Nichol did not intend to sabotage Sherman's campaign. In fact, as he jestingly told Garfield, "If I keep on I will soon have *myself* convinced that his nomination is absolutely essential. . . ." He did, however, contrive to keep an eye out for Garfield's interests even while he was off on Sherman's business. Assigned the job of organizing the Sherman forces in Wisconsin, he was careful to plant the suggestion of a switch to Garfield in case the national convention should deadlock. In February, former Wisconsin lieutenant-governor and congressman Thaddeus Pound called on Garfield to explain the plan, apparently unaware that its details were already familiar. Garfield's reply was proper but not unduly discouraging. He assured Pound that "whatever happened, I should act in perfect good faith towards Mr. Sherman and do nothing that would in the slightest degree interfere with his chances for success. At the same time I would consider such suggestions as he [Pound] might make. . . ."10

Meanwhile, in Philadelphia, Wharton Barker had been plugging away industriously on Garfield's behalf. Barker was never quite as influential as he claimed to be. Despite his promises, he was not able to pry a majority of the Pennsylvania delegation away from Grant, though he did secure some delegates. Nor do his later claims of having secured covert Garfield endorsements from both Conkling and Hayes ring completely true. He also boasted of having lined up support in Connecticut, Massachusetts, New York and New Jersey, support which never materialized at the convention. Still, he did manage to organize an anti-third-term movement in his native state that substantially weakened Grant's (and Cameron's) strength. The immediate beneficiary of this revolt was Blaine, but Barker confidently assured Garfield, "we understand how to move so as to kill him. . . ." When Grant and Blaine deadlocked, Barker predicted, the convention would turn to Garfield.

A practical businessman like Barker would not have invested all this time and energy to promote the fortunes of an unwilling candidate. Garfield, however, was careful to give no overt encouragement to his schemes. For the record, he told Barker, as he had told Pound earlier, that "I would not be a candidate, and did not wish my name discussed in that connection . . . that I was working in good faith for Sherman and should continue to do so." Barker humored his qualms. "Be loyal to Sherman before and in the convention," he advised, "and your friends will do far more for you than you could do for yourself."[11]

Garfield was torn. He did want to be president, but he did not hunger for the office with the fierce intensity of, say, Blaine. Instead, he trusted to his destiny, convinced that fate had marked him out for the White House. If it was not in 1880, it would be yet to come. He could wait; he was not yet fifty. Still, if Wharton Barker or Tom Nichol should choose to play destiny's agent, Garfield would not interfere. Neither, however, could he help them, for Sherman had him neatly boxed in. Garfield had no particular fondness for Sherman as a person, nor did he think he had much of a chance to win the nomination. He supported him only as the best means to keep the state delegation united against Grant. Still, Sherman had to be appeased if only, as Charles Henry warned, "so that he cannot say that he lost it on account of Garfield's friends." It was an awkward dilemma. If Garfield stood by Sherman, as he had promised, he risked going down with a losing candidate and, what was even worse, helplessly watching as Grant triumphed. If he struck out for himself, he risked alienating Sherman forever. Faced with this unpalatable choice, he preferred to drift, placing himself in the hands of what his wife once mystically hailed as "the benign care of the far-seeing spirit . . . preserving you for that time when you shall become

> The pillar of a people's hope
> the centre of a world's desire."[12]

457

But while destiny was marking time, Sherman's demands were growing ever more pressing. Not content with a public endorsement, he now insisted that Garfield take a more active role in his campaign. Sherman was especially worried about northern Ohio, and with good reason. A poll in Sherman's home district had uncovered a surprising amount of hostility. "Cold and selfish" was reported to be the general verdict. Garfield's own district was even less enthusiastic. There the opposition to Ohio's would-be favorite son was so intense that it positively embarrassed Garfield. If he could not control his own friends, he realized, "It would almost certainly be said that I had gotten up a division so as to break Sherman's strength and pave the way for a movement in my own favor."

Near the end of February, Sherman ordered Garfield back to Ohio to force his wavering friends into line. At a meeting in Cleveland, Garfield pleaded with local leaders to send a united Sherman delegation in order to stop Grant. He was not successful. His friends reportedly expressed their objections to Sherman "in the plainest Saxon," insuring that, despite Garfield's efforts, the delegation would be split. At least two delegates among his friends were implacable in their opposition. John Beatty intended to vote for Blaine, he explained, "not that he likes him but because B is the most available club he can find to hit Sherman with." Another delegate, Garfield's old army buddy Lionel Sheldon, was even more adamant. His feud with Sherman dated back to his carpetbagger days in Louisiana, and now he gleefully anticipated revenge. When solicited for support, he replied with a crude but pungent classical allusion: "Herodotus says that some of the Asiatics were in the habit of having connection with dead women. I presume the supporters of Sherman feel a similar enthusiasm."[13]

Sherman was disappointed and a trifle suspicious after the failure of the Cleveland unity mission, but he had fresh plans to enable Garfield to redeem himself. He now informed Garfield that he would have to attend the convention as a delegate-at-large and there serve as Sherman's floor manager. This demand disturbed Garfield. He did not want to go to Chicago but neither did he want to offend Sherman. Against

458

his will he was being drawn step by step into the false position of chief spokesman for a candidate he did not really support. Burke Hinsdale, a clergyman, a moralist and a liberal, could not understand his friend's hesitation. "If," he suggested virtuously, ". . . men are to propose candidates publicly that they are opposed to privately—if politics consists largely of 'throwing dust'—then you can decline to be a delegate. But if politics be a sincere affair, I do not see how you can refuse." Wharton Barker, on the other hand, argued that it was Sherman who was guilty of insincerity. "Sherman evidently believes that if you can be side-tracked, the road will be opened to him. No honorable man would have sought to take advantage of you in this manner."

Honorable or not, Sherman's insistence that Garfield lead his forces at Chicago was not wise. This was the sort of responsibility which should have been entrusted only to someone in whom he had total confidence. Yet Sherman did not really trust Garfield, fearing that "at critical moments he wavers when firmness is indispensable." He knew of Garfield's presidential prospects. He had even encouraged them. More than once Sherman had promised that if his own presidential bid failed he would try to transfer his strength to Garfield. Even Miles Standish had not been so obliging to John Alden.[14]

To compound his error, Sherman chose Governor Charles Foster to be the other delegate at large. Foster was an avowed Blaine supporter who could hardly be expected to give Sherman his best efforts so long as Blaine was in the field, but at least Foster did not harbor presidential ambitions of his own. His sights were more modestly set on the vice-presidency. Incredibly enough, Sherman encouraged these hopes, promising to support a Blaine-Foster ticket if his own campaign faltered.[15] Perhaps Sherman thought he was being clever, but the result was to place his fortunes in the hands of two men who could succeed only if he failed. It was an unfair burden to place upon Garfield and Foster. No matter how diligently they might work for Sherman, they would inevitably be suspected of shirking if Sherman should lose.

As the convention drew nearer, that possibility seemed increasingly likely. Robert Ingersoll spoke for many Republi-

459

cans when he declared that "should Sherman be the only candidate before the Convention, the Convention would adjourn and advertise for proposals." Sherman himself adopted a pessimistic tone in private, talking less of victory than of the prospects for an honorable defeat. Blaine was equally discouraged. A week before the convention, he told Garfield that he expected Grant to be the victor at Chicago. Garfield agreed, but he was prepared to do his duty in what seemed like a lost cause.[16]

On May 25, Garfield delivered what would prove to be his final speech to the House he had entered so many years before. That evening he called on Secretary Sherman for last-minute instructions. In addition to everything else, Sherman was now insisting that Garfield place his name in nomination. When Garfield asked the candidate which of his virtues should be stressed in the nominating speech, Sherman suggested that his outstanding trait had always been "courageous persistence in any cause he had adopted." Garfield, who had often indulged in snide remarks about Sherman's "wobblings," diplomatically said nothing.[17]

Sherman's unwilling spokesman looked forward to his forthcoming Chicago ordeal with apprehension. "I go with much reluctance," he said, "for I dislike the antagonisms and controversies which are likely to blaze out in the convention." His own ambitions he reluctantly put aside. On the eve of his departure he assured a friend that he was determined to do everything in his power to aid Sherman and would squelch any movement aiming at his own nomination. The friend scrutinized Garfield carefully as he said this and was convinced of the "absolute sincerity" of the pledge. It hardly mattered. Garfield had already allowed his forces to be set in motion and they could not now be recalled. Sincere or not, this dark horse was still in the running.[18]

Garfield arrived in Chicago a week before the opening of the convention but already the city was a swirling, hectic madhouse. Each incoming train disgorged a fresh load of Republicans who scrambled for hotel rooms, roamed the corridors looking for familiar faces, crowded the lobbies spreading the latest rumors and sampled the local liquors

460

with a diligence worthy of a Democratic gathering. From out of this chaos one fact emerged clearly—the impending contest would be a struggle between Grant and the field. In such a battle the Grant forces held the advantage. They were a compact, disciplined band while their opponents were leaderless and divided. The Grant men also had a plan which, if not thwarted at the very outset, could insure their success. Their strategy was based on simple arithmetic. They could count on slightly over three hundred delegates, but 379 votes were needed for the nomination. Within the three large Grant delegations of Pennsylvania, New York and Illinois, however, there were some sixty dissidents who refused to be bound by their pro-Grant instructions. If the Convention could be induced to adopt the so-called "unit rule," whereby each state cast its entire vote according to the will of the majority of the delegation, then these dissidents could be forced, willy-nilly, into the Grant column, virtually insuring his nomination. Unwilling to risk the uncertainties of persuasion, the Grant men had decided to impose the unit rule by a fait accompli. Don Cameron, Chairman of the National Committee, would call the convention to order and entertain nominations for the Convention's permanent chairman. In so doing, Cameron would rule that the unit rule applied in this first vote to organize the convention. This would insure a pro-Grant presiding officer who would then apply the unit rule to all subsequent business of the convention, including the presidential nomination.

Word of the plot leaked out, and at a stormy all-day meeting of the National Committee Cameron refused to disavow the scheme. His stubborn silence in the chair was so exasperating that at least one committeeman was ready to pitch him out the window, while less violent men threatened to depose him as chairman. Garfield was not a member of the National Committee but he was active in the fight against the unit rule. Publicly, he denounced it as a combination of Tammany Hall tactics and Confederate states-rights theory, while privately he persuaded the Sherman and Blaine forces to unite in foiling the plot by supporting Massachusetts Senator George Frisbie Hoar, an Edmunds backer acceptable to all factions, for the

461

post of convention chairman. Hoar, it was agreed, would allow the convention itself to decide whether to follow the unit rule. Rather than face a humiliating defeat at the outset, Cameron backed down. The unit rule was, for the moment at least, put aside and the Grant forces had clearly lost round one. The main contest, however, was still to come.[19]

At five minutes after one on the afternoon of June 2, a subdued Donald Cameron raised a gavel fashioned from the door sill of Abraham Lincoln's Springfield home and, with three smart raps, called the Republican National Convention into something resembling order. The immense, flag-draped auditorium, as wide as a city block and twice as long, was crammed with over 15,000 delegates and spectators, few of whom could possibly have caught more than an occasional whiff of oratory from the distant platform. Few speakers could conquer the hall's vast spaces, much less cut through the noise of the constantly milling crowd, the huffing of nearby locomotives and the roar of the rain on the wooden roof. Only Conkling and Garfield were loud enough and tall enough to command the attention of the horde of confused delegates. Neither had ever been delegates to a national convention before but they dominated this one. They were the popular favorites as well. Every time either of them entered the packed hall he was greeted by enthusiastic cheers from the galleries.

These cheers were not exactly the spontaneous tribute they may have seemed. Wharton Barker had taken the precaution of planting a claque in the spectators' stands. Posting himself conspicuously behind the speaker's platform, Barker signaled his cheerleaders to applaud on cue. Garfield obligingly made a point of always entering the convention hall late, thus managing to call attention to the staged ovation. The Sherman forces could not suppress a touch of suspicion over Garfield's unexpected emergence as a popular hero. "There is treachery over there," a delegate muttered, pointing to the Ohio contingent. Garfield was aware of this suspicion and did his best to allay it. Warner Bateman, who of all the Ohio delegates was the most devoted to Sherman, later insisted that Garfield, "in his conciliatory and philosophic way," had been perfectly loyal to Sherman throughout the Convention. He could not,

462

however, say as much for Foster. "I do not think he gave you an hour of honest service during the whole time he was in Chicago," Bateman told Sherman.[20]

The smooth Ohio governor seemed deliberately to avoid the other Sherman leaders, preferring to spend his time in the company of Blaine supporters, whose hints of the vice-presidency left Foster positively purring with satisfaction. He was also spotted passing money and instructions to a certain Miss Dora, "a loud, coarse, vulgar woman," who was reputedly able to procure, among other things, the votes of Southern delegates.[21] Such behavior could not help reflecting upon Garfield, who was Foster's traveling companion and Chicago roommate. At first glance, such suspicions seemed pointless; the nomination of any Ohioan, whether Garfield of Sherman, would be equally fatal to Foster's vice-presidential hopes. If, however, Foster was really aiming for the Senate, then the nomination of Garfield would clear the way for him "to step into Garfield's new senatorial shoes before he wears them." Speculation on the subject was so widespread that a brash reporter bluntly asked Tom Nichol, who was running the Sherman rooms at the Grand Pacific Hotel, "Is Foster heart and soul for Sherman?" To which Nichol smoothly replied, "I am as well satisfied of Foster's sincerity toward Sherman as of my own." Nichol was enjoying a little private joke at Sherman's expense. As the originator of the Garfield-for-President boom, he was hardly in a position to speak of loyalty.[22]

That boom was now exceeding Nichol's happiest expectations. Each day's newspapers brought fresh reports of "a Garfield tide rising in the West." Even before the convention opened he was rumored to be the second choice of both Blaine and Grant supporters. From the day he arrived in Chicago, Garfield was surprised and embarrassed by the many delegates from all sections who offered their support. Secretly flattered, he informed his wife, "that without any act or word of mine to induce it, there has been growing hourly a current of opinion, which, were Ohio and I honorably free might nominate me." He prudently decided, however, to "do nothing and ask nothing—far better pleased to have nothing but the knowledge that

many desire me." Besides, he had been cast in the forthcoming
floor battles as the champion of the anti-Grant forces, a role
that could only lead to conflict with Conkling. "If I win that
fight, it will be likely to embitter him and his followers against
me. If I lose it the convention will lose interest in me. So I am
between two fires," Garfield concluded, in an odd admission
from a man who was insisting he was not a candidate.[23]

The first day of the convention was spent in shadow-boxing,
as both sides gingerly tested the limits of their strength. A
roll-call vote on adjournment showed that the Grant forces,
as had been expected, were able to muster slightly over
three hundred votes. The next day, June 4, immediately after
the opening prayer, Conkling boldly grasped for the initiative.
He moved the adoption of a loyalty oath which would bind
all delegates to support the convention's choice. This was
designed to rebuke those anti-third-term diehards who had
been threatening to bolt the party, as they had in 1872, should
Grant again be nominated. Rolling with the punch, the Blaine
and Sherman leaders chose not to contest Conkling's motion,
which passed, 716 to 3. Pressing his advantage, Conkling then
moved that those three West Virginia delegates who had
voted against his resolution be expelled from the convention.

This, Barker realized, was Garfield's opportunity. From his
prompter's spot behind the platform, he signaled for Garfield
to rise, but the signal was lost in the tumult at the conclusion
of Conkling's speech. Barker's friend and coconspirator,
Wayne McVeagh, rushed close to the platform and, in a voice
loud enough for Chairman Hoar to overhear, indicated that
Garfield had something to say. As Hoar looked toward the
Ohio delegation, Garfield finally caught Barker's frantic
arm-waving and slowly rose, "screwing himself, as it were, to
his feet."[24] In his most solemn and emphatic manner he
declared, "I fear this Convention is about to *make a mistake*."
"That ends Garfield," a Grant supporter muttered, but he
was wrong.[25] In a brief, conciliatory appeal, Garfield calmed
the ugly mood of the Convention, saved the seats of the West
Virginians and thrust himself into the limelight as the champion of party unity. Conkling hastily withdrew his resolution
of expulsion and slipped Garfield a sarcastic little note,

requesting that "Ohio's real candidate and dark horse come forward." Barker was delighted. "Nothing but a blunder on your part," he assured his candidate, "can now prevent you from receiving the nomination for President from this convention."[26]

No man could predict with such confidence just what this convention might do. As the days wore on it seemed as if the Republican Party was on the verge of spinning out of control. Some feared that the convention might end in a full-scale riot, or perhaps a deadlock like the ill-fated Democratic meeting of 1860. Each fresh confrontation, over the seating of disputed delegates, the adoption of the rules, or the framing of a platform, screwed the tension one notch tighter until it exploded in a scene that to Garfield belonged not in America "but in the Sections of Paris in the ecstasy of the Revolution." It was touched off by Emory Storrs of Chicago, whose speech happened to mention the leading candidates by name. This was the signal for pandemonium as the followers of Blaine and Grant tried to outdo each other in alternating demonstrations. For an hour and a half first one side, then the other, went crazy. Normally sober men stood on tables and chairs screaming, cheering and singing innumerable verses of *John Brown's Body*. They waved hats, umbrellas, overcoats and, on the platform, Robert Ingersoll waved a huge red shawl for the greater glory of Blaine. Even Conkling swallowed his dignity and fluttered a silk handkerchief for Grant. Flags and banners were ripped from the walls to be waved; boards were pried from the floor to be banged on benches. An immense woman from Brooklyn climbed onto the platform to bellow "Blaine, Blaine, James G. Blaine" until she was forcibly dragged from the hall. When the din finally subsided, a dazed Emory Storrs could still be seen standing on the platform with his collar torn off and his cravat draped over one shoulder as he contemplated the chaos he had unwittingly evoked.[27]

No amount of tumult and shouting could disguise the fact that the Grant forces were losing every skirmish. They lost the credentials struggles even though Logan swaggered and blustered in high style as he tried to bully the convention

465

into accepting his patently fraudulent delegates. More important, they lost the floor fight for the unit rule. This was Garfield's particular responsibility. As chairman of the rules committee, he had presided over a three-hour meeting that finally resolved to support the right of each delegate to cast his own vote, regardless of state instructions. "This," he realized, "will encounter the fury of the Grant men," who could be expected to wage a desperate fight when the committee report reached the convention floor. His tact and courtesy while winning that struggle, however, contrasted so favorably with Conkling's arrogance and Logan's boorishness that it further enhanced Garfield's esteem in the eyes of his fellow-delegates.[28]

The platform represented yet another defeat for Conkling and his followers. Despite their objections, it endorsed the record of the Hayes administration although, as reported out of committee, it did discreetly omit any reference to civil service reform. When a motion was made to remedy that neglect, one frustrated Grant supporter finally lost patience. "What are we up here for?" he indignantly asked. "I mean that members of the Republican party are entitled to office, and if we are victorious we will have office." The delighted cheers that greeted this outburst showed where the delegates' hearts were, but prudence prevailed and the party solemnly adopted a plank advocating civil service reform, though wisely avoiding a roll-call vote on the matter.[29]

Defeated in every major encounter, the Grant leaders resorted to delaying tactics, hoping to stall until delegates grew tired, short of funds and irritable enough to accept Grant out of sheer weariness. The convention chairman, George Frisbie Hoar, a deceptively mild-looking old gentleman, would tolerate none of this. Using his gavel "as a blacksmith would use a sledge," he kept the proceedings moving at a respectable clip so that by the evening of June 5 the time for nominations could no longer be deferred.[30]

Blaine won the honor of being placed in nomination first. It was a hollow victory. Four years before, his nominating speech by Robert Ingersoll had provided one of the great moments of American political oratory, but this year, fearing

466

the taint of Ingersoll's atheism, Blaine had entrusted his fortunes to an obscure Michigan industrialist, James F. Joy. The hapless millionaire began with mumbled regrets that he had been chosen for this duty. As he stumbled through a speech full of platitudes and inaccuracies, the Blaine supporters grew increasingly restless and when, at the conclusion, he placed in nomination "that eminent statesman, James S. Blaine," they shouted in dismay: "G. you fool, G.!"[31]

Next came a brief speech nominating Minnesota's favorite son, William G. Windom, and then it was Conkling's turn. He shot down the aisle like "a racehorse when the word 'go' is given," and, disdaining the platform, vaulted onto a reporters' table to deliver the speech of his career. Normally, a nominating speech followed a stereotyped pattern, as the orator tried to build up enthusiasm until it exploded at the end of the speech when he finally let drop the name of the candidate. Conkling, however, had so much confidence in his powers that he could begin with an oratorical bombshell which lesser men might reserve for a climax. "He folded his arms across his swelling breast," a hostile newspaperman reported, "laid his head back with a kingly frown upon his cleanly washed face, and settling upon his left foot with a slight stamp of his right," began to recite "with slow and thrilling utterance," a familiar bit of doggerel:

> When asked what state he hails from,
> Our sole reply shall be,
> He comes from Appomattox,
> And its famous apple-tree.

As expected, this reference to the scene of Grant's finest hour touched off a ten-minute explosion of enthusiasm, which Conkling was able to sustain, and even intensify, as his speech progressed. Not content, however, with praising Grant in the most extravagant terms, Conkling could not resist sniping at the rival candidates. He sneered at Sherman's use of patronage, mocked Blaine's private telegraph wires, and insulted the independents as "charlatans, jayhawkers, tramps and guerrillas." He brushed aside objections to a third term as hypocrisy: "Nobody now is really disquieted by a third term except those hopelessly longing for a first term, and their dupes and coadjutors." Unruffled by the chorus of hisses and boos he had provoked, Conkling imperiously sucked on a lemon until the howls subsided and then launched a fresh series of taunts. He sat down to a quarter-hour ovation that matched the hysteria of the previous day's outburst and which left the convention hall emotionally drained.[32]

Garfield was scheduled to follow with a speech nominating Sherman. He walked slowly down the aisle as he pondered how best to regain the attention of this crowd after Conkling's virtuoso performance. In the press of convention business he had neglected to prepare a speech beforehand and now, at the most conspicuous occasion of his public career, he found himself dependent solely upon the inspiration of the moment. As he mounted the same reporters' table Conkling had just vacated, he decided upon a strategy of carrying the convention away from Conkling's contrived emotionalism. He began softly, dredging up from his memory an image he had employed seven years before.

> . . . as I sat in my seat and witnessed this demonstration, this assemblage seemed to me a human ocean in tempest. I have seen the sea lashed into fury and tossed into spray, and its grandeur moves the soul of the dullest man; but I remember that it is not the billows, but the calm level of the sea, from which all heights and depths are measured. . . .

> Gentlemen of the Convention, your present temper may not mark the healthful pulse of our people. When your enthusiasm has passed, when the emotions of this hour have subsided, we shall find below the storm and passion that calm level of public opinion from which the thoughts of a mighty people are to be measured, and by which their final action will be determined.

> Not here, in this brilliant circle where fifteen thousand men and women are gathered, is the destiny of the republic to be decreed for the next four years. Not here . . . but by four millions of Republican firesides, where the thoughtful voters, with wives and children about them, with the calm thoughts inspired by love of home and country, with the history of the past, the hopes of the future, and reverence for the great men who have adorned and blessed our nation in days gone by,

468

burning in their hearts—*there* God prepares the verdict which will determine the wisdom of our work tonight.[33]

George Frisbie Hoar would later declare that though he had heard many great public speakers, this was "the finest and happiest" stroke of oratory he had ever witnessed. In less than five minutes Garfield had turned the convention around. Calmed now, the vast assemblage listened attentively to his pleas for party unity. As he went on to describe the qualities needed by the next president, more than one man in the audience thought the description fit the speaker. "And now, gentlemen of the Convention," he asked rhetorically, "what do we want?" And a voice from the gallery (which probably belonged to one of Barker's claque) shot back, "We want Garfield." Shrugging off the interruption, Garfield finally worked his way around to Sherman. Afterwards, he would be criticized for not praising Sherman highly enough. This would remind him of a story Lincoln used to tell about a boy he saw making a church out of mud. Why don't you make a preacher too, Lincoln asked. "Laws," said the boy, "I aint got mud enough." Garfield did the best he could with what he had to work with, praising Sherman's solid, if not exciting achievements in sober, yet alluring, colors. Had it not been for his unfortunately lame conclusion, Garfield would not have given even the most ardent Sherman supporter any grounds for complaint. Perhaps intending to counter Conkling's excessive adulation of Grant, he deliberately underplayed his peroration. "I do not present him as a better Republican or a better man than thousands of others that we honor," Garfield concluded, "but I present him for your deliberate and favorable consideration. I nominate John Sherman of Ohio."[34]

There were other nominating speeches yet to be made, but Conkling and Garfield had clearly stolen the show. From the talk of the weary delegates who filed out of the hall near midnight, one would have thought theirs were the only two speeches that had been made and Garfield's, on the balance, had been received more favorably. He had risen one more notch in the estimation of the men who would soon be called upon to choose a candidate.[35]

The next day was a Sunday. The convention lay adjourned for the Sabbath, but for the delegates it was hardly a day of rest. The anti-Grant coalition which had dominated the proceedings thus far was beginning to unravel. So long as the question was one of stopping Grant they could stand together, but now that the time for balloting was drawing near their common front began to crumble. Despite a day full of caucuses and consultations, whispered meetings and angry confrontations, no common strategy could be agreed upon. Neither the Blaine nor the Sherman men would give way to the other. As the prospect of a deadlock mounted, the pressure on Garfield increased. From the Mississippi delegation came promise of support if he would only give the word. In the afternoon, Benjamin Harrison of Indiana called on Garfield's hotel room to urge his candidacy, and in the evening a New England delegation formally made the same request. To all such pleas Garfield gave the same correct response: "I am going to nominate John Sherman; I am going to vote for him and I will be loyal to him. My name must not be used." This seemed definite enough but, as the next two days would show, it would take more than a denial to eliminate Garfield.[36]

Monday was hot; the sweaty delegates tramped into the steaming hall looking "as though they had slept in the lake and been dried through a wringer."[37] At ten o'clock Hoar ordered the call of the states to begin. When New York was reached, Conkling demanded that the delegation be polled. He wanted those rebels who had gone back on their pledged word by defying the state instructions for Grant, to stand up and be counted under his baleful eye. The first few insurgents mumbled their vote and quickly sat down, but Judge William H. Robertson, who had earned Conkling's special enmity by leading the bolt, defiantly shouted out his vote for Blaine to the applause of the galleries. All in all, seventeen New Yorkers recorded their votes for Blaine and two for Sherman—votes that would have been Grant's had the unit rule prevailed.

The first ballot disclosed a pattern that would be followed with only minor variations for the rest of the day. Grant led the pack with 304 votes. Of these, 176 were from south of the Mason-Dixon Line, a region rich in delegates but which would likely prove barren of Republican electoral votes come November. The three Northern boss-controlled states contributed 107 votes to the Grant column, leaving only twenty other scattered votes from the rest of the North and West. Had the unit rule been applied to all the states, Grant would have received 378 votes, only one short of victory. Blaine pressed hard at Grant's heels with 284 votes. His support was much more broadly based than his rival's; only thirty-four of his votes were from the South, the rest were all from potentially Republican areas. Sherman was a poor third, with ninety-three votes. Ohio was responsible for thirty-four of that total and the notoriously purchasable Southern delegates accounted for forty-seven more, leaving only twelve Sherman votes scattered in small pockets of the North. The Sherman managers, however, counted on picking up another sixty or seventy votes from the Blaine camp at the proper psychological moment.[38] The dark horses trailed far behind. Only two of Edmunds's thirty-four votes were from outside New England and almost all of Washburne's thirty supporters were concentrated in Connecticut, Illinois and Wisconsin. Windom claimed Minnesota's ten votes and nothing more.

On the second ballot, Wharton Barker played another of his little tricks. He instructed a Pennsylvania delegate, W. A. Grier, to cast a vote for Garfield. "If Garfield were placed in nomination in a speech," Barker reasoned, "he would be compelled to forbid the use of his name, but he need pay no attention to a vote." When the vote was announced it created only a minor stir and Garfield himself ignored it with studied indifference. Yet throughout the long, frustrating day that one vote hung on as a subtle reminder to the deadlocked delegates that an alternative was available.[39]

Ballot followed ballot with monotonous succession. Twenty-eight times Clisbee, the recording clerk, droned out the call of the states and each time the deadlock persisted. With remarkable tenacity, the ranks of the candidates held firm throughout the day. After time out for dinner, the ordeal was resumed under the glow of gas jets, but no significant change could be seen. After the twenty-eighth ballot the leading candidates were all within five votes of where they had started, twelve

471

long hours before. It was almost ten o'clock. The Grant forces, confident of their staying power, were prepared to sit all night, but they were outvoted and the Convention adjourned until the following morning.

That night the exhausted anti-Grant leaders drifted in and out of Sherman headquarters at the Grand Pacific, seeking to find in the traditional smoke-filled room some way out of their deadlock. It was hopeless. The Sherman spokesmen demanded that the Blaine leaders give way to them but the Blaine leaders, though clearly demoralized, refused. They maintained, with reason, that it was absurd for 285 votes to go to ninety-five. The Sherman people, for their part, argued that Blaine had already shot his bolt and now it was their candidate's turn. So the argument went, back and forth along well-worn grooves, without a resolution. Nor was any resolution really possible. The truth was that neither the Sherman nor the Blaine leaders could control their votes firmly enough to transfer them in a block. Many Blaine supporters, especially those in New York, actually preferred Grant to Sherman. Blaine's withdrawal could let loose enough of these votes to put Grant over the top. Sherman's Southern votes were even more precarious. If Sherman should pull out they would, most likely, go not to Blaine but to the highest bidder. The dispirited meeting finally broke up at three o'clock in the morning without any common plan agreed upon for the coming day's battle. The only faint hope to emerge for Sherman was the promise that some Massachusetts Edmunds supporters would switch to him in the morning, and might start a bandwagon rolling.[40]

With the anti-Grant forces in such disarray, the pressure on Garfield mounted. By Monday night his support was so widespread that nothing could stop it but Garfield himself. "General, they are talking about nominating you," a friend warned. "My God, Senator, I know it, I know it! and they will ruin me," Garfield replied in agitation. "I am here as a friend of Sherman, and what will he and the world think of me if I am put in nomination? I won't permit it."[41]

The next morning, as Garfield was walking to the convention hall, a friend asked, "Well, General, who is going to win

472

the battle of the wilderness?" "The same little man that won the first will win it," Garfield replied, "and I am afraid it will mean the destruction of the Republican party." The Stalwart leaders, exuding confidence, openly boasted that Grant would be nominated before lunch. There was an element of bluff in their boast. Actually, Conkling and Cameron, in something approaching desperation, were trying to buy support with promises of cabinet posts and finding no takers.[42]

The voting resumed with the twenty-ninth ballot. True to their promise, the Massachusetts delegation switched a block of votes to Sherman, but no bandwagon followed. After the thirtieth ballot Sherman's tally began to drift slowly downward, proof that his name could arouse no enthusiasm. Blaine's friends now began passing eager little notes to Garfield, begging him to desert Sherman's sinking ship for their own, but Garfield ignored their pleas and the convention remained locked in its by-now familiar pattern. In desperation for a fresh face, someone cast a vote for Philip Sheridan, but that old soldier dashed from the spectators' gallery as if he were refighting the Battle of Winchester in order to decline the honor. Hoar indulgently allowed him to break the usually iron-clad rule against interrupting a roll call but he sternly warned that the privilege would be granted "to no other person whatsoever."[43]

Meanwhile, off in a corner of the convention floor, the Wisconsin delegation was huddled in an important caucus. Aside from a determination to thwart Grant, these delegates had come to Chicago with no particular preference for any candidate. There was some Blaine and Washburne sentiment but it was lukewarm at best. For months, however, Nichol, Rusk and Pound had been assiduously cultivating the notion of Garfield as a dark horse and had reached a "tacit" understanding that they would break for him "at the proper time." Now J. B. Cassoday, head of the delegation, was urging that the time had arrived. Most of the anti-Grant delegates were willing to try the experiment, but Cassoday was well aware that a declaration for Garfield would fall as flat as the Massachusets switch to Sherman earlier in the morning unless it were immediately followed by some other states.[44]

Benjamin Harrison of Indiana seemed the most promising ally. After the futile conferences of the night before he had been heard to say that he could not endure the suspense much longer and intended to end it one way or another. When Cassoday stepped over to the Indiana section to explain his plan, the tight-lipped Hoosier replied, "We'll see," which Cassoday interpreted as assent. He then conferred with August Brandegee of Connecticut who insisted on one last effort for Washburne. This was agreeable to both Harrison and Cassoday so, on the thirty-second ballot, seven Blaine votes from Indiana and Wisconsin switched over to Washburne. The gesture was wasted. Washburne picked up no further support on the thirty-third ballot, which convinced the Wisconsinites that he was a "dead duck." Cassoday polled the delegation while the thirty-fourth ballot was underway. The hasty poll was completed just as the clerk called for Wisconsin. Cassoday rose to his feet. "Wisconsin casts two votes for General Grant, two votes for James G. Blaine and," Cassoday paused briefly and then his voice rang out "as clear as a bugle note," as he dramatically shouted, "SIXTEEN VOTES FOR GENERAL JAMES A. GARFIELD!"[45]

For a moment the huge chamber hung suspended in astonished silence, then it erupted with tumultuous cheers. "The popular chord had been touched as if by the wave of a magician," a proud Wisconsinite recalled. Garfield, "pale and dumbfounded," struggled to his feet with a point of order. "No man has a right without the consent of the person voted for, to announce that person's name and vote for him in this convention. Such consent I have not given—" At that point Hoar smashed down his gavel and ordered Garfield to be seated. Technically, Hoar was quite right. He had earlier served plain notice that he would permit no interruptions and, furthermore, Garfield's objection should properly have been cast as a point of personal privilege rather than a point of order. Hoar was not, however, concerned with such parliamentary technicalities at this moment. He had been convinced for days that Garfield represented the only salvation for the badly divided Republican Party and he had no intention of letting this opportunity be lost. He immediately ordered that the

474

balloting be resumed and Garfield sank back in his chair to watch the astonishing scene that was being played around him.[46]

On the next ballot, Indiana, as Harrison had promised, wheeled into line behind Wisconsin, throwing twenty-seven of its thirty votes to Garfield, whose total now reached fifty. Was this the break that had been so long awaited? An air of intense, almost painful excitement gripped the hall as the thirty-sixth ballot began. Early in the balloting nine Connecticut votes shifted to Garfield and then seven from Illinois and then all twenty-two from Iowa, and the stampede was on. To one astonished spectator, it almost seemed as if a supernatural force had taken possession of the convention, "as you have seen a mist or a cloud come down a mountain side, covering the valley. . . ." Men who had not given Garfield a thought found themselves giving him their vote lest they be left behind in the rush. Hoar could barely preserve order over the confusion. Eugene Hale of Maine passed him a note asking for advice. "Go for Garfield" was the Chairman's terse reply. Maine's switch was the signal the Blaine forces had been looking for, and they clambered aboard the Garfield bandwagon with enthusiasm. Nevada's Stalwart Senator Jones pushed his way to Conkling with an audacious suggestion: stop the Garfield boom by throwing the New York vote to Blaine. Conkling objected that there was not enough time to poll the delegation. "Cast the vote and poll the delegation afterward," Jones shouted, but it was too late. Even as they spoke, New York was called and Conkling stayed with Grant. The Stalwarts, true to their nickname, held firm. When their lines threatened to waver, General Beaver, a grizzled, one-legged old soldier, hopped onto a chair and, balancing himself with his crutch, shouted: "Grant men, steady! steady!" The command passed down the Grant column which pulled itself together for its last, hopeless stand.[47]

Over in the Ohio delegation, an argument was in progress. Garfield was trying to persuade his fellow-delegates to stand by Sherman. "If this convention nominates me," he pleaded, "it should be done without a vote from Ohio." Just then, Governor Dennison was handed a telegram. He ripped it open

475

and exclaimed to the delegates, "Sherman tells us to go for Garfield." "That settles it," they shouted. "Cast my vote for Sherman," Garfield begged, but in vain. Ohio was recorded solidly for Garfield.

His protest ignored, Garfield slumped in his seat, "pale as death" but possessed by an almost uncanny calm. Though the vast hall rocked to the rhythm of ten thousand voices chanting his name, Garfield himself seemed, to one observer, "the only sober man in the whole crowd." When the recording clerk read out the vote of Ohio, Garfield turned to a friend and inanely remarked: "Did you know that Clisbee was a classmate of mine at college?" Meanwhile, well-wishers were pushing over chairs and elbowing each other aside in their eagerness to be near the new hero. "They have nominated you," screamed one as he hugged him for joy. "Does it look so?" Garfield replied, with such cool detachment that some suspected he was in a daze. Actually, he was in complete control of his emotions and well aware of what was taking place. Spotting a newspaperman nearby, he carefully explained: "I want it plainly understood that I have not sought this nomination and have protested against the use of my name. . . . [Nonetheless] a nomination coming unsought and unexpected like this will be the crowning gratification of my life."[48]

Wisconsin, the state that began the landslide, had the honor of finishing it. When it was announced that her vote had put Garfield over the top, the hall went wild. For half an hour men screamed themselves hoarse, drowning out the thunder from the six cannon posted outside. Hats and coats were recklessly tossed in the air and ladies waved their handkerchiefs until the galleries looked like a billowing sea of linen. Ten thousand voices broke into a jubilant chorus of "Rally Round the Flag" as state banners were paraded around the floor and carried to the Ohio delegation as tribute.

Only the Grant men sat silent and sullen in their seats. With a discipline born of desperation, they had held firm and gone down with their ranks intact. Despite the stampede, the Stalwarts gave Grant 306 votes on the last ballot and the "immortal 306" would henceforth congratulate themselves at annual reunion dinners. For the present, however, they constituted an embittered party within a party, serving notice that the path of the newly-chosen Republican standard-bearer would not be an easy one. The Stalwart leaders made the customary gestures to party unity in poor grace. Conkling, his golden voice reduced to a choked whisper, moved that the nomination of Garfield be made unanimous and Logan seconded the motion in a bilious speech that neglected to mention Garfield by name. By this time, the candidate himself had been hustled back to the quiet of his hotel bedroom where he sat, fingering a freshly-minted Garfield-for-President badge as he reflected on the extraordinary turn of fortune's wheel.[49]

The put-up job had succeeded. Or had it? Could Nichol or Barker or anyone else legitimately claim credit for engineering Garfield's astonishing victory? They had certainly predicted this outcome and, each in his own way, had maneuvered to bring it about. But how effective had all their plotting been? Barker's claques and planted votes did help to publicize Garfield but these tricks, clever though they may have been, were just window dressing; there is no proof that they swayed a single delegation. Barker was not even in Chicago when the convention turned to Garfield, having been called away on urgent business with the Czar of Russia before the balloting began.

Nichol, Rusk and Pound had been somewhat more effective. All had been active in buttonholing delegates throughout the convention, but their most significant work had been with the Wisconsin delegation. Even there, however, their influence had not been as decisive as they seemed to think. As late as the thirty-second ballot, the Wisconsinites had been ready to go for Washburne. Only when that move failed did they turn to Garfield, and not from any long-nurtured plot but as an impulsive effort to break an intolerable deadlock. "It is absolutely certain that no delegate outside our own delegation suspected that anything of the sort was about to happen," testified Andrew Jackson Turner, father of the future historian and himself a Wisconsin delegate. "They could not have done so, for we didn't know ourselves what we were going to do until a moment before." The plotters may have plowed the ground and planted the Garfield seed in the minds of the Wisconsinites, but then they sat back and let nature take its course. Whatever happened thereafter owed more to the logic of events and to the accident of Garfield's presence on the scene than to any underground machinations.[50]

Nor were the conspirators particularly effective in mobilizing Garfield support in other delegations. A former Eclectic student, Charles W. Clarke, who was now in the Mississippi delegation, was eager to help his old teacher but he could find no one to turn to for advice. "There was no plan or combination or scheme to nominate him," Clarke insisted, "if there had been I should have been in on it, for it was generally known that I was a Garfield man voting for Grant. . . ." Benjamin Harrison who, next to the Wisconsinites, was the man most responsible for starting the Garfield landslide declared that no Garfield supporter had ever contacted him. "If he or any friend for him had been secretly working for his nomination," Harrison argued, "there was no place they would more surely have come than to our delegation being informed of our willingness to support him." After much reflection, Warner Bateman reported much the same conclusion to Sherman. "If there was any scheme in [the] Garfield movement," Bateman decided, "there were few parties to it" and its success was due entirely to the inability of the anti-Grant forces to unite behind a candidate.[51]

Sherman was not satisfied with this explanation and would brood for the rest of his life over Garfield's supposed treachery. It rankled to think that he had been deprived of the nomination by his own emissary. Yet no one who was at Chicago (with the exception of Warner Bateman) seemed to think that Sherman ever had a chance. George Frisbie Hoar, who was ideally situated to know, concluded flatly that Sherman's nomination was "absolutely impossible." Even if Garfield had managed, through some heroic act of self-denial, to decline the nomination, Sherman's cause would not have profited. The prize would have gone to someone else, most likely Grant.[52]

If Garfield had really been plotting to bring about his own nomination it was done with such finesse as to deceive

478

almost everyone at Chicago. The many Republicans who tried to persuade him to be a candidate were invariably impressed with the vehemence with which he rejected the suggestion and by the apparent sincerity with which he insisted that he wanted to make his mark in the Senate before aiming at the White House.[53] He certainly did not act like a man who wanted to be president, and when the nomination came he accepted it without joy. Perhaps he had his wife's admonition in mind. "I don't want you to have the nomination merely because no one else can get it," she had said. "I want you to have it when the whole country calls for you. . . ."[54] In any event, pushing himself forward for office simply was not Garfield's way. His peculiarly passive personality demanded that the office seek him out. He had even elevated this quirk to what he called "the law of my life" and, after following it for over thirty years, he had grown superstitiously certain "that should I violate that law I would fail." Many years earlier, when pressed to take charge of the Eclectic Institute, he had replied: "If the Presidency is thrust upon me, I shall do as I please about accepting."[55] That just about summed up his position in 1880. In brief, here was a man who managed to be standing out in the open when lightning struck. Could he be blamed if he just happened to be carrying a lightning rod at the time?

By most standards, therefore, Garfield could be exonerated of the charge of deliberate treachery to Sherman. He himself, however, indicated that a higher standard should be applied. Late in the evening of June 8, when he was officially "notified" of the convention's choice, he assured the notification committee that he was aware of his delicate position, "especially so in view of the fact that I was a member of your body—a fact that could not have existed with propriety had I the slightest expectation that my name would be connected with the nomination for the office." Sherman could be excused for thinking that Garfield here protested overmuch. Considering that Garfield had known of plans to nominate him for almost a year and a half and had done nothing to discourage them, and that he had even cooperated with the plotters in petty ways, his blanket disavowals seemed less than sincere. His melodramatic insistence that rather than be thought untrue to Sherman he would prefer to be "shot to death by the inch" —a statement that gains extra poignancy considering that precisely such a grisly fate did await him—perhaps indicated that Garfield could not suppress a certain nagging guilt over his victory at Chicago.[56]

Immediately after the nomination, Garfield's friends moved swiftly and smoothly to heal the bruised feelings of his disappointed rivals. Nichol and Foster made the unprecedented gesture of assuming Sherman's campaign expenses to the tune of about $1,500, for which Bateman, and presumably Sherman, were properly grateful. The Stalwarts could not be bought off so cheaply. By both logic and tradition the defeated faction was entitled to the vice-presidency. Governor Dennison, a likeable "old granny" grown crotchety and vain, took charge of the vice-presidential negotiations. He first tendered the honor to Levi P. Morton, an eminently respectable New York banker. Morton was tempted, but prudently consulted Conkling first. When the Great Man let it be known that he hoped no friend of his would accept, Morton hastily backed off. After other refusals, Dennison finally told the New York delegation he would abide by their choice.[57]

The New Yorkers caucused (with Conkling absent) and settled upon Chester Alan Arthur. A fine figure of a man, tall, courtly and possessing elegant, expensive tastes, Arthur was able and personally honest. In the eyes of the public, however, he was stamped as a typical machine politician because of his stubborn opposition to civil service reform as Collector of the Port of New York, a stand which had cost him his job and had led to the feud between Conkling and Hayes. He was also considered little more than Conkling's stooge, and it was generally assumed that Conkling had dictated his nomination to spite the Hayes administration. Actually, Arthur had been selected without Conkling's knowledge. Later in the afternoon he found the Senator, pacing up and down and talking to himself, and informed him that he had been offered the second place on the ticket. Conkling imperiously shot back, "Well, sir, you should drop it as you would a red hot shoe from the forge." Arthur winced but held his ground.

"The office of the Vice President is a greater honor than I ever dreamed of attaining. . . . In a calmer moment you will look at this differently." Conkling coldly replied, "If you wish for my favor and my respect you will contemptuously decline it." Arthur looked him straight in the eye and said, "Senator Conkling, I shall accept the nomination and I shall carry with me the majority of the delegation."[58] Conkling stalked out in a rage, but by the time the evening session was called to order he had regained control of his emotions and was prepared to acquiesce in his friend's nomination.

The selection of Arthur did not sit well with the reform wing of the party. They gave over 280 votes to a scattering of more acceptable candidates, including eight votes for Mississippi's Blanche K. Bruce, the first Negro to be so recognized by a major party. Sherman took the nomination of Arthur as a personal affront. "The only reason for his nomination," he sniffed, "was that he was discharged from an office that he was unfit to fill." He feared it would sink the whole ticket, but William E. Chandler, a better judge of both men and politics, was more hopeful. "Arthur is able," he reflected, "and the concession, if one was to be made . . . was the best one. . . ."[59]

Its work done at last, the Seventh Republican National Convention dissolved. The delegates returned to their scattered homes, still astonished at the unexpected fruit of their labors. Rutherford B. Hayes, whom Garfield had once described as the most optimistic man in public life, was delighted with its work. "What other Convention in all our history can show as much good and as little harm?" he asked. Others, who had more accurately measured the depths of party factionalism which this Convention had revealed, were less confident. "On the day the delegates turned their backs on Chicago and their faces toward home," declared one experienced political reporter, "Garfield was a beaten man. . . ."[60]

CHAPTER TWENTY-TWO

A BUSY, PLEASANT SUMMER

The return from Chicago was a triumphal caravan. Good natured crowds lined the route of the special flag-draped train, curious for a glimpse of the new hero. At Cleveland tens of thousands jammed the depot to cheer his arrival. At Burton he was greeted with trumpets and cannon blasts and at Chardon he made his way in an open carriage through a blizzard of rose petals. At Hiram, with all the memories it evoked, his wife's carriage met his own and from there, at last, he headed home.

And home, according to protocol, was where he was to stay, in decent obscurity until the election was over. Americans expected their presidents to rise above the vulgarities of partisan campaigning. Horace Greeley had flouted this prejudice by taking the stump on his own behalf only to be soundly beaten by the silent Grant. The lesson was not lost on Garfield or his party. Having nominated one of the great stump speakers of the day, the Republican party bowed to convention and kept him muzzled. Garfield's only function, insisted Rutherford B. Hayes, should be "to sit crosslegged and look wise until after the election. . . ." The taciturn President enjoined complete silence on his would-be successor: no speeches and, above all, "absolute and complete divorce from your inkstand . . . *no letters to strangers*, or to anybody else *on politics.*"[1]

One exception to this rule was permitted—the traditional Letter of Acceptance. This document was based on the quaint fiction that, since the office sought the man, the candidate needed a month or so to decide whether he would accept the proffered nomination. The custom did have the merit of allowing the candidate to stake out a platform of his own and as such it was examined by the public with close attention. Its preparation demanded equal care. Garfield canvassed the party leaders for suggestions. From their response it was clear that two issues would require particularly sensitive treatment: Chinese immigration and civil service reform. On the West Coast, hatred of the Chinese ran so deep, Garfield was warned, that a candidate who failed to oppose the Yellow Peril with sufficient vigor would have only the proverbial Chinaman's chance of carrying the Pacific states. Garfield bowed to their advice and inserted in his acceptance letter a sharp attack on Chinese immigration, calling it "too much like an importation to be welcomed without restriction; too much like an invasion to be looked upon without solicitude." His proposed remedy—treaty revision rather than summary deportation—was too tame to satisfy the California demagogues completely, but Garfield had no cause to doubt that his gesture had laid the issue to rest for the duration of the campaign.[2]

Civil service reform was a more ticklish matter. The reform wing of the party had made an endorsement of Hayes's policy the touchstone of their support. These Independents (or "Scratchers" as the party regulars derisively called them) constituted that college-trained, upper class, moralistic elite who placed issues above party regularity. Blaine could contemptuously dismiss them as "noisy but not numerous, pharisaical but not practical, ambitious but not wise, pretentious but not powerful," but even he had to admit that they exerted an influence far out of proportion to their meager numbers. They had long considered Garfield as almost one of their own and he, in turn, counted on their support. That support, however, could prove dangerous if it drove away Conkling and his friends. On the other hand, anything that looked like a surrender to the machine politicians could disillusion the reformers.

Torn between the expectations of the Independents and the demands of the Stalwarts, Garfield scarcely needed William

E. Chandler's advice that in this instance it might pay "to stoop a little to conquer much."[3] Besides, he had never been wedded to Hayes's particular brand of civil service reform.[4] It was not difficult, therefore, for Garfield to draft a civil service statement sufficiently vague and contradictory to minimize trouble. He endorsed the goal of civil service reform but in the next breath he promised to make no appointments without consulting local party leaders. This might seem inconsistent, but at this stage, as Garfield bluntly admitted, it was better "to run the risk of being stupid than to risk awakening unnecessary controversies." Despite his ingenuity, the reformers felt vaguely betrayed. Hayes was disappointed, Carl Schurz was "disgusted," and E. L. Godkin of *The Nation* denounced the letter as cowardly and "unworthy." Garfield, however, was willing to bear up under their disapproval if that was the price necessary to appease the Stalwarts.[5]

Simple arithmetic dictated Garfield's strategy. Victory required a minimum of one hundred and eighty-five electoral votes, precisely the number Hayes had gained four years earlier. Of that 1876 total, however, nineteen votes had been obtained in the deep South under circumstances that were not likely to be repeated. Faced with the certain loss of these votes in the South, Garfield needed to find an equivalent number somewhere else. The most likely prospects were three Northern states that had been lost by Hayes but which could yet be redeemed: Connecticut with six votes, Indiana with fifteen and New York with thirty-five. New York could be carried by organization and Indiana by money, but a divided party could command neither. An accidental nominee, Garfield had no organization of his own nor had he the confidence of the large donors. He was forced to rely upon the organizations and the contacts of others. Unless he had the active cooperation of the leaders he had just humiliated at Chicago, he was a beaten man.

The immediate outlook was not encouraging. All the disappointed candidates were acting sulky. Grant was threatening to sit out the campaign in the Rocky Mountains, Sherman was inwardly seething with each fresh report of Garfield's "treachery" at Chicago, and even Blaine could not conceal a touch of satisfaction as he predicted: "Garfield will be beaten."[6]

Blaine and Sherman could be expected to swallow their hurt in due course, but Conkling and his friends were more stubborn. The haughty New York chieftain made no secret of his reluctance to campaign for the ticket. "But for the disgrace," he sniffed, "I would rather spend the time required in Mohawk Street jail. . . ." Garfield tried to mollify him. The Acceptance Letter was an oblique form of appeasement, but Conkling demanded more direct assurances. Shortly after the Convention, Garfield made a quick trip to Washington to tidy up his affairs. While there, he pointedly called on Conkling's hotel but, finding the Senator not at home, he left his regrets. This simple note was drafted and revised with all the care normally given to a state paper, but all in vain. When the proud senator learned that Garfield had been seen consorting with the notorious reformer, Carl Schurz, he took it as a personal affront and refused to answer the note. Now it was the spurned candidate's turn to show pride. "I have made all reasonable personal advances for harmonious action," Garfield complained, and he vowed to make no further overtures. Someone else would have to break this impasse and bring the two men together.[7]

This was the sort of opportunity Stephen W. Dorsey had been waiting for. Dorsey was the new secretary of the Republican National Committee. His appointment, which had been engineered by the Stalwarts, demonstrated how little control Garfield actually exerted over the party he was supposed to be leading. The defeat at Chicago had not destroyed the Stalwarts. On the contrary, having lost the nomination, they redoubled their efforts to hold onto the party organization. Immediately after the convention adjourned, at a routine meeting of the National Committee, the punctual Grant men had arrived before their opponents and very nearly succeeded in taking over the whole committee before Garfield's friends drifted in, just in time to avert the attempted coup. Nothing further could be done until the Committee met again in New York at the beginning of July. In the meantime, the unorganized party had to waste a valuable month while its factions maneuvered to win the key positions of chairman and secretary. Garfield rather diffidently offered four equally suitable names for chairman, none of which aroused any enthusiasm in the Grant camp. As a concession to them, he suggested that Thomas Platt of New York be made secretary, despite Platt's reputation as one of Conkling's chief "fuglemen." The Stalwarts, however, insisted that Platt be made Chairman.

The problem was turned over to a special subcommittee composed of John Murray Forbes, representing the Independents, William E. Chandler, representing the Blaine men, and John Logan for the Stalwarts. Significantly, there was no spokesman for Garfield, since there was no one high in the party's councils who could be considered a Garfield man. Chandler and Forbes quickly settled on Marshall Jewell, a wealthy Connecticut industrialist, for Chairman. Although honest and respectable, Jewell was an irresolute old fuddy-duddy, whose chief recommendation seemed to be that he was the only man on Garfield's list willing to take the job. His chief drawback was the enmity of Grant, which prompted Logan to resist the appointment by throwing one of the spectacular temper tantrums for which he was famous. To pacify him, the other committee members agreed to allow Logan to choose the secretary. Logan picked Dorsey. Forbes then recommended his selection to the full committee, even though he knew nothing about the nominee's background. His ignorance, however, did not last long. Some committee members took him into the lobby and whispered that in the Senate Dorsey's vote was known to be for sale and (what was even worse) "often not for a very high price." Forbes tried to get back to the committee room to withdraw the nomination but was detained in the corridor by Platt. By the time Forbes shook himself loose, the meeting was adjourned and the conduct of the forthcoming campaign had been placed in the hands of one of "the worst machine men in the whole party."[8]

The same energy and lack of scruples that in the past had enabled Dorsey to conjure up a railroad out of "trickery, hocus-pocus and ledgerdemain," then parlay its treasury into the purchase of a Senate seat from Arkansas while the unfinished road slid into bankruptcy—these talents were now to be placed at Garfield's disposal. Ambition spurred Dorsey to make the most of the opportunity. "I have sense enough to know that if I want anything," he said, "the way to get it is to show myself entitled to it by the management of the canvass." He chafed under the plodding direction of a fuss-budget like Jewell, and maneuvered to elbow the party chairman out of his way. "Poor old Jewell" was left so bewildered that he could no longer tell whether he was running the campaign or not. "Dorsey's running it himself I guess, or all creation's running it, I don't know which," he plaintively confessed.[9]

Dorsey impatiently yearned to take campaign matters into his own hands. "We are about where we were the day we organized. No money has been raised, nor general organization effected, and, in fact, little or nothing accomplished," he burst out in vexation late in July. Actually, in his own quiet and methodical way, Jewell had been laying the foundation for an effective canvass, but Dorsey, eager for some tangible results (and not averse to a little personal publicity) demanded more spectacular action. He blamed the languishing campaign on the continued estrangement between Garfield and Conkling. The New York party workers, he warned, would continue to sit on their hands until Conkling gave the order to march. Even more important, as Dorsey explained to Whitelaw Reid, powerful New York bankers and railroad men trusted Conkling's judgment and could see no reason for "throwing away their money" on a lost cause without his endorsement. The only remedy, Dorsey insisted, was for Garfield to come to New York to set Conkling's mind at ease. A fifteen minute chat would do the job, he claimed.[10]

Reid was not completely convinced and neither was Garfield. Would not such a visit be construed by the Independents as a surrender to the machine, he wondered. Dorsey was appalled that Garfield should even consider the views of such "featherheads." A conference with Conkling, he insisted, was a "duty" the candidate owed the party, "regardless of what Mr. Jewell says or Mr. George Wm. Curtis or Mr. Anybody else." When Garfield continued to balk at the prospect of going to "Canossa," Dorsey abruptly settled the matter for him. Taking advantage of Jewell's temporary absence from headquarters, Dorsey sent out invitations to over a hundred prominent Republicans (including the New York Stalwarts) to meet with the candidate on August 5 at the Fifth Avenue Hotel. *"I am going ahead in this matter . . .,"* he informed Garfield, who now found himself confronted with a fait accompli. How unreasonable, Garfield grumbled, "that so much effort should be made to conciliate one man," but he had no choice except to pack his bags and join the Republican pilgrimage to Fifth Avenue.[11]

Accompanied by his ever-loyal crony, Major Swaim, Garfield forsook the silent role in which he had been cast and embarked upon a hazardous journey fraught with "serenades and speechmaking and like perils." He sought safety in statesman-like blandness, praising every town he passed, admiring the virtues of its citizenry and the beauty of its sunsets, but begging off from political discussions that might "offend the proprieties of the occasion." The formula seemed to work, for the crowds grew larger at each whistle-stop until by the time the train reached Buffalo the candidate was "hushed . . . into something like awe" by the densely-packed human mass that hailed his passage. Local Republican politicians, even those loyal to Conkling, hastened to hop aboard Garfield's coach to bask in the attention of the crowds he had collected.[12]

His spirits buoyed by this reception, Garfield reached New York City full of confidence for the next day's confrontation. Two problems had brought him to this city: money and patronage. The first was dealt with at a special gathering convened at Whitelaw Reid's home the evening of Garfield's arrival. The city's leading capitalists (as they were not yet ashamed to call themselves) had been invited to hear Garfield's views on the campaign. He was frank but pessimistic. Victory was doubtful, he admitted, without their prompt and generous support. His plea was met with sympathetic generalities until Levi P. Morton stepped into the breach to propose a special campaign fund, to be administered "independent of politicians." For his pains, Morton found himself saddled with the management of this secret fund. This was an unwanted responsibility since it was bound to conflict with his other role as party finance chairman. Despite this complication, securing Morton was a welcome coup for Garfield. It brought into his camp one of Conkling's most respected followers and raised hopes that Conkling himself might not be far behind.

Almost every Republican of note was at the Fifth Avenue Hotel the next day. Blaine was there and made a speech; so did Sherman and Logan and a host of lesser lights. Only Conkling was missing. It was like a wedding party without the bride. Some thought that Blaine had scared Conkling off; others suspected that it was the presence of George William Curtis that had driven him away. Conkling himself later claimed that he was unwilling to be shut up in the same room with so untrustworthy a man as Garfield but this must have been an afterthought, for at the time Conkling let it be known that he would be available to receive the candidate at his Coney Island retreat. Garfield had now reached the limit of his patience. Having come this far to meet Conkling, he refused to go one step further, declaring that "if the Presidency is to turn on that, I do not want the office badly enough. . . ."[13]

Any negotiations would have to be conducted with Conkling's embarrassed lieutenants. Actually, this arrangement did not greatly displease Garfield. He saw it as an opportunity to drive a wedge between the New York Stalwarts and their chief. This was not as unlikely a prospect as it might seem. Conkling was losing interest in politics and was sustained in the struggle mainly by pride and spite. The younger men, such as Tom Platt, still had careers to make and, despite their protestations of loyalty, were not eager to follow their leader into defeat. They promised Garfield the full support of the New York organization. In return, they wanted to be assured that Garfield would not ignore them when distributing patronage, as Hayes had done. The newspapers would later make much of this so-called "Treaty of Fifth Avenue," but in reality nothing so formal was negotiated. Garfield was perfectly willing to agree that neither Schurz nor Sherman (both of whom the New Yorkers detested) would be retained in his cabinet, and he promised to end the patronage war Hayes had waged against the New York organization, but this

489

hardly constituted a treaty. "There was nothing in the treaty," Garfield's private secretary later confided, "except that [Garfield] was indiscreet in having let himself be cornered in a room where general conversation upon such matters took place."[14]

The results of the meeting were transmitted to Conkling, who had no choice but to abide by the arrangements his subordinates had made in his absence. Conkling was learning one of the paradoxes of power—that a leader needs followers more than they need him. With unaccustomed meekness, he placed himself "in the hands of his friends" and agreed to do whatever they might ask. What they asked was that he raise his golden voice for Garfield at political rallies and meetings. "If you insist," he finally agreed, ". . . I shall carry him through." With Conkling's capitulation came also his host of followers, those who "stand around and watch Conkling as little dogs watch their master when he is in a bad mood—waiting for him to graciously smile, and they will jump about with effusive joy." He did smile and they jumped eagerly. "The campaign in the State of New York was from that moment pushed with the most untiring and sleepless energy," Platt boasted. "No equally exhaustive and 'red hot' canvass was ever before made. . . . The organization of the party did its whole duty. . . ." The New Yorkers were galvanized into all this action by something more tangible than Platt's sense of "duty." The Fifth Avenue Conference had left them painfully aware that, as Blaine vividly put it, they could ill afford to scuttle a ship on which they were passengers. This lesson alone made the conference worthwhile and justified Reid's happy conclusion that "it turned all our way . . . and that the only one in any way injured by it was Mr. Conkling himself."[15]

Garfield had reason to be pleased with his New York labors. He had surmounted the hazards of the occasion and could now run the gantlet of admiring crowds and return to the safety of home. His voice was hoarse and his right hand swollen but his conscience was clear: "No trades, no shackles and as well fitted for defeat or victory as ever," he reflected with satisfaction. Many people would have been puzzled if they could have read this disclaimer in Garfield's diary. Levi P. Morton, for one, certainly expected some reward for

490

his fund-raising services. Precisely what he expected, however, was never spelled out, an omission that was bound to cause confusion and hurt feelings later on. Similarly, Garfield's promises to the New York Stalwarts carried the seeds of future misunderstanding, a misunderstanding that was compounded by Garfield's deliberate ambiguity, the circus-like atmosphere of the conference and, to a degree, the wishful thinking of the Stalwarts themselves. Garfield may have thought that he escaped from New York untramelled by pledges, but conflicting tales of promises given and broken would follow him into his troubled presidency. It would be whispered that, in return for campaign contributions, he had given Jay Gould and other railroad men the right to choose his Supreme Court appointments, and, in addition, had guaranteed that a syndicate of New York bankers, headed by Gould and Morton, would be given exclusive rights to handle the next issue of government bonds. The first of these charges was a distortion, the other a malicious invention, but in after years they would cloud the fact that the Fifth Avenue Conference had been a personal triumph for Garfield. It marked the turning point of the campaign.[16]

At this stage, the Republican campaign certainly needed to turn. Big city gamblers were giving odds against Garfield's winning his home state, much less the presidency. While Republicans had been trying to decide whether or not to speak to one another, the Democrats had stolen an early lead. "For the first time in twenty years the Democracy did not blunder," warned one alarmed Republican upon hearing of the nomination of General Winfield Scott Hancock. "Hancock the Superb," hero of Gettysburg, was a shrewd and unexpected selection in this season of dark horses. His portly presence on the ticket was bound to neutralize the favorite Republican theme of the "bloody shirt" by casting an aura of patriotic respectability over the one-time party of rebellion. True, Hancock's civil experience was negligible but the party of Grant could hardly make much of an issue of that failing. Furthermore, Hancock lived in New York, while his running-mate, William H. English, a rich but miserly Hoosier, could be expected to add strength in the other pivotal state of Indiana.[17]

Having chosen a candidate without a record, the Demo-

491

crats were free to vilify that of their opponent's. Ignoring the more lofty issues of public policy, they concentrated their fire on Garfield's personal character. His entire career was dredged to prove his unfitness for the White House, but the DeGolyer Pavement scandal and Crédit Mobilier provided the juiciest themes. To memorialize Crédit Mobilier, they adopted the number 329 as a battlecry, scrawling that mystic figure on buildings, barns, fences, sidewalks and (with peculiar aptness, considering the level to which their campaign had sunk) gutters. Garfield would not stoop to respond to "this blackguard campaign," even though some nervous advisers suggested he issue a public defense. All his life, he had been reluctant to answer personal attacks by parading his own virtue, and he saw no reason to break this habit now. He trusted that time and the good sense of the electorate would counteract the Democrats' tactics.[18]

The first test would come with the September elections in Maine. These contests, like those in the October states of Indiana and Ohio, were purely local but they were regarded by some as reliable portents of the general election in November. The Maine situation was complicated by a fusion between Democrats and Greenbackers, but Blaine, who was running the show, was confident of a six to ten thousand vote majority. Instead, the Republicans lost. Blaine tried to excuse his poor showing with the claim that the Democrats had poured $100,000 into the state at the last moment, but most observers interpreted the defeat as a revolt against Blaine's high-handed, dictatorial management. "He has saddled and ridden the party for twenty years," said one, "and now it has thrown him." Garfield was not so much concerned with assigning blame as he was with minimizing the effects of the bad news on Republican morale. He urged the party to turn this setback into the equivalent of the first Battle of Bull Run—a painful but salutary warning against complacency.[19]

Blaine, unchastened by his responsibility for the distressing events in Maine, was as free as ever with advice. He insisted that the party's salvation was to find new issues to stir the voters. Up to this point the campaign had stressed two basic themes: Garfield's personality and the old reliable bloody shirt. Rutherford B. Hayes reasoned that about every twenty years Americans were ripe for an election waged on personalities. Garfield, he suggested, was the ideal candidate for such a campaign, "because he is the ideal self-made man." The President envisioned a canvass conducted with all the hoopla of the famous Log Cabin campaign of 1840. Garfield's inspirational rise from obscurity should be trumpeted across the nation. "Let it," Hayes urged, "be thoroughly presented— in facts and incidents, in poetry and tales, in pictures, on banners, in representations, in processions, in watchwords and nicknames." The public was deluged with campaign biographies bearing such Horatio Alger-like titles as *From the Log Cabin to the White House* or *From the Tow Path to the White House*. Even Horatio Alger himself allowed his art to imitate life by writing *From Canal Boy to President*. Garfield proved to be his party's greatest asset. Almost four million copies of his various speeches were circulated, nearly one for every Republican voter.

Less than two years earlier, Garfield had publicly buried the bloody shirt. "The man who attempts to get up a political excitement in this country on the old sectional issues," he had warned, "will find himself without a party and without support." Now he was disregarding his own advice. Over a half million copies of his inflammatory "Revolution in Congress" speech were being circulated and Garfield himself helped fan the embers of sectional hatred. Addressing a Pennsylvania audience, he contrasted their true Americanism with the "bastard civilization" of the South, still "steeped to the lips with treason and disloyalty." Unedifying though this sort of thing might have been, it seemed to be what rank-and-file Republican voters expected of their candidate. The old issue of North versus South was the only one to arouse widespread enthusiasm from Garfield's correspondents. As one put it: "I think the Blue will triumph over the Gray as it done at Appomatick Court House." He spoke for millions whose politics had been shaped by the feuds of the past.[20]

Blaine, on the other hand, envisioned a party that could speak to the aspirations of the new industrial age by stressing economic issues, especially the tariff. Shortly after the Maine elections, he burst into party headquarters and, with his customary brisk enthusiasm, cried out: "fold up the bloody shirt and lay it away. It's no use to us. You want to shift the main issue to protection. Those foolish five words of the Democratic platform, 'A tariff for revenue only,' give you the chance." Under the banner of the protective tariff, the Republicans could transform themselves from the party of the Union to the party of prosperity. This strategy was aided by the return of good times. With bankruptcies at their lowest rate in five years and the vexing currency question apparently laid to rest by specie resumption, the Republican claims gained plausibility.

Hancock played right into their hands. In a newspaper interview, he cryptically dismissed the tariff as "a local question." "That," chuckled a delighted Republican, "is one interview too many." Even though Garfield had said virtually the same thing on a number of occasions, his friends gleefully seized upon Hancock's statement as fresh proof of his ignorance. Cartoonist Thomas Nast portrayed a befuddled general plaintively asking, "Who is Tariff, and why is he for Revenue Only?"[21]

By stressing economic issues, the Republicans hoped to convince the business community that its interests would continue to be well guarded. In return, it was hoped that the grateful businessmen would loosen their purse strings to fill the party treasury. Despite the New York conference, the large donors were still holding back. "There are some people you know," Jewell reminded the candidate, "who want to be on the winning side; some of our most valuable friends have about made up their minds that the other side is to be the winner. . . ." The Maine election further discouraged these potential donors, as well as leaving the National Committee's bank account embarrassingly overdrawn. Yet a political campaign, as Judge Hoar once cynically remarked, "cannot be run with merely a barrel of music and a monkey." It took money, far more money than the public realized, to elect a national ticket. There was nothing necessarily sinister in the use of all this money. Even the honest and legitimate requirements of politics swallowed money in vast quantities. Barbecues in the South, clambakes in New England, parades and rallies in the cities, were all necessary but expensive. First, the voters had to be located. This required elaborate and expensive surveys. In New York City alone a list of 300,000 names was drawn up and organized precinct by precinct. Then documents had to be printed and placed in the proper hands. Over twelve million documents were circulated by the Republicans in the campaign of 1880.[22] Then on Election Day voters had to be brought to the polls. In the South, the poll tax often had to be paid, while in all states the voting booth had to be watched with care to avoid skulduggery. A seasoned party professional itemized some other expenses:

The New York Headquarters bill, with its Fifth Avenue or other rooms for four months, its staff of correspondents and travelling agents for canvasses, is always a heavy item. Public speakers sent over the country by the national committee are not often paid for their speeches, but their expenses are usually paid out of the fund and are apt to be large,—travelling, as they do, in palace cars and living in first-class hotels; and they cannot well be scrutinized carefully through vouchers or by auditors. Flag-raisings, torchlight processions and bands of music swallow the fund fast. . . . Newspaper advertisements are sometimes very costly indeed; extra copies of papers foot up a heavy bill; as does the distribution of campaign matter from headquarters; the newspaper supplement, or broadside, often going in the same wrappers without additional postage, is a very valuable method, and in proportion to its value is not a costly one; but there is abundant room to spend money legitimately in this way.[23]

To make the financial picture even more bleak, one traditional source of funds—the assessment of government officeholders—was now illegal under Hayes's civil service reform decrees. Squeezing "milk" from the docile corps of federal workers was one of the more traditional, though less savory, methods of political fund-raising. Eight years earlier, Garfield had condemned the practice as "shameful," pointing out that the money thus raised "in many cases never gets beyond the pockets of the shysters, the hangers-on, and the mere camp-followers of the party." Much to the reformers' delight,

Hayes had outlawed such political assessments. In their stead, however, he tolerated the soliciting of "voluntary contributions," a distinction which deceived no one but which seemed to satisfy Garfield. "Old boy," he enthusiastically urged a collector of such contributions, "do all you can to raise the *sinews of war*."[24]

In every government office, officious collectors with little black books in hand tried to browbeat clerks into making their donations. In New York, Chester Alan Arthur personally supervised the collections with merciless rigor. Despite his professions of sympathy for civil service reform, John Sherman made certain that each Treasury Department worker came to the aid of his party, but in the Interior Department, Carl Schurz kept throwing the collectors out of this office. Jay Hubbell, chief of this fund-raising operation, was reduced to a steady stream of profanity as he saw at least $20,000 slip out of his hands from Interior alone. He warned that if Schurz's attitude should prove contagious it might cost the party $100,000 more. "Cant you capture a few first class millionaires," he asked Garfield, "and clip them in for loose change?"[25]

To snare the elusive millionaire, however, required the proper bait, and this season, as Whitelaw Reid informed Garfield, "The real anxiety of these people is with reference to the Supreme Court." The previous year, the Court had upheld, by a five to three decision, a law that would have compelled the Union Pacific Railroad to set aside a portion of its profits in order to pay off its debt to the government. This decision, coming on the heels of the celebrated Granger Cases, raised the specter of massive federal regulation of private corporations unless this "revolutionary" judical tendency could somehow be reversed. With three seats soon likely to fall vacant, the next president would have the power to reshape the bench to his own philosophy. Garfield's public record, however, was not likely to assuage the fears of railroad magnates. His wartime opposition to the Camden & Amboy monopoly, his attacks on Jay Gould in connection with the great Gold Panic, his repeated warnings that the state must choose between controlling the railroads or being controlled by them, and his recent proud advocacy of the Reagan Bill to regulate interstate commerce, all seemed to betray a disturbing lack of sympathy for the sanctity of private corporations.

Apparently the New York conference had done nothing to allay these doubts (thus putting to rest the charge that Garfield sold Supreme Court appointments in Whitelaw Reid's living room), for the railroad men persisted in their efforts to pin Garfield down. Using Reid and Jewell as intermediaries, Gould, Collis P. Huntington and Cyrus Field dropped enticing hints of large campaign donations in return for the proper guarantees. Gingerly, as if avoiding a trap, Garfield responded with cautious generalities. He had his friend Charles Foster write a letter to Senator Preston Plumb who was, in turn, authorized to show it to the railroad men. "You can assure such friends," Foster declared, with Garfield's prompting, "that the General has the highest possible regard for the sacredness of vested rights. . . ." As evidence, Foster cited a paragraph which had been omitted from the Acceptance Letter "from motives of campaign discretion," in which the candidate pledged to avoid "any policy which will prevent capitalists from extending our great railroad system."[26]

Garfield could not squirm off the hook this easily. Reid wrote back in disappointment that his friends expected a more precise response. He forwarded copies of the controversial dissent along with the Court's majority opinion, demanding that Garfield indicate which opinion he supported. "If the former," Reid bluntly declared, "then I will go out at once, on the matter we have spoken of, and am sure my visit can do great good. If the latter, I don't see that I can render any other service than to keep pounding away on the [news] paper. . . ." Under this sort of pressure, Garfield finally agreed that "as a lawyer" he did sympathize with the dissenting opinion, but this was not enough of a capitulation to satisfy Reid's friends. They now demanded the right to pick Garfield's Supreme Court nominees. This, at last, was too much. "My life has been so earnestly devoted to the public good," Garfield angrily retorted, "that I cannot tolerate the suggestion of giving bonds that I will not act otherwise hereafter. I do not care enough for the presidency to assume its functions under any bonds but my conviction of duty." But, in the next breath, he swallowed these brave words by promising, in effect, to give Reid and his friends veto power over his Supreme Court choices. This was all they wanted to hear and within the week Reid could happily report, "It has all worked out right."[27]

The grateful railroad men proceeded to do their duty, as did other segments of the business community. In Pennsylvania, Wharton Barker was able to tap the Union Leagues for over $100,000 by stressing Garfield's soundness on the tariff, while in Ohio, Charles Foster managed to collect almost $50,000 more. Morton's "special work" was moving along nicely and in other states busy fund-raisers were filling the party coffers. With finances assured, the campaign at last began to hum. Meetings, parades, rallies and speeches carried the Republican message to every crossroads village. The bustling confusion of an active campaign was reflected in the hundreds of anguished telegrams streaming into party headquarters telling of cancelled appointments, speakers unable to address meetings and frantic efforts to line up other speakers. One distraught party chairman from Brazil, Maryland, faced with the prospect of a speakerless rally, prayed, "FOR GOD'S SAKE SEND US INGERSOLL," forgetting that such an appeal would scarcely move the great atheist.[28]

While the campaign raged across the land, the candidate himself played the country gentleman amid the rustic simplicity of his Mentor farm. Enlarged from one-and-a-half floors to three by a timely renovation, the house was now able to accommodate some of the visitors who descended upon "Lawnfield" (as the newspapers grandly dubbed the farm, much to its owner's amusement). The upstairs library was converted into campaign headquarters; the little cabin in the back was linked by telegraph wires to party nerve centers and even the hay loft was pressed into service as a makeshift bedroom for Harry and Jim when overnight company preempted their own beds. Mentor had never seen such excitement. The daily deluge of newspaper reporters and distinguished guests placed the little town at the very center of national attention. Despite the floodlight of publicity which followed his every move, Garfield attempted, with some success, to lead a normal life. Visitors were charmed by scenes of unpretentious domesticity: Garfield's aged mother rocking on the back porch, pitting cherries; the candidate himself perched on a window sill playing the hose on his naked sons; the entire family playing word games around the dinner table.[29]

This was the first summer in over twenty years in which Garfield was not called upon to campaign somewhere. It seemed strange, and somehow unnatural, for Garfield to be sitting peacefully on his front porch while a congressional campaign was being waged in his old nineteenth district. For eighteen years this had been virtually his fief, and it galled him to see it pass into the hands of someone else. What was even worse, the new Republican nominee was that same Judge Ezra Taylor of Warren who had once borrowed money from Garfield and then promptly deserted him at the first hint of the Crédit Mobilier scandal. Garfield's true friends were disgusted at the choice of Taylor and whispered darkly that "in one term drink will 'finish him,' " but even that comfort was denied them. Taylor would hold his congressional seat with distinction for the next thirteen years.[30]

Local affairs, however, were merely a minor distraction and hardly prevented Garfield from making the most of the leisure which propriety imposed upon a presidential candidate. Five thousand pieces of mail awaited his attention, with a hundred more arriving each day. A steady torrent of callers pressed their good wishes upon him at tedious length. Yet even so, the candidate found time to supervise his farm, romp with his boys, play croquet on the lawn or simply sit by the fire and contemplate the latest theories on the creation of the universe. Much to his surprise, Garfield found himself actually enjoying a "busy though pleasant summer."[31]

Guilty over enjoying himself at home while others were laboring on his behalf, Garfield grew restless. "If I could take the stump and bear a fighting share in the campaign I should feel happier," he said. Actually, there was no need for him to go forth to meet the voters; every passing train brought the voters to his own front door. To each delegation Garfield gave a gracious little speech and light refreshments. One day

499

it might be seven cars full of Germans; the next, 1,880 members of the Indianapolis Lincoln Club, all garbed in identical linen dusters and three-cornered straw hats. One rainy afternoon a trainload of nine hundred ladies marched from the station, presenting the delightful spectacle of a mile of black umbrellas bobbing slowly down the road. The most emotional moment of this campaign was provided by the Jubilee Singers of all-black Fisk University. As they sang their mournful spirituals, the little audience that had gathered in the parlor began to weep openly. Garfield, too, was deeply moved. These were the songs he had heard from the slaves in army camp so many years before, and now the old memories of wartime rose again as he stood before his fireplace to deliver some brief remarks. He began softly, but at the conclusion he pulled himself erect and in a ringing voice declared: "And I tell you now, in the closing days of this campaign, that I would rather be with you and defeated than against you and victorious." In the report prepared by his secretary for the press, this pledge was prudently omitted.[32]

The undisputed high point of the front-porch campaign was reached on the day Roscoe Conkling and a group of distinguished friends dropped in for a cup of tea. Once his initial reluctance to campaign had been overcome, Conkling had proven a hard and effective worker. Just whom he was working for, however, remained open to question. He managed to deliver twenty speeches from New York to Indiana without finding anything more flattering to say about the head of the ticket than that he might make a "competent" president. Garfield was deeply offended by this lack of courtesy and suspected that Conkling was less interested in pushing Garfield in 1880 than Grant in 1884. This suspicion was strengthened by Conkling's insistence that Grant accompany him on his campaign tour. The old hero had been coaxed down from his Rocky Mountain hideaway by the plea of party unity. Public speaking was torture to him, but, "like the good soul he is," Grant grimly subjected himself to the ordeal.

Late in September, Grant and his friend were invited to address a "Monster Rally" at Warren, Ohio. Since Conkling refused to subject his voice to the strain of open air oratory,

500

a vast wooden "Wigwam" was erected for the occasion. Forty thousand people braved a thunderstorm to hear the general talk for seven minutes and the senator for two hours. Afterwards, to give vent to their enthusiasm, the crowd attempted to unhitch the horses from Conkling's carriage and pull it themselves through the streets. "It was a great day for Warren—a great day for Ohio," declared a local newspaper. It was not, however, a great day for Garfield. Here, in the heart of the nineteenth district, Conkling had studiously avoided mentioning Garfield "in any generous way." This "narrow and unmanly" behavior seemed bad enough but, to compound the insult, Conkling intended to avoid paying the candidate at nearby Mentor the expected courtesy call. Simon Cameron overruled this plan and at his insistence Conkling, Grant, Logan and the Camerons, father and son, stopped off at "Lawnfield" on their way west.[33]

Tom Platt, who was not there, left a vivid description of the event: Garfield, hatless, rushing out in a rainstorm to embrace Conkling and blubber, "Conkling, you have saved me. Whatever man can do for man that will I do for you!" Those who were there, however, insisted that no such scene occurred. Instead, the company was ushered into the house, served a light snack, introduced to a number of local notables and sent on their way within an hour. According to Platt, Conkling extracted a pledge that all New York patronage would go to his friends. This Treaty of Mentor was supposed to be something on the order of a Midwest ratification of the alleged Fifth Avenue Treaty but the evidence clearly indicates that no such deal was even considered. Garfield's secretary vehemently branded the story "a deliberate lie." Garfield himself insisted that he held no private conversations with anyone and, with two hundred guests milling around, it was unlikely that he could have had much opportunity to do so.[34]

Except for his foray into New York and a few innocuous side trips to county fairs and veterans' reunions, Garfield remained immured in Mentor throughout the campaign. Physically isolated, he managed nonetheless to maintain a constant watch over the progress of that campaign. Not only was

501

he supplied with "the most minute and comprehensive reports" of each day's activities but he was also responsible for the single most important strategic decision of the campaign—the allocation of priorities.

Not even Republican resources could be stretched so thin as to make a fight on every front. The Southern states were reluctantly left to their own devices as the party concentrated its ammunition on the key Northern contests. Of these, the most strategic, Garfield decided, was the October election in Indiana. He vigorously pressed this view on the party managers, insisting that "If we carry Indiana the rest will be easy." He pursued his argument with a military analogy, reminding those New Yorkers who wanted to spend their money closer to home that "Napoleon won the siege of Toulon by announcing that Toulon was not in the city but on the point of land projecting in the bay. He planted a battery there that compelled the abandonment of the city by his enemy. So now the Republicans ought to see that, politically speaking, New York is in Indiana and the capture of the latter state in October ensures New York in November." Republican leaders, including Conkling and his friends, bowed to the candidate's desires and a massive effort was launched to carry Indiana.[35]

It promised to be an uphill fight. Four years earlier Tilden had carried the state by over six thousand votes and in 1878 the Democrats had widened that lead even further. Soundings taken in September of 1880 indicated that the Democratic grip on Indiana had not slackened. Garfield had chosen to give battle on the enemy's high ground but he felt he had a few secret weapons of his own. One was the disorganized state of the opposition. Indiana Democrats had entrusted their campaign to vice-presidential nominee English, a political Rip van Winkle who had been hibernating in his bank for the past twenty years. He ran the sort of campaign that might have been fashionable in the 1840s, while the more up-to-date party regulars, envious of his sudden rise from obscurity, stayed on the sidelines. Economic issues, such as farmer and labor grievances, were ignored, and assistance from the Greenbackers was disdainfully repulsed.[36]

The Republicans, in contrast, displayed remarkable flexibility. Unhampered by considerations of ideological consistency, they were able to harness the most disparate forces to their cause. Even though Garfield had regarded the Greenbackers of Maine as dangerous communists and anarchists, he raised no objection to a covert alliance with their party in Indiana. At the very same time, the resourceful Republicans were able to work the other side of the street by accepting aid from the notorious Standard Oil Corporation. This mammoth company employed two thousand woodcutters in southern Indiana who could be mobilized for political work if the central office in Cleveland raised no objection. Garfield was asked to use his influence with John D. Rockefeller to secure permission. Actually, he had no influence. Even though they lived only a few miles apart they moved in different circles. Garfield not only had never met the tycoon, he somehow thought that his name was "Rockafeller" (Swaim called him "Rockfelter"). Discrete inquiries, however, indicated that the corporation was *"all right,"* and willing to help. Secrecy was enjoined, lest word leak out to the oil districts of Pennsylvania where the very mention of Standard Oil would "cut like a knife." Otherwise, there was no objection to adding the forces of Standard Oil to the political arsenal Republicans were assembling in Indiana.[37]

Garfield's most cherished weapon in this campaign was forged in his own church—one more example of that Disciple connection which he had successfully exploited throughout his career. Over twenty-five thousand Indiana voters gave their allegiance to the Brotherhood. A concerted campaign to woo them might, it was estimated, make a difference of five thousand votes, nearly enough to neutralize the Democratic lead. Garfield's ministerial friend, Burke Hinsdale, was put in charge of an operation to mobilize the Campbellite network. Four hundred preachers were pressed into service to praise Garfield from the pulpit and a quarter million pieces of campaign literature, ten for each voter, were stuffed into the mailboxes of Indiana Disciples. All this effort was surprisingly inexpensive (only a few thousand dollars), but both Hinsdale and Garfield expected a substantial return from the investment. Dorsey, however, contemptuously dismissed the project, insisting that if Indiana were to be saved it would be by money rather than by prayer.[38]

Dorsey was in charge of the less holy aspects of the Indiana campaign. At New York headquarters he and Jewell had been at such constant loggerheads that it was thought best to ship Dorsey off to the West, partly to keep him out of Jewell's hair and partly because his peculiar expertise was needed in Indiana. Jewell was deliberately kept ignorant of his subordinate's activities. Funds for Indiana bypassed the national office and went straight from Morton to Dorsey, while Jewell pathetically shuffled papers at the Fifth Avenue Hotel and tried to preserve some shreds of dignity. The Chairman "has been badly used in the whole business," Garfield was told, but Jewell himself claimed he would be content if this humiliating arrangement helped to carry Indiana.[39]

Dorsey was in his element in this corrupt, free-wheeling state. Using all his ample executive ability, he set up a complex scheme of organization that blanketed Indiana with a crazy-quilt pattern of overlapping jurisdictions. An organization of the scope he had in mind would not come cheaply, but Dorsey guaranteed that the money would be well spent. Morton responded generously, although not with anything like the $400,000 Dorsey later boasted of having spent. The true costs for the October election were closer to $70,000 but this was ample, considering that the opposition spent only about $50,000. Dorsey gave the party its money's worth. His army of agents burrowed into every township and precinct, sending daily detailed reports of every wavering voter, every purchasable vote and every suspicious-looking stranger. Convinced that the Democrats intended to steal the election, Dorsey and his associates prepared cunning countermeasures to forestall the anticipated frauds. "If the Democratic party can put up any jobs on us this year," he confidently boasted, ". . . I for one will be willing to throw up the sponge." Poll watchers were trained to prevent ballot stealing and stuffing, and supervisers were hired to watch the poll watchers. Negroes, who might be intimidated by Democratic thugs, were given protection, at least until they had cast their vote. The use of "professional repeaters" was discouraged by the distribution of voter lists for every county to each poll watcher. Dorsey's greatest fear, however, was that the wily Democrats would sneak out-of-state voters into Indiana. Railroad inspectors and Pinkerton agents were hired for detective work. They followed anyone who entered the state carrying cheap luggage, they infiltrated saloons to pump drunks, and they wormed their way into Democratic strongholds to sniff out plots.[40]

These spies uncovered little concrete evidence to support Dorsey's fears. On the contrary, their reports indicated that the Democrats were chiefly preoccupied with the fear of Republican frauds.[41] These fears had some basis. Republican managers did display a disturbing familiarity with the fine points of various electoral frauds and Dorsey himself in a candid moment, had earlier declared, "I believe in fighting the devil with his own fire." One need not believe the Democrats' story that a blizzard of crisp new two dollar bills descended upon the state "like snowflakes" on election day to suspect that Dorsey's hands might not have been entirely clean. Burke Hinsdale, who admittedly was easily shocked, openly doubted whether there was "any uncleaner nest of political birds in any state capital in the last campaign" than the one which had taken roost in Indianapolis. Even a seasoned and cynical party regular, however, shuddered when he realized that "some of our worst men" had taken charge in Indiana. "If they do not cover the party with disgrace I shall be thankful," he said.[42]

Victory dissolved these misgivings into euphoria. In the October election this recent Democratic stronghold gave the Republicans majorities of five to seven thousand votes, and the party could, for the first time since the convention, look forward to November with confidence. "The rest is form," Robert Ingersoll assured Garfield. "Your inauguration has commenced."[43]

Such confidence was premature; the opposition might still have some last-minute trick up its sleeve. There was ample precedent. In 1844, for example, when James K. Polk was running for president, a Northern newspaper had printed a fraudulent story that a traveler named Roorback had seen slaves hideously branded with the initials J. K. P. From that time on, any election-eve hoax was termed a roorback and political managers lived in fear of being victimized by such a device. In October of 1880 Garfield found himself the target of a classic roorback. Five days after the Indiana election, the editor of a New York scandal sheet, quaintly called *Truth*, found an odd-looking envelope on his desk. It contained a letter on House of Representatives stationery dated January 23, 1880 and addressed to one H. L. Morey of the Employers Union in Lynn, Massachusetts and signed by J. A. Garfield.

Yours in relation to the Chinese problem came duly to hand.

I take it that the question of employees is only a question of private and corporate economy, and individuals or companys [*sic*] have the right to buy labor where they can get it cheapest.

We have a treaty with the Chinese government, which should be religiously kept until its provisions are abrogated by the action of the general Government, and I am not prepared to say that it should be abrogated until our great manufacturing and corporate interests are conserved in the matter of labor.

If genuine, such callous antilabor sentiments could do Garfield serious damage, especially on the West Coast. The letter was shown to prominent Democrats, most notably Abram Hewitt. Hewitt was a friend of Garfield's who had recently given him a prize bull for the Mentor farm and who was familiar with both his views and his handwriting. Partisanship now enabled him to rise above mere friendship. He examined the letter and declared it to be genuine, a position he would vocally maintain until Election Day. A more judicious scrutiny could have revealed some disturbing points, such as the quite uncharacteristic mistakes in spelling and punctuation. The handwriting, though superficially similar to Garfield's, betrayed certain glaring differences, especially in the signature. Garfield always placed periods after his initials, but the writer of the Morey letter ran *J* and *A* together. Nor did Garfield ever dot the *r* in his name so that it looked like an *i*. Hewitt could have given Garfield credit for knowing how to spell his own name. Further investigation, moreover, could have disclosed that there was no Employers Union at Lynn. Nor, for that matter, was there any such person as Henry L. Morey.

With Hewitt's endorsement secured, *Truth* felt confident enough to publish the damaging letter on October 20. An immense number of copies were run off, with one hundred thousand sent to California alone. Jewell was caught asleep at the switch. With his customary lack of acumen, the party chairman dismissed the matter as inconsequential. "It is a harmless affair if genuine and no denials have been made," he assured Garfield, leaping to the astounding conclusion: "I rather imagine that it is a letter you wrote and kept no copy." But with New York "ablaze with excitement" over the issue, Jewell belatedly awoke to the fact that the letter was capable of doing serious damage. He begged Garfield to issue a clear and speedy denial.[44]

Garfield was reluctant to defend himself. For one thing, he still hoped to get through this campaign without having to break his self-imposed rule of silence in the face of slander. For another, it was possible that he *had* written the letter, or that some secretary had issued it over his name. He authorized Jewell to denounce the letter as "a bald forgery" but he issued no statement of his own. In the meantime, he dispatched George Rose to Washington to comb his files. Not until Rose reported that he could find no evidence of any such letter did Garfield feel free to issue a personal denial in his own hand. Reproduced in facsimile in newspapers across the country, often side-by-side with the forgery, it gave the public a chance to judge the controversy for itself.

Five days elapsed between the publication of the Chinese Letter and Garfield's denial and during that interval the opposition loudly denounced Garfield's silence as evidence of guilt. Had the election been held immediately, the Democrats might have profited, but whoever was responsible for the forgery neglected the basic principle of the roorback—proper timing. The editor of *Truth* tried to string the excitement along for a few days more by entrapping Jewell into what looked like an attempt to suppress evidence, but the tide of public opinion was clearly running in Garfield's favor. Except for the West Coast, he probably gained more from the episode than he lost. Even his old enemy, Charles A. Dana, advised the voters to punish the Democrats for having indulged in such tactics. The roorback had boomeranged and Garfield, in a whimsical

Voters could compare this widely-circulated facsimile of the Morey letter with a genuine sample of Garfield's handwriting (opposite) and draw their own conclusions.

Telegram

MENTOR, OHIO. Oct 23. 1880.

Hon Marshall Jewell
241 Fifth Avenue N.Y.

Your telegram of this
afternoon is received. Publish my
dispatch of last evening if you think
best. Within the last hour, the mail
has brought me the lithographic
copy of the forged letter. It is the
work of some clumsy villain, who
cannot spell, — nor write English.
nor imitate my hand-writing.
Every honest and manly democrat in America who is familiar
with my hand-writing, will denounce
the forgery at sight— Put the case
in the hands of able detectives at
once, and hunt the rascals down

J. A. Garfield.

mood, suggested that the motto of the campaign should read, "Memento Morey."[45]

At the height of the crisis, Garfield had ordered Jewell to put the case in the hands of able detectives and "hunt the rascals down," but the rascals, whoever they were, remained uncaught. For a time it seemed that a scribbler on the staff of *Truth* was the guilty one. Indictments were drawn but the case against him petered out for lack of evidence. Others traced the hoax to the doorstep of the Democratic National Committee, claiming that a wily, though insignificant, Democratic hanger-on had perpetrated the fraud, but again the evidence was too inconclusive to warrant conviction. Whoever may have been the culprit, it seems likely that neither *Truth* nor the Democratic party were entirely without complicity. Both later apologized. *Truth*, facing a lawsuit, tendered handsome regrets, and Hewitt personally contributed a hundred dollars towards the prosecution of the "wicked" forger. By that time, of course, the election was over and the damage had already been done.[46]

Election day was clear and sunny across the nation and all reports indicated a large and peaceful turnout. An unnatural calm settled over Mentor, allowing Garfield to catch up on his mail and oversee the fall planting before he walked, in the old tradition of republican simplicity, to the Town Hall to cast his vote. On the way home he stopped by the cheese-seller to settle accounts and then he relaxed at home in the company of a small group of friends and neighbors to await the returns. The telegraph in the little office behind the house clicked merrily away all evening, bringing cheering news from almost every Northern state. By eleven o'clock it was learned that New York was safe and at three o'clock in the morning the candidate could go to bed, secure in the knowledge that he would awake the next morning president-elect.[47]

In the post-election calm, Garfield could analyze the full extent of his victory. Some obvious conclusions were bound to emerge as he pondered the returns. For one thing,

The election was close. Garfield's plurality over Hancock was only 7,368 votes, or less than one-tenth of one percent of the total vote cast.[48] If the vote of the minor parties is taken into account, Garfield's total drops to only 48.3 percent of the tally. The Greenback party, led by General James B. Weaver, pulled over three hundred thousand votes, mostly in the Midwest, while the Prohibitionists managed to attract over ten thousand voters, even though their candidate, General Neil Dow, privately indicated that he favored Garfield.[49] These totals might seem insignificant, but with the major parties so evenly balanced, the splinter parties could be decisive in a close election. This even political division manifested itself at all levels of the election. It was reflected in the composition of the next House of Representatives, where the Republican majority would be less than a dozen seats, and even more so in the Senate, which would be exactly tied. It was certainly reflected in some of the critical states. New York was carried by slightly more than twenty thousand votes, while New Jersey, where the opposition of the influential Pennsylvania Railroad may have been decisive, was lost by only two thousand. The Democrats won Delaware by about a thousand votes and their margin in Nevada, where the Morey Letter carried some weight, was even less. The forgery was probably responsible for Hancock's success in California, which he carried by only twenty-two votes! The closeness of the election, however, was in some ways deceptive, for, looked at in another light,

The result was decisive. Four years earlier, at the height of the Hayes-Tilden controversy, Garfield had gloomily predicted that the nation would never enjoy another uncontested election. Yet, despite Democratic grumblings of fraud, Garfield's victory went unchallenged because of his overwhelming lead in the electoral college. The Republicans could claim 214 electoral votes to the opposition's 155. Even though their popular margin was small, it was concentrated in the large, critical states, pointing up the fact that,

Republican support was sectional. The party carried every Northern state except for New Jersey, Nevada and California. The Democrats, for their part, captured every one of the old slave-holding states, thereby converting the "Solid South" into a political reality and laying to rest, at last, Hayes's dream of a native, white, respectable Southern Republican

511

organization. It also made that dream unnecessary, for by demonstrating that the party could win without the South, it enabled the Republicans to concentrate on promising national issues, such as the tariff, unencumbered by any lingering concern over the fate of the Negro. Democratic success in the South was achieved through the wholesale, blatant disenfranchisement of the Negro. The process can be seen in a typical Southern county. In 1872, Yazoo County, Mississippi, had cast 3,355 votes, 2,433 of which were Republican. In 1880, the vote dropped to 2,288, with only 155 recorded as Republican. By 1892, despite an increase in population, only 854 voters would bother to cast their ballots and only three lonely Republicans could be found in the whole county. Yet even with this decrease in Southern voters, the national turnout in 1880 was the largest yet recorded. An unprecedented seventy-eight percent of the eligible voters went to the polls, many of them attracted by the personalities of the candidates, which indicated that, to a significant extent,

Garfield's triumph was personal. Instead of taking the passive role that had been urged upon him, he took charge of his own campaign, making the key decisions and making them correctly. Unlike Hancock, Garfield made no blunders. Not only did his fresh personality prove appealing to the voters, but his conciliatory manner preserved party harmony. If any of the other candidates at Chicago had been nominated, their disappointed rivals would very likely have scratched the ticket in sufficient numbers to bring about defeat. Given the closeness of the vote and the size of the turnout, it was obvious, in retrospect, that only a candidate able to command the support of all Republican factions could have won. This meant that, for the moment at least, Garfield was indispensable. It also imposed upon the president-elect the heavy responsibility of keeping his party intact by balancing all its factions.

Whichever way Garfield looked at it, it was a famous victory. An accidental nominee, he had taken a party whose prospects had seemed hopeless and led it to success. In the process, he had achieved the pinnacle of his personal ambition earlier than he had ever imagined possible.

Why, then, was he so unhappy? Instead of the exhilaration

512

one might expect, Garfield found himself oppressed by "a tone of sadness running through this triumph which I can hardly explain."[50] He acted increasingly distant and preoccupied, and friends noted that his once jovial face seemed perpetually set in "a sad and weary earnestness of expression which he never had before." He begged these friends to bear with him for awhile, but in his heart he knew his life would never be the same. "Your real troubles will now begin," predicted Carl Schurz, and Garfield secretly agreed. As he cast a backward glance over the events of the past year, he was filled with "the sad conviction that I am bidding goodbye to the freedom of private life and to a long series of happy years which I fear terminate with 1880."[51]

513

CHAPTER TWENTY-THREE

JUSTICE AND JUDGMENT

Drafted for a more leisurely era, the Constitution of the United States allowed four months to elapse between the election of a president and his inauguration. During this long pause Garfield had only two tasks to perform: write a speech and appoint a cabinet. As it would turn out, he would need every minute of the time.

He started slowly, determined (as Lincoln had once put it) "to take a bath in public opinion" before committing himself. Instead of a bath, he found himself in danger of drowning. Each day's mail brought a tidal wave of congratulations and well-intentioned advice, usually coupled with a plea for office. "I wood liuke to be in the Kustim Hous," announced one hopeful. Most expected some reward for their campaign services, ranging from the Washington man who modestly offered to settle for a $2.90 loan, to Thaddeus Pound of Wisconsin, who had somehow convinced himself that his activities at the Chicago Convention entitled him to a seat on the cabinet. When Pound's hopes were dashed by Mrs. Garfield, who had learned of an ancient scandal involving his wife, the rejection struck him "like an iceberg," but after a good cry the frustrated cabinet minister reconciled himself to his loss like a. man.

Some, more stubborn, insisted on pleading their case in person. Throughout the long, gray Ohio winter, delegations of office seekers presented themselves at Garfield's doorstep for inspection. Few were quite as doggedly determined as the Disciple woman anxious for the Cincinnati Post Office who dismissed her carriage at the door and settled down for a full day's visit with "Brother Garfield." Even more irritating was the life insurance salesman who consumed much of the president-elect's day before disclosing the purpose of his call. That same evening, four old friends dropped by. Garfield pointedly told them how thoughtless callers were wasting his time, but they obtusely lingered on to sympathize. "I think it is too bad to bore any body to death," old Eliza grumbled, and even Garfield realized that if he kept on at this rate he would be "eaten up" by the demands of his voracious friends. "There are fifty million of us," John Hay reminded him. "You can't give us all a first rate office. . . . Do what *you* think is right."[1]

That was precisely the problem. Garfield did not yet know his own mind. Thrust into the presidency by a series of accidents, he had not yet had time to chart his own course. Someone like Blaine who would yearn for the White House for half a lifetime, might at least know what to do if he ever got there, but not Garfield. His unexpected elevation left him more than ever dependent on the advice of friends. Yet, now that he needed them most, even his friends could no longer be entirely trusted. ". . . Almost everyone who comes to me," he suspected, "wants something . . . and this embitters the pleasures of friendship." Always anxious—sometimes morbidly so—for the good opinion of others, Garfield was saddened by the social isolation which his new life imposed. "I fear it remains for me to make my pathway over the wrecks of human hearts," he sighed.

Already two of his oldest friendships had fallen casualties of politics: Jere Black and William Rosecrans. For over fifteen years Black and Garfield had risen above partisanship to genuine affection, but his friend's latest good fortune was finally too much for an unregenerate Democrat like Black to bear. Convinced that even "a very inferior Democrat" would be preferable to "the best and ablest" of Republicans, Black had campaigned against his old friend with a bitterness that seemed "mean beyond expression." John Hay urged that Garfield drop "that infamous old blackguard," and Garfield, hurt more than he cared to admit by Black's unexpected treachery, reluctantly complied.[2]

Rosecrans was an even sadder story. Over the years Garfield had patiently defended his old commander's reputation and, from time to time, had done him small favors. Now a resident of California, Rosecrans was still drifting from career to career, trying to live down his fatal mistake at Chickamauga. In the fall of 1880, he tried an unsuccessful run for Congress on the Democratic ticket. When rivals dredged up his wartime praise of Garfield in an effort to embarrass him, Rosecrans ungraciously disassociated himself from his earlier statements. "Seventeen years is a long period," he explained, "and many a splendid young man, in less time, has descended from honor to infamy, and mortified admiring and devoted friends . . . by being put in the penitentiary." Shortly after this, Rosecrans (never noted for his sensitivity) had the cool nerve to send Garfield a fawning letter asking for another favor. Garfield brusquely replied that his "wicked and unjust" campaign accusations constituted "an insuperable barrier to the restoration of our old relations," and with that, another link to his past was severed. There was not time for regrets. As he told a literary society that was importuning him to deliver an address on The Annals of Tacitus, it was impossible to devote any time "to subjects more ancient than eighteen hundred eighty one."[3]

That year was almost upon him and he had, as yet, made no discernible progress in forming his administration. It should not have been all that difficult. There were, after all, only seven cabinet positions to be filled. The most important, all agreed, were State and Treasury. The first had the most prestige; the other had the most patronage. Interior and the Post Office were also prized for the patronage plums at their disposal, while Army, Navy and Justice were considered only slightly less desirable. A cabinet, however, was more than the sum of its parts. It was, ideally, a microcosm of the party. As such, the cabinet had to be considered as a unit, not as a conglomeration of department heads, however talented.

Administrative talent, in fact, was one of the least significant considerations. In the previous administration, to take an

516

extreme example, Hayes had selected Richard Thompson of Indiana to head the Navy Department even though he had never been aboard any vessel larger than a rowboat. When he finally toured a warship, he was astounded. "Why, the durned thing's hollow!" he exclaimed. Garfield, too, never put mere expertise above politics in choosing his cabinet members. "How much trouble you would save yourself," Carl Schurz suggested, "by just picking out the fittest man for each place and then going ahead to make a good business administration . . . ," but this was advice Garfield could not afford to follow. As the custodian of a party that had narrowly escaped self-destruction, he felt an overriding obligation to preserve party unity.

Blaine urged a different course. As he saw it, the Republican party was divided into three factions. One was made up of the so-called Independents, those impractical "upstarts" who paraded as reformers but who were actually "conceited, foolish, vain, without knowledge of measures, ignorant of men." They constituted nothing more than a noisy nuisance and could be safely ignored by the new administration. "I could handle them myself without trouble," Blaine volunteered. On the other hand were the self-styled Stalwarts, those who had supported Grant at Chicago and who, Blaine warned, were "absolutely determined" to try again for Grant in 1884. This group included "all the desperate bad men of the party," and they too ought to be excluded from power, lest they disgrace the administration. Even so, it would not be wise to wage open war on the Grant supporters. "They must not be knocked down with bludgeons. They must have their throats cut with a feather." Since Blaine dismissed the reformers as impotent and the Stalwarts as evil, this left only the third group, which he termed, "only for convenience," the Blaine Section, and he advised Garfield to draw his cabinet exclusively from that faction.[4]

Garfield agreed with Blaine's analysis but rejected his advice, choosing instead to continue his efforts to construct a balanced administration in which all factions would be represented. This would require singularly dexterous juggling. In addition to balancing factions, he would also have to take geography into account by satisfying the claims of New England, the Midwest, the Great Plains and, if Hayes's policy were to be continued, the South. Beyond this, it would be necessary to appease the leaders of the great Republican states, particularly New York, Pennsylvania and Illinois. In addition to these considerations, a cabinet appointment could also be treated as hard political currency to redeem an old debt or as a binder for future performance.

In this complex jigsaw puzzle, each piece was called upon to fill many blanks. This was why Wayne McVeagh, a Philadelphia lawyer, seemed irresistible. He carried endorsements from both Carl Schurz, the leading reformer, and Don Cameron, the Stalwart boss of Pennsylvania (and, not incidentally, McVeagh's brother-in-law). Furthermore, McVeagh had been an accomplice of Wharton Barker's at Chicago. With this one stroke, Garfield could pay off a convention debt, gratify the reformers, please a boss and recognize an important state. Even Blaine had to admit that there was "no other cabinet stone . . . that will kill as many dogs at one throw," and McVeagh assumed a prominent place on Garfield's ever-lengthening list of cabinet possibilities.[5]

Another intriguing suggestion came from John Logan, the flamboyant Illinois chieftain. The Midwest was certainly entitled to at least one, and possibly two, cabinet slots. Garfield's first choice had been Indiana's Benjamin Harrison, who had displayed such cool competence at Chicago, but Harrison seemed unwilling to leave the Senate. Logan's novel recommendation was Robert Todd Lincoln, son of the late president and currently a rising Illinois lawyer. Garfield was receptive to any respectable appointment that might bind Logan to his administration and, furthermore, any association with the magic Lincoln aura was bound to be popular with the country. Harrison objected that young Lincoln was too small for the job, but Garfield was more interested in the name than the man, and so Lincoln joined McVeagh somewhere near the top of Garfield's list.[6]

At the very head of that list stood the name of James G. Blaine. Massachusetts reformers might object to his filling the New England slot, but who could better represent the

Blaine Section than Blaine himself? It was an obvious choice but a risky one. Garfield hardly needed the many warnings that the senator from Maine could be ambitious, vain, devious and unstable.[7] For eighteen years, ever since that day they had both first entered Congress, their careers had twined and intertwined and by now they knew each other too well to harbor illusions. Despite their occasional disagreements, Garfield looked up to Blaine as a friend and leader, but his admiration was tinged with distrust. He was certainly aware of his friend's shortcomings but he also wanted to harness all that energy and brilliance to the new administration. Blaine, however, had always been the dominant partner. Could he adjust to a new relationship? Garfield proposed to find out.

Over breakfast one day late in November, Garfield bluntly told Blaine that no cabinet offer could even be considered unless he put aside his presidential ambitions. "I ask this," Garfield explained, "because I do not propose to allow myself nor anyone else to use the next four years as the camping ground for fighting the next presidential battle." Two disappointments had cooled the Plumed Knight's presidential ardor, and he wistfully conceded that he would never again seek the Republican nomination. No doubt he meant it sincerely, but he would be saying much the same thing every four years for the rest of his life and would, nonetheless, somehow manage to be an active candidate at every Republican convention. Garfield, however, took his friend's pledge at its face value and tendered him the State Department. It was not a definite offer, and no final answer was expected immediately. At first Blaine seemed loath to leave the Senate, but both men were aware that he was losing his grip on the Maine party and that the time had come for him to move on.

Nothing was concluded, but Garfield rose from the breakfast table hopeful that he had found a "premier" for his administration. This impression was strengthened when Blaine began to fill his letters with detailed advice on foreign policy coupled with the most shameless flattery of Garfield's wife— a subject and a lady he had not taken any particular notice of hitherto. By mid-December he informed the president-elect that he was "inclined" to accept, and a few days later it was definite. "In accepting this important post I shall give all that I am and all that I can hope to be, freely and joyfully to your service!" Significantly, Blaine's acceptance letter betrayed not a hint of foreign policy but was instead concerned almost exclusively with plans for securing Garfield's second term.[8]

Garfield received Blaine's acceptance with relief, asking only that the decision "be known to nobody but ourselves and our good wives" until he was ready to make a formal announcement. Rumors of the appointment, however, continued to fly. Blaine tried to dissemble, but he was constitutionally unable to keep a secret for long. By late December, it could no longer be hidden. The Maine legislature was about to choose a United States Senator and Blaine's two best friends in the state, Eugene Hale and William Frye, were locked in bitter rivalry for the position. If Blaine would resign his seat for the cabinet, however, room could be found in the Senate for both his friends. Otherwise, if the matter were postponed, it might lead to the selection of a Democrat, which would allow the Senate to fall into the hands of the enemy. To avert this calamity, Garfield was compelled to release Blaine from his vow of silence.[9]

When the news became public that Blaine was to occupy the first place in the new cabinet, it convinced the habitually suspicious Stalwarts that their most hated rival was about to dominate the incoming administration. As a counterweight to Blaine's expected influence, Conkling demanded nothing less than the right to name the Treasury Secretary. There was more than prestige at stake. The Secretary of the Treasury was in charge of the New York Custom House, an agency which in its recent heyday had given jobs to over 1,500 of the party faithful and had enabled the Collector of the Port, Chester Alan Arthur, to enjoy an annual remuneration of almost $100,000—twice the salary of the President of the United States. It had been these abuses that had led President Hayes to replace Arthur with Edwin A. Merritt, which, in turn, had led to the breach between Conkling and Hayes.

Garfield wanted to heal that breach, but the Treasury Department seemed too steep a price to pay, particularly since Conkling's choice, Levi P. Morton, was unacceptable. Garfield had nothing against Morton personally. Quite the contrary, he was duly grateful for the New York banker's heroic fund-raising efforts during the late campaign and fully intended to offer some fitting reward. The Treasury Department, however, was out of the question. For one thing, it was illegal. Anyone who engaged in banking and the sale of government securities was specifically prohibited from holding a high Treasury post. This seemed to eliminate Morton. Yet, even if the law could have been evaded (as surely it could have been, given a minimum of ingenuity), Morton still would have to be ruled out on grounds of political prudence. Western Republicans could be expected to howl with fury if the Treasury Department were handed over to a Wall Street banker with such close ties to the notorious Jay Gould.

Conkling was unmoved by these arguments. He insisted that Garfield had promised the Treasury to Morton at the Fifth Avenue Conference the preceding August, and he demanded that Garfield keep his end of the bargain.[10] The accusation was based, necessarily, on rumor and hearsay, but the only Stalwart in a position to know the truth—Morton himself—never reproached Garfield directly. Instead, he based his claim on second-hand evidence: "upon reports of conversations with you by Senators Plumb, Dorsey, Cameron (Simon) and others that I could have the position of Secty. of Treasury." Neither Plumb nor Dorsey, however, would back Morton's claim, while Donald Cameron told friends that he knew all about the matter and that Garfield's version was the correct one. In view of this support, Garfield's position gains credence. He maintained all along that he had merely mentioned a list of possible offices to Morton, including a cabinet post or a first class diplomatic assignment, but he vigorously repudiated the notion of any binding commitment. "I will not tolerate, nor act upon any understanding that anything has been pledged to any party state or person," he emphatically concluded.[11]

Despite his irritation over this "unfortunate misunderstanding," Garfield still intended to do right by Morton. Near the end of December, an opportunity seemed to present itself.

521

President Hayes informed his successor that the Secretary of the Navy was about to resign. If Morton would accept the post, with the understanding that he would carry over into Garfield's cabinet, would not that neatly "cut the Gordian knot?" Conkling had intimated to some that he would not seriously object to such an arrangement, though others, who knew the imperious New York senator well, warned that the offer of a minor cabinet post to his state would be regarded as "a spit in the face." Garfield was prepared to hazard that reaction. He had his friends sound out Morton on the Navy Department but they reported that the New York banker was too deeply involved in the pending Senate race to consider anything less than the Treasury. If his Senate hopes should be dashed, he might, however, think better of the Navy.[12]

Formation of the new cabinet would simply have to wait until New York affairs were settled, if affairs in that turbulent state could ever be considered settled. To an outsider, New York politics might seem merely "disgusting child's play, or pouting and making faces,' but to an insider it was a grim, serious business. At the moment, the selection of a United States senator threatened to tear the party organization apart. The seat had originally been slated for Chester Alan Arthur, but his elevation to the vice-presidency had thrown the race wide open, with three Conkling proteges contending for the honor. In addition to Morton, Thomas Platt of New York City and Richard Crowley of Buffalo were in the race. Governor Cornell seemed to be backing Platt, while Arthur was managing Crowley's campaign, but Conkling stood aloof, unwilling to support one of his followers at the expense of another. Some suspected that his insistence on Morton for the Treasury was primarily designed to remove one candidate from this cluttered senatorial field. This suspicion was fortified when a delegation of New Yorkers, including Cornell and Crowley, showed up at Mentor to urge Garfield to provide a suitable cabinet post for Morton before the Senate contest was settled. Garfield refused, but in refusing he indicated that he would keep his hands off the pending Senate race. "I think N.Y. politics are first rate things for an outsider to let alone," Marshall Jewell advised, and Garfield evidently agreed.[13]

522

Blaine did not. He was incapable of resisting any opportunity to strike at Conkling and he realized that the New York
senatorial tangle gave him a rare opportunity indeed. With
Conkling's followers split three ways, the anti-Conkling minority in the legislature now held the balance of power. Working
with Judge William Robertson, who had led the antimachine
revolt at Chicago, and with Whitelaw Reid, editor of the *New
York Tribune*, who aspired to build his own state machine,
Blaine cooked up a plan. They persuaded Chauncey M.
Depew, a noted railroad attorney and after-dinner speaker, to
enter the race. Depew did not especially want to be a senator,
but Blaine and his friends promised that he had no chance of
winning; he was merely to hold the anti-Conkling forces
together in order to prolong the stalemate. Any lingering reluctance was overcome when Blaine solemnly assured Depew
that Garfield himself wished it.

Next, Blaine took steps to insure that his troops in the
legislature would stand firm. He drafted an announcement
which Reid printed as a special editorial in the *Tribune*.
Speaking "by authority," the anonymous editorialist declared
that the incoming administration "will not permit its friends to
be persecuted for their friendship." Specifically, this meant
that those who defied Conkling "shall not suffer for it, nor
lose by it." Most readers assumed that the "authority" referred to was Garfield's, but the president-elect had not seen
the statement in advance nor, for that matter, did he fully understand it. He was led to believe by Reid that the editorial's
intent was to serve notice that Garfield did not intend to "meddle" in the senatorial contest. At the same time, Reid was busy
in Albany drumming up support for Depew in the president-
elect's name.[14]

As anticipated, the strain imposed by the senatorial election
was more than Conkling's organization could bear. Platt
cracked first. He approached Depew and asked why he had
entered the race. To see to it that New York would have a
senator who would support the incoming administration,
Depew replied. "Very well," said Platt, "I will do that."
Depew called his supporters together and made Platt repeat
his pledge. They pushed him hard but Platt gave way on every

point. No, he would not allow the anti-Conkling men to be crushed or ignored. Yes, he would support the incoming administration and help confirm all its appointments. Would that support extend even to "so extreme a case" as Judge Robertson, he was asked. He declared that it would, and, with that, Depew's twenty votes were transferred to Platt who was promptly elected.[15]

Blaine's friends were delighted. They happily envisioned a recasting of the New York Republican machine, "with our fellows in and a united party, minus Conkling, who won't last forever!" Platt was properly grateful to his new allies. "I am yours to command;" he told Reid, "draw on me at sight." Conkling was furious. He assumed that Garfield had engineered the whole business, in flat violation of his promise to Crowley not to interfere. Morton was hurt and bewildered. "I have lost a seat in the Senate—my great ambition," he complained, "—solely on account of the belief of the leaders in N. Y. . . . that I could have the position of Secty of the Treasury. . . ." He hinted that the pain caused by this loss could be soothed by the offer of a post in the government, and there was every indication that he would settle for something less lofty than the Treasury Department.[16]

Having ruled out the East, Garfield turned to men of the West to fill the vexing Treasury post and his eyes lit upon Minnesota's favorite son, Senator William Windom. The suggestion was endorsed enthusiastically by both Sherman and Hayes but it threw Blaine into a dither. "He wont do at all," Blaine flatly declared, insisting that Windom was incompetent. "He is profoundly and absolutely ignorant of our finances except as Appropriation Bills teach—which is nothing and on the wrong side. Any darned . . . fool can spend money!" Blaine snorted, forgetting for the moment that Garfield's own financial reputation had been built as chairman of the House Appropriations Committee. Furthermore, Blaine warned that Windom "has the Presidential bee in his bonnet *terribly*, and would be looking to that all the time." Since his own bee had ceased to buzz, Blaine felt free to proffer disinterested advice. "I shall never urge a man upon you for the Cabinet," he promised, "but I will not hesitate to protest against wrong men. I think that is a good distinction for me to observe."

524

It was not a distinction he could long maintain, particularly since he knew of just the right man for the Treasury Department—Iowa's powerful senator, William B. Allison, who enjoyed both Blaine's friendship and Conkling's trust. Unlike Windom, Allison was endowed with a catalogue of virtues reminiscent of a Boy Scout: "He is true, kind, reasonable, fair, honest and good . . . methodical, industrious and intelligent. . . ." Such a paragon, Blaine concluded, "will be as devoted to you as your wife will be." Garfield was impressed, but not completely convinced. He could not forget that in the past Allison had displayed a disturbing sympathy for inflationary measures. These suspicions could not be dispelled by a personal interview with Allison nor by Blaine's ingenious suggestion that the best man to fight inflation was one who had the confidence of the inflationists. Yet, so strong was Blaine's influence that Garfield retained Allison's name on his cabinet list, despite his own reservations.[17]

Not content with pushing for his friend Allison, Blaine continued to press advice on Garfield at every opportunity. "If you can only restrain his immense activity and keep him from meddling . . . you will have a brilliant Secy.," Sherman predicted, without much hope that it could be done. Blaine was irrepressible; advice flowed from his pen in gushing torrents. Within a matter of weeks he managed to put forward a dozen different names for the cabinet and tried to veto a dozen more, giving rise to fears that the incoming administration would be stocked exclusively with friends of the Secretary of State—fears that were bolstered by the indiscrete "crowing of Blaine's fool friends." Blaine himself scoffed at the notion. "As to my disposition to dominate that is *mere rot.* . . . My efforts at domination will cease when I urge upon you honest and disinterested counsel." Actually, Garfield did listen to others—Sherman, Hayes, Logan, Grant, even (despite provocation) Conkling—as often as to Blaine. The difference was that Blaine was so much more insistent that he could not be ignored. He lived perpetually on the thin edge of hysteria, and each day brought its fresh crisis that required immediate action. Garfield tried to keep his balance, but how could he resist a steady stream of entreaties made so earnestly by one who insisted that his sole concern was Garfield's welfare?[18]

525

The sheer energy of the man could be intimidating. Garfield sometimes found himself acceding to requests he would have instantly dismissed had they come from anyone else. Late in February, for example, Garfield sent Blaine a letter regretting that he could not appoint Stephen B. Elkins to a high government post since he came from a territory rather than a state. This seemingly innocuous communication was odd in a number of respects. For one thing, Garfield had never considered appointing Elkins to anything. For another, the letter had, in fact, been drafted by Blaine himself. Garfield obligingly sent it back, over his own signature, as "a favor." It left Elkins with the impression that Blaine was a loyal friend whose efforts were unfortunately obstructed by the president-elect. That Garfield would lend himself to this deception did him no credit, but Blaine's boyish zest for intrigue was sometimes hard to resist. He enjoyed playing the conspirator, solemnly marking his letters with a private code which he soon forgot how to use. He saw deep plots everywhere, usually directed by Conkling, whom he envisioned as a superman of intrigue.[19]

Faced with such a sinister opponent, Blaine felt justified in concocting the most audacious schemes to thwart his rival. Late in January, for example, he threw out a daring suggestion for the Treasury Department. Why not offer the job to Conkling himself? Blaine's friends were so dazzled by this proposal that they at once passed it on to Garfield, pointing out that if Conkling accepted "you have him fairly harnessed to your car." If, as was more likely, he should decline, "then his mouth and the mouths of all his friends are forever sealed." Garfield was receptive, for he had been toying with the same idea himself but, unlike Blaine who intended only to embarrass Conkling with an insincere offer, Garfield was in earnest. ". . . What would you say to exchanging seats," he proposed to Blaine, "—you for Treas, he for State?" When Blaine realized that his little *jeu d'esprit* was being taken seriously, he rapidly backed away from the plan. Upon cool reflection, he now told Garfield, he had decided that Conkling's presence "would act like strychnine upon your admin.—first bring convulsions and then followed by death." That seemed final enough, and so an interesting, but probably unworkable, idea was abandoned, much to Blaine's relief.[20]

Blaine had not, however, run out of ideas concerning Conkling. He now insisted that Garfield invite the New York boss to Mentor. The genesis of this proposal was a typically convoluted one. Actually, it was Blaine who wanted to confer with the president-elect. Garfield, however, was unwilling to go east for fear of being forced to testify at the trial of a suspected perpetrator of the Morey fraud. His wife was safe from subpoenas, so she was secretly whisked into New York under an assumed name for a preinaugural shopping spree. While her husband fretted alone at home, she was being measured by the dressmakers and prowling the stores for bargains, picking up such prizes as slightly soiled underpants for the president-elect, marked down from eighteen to only ten dollars a pair. While in New York, "Mrs. Greenfield" (as she was called for security reasons) stayed at the home of Whitelaw Reid. Both Reid and Blaine took advantage of this opportunity to fill their guest's ear with lurid tales of how "the Conkling clique" ridiculed and belittled her husband. Lucretia was duly incensed. The only way to deal with the Stalwarts, she wrote home, was to "fight them *dead*. You can put every one of them in his political grave if you are a mind to. . . ."[21]

Blaine wanted to pursue these arguments further with the head of the house in person. If Garfield could not come to him, Blaine would have to go to Mentor. Such a meeting, he realized, would only reinforce the fears of Blaine's supposed domination. If, however, Conkling should be invited first, then he would have no reason to complain that Garfield was showing Blaine preference. "He will not come," Blaine confidently assured Garfield, but an invitation (however insincere) would look good on the record and would clear the way for Blaine's visit. As it turned out, Blaine did not get to Mentor after all. He was confined to his room by an untimely attack of gout, which the newspapers obligingly reported as "rheumatism" since, as Blaine explained, "gout is associated in the public mind with drinking and high living of neither of which I am at all guilty."[22]

Conkling, however, accepted the call to Mentor, contrary to Blaine's prediction. As a result of Blaine's petty scheming, Garfield found himself saddled with a caller he did not want to see and to whom he had nothing to say. It had all the

makings of an unpleasant confrontation and Garfield's apprehensions were certainly not dispelled when he read Conkling's acceptance note which slyly concealed a threat within
its stiffly-worded courtesies. "I need hardly add," Conkling
had concluded ominously, "that your Administration cannot
be more successful than I wish it to be, nor can it be more
satisfactory to you, to the country, and to the party than I will
labor to make it." Despite Garfield's forebodings, the meeting
was frank, amiable and "conducted in excellent temper."
Conkling arrived on February 16 and stayed for eight hours.
Their discussion was confined to cabinet matters. Conkling
made no demands; Garfield made no promises. Yet, even
though no formal agreement was reached, there seemed, to
Garfield at least, a meeting of minds that augured well for
future relations. "I think much better of him than I expected
to," Garfield reported afterwards, "and I shall be somewhat
surprised if he has not carried away the same impression."

Garfield was deceiving himself. The inconclusive conference had left Conkling puzzled and disappointed. He had half
expected to be tendered a cabinet post himself or, failing
that, the right to name his choice. Instead, he was informed, in
a "trifling and undecided manner," that Levi P. Morton was
not acceptable for the Treasury—a piece of stale news which
hardly warranted a special journey from New York to hear
again. He was then asked about the character and fitness of
New York Judge Charles F. Folger. At this Conkling
bristled. "Do you contemplate offering him a cabinet position?" he asked. "If such is your purpose, I would like to
advise that the Treasury is the only post which would satisfy
New York, and that our state would prefer to be passed altogether if it could not obtain the department to which its
rank and service entitled it." His host dropped the subject
and offered to escort him to tea. "To tea! tea! tea!" Conkling's lips would later curl at the memory of the insipid
beverage. At the time, however, he was secretly elated, for he
was convinced that the coveted Treasury would be offered
Folger, and upon returning to New York he so informed his
friends. Instead, Folger was summoned to Mentor and offered the Justice Department with the hint that in a "con-

tingency" the Treasury might follow. Conkling felt betrayed. "Was it only to find out what I would like," he raged, "and then do just the opposite, that this man Garfield called me to Mentor? Was it only to make his indifference to my wishes more marked that he summoned Folger, whose character he had impugned, the moment my back was turned, to offer him an office lesser in dignity than that which I had said New York was entitled to?"[23]

Blaine was equally distressed. The fact that Folger was even being mentioned in connection with the Treasury Department inspired panic among Blaine and his friends, who bombarded Garfield with the most dreadful rumors regarding the judge's character. He was a drunkard, they reported, a tool of Tammany Hall, corrupt, "a most dangerous man in any political place where there is temptation." From their warnings it might seem that Folger's proper place was the penitentiary, but they were willing to let him take the Attorney-Generalship instead—anything to keep him out of the Treasury. The beleaguered judge spared Garfield further embarrassment by declining the offer. Unable to stand up against Conkling's wrath and Blaine's attacks, Folger reluctantly asked Garfield to withdraw his name from further consideration.[24]

It was now the last week of February. On March 4, Garfield would have to take his oath of office and move into the White House, yet he was no nearer to solving his two most vexing cabinet problems—the Treasury Secretary and the New York tangle—than he had been on the day of his election. His other chore, the inaugural address, lay half-finished on his desk. Garfield had always been a slow, painstaking writer. A fluent correspondent and a facile orator, he approached the composition of a formal essay or speech with a caution bordering on paralysis. Each sentence had to be carefully polished before he would allow himself to proceed to the next. "I sometimes think no one will ever appreciate the work [I] put into a page," he sighed. This speech would be more important than most and thus required special care in its preparation. He began in December by reading the inaugural speeches of all his predecessors. Essentially a scholar at heart, Garfield found in such academic diversions an excuse to avoid an unpleasant task. By late January, it could be postponed no longer. He had learned nothing from his historical survey except that a diet of inaugural addresses, other than Lincoln's, made for dreary reading. "Doubtless mine will be also," he suspected, with good cause. By February, he had become so "jaded" that the very thought of the speech filled him with "an unusual repugnance." He toyed with the novel idea of omitting an inaugural address altogether, but the force of custom was too strong and he finally began to patch together a first draft.[25]

Too often for coincidence, Garfield was forced to abandon work on his speech by the onset of crippling headaches. Even his dreams were haunted with apprehensions of his impending ordeal. He dreamed one night he was on a canal boat again, riding to attend some great ceremony. (Had he been reading his campaign biography, *From Canal Boy to President*?) Then the boat started to sink in a storm. (Lincoln, too, had recurring dreams of the Ship of State.) He leaped ashore and turned to watch the sinking boat, when he noticed Chester Alan Arthur still aboard, lying on a couch, pale and sickly. He could not be saved. Garfield wandered in the storm, naked and alone, through hostile country, until an old Negro woman nursed and comforted him as if he were a child. Then he woke. Most politicians dreamed of the presidency; Garfield had nightmares.[26]

The calendar brought him back to reality. He was scheduled to leave for Washington on the 28th of February. Jacob Dolson Cox had wisely advised his old roommate to settle his cabinet slate firmly and finally before arriving at the capital. "The pulling and hauling there utterly prevents calm thought, and one is in danger of being in . . . a panic or a rush when all former thinking is lost sight of, and a haphazard arrangement adopted on the spur of the moment," warned Cox, who had seen it all happen in the hectic early days of the Grant administration. That was not a precedent Garfield cared to emulate. Putting hesitation aside, he hammered a cabinet together and, in the closing hours of February, sent out telegrams to the men of his choice informing them of their selection. Blaine, of course, needed no such notification; some of the others were taken by surprise. Robert Todd Lincoln and Wayne McVeagh had been high on Garfield's list for months, yet neither had been formally contacted until this, the very last moment. Young Lincoln accepted the War Department with thanks, but McVeagh had reservations about the Attorney-Generalship. He accepted it for the moment, however, because to refuse might embarrass the President at the outset of his administration.[27]

As late as February 27, Garfield was still undecided about the Interior Department. His list had boiled down to two Iowans: Allison, who was recommended by Blaine; and Samuel J. Kirkwood, who was recommended by Allison. The choice went to Allison, who declined by return mail, leaving a gaping hole in the cabinet that would have to be patched up within the next few days, exposing Garfield to that last-minute "pulling and hauling" that Cox had warned against.[28] The Southern representative required another hasty, last-minute decision. When Hayes had first appointed a Southerner to the cabinet, Garfield had disapproved. Four years later, the failure of that experiment could be read in the meager Republican Southern vote. Despite this evidence, Hayes urged Garfield to continue, and Garfield, unwilling to give the appearance of repudiating his predecessor's pet policy, reluctantly agreed. Finding a suitable candidate from the horde of obscure hopefuls proved a vexing chore. Each seemed to have some serious disqualification. "One by one my southern roses fade," Garfield sighed, as he searched for "a magnolia blossom that will stand our northern climate." By the end of February, the choice had narrowed down to two names, and his lack of enthusiasm for the whole idea could be gathered from the fact that one of them was his old army buddy, Don Pardee. Even though he had settled in Louisiana after the war, Pardee was no more southern than Garfield himself. Finally, Pardee was dropped, and Garfield was left with William H. Hunt, a much-married Louisiana judge about whom no one seemed to know very much, including Hayes who had recommended him. Hunt was tentatively slated for the Post Office Department, but a formal offer was postponed for the time being.[29]

531

The Treasury Department, which had given Garfield more than its share of headaches over the past few months, seemed finally settled when he decided to choose William Windom, despite Blaine's objections. As a concession to his Secretary of State, however, Garfield agreed to defer a definite offer to Windom, a decision which would open the way for more headaches to come. The most knotty problem of all—finding the proper place for New York—was finally resolved with the offer of the Navy Department to Levi P. Morton. For months, Morton's New York friends had been insisting on the Treasury Department or nothing. That Morton himself found such a stark alternative unpalatable was evidenced by the alacrity with which he accepted Garfield's lesser offer. Blaine's friends were delighted at their success in detaching Morton from Conkling's grasp. ". . . Conkling is at once utterly foiled and left without any cause of quarrel," crowed Whitelaw Reid, a trifle prematurely as it would turn out.[30]

With the long agony of cabinet-making apparently over, Garfield was ready for his final journey. He felt no elation at the prospect before him. Quite the contrary, his heart was filled with sadness and foreboding. "I know I am bidding goodbye to my old freedom," he confessed, but he kept his true feelings concealed as he said goodbye to the crowd of friends and neighbors who had gathered at the railroad station. After an exchange of speeches, the Lane Cornet Band struck up a patriotic air and the president-elect and his party boarded the train. He stood on the observation car, bowing and waving, as Mentor and his former life slowly receded into the distance.[31]

A light snow was beginning to fall when the train pulled out. As it chugged east, both the snow and the welcoming crowds grew thicker, but when it reached Washington, at nine o'clock on the morning of March 1, the sun was shining brightly. President Hayes's son, Webb, was waiting at the depot to escort young Abram and old Eliza Garfield to their rooms at the White House. The rest of the family took temporary quarters at the Riggs House, a hotel where they could receive visitors freely without embarrassing the outgoing President. Among the first of these callers, predictably, was

James G. Blaine. Blaine was still "up in arms" against Windom and used his considerable powers of persuasion to induce Garfield to reconsider Allison. Caught in the spell of Blaine's magnetism, Garfield quite forgot his original reasons for preferring Windom. He withdrew the offer and sent feelers to Allison instead. Garfield had been in Washington for only a few hours, and already his laboriously constructed cabinet slate was beginning to crack.[32]

While Blaine was working to put his friends on the cabinet, Conkling was striving to keep his friends off. He regarded Morton's acceptance of the Navy Department as an act of gross insubordination and ingratitude. Determined to put his "unwise friend" in his proper place, Conkling dispatched Congressman John H. Starin to fetch the banker in the middle of the night of March 1. Morton was sick in bed, but the versatile Starin, who had once been a pharmacist, whipped up a potion that put Morton back on his feet. The would-be cabinet minister made his groggy way to "the morgue," as Conkling's rooms at Fourteenth and F were ominously called. There he found Conkling and Arthur waiting to denounce his treachery. The vice-president-elect apparently saw no impropriety in sabotaging his own administration. Morton was in no condition to stand up to this pressure. At four o'clock in the morning, he caved in, scrawled a note of withdrawal and crawled back into bed, his cabinet career over before it had begun.[33]

It was Wednesday morning. The inauguration was only forty-eight hours away and the cabinet was shifting around "like a kaleidoscope." Of the original lineup, only Blaine, Lincoln and McVeagh were still at their posts. Windom was out, Morton was worse than out, and Allison was out of the Interior but not out of the running. Blaine was in his element. He gleefully "patched up a new deal" which moved Hunt to the Interior, gave the Navy to a nonentity who had not hitherto been considered as cabinet material by anyone, and put Allison in charge of the Treasury—the goal towards which Blaine had unceasingly worked for months. To tie the whole package together, Thomas L. James of New York as Postmaster General would represent the Empire State's Stalwarts in lieu of Morton. Garfield acquiesced to all of Blaine's suggestions. He was too bewildered by the rapid cabinet turnover to come up with any better alternatives on the spur of the moment.

Blaine's support of Thomas James represented an abrupt about face. Garfield had been considering James since early in November. As postmaster of New York City, James had earned such an outstanding reputation for honesty and efficiency that he was an obvious candidate for Postmaster General. The only question in Garfield's mind was whether James could cut the "political umbilicus" which bound him to Conkling and stand on his own feet. Blaine at first thought not. As recently as February he had described James as nothing more than Conkling's faithful tool, who could be expected to relay any cabinet secrets back to his master. Now, however, Blaine was perfectly willing to risk this "spy" as a cabinet colleague, "if that concession to New York would secure in turn an agreement to Allison in the Treasury." Actually, there was little risk. James had already assured Reid of his independence. To make doubly sure, Garfield's friends intended to detach James from Conkling by demonstrating that he owed his appointment to them alone, and not to the New York boss. James was quietly smuggled into Washington without Conkling's knowledge on the morning of March 3. Reid and Blaine then whisked the "embryo Postmaster General" over to the Riggs House to meet Garfield, who wanted to "measure" his future post office chief for himself. Garfield pointedly asked if James could give the incoming administration his undivided loyalty, and James firmly and earnestly said that he could. Next, Platt was called in and asked if he had any objection to the appointment. This was a formality. In January, Platt had already promised to support all administration appointments as the price of his Senate seat. He could not now go back on his word. James was then hustled out of town on the afternoon train before Conkling could subject him to the same treatment he had given Morton.[34]

Platt immediately dashed over to the "morgue" to break the news. He found Conkling and Arthur enjoying a late breakfast. When they heard his story they lost their appetites. Abandoning breakfast, Conkling stormed into the Riggs House, with

Arthur and Platt in tow. Garfield ushered them into his bedroom for a private chat, but Conkling was too wrought up for
conversation. He seized the floor and began to deliver a formal
oration to an audience of three. Platt and Arthur listened in
rapt admiration as the master delivered what "for invective,
sarcasm and impassioned eloquence" was the speech of his life.
Garfield did not try to interrupt his guest's harangue. "He had
it in him and it came out of him," and nothing could stop the
passionate flow of words. As Conkling paced the floor, Garfield sat on the edge of his bed and watched the performance
with amused detachment, paying less attention to the words
than to the speaker's mannerisms: "deliberate, intense, and at
times angular, and at times graceful." Conkling's speech dealt
mainly with persons rather than principles, "and much of it
was about himself," Garfield dryly recalled. After about an
hour, Conkling abruptly ran down. His host made no reply and
the one-sided interview was over.[35]

Garfield could face Conkling's wrath so calmly because he
knew how futile it was. He now had acceptances from both
James and Allison safely in hand, and he knew that Conkling
could make no public objection to their appointment. The cabinet, at last, seemed settled; the inaugural address was not.
Garfield had become so dissatisfied with his laboriously composed speech that he finally decided to junk it and start over
again from scratch. He always worked best under the pressure
of a deadline, but this time he was cutting his margin perilously
thin. All this last-minute cabinet shuffling had left him little
time for calm reflection. On the evening of March 3, with the
speech still unwritten, he allowed himself to be inveigled into
attending a time-consuming Williams College class reunion.
By the time he got around to finishing his speech, it was two
thirty in the morning of the 4th. He was not satisfied with his
work but it would simply have to do.

Inauguration Day dawned cold and blustery. An all-night
snowfall blanketed the city and the parade route was churned
into slush. At various assembly points along that route sixteen
thousand shivering marchers had been milling about for half
the night, trying to keep warm as the cruel wind pierced their
dress uniforms. Every downtown dry goods store was stripped

of boots and overshoes within minutes of opening for business. Back at the Riggs House, Garfield stared glumly out the sleet-streaked windows. He had more on his mind than the weather: the cabinet had come unraveled again.

After a night's reflection, Allison had decided to withdraw yesterday's "hasty promise" regarding the Treasury Department. He had never really wanted to accept it, but he had allowed his resistance to crumble momentarily under Blaine's persuasive onslaught. A cabinet post would remove Allison from the Senate just when he was on the verge of becoming the unquestioned leader of that body. Furthermore, Iowa politics was in a turmoil, and it had been decided that the party could not stand the strain of choosing another senator at this time. The most pressing reason, however, was personal: Mrs. Allison was undergoing a severe nervous collapse which had sent her shuffling in and out of various mental institutions, and would soon lead to suicide attempts. She was in no condition to be subjected to the glare of publicity that surrounded a cabinet minister's wife. Once Allison was free from Blaine's spell, the force of these arguments was renewed, and he thought better of his promise to accept.[36] Blaine was understandably upset at the wreck of his plans. "I am disgusted with human nature," he bitterly declared, but the fault was his own. Before destroying Garfield's carefully arranged cabinet, the least he could have done was to make certain that his pet candidate was available. Garfield retained his composure despite the damage done by Blaine's irresponsible meddling. "Surprises will never cease," he philosophically observed, "but the world is wide enough to find in it a man for the Treasury." Blaine's world, apparently, was not quite wide enough to include Windom, for he now pulled a fresh name out of his hat, Walter Q. Gresham of Indiana. Emissaries scurried all over the capital to explore this new plan, but it was growing late. In thirty minutes Garfield was due at the White House to begin a full day of ceremonial.[37]

Promptly at ten thirty, the President's carriage rolled up to the hotel door to carry his successor to the White House. There they were met by a committee of senators who were to escort them up Pennsylvania Avenue to the Capitol for the swearing-

536

in ceremonies. The Avenue was decked out in holiday finery: government office buildings were draped with patriotic bunting, while flags and banners fluttered from every street corner. Thirty-eight arches, one for each state, spanned the line of march, dominated by the Union Arch, a gaudy, gothic wooden structure that was, even to contemporary eyes, remarkably ugly. Row upon row of temporary bleachers lined both sides of the parade route to accommodate the sightseers who had descended upon the city. These visitors had driven up the price of hotel rooms to thirty-five dollars a day, for those lucky enough to find them. Despite the weather, the benches were beginning to fill up, hours before the parade. The scene was marked by good-natured confusion: peanut vendors wandered through the throng; street-cleaners pushed slush off to one side of the road; lost groups of paraders searched up and down for their companions; and cold, unhappy children added a shrill note of protest to the festivities. The stands were almost full by the time the presidential party drove down the Avenue. With propitious timing, the wind died down and the sun broke out from behind the clouds just as the hero of the hour passed by, bowing and waving his new silk hat to the multitudes. The outgoing President sat, as protocol required, on the left; the incoming one on the right. On the return trip, their positions would be reversed.[38]

At the Capitol, the expiring Congress was winding up its business, marking time until noon. The Senate chamber was filled to overflowing with distinguished guests: Supreme Court justices in their black robes; the Diplomatic Corps in their glittering sashes and medals; and generals and admirals in full dress regalia. Among the military observers, the popular favorite was clearly General Winfield Scott Hancock, whose appearance brought prolonged cheers from the galleries. Last November's loser outwardly seemed "fat, substantial and philosophic," but he could scarcely help reflecting on how close he had come to being today's guest of honor instead of a mere spectator. In the gallery, all eyes were on the Garfield women. Fourteen year old Mollie sat primly, trying to look as grownup as possible despite the girlish ribbons trailing down from the back of her hat. Her grandmother was dressed in black silk.

537

Under her demure bonnet, her bright eyes darted briskly, taking in everything. Lucretia carried a purple bouquet and wore green velvet, trimmed with lace. She appeared tired and nervous, but actually she was in something like a trance, seeing and hearing little except her husband. He arrived precisely at noon (thanks to a little jiggling of the Senate clock), arm in arm with his predecessor. To Lucretia, her husband seemed "almost superhuman," but to more detached observers he appeared visibly pale and worn. The outgoing President, on the other hand, was wreathed in a "sweet and lamblike" smile. For months he had been acting like a man about to be reprieved. ". . . Out of a scrape," he kept chuckling, "out of a scrape."[39]

When all had been seated, it was Arthur's turn. Looking dapper but nervous, the Vice-President made a modest little speech to the senators and took his oath of office while Conkling beamed. The entire company then formed a procession that marched out of the Senate, through the Rotunda and outdoors to the East Portico. The broad staircase was now covered by a wooden platform capable of holding perhaps two thousand people. The capitol grounds in front of this stand were packed with a dense multitude. To Lucretia, this immense throng was "the greatest human spectacle" she had ever beheld. "I have once or twice seen as large a number of people gathered in a moving swirling crowd," she said, "but this was grand in its unity." That vast sea of upturned faces strained for a glimpse of the tall, balding, full-bearded man who took his place in a chair once occupied by George Washington. He sat there for about five minutes, staring gravely into space. As he waited the color came back to his face and the weariness seemed to drop away. There was no small talk on the platform and almost no movement in the crowd. When he was ready, Garfield rose to his feet without any fanfare or introduction, took his scarcely-dry manuscript from his pocket and began to read in a harsh, penetrating voice.

"Fellow-citizens,—We stand to-day upon an eminence which overlooks a hundred years of national life,—a century crowded with perils, but crowned with the triumphs of liberty and law." A brief, conventional and optimistic review of that century followed. The speaker was accustomed to outdoor orations; he spoke slowly and clearly but even so most of the vast audience could see only the moving of his lips. They applauded anyway, every time he paused for breath. He asked for an end to the bitter feelings arising from the Civil War and a final acceptance of the results of that war. In particular, he dwelt at length on the new role of the Negro in American life. The Negroes in the crowd, who were somewhat fewer but noticeably better dressed than at previous inaugurals, cheered as the speaker praised their efforts to enjoy "the blessings that gather around the homes of the industrious poor." He promised to protect their newly-won rights, especially the right to the ballot. There can be no middle ground between slavery and full equality, he insisted. "There can be no permanent disenfranchised peasantry in the United States. Freedom can never yield its fulness of blessings so long as the law or its administration places the smallest obstacle in the pathway of any virtuous citizen." For the eventual solution of the racial problem, the onetime Professor of Ancient Languages at the Western Reserve Eclectic Institute pinned his hopes on "the saving influence of universal education."

This was the emotional high point of the address. What followed, however sincerely intended, betrayed its hasty composition by the flatness of its tone and the conventionality of its subject matter. He praised the farmer. He praised industry, and promised to promote the interests of both. He promised to uphold the integrity of the dollar, to maintain strict economy in government expenditures and faithfully to execute the laws. The only jarring note was a passionate and unexpected denunciation of the Mormons. Otherwise, all was bland and inoffensive. Hayes thought it "sound and admirable," but the *London Telegraph*, which was disappointed by its neglect of foreign affairs, bluntly pronounced the speech dull. The audience, however, was disposed to be enthusiastic in its response. Among the most enthusiastic, surprisingly enough, in view of his performance of the preceding day, was Roscoe Conkling, who had insinuated himself directly behind the speaker and ostentatiously applauded his every remark.

As he neared the end, Garfield began to grow hoarse. He turned away from the raw wind and addressed his concluding remarks to the guests on the platform. The civil service, he declared, must be regulated by law. "I shall," he pledged, ". . . ask Congress to fix the tenure of the minor offices of the several Executive Departments, and to prescribe the grounds upon which removals shall be made during the terms for which incumbents have been appointed." With the obligatory invocation of the support and blessing of the Almighty, Garfield's inaugural address drew to a close. When the cheering had died away, he turned to Chief Justice Waite, placed one hand upon a Bible, raised the other to the sky, and swore the oath prescribed by the Constitution. He then pressed his lips to the book where it had fallen open—at the twenty-first chapter of Proverbs: "To do justice and judgment is more acceptable to the Lord than sacrifice." And then James Abram Garfield, twentieth President of the United States of America, bent to kiss the frail old woman who, fifty years earlier, had borne him in a rough log cabin, had reared him without the guiding hand of a father and had started him on the road which led, who could say how, to this place and this moment.[40]

The rest of the day was given over to celebration. First, the outgoing tenant of the White House gave one final lunch in honor of his successor. Packing crates and boxes were piled high behind the staircase as the Hayes family prepared to take its leave and turn the mansion over to its new occupants. The transition was free of the rancor that usually marred such occasions. As Garfield gratefully acknowledged in his bread-and-butter note the next week: "I know of no case, unless it may have been at the occasion of Van Buren's, when the transfer of an administration was attended with such cordiality of personal and political friendship. . . ."

Then came the parade. No such array of marching men had been seen in Washington since the Grand Review of the Union Army at the end of the Civil War. Grand Marshall William Tecumseh Sherman, astride a spirited white stallion, presided over the procession. The Avenue was dry now; sun and street-cleaners had done their job well. For two hours, uniformed men marched or rode past the reviewing stand to receive the salute of their new President. By European standards, the parade was not very impressive. Most of the marchers were militia men, whose gait lacked the smart precision of the handful of regular soldiers sprinkled among them. The President, a one-time citizen-soldier himself, did not seem to mind; he appeared to be enjoying himself immensely. He, and the other spectators, roared with special appreciation at the antics of Jack Haverley's Mastodon Minstrels, then playing at the National Theater, who had wormed their way into the parade and refused to be ejected. A more ominous intruder was the hearse that had somehow gotten caught up in the parade and rolled grimly along, reminding the superstitious of similar omens that had attended Lincoln's second inaugural.[41]

After the marching came the dancing. The Inaugural Ball was held in the new Smithsonian Museum. The decor was dominated by a colossal plaster statue of the Goddess of Liberty, holding that new-fangled wonder, the electric light, in her upraised hand. Beneath that statue, thousands of revelers danced and swirled while thousands more, without tickets, lined the grounds to gawk. Only seven Negroes were among the ticket-holders. When two of them had the impertinence to join the dance, they were silently rebuked by the other dancers, who walked off the floor, leaving the Negroes and the Goddess of Liberty, for the moment, in undisputed possession of the empty ballroom. The presidential party arrived at about nine o'clock. Garfield was in full evening dress; Lucretia wore a pearl-gray silk gown. Even though the Marine Band obligingly played the President's favorite airs from Gilbert and Sullivan, he did not dance. He had never learned how; the subject had not been part of the Eclectic's curriculum. Instead, he stood at the reception line and shook an endless stream of hands until eleven o'clock. His departure did not dampen the gaiety of the party. The sounds of polkas, waltzes and quadrilles continued to fill the night air, while between dances the hungry guests helped themselves to 1,500 pounds of turkey, 100 gallons of oysters and 250 gallons of coffee.[42]

While his friends were dancing the night away in his honor, Garfield was still hard at work, trying to put the pieces of his broken cabinet together again. Neither Gresham nor any other of Blaine's last-minute suggestions for the Treasury Department had proved feasible, so Garfield was compelled to fall back upon his own original first choice, William Windom. The Minnesotan was waiting at the White House when Garfield returned from the ball. After an hour's conversation an offer was made and Windom seemed agreeable. With Windom secured, everything fell back into place. Hunt could be moved over to the Navy and Kirkwood restored to the Interior, now that Allison's refusal had made room for his fellow Iowan. Except for the substitution of James for Morton, the final slate was virtually identical to the one Garfield had carried away from Mentor.

It was twelve-thirty. Faint strains of music could still be heard from across the Mall, but the weary President paid no attention. Troubled neither by premonitions of the future nor by "the shadows of the last eighty years" which his wife imagined still hovered over their new home, he was lost in a deep, dreamless sleep.[43]

In the morning, the Garfield Administration would begin.

CHAPTER TWENTY-FOUR

THE PORCUPINE ADMINISTRATION

John Hay, who had once served as Lincoln's private secretary and who had since kept close watch on Lincoln's successors, had high hopes for the success of this new administration. What with youth, genius, education and experience, Garfield entered office, according to Hay, the best-trained, best-equipped president since John Quincy Adams. It was an unfortunate comparison: Adams for all his brilliance had been such a spectacular failure that even his own grandson was bound to admit that "the old gentleman's" presidency had been a "lurid" one. Garfield's record seemed to preclude a similar disaster. Seventeen years in Congress, four of them spent at the helm of the Appropriations Committee, had given him an unparalleled knowledge of the inner workings of the government. Could he now put that knowledge to use? Much would depend on whether he could rise above his limited conception of the nature of his new office.[1]

Having been called to the presidency almost by accident, Garfield had never thought about the office in any systematic way. Still, no politician is quite immune to the half-wistful daydream: "If only I were running things . . . ," and Garfield was probably no exception. He kept all such thoughts to himself, but from a few scattered remarks made over the years, Garfield had dropped hints of what sort of president he intended to be, if ever given the chance. His view of the presidency was a negative one, quite in keeping with the laissez-faire principles he had imbibed in his formative years. The whole duty of government, he had once declared, was merely "to keep the peace and stand out of the sunshine of the people." Long years as a congressman had fortified his suspicion of presidential power. "While it is made the constitutional duty of the President to recommend to Congress such measures as he considers for the public good," Garfield once declared, "it was never intended that he should dictate to Congress the policy of the government, nor use the power of his great office to force upon Congress his own peculiar views of legislation." On the other hand, he argued that the president was entitled to exercise a free hand in appointing men to public office without undue interference from Congress, especially from that "vicious" practice known as senatorial courtesy.[2]

In short, Garfield divided the duties of the presidency into two parts: public policy and personnel. In dealing with the first category the president was expected to follow the lead of congress; in the second, congress should follow the president. Yet, ironically, this division of labor required the sort of temperament which Garfield frankly acknowledged he did not possess. As he saw it, his character was strong precisely where a president was expected to be weak, and vice versa. "I love to deal with doctrines and events," he admitted. "The contests of men about men I greatly dislike." Unless he could somehow manage to reconcile his views of the presidency with his personal predelictions, his time in the White House was not likely to be a happy one.[3]

I

That house itself (which Garfield preferred to call by its formal name, The Executive Mansion) was in a state of shabby disrepair. Four years of neglect by a stingy Democratic congress which had refused to appropriate funds to house what it regarded as a usurper had left the drapes in tatters and the carpets so threadbare that Mrs. Hayes constantly had to rearrange her furniture to cover over the worst spots.[4] Despite its deficiencies, the historic old mansion was so much more grand than anything the Garfield family had ever known that they settled into their new quarters with relish.

The President's mother was put up in a "cozy and home

like" room from which she emerged at meal times, a lace-
bonnetted wisp of black tafetta, clinging to her son's arm.
Her grandchildren quickly made themselves at home. Mollie
was at first overwhelmed by her new surroundings. "When I
got here," she gushed, ". . . and saw the city so crowded I
just said 'My goodness I'll take the next train for Cleveland,
if this is the way things are going on,' " but in no time at
all she was comfortably banging away at her lessons on the
White House grand piano and presiding over formal lun-
cheons for her girl friends. Her younger brothers, lively and
more than a little spoiled, turned the White House into a play-
ground. Irvin was a special terror. In bad weather he would
bring his high-wheeled bicycle indoors and careen down the
staircase and through the corridors, gouging chunks from the
historic wainscotting and scattering the lines of anxious office seekers waiting for an audience with his father. The
older boys were more sedate. Both Harry and Jim had been
taken out of school and placed under tutors to prepare them
for college (Williams, of course) in the fall, and were too busy
for much mischief. Harry was so absorbed by a puppy-love
romance with his teenage sweetheart, Lulu Rockwell, that he
hardly even seemed to notice his glamorous new surroundings.[5]

Harry's parents fretted nervously over this adolescent passion, so foreign to their own experience, but both had more
pressing problems to contend with. His mother, hitherto a
somewhat mousey stay-at-home, had to manage the tremendous transition to First Lady, the social arbiter of Washington
and ultimately the nation. She turned to the wife of the Secretary of State for counsel. In the past Lucretia had been "just
a little" afraid of Mrs. Blaine's sharp tongue and imperious
manner but now she took refuge in her new friend's brisk self-
assurance when Washington busybodies criticized each trivial
departure from Mrs. Hayes's precedents. The most vexing social problem left over from the previous administration was
Mrs. Hayes's well-publicized policy of banishing wine from
the White House table. This practice, which had won her the
devotion of the temperance advocates and the derisive nickname "Lemonade Lucy" from the scoffers, presented the new
administration with its first crisis. For months Hayes had

been badgering his successor on this question and had even warned that the restoration of wine might cause Republican defeat at the next election.[6]

Garfield had no strong feelings one way or the other on the matter. Although he generally preferred a wholesome glass of milk with his meals, he was not averse to an occasional sip of champagne. What made the whole business so delicate was the extraordinary expectations his election had raised in the breasts of God-fearing Republicans across the land. Many, as Burke Hinsdale informed his friend, "hold that you have been divinely called and sent, as Saul was to the Gentiles." Frances Willard, the guiding spirit of the Women's Christian Temperance Union, was in something close to ecstasy. "To think that *my candidate* could have been chosen! . . . The only man . . . who spoke of God, of Home, of the mothers, wives and daughters . . . is to be the next President of the Great Republic! Verily, 'There is a God in Israel!' " Such enthusiasm embarrassed Garfield, who was privately more than a little nettled at the "impertinence" exhibited by these fanatics. Still, it might be prudent to submerge his own feelings and bow to their demands rather than disappoint his admirers. He turned to Blaine for advice.[7]

The Secretary had no hesitations. He urged Garfield to make his administration a brilliant social, as well as political, success and sneered at Mrs. Hayes for having imported into the White House "the usages of village society." In this, as in so many other matters, Blaine's voice would be decisive. Nonetheless, Frances Willard tried to force the issue by marching a delegation of fifty temperance ladies into the East Room. Their ostensible purpose was to present the new President with a full-length portrait of Lucy Hayes, but while they had him captive they pressed their abstinence views upon him. In a similar confrontation a few years later, Chester Alan Arthur would respond: "Madam, I may be President of the United States, but my private life is nobody's damned business." Garfield, compelled by circumstances to be more discreet, sidestepped the issue. He praised their principles in generalities but he pointedly insisted upon "the absolute right" of each family to control its affairs according to its own convictions. Which meant, in effect, that wine from the well-stocked (and by now, well-aged) cellar that Grant had thoughtfully left behind would be free to flow once more.[8]

Garfield himself would never have an opportunity to savor that cellar's contents. His brief presidency did not coincide with the social season, so there were no White House state dinners during his tenure. The only formal social affairs were a grueling series of receptions held in the first weeks of his term. For four days in a row he and his wife stood at the head of seemingly endless receiving lines, shaking hands and mumbling ritual greetings. On one day it was the diplomatic corps, on the next, the military officers, and finally the doors were thrown open "for all the great roaring world" to enter. "Before the first hour was over," Lucretia said, "I was aching in every joint, and thought how can I last through the next long sixty minutes." But she found a second wind and even though "nearly paralyzed" by the ordeal she became caught up in the glamour and glitter of these occasions. Under the flattering glow of gaslight the old mansion lost much of its shabbiness, the profusion of fresh-cut flowers from the White House conservatory gave it a welcome touch of spring, and even the First Lady herself seemed to blossom.

All this glamour carried a steep price tag. Under Hayes a formal reception could run as much as $2,400, while a state dinner (even without wine) had to be budgeted at over thirty dollars per plate. Total White House expenses seldom ran less than $35,000 a year. Much of this cost, of course, was borne by the government, but Hayes was continually digging into his own pocket for extras. Hayes could afford it—he was a millionaire, possibly the wealthiest president of the nineteenth century—but Garfield had little to draw on other than his presidential salary of $50,000 a year. Nothing in his past experience had prepared him for the responsibility of managing a mansion with a domestic staff of nearly fifty. Little wonder that these servants at first thought their new master cold, aloof and, in money matters, "dreadfully close."[9]

The White House staff was large enough to operate a good-size hotel. With ten gardeners, five messengers (two on horseback), cooks, bakers and even its own barber, the mansion was virtually self-sufficient. There was also a fully-equipped stable, the presence of which proved something of an embarrassment to Garfield since he had neither horse nor carriage to put in it. After a lifetime of public service and despite constant accusations of corrupt, ill-gotten wealth, Garfield had never been able to afford either of these luxuries. The lack of a carriage was solved when Hayes graciously left behind his own elegant $1,150 landau on temporary loan. He also offered to sell his matched team of horses. This gesture was somewhat less gracious than it seemed, for when Garfield consulted a veterinarian he learned that Doc was lame, Ben was blemished and both animals showed such signs of hard use that "Whoever buys them now is getting the skim milk, the present owner has had the cream."[10]

In spite of its many headaches, life in the White House had some compensations. For one thing, being president meant that Garfield could work at home. His day began at seven. By breakfast time he had already digested the morning papers and was ready to tackle his correspondence. The vast bulk of this mail did not, of course, require his personal attention. At least ninety percent of it consisted of routine job applications which his secretaries routinely bundled off to the appropriate government departments. Personal or official correspondence was winnowed out from this chaff and placed in separate files.

Another folder was reserved for what was called "the eccentric file." This was crammed with messages from unhinged patriots, ranging from a mad scientist (appropriately named Frankenstein) who had just discovered the principle of Reciprical Identity, to a Tennessee preacher whose new system of scriptural science was guaranteed to unite all Christendom. There was something about the office of the presidency that attracted such pathetic cranks. "I am followed by Russian despots to be shot by private treaty without any provocation whatever. Protect me," begged one. "Have discovered long sought for perpetual motion," exulted another. "Comes out in dead weight and leverage. Please protect me in patent office."[11] Others, more ominously, babbled of obscure catastrophes, or even threatened to blow up the White House. In later years, after sad experience, all such threats would be taken very seriously, but now they were regarded merely as amusing tidbits for the delectation of clerks and passing journalists.

The President's time, of course, was not taken up with such trifles. Only the most pressing matters were brought to his attention and he usually reserved the hour following breakfast to dictate replies to his private secretary. Finding such a secretary had been a particularly difficult quest. In all his years as Congressman, Garfield had never been able to afford a full-time secretary of his own. Instead, he had been forced to make do with the part-time services of George U. Rose. Rose was almost one of the family. After so many faithful years of underpaid service he assumed that he would follow his boss into the White House, but Garfield had other ideas. He hoped to elevate the post of private secretary to something approaching cabinet status, and for that he needed someone with more glamour than loyal, lackluster old Rose—someone, in fact, like John Hay. But Hay, who moved on easy terms of equality with the likes of Blaine, Whitelaw Reid and Henry Adams, and whose ambition to be Secretary of State would one day be gratified, had no desire to go back to the same post he had held twenty years earlier under Lincoln. He cloaked his refusal in the supercilious irony that his circle affected. ". . . Contact with the greed and selfishness of office seekers and bulldozing Congressmen is unspeakably repulsive to me," he claimed, as he deprecatingly insisted that he was temperamentally "not fit for public office." Actually, he was deeply disappointed, for he had hoped for a more important position in the new administration. After Hay's refusal, Garfield turned to his old crony, Lionel Sheldon, but Sheldon, who lacked Hay's elegant manner, bluntly told his friend that he wanted a job that paid more money.[12]

Meanwhile, it began to dawn on Rose that he was to be left behind. "All this is like a dream to me," he moaned in stunned disbelief as he reproached Garfield with memories of happier days. "You have lavished the warmest expressions of friendship, you promised me at the earliest opportunity to take me wholly with you and pay me a much better

549

salary. . . . Through all these long years you have often placed your hand upon my shoulders and sympathized with me because of the late hours I worked. . . . Your little ones have called me Uncle, their arms have clasped me in affectionate embrace. . . . I am indignant. I am hurt. . . . God grant that your administration may be a glorious success. I am of small account compared to that, and shall quietly, but with a broken spirit, plod along." All that he asked now was that Garfield appoint an outstanding private secretary whose obvious distinction would lessen his own humiliation.[13]

Instead, Garfield selected a man younger and even less experienced than Rose. Joseph Stanley Brown (the hyphen would come later) was scarcely twenty-four years old. Despite his youth and inexperience, Brown had made himself particularly useful at Mentor during the presidential campaign by his energy, tact and boyish enthusiasm. When the negotiations with John Hay broke down Garfield brought the young man along to the White House, at first as a temporary expedient but by late March as private secretary in name as well as in fact. There he presided over the small staff of only half a dozen clerks who were kept busy clipping newspapers, recording appointments, handling correspondence, and generally arranging the President's day. To be passed over in favor of a mere boy was the final blow to Rose's already wounded pride, but at least one person was made happy by Brown's appointment. Mollie had been harboring a secret crush on the young secretary for almost a year. "Isn't he cool," she giggled. Now, the thought of seeing him daily under her own roof was almost more than she could bear. "Just think of it," she confided to a school friend. "Whew!!!"

By about ten o'clock each morning the President and his young secretary had cleared the desk of mail and it was time to throw open the doors to the public. In the early days of the administration the line of callers snaked through the halls of the White House and stretched out to Pennsylvania Avenue as literally thousands patiently filed through the Oval Office to pay their respects and, while there, remind the President that they were available to serve their country if needed. To the fastidious John Hay, it seemed as if the marble corridors echoed to "the sound of beasts at feeding time" as the hungry office-seekers prowled in search of jobs.[14]

Over one hundred thousand civilians were employed by the federal government.[15] All of them owed their appointment, in one degree or another, to political influence, and it was expected that a substantial portion would be replaced by each incoming administration. Any new president, consequently, found himself at the outset of his term the target of a frightening barrage of fear and greed. Years earlier, Tocqueville had observed that "of all people in the world, the most difficult to restrain and to manage are a people of office-holders." Now Garfield was rediscovering this for himself. Office-seekers tormented his days and haunted his dreams. They laid siege to his office and they accosted him on the street. The steady stream of supplicants was almost more than he could bear. "These people would take my very brain, flesh and blood if they could," he groaned.[16] "My God!" he asked after a particularly trying day, "What is there in this place that a man should ever want to get into it?" At night the harassed President tossed in his bed, oppressed with the suspicion that he was "wholly unfit" for his job. His training in public life had been devoted to issues and ideas, and now he found his time taken up with deciding "whether A or B shall be appointed to this or that office." "My services ought to be worth more to the government than to be thus spent," he declared. The only solution seemed to be some sort of civil service reform.[17]

Garfield was not a civil service reformer in the usual sense of the term. He had no quarrel with the spoils system on principle. Quite the contrary, he unblushingly provided so many government jobs for his old friends that the civil service list read like the 42nd Regiment's muster roll or a Hiram class reunion. Don Pardee was made a federal circuit judge, while Lionel Sheldon was sent off to New Mexico to be territorial governor. David Swaim was elevated to Judge Advocate General of the army[18] and Charles E. Henry's faithful service entitled him to be U.S. Marshall for the District of Columbia.[19] Burke Hinsdale would have joined this roster had the President lived long enough to keep his promise of a dip-

lomatic mission to Hawaii. Those who had helped Garfield
win the presidential nomination were now rewarded. Thomas
Nichol was nominated as Commissioner of Indian Affairs
and Wisconsin's Jere Rusk was named charge d'affaires to
Paraguay and Uruguay,[20] while W. A. Grier who had cast
that lonely initial vote for Garfield at the convention was
made Third Assistant Postmaster General. Even relatives were
taken care of, as Ballou and Letcher cousins were sent to
staff western land offices. Sometimes an appointment could
even be made on sheer impulse. In mid-April the President
was relaxing with a copy of Lew Wallace's popular new novel, *Ben Hur*. Wallace had just been nominated to a diplomatic post in Latin America, but the novel gave the President a better idea: why not send its author to Constantinople
instead, to gather material for a sequel?

Such happy inspirations were rare. There simply were
not enough friends or relations to fill one hundred thousand
jobs. A president needed some sort of guidance, and the traditional network of patronage recommendations no longer
seemed adequate for a government as large as this. Garfield
opposed the patronage system not because it fostered corruption but because it was ineffective. What he most resented
were the demands it made on his time. Instead of the "vital,
useful activity" he yearned to perform, his days were frittered away on trifles. "Four years of this kind of intellectual
dissipation may cripple me for the remainder of my life," he
said. ". . . Some Civil Service Reform will come by necessity after the wearisome years of wasted Presidents have
paved the way for it."[21]

To relieve a bit of this burden, he ordered Postmaster
General Thomas James to devise a better system. The Post
Office alone accounted for almost half of the available government jobs. Under the previous administration, despite President Hayes's well-publicized reform sentiments, these jobs
had generally been awarded for political loyalty. James, however, wanted the Post Office to be run in an efficient, businesslike manner. As postmaster of New York City he had
earlier tried the experiment of promotion by competitive exam
and removal only for cause. Now, with Garfield's encouragement, he planned to apply these same reforms nationwide.[22]

The President himself had promised in his inaugural address to submit a civil service reform proposal to Congress at the appropriate time. Time, of course, would run out all too quickly for this administration, but the outlines of Garfield's unsubmitted proposal seem clear. He would have advocated secure job tenure for all minor office-holders, not for life, as the doctrinaire reformers urged, but for a fixed period, preferably four years. In this way he hoped to relieve the anxiety of the office-holders which would, in turn, relieve some of the pressure placed on the president.

Such a proposal would not have satisfied the simon-pure reformers who hoped to create a permanent corps of government workers divorced from politics. Nor, on the other hand, would it please the politicians. Blaine, for one, dismissed all this talk of civil service reform as "humbug." He frankly enjoyed manipulating the patronage and tried to instruct the President in the fine points of the game. He teased his friend that automatic reelection by the dependable 19th District had so spoiled him that he did not know what personal opposition was nor how to handle it. Blaine was perfectly willing to teach Garfield how.[23]

Newspapers enjoyed poking fun at the supposed contrast between the naive, idealistic President and his practical-minded Secretary of State.

There are times, my dear Mr. Secretary [Garfield was pictured as saying], in the history of men and nations when they stand so near the veil that separates mortals from immortals, time from eternity and men from their God that they can almost hear the breathings and feel the pulsations of the heart of the Infinite.

I dare say that's so, General Garfield [Blaine was imagined as replying]: but I don't know anything about that. What I'm after now is the Oshkosh Post Office.

Actually, this imaginary exchange was not as far-fetched as it may have seemed. Blaine was obsessed by patronage matters and used his influence with the President to punish Grant's friends and reward his own. With a perfectly straight face he predicted the direst consequences if his advice should be ignored. Appointment of a Logan crony as Federal Marshall in Illinois, for example, would be "political suicide," whereas failure to appoint a distant relative of Blaine's as the Helena postmaster "would be strangling the last chance to make Montana Republican."[24]

Blaine's constant presence at the White House was a source of concern to those who feared that the President might fall under his spell. "If you can only restrain his immense activity," advised John Sherman, ". . . you will have a brilliant Secy." Sherman was asking the impossible. There was too much energy in Blaine to be pent up in the duties of any one office; it simply had to spill over. Never stingy with advice, Blaine took it upon himself to instruct Garfield in everything from social protocol to the proper timing of news releases, sprinkling his lengthy letters with such fatherly injunctions as "Take care of yourself and see nobody after lunch." An incurable busybody, Blaine had to know everything that was going on, and to make certain that nothing escaped his eye, he even (so some suspected) planted spies in the White House staff to keep him fully posted. Such precautions were unnecessary. Garfield had no secrets from Blaine. On cabinet days the two would confer privately before the meetings. Blaine would then slip out a side door, scurry around to the front and breeze into the President's office with his fellow cabinet ministers as if he had just arrived. When unable to attend cabinet meetings, Blaine would send the President detailed instructions on how to proceed in his absence.

Such undue influence alarmed John Sherman, who had seen the Hayes administration come to grief because of Secretary of State Evarts's meddling in New York custom house appointments. To spare Garfield similar anguish, Sherman offered a simple piece of advice: "One rule is essential to your comfort, that the head of one Dept. shall not meddle with or interfere with Appointments to office in another Dept." This seemed reasonable, and at his first cabinet meeting Garfield laid down just such a rule. Blaine, however, acted as if the rule was not intended to apply to him. So long as his meddling was confined to postmasterships and other petty offices, the damage, if any, was minor, but inevitably his attention turned to bigger game. When it did, it embroiled the administration in a series of battles which would shake the Republican Party to its very foundations.[25]

II

Blaine's first target was the Justice Department. Attorney General Wayne McVeagh was certainly no friend of the Secretary of State. A man of conspicuous independence who had built a reform reputation into his political stock-in-trade, McVeagh had twice opposed Blaine's presidential ambitions and could be expected to continue to resist his famous magnetic spell. Blaine hoped to neutralize McVeagh's influence by installing his own close friend, William E. Chandler, in the second most important position in the Justice Department, Solicitor General.

Blaine and his friends began a well-orchestrated campaign to persuade the President of Chandler's merits. Garfield needed little persuasion. He could hardly have forgotten the thousand dollar campaign contribution Chandler had tendered in the bleak year of 1874, although the most telling argument seems to have been the desirability of balancing off McVeagh with a true friend of the Negro, such as Chandler, in the handling of Southern affairs.[26] As an abstract proposition, the appointment had merit. Chandler was neither a spoilsman nor a party hack, but was instead a man of exceptional ability and unexpected depths, whose private musings anticipated Freud and whose public services would later include the renovation of the American navy. The only problem was that Chandler had managed to accumulate a long list of political enemies over the years, one of whom was McVeagh himself. The Attorney General still bristled at the memory of some harsh words Chandler had thrown in his face years before, and the prospect of having this old enemy foisted upon him was more than McVeagh could bear.[27]

Despite Blaine's repeated assurances that *"He will not resign,"* McVeagh did just that. When he learned that Chandler's nomination had been sent to the Senate, the Attorney General stormed into the White House, accompanied by his brother-in-law, Senator Don Cameron, and a group of Pennsylvania politicians. Their argument with the President raged back and forth throughout the afternoon and into the dinner hour. Lucretia had to send Crump, the White House steward, to the library three times to remind her husband that guests were waiting at the table. The third time he arrived just as McVeagh was slamming his fist on the desk, demanding that the nomination be withdrawn. This was the only time Crump ever saw the President lose his temper, and it left him shaken. With an expression Crump had never before beheld "on any human face," Garfield swore a mighty oath and slammed *his* fist down with a "sledge hammer blow." "No gentlemen," he growled, "by God, *I will not do it!*", and with that he rose, bowed to his guests and descended to dinner.[28]

The very next day the President began to have second thoughts. Blaine attempted to stiffen his resolve by turning the quarrel into a matter of constitutional principle. "You can never surrender (without fatal compromise of your own power and dignity) the right to nominate the great officers in the various departments," he insisted. If McVeagh would not bend, Blaine was willing, almost eager, to see him resign, even though that would shatter Garfield's carefully constructed cabinet. With typical hyperbole, Blaine calculated that a Chandler was "a thousand" times more valuable than a McVeagh. In a political sense, of course (as Blaine neglected to point out), the calculation ran the other way. The resignation of McVeagh would offend, perhaps irreparably, both the reform element and the powerful Cameron family, while the addition of Chandler would bring no new allies to the administration to compensate for these losses.

Faced with these considerations, Garfield began to realize that the Chandler nomination *"may* prove to have been a mistake" and, shaking free from Blaine's influence, he worked out a face-saving compromise: McVeagh would stay on, Chandler's name would not be withdrawn, but Chandler was induced to promise that if confirmed he would decline to serve. That seemed to satisfy McVeagh, but it exposed the President to an unnecessary humiliation since, as it turned out, Chandler never had an opportunity to decline the position. His nomination as Solicitor General was decisively defeated in the Senate, 24 to 19, by a coalition of Southern

Democrats and disgruntled reform Republicans. By that time, however, the whole Chandler tempest had been overshadowed by another and far more serious Blaine-inspired controversy —this time with Conkling.[29]

After so many bitter years this feud between Conkling and Blaine was no longer merely a personal quarrel. It had risen above its petty, half-forgotten origins and had now become a symbolic duel to determine the destiny of the Republican party. Conkling represented a faction and a state; Blaine thought in national and even continental terms. Conkling looked to the past, to a restoration of Grant and all he stood for; Blaine looked to the future, to the problems of an industrialized America with the trials of the Civil War put behind it. Both men were flawed, but Conkling's flaws were those of pettiness, while Blaine's were the result of excess. If it had to come to a choice, there was no question as to which of the two Garfield would support, but he was hoping that such a choice could be avoided. In spite of Conkling's insults and Blaine's ingratiating flattery, the President remained committed to the ideal of a balanced administration that would satisfy all Republican factions.

Success for this strategy depended on Conkling. If, as some suspected, the New York boss would settle for nothing less than total domination, then all of Garfield's efforts at appeasment were bound to fail. Conkling's high-handed behavior over the past few months was hardly designed to inspire feelings of party harmony, but Garfield refused to be drawn into a fight. "I will not begin a war," he declared, "—but I will try to be prepared for one, if it must needs come." Despite provocation, he leaned over backwards to show signs of good faith, even to the extent of appointing Levi P. Morton as Minister to France, after Conkling's weak-kneed banker friend had twice backed out of Garfield's cabinet. Displaying a patience that some construed as amiable weakness, the President tried to placate the New York Senator with patronage. This was the surest way to Conkling's heart. "He never interests himself in anything but personal antagonisms," John Sherman observed, "he never rises above a Custom House or a Post Office."[30]

On Sunday evening, March 20, Conkling was invited to the

White House for the first time in over four years. The meeting was surprisingly amiable. For over two hours, he and the President reviewed the New York scene, trying to arrive at an equitable distribution of the political loaves and fishes. Conkling, of course, wanted the choice morsels reserved for his followers, but Garfield insisted that those "protestants" who had defied Conkling's rule at Chicago were entitled to their share of the spoils. Conkling suggested that if these bolters had to be rewarded it should be with foreign appointments, and he offered to go into the Senate cloak room and "hold his nose" while they were being confirmed. The President replied that his New York friends did not deserve "exile" but rather an honored place in the affairs of their own state. Just what place they should have was open to negotiation, but Garfield insisted that, at the very least, something should be reserved for William H. Robertson, the leader of the state's anti-Grant forces at the convention. Garfield proposed that Robertson be named district attorney or collector of internal revenue, but Conkling raised objections to both suggestions and the conversation drifted on to other topics.

As the Senator was about to take his leave, he asked what the President intended to do about the New York Custom House. Since the present Collector, Edwin A. Merritt, still had two years left to serve, the matter hardly seemed urgent. Garfield brushed the question aside, saying something to the effect that he intended to take it up at a later date. Conkling thought that this implied a promise to consult with him, an implication which Garfield later denied. At the moment, however, this ambiguity was scarcely noticed and Conkling returned to his lodgings convinced that he and "that man Garfield" might be able to work in harmony after all.[31]

That conviction was fortified two days later when the President, true to his word, submitted the names of five New York Stalwarts to the Senate for confirmation. All were loyal members of the Conkling machine, including Stewart L. Woodford, who had made the nominating speech for Conkling at the Republican convention of 1876, Woodford was now to be rewarded with another term as United States Attorney for New York's Southern District, the most lucrative position in the state. When Blaine discovered that the President had reached such a cozy accomodation with his chief rival he felt a sharp pang of personal betrayal. The reappointment of Woodford was an especially bitter blow, for Blaine had privately earmarked Robertson for District Attorney and had already sounded out his New York friend to see if he was interested in that position. That very day, despite the agony of an abscessed tooth, the Secretary hastened to the White House, arriving at dinner time. The President was called away from the table "for one moment only," but the moment stretched out through two or three courses. After his talk with Blaine, Garfield returned to his dinner visibly distraught. The color was drained from his face, and he picked at the remainder of his meal in a silent and preoccupied mood. No one dared ask what the trouble might be, but later, when alone with his wife, he explained: "I have broken Blaine's heart with the appointments I have made today. He regards me as having surrendered to Conkling."[32]

Blaine, in fact, felt so heartbroken that he had threatened to resign. Faced with the breakup of his administration as well as the loss of a valued friend, the President was open to any suggestion that might undo some of the consequences of his hasty courtship of Conkling. At ten o'clock that evening Blaine returned to the White House with a plan. Its key element was Robertson. If the district attorneyship was no longer available, then something equally desirable would have to be found for Blaine's friend. The only comparable office at the President's disposal was Collector of the Port of New York.

This was no ordinary government job but was, perhaps, the most sensitive political appointment in the nation. With a force of fifteen hundred workers at his command, whoever controlled the New York Custom House was bound to be a potent force in the affairs of his state and party. In recent years the Collectorship had been the object of fierce political controversy. When Chester Alan Arthur had been removed from the position by President Hayes for tolerating lax and corrupt practices, Conkling had declared war on the administration and had successfully defeated Hayes's first choice for replacement by appealing to the principle of "senatorial courtesy." This practice, which in effect gave any administration senator veto power over a federal appointment in his state, suffered its first major setback when Hayes was able to secure the confirmation of his next choice, Edwin A. Merritt, a victory that reformers extravagantly hailed as the dawn of a new era. Now Blaine was proposing to reopen the whole controversy by dismissing Merritt in mid-term for no other reason than to make room for Robertson.[33]

Like so many of Blaine's schemes, this one became overly complicated. In order to blunt the reformers' anticipated outrage over the dismissal of Merritt, a place had to be found for the Collector. This set in motion a game of musical chairs, a game that Blaine cleverly constructed so as to provide fresh humiliation for Conkling at every step of the way. Merritt would go to London, as consul general, a transfer which could be portrayed as a promotion. The current consul general, Adam Badeau, Grant's wartime companion and peacetime biographer, would, in turn, be moved to Denmark, as charge d'affaires. Technically, this move too could be considered a step up, but in actuality it was a slap at Grant. Badeau was happy in London, and Grant had specifically requested that he be retained there.[34] To compound the insult, the present incumbent at Copenhagen, Michael J. Cramer, was Grant's brother-in-law. To make room for Badeau, Cramer was now shuffled off to Switzerland where he, in turn, bumped Nicholas Fish, the son of Hamilton Fish, who had been Conkling's first sponsor and Grant's trusted Secretary of State.

The President went along with everything Blaine suggested. On the very next day, March 23, all of the proposed nominations were forwarded to the Senate in such haste and secrecy that none of the principals, including even Merritt and his superior, Secretary of the Treasury Windom, could be afforded the courtesy of advance notification. Blaine tried to brace the President for the expected storm. "Your work of today," he declared, "creates a splendid impression." If a few Stalwarts complain, he said, "it only shows their utter unreasonableness and discloses the design that would have used *your* admn. to crush *your* friends," and he advised Garfield to stand as firm as if he were refighting Chickamauga. Blaine evidently forgot that Garfield's side had *lost* the battle of Chickamauga, through rashness in the face of a superior force.[35]

Despite Blaine's soothing assurances, the storm raised over this batch of appointments was far fiercer than anticipated. The Stalwarts, of course, were nearly speechless with indignation. "Perfidy without parallel," sputtered Conkling, and his partner Platt threatened that "There will be hell before Judge Robertson is confirmed." Former president Grant protested that "I ought not to be humiliated by seeing my personal friends punished for no other offence than their friendship and support," and he angrily broke off all relations with the President. "Garfield," he grumbled, "has shown that he is not possessed of the backbone of an angleworm. I hope his nominations may be defeated."[36]

Criticism from this quarter was to be expected; more alarming were the rumblings heard from normally friendly voices. The reform element, fearing that Merritt's dismissal signaled a reversal of Hayes's civil service policy, found itself in a strange and uncomfortable alliance with Conkling as both, for different reasons, objected to the President's new appointments. Old reliable senators who normally could be counted on for support, such as William Allison and John Sherman, joined in the opposition, and even such dependable Blaine followers as Hale and Frye of Maine were urging that Robertson be withdrawn. Closer to home, this new crisis created fresh cracks in Garfield's already crumbling cabinet. Postmaster General James joined with Arthur, Platt and Conkling in sending a formal remonstrance to the President and, to show he meant business, James "regretfully" resigned from the cabinet.

Within three days, three members of the cabinet had threatened to resign—Blaine, McVeagh and now James—while a fourth, Windom, had ample grounds for following suit. Only three weeks old, the Garfield administration was already on the brink of a collapse unprecedented in the history of American government. The stormy Hayes years seemed almost placid in comparison. According to Senator Dawes, "The last Administration was a sort of dove; this is more like a porcupine."[37]

The beleaguered President moved to repair the damage before it was too late. In what amounted to a virtual repudiation of Blaine's advice, he placated McVeagh by scuttling Chandler, and simultaneously sought a similar accord with

Conkling. Bypassing Blaine, Garfield now turned to Postmaster General James (who had reconsidered his hasty resignation), and together they devised a plan that could satisfy both honor and the Stalwarts. Merritt would be retained as Collector for the time being; Robertson would be named District Attorney (which had been Blaine's original intention); Woodford would be rewarded with a diplomatic post in a sunny climate; and Grant's overseas friends would be able to hold onto their jobs. All that the compromise needed was Conkling's blessing, and with that formality obtained the crisis would be at an end.

A conference was arranged with the President for the very next evening. When James and other peacemakers called to escort Conkling to the White House, they found the haughty senator in an unusually playful mood. "How are the envoys extraordinary tonight?" he asked, and they replied in the same bantering tone. Conkling had good reason to be so jovial: his chief rival thwarted; he himself negotiating with the President on terms of equality, as sovereign to sovereign—it was a triumph to be savored. Still beaming, the senator was just buttoning up his gloves, ready to leave, when a telegram arrived. He tore open the envelope, deciphered the message and scowled for a moment. Then suddenly crumpling the telegram, he threw it on the table, turned to his guests and announced: "Gentlemen, I won't go! I'm no place-hunter and I won't go!"

The message was from New York's Governor Alonzo Cornell, asking Conkling not to oppose Robertson's nomination. This seemingly innocuous request shattered Conkling's mood. Such disloyalty from a trusted subordinate was a chilling reminder of how fragile power could be. Moreover, the injection of petty politics demeaned the grandeur of the occasion and reduced it to a vulgar bickering over spoils. It seemed to shrink Conkling from a sovereign to a supplicant, a deflation which the great man's ego could not endure. His friends tried to jolly him back to his earlier mood, but it was no use. Conkling's triumph had soured and the heady sense of elation could not be recaptured. He kept muttering that he was no place-hunter and finally the negotiators left in disgust.

They returned to the White House to find the President fuming at having been kept waiting for over an hour and a half. When he saw that they had returned without the guest of honor and realized that Conkling had once again humiliated him, just as he had done at the Fifth Avenue Conference, his patience. finally snapped. Ever since the nomination Conkling had snubbed him, reviled him, hectored and belittled him. Personal insults could be endured, but this was an affront to Garfield's great office and could not be borne. "I owe something to the dignity of my office and to my own self-respect," he told the embarrassed negotiators. Rather than withdraw Robertson's nomination now, he vowed, "I will suffer myself to be dragged by wild horses." The war had begun.[38]

It promised to be "no rose-water war." To Whitelaw Reid the impending showdown represented not only the turning point in Garfield's administration but, more dramatically, "the crisis of his fate." The President did not flinch from such a prospect. After the dreary patronage squabbles in which he had been enmeshed, he actually looked forward to some "first class rows" to clear the air. Blaine and his friends eagerly egged him on. "Conkling's insolent course," they declared, "must not be allowed to triumph."[39] Blaine's camp had good reason to be so eager for battle: they had almost thrown away their influence with the President and had only been narrowly saved by Conkling's stubborn pride, which had driven the President back into the arms of Blaine. Now they wanted to press their advantage. Yet actually, despite all appearances, Garfield was not merely fighting Blaine's battle. Blaine's goal was personal: to destroy Conkling as a political force. Garfield, however, thought that he was contending for a principle.

The Robertson appointment, which had begun as an impulsive gesture to placate Blaine, was now transformed into a constitutional test of the limits of presidential power. "It had better be known, in the outset," Garfield declared, "whether the Pres. is the head of the government, or the registering clerk of the Senate." Compared to this momentous question, Robertson's personal fate seemed trivial. Even though Garfield privately admitted that the appointment had probably been "a great mistake," he was now committed to see it through.

The time for compromise had passed. "Robertson may be carried out of the Senate head first or feet first," Garfield insisted. "I shall never withdraw him."[40]

Such audacity and determination seemed to many entirely out of keeping with Garfield's usually affable behavior, and they suspected that the hand of Blaine was directing the President's every move. But no one who had followed Garfield's career closely should have been surprised. For almost a decade he had repeatedly assailed senatorial courtesy as "one of the most corrupt and vicious practices of our times. It virtually robs the President of his power of appointment and puts a dangerous power in the hands of the Senate." He regarded abuses as inevitable under a system in which the Senate enjoyed the power, but the president had to bear the responsibility. Garfield's remedy was simple. As early as 1872 he had proposed: "Let it once be fixed and understood that neither Senators or representatives, singly or combined, can dictate appointments to the Executive, and then again, as in former days, the whole responsibility of the selection of officers will justly rest upon the President and the heads of departments." Some president, he urged prophetically, "ought to make an open contest with the Senate on this subject." Now Garfield found himself engaged in such a contest. The Robertson controversy provided him with a challenge that was almost tailor-made to fit his conception of the presidency. "Summed up in a single sentence this is the question: shall the principal port of entry in which more than 90% of all our customs duties are collected be under the direct control of the Administration or under the local control of a factional Senator." To shirk this challenge, he feared, would hobble himself and his successors by depriving them of that independence in making appointments that he considered the essential function of the presidency.[41]

Looked at in broader perspective, his goal was to redress the balance of American government by halting that steady drift of power to the Senate that had been such a striking feature of national politics for over a generation—a trend that the trial of Andrew Johnson had so graphically illustrated. Grant had been unwilling and Hayes unable to reverse this trend. Left to his own devices, Garfield would probably have recoiled from the messy battle such a stand required, but under the prodding of Conkling and Blaine he had been forced to begin a fight that was not of his choosing. Garfield had, unwittingly, taken the first step towards that steady accretion of presidential power that would in later years transform the whole nature of the office. The path upon which he had been pushed led straight to the twentieth century.

Garfield's quarrel was not with Conkling alone, but with the entire Senate. Had Senators been able to respond immediately to his challenge, their instinctive reaction would most likely have been to rally behind one of their own and support Conkling's prerogatives. Instead, the Senate sat helplessly paralyzed by a filibuster. This filibuster began on the same day that the controversial nominations had been submitted, but otherwise they were unrelated. The Senate's problem was really a reflection of the national political stalemate revealed by the preceding November's election. It was compounded by another unresolved national issue, the Southern Question. Now both issues came to a head at once, leaving the Senate immobilized and impotent.

Garfield's narrow margin over Hancock, a matter of only slightly more than seven thousand votes, was an accurate measure of the delicate equilibrium between the two major political parties. That same equilibrium accounted for the deadlock in the Senate, where thirty-seven Democrats glowered across the aisle at exactly the same number of Republicans. Under these circumstances, two so-called Independents held the balance of power. One was David Davis of Illinois, who was pledged to vote with the Democrats. His support would enable them to organize the Senate and control its committees unless it could be neutralized by the other independent, General William Mahone, the Virginia Readjuster. Though he weighed in at less than a hundred pounds, even with his flow-- ing gray whiskers and high pompadour, "Little Mahone" could tip the scales of the Senate in whichever direction he chose. For months he had been dropping broad hints that he could be induced to choose the Republican side. Garfield had temporized, but now the decision could no longer be delayed.

It was a painful decision, for it forced Garfield to come to

565

grips with the Southern Question before he was ready. The Solid South was an ill for which he suspected no speedy cure was possible. Only time, patience and "the blessings of general education and business enterprise" could bring that region out of the darkness of feudalism and into the light of the nineteenth century. In the meantime, the interests of the Republican party had to be protected. In the South that party was a tattered remnant. With the Negro disenfranchised, its future was bleak unless some new base of party support could be constructed. Hayes had tried to woo Southern Democrats with patronage, but Garfield had no intention of continuing that "dreary failure." Nor was he tempted by a suggestion from Georgia's senator, Ben Hill. Hill, a prewar Know Nothing, urged that the existing party system be scrapped and that Garfield emerge as the leader of a new National Union Party representing like-minded men of all sections. Instead, Garfield decided to maintain the regular party organization in the South and funnel patronage through the various state chairmen until a better solution presented itself.[42]

The emergence of Mahone offered another alternative. In Virginia, Mahone had created the Readjuster Party out of an amalgam of dissident Democrats and Negroes by subordinating racial issues to economic ones. Their objective was to scale down the oppressive state debt with which Virginia had been saddled. This was the first crack in the Solid South since the end of Reconstruction, but Garfield was reluctant to exploit it. For one thing, support for Mahone meant the abandonment of whatever Republican Party was left in Virginia. For another, "readjustment" seemed to smack suspiciously of "repudiation," of course abhorrent to Garfield's well-honed sense of fiscal orthodoxy. His first reaction was to have nothing to do with a movement which, in his view, had "inflicted a serious if not fatal wound upon the honor and prosperity of Virginia." The critical condition of the Senate, however, prompted a reevaluation of his initial prejudice. If Virginia were truly bankrupt, Garfield now conceded, then some sort of debt readjustment might be proper, provided it was performed honestly and economically. "If that is Mahone's position, followed up in good faith it is defensible."

Mahone's friends assured the President that this was indeed
Mahone's position, and the door was now open for an alliance that could control the Senate.[43]

Mahone's cooperation did not come cheaply. Five choice
Senate committee posts were bestowed upon the Virginia
maverick, and Republicans in Virginia were urged by the
President to cooperate with the local Readjuster organization.
In addition, upper chamber Republicans agreed to support
two of Mahone's cronies for high administrative posts in the
new Senate. On March 23, George C. Gorham, editor of the
National Republican, was nominated for Secretary of the
Senate and Harrison H. Riddleberger of Virginia for Sergeant-at-Arms. At this latest concession, the Democrats finally drew the line. Rather than permit Mahone's apostasy
to be so lavishly rewarded, they began a filibuster. The Republicans, equally stubborn, refused to desert their new-found
friends, even though it meant that Senate business would
grind to a halt. The President reluctantly went along. "As an
original question," he said, "the appointment of the officers
was not a sufficient ground for the struggle now going on in
the Senate. But when our friends have secured all the Committees by the help of Mahone they ought to stand by him until
he is reasonably satisfied."[44]

So long as the filibuster continued to drone on, no action
could be taken on Garfield's controversial appointments.
During that time Conkling and the President were locked in
mortal combat to sway the Senate. The initial advantage was
all with Conkling. His chief asset was his imperious will. Even
fellow-senators cringed before his wrath. "Conkling seems to
have a magic influence over them," John Hay observed disdainfully. "They talk as bold as lions to me, or anybody
else—and then they go into caucus or the Senate, and if he
looks at them they are like Little Billee in the ballad." The
Senate Republican caucus, Reid reported, was "completely
under Conkling's thumb." At one such caucus, according to
Senator Dawes, his colleagues sat spellbound while Conkling
"raged and roared like a bull of Bashan for three mortal
hours." This was the speech he had been rehearsing for
months before captive audiences of newsmen and rapt cronies

until each rounded period was suitably polished. He dwelt at length on "the base ingratitude" of Garfield and recounted in detail the many "shameful" treacheries committed by Robertson, Blaine and the President. Dawes was entranced: "I had never heard anything which equaled this effort for flights of oratorical power—genuine eloquence, bitter denunciation, ridicule . . . and contempt. . . ." Finally the oration drew to a close with a lofty appeal to the grandeur of the Republican Party, an appeal which was marred by a spiteful touch of blackmail. "I have in my pocket," Conkling announced, "an autograph letter of this President . . . which I pray God I may never be compelled in self-defense to make public; but if that time should ever come, I declare to you, his friends, he will bite the dust."[45]

This revelation produced its expected sensation. Dawes immediately dashed over to the White House, but the President had evidently been forewarned. He pulled a copy of the mysterious letter from his pocket and handed it to Dawes for inspection. It was a brief note written during the heat of the presidential campaign to Jay Hubbell, chairman of the Republican Congressional Committee. "Please say to [Assistant Postmaster General Thomas A.] Brady that I hope he will give us all the assistance he can. I think he can help effectively. Please tell me how the Departments generally are doing." This cryptic message was hardly the bombshell Conkling had led Dawes to expect, but it did pose some potential embarrassments. For one thing, clouds of scandal were beginning to gather around Brady's head. In the hands of enemies, the Hubbell letter might be used as "evidence" that the President was involved in Brady's crooked schemes. Actually, Garfield had merely been trying to spur Hubbell's efforts to raise campaign funds from government workers, including those in Brady's department. From the reformer's point of view this concern with dunning contributions from hapless clerks might seem reprehensible, but by no stretch of the imagination could it be considered criminal.

Relieved, Dawes urged that the letter be published immediately in order to spike Conkling's guns. Garfield agreed, and was about to hand it over when Blaine walked in. "Here,

568

Blaine," the President said, waving the letter, "is where I have been slopping over again." Blaine, whose antipathy to publishing private correspondence dated back to the Mulligan letters, at once vetoed Dawes's suggestion, and the President, much to Dawes's dismay, submissively followed his Secretary's advice. The advice was sound. When Conkling did publish the letter it seemed like an act of desperation that did Conkling more damage than it did Garfield.[46]

Despite its harmless outcome, this episode, piled on top of the other embarrassments of the administration, left Dawes despondent. "It is not three months," he said hopelessly, "and the whole party is by the ears. Folly, folly, folly—" His gloom was shared by many Republican leaders who blamed the President for the party's disarray. "He does not seem to have the confidence and nerve to take charge of his administration," one former sympathizer reluctantly concluded. To another former friend Garfield was revealed as "morally . . . invertebrate. He had no bony structure." "Of course," concluded a political reporter, "all this lets G. out of the chance of a renomination."[47]

What they failed to realize was that in the wide world outside of Washington Garfield was emerging as a hero in the eyes of the public at large. Far from seeming vacillating or timid, Garfield was generally perceived as courageous and decisive. His apparent boldness in striking at boss rule and senatorial courtesy reminded the voters of the good old days of Andy Jackson. Garfield was discovering the latent power of the president to personalize issues. Outside of Washington few cared much about senatorial perogatives or even about the collectorship of the port of New York. But to a people hungry for leadership this president, at last, seemed to be supplying it. Garfield was winning the battle for public opinion. Even in Conkling's home state 94 newspapers supported the President, while only 18 defended the senator.

As Republican senators began to realize this, support for Conkling's position began to dwindle. Sherman was induced to abandon his earlier neutrality and now took command of the pro-Robertson forces. Other senators grew uncomfortably aware that a newly-installed president, with the bulk of his favors yet to bestow, was not to be trifled with. Support for Robertson was turned into a test of loyalty to the Administration, and those who opposed the nomination, the President coldly announced, "will henceforth require letters of introduction to the White House." The message was not lost on wavering Republican senators, who began to slip quietly away from Conkling's camp.[48]

By early May, the President felt confident enough to force the issue. The first step was to bring the filibuster to an end. This was easy enough. The only obstacles were Gorham and Riddleberger, and the daily attacks being leveled on the Administration by Gorham's pro-Conkling newspaper, *The National Republican*, had not endeared its editor to the President. With Garfield's approval, both Gorham and Riddleberger were abandoned and the Democrats, in turn, abandoned their filibuster on May 4. The Senate could now turn its attention to the immense backlog of nominations that had accumulated during its weeks of enforced idleness.

Conkling thrashed about, seeking some further opportunities for obstruction before Robertson's name would come before the Senate, but time and the patience of his colleagues were beginning to run out. In caucus he no longer bullied, but instead pleaded, in an almost pathetic manner, that he be spared further humiliation. He asked for postponement, then he asked for delay, and then he suggested various compromises, but to no avail: the impending showdown could not be averted. Conkling had one last trick at his disposal. The Senate usually acted on nominations in the order in which they had been submitted. It might yet be possible to confirm all his New York friends and then move for adjournment without having acted on Robertson's case. Garfield, however, had anticipated this maneuver and was determined to withdraw all the New York nominations except for Robertson if that should prove necessary. The strategy had been devised by Blaine. "I never felt clearer in my life in urging a suggestion than I do in this case," he said. "I *know* by inspiration that it will work like a charm."[49] On May 5, a special White House messenger was dispatched to the Capitol, carrying under presidential seal the withdrawal of five New York nomi-

570

nations, all friends of Conkling. "This will bring the Robertson nomination to an issue," Garfield explained. "It may end in his defeat; but it will protect me against being finessed out of a test." Blaine was ecstatic. "Glory to God—" he exclaimed to Garfield, "Victory is yours, sure and lasting." The Stalwarts were downcast. When the message was read to the Senate, Conkling turned pale, Logan gnashed his teeth and Vice-President Arthur stared glumly into space as he absently tore an envelope into little pieces.[50]

None of them had better reason to be upset than Platt. The junior senator from New York was caught in a cruel dilemma. He owed his political career to Conkling, and Conkling was a harsh master who expected total loyalty. On the other hand, Platt owed his Senate seat to a promise he had made back in January to Whitelaw Reid and others. Then he had gladly promised to support all of Garfield's appointments, up to and specifically including Judge Robertson. Now, unless some escape could be devised, Platt would be forced to choose between appearing an ingrate or being exposed as a welsher; either choice could destroy his political future. He tried to wriggle out of his promise, claiming that he was not bound to support a nomination unless he had been consulted in advance, but Garfield easily demolished that argument. Suppose Platt had been consulted, the President asked. "Would he have then voted for Robertson? If yes, on what ground of reason can he now vote no? In either case he would vote, not on the merits of the nominee but on the wholly irrelevant question of his being consulted." All that now stood between Platt and dishonor was the dim possibility that Robertson's name might somehow be prevented from reaching the Senate floor, and with his bold action of May 5 Garfield had eliminated even that last hope.

With an audacity born of desperation, Platt hit upon the only way out of his dilemma—resignation. For this, Conkling's cooperation would be essential, so Platt carefully explained his plan in terms calculated to play on his senior colleague's vanity. "We have been so humiliated as U.S. Senators from the great state of New York," he said, "that there is but one thing for us to do—rebuke the President by immediately turning in our resignations and then appeal to the Legislature to sustain us." Conkling was receptive. He had already half-decided to give up politics in order to spend the rest of his life making money and "wreaking his revenge" on his many enemies. What better way to end his public career than with a grand theatrical gesture of renunciation?[51]

The gesture, however, fell flat. Rather than a heroic act of self-denial, Conkling's resignation was regarded as "a freak of insanity." It evoked laughter rather than dismay. "A great big baby boohooing because he can't have all the cake and refusing to play any longer runs home to his mother. That is all there is to it," said Dawes in disgust.[52] Most of the ridicule was directed at Conkling, but "his serf Platt"[53] had to endure the humiliating (and misleading) nickname "Me too" for the rest of his life. Fellow senators, however, were not amused. Angry at the trifling manner in which the New Yorkers had abandoned their posts, they rebuked the two deserters with a swift and decisive confirmation of Robertson on the 18th of May.

Blaine urged Garfield to follow up this victory with a mass purge of Stalwarts from office, but the President magnanimously resubmitted the names of most of Conkling's New York friends, thinking it best, he explained, "not to bend from the course I had started upon—to recognize fairly both wings of the party." Blaine could not hide his disappointment. "Some blunders you know are worse than crimes," he reminded his friend, "—I fear this is one." Blaine was so captivated by the love of battle that he failed to realize that the war had already been won. The President had amply demonstrated the independence and authority of his office. The senator who had tried to destroy him was himself destroyed; there was no point in pursuing his followers beyond the grave.[54]

So came to an end the public career of "the great American quarreler," Roscoe Conkling. He would linger for awhile, but it would not be the same. "That Olympic brow will never again garner up the thunders of yore," John Hay predicted smugly. Instead, Conkling would simply fade away, leaving behind at last, like some perverse Cheshire cat, only "the ghost of a sneer."[55]

III

While the Robertson drama was being played out to its climax, the President could not afford to neglect the routine burdens of his office. Even so, there were occasional opportunities for relaxation. One informal White House evening in May was especially memorable. The guests were all treasured friends. The most conspicuous was General Sherman, mellowed now with age into something of a bon vivant, who had collected a rapt circle of admiring ladies for his familiar war stories. The President arrived late, "with a quick step and a hearty manner," and instantly stole away Sherman's audience. "How grand he is!" one of the women whispered. "How can they speak about him so? . . . Talk about your canal boys!" The First Lady had a touch of the chill. She sat close to the fire, smiling wanly as she soaked up its warmth and basked in the good company. It was her last happy moment in the White House.

The next morning the "chill" turned into malaria. Lucretia's fever soared to 104°, her pulse raced at 100 beats a minute and her hair fell out in patches. For a time it seemed as if she could not possibly live. Night after night, her distraught husband paced the empty White House corridors, sinking at last to his knees on the floor of the Red Room. His anguished moans woke the domestic staff who tiptoed to the door to see the President alternately praying and sobbing. His prayers were answered; Lucretia passed the crisis, though she would remain dangerously weak for another month.

The First Lady's illness began on May 4, the same day that the Senate filibuster was broken. Preoccupied with his family crisis, the President could pay only fitful attention to the last critical stages of the struggle with Conkling. Instead, he devoted his energies to nursing his wife back to health—"all my thoughts center in her, in comparison with whom all else fades into insignificance." He personally stayed by her bedside, attending to her needs and, as she improved, carried her in his arms from room to room. By the end of May she was clearly out of danger and her grateful husband sensed that "a deep current of happy peace flows through every heart in the household." To complete her convalescence, Lucretia was sent to a summer house at Long Branch, New Jersey, where she could regain her depleted strength under a bracing sea breeze.[56]

With his wife on the mend and his chief rival in limbo, it was time for the President to take stock of his administration. Despite the political storms of the past months there had been many solid achievements that promised well for the future.

The most striking activity, as might be expected, came out of Blaine's office in the new State Department building next to the White House. Traditionally, the State Department had been run along gentlemanly, somnambulent lines, with only a dozen or so clerks. Blaine's predecessor, the easygoing William Evarts, had based his administration on "the great truth that almost any question will settle itself if you only leave it alone long enough." "There are just two rules at the State Department," he had boasted, only half in jest, "one, that no business is ever done out of business hours; and the other is, that no business is ever done *in* business hours."[57]

Blaine, with his superabundance of nervous energy, could hardly be expected to operate at this leisurely tempo. With his presidential ambitions apparently laid to rest, he now intended to make his mark in history as a brilliant foreign secretary. Opportunities for diplomatic distinction, however, were decidedly limited. America was at peace with the world (which was providential, considering the shabby state of the army and navy), and nothing disturbed the tranquillity of relations with Europe except for the usual routine quarrels caused by a few Irish-Americans languishing in English jails, and the perennial dispute as to whether American pork was fit for European consumption. Such unheroic matters could hardly satisfy Blaine's ambitions. Fortunately, a fresh field for diplomatic endeavor presented itself—Latin America.

In 1881 controversies abounded south of the border: Mexico and Guatemala were on the brink of war over possession of a disputed border province; Costa Rica and Colombia were locked in a similar dispute, as were Argentina and Chile. France was threatening to intervene in Venezuela in order to collect its share of the foreign debt, while both England and the United States were beginning to have second thoughts about the thirty-year-old Clayton-Bulwer agreement for joint control over the (as yet unbuilt) Isthmian canal. Overshadowing all else was the bloody War of the Pacific, in which an aggressive Chile was on the verge of subjugating both Bolivia and Peru.[58]

To each of these crises Blaine felt that the United States had to make some response, if only to forestall European intervention and the consequent weakening of the Monroe Doctrine. Beyond that, he hoped that increased American prestige in the region would attract a greater share of South America's trade from Europe to the United States. To these ends, a flurry of diplomatic activity was set in motion in a dozen Latin American capitals, but even this unprecedented bustle from the formerly lethargic State Department failed to satisfy Blaine. "Instead of friendly intervention here and there," he explained, "—patching up a treaty between two countries today, securing a truce between two others tomorrow; it was apparent to the President that a more comprehensive plan should be adopted if war were to cease in the Western Hemisphere."

The "comprehensive plan" was nothing less than a fundamental reorientation of American foreign policy. The United States was now to assume the moral and political stewardship of the hemisphere. Renouncing further territorial expansion, the United States expected all American nations to follow its example and peacefully preserve the status quo. For its part, "as the strong but disinterested friend of all our sister states," the Northern big brother promised to exert its influence "for the preservation of the national life and integrity of any of them against aggression whether this may come from abroad or from another American Republic." A new era of peaceful arbitration under the benevolent guidance of the United States would commence, an era which Blaine planned to inaugurate with a grand Pan-American conference to be held at Washington.[59]

Nothing came of these plans. After Garfield's untimely death, his successor would cancel the Pan-American conference and dismiss Blaine from the cabinet. Even if Blaine had been granted the opportunity, it is unlikely that he could have completed his grand design. Too full of nervous impatience to be a proper diplomat, Blaine's heavy-handed meddling usually managed only to alienate the governments he dealt with. For

575

all his pains, only the relatively minor Argentina-Chile dispute responded to Blaine's efforts at mediation; elsewhere his efforts only aroused resentment. Nor was there any significant increase in trade with South America.

The execution may have been inept, but the grandiose sweep of the conception later won praise as the opening of "a new era" in American foreign policy. Whose conception was it? Blaine himself repeatedly gave Garfield credit for shaping his Latin American policy but this is usually dismissed as polite rhetoric, and it is generally assumed that the Secretary rather than the President was responsible for the attempt to reorient America's relations with the world.[60] The record would seem to indicate otherwise. In his long career Blaine had scarcely displayed any interest in foreign affairs, except for his obsession with Chinese immigration which was, of course, fundamentally a domestic issue. Garfield, on the other hand, had been concerned with international questions for over a decade. His public and private statements disclose that he had already developed in embryo the main features that were to distinguish the foreign policy of his administration. It had been Garfield, not Blaine, who had advocated the principle of international arbitration which the Pan-American conference was designed to foster. In 1878, for example, Blaine had urged Congress to reject the findings of the Halifax Commission, whereas Garfield had strongly advocated compliance. Two years earlier he had hailed the adjudication of the *Alabama* claims in extravagant terms, urging that the principle of international arbitration be extended.[61]

As early as 1872 Garfield had publicly urged that the nation's ties with its southern neighbors be strengthened. Four years later he developed this theme at length in a speech that forecast the principal policy of his administration. In response to a congressional threat to abolish a number of diplomatic posts in Latin America, Garfield replied: "I would rather blot out five or six European missions than these South American ones. . . . They are our neighbors and friends."[62] In succeeding years he repeatedly stressed the importance of cultivating closer Latin American ties.[63] In the day-to-day operation of State Department affairs Garfield may have given Blaine a free hand, but the broad policy decisions bore the President's unmistakeable stamp.[64]

Garfield's new departure in foreign policy was a promising experiment, but the promise was unfulfilled. His economic policy, however, could boast at least one notable achievement: the successful refunding of the national debt. Almost two hundred million dollars of mainly six percent government bonds were scheduled to fall due by July 1. Since the Congress had made no provision for refunding this debt, Garfield had to decide whether to proceed on his own or call an extra session of Congress. After wrestling with the problem, the President decided not to risk the political uncertainties of an extra session. Instead, he would gamble that the Treasury Department could refund out of its own resources. The six percent bonds were called in and the owners were given the option of holding them at 3½ percent interest. Almost ninety percent of the bond holders elected the lower interest rate, with an annual savings to the taxpayers of over ten million dollars. The loan proved so attractive that the government was able to bypass the traditional bankers' syndicate and deal directly with the public.

Secretary of the Treasury Windom won considerable acclaim for this financial coup. Refuting Blaine's pre-inaugural animadversions, Windom displayed remarkable competence and ingenuity. "Secretary Windom is cautious and careful," declared John Sherman, "and has done the very best for the public that is possible." The President's role in this "brilliant feat of financeering" was generally overlooked, but the truth was that Windom had only been carrying out Garfield's policy. The President closely supervised the refunding operation from its original conception to its successful conclusion, and its essential features had all been foreshadowed in Garfield's congressional speeches years earlier. In 1878 and again in 1879 Garfield had urged the public sale of government bonds, rather than private sale to banks or wealthy syndicates, as the surest means of giving the mass of Americans a stake in the financial integrity of their country.[65]

Many of Garfield's contemporaries tended to deride his capacity for presidential leadership. It was fashionable to insinuate that Blaine was the cunning mastermind while the President himself was "nothing more than a big, confused New-foundland dog."[66] The record proves otherwise. All the key decisions of this administration—foreign policy, economic policy, even the struggle against senatorial courtesy—were made by Garfield, and in each case the guiding principle can be traced to ideas he had expressed years earlier. Whatever intellectual consistency this administration had, it owed to Garfield himself. This president was master in his own household.

With the approach of summer, the Porcupine Administration had shed most of its quills and settled into a more placid routine. One cloud yet lay on the horizon. It came from the Post Office where, the President was warned, "there are cunning preparations being made by a small cabal to steal half a million a year during your Administration." The source of the trouble was the so-called "star route" service.

In the lightly-populated Western regions, conventional mail delivery was impractical. Special contracts had to be granted to insure that these routes were serviced with "certainty, celerity and security," a formula so often repeated that postal clerks usually substituted three asterisks, or stars, for the key words. These star route contracts were perfectly legal, but they carried an intriguing potential for fraud. The scheme worked like this: a contractor would secure a route with an unrealistically low bid. Congress would then be asked to permit increased service. Such petitions were seldom denied, but the increased compensation for this expedited service was computed by a complex formula that permitted extravagant profits. As a knowledgeable friend of Garfield's explained: "A route 100 miles long, time 50 hours, would be—say—$500. Double the distance would be $1000, but double the *speed*, i.e., reduce the time to 25 hours would give the contractors under the law several thousand dollars." In this way "a route through sage brush and desert 800 miles once a week and 2 miles an hour at say $10,000 would be over one hundred thousand [dollars] when expedited to 6 trips a week and 5 miles an hour."[67]

Congress had erected safeguards to prevent gross fraud, but information was coming to light that seemed to indicate that these safeguards had been overriden by what smacked of bribery and collusion. "The P.O. Dept. in some of its most important bureaus has been a nest of very unclean birds under Hayes," Blaine concluded. Since all this suspected fraud had taken place during the previous administration, Garfield would seem to have little cause for alarm. Actually, the scandal touched him closely, for the prime suspect was his erstwhile campaign manager, Stephen W. Dorsey.

Since the election, Dorsey had been busy publicizing his contribution to Garfield's success. His most ambitious puffery had been a gala testimonial dinner held at Delmonico's in February (which, according to rumor, he himself had paid for and arranged). The president-elect had been invited to attend what the guest of honor promised would be "the greatest thing of the kind ever held in this city," but Garfield prudently sent his regrets. The dinner turned into an expensive, tasteless tribute to corruption. With the blessing of Henry Ward Beecher and the approval of a host of Stalwart luminaries, including Grant, Dorsey's campaign irregularities were both exaggerated and glorified. The evening's high point was a maundering, semi-inebriated speech by the vice-president-elect in which Arthur attributed the Indiana victory to "perfect organization and a great deal of—" The audience gleefully shouted "Soap!" but Arthur, noting reporters present, smirkingly concluded his sentence with "tracts and political documents."[68]

Garfield was puzzled by this strange episode, but his friends understood its significance. Blaine explained that "the true intent and meaning of the Dorsey dinner in N.Y. was (by increasing Dorsey's prestige) to enable him to make demands of the Administration which will in the end, modestly center in the Second Ass't Postmaster Generalship. . . ." Chandler was even more outraged at "the gross want of sense, propriety and taste which prepared a public celebration and glorification of the use of money to carry elections." He predicted that "The evidently desired sequel of all this apotheosis of corruption is to be the plunder of the government. . . . The 'Star Service' is the grand prize which is to nourish them and to furnish the scandals of the next presidential fight."[69]

Ever since July, Garfield had been hearing rumors of Dorsey's corrupt involvement in Post Office affairs, but the Arkansas senator himself stoutly denied ever having had "the slightest interest in any contract or business with the Post Office dept., or with any other departments of the government."[70] This was an unblushing lie. Dorsey was up to his ears in star route contracts, and so were his brother, his brother-in-law and numerous friends and relations. One typical Dorsey route had originally been obtained for $2,350 but had been "expedited" to the tune of $70,000 per year. Further evidence seemed to indicate that Dorsey's ring had enjoyed special consideration from Second Assistant Postmaster General Brady who, in return for his services, had reserved a percentage of the profits for his own pocket.

On March 9, only five days after his inauguration, the President called Postmaster General James into his office. He informed James of the rumors and insisted that a thorough investigation be launched immediately. Within a few weeks James had learned enough to realize that he was facing a scandal of such monumental proportions that its exposure could seriously damage the fortunes of the Republican party. Should he pursue the probe, he asked, even if it cost the party control of the Senate? The President thought for a moment, walked across the room and turning to James, replied firmly: "I have sworn to execute the laws. Go ahead regardless of where or whom you hit. I direct you not only to probe this ulcer to the bottom, but to cut it out."[71] Under the circumstances, of course, Garfield could have given no other answer, but his sincerity was soon demonstrated when he ordered a purge in the Post Office Department which eliminated Brady. As further indication that he meant business, the President hired a corps of detectives to prepare the case against Dorsey. Some of these sleuths, unfortunately, were almost as unsavory as their quarry, but by June they had unearthed enough evidence that Attorney General McVeagh could begin planning to take the case to trial in the fall.[72]

For the time being, however, justice would have to wait. With the Senate in adjournment for the summer, the semi-deserted city slowed its pace to a crawl and even presidents could dream of a holiday in the country. The First Lady was already at the seashore, recuperating from her illness. In late June her husband joined her briefly and then returned to

Washington to clear his desk for the anticipated summer vacation. He was scheduled to leave on the second of July.

The evening before his departure he strolled across Lafayette Square to pay a call on the Secretary of State. Absorbed in his plans, he did not even notice the shabbily-dressed, wild-eyed man who dogged his steps all the way to Blaine's door. Half an hour later, when the President emerged, arm-in-arm with Blaine, that same man was skulking in a nearby alley, his right hand jammed in his pocket where it nervously clenched a .44 caliber snub-nosed revolver. Charles J. Guiteau was stalking his prey.[73]

CHAPTER TWENTY-FIVE

STRANGULATUS PRO REPUBLICA

It was sometime between eight-thirty and nine o'clock on the evening of May 18, 1881 that the inspiration first struck Charles Julius Guiteau. As inspirations go, this one was not particularly dramatic; there were no mystic visions or heavenly voices in the night. Instead, as he was tossing restlessly on his cot in a Washington boarding-house it flashed through his mind with the force of conviction that President Garfield had to be "removed." At first the idea horrified him, but he could not shake it loose: "it kept growing upon me, pressing me, goading me," until, as he later explained, he finally accepted the fact that God had selected him as the instrument of the President's removal. For weeks this "irresistable pressure" continued to mount, drawing him nearer and nearer to his appointed victim.[1]

They resembled each other in some curious ways. Each had lost a parent at an early age; each in adolescence gave allegiance to a heterodox religious brotherhood. Both believed in the success ethic, the faith that in America worldly success could crown the efforts of even the most humble. In pursuit of that success each turned his hand to various callings: politics, religion and the law, but where Garfield made success, Guiteau found only failure. In both their backgrounds and aspirations they had more in common than either would have been willing to admit; in some respects the assassin reflected a grotesquely twisted image of his victim.

The actual course of their careers could not have been more different. Guiteau was born in Freeport, Illinois in 1841. Sickly as an infant, he developed into a hyperactive child, unable to sit still for five minutes even when offered a dime as a reward. His mother was a chronic invalid who seldom ventured outside the house. She died when Charles was seven. "I have always felt I never had a mother," he later complained. His father was a stern disciplinarian who beat his son in a vain effort to cure a childish speech defect. A nervous strain seemed to run through the family. Uncle Abram was generally considered "a little weak in the upper story." Cousin Abigail ("Foolish Abby") would sidle up to visitors and repeatedly whisper, "Do you love Jesus?" until led away. She died in an asylum, as did Cousin Augustus, who was deranged by a business disappointment, and Uncle Francis, who had been thwarted in love and then totally unhinged by a cruel practical joke. Other cousins, aunts and uncles met the same unhappy end, as did Charles's only sister, Frances. Their father, Luther W. Guiteau, was a respected banker and local political figure who had but one apparent eccentricity: he was convinced that he would never die.

He had arrived at this comforting conclusion from a study of the works of John Humphrey Noyes, the prophet of Perfectionism. Noyes, in such books as *The Berean*, argued that the Second Coming had already taken place during the Roman capture of Jerusalem in 70 A.D. while everyone involved had been too preoccupied to notice. This being the case, men are already living in the prophesied Millennium where sin is an illusion, death can be overcome and mankind can make itself perfect. Noyes did more than merely preach this doctrine; he put it into practice in a remarkable community which he established at Oneida, New York. There, the consequences of human perfectability were thoroughly explored in a new style of living, of which the most notorious feature was known to the initiates as "complex marriage" but condemned by the imperfect world-at-large as "free love." The senior Guiteau sympathized with the Oneida community from afar, but neither his first nor second wife would allow him to join. Instead, he tried to raise up his children in the doctrine. Charles hardly needed Noyes's theology to persuade him that he was perfect; even as a young man in Freeport he displayed such an "offensive egotism" that he had not a single friend in town. At the age of nineteen he tried to prepare himself for college, but he soon grew discouraged and began to immerse himself in the Bible and the *Berean*. Before long he found himself not at college but at Oneida, drawn there, he maintained, "by an irresistable power which I was *not at liberty to disobey*."[2]

At first all went well. Charles rapidly contracted three "spiritual marriages" and was confirmed in his faith that this was indeed "the kingdom of God on earth." But before long his eccentric behavior and unabated egotism so repelled the Oneida sisterhood that he was compelled to live "practically a Shaker," i.e., celibate, for the rest of his stay. Notwithstanding these rebuffs, he was convinced that he was destined to replace Noyes as community leader, then become President of the United States and ultimately ruler of the world. For these pretensions he was rebuked and ridiculed at the community's nightly sessions of "free criticism" until he could stand it no longer.

To make matters worse, Guiteau realized with horror that "They wanted to make a hard-working businessman out of me." In addition to inventing a new technique of sexual intercourse, the versatile Noyes had helped build a better steel trap. After working in the packing room for several years, Guiteau beat a path from its door, leaving Oneida for New York City in the dead of night rather than face another communal mutual-criticism session.

As his coming was inspired by God, so was his going forth. He did not intend to desert the community, he explained, but merely planned to carry its message into the world by establishing a daily religious newspaper in New York. This was an idea with which Noyes had repeatedly toyed, but Guiteau insisted the conception was his alone: "I say boldly that I claim *inspiration*. I claim that I am in the employ of *Jesus Christ & Co.*, the very ablest and strongest firm in the universe. . . ." When cynical newspapermen laughed at the project, however, Guiteau dropped it and dissolved the firm. He then attempted to make his fortune by blackmailing the Oneida community for five thousand dollars, threatening to expose how "nightly, innocent *girls* and innocent young women are sacrificed to an experience easier imagined than described."

Extortion, however, proved as unrewarding as piety, so Guiteau turned his talents to the law. Standards of admission to the Chicago bar were not particularly rigorous. Guiteau was asked three or four questions, answered more than half correctly and was entitled to call himself a lawyer. He seems to have argued only one case. Assigned to an open-and-shut case of petty larceny, he insisted on making a full-blown speech to the jury. For the better part of an hour, he screamed and rambled incoherently, raving of God and the rights of man and shaking his fist at the jurors who then hastily convicted his client without even bothering to leave the jury-box. After that he followed a less demanding branch of his profession— chasing bad debts. For a time, he did well. He had a surface air of plausibility which commended him to clients, and a dogged perseverence that made him the bane of debtors. Unfortunately, he also had the habit of pocketing the debts he collected, which severely limited his repeat business. By 1871 he had exhausted Chicago's possibilities and decided to relocate in New York City. His bride accompanied him.[3]

Annie Bunn was a timid young librarian who worked at the YMCA which Guiteau frequented. She was attracted by his piety: he neither drank, smoked nor swore and was always conspicuous at prayer meetings. As a husband, however, he was a tyrant. If his wife dared contradict him, he would kick her out of doors, or lock her all night in an unheated closet. They never had a home, but instead moved from one boarding house to another, often in the dead of night, to avoid paying the rent. Guiteau was an effective hounder of deadbeats because he knew all the tricks of the trade himself. A trail of unpaid loans and boarding house bills marked every step of his career. Although he always like to live in style, he resented having to pay for it. "The world owes me a living," he repeatedly insisted.

In 1872 he began to neglect his business for politics. He wrote a speech supporting Horace Greeley for president which

585

he delivered at various campaign rallies. His services went virtually unnoticed, but he confidently expected to be rewarded with a first-class government job in the Greeley Administration, preferably Minister to Chile. He would constantly preen himself before the mirror, asking his wife: "Don't you think I would look like a good Foreign Minister?" Greeley's defeat crushed these hopes but not his ambition for fame. "If I cannot get notoriety for good," he told an associate, "I will get it for evil." When pressed to explain, he said, "Well, I will shoot some of our public men."[4]

After 1872 his career began to run downhill. In 1873 he lost his wife. She had been taught that a woman's duty was to submit to the husband God had sent her, but after nursing Charles through a bout of syphilis contracted from one of the "lewd women" he regularly frequented, Annie had finally had enough and sued for divorce. In 1874 he lost his business. After the New York *Herald* printed an article exposing his collection frauds, clients shunned his services. Without a family, without an income, he drifted from hotel to hotel until finally his luck ran out and he was thrown in jail. After a month in "the Tombs," as New York City's jail was grimly called, he was bailed out by his brother-in-law who took him to Wisconsin to live. Guiteau's sister was appalled at his wild, gaunt appearance, but her sympathy vanished the day he took after her with an axe. She called in a local doctor who agreed that Charles should be committed to an asylum, but before he could be put away he slipped across the state line to Chicago.

There he again became obsessed with religion. In a furious fit of inspiration he wrote a book which he called *The Truth: A Companion to the Bible*. The book's central revelation was the discovery that the Second Coming had already taken place in 70 A.D. in the clouds over Jerusalem. "A new line of thought runs through this book," Guiteau proudly proclaimed but, in fact, *The Truth* was simply a plagiarism of *The Berean*, a resemblance Guiteau stubbornly refused to acknowledge even when identical passages from both books were pointed out to him. He hawked *The Truth* on street corners for twenty-five cents a copy and then, convinced that like St. Paul he had been called upon to preach to the Gentiles, he took to the road. "The Little Giant from the West," as he billed himself, criss-crossed the country giving disjointed, rambling lectures on the Second Coming, Paul the Apostle and (a special favorite of his) "Some Reasons Why Two-Thirds of the Human Race are Going Down to Perdition." He traveled light, skipping town whenever his rent came due and once leaping from a moving train to avoid an irate conductor. His audiences were tiny and their response invariably hostile but he ignored their jibes with sublime indifference. It was perhaps the happiest time of his life.

After three years of this itinerant evangelism he finally grew discouraged. "There is no money in theology," he decided. The reason was plain: "A great many people are perfectly willing to pay fifty cents to hear that there ain't any hell, but they don't like to hear that there is one." He retired from the pulpit and turned again to politics. It was 1880. A presidential campaign was about to begin and Guiteau was caught up in the general excitement. Hoping to be of service, he dusted off his old speech for Greeley and converted it into a speech for Grant, the expected nominee. When the party turned instead to Garfield, Guiteau was unfazed. He tacked on a paragraph extolling the candidate, changed the title to "Garfield against Hancock" and had hundreds of copies printed.[5]

This speech, of which he was so proud, was a three-page collection of childish cliches. It began with a review of the great figures of the Republican past: Wendell Phillips, "the silver-tongued orator of Boston;" Henry Clay, "he of matchless eloquence;" Harriet Beecher Stowe, author of that "matchless work of fiction," *Uncle Tom's Cabin*. With the election of "the immortal Lincoln" the Confederates captured "some of our forts and emoluments [sic] of war." The North was stirred "to its depths." "To arms! to arms! resounded all over this broad land. Thousands of brave boys went forth to battle, to victory or to death." Guiteau then inserted a paragraph in praise of Grant, "renowned in war and peace," and at last turned apologetically to Garfield. "Some people say he got badly soiled in that Credit Mobilier transaction, but I guess he is clean-handed. . . . He is a high-toned,

587

conscientious Christian gentleman." Then, on to the triumphant peroration:

> Ye men whose sons perished in the war! what say you to this issue? Shall we have another war? Shall our national treasury be controlled by ex-rebels and their Northern allies, to the end that millions of dollars of Southern war claims be liquidated? [Guiteau was particularly proud of this point: "it was *this* idea," he wrote Garfield, "that resulted in your election"] If you want the republic bankrupted with the prospect of another war, make Hancock President. If you want prosperity and peace, make Garfield President, and the republic will develop till it becomes the greatest and wealthiest nation on the globe.

Guiteau never actually delivered this speech, yet he was somehow convinced that it was responsible for Garfield's victory. Its "success" persuaded him that he was now well launched upon a political career that would lead him to the White House. Filled with a sense of his own importance, he spent the summer haunting party headquarters at the Fifth Avenue Hotel, using the stationery, reading the newspapers and giving familiar greetings to the great men of the party. To each, he gravely handed a copy of his speech, as if it were a calling card. He made of himself, in short, a nuisance and a laughing-stock, but Guiteau was oblivious to ridicule. He imagined that all the politicians who said "Good morning" to him were close friends and he interpreted their polite acknowledgments of his speech as endorsements of its merit.[6]

For his contribution to Garfield's victory, Guiteau expected a suitable reward. His first choice was Minister to Austria. Even before election day he staked his claim to that office by sending Garfield a copy of his speech. "Next spring," he added, "I expect to marry the daughter of a recently deceased New York Republican millionaire and I think we can represent the United States Government at the Court of Vienna with dignity and grace." This heiress was a product of Guiteau's imagination, as was the impressive list of references he appended to his application: U.S. Grant, John Logan, Emory Storrs and Henry Ward Beecher—men who scarcely knew Guiteau well enough to nod when they passed him on the street. Guiteau had drifted so far from reality that he regarded his appointment as a certainty. "I presume it will go through the Senate almost as a matter of course," he concluded confidently. "I will get Logan, Conkling, and the rest of them to put it thru. . . ."

Shortly after this, Guiteau discovered that the Austrian Ministry was unavailable, so he lowered his sights a notch to consul general at Paris, sending Garfield another copy of his speech as a reminder. "There is nothing against me," he assured the president-elect. "I claim to be a gentleman and a Christian."[7] Suspecting that this might not be sufficient recommendation, he decided to go to Washington to press his claim in person. He arrived the day after the inauguration, one more drop in the torrent of office-seekers that was then inundating the capital. Outwardly he displayed the same serene, single-minded confidence that had characterized all his earlier ventures, but actually he was in something close to desperation. He had less than five dollars in his pocket and his only shirt was on his back. Guiteau was near the end of his rope; this would be his last chance for fame and success. He was determined to make the most of it. On March 8 he joined the long line of hopefuls at the White House. When he was finally ushered into the President's office he wasted no time. He whipped out yet another copy of his speech, wrote "Paris Consulship" on the cover and handed it to Garfield. After a few words he withdrew, leaving the President staring in perplexity at the speech. When Guiteau next called at the White House he was told by a clerk that his application had been forwarded to the State Department. Guiteau then tracked down Blaine, catching him at last in a State Department elevator. Between floors he stated his business and left a copy of his speech as a memento. To prod Blaine and Garfield into a quick decision, Guiteau prepared a petition on his own behalf and buttonholed Harrison, Conkling, Logan and other Republican leaders to sign it. No one ever did, but Guiteau could not be discouraged. One evening he barged into Logan's rooms and would not leave until the senator had promised to "mention" his case to Blaine. Logan thought his visitor was "a little off in his head," but Guiteau was convinced that Logan was now his firm ally.

589

Now began the long vigil. Almost every day Guiteau would shuttle back and forth between the State Department and the White House, clutching his bundle of papers. At the State Department, Blaine or a clerk would brush him off with some polite evasion which anyone less obtuse would have recognized as a dismissal. At the White House, Guiteau's regular appearance fell into a routine. He would send his card in through the gatekeeper and, after a suitable delay, the stereotyped answer would come back: "Mr. Guiteau, the President says it will be impossible for him to see you today." It was the "today" that kept him coming back; perhaps tomorrow would be different. Months passed in this fashion. His clothes grew shabby. He had no socks and he wore his coat collar turned up to conceal his ragged shirt. His haggard face seemed pinched with hunger, yet his eyes burned with exultation. Convinced of his destiny, he persevered through March and April. By that time he was no longer even bothering to sign his almost daily letters to the President, on the assumption that "C.G." was sufficient identification between such good friends. Actually, none of his notes to Garfield or Blaine reached their destination; they were intercepted by alert secretaries and filed with the other crank mail.[8]

By the middle of May, even Guiteau's confidence began to crack. On the 13th he got into a row with a White House usher which resulted in his banishment from the waiting-room. The very next day, he found himself the target of Blaine's wrath. "Never speak to me again on the Paris consulship as long as you live," the badgered Secretary finally exploded. That was on Saturday. On Monday, Conkling and Platt resigned from the Senate. On Wednesday night, May 18th, as Guiteau lay brooding over the political situation, the inspiration flashed through his brain "that if the President was out of the way every thing would go better."[9]

The newspapers seemed to confirm Guiteau's revelation. This was the peak of the Robertson controversy and the columns of the Stalwart press were filled with furious denunciations of the administration: "The Democrats are exultant. . . . Madness has ruled for three months. . . . All this will lead to Democratic success—to a restoration of the Bourbons

590

—to disaster—perhaps to ruin." These editorials preyed upon Guiteau's mind, convincing him that his own disappointment was but another indication of the President's treachery. "Gradually, as the result of reading the newspapers," he explained, "the idea settled on me that if the President was removed it would unite the two factions of the Republican party, and thereby save the Government from going into the hands of the ex-rebels and their northern allies." It was patriotism, not revenge, which motivated him, he insisted. "In the President's madness he has wrecked the once grand old Republican party and for this he dies." While he was wrestling with his inspiration, Guiteau gave the President a final chance to redeem himself. On May 23 he sent Garfield a warning: ". . . Mr. Blaine is a wicked man, and you ought to demand his *immediate* resignation; otherwise you and the Republican party will come to grief." It was ignored, and Guiteau began to plan in deadly earnest how to carry out his act of "political necessity."[10]

His preparations were thorough and methodical. Anticipating that a sudden demand for his book would follow the assassination, he first spent two weeks preparing a revised and expanded edition of *The Truth*. With his literary labors out of the way, Guiteau could turn to more practical measures. He borrowed some money from an acquaintance and went shopping for a pistol. For ten dollars he purchased a powerfull little .44 caliber ivory-handled revolver known as the British Bulldog. Guiteau could have bought a wooden-handled model for a dollar less, but he thought that the fancier model would look more imposing in the museum case it was destined to occupy. He had never handled firearms before, in fact he was afraid of them, but he screwed up his courage for a practice session. On the bank of the old city canal there was a mud flat which was sometimes used for target practice. He took aim at a little tree growing in the water, pulled the trigger and was almost knocked off his feet by the unexpected recoil. The tree was left in splinters. He never hit his practice target again, but for the sort of shooting he had in mind expert marksmanship would not be necessary.

Next, Guiteau decided to inspect the jail. He was looking

for security as well as comfort, some place strong enough for protection against the misguided mob which might well try to lynch him. This was merely a temporary precaution, for he was convinced that once the public understood his motives they would hail him as a patriot and savior. To explain these motives, he drew up a series of statements. One was to General Sherman, asking that he call up the troops to protect the jail. Another was to the New York *Herald*, permitting them to print *The Truth*. (He thoughtfully included some reviews and a brief autobiographical introduction along with the manuscript.) Others were designed to justify his deed, which he always referred to in the past tense, as if it were already part of history:

> The President's tragic death was a sad necessity, but it will unite the Republican party and save the Republic. Life is a fleeting dream and it matters little when one goes. A human life is of small value. During the war thousands of brave boys went down without a tear.

> I presume the President was a Christian and that he will be happier in Paradise than here.

> It will be no worse for Mrs. Garfield, dear soul, to part with her husband this way than by natural death. He is liable to go at any time any way.

> I had no ill-will toward the President

> His death was a political necessity

> I am a lawyer, theologian, and politician.

> I am a Stalwart of the Stalwarts.

> I was with General Grant and the rest of our men in New York during the canvass.

>   . . .

> I am going to the jail.

With these preliminaries out of the way it was time for the hunting season to begin. Guiteau tracked the President during the entire month of June, waiting for the perfect time and place. He ruled out the White House: it was too crowded, and besides, Guiteau was no longer allowed inside. Elsewhere, however, the President was a tempting target. He had no Secret Service to protect him, not even a bodyguard. Americans still believed that political assassination was some exotic custom practiced only in despotisms, such as Russia, whose Tsar had been blown to bits only a few months before. The leader of a Republic, it was felt, should be able to walk freely among the people he served. Garfield himself would have it no other way. Always a bit of a fatalist, he believed that "Assassination can no more be guarded against than death by lightning; and it is not best to worry about either."[11]

This attitude simplified Guiteau's mission. He seldom left his room now without stuffing his loaded pistol in his pocket, in the hope of finding some opportunity of using it. One Sunday he followed Garfield to church. What better place, he thought, "to remove a man than at his devotions." He peered through the window at the President's pew, but the angle of fire seemed too difficult for a marksman of his limited abilities. Disappointed but not discouraged, Guiteau searched for a better opportunity. While he waited, his mind churned with eager anticipation: "I thought just what people would talk and thought what a tremendous excitement it would create. . . ." Later that week, the newspapers reported that the President and his wife would leave for Long Branch, New Jersey on the morning of June 18. The railroad depot struck Guiteau as an ideal location. He arrived early, his bundle of papers in one pocket, his revolver in the other, but when he saw the invalid first lady he lost his nerve. "Mrs. Garfield looked so thin, and she clung so tenderly to the President's arm, that I did not have the heart to fire upon him." Guiteau was a sentimental assassin.

When the President returned from New Jersey on the 27th, Guiteau was back at the depot with his papers and revolver. It was a hot, muggy day, not really suitable for an assassination. "I did not feel like it," Guiteau explained, and he went back to his hotel to cool off. He dogged the President's steps for the rest of the week. Each day brought fresh opportunities but also fresh excuses for inaction. Time was running out; on Saturday, July 2, Garfield was scheduled to leave

Washington for a summer-long vacation. Friday evening, while Guiteau was sitting on his usual park bench across from the White House, he saw the President walking alone, across Lafayette Square. Guiteau rose from his bench and began to follow but before he could get close enough to shoot, Garfield was already inside Blaine's front door. Guiteau waited in a nearby alley for about half an hour, but when the President emerged Blaine was at his side. Guiteau was shocked to see them "just as cozy and chatty and hilarious as two schoolgirls." It confirmed his impression that Garfield had "sold himself body and soul to Blaine, and that Blaine was using Garfield to destroy the Stalwart element of this nation." Yet, even though the pistol was primed, for some reason Guiteau could not bring himself to fire it.

He arose at four o'clock the next morning, determined to be more resolute. After a good breakfast and a stroll to enjoy the morning air, he took a cab to the Baltimore & Potomac station. There he engaged a hack to drive him in the direction of the jail. He told the driver to wait and then entered the station. Stopping at the newsstand, he left his bundle of papers in a spot where they were bound to be discovered and then stepped into the men's room to inspect his pistol. All was in order, so Guiteau took up a strategic position by the ladies' waiting-room where he could keep an eye on all the entrances. He would not have long to wait; it was now about twenty minutes after nine and the train with the President's special car was scheduled to leave at nine-thirty.[12]

The President had arisen that morning in an unusually good humor. A vacation lay ahead of him and his troubles seemed safely behind him. The major source of those troubles, Roscoe Conkling, was in Albany seeking vindication and finding only humiliation. The haughty ex-senator had been persuaded, against his better judgment, to campaign for reelection, but his hold on his former followers had crumbled. It was almost pathetic to see him wheedling support from men he was accustomed to command and soiling his immaculate hands with "the dirty work of a ward politician." Garfield, however, wasted no sympathy. "Suicide is the chief mode of political death, after all," he coldly observed upon learning of Conkling's failure to win reelection. The former junior senator, Thomas Platt, suffered even greater indignity. One night, near the end of June, after a hard day of campaigning, he was relaxing in an Albany hotel room. Someone maliciously propped a stepladder against the room's transom window, enabling smirking newsmen to discover just whom Platt was relaxing with. It was not his wife. Platt withdrew from the Senate race on the morning of July 2, just as Garfield was preparing to leave for his holiday.[13]

Garfield was unaware of this development, but his spirits were already so exuberant at the prospect of his imminent escape from Washington that they spilled over into raucous horseplay. Up in Harry's room, the President of the United States turned handsprings over his boy's bed and then tossed both his grown sons about, to the tune of "I mixed these babies up," from his favorite, *Pinafore*. He was still laughing as he shook hands with the White House staff lined up to bid him farewell, and then he stepped into the carriage bound for the depot.[14]

Blaine was on hand to keep the President company for the drive, while Harry and Jim followed in a second carriage. During the brief ride, Garfield and Blaine chatted about their summer plans. The President had a busy summer ahead of him. First, he would pick up his wife and daughter in New Jersey. There they would be met by millionaire Cyrus Fields, whose yacht was waiting to steam to his castle at Irvington-on-the-Hudson. Then the President would go to New England to drop his sons off at Williams College and pick up an honorary degree. After spending the rest of the summer at his Mentor farm, he was scheduled to take part in the centennial ceremonies at Yorktown and then to tour the South. At Atlanta, he planned to deliver a major speech unveiling his Southern and racial policies. He was just beginning to discuss this speech with Blaine when the carriage rolled up to the entrance of the Baltimore & Potomac station.[15]

Garfield had never liked this station. He had once described it as "a nuisance which ought long since to have been abated," but by now it was such a familiar nuisance that he paid scarcely any attention to his surroundings as he walked, still deep in conversation with Blaine, towards the train platform. Their path took them through the ladies' waiting-room, close by the spot where Guiteau was lurking. They were no more than half-way across the room when Guiteau came up from behind the President, extended his pistol at arm's length and fired into Garfield's back from less than a yard away. The President's hat flew off his head, he threw his arms in the air and cried, "My God! What is this?" Guiteau said nothing, but took two steps forward and fired once more as Garfield was half twisting, and half falling. With the second shot the President crumpled to the carpet and Guiteau wiped off his pistol and put it back in his pocket.

Pale but calm, Guiteau turned to escape in his waiting cab to the safety of the jail. Before he could reach the door he was grabbed by police officer Patrick Kearney. By now the stunned crowd was beginning to comprehend what had happened and cries of "Lynch him!" could be heard. Kearney promptly hustled the assassin out of the depot to the police station, a few blocks away. Guiteau offered no resistance. "I am a Stalwart," he earnestly explained to Kearney as they were crossing the street. "Arthur is now President of the United States." Later, when the jail door slammed behind him, Guiteau at last felt free. With the pressure of his inspiration lifted, he was "light-hearted and merry . . . because I had been true to God and the American people." That night he enjoyed his first peaceful sleep in six weeks.[16]

Meanwhile, at the railroad depot, the President was lying on the floor in a pool of vomit. His head was cradled in the lap of the ladies' room matron who stroked his face while tears streamed down her own cheeks. Garfield was conscious, but he exhibited all the signs of severe shock: his pulse was faint and irregular; his breathing was shallow and labored; his face pale and expressionless. Although bathed with sweat, he complained of a cold, prickly sensation, especially in his legs and feet. One bullet had merely grazed his arm, the other (whether the first or second shot was never determined) had entered about four inches to the right of the spine, shattered the eleventh rib and burrowed its way into his body, coming to rest somewhere within the President's ample frame.

To determine the track and location of that bullet, doctors poked and probed the wound with their unwashed fingers and instruments, but with no success. Their initial conclusion was that the bullet had penetrated some organ, possibly the liver. This, plus the apparent signs of internal bleeding, seemed to indicate that the President would not live out the day. Garfield evidently concurred. When a doctor tried to cheer him with an optimistic prognosis, Garfield gravely replied, "I thank you doctor, but I am a dead man."

By now he had been placed on a mattress and carried upstairs. There his wound was dressed, amid scenes of hysterical confusion. A score or more of doctors were milling about, suggesting remedies but each afraid to take the initiative. Jim was bawling uncontrollably while his brother Harry bravely tried to give comfort. Blaine kept trying to make himself useful but only managed to get in the way until he finally broke down and wept. Of the other cabinet members present, none was more visibly affected than Robert Todd Lincoln. "How many hours of sorrow I have passed in this town," he said as his mind flashed back sixteen years to a similar scene. The patient himself was one of the few calm men in the depot. Revived from his initial shock by a bit of brandy, he insisted quite sensibly that he be taken home. Mattresses were ripped from a nearby Pullman car and piled onto an express wagon. The President was gently placed in this improvised ambulance and driven slowly back to the White House he had left in such high spirits only an hour before.[17]

Strong arms tenderly carried the wounded President to an upstairs bedroom. Garfield bravely made a show of confidence, blowing a faint kiss to Mrs. Blaine and assuring his son Jim that "the upper story was not hurt; it was the hull." Despite these pathetic gestures, the sick-room was filled with a sense of bleak despair. Friends and colleagues of the stricken man shuffled by to pay what they expected to be their last farewell. Most burst into tears and had to be led away. The doctors who hovered about the President's bedside did nothing to dispel the gloom. "He is dying," said one. "Look at his eyes; they

597

are becoming fixed." "Why don't we do something?" asked another helplessly. No use, replied another, he cannot live out the hour. All this was taking place within earshot of the wounded man, plunging his spirits dangerously low. Tearfully, he prayed that he might at least be spared long enough to see his wife once more.[18]

Lucretia was in New Jersey with Mollie, packed and ready for her husband's arrival, when the telegram came from Washington. A special train was at once placed at her disposal. As it was speeding across the coastal plain, the other members of the scattered Garfield family were being shielded from the tragic news. The President's mother was in Ohio to attend the funeral of his cousin Cordelia and Uncle Thomas who had died in a train accident. It was feared that another shock would be too much for her, so she was lured on a pretext to the country, far from the cries of paperboys. When the news was gently broken to her the next day she gasped, "Oh Lord help me!" but otherwise displayed remarkable calm. Young Irvin and Abe were on the train to Mentor the morning their father was shot. Alert conductors tiptoed through each car, explaining the situation in whispers, and station-masters along the route were warned by wire to banish newspapers and loose talk. The conspiracy of silence succeeded; the boys did not learn of their father's condition until they had reached the comforting surroundings of their own home.[19]

Throughout the long afternoon Garfield clung doggedly to life, despite the assurances of twenty-five or thirty physicians that his condition was hopeless. He continued to vomit every half-hour and his vital signs continued to diminish, but his mind remained alert. All his thoughts were focused on his wife, who arrived shortly after seven, so overcome by grief that two men had to support her from her carriage to the sickroom door. Once inside that door, however, she shook off her despair and put on an air of courage she did not possess. When her husband began to tell her how to bring up the children in his absence, she cut him short: "Well, my dear, you are not going to die as I am here to nurse you back to life; so please do not speak again of death."

That night the President slept well, in between vomiting

spells, and the next morning confounded the doctors by appearing cheerful and rested. His pulse and temperature were
near normal. With the spontaneous resumption of bowel movements and urination, it was clear that neither the kidneys, intestines nor peritoneum had been injured. The earlier fears of
liver damage and internal hemorrhage now seemed groundless, and, for the first time in twenty-four hours, the doctors
could allow themselves to hope for his recovery.[20]

It was Sunday morning and every church in the nation was
offering up prayers for the President's safety, while every
preacher had a ready-made topic for his sermon. In the face of
tragedy, all political and sectional differences were, for the moment swept aside, to be replaced by an awesome unity of grief
and affection. A nation which had avidly followed the mock
battles of politics, realized with a guilty shock that sham battles
can create real casualties. No event since the Civil War had
summoned forth such universal dismay and apprehension.

Part of the apprehension was caused by the possibility that
Chester Alan Arthur might assume the presidency. Arthur's
behavior since the inauguration had not been the sort to inspire
public confidence. Throughout the troubled administration he
had continued to room with Conkling and slavishly assisted the
senator in ways that many regarded as beneath the dignity
of the vice-presidential office. Arthur made no secret of his
contempt for Garfield, and even before the assassination
newspapers were depicting the "heir-apparent" as viewing
with satisfaction "the efforts which the office-seekers are making to kill off the man who stands between him and the coveted prize." These suspicions were only reinforced by Guiteau's wild boasts to Kearney at the time of the shooting. Had
Garfield died immediately after the assassination, it is unlikely that the country would have accepted Arthur as President. Most would have agreed with Rutherford B. Hayes
that Garfield's death would amount to a "national calamity."
"Arthur for President! Conkling the power behind the throne,
superior to the throne! The Republican party divided and defeated,"—Hayes was appalled at the prospect.[21]

For the time being, however, such a prospect seemed increasingly unlikely as the daily bulletins issued by the White

House doctors grew more optimistic. These bulletins were eagerly followed by a public hungry for any scrap of information that issued from the sick-room. Day after day, the newspapers were filled with the most minute clinical details of Garfield's condition. "I should think the people would be tired of having me dished up to them in this way,"[22] Garfield said, but they were not. Wounded and helpless, Garfield had become what he could never have been in health—a genuine folk hero. "The whole country has been agonized about the President, and is almost deifying him already," William Chandler observed. "This worship will make him all-powerful if he lives." In his struggle with Conkling, Garfield had demonstrated the political power inherent in his office. Now, in his struggle with death, he revealed the power of the president to rise above politics to become a symbol of national unity. "Gen. Garfield will arise from his bed the most popular man in America," predicted a political observer.[23]

Such speculation was fruitless; despite the optimistic tone of the early bulletins, Garfield was never to rise from his sickbed. Instead, for eighty days he would slide slowly towards death, while the nation watched with horrified fascination. From time to time, deceptive rallies would inspire false hopes, but from the very beginning of his ordeal, Garfield's fate was sealed. For the first three weeks, however, hopes for his recovery ran so high that the navy began to fit out the steamer *Tapaloosa* as a floating hospital for the President's expected convalescence. His symptoms showed steady improvement: the fever slowly abated, while his appetite gradually increased. From time to time, he even felt strong enough to sit up. On one such occasion, he asked for a pencil and a clip board. He scrawled his name and then thought for a moment and wrote beneath it an enigmatic Latin phrase, "Strangulatus pro Republica"—tortured for the republic. Most of the time, however, the President remained helpless on his back. Attendants had to shift his position fifteen to twenty times a day to prevent bedsores, rub his numb feet, feed and clean him as they would an infant. Through all these indignities the patient remained cheerful and alert. He never complained during the painful daily routine of dressing and probing the wound, and after each session he would solemnly shake the doctors' hands and politely murmur, "Thank you, gentlemen." Sometimes he would even make little jokes, but it was noticed that he himself never smiled.[24]

In truth, he had little to smile about. For one thing, he was lonely. The doctors had surrounded his bed with screens and stationed soldiers at every door. Few visitors were allowed to penetrate these barricades. "He might as well be within stone walls a prisoner," one of them reported. Garfield's wife, of course, was in nearly constant attendance, but her husband begged in vain for Blaine and other masculine comrades. Isolated by well-meaning doctors, the gregarious President was starving for companionship. He was starving in the literal sense as well. After the shock to his nervous system, his stomach (fluttery even in the best of times) rebelled at solid foods. The doctors were forced to put him on a liquid diet: lime water to soothe his digestion and fresh milk from a cow that was put out to pasture on the White House lawn. Under this austere diet Garfield clung to life but lacked the strength to rebuild his ravaged body. He longed for the foods of his childhood, squirrel soup and Minerva Austin's hard little biscuits, but was compelled instead to subsist on oatmeal, which he detested. One day, learning that Sitting Bull was starving, he snapped, "Let him starve." Then he corrected himself as he thought of a crueler torment: "Oh no, send him my oatmeal." By the middle of July, however, he was able to keep down an occasional steak or lamb chop, but usually he merely picked at his food to humor the doctors.[25]

In addition to his other afflictions, the President was hot. As the temperature and the humidity both soared into the upper 90s, his discomfort became acute. Suggestions for cooling the sick-room poured in from all over the country, most of them involving either the punkah, a fan used in India, or large blocks of ice. Ice was tried, but it only managed to add to the humidity without appreciably lowering the temperature. The problem was brilliantly solved by a group of Navy engineers who, with the aid of scientist Simon Newcomb, invented and installed what may well have been the world's first air-conditioner. The device consisted of a blower which forced air over a large chest containing six tons of ice. The cool air was then dried as it

601

passed through a long cast-iron box filled with cotton screens. The end of this box was connected to the sickrooms heat vent, from which poured a steady flow of air that averaged about twenty degrees cooler than the outside temperature.[26]

During these early weeks, the doctors' major worry seemed to be the mystery of the missing bullet. This preoccupation was a mystery in itself, since the bullet had obviously become encysted and was doing no harm. Even if it had been found, there was no way to extract it without killing the patient in the process. Nonetheless, they continued to poke dirty fingers and instruments into the President's wound, concluding at last that the ball had been deflected downward and to the right after hitting the ribs, lodging finally in the muscles of the right groin. This diagnosis seemed to be confirmed by the discovery that a flexible catheter passed through the wound could drop unobstructed for a distance of almost twelve inches in a direct line with the supposed location of the bullet. The latest devices of modern science seemed to support the doctors' guess. Professor Alexander Graham Bell assembled an ingenious contraption designed (like twentieth-century mine detectors) to locate buried metal. When tried on the President the results were inconclusive because of interference from the metal bed springs, but the tell-tale clicks seemed to intensify in the neighborhood of the right groin.[27]

The track leading to that area was washed and drained daily with a mild antiseptic solution, yielding considerable quantities of "healthy pus." Despite this constant attention, it stubbornly refused to heal. The reason became clear only after the autopsy when it was belatedly discovered that both the doctors and Alexander Graham Bell had been deceived. The actual course taken by the bullet was to the *left*. In its passage it was deflected off the ribs and through the spinal column, ripping a jagged hole through the first lumbar vertebra, but missing the spinal cord. Its force spent, the bullet lodged behind the pancreas, only two and a half inches to the left of the vertebrae. What had been mistaken for the track of the bullet turned out to be merely a channel of pus formed by some secondary infection, possibly even caused by the doctors themselves with their persistent, unsanitary probing.

602

It was this possibility which led Guiteau to deny that he killed Garfield. "The doctors did that. I simply shot at him," he insisted.[28] Others accepted Guiteau's conclusion, if not his logic, and blamed the doctors for Garfield's death.[29] ". . . Had the President been but an ordinary citizen," it was later alleged, "less persistent treatment might have allowed recovery." It was hardly necessary, however, to place the blame on the doctors when more obvious sources of infection were already festering within Garfield's body. The putrefying fragments of shattered vertebrae were by themselves sufficient to cause blood poisoning without any further assistance from the germs on Doctor Bliss's finger.[30]

The first signs that Garfield might be harboring a deep-seated infection appeared on July 23. Up to then the President's steady recovery had been encouraging, but on that day he was stricken with chills and convulsive tremors. After these "rigors," his fever soared to 104° and his vomiting was renewed. The next day it was decided to operate on an ugly pus sac that had appeared below the wound. An inch and a half incision was made through this sac, a drainage tube was inserted and, while they were at it, the surgeons set Garfield's broken rib. All of this was done without any anesthetic, but Garfield neither flinched nor murmured.

The result seemed to justify the pain. The President steadily gained ground and by the 29th of July was strong enough to preside over a brief cabinet meeting held at his bedside. This meeting was strictly pro forma; the department heads were under doctor's orders to discuss nothing which might disturb the patient. Fortunately for the country, the government virtually closed up shop every summer. Only one piece of official business required the President's attention during his entire illness, an extradition paper to which he signed his name. Otherwise, the nation discovered, to its surprise, how smoothly it could run for a while without a president.[31]

The government could not, of course, drift leaderless indefinitely, yet there was neither precedent nor law available to resolve the situation. Garfield's incapacity dramatized a hitherto unappreciated flaw in the Constitution: the lack of any mechanism to certify whether a president was, in fact, unable to

603

"discharge the Powers and Duties of the said Office." Blaine reportedly proposed a drastic solution. He suggested that the cabinet declare Arthur acting president until Garfield either died or recovered. For this he was assailed as a ghoulish schemer plotting to ingratiate himself with the next president but, in truth, Blaine's suggestion was not improper, only premature. If Garfield had lingered on until Congress was scheduled to meet in December, some similar action certainly would have been required. In any event, Blaine's initiative was vetoed by Arthur, who had little desire to be president and even less to force himself upon the office. Arthur was rising in the public estimation. During the protracted crisis he displayed a propriety, dignity and poise that dispelled the initial apprehensions and paved the way for the peaceful acceptance of his succession.[32]

The likelihood of that succession grew stronger with each passing day. Garfield was dying. He took so long about it that the doctors and the public were lulled into false confidence, but there could be no doubt as to the ultimate end. From each crisis he emerged weaker than before. On August 8, more surgery was required, this time with the help of ether. Garfield had barely recovered from this operation when his feeble digestive system broke down altogether. Unable to eat, sleep, or do anything but vomit, Garfield weakened dangerously. The desperate doctors tried to rebuild his strength with "nutrient enemas," a sort of eggnog forced into the intestines through the rectum, but they only managed to stabilize his condition at a low level. Normally a strapping two hundred pounds or more, Garfield had shriveled to only 135 pounds. His face was still full, but hidden under the bedcovers his puny legs and chest gave proof that the President was wasting away. Then a fresh crisis appeared from an unexpected quarter. The right parotid gland, a salivary gland located behind the ear, became painfully swollen and infected. This was the clearest sign yet of blood-poisoning and it was followed by frightful complications. A torrent of mucus and pus from the infected regions flowed into the patient's mouth, nearly drowning him in his own secretions. The right side of his face was paralyzed and sagging and, even more distressing, his grip on reality slackened. Under the spell of feverish hallucinations he rambled deleriously of his Mentor home and his childhood. On the 26th of August the newspapers proclaimed his imminent death, yet somehow he rallied once more. After the infected gland was lanced his mind cleared and he even began to retain some solid food.[33]

By the first of September, the heat and boredom of his sickroom had become intolerable, and Garfield begged for a change of scene. The *Tapaloosa* was now ready for its distinguished patient but the patient was no longer strong enough for a cruise. Disappointed, Garfield still longed for the sea, which in his mind had ever possessed almost mystic, healing powers. "I have always felt that the ocean was my friend," he had once said, "and the sight of it brings rest and peace." Somewhat reluctantly, the doctors agreed to allow him to be transferred to Elberon, New Jersey, near the President's favorite seaside resort of Long Branch. The transfer was carried out with all the precision of a military operation. Shortly before six o'clock on the morning of September 6, Garfield was placed on a stretcher and carried to a waiting van which then rolled through empty streets from which all traffic had been diverted. The President was weak but excited and even managed to wave at some of the silent spectators who lined the sidewalk. At trackside, the horses were unhitched (to prevent shying) and the wagon gently pushed by hand to the train's entrance. This train had been especially modified for its mission. The engine burned only anthracite coal to reduce smoke and fumes. The seats had been ripped out of the President's car to make room for an ingeniously designed bed that floated on heavy-duty springs. Boxes of ice were placed under the bed and, as a further cooling measure, a false ceiling was installed to allow air to circulate between it and the roof. A pilot engine preceded the train to warn approaching trains to stop, lest their noise disturb the passenger. As a final precaution, houses at strategic points along the route were equipped as emergency medical shelters in case the trip had to be cut short.

The journey of over 230 miles was accomplished in seven hours, at speeds ranging up to sixty miles per hour. As the

605

train smoothly sped to its destination it passed hushed throngs standing with their bowed heads uncovered. Almost all activity across the nation had been suspended for the morning, and in most states the day had been declared an official day of prayer. Shortly after one o'clock in the afternoon, the train reached its destination, the Franklyn Cottage, a gracious twenty-room summer house on the seashore. The night before, over two thousand volunteers had labored by the glare of calcium lights to construct a 3,200 foot spur connecting the main line to the very door of the "cottage." The President's car was uncoupled and pushed by hundreds of hands along this spur and the President himself was carried to an upstairs bedroom facing the ocean.[34]

For the next two days it seemed as if all of this effort had been wasted. The Jersey shore roasted under a record heat wave with temperatures up to a hundred degrees, rendering it even more oppressive than the city from which Garfield had fled. But after the heat spell had been broken by a welcome summer storm, the patient was allowed to be propped up before an open window where he could gaze at the waves. "This is delightful," the grateful President murmured, ". . . the fishermen at sea, the vessels on the ocean, and the bathers on the surf. . . . I am myself again." In these benign surroundings he rallied once more. Dr. Bliss was so encouraged that he dismissed half of his staff, leaving the bulk of the nursing duties in the unprofessional but devoted hands of the President's old card-playing cronies of army days, Almon F. Rockwell and David Swaim. The world was about to see the most miraculous cure in medical history, Dr. Bliss rashly predicted, but the distinguished consulting physician, Dr. D. Hayes Agnew had no such illusions. "The President may live the day out, and possibly tomorrow," he confided to a friend, "but he cannot live a week."[35]

Agnew's prognosis was all too accurate. By the 15th of September the President began to sink once more. The melancholy procession of chills, fever, vomiting and irregular pulse was resumed, with two new and ominous symptoms added: a violent, hacking cough which indicated pneumonia, and severe, painful spasms near the heart, similar to those of angina

606

pectoris. On the morning of September 19 it seemed as if the end was at hand. Garfield's temperature climbed to 108.8° and his pulse fluctuated wildly between 106 and 143 beats to the minute. Yet, once again he rallied and by afternoon his condition was comfortable and his mind was clear. That evening he gave Rockwell an impish look and wistfully pantomimed dealing a deck of cards.

Around ten o'clock that night, shortly after Rockwell had been relieved by Swaim, Garfield suddenly awoke. He asked for water and then began to claw at his chest. "O Swaim," he moaned, "this pain!" and then sank back, unconscious. Dr. Bliss was immediately summoned. He entered the sickroom on the run and at once grasped the situation. "My God, Swaim!" he said, "the President is dying!" The President's wife arrived an instant later. "Oh! why am I made to suffer this cruel wrong?" she cried. One by one the other members of the household quietly assembled around the deathbed. The only light was from a candle held by the President's bodyservant, Dan; the only sound, Garfield's husky, labored breathing. Dr. Bliss could find no pulse at the wrist, but by placing his ear over Garfield's heart he could detect a faint, fluttering murmur which gradually weakened and subsided. At 10:35 even that faded into silence and Dr. Bliss raised his head and whispered, "It is over."[36]

At the autopsy the next day a mass of dark, coagulated blood, about the size of a man's fist, was discovered in the abdominal cavity. This hemorrhage was traced to a rent in the splenic artery, which had apparently been nicked by the bullet. An aneurysmal sac, about the size of an egg yolk, had formed a protective bypass around this wound, but as the patient weakened the sac had disintegrated and at last ruptured. This escaping blood had been the source of the chest pains Garfield had suffered in his last days and, according to the doctors, was the immediate cause of his death. Some medical observers disputed this conclusion, but it hardly mattered. If, by some miracle, Garfield had survived the burst aneurysm he would have died from blood-poisoning. Had he managed to escape blood-poisoning, he would have died from the pneunomia that was beginning to attack his weakened

607

frame. Had he overcome all these hazards and somehow lived, he would have spent the rest of his days a hopeless cripple. That Garfield understood this better than did the doctors was evidenced shortly before his death when he solemnly declared: *"my work is done."*[37]

Chester Alan Arthur learned of Garfield's death from a newspaper reporter who rang the bell of Arthur's New York townhouse about midnight to deliver the long-expected, yet startling, news. "I hope—my God, I do hope it is a mistake," Arthur stammered, his voice cracking with emotion, but the rumor was confirmed a few moments later with the arrival of a telegram from the cabinet. Someone looked up the official oath of office and Judge Brady of the New York Supreme Court was roused from bed to administer it. The next morning President Arthur went to Elberon to pay his respects and give his approval to the arrangements for his predecessor's funeral.[38]

The same special train that had brought Garfield to Elberon now carried his body home. Swathed in black crepe, the little train retraced its earlier journey, past a route lined with bareheaded mourners. Flags at half mast fluttered sadly from each passing window, and at Princeton the tracks were strewn with a blanket of flowers. A steady clang of church bells tolled the train's mournful passage. At Washington the coffin was transferred to a hearse which ever so slowly made its way to the Capitol while the Marine Band droned "Nearer, my God to Thee." The body lay in state for two days in the Rotunda, beneath that same dome which had sheltered Garfield for seventeen years. Over seventy thousand people filed by the open coffin, some waiting in line for three and a half hours for a last glimpse of the fallen leader.

The coffin was then returned to the train for the last leg of its homeward journey; this time to Cleveland, where preparations were underway for an elaborate funeral pageant. Much of this route was traversed at night, but the trackside crowds of mourners were undiminished. At Altoona, they held pine torches whose eerie flickerings briefly illuminated the silent train as it flashed by. In Cleveland, an immense pavilion had been erected on the Public Square to house the President's remains. Nearly a hundred feet high, capped by a twenty-four foot angel balanced atop a gilt ball, this pavilion was draped with black velvet and festooned with two carloads of flowers. There Garfield lay in state, only blocks from the riverfront where thirty-three years earlier a drunken ship's captain had thrown him off his boat with jeers and curses.

One hundred and fifty thousand people (virtually equivalent to the entire population of Cleveland) passed by this bier. On the morning of the next day, September 26, an honor guard carried the casket to a funeral car drawn by twelve black horses. The cortege rolled up tree-lined Euclid Avenue, past the neighborhood where Garfield had once hoped to live and wound its way for three hours, through intermittent thundershowers, to Lakeview Cemetery, five miles away. There, on a high knoll within sight of the same waves that had so delighted him as a boy, James A. Garfield was laid to rest, just a few weeks short of what would have been his fiftieth birthday.[39]

The flower-laden vault that housed his remains was only temporary. On its site would soon rise a one hundred and eighty foot Romanesque turret lavishly decorated with mosaics and bas-relief, illustrating every phase of Garfield's career. This memorial would cost $225,000, most of which was raised by popular subscription.[40] Inside was a memorial shrine, dominated by a heroic statue of the late President, carved from a solid block of Italian marble. A winding staircase led to a gloomy basement crypt which housed his bronze casket.

A place in that crypt next to her husband was reserved for Lucretia, but she would not occupy it for another thirty-seven years. She would live out those years at Mentor, writing letters on black-bordered stationery, arranging her husband's memorabilia and watching over the careers of her active children. Mollie, in proper storybook fashion, would marry her "cool" Mr. Stanley-Brown as soon as she was of age. Her brothers would each lead remarkably useful and productive lives. Irvin became a prominent Boston lawyer, and little Abe, displaying the only artistic bent in the family, would be a successful Cleveland architect. After graduating from Williams, Harry and Jim would form a law firm of their own

609

which dissolved when each went on to prominence in public life. Jim followed politics, becoming a member of the U.S. Civil Service Commission, Commissioner of Corporations and, ultimately, Secretary of the Interior in Theodore Roosevelt's cabinet. Harry was more academically inclined. He became a professor of political science at Princeton University, whose president, Woodrow Wilson, later called upon him to preside over the U.S. Fuel Administration during World War I. For twenty-six years Harry held a job his father would undoubtedly have envied above all others and which he might even have filled had he lived—President of Williams College.

The other supporting players in the Garfield drama lived out their remaining days with varied fortunes. Chester Alan Arthur, as President, first renovated the White House, carting away wagonloads of priceless antiques. Then he overhauled the cabinet, dismissing all of Garfield's choices except Robert Todd Lincoln. Arthur's major accomplishment as president, the passage of a civil service reform act, was not, ironically, of his own doing but was rather conceived as a memorial to his predecessor, whose death was somehow attributed to the operations of the spoils system.

James G. Blaine would ultimately get another opportunity, as Secretary of State under Harrison, to put his cherished Pan American Union into reality, but in his great goal, the presidency, he would be continually frustrated. He came the closest in 1884, winning the nomination but losing a heartbreakingly close election.

Roscoe Conkling receded into private life, spurning Arthur's offer of a Supreme Court seat. All he asked of the President was that Robertson be fired, but when Arthur refused, Conkling angrily broke off relations and turned instead to making his fortune as a railroad lawyer. In 1884, when someone injudiciously asked him to speak for Blaine, he replied, "No, thank you, I don't engage in criminal practice,"—a magnificent curtain line to a career that was essentially threatrical. His less flamboyant junior colleague, Thomas Platt, patiently mended his fortunes after his Albany embarrassment and ultimately became undisputed boss of the New York Republican organization, ruling with a firmer hand than Conkling ever could.

Other fortunate survivors of the Garfield years included the star route scoundrels, who escaped jail thanks to a hung jury thoroughly confused by attorney Robert Ingersoll. Lacking such able legal talent, Charles Guiteau went to the gallows after a lengthy, unruly trial. Convinced to the end that his inspiration had come from God, Guiteau faced the hangman while chanting a childish hymn of his own composition, "I am going to the Lordy." The late President's doctors fared but little better than his assassin. All had their fees slashed by a stingy Congress, and some of them, including Dr. Bliss, died soon after their most famous patient, from causes directly related to their ordeal over the President's bedside.

As the years passed, bringing new issues and new heroes, Garfield's image slowly faded from public consciousness. The tremendous outpouring of grief and adulation occasioned by his death could not be long sustained and gave way in due course to indifference. By the twentieth century, according to novelist Thomas Wolfe, Garfield and his contemporaries had become "the lost Americans: their gravely vacant and bewhiskered faces mixed, melted, swam together. . . . Which had the whiskers, which the burnsides: which was which?" Such obscurity was the fate Garfield most dreaded. "Old boy!" he had asked Rockwell as he lay dying, "do you think my name will have a place in human history?" To which Rockwell replied: "Yes, a grand one, but a grander place in human hearts," —a judgment which was not, after all, so very different from Guiteau's patronizing evaluation: "Garfield was a good man, but a weak politician."[41]

Both friend and assassin did Garfield an injustice. True, his accomplishments were neither bold nor heroic, but his was not an age that called for heroism. His stormy presidency was brief and, in some respects, unfortunate, but he did leave the office stronger than he found it. As a public man he had a hand in almost every issue of national importance for almost two decades, while as a party leader he, along with Blaine, forged the Republican Party into the instrument that would lead the United States into the twentieth century. These were sufficient achievements by most standards, but not by Garfield's own, more demanding, measure of greatness which asked of a man,

611

"Did he drift unresisting on the currents of life, or did he lead the thoughts of men to higher and nobler purposes?" Garfield drifted. "My life," he realized quite early, ". . . has been made up of a series of accidents, mostly of a favorable nature. . . . I am perpetually in a series of unexpected fixes, not at all sure how I shall come out or always clear how I *ought* to come out."[42]

Little wonder that Garfield would be remembered more for what he was than for what he did. His career seemed to embody the national ideal of the self-made man, rising from log cabin to White House in unbroken ascent, propelled to success by character, piety and ability—a living exemplar of the blessings of adversity. Yet, far from being a simple, inspirational success story, Garfield's life was actually tangled in contradictions: a pacifist turned soldier, an educator turned politician, a preacher turned economist, a man of essentially literary tastes cast in the role of party chieftain, a husband who, at length, fell in love with his wife, and a man racked by self-doubts who was, at the same time, convinced of his high destiny. And, above all, the central contradiction of his career: here was a misplaced intellectual thrown onto the stage of public life, moving restlessly between the worlds of action and introspection, drawing strength from each but at home in neither.

Garfield often liked to cite a saying of George Canning's that struck him as peculiarly appropriate to his own circumstances: "My road must be through character to power." In his own career Garfield tried to live by that motto and in so doing demonstrated that not all that glittered in the Gilded Age was gilt.

In Garfield's favorite poem, Tennyson's "In Memoriam," there was a passage to which he often turned:

> Dost thou look back on what hath been,
> As some divinely gifted man,
> Whose life in low estate began
> And on a simple village green;
>
> Who breaks his birth's invidious bar,
> And grasps the skirts of happy chance,
> And breasts the blows of circumstance,
> And grapples with his evil star;

Who makes by force his merit known
And lives to clutch the golden keys,
To mould a mighty state's decrees,
And shape the whisper of the throne;

And moving up from high to higher,
Becomes on Fortune's crowning slope
The pillar of a people's hope,
The centre of a world's desire;

Yet feels, as in a pensive dream,
When all his active powers are still,
A distant dearness in the hill,
A secret sweetness in the stream, . . .

In these now-faded verses, did he read his own epitaph?

NOTES

1. CHAOS OF CHILDHOOD

1. Virtually all the information concerning Garfield's parents and his early life comes, either directly or indirectly, from his mother. Especially valuable is a series of reminiscent letters she wrote her son from 1868 to 1870. I have cited this particular series of letters as they are found in Theodore Clarke Smith's 1925 study of *The Life and Letters of James Abram Garfield*. For many years Smith's comprehensive biography was the standard life of Garfield. Unfortunately, his judicious selection of documents is too often marred by careless or garbled citations and must be used with caution. Two other sources have proved especially useful for the early portions of this chapter. The first is an unfinished fragment by President Garfield's widow, Lucretia Rudolph Garfield, entitled "A Rough Sketch of an Introduction to a Life of General Garfield," which she began in 1887 and laid aside soon after, without going further than her husband's boyhood. The manuscript was in the possession of Mr. Edward Garfield of Cleveland, Ohio, whose many kindnesses included an opportunity to examine this and other papers before they were placed in the Library of Congress. Most of the printed biographies from the nineteenth century are worthless for Garfield's youth but the least untrustworthy of the group is *The Life of James Abram Garfield* by Jonas Mills Bundy which seems to contain reasonably reliable (although somewhat romanticized) information apparently derived from interviews with Garfield's mother.

2. Bundy, *Life of Garfield*, p. 5; Smith, *Life and Letters of Garfield*, I, 2. For more detailed genealogical information see a letter by Garfield to Mrs. Mary Garfield Bassett, January 15, 1877, in the Letterbooks, Garfield Papers, LC.

3. "Note taken July 13, 1871 by J. A. Garfield from the statements of Eliza Garfield," Garfield Papers, LC. The biographies of Garfield tell a much more sentimental story. In their account (which apparently had the blessing of both Garfield and his mother), Abram Garfield's childhood

sweetheart became Eliza and Abram's journey to Ohio was done with the express purpose of making her his wife. In this, and other instances, Garfield's mother was not above romanticizing the details of her early life. See, for example, Bundy, *Life of Garfield*, p. 6.

4. Hawley, *Journal of a Tour*, pp. 27, 41, 56; see also Hatcher, *Western Reserve*, Chapters 7 and 8.

5. Rose, *Cleveland*, Chapter 5; Hatcher, *ibid.*, p. 111.

6. Eliza Garfield to James A. Garfield, December 23, 1868, in Smith, *Life and Letters of Garfield*, I, 3.

7. Eliza Garfield to James A. Garfield, March 31, 1870, in *ibid.*, pp. 5-6; nephew cited on p. 23; see also Bundy, *Life of Garfield*, p. 57.

8. Eliza Garfield to James A. Garfield, December 27, 1868, in Smith, *Life and Letters of Garfield*, I, 4; see also Hatcher, *Western Reserve*, Chapter 10.

9. Riddle, *Life of Jas. A. Garfield*, p. 27.

10. Eliza Garfield to James A. Garfield, March 31, 1870, in Smith, *Life and Letters of Garfield*, I, 5.

11. The most recent study of the growth of the Disciple movement in Ohio is *Buckeye Disciples* by Henry K. Shaw. Less critical older accounts which are still useful are: Amos S. Hayden, *Early History of the Disciples in the Western Reserve*, and Alanson Wilcox, *History of the Disciples of Christ in Ohio*.

12. Eliza Garfield to James A. Garfield, March 31, 1870, in Smith, *Life and Letters of Garfield*, I, 9; Bundy, *Life of Garfield*, p. 9.

13. Eliza Garfield to James A. Garfield, March 31, 1870, in Smith, *Life and Letters of Garfield*, I, 5; Bundy, *Life of Garfield*, pp. 9-10.

14. Garfield to his mother, April 21, 1854; November 19, 1855; Lucretia Garfield, "A Rough Sketch . . . of General Garfield," all in the Garfield Papers, LC; Bundy *Life of Garfield*, pp. 13-14.

15. Donn Piatt and Jeremiah S. Black, cited in Smith, *Life and Letters of Garfield*, II, 936; C. R. Williams (ed.), *Diary of Rutherford B. Hayes*, IV, 110.

16. This account of the remarriage and subsequent divorce of Garfield's mother is based on records in the Cuyahoga County Courthouse, Cleveland, Ohio. Due to the scanty nature of these records and the anarchic spelling habits of the era, it is not possible to nail down what happened with complete certainty. The Marriage Records in the License Bureau, volume 4, p. 142, record a marriage between Alfred "Belding" and Eliza "Guiffield" on April 16, 1842 in Bedford, Ohio. In the Records of the Court of Common Pleas of the State of Ohio, Cuyahoga County, for the October Term, 1850, volume 54, p. 441, can be found the divorce of Alfred and Eliza "Belden," who were married in Bedford on the same day as Belding and Guiffield. It is, of course, conceivable that all this had nothing to do with Garfield's mother, but this supposition is extremely unlikely, especially since such collateral evidence as does exist reinforces the court records. In his diary for January 17, 1881, Garfield mentions a Warren Belden

as "the man with whom mother made an unfortunate marriage 36 years ago. [That would be 1844 or 1845, a pardonable error.] They separated in less than two years. . . ."

17. Diary, January 17, 1881, Garfield Papers, LC.

18. Garfield to J. H. Rhodes, November 19, 1862, Garfield Papers, LC.

19. Diary, July 30, 1853; Phebe Boynton to Garfield, April 30, 1853; Lucretia Garfield, "Rough Sketch . . . of General Garfield," all in the Garfield Papers, LC; Bundy, *Life of Garfield.* p. 15.

20. Cited in Smith, *Life and Letters of Garfield*, I, 19-20; see also Bundy, *Life of Garfield*, pp. 13-14 and the Garfield Diary for May and June 1848, Garfield Papers, LC.

21. Cited in Smith, *Life and Letters of Garfield*, I, 21.

22. *Ibid.*

23. Amos Letcher cited in *ibid.*, I, 23; see also Garfield Diary, August 30, 1848; Garfield to Lucretia Rudolph, February 25, 1855, Garfield Papers, LC.

24. Garfield to his mother, November 19, 1855; Lucretia Rudolph, "Rough Sketch . . . of General Garfield;" Garfield Diary, March 6, 1849, Garfield Papers, LC.

25. Garfield to J. H. Rhodes, November 19, 1862, Garfield Papers, LC.

2. A VERY PULPY BOY

1. Hinsdale, *Garfield and Education*, p. 69.

2. *Pioneer History of Geauga County*, p. 100.

3. Green, *Hiram College*, pp. 35-36; Diary, May 24, 1850, Garfield Papers, LC.

4. Diary, August 8 and 24, 1849, Garfield Papers, LC.

5. *Ibid.*, October 29, 1849.

6. James A. Garfield to Thomas Garfield, August 16, 1849, Garfield Papers, LC.

7. Diary, October 15 to October 22, 1849, Garfield Papers, LC.

8. In Hinsdale, *Garfield and Education*, p. 48.

9. Diary, October 5, 1850, Garfield Papers, LC.

10. *Ibid.*, December 31, 1880.

11. Riddle, *Life of Jas. A. Garfield*, p. 73; Sherman, *Recollections*, II, 807.

12. Hinsdale, *Garfield and Education*, pp. 49-50; Diary, October 22, 1849, Garfield Papers, LC. For a description of a rural Ohio school which Garfield thought was much like his own experiences, see Albert Gallatin Riddle's 1873 novel, *Bart Ridgely.*

13. Diary, February 28, 1850, Garfield Papers, LC.

14. *Ibid.*, March 4, 1850.

15. *Ibid.*, May 1, 1850.

16. *Ibid.*, March 23, 1850.

17. *Ibid.*, October 1, 1850.

18. *Ibid.*, 15 [March, 1854], Garfield Papers, OHS; Garfield to Harmon Austin, May 1, 1864 in Smith, *Life and Letters of Garfield*, II, 932.

19. Diary, 11 [March, 1854], Garfield Papers, OHS; Diary, May 19 and August 18, 1850, Garfield Papers, LC.

20. Diary: September 6, 1850; September 29, 1850; October 2, 1850; February 28, 1851; July 4, 1851; July 4, 1852; August 17, 1852, Garfield Papers, LC.

21. *Ibid.*, July 2, 1850; June 28, 1853.

22. *Ibid.*, October 11, 1850; March 28, 1850; August 8, 1850; August 17, 1850; A. W. Stiles to Garfield, January 7, 1880, Garfield Papers, LC.

23. Diary, January 21 and April 16, 1851, Garfield Papers, LC; Henry, *Captain Henry*, pp. 68-69.

24. Garfield to Harriet, Phebe and Cordelia Boynton, March 30, 1851, Garfield Papers, LC.

25. In Fuller, *Reminiscences*, p. 43.

26. *Ibid.*, p. 4. This was the problem so "baffling" to the best teachers of Belmont and Muskingum counties: "A man had a ditch to dig, 100 rods in length, for which he was to pay 100 dollars. He let the job to two men, one to dig for 87 1/2 cents per rod and to dig enough to amount to $50. The other was to dig the rest at $1.12 1/2 cents per rod. Required: the number of rods that each must dig?" Diary, May 26, 1851, Garfield Papers, LC.

27. See Treudley, *Prelude to the Future* and Green, *Hiram College*.

28. Speech of Garfield's delivered on November 14, 1851, in Fuller, *Reminiscences*, pp. 36-38; Address of Garfield's at Hiram College, June 1880, in Hinsdale, *Garfield and Education*, p. 19; Garfield, "Life and Character of Almeda A. Booth," in *ibid.*, p. 391.

29. Hinsdale, *Garfield and Education*, pp. 35-36; Davis, *Garfield of Hiram*, p. 63.

30. Fuller, *Reminscences*, pp. 47, 31, 65; Sarah J. Cooper to Garfield, March 7, 1874, Garfield Papers, LC.

31. Diary, September 5, 1850, Garfield Papers, LC; Green, *Hiram College*, p. 395. For a full description of the origins of the various literary and debating societies at Hiram, see Garfield to B. A. Hinsdale, May 11, 1875, Garfield Papers, LC.

32. Fuller, *Reminiscences*, pp. 52-54.

33. Diary, February 11, 1852, Garfield Papers, LC.

34. *Ibid.*, title page inscription for 1851.

35. *Ibid.*, March 31, 1852.

36. *Ibid.*, April 17, 1851.

37. *Ibid.*, July 7, 1854.

38. *Ibid.*, June 28, 1874; see also September 2, 1875.

39. *Ibid.*, June 24, 1854; Green, *Hiram College*, p. 41; Garfield, "Life of Almeda Booth," in Hinsdale, *Garfield and Education*, pp. 365-426.

40. Diary, July 17, 1852, Garfield Papers, LC.

41. *Ibid.*, April 9, 1852; Garfield to Mary Hubbell [July 24, 1852?], Garfield Papers, LC.

42. Fuller, *Reminiscences*, pp. 71-72; Garfield to Fuller, January 19, 1853, *ibid.*, pp. 72-74.

43. Garfield to Fuller, December 17, 1852, *ibid.*, 71.

44. Garfield to Mary Hubbell, February 27, 1853; Henry Boynton to Garfield, June 7, 1855; Diary: December 31, 1852; February 27, 1853, all in the Garfield Papers, LC.

45. Diary, January 25, 1853; December 18, 1852; April 10, 1853, Garfield Papers, LC; Garfield to Fuller, April 9, 1853, Fuller, *Reminiscences*, p. 76.

46. Wilber to Garfield, January 10, 1854, in Fuller, *Reminiscences*, p. 76.

47. Garfield to Mary Hubbell, May 29, 1852 and April 25, 1852, Garfield Papers, LC.

48. Garfield to his mother, July 29, 1853; Diary, August 26, 1851, Garfield Papers, LC.

49. Diary, July 25, 1853; April 3, 1853, Garfield Papers, LC.

50. Garfield to Lucretia Rudolph, March 3, 1854, Garfield Papers, LC.

51. *Ibid.*, November 16, 1853.

52. Diary, January 22, 1852, Garfield Papers, LC; Fuller, *Reminiscences*, p. 57.

53. Diary, December 31, 1853, Garfield Papers, LC.

54. *Ibid.*, June 24, 1854.

55. Lucretia Rudolph Diary, June 24, 1854, manuscript lent to author by Mr. Edward Garfield of Cleveland, Ohio.

56. Garfield to Phebe Boynton, May 30, 1854, Garfield Papers, LC.

57. Diary, August 2, 1853; Charles Wilber to Garfield, April, 1854, Garfield Papers, LC.

58. Diary, June 23, 1854, Garfield Papers, LC.

59. *Ibid.*, July 3, 1853.

60. *Ibid.*, July 2, and July 5, 1853.

61. Henry, *Captain Henry*, p. 76; Fuller, *Reminiscences*, p. 120.

62. Diary, June 23, 1854, Garfield Papers, LC.

63. *Ibid.*, June 22, 1854.

3. ON ONE END OF A LOG

1. Diary, July 11, 1854, Garfield Papers, LC.

2. *Ibid.*, July 17, 1854; Perry, *Williamstown*, p. 821; Rudolph, *Mark Hopkins and the Log*, p. 66; Ingalls, *Writings*, p. 403.

3. Or words to that effect. The genesis of the aphorism has been diligently reconstructed by Carroll A. Wilson, who concludes that at the Delmonico dinner of December 28, 1871 Garfield did, indeed, praise Mark Hopkins, but not in the words later attributed to him. According to Wil-

son's ingenious emendation, Garfield placed Hopkins and the student in a log cabin, rather than on the familiar log. The remark passed virtually unnoticed until, as Wilson believes, John J. Ingalls, with his superior gift for phrasemaking, refined Garfield's crude epigram into its present well-known and pithy form. Wilson, "Familiar Small College Quotations."

4. Garfield to Lucretia Rudolph, July 30, 1854; Garfield to his mother, July 22 and August 2, 1854, all in the Garfield Papers, LC; Garfield to C. E. Fuller, July 30, 1854, Fuller, *Reminiscences*, p. 132; Garfield to Mary P. Watson, September 16, 1854, in *ibid.*, pp. 150-51.

5. Garfield to C. E. Fuller, August 22, 1854, Fuller, *Reminiscences*, p. 137. A summary of the speech can be found in Cabot, *Memoir of Ralph Waldo Emerson*, II, pp. 757-59. It is a typically Emersonian plea for the scholar to rise above vulgar materialism. All that Garfield seems to have gotten out of this was a half-remembered phrase, which Emerson may or may not have employed: "Mankind is as lazy as it dares to be." See Atkinson, *Industrial Progress*, p. 11.

6. Garfield to C. E. Fuller, July 30, 1854, Fuller, *Reminiscences*, p. 133.

7. Garfield to C. E. Fuller, July 16, 1854, *ibid.*, p. 128.

8. Garfield to C. E. Fuller, January 28, 1854, *ibid.*, p. 104; Garfield to J. H. Rhodes, November 19, 1862, Garfield Papers, LC.

9. Wilber cited in Hinsdale, *Garfield and Education*, p. 141; Bundy, *Life of Garfield*, p. 38.

10. Garfield to C. E. Fuller, July 30, 1854, Fuller, *Reminiscences*, p. 133; Benjamin, *Life of a Free Lance*, p. 142.

11. Bundy, *Life of Garfield*, p. 40.

12. *Ibid.*, pp. 37, 40; Benjamin, *Life of a Free Lance*, p. 142.

13. Henry, *Captain Henry*, p. 93.

14. Garfield to Lucretia Rudolph, November 1, 1855, Garfield Papers, LC.

15. Ingalls, *Writings*, p. 397.

16. *Ibid.*; Bundy, *Life of Garfield*, pp. 39, 41.

17. The entire poem can be found in Fuller, *Reminiscences*, pp. 199-202. The Equitable Fraternity was later transformed into Delta Upsilon, and Garfield was an active alumnus for a time during the 1870s.

18. Garfield to C. E. Fuller, November 2, 1855, Fuller, *Reminiscences*, pp. 210-11; Diary, November 8, 1855, Garfield Papers, LC.

19. A. L. Perry to B. A. Hinsdale, October 25, 1881, Hinsdale Papers, WRHS; Scudder, *Life of David Coit Scudder*, pp. 67-68.

20. See: Perry, *Williamstown*, p. 504, pp. 595-96; Bascom, *Things Learned*, pp. 100-03; Rudolph, *Mark Hopkins and the Log*, pp. 27-29.

21. Garfield to Lucretia Rudolph, April 7, 1855, Garfield Papers, LC.

22. Garfield to C. E. Fuller, March 13, 1855, Fuller, *Reminiscences*, p. 181; Perry, *Williamstown*, p. 821; Ingalls, *Writings*, p. 397; Benjamin, *Life of a Free Lance*, pp. 141-42; Hopkins cited in Bundy, *Life of Garfield*, p. 33; Mark Hopkins to Edmund Kirke, May 26, 1865, Garfield Papers, LC.

23. Garfield to Lucretia Rudolph, December 31, 1854, Garfield Papers, LC.

24. Diary, September 10, 1855, Garfield Papers, LC.
25. Philip [————?] to Garfield, June 28, 1854, Garfield Papers, LC.
26. Diary, September 10, 1855, Garfield Papers, LC.
27. Lucretia Rudolph Diary, August 5 and September 4, 1854; September 7, 1855.
28. Diary, September 11, 1855, Garfield Papers, LC; see also Lucretia Rudolph Diary for September 12, 1855.
29. Garfield to Lucretia Rudolph, September 18, 1855, Garfield Papers, LC.
30. *Ibid.*, December 8, 1855; May 12, 1856; Diary, September 10, 1855, Garfield Papers, LC.
31. Perry, *Williamstown*, pp. 603-07; Rudolph, *Mark Hopkins and the Log*, pp. 47-52.
32. Mark Hopkins to Edmund Kirke, May 26, 1864; Garfield to Lucretia Rudolph, November 10, 1855, both in the Garfield Papers, LC; student cited in Rudolph, *Mark Hopkins and the Log*, p. 49.
33. Garfield to C. E. Fuller, May 13, 1854, Fuller, *Reminiscences*, p. 114; Garfield to Lucretia Rudolph, July 30, 1854, Garfield Papers, LC.
34. Cited in Smith, *Life and Letters of Garfield*, I, 98. When Garfield's puzzled friends read the article they demanded an explanation, causing Garfield to back away from some of its more extreme implications. See Garfield to C. E. Fuller, May 31, 1856, Fuller, *Reminiscences*, p. 222.
35. Diary, November 2, 1855, Garfield Papers, LC; see also Bundy, *Life of Garfield*, p. 40; Garfield to William Boynton, March 21, 1865, Garfield Papers, WRHS. Disciples back on the Western Reserve were also beginning to attack slavery, leading to considerable friction between the Hiram church and Alexander Campbell at Bethany, Virginia.
36. Garfield to Barbara Fiske, December 31, 1855, in undated newspaper clipping, Garfield Papers, LC.
37. Garfield to Phebe Boynton, April 4, 1855, *ibid.*
38. Garfield to Lucretia Rudolph, September 13, 1854, *ibid.*
39. *Ibid.*, May 4, 1856.
40. *Ibid.*, May 18 and June 15, 1856.
41. *Ibid.*, November 10, 1855; T. Brooks to Garfield, January 6, 1856, Garfield Papers, LC.
42. Garfield to Lucretia Rudolph, March 3, 1856; A. S. Hayden to Garfield, July 28, 1855 and May 24, 1856, all in Garfield Papers, LC.
43. Garfield to Lucretia Rudolph, February 3, 1856, *ibid.*
44. *Ibid.*, July 6, 1856.
45. Garfield to C. E. Fuller, February 11, 1856, Fuller, *Reminiscences*, pp. 216-17.
46. Garfield to Lucretia Rudolph, May 25, 1856, Garfield Papers, LC.
47. Fuller, *Reminiscences*, p. 236; graduation address in Hopkins, *Teaching and Counsels*, p. 101.

4. THE DECISION MUST COME

1. Garfield to C. E. Fuller, September 8 and December 14, 1856, Fuller, *Reminiscences*, pp. 238, 241; Garfield to his mother, October 2, 1856; Garfield to Lucretia Rudolph, November 13, 1856, both in the Garfield Papers, LC.

2. Charles Wilber to Garfield, July 24, 1857, Garfield Papers, LC.

3. Garfield to Lucretia Rudolph, November 13, 1856, Garfield Papers, LC; Green, *Hiram College*, p. 163.

4. Garfield to C. E. Fuller, February 3, 1857, Fuller, *Reminiscences*, p. 244; Hinsdale, *Garfield and Education*, p. 74. Garfield is usually referred to as a lay preacher. Actually, he was a regularly ordained minister who was entitled to perform marriages and who was usually addressed as "the Reverend James A. Garfield." See Certificate of Ordainment, September 18, 1858 in the Garfield Papers, LC.

5. "Some Recollections of Early Hiram," unsigned typescript by B. A. Hinsdale, Hinsdale Papers, WRHS; see also Charles Wilber to Garfield, April 11, 1857, Garfield Papers, LC.

6. Amos S. Hayden, Farewell Address, cited in Green, *Hiram College*, p. 93; see Norman Dunshee to Garfield, November 13, 1855 and February 12, 1856, Garfield Papers, LC, for evidence that Dunshee tried to undercut President Hayden's authority and regarded himself, somewhat smugly, as the real head of the school.

7. Garfield to C. E. Fuller, August 30, 1857, Fuller, *Reminiscences*, p. 256.

8. Garfield to Lucretia Rudolph, May 18, 1857, Garfield Papers, LC.

9. Garfield to C. E. Fuller, August 30, 1857; January 16, 1858, Fuller, *Reminiscences*, pp. 256, 267.

10. Hinsdale, *Garfield and Education*, p. 53; Green, *Hiram College*, pp. 105-06; Henry, *Captain Henry*, p. 76; Treudley, *Prelude to the Future*, p. 84; letter from "Incog." in *Portage County Democrat*, May 19, 1858; Garfield to Harmon Austin, November 9, 1857; Diary, November 8, 1857, both in Garfield Papers, LC.

11. "Elements of Success," speech by Garfield, delivered June 29, 1869, copy in Garfield Papers, LC; see also speech at Hiram, June 14, 1867, in Hinsdale, *Garfield and Education*, pp. 275-315.

12. Green, *Hiram College*, p. 111; *Portage County Democrat*, April 7, 1858. For a schedule of student fees and living expenses, see the issue of February 3, 1858.

13. For a complete faculty salary schedule, see Green, *Hiram College*, p. 383; for an explanation of Everest's dismissal from Bethany College which reveals the extent of the split in Disciple ranks on the slavery question, see Norman Dunshee to Garfield, February 12, 1856, Garfield Papers, LC; see also *Portage County Democrat*, June 16, 1858; Hinsdale, *Garfield and Education*, p. 51.

14. Speech at Hiram, June 14, 1867, in Hinsdale, *Garfield and Education*, pp. 282-83.

15. *Ibid.*, pp. 53, 58, 64-65.
16. Garfield to Lucretia Rudolph, June 29, 1868; Diary, August 11, 1857, August 10, 1858, all in Garfield Papers, LC.
17. Diary, October 3, 1857, Garfield Papers, LC.
18. Garfield to C. E. Fuller, January 16, 1858, Fuller, *Reminiscences*, pp. 267-68.
19. *Ibid.*, March 23, 1858, p. 269; Diary, April 14, 1858; Garfield to Lucretia Rudolph, June 29, 1858, both in Garfield Papers, LC.
20. Garfield to B. A. Hinsdale, December 16, 1858, Garfield Papers, WRHS; Diary, April 14, 1858; C. D. Wilber to Garfield, July 25, 1858, both in the Garfield Papers, LC.
21. C. D. Wilber to Mary Learned, October 26, 1857, Garfield Papers, LC.
22. Diary, November 19 and October 12, 1847, Garfield Papers, LC.
23. Diary, April 17, 1858, September 26, 1875; Garfield to Lucretia Rudolph, September 26, 1875, all in the Garfield Papers, LC.
24. Diary, November 11, 1858, *ibid.* The entire entry consists of a laconic statement that he was married, without further comment.
25. Garfield to J. H. Rhodes, January 8, 1859; Diary, December 31, 1858, both in the Garfield Papers, LC.
26. Garfield to J. H. Rhodes, December 4, 1858; Garfield to B. A. Hinsdale, December 16, 1858, both in Garfield Papers, LC.
27. Garfield to J. H. Rhodes, January 8, 1859; see also, Diary, December 31, 1858, both in the Garfield Papers, LC; Henry Boynton Diary, December 28, 1858, WRHS.
28. S. W. Collins to Garfield, February 4, 1859; Garfield to J. H. Rhodes, February 3, 1859, both in Garfield Papers, LC; "war into Carthage" cited in Smith, *Life and Letters of Garfield*, I, 126.
29. Garfield to J. H. Rhodes, December 4, 1858, Garfield Papers, LC.
30. "Croakers" cited in Hinsdale, *The Eclectic Institute*, p. 15; Diary, October 3 and October 13, 1857; Garfield to J. H. Rhodes, February 3, 1859, Garfield Papers, LC. Had Garfield's proposed chess meets been held, they might well have been the first organized intercollegiate chess in the United States. Garfield's fondness for the game led him to recommend it to his students as an antidote for overly abstract study. "Frequently lay aside Emerson and study Morphy," he suggested. Garfield to J. H. Rhodes, October 6, 1858, Garfield Papers, LC.
31. A. S. Hayden to Garfield, August 26, 1858, Garfield Papers, LC. On September 14, Hayden abjectly retracted the insinuation in an effusive letter to "Beloved Bro. Garfield."
32. Diary, May 4, 1858; See 1858 receipt from a brewer to "Rev. J. A. Garfield," with penciled notation by J. Stanley-Brown, all in Garfield Papers, LC.
33. See: Garfield to C. E. Fuller, March 23, 1858, Fuller, *Reminiscences*, p. 270; Diary, October 5, 1857, Garfield Papers, LC; Green, *Hiram College*, pp. 155-56n. The boys involved were expelled.
34. Garfield to Isaac Errett, May 3, 1859, in Lamar, *Memoir of Errett*,

I, 220; Garfield to Harmon Austin, March 30, 1859; J. H. Jones to Garfield, April 20, 1859, both in Garfield Papers, LC.

35. Garfield to J. H. Rhodes, May 14 and April 15, 1859, Garfield Papers, LC.

36. Garfield to Harmon Austin, May 21, 1859; Garfield to J. H. Rhodes, May 29, 1859; Harmon Austin to Garfield, May 28, 1859, all in Garfield Papers, LC.

37. Garfield to J. H. Rhodes, April 15, 1869, *ibid.*

38. Diary, June 29, 1859, *ibid.*

39. Garfield to J. H. Rhodes, April 15 and June 20, 1859, *ibid.*

40. W. J. Ford to Garfield, July 16, 1859, *ibid.*

41. Harmon Austin to Garfield, March 3, 1859; Brown cited in W. J. Ford to Garfield, July 16, 1859, *ibid.*

42. Diary, August 22, 1859, *ibid.*

43. J. T. Smith to Garfield, August 19, 1859; Cannon to Garfield, August 19, 1859; Diary, August 22, 1859, *ibid.*

44. *Portage County Democrat*, August 31, 1859; Diary, August 23, 1859, Garfield Papers, LC.

45. Cited in Land, "John Brown's Ohio Environment."

46. G. P. Udall to Garfield, September 27, 1859, Garfield Papers, LC; *Portage Sentinel*, September 14, 1859.

47. Jackson, Little, *et al.* to Garfield, September 5, 1859, Garfield Papers, LC; Garfield to Jackson, Little, *et al.*, September 12, 1859, *Portage County Democrat*, October 5, 1859.

48. *Portage Sentinel*, October 5, 1859; *Portage County Democrat*, October 5, 1859.

49. *Portage Sentinel*, September 14 and 21, 1859.

50. *Summit Beacon*, in *Portage County Democrat*, September 14, 1859; *Portage Sentinel*, October 5, 1859.

51. *Portage County Democrat*, September 14 and 28, 1859.

52. *Ibid.*, October 5, 1859.

53. *Ibid.*, October 19, 1859.

54. Garfield to C. E. Fuller, November 19, 1859, Fuller, *Reminiscences*, p. 286; Lamar, *Memoirs of Errett*, I, 207. For advice in a similar vein see Charles Loos to Garfield, August 23, 1859, Garfield Papers, LC.

55. In W. J. Ford to Garfield, August 30, 1859, Garfield Papers, L.C.

5. A RISING MAN

1. Garfield to J. H. Rhodes, January 1, 1860 [misdated 1859]; see also Garfield to his wife, December 31, 1859, both in Garfield Papers, LC.

2. On Cox, see his autobiography, *Military Reminiscences* and short sketches by Whitelaw Reid and James Ford Rhodes in *Ohio in the War* and *Historical Essays* respectively. The typescript of a rambling, uncritical and unfinished attempt at a biography by William C. Cochran is on deposit at the Oberlin College Library.

3. Garfield to Harmon Austin, February 5, 1860, Garfield Papers, LC: J. D. Cox, "Oration on . . . Garfield," p. 96.
4. Garfield to B. A. Hinsdale, January 22, 1860, Garfield Papers, WRHS.
5. Garfield to C. E. Fuller, January 7, 1860, Fuller, *Reminiscences*, pp. 290-91; *Cincinnati Commercial*, in *Portage County Democrat*, January 11, 1860.
6. *Portage County Democrat*, January 18, 1860.
7. Garfield to J. H. Rhodes, January 21, 1860, Garfield Papers, LC. The opposition to the library tax came mainly from rural districts. See Aldrich, "History of Ohio . . . Library Legislation," pp. 50-56.
8. *Portage County Democrat*, January 25, 1860.
9. *Ibid.*, January 11, 1860; Diary, December 2, 1859, Garfield Papers, LC.
10. Bratton, "Unionist Junket," pp. 64-81.
11. Garfield to J. H. Rhodes, January 21, 1860, Garfield Papers, LC.
12. *Ibid.*, January 24 and 25, 1860.
13. *Portage County Democrat*, February 1, 1860.
14. *Ibid.*; L. W. Hall to Garfield, January 26, 1860; see also W. J. Ford to Garfield, February 13, 1860, both in the Garfield Papers, LC.
15. Garfield to Hinsdale, January 22, 1860, Garfield Papers, WRHS; Reid, *Ohio in the War*, I, 26.
16. Garfield to Charles Whittlesey, January 18 and March 1860, Garfield Papers, WRHS.
17. *Portage County Democrat*, February 15, 1860.
18. Unidentified newspaper cited in Smith, *Life and Letters of Garfield*, I, 149.
19. *Cleveland Leader* cited in *Portage County Democrat*, January 25, 1860.
20. *Cincinnati Commercial*, February 27, 1860, cited in *ibid.*, March 7, 1860.
21. L. H. Hall to Garfield, March 16, 1860; J. D. Cox to Garfield, April 4, 1860, both in Garfield Papers, LC.
22. Garfield to his wife, February 12, 1860; Lucretia to James Garfield, March 18, 1860, *ibid.*
23. Lucretia to James Garfield, February 3, 1860, *ibid.*
24. Garfield to his wife, November 11 and December 26, 1862, *ibid.*
25. *Portage County Democrat*, July 11, 1860.
26. J. D. Cox to Garfield, June 9, 1860; W. T. Bascom to Garfield, June 15, 1860, both in the Garfield Papers, LC; *Cincinnati Commercial*, in *Portage County Democrat*, June 20, 1860.
27. *Portage County Democrat*, September 12, 1860; see also Garfield to C. E. Fuller, October 3, 1860, Fuller, *Reminiscences*, p. 294.
28. *Portage Sentinel*, September 12, 1860.
29. W. T. Bascom to Garfield, September 13 and 19, 1860; J. D. Cox to Garfield, April 25, 1860, all in the Garfield Papers, LC; newspapers cited in *Portage County Democrat*, October 10 and 17, 1860.

30. *Portage County Democrat*, September 12, 1860.

31. Henry, *Captain Henry*, p. 97.

32. Diary, November 6, 1860, Garfield Papers, LC. The presidential vote in the 26th Ohio Senatorial District was:

	Lincoln	Douglas	Breckenridge	Bell
Portage	3,065	1,970	117	13
Summit	3,607	1,785	97	16
	6,672	3,755	214	29

33. Garfield to B. A. Hinsdale, January 5, 1861; see also *ibid.*, January 22, 1860, both in Garfield Papers, WRHS.

34. B. A. Hinsdale to Garfield, January 26, 1861, *ibid.*

35. *Portage County Democrat*, December 5, 1860; Garfield to his wife, January 13, 1861, Garfield Papers, LC.

36. Garfield to J. H. Rhodes, January 26, 1861, *ibid.*

37. *Portage County Democrat*, January 31, 1861; Cochran, *Political Experiences of . . . Cox*, I, 592.

38. *Portage County Democrat*, February 6, 1861.

39. *Ohio State Journal*, January 28, 1861, in *ibid.*

40. Garfield to his wife, February 9, 1861, Garfield Papers, LC.

41. J. D. Cox to Garfield, May 29, 1860, Garfield Papers, LC; see also: Garfield to Hinsdale, January 22, 1860, Garfield Papers, WRHS; Garfield, "My Experience as a Lawyer," p. 565; Riddle, *Life of Jas. A. Garfield*, pp. 50-51, 358-59; *Portage County Democrat*, February 6, 1861. In his novel, *Bart Ridgley*, Riddle describes an interview between a young law student and an experienced lawyer which seems to be very similar to the interview between Riddle and Garfield.

42. Garfield to his wife, February 17, 1861, Garfield Papers, LC; Garfield to B. A. Hinsdale, February 17, 1861, Garfield Papers, WRHS.

43. Garfield to his wife, February 17, 1861, Garfield Papers, LC.

44. Garfield to B. A. Hinsdale, February 17, 1861, Garfield Papers, WRHS.

45. Garfield to his wife, January 27, 1861 and March 30, 1862, Garfield Papers, LC.

46. *Ibid.*, March 24, 1861; see also: *ibid.*, March 19, 1861 and Garfield to S. D. Page, March 16, 1861; Sherman, *Recollections*, I, 232-33; Oberholtzer, *Jay Cooke*, I, 131; Reid, *Ohio in the War*, I, 737. According to Reid, "Garfield, Cox and Monroe, the Radical triumvirate of the State Senate, threw their influence in favor of the Conservative John Sherman as against the Radical Schenck, and decided the contest." Reid offers no proof for this assertion and, since the records of the caucus were secret, it is not impossible that the election of Sherman was decided by such a last-minute switch by Garfield. However, since Garfield's correspondence at the time is particularly bitter towards Sherman, and since he retained the friendship of Dennison, it seems likely that Reid's account of the election is mistaken.

47. Garfield to his wife, March 10, March 14, April 7, 1861, Garfield Papers, LC.
48. *Ibid.*, March 10 and April 7, 1861.
49. Cox, *Military Reminiscences*, I, 1; *Cincinnati Gazette*, January 15, 1880.

6. COLONEL GARFIELD

1. Cox, *Military Reminiscences*, I, 6.
2. Garfield to his wife, April 14, 1861, Garfield Papers, LC; Fuller, *Reminiscences*, pp. 302-03.
3. Cox, *Military Reminiscences*, I, 7.
4. Garfield to J. H. Rhodes, April 14, 1861, Garfield Papers, LC.
5. Diary, July 28, 1857; Garfield to [F. A. Williams], March 23, 1861 (typed copy), Garfield Papers, LC.
6. Garfield to his wife, May 5, 1861; see also Garfield to J. H. Rhodes, April 17, 1861, both in Garfield Papers, LC.
7. Reid, *Ohio in the War*, I, 21, 744.
8. *Portage County Democrat*, May 1, 1861; Garfield to J. H. Rhodes, February 18, 1861, Garfield Papers, LC.
9. Garfield to J. Q. Smith, July 28, 1861, Garfield Papers, LC.
10. *Ibid.*, May 30, 1863; Garfield to L. Day, August 30, 1861, *ibid.*
11. *Portage County Democrat*, April 24, 1861.
12. S. T. Loomis to Garfield, April 28, 1861; see also: telegram from J. H. Clapp to Garfield, April 29, 1861; Garfield to his wife, April 28, 1861, all in the Garfield Papers, LC.
13. Reid, *Ohio in the War*, I, 35; Garfield to J. H. Rhodes, April 30, 1861; Garfield to Governor Dennison, May 3, 1861, both in the Garfield Papers, LC.
14. Shurtleff, "Year with the Rebels," pp. 389-90; Reid, *Ohio in the War*, I, 833; Wm. Bouler to Garfield, April 29, 1861; Garfield to his wife, May 5, 1861; L. W. Hall to Garfield, May 6, 1861, Garfield Papers, LC.
15. Garfield to J. H. Clapp, June 28, 1861; see also Wm. Bascom to Garfield, May 20, 1861 and memo of May [20?] of a proposed staff of the 19th Ohio which lists Garfield as colonel, all in the Garfield Papers, LC.
16. *Portage Sentinel*, May 29, 1861.
17. Wm. Bascom to Garfield June [11?], 1861; Garfield to Governor Dennison, June 18, 1861, both in the Garfield Papers, LC.
18. Garfield to Harmon Austin, June 28, 1861, Garfield Papers, LC; Garfield to B. A. Hinsdale, July 12, 1861, Garfield Papers, WRHS. A colonel was paid $218 a month, plus rations for himself, servants and two horses. He had to furnish his own uniform.
19. Garfield to B. A. Hinsdale, July 12, 1861, Garfield Papers, WRHS; Governor Dennison to Garfield, July 27, 1861, Garfield Papers, LC.
20. J. H. Rhodes to Garfield, 1861, n.d., Garfield Papers, LC; Henry,

Captain Henry, pp. 92, 101; Mason, *42nd Ohio*, pp. 42-43; Garfield, "My Campaign," p. 526; Squire, *A Few Recollections*, p. 15.

21. Henry, *Captain Henry*, p. 101. For sketches of Sheldon and Pardee see, Mason, *42nd Ohio*, pp. 21-35.

22. Garfield to his wife, November 4, 1861, Garfield Papers, LC.

23. *Ibid.*, August 22, 1861; see also, Garfield to L. Day, August 30, 1861 and Garfield to "The Friends at Home," August 19, 1861, all in the Garfield Papers, LC.

24. Garfield, "My Campaign," p. 525; Garfield to "The Friends at Home," August 19, 1861; Garfield to J. H. Rhodes, August 31, 1861, both in the Garfield Papers, LC.

25. Henry, *Captain Henry*, p. 102; Mason, *42nd Ohio*, p. 43.

26. Garfield, "My Campaign," pp. 526-27; Garfield to J. H. Rhodes, August 31, 1861, Garfield Papers, LC.

27. Garfield to his wife, September 28, 1861, "4 o'clock a.m.," Garfield Papers, LC; Mason, *42nd Ohio*, p. 43.

28. Mason, *42nd Ohio*, p. 29.

29. Garfield to J. H. Rhodes, October 26, 1861, Garfield Papers, LC.

30. See, Lamar, *Memoirs of Errett*, I, 247.

31. J. H. Rhodes to Garfield, October 16, 1861, Garfield Papers, LC.

32. Garfield to his wife, December 9, 1861; Garfield to J. H. Rhodes, August 31, 1861, both in Garfield Papers, LC. Much to his dismay, Garfield discovered that since his pay dated only from the time his regiment was finally completed, he had donated his services to his country for over four months. Garfield to his wife, November 23, 1861, Garfield Papers, LC.

33. Bond, *Under the Flag of the Nation*, pp. 12-13; see also Mason, *42nd Ohio*, p. 46.

7. The Hero of the Sandy Valley

1. Nicolay and Hay, *Works of Lincoln*, VI, 360. For a discussion of Kentucky's "neutrality" see Coulter, *Civil War in Kentucky*.

2. See the sketch of Buell in Reid, *Ohio in the War*, I, 695-724.

3. *War of the Rebellion: A Compilation of the Official Records of the Union and Confederate Armies*, Ser. 1, IV, 225-30. Hereafter cited as *O.R.*; since all citations, unless otherwise noted, are to series 1, the series number will be omitted.

4. Garfield to J. H. Rhodes, December 17, 1861; see also Garfield to his wife, December 16, 1861, both in Garfield Papers, LC.

5. Garfield to his wife, December 16, 1861, 11:45 p.m., Garfield Papers, LC.

6. Garfield, "My Campaign," p. 527. This account must be used with care since it was a hastily dictated memoir prepared for political publicity. The dates are incorrect, as are many of the details.

7. *Ibid.*, pp. 527-28.

8. *O.R.*, VII, 22-23, 25-27, 503-04; Garfield to his wife, December 16, 1861, 11:45 p.m., Garfield Papers, LC.

9. Garfield to J. H. Rhodes, December 17, 1861; Garfield to his wife, December 20, 1861, both in the Garfield Papers, LC; Garfield, "My Campaign," p. 528.

10. Bond, *Under the Flag*, pp. 13-14.

11. Mason, *42nd Ohio*, pp. 53-55.

12. *Ibid.*, pp. 54, 55-57; Bond, *Under the Flag*, pp. 14-15.

13. Garfield to his mother, January 26, 1861, Garfield Papers, LC; Mason, *42nd Ohio*, p. 55; Garfield, "My Campaign," p. 529.

14. Humphrey Marshall to Alexander Stephens, December 13, 1861, Humphrey Marshall Papers, Filson Club, Louisville, Ky. I am indebted to Mr. Jon Kaliebe who kindly allowed me to examine an unpublished paper, "The Big Sandy Campaign," from which this and other references to the Marshall Papers are taken.

15. Johnson and Buel, *Battles and Leaders*, I, 397; *O.R.*, IV, 495; VII, 43.

16. Kaliebe, "Big Sandy Campaign"; Johnson and Buel, *Battles and Leaders*, I, 394; Shakers cited in Eaton, *History of the Confederacy*, p. 95.

17. *O.R.*, VII, 43, 45; Johnson and Buel, *Battles and Leaders*, I, 395-97; Humphrey Marshall to Alexander Stephens, December 23, 1861, Marshall Papers, Filson Club.

18. *O.R.*, VII, 43. Marshall's recruiting efforts were disappointing. As he later disgustedly observed, "It was wonderful to see how ignorant, how apathetic, how utterly unconscious of the despotism which guarded their moral nature these people were. . . . Some times they would join a company and desert before they had marched twenty miles." *O.R.*, LII, pt. 2, 284; Johnson and Buel, *Battles and Leaders*, I, 394.

19. *O.R.*, VII, 46.

20. *Ibid.*, 25-26, 27, 32; Garfield, "My Campaign," p. 529; Garfield to his wife, January 1, 1862, Garfield Papers, LC.

21. Garfield to Wallace Ford, February 14, 1862, DeCoppett Collection; Garfield to his wife, January 1 and 13, 1862, Garfield Papers, LC.

22. Reid, *Ohio in the War*, I, 747n; *O.R.*, VII, 26.

23. *O.R.*, VII, 27-28; Mason, *42nd Ohio*, pp. 59-60; Garfield, "My Campaign," pp. 530-31; Garfield to his wife, January 18, 1862, Garfield Papers, LC.

24. Garfield to his wife, January 13, 1862, Garfield Papers, LC.

25. *Ibid.*; Bond, *Under the Flag*, p. 17; Mason, *42nd Ohio*, p. 65; *O.R.*, VII, 28.

26. Garfield to his wife, January 13, 1862, Garfield Papers, LC; *O.R.*, VII, 28-30; Bond, *Under the Flag*, p. 18.

27. Garfield to his wife, January 26, 1862, Garfield Papers, LC; Mason, *42nd Ohio*, p. 67.

28. *O.R.*, VII, 52.

29. *Ibid.*, 30; Garfield to his wife, January 13, 1862, Garfield Papers, LC; Mason, *42nd Ohio*, p. 67.

30. Garfield to his wife, January 13, 1862, Garfield Papers, LC; *O.R.*, VII, 56.

31. Garfield to his wife, January 13, 1862, Garfield Papers, LC; Mason, *42nd Ohio*, p. 69; see also: *O.R.*, VII, 46-48; Johnson and Buel, *Battles and Leaders*, I, 396.

32. Henry, *Captain Henry*, p. 113; *O.R.*, VII, 56.

33. Garfield to his wife, January 13, 1862, Garfield Papers, LC; Mason, *42nd Ohio*, pp. 72-73; Henry, *Captain Henry*, pp. 113-14.

34. Garfield to his wife, January 13, 1862, Garfield Papers, LC; *O.R.*, VII, 31.

35. Garfield to his wife, January 13, 1862, Garfield Papers, LC; *O.R.*, VII, 29, 31; Henry, *Captain Henry*, p. 113; Bond, *Under the Flag*, p. 19; Marshall's estimate is in *O.R.*, VII, 48.

36. Garfield to his mother, January 26, 1862, Garfield Papers, LC; Howells, *Years of My Youth*, pp. 205-06.

37. Speech at the Cleveland Sanitary Fair, February 22, 1864, in *Portage County Democrat*, March 2, 1864; Lerner, *Mind and Faith of Holmes*, p. 16.

38. *O.R.*, VII, 31, 56; Bond, *Under the Flag*, p. 19; Proclamation cited in Smith, *Life and Letters of Garfield*, I, 193.

39. J. H. Rhodes to Garfield, February 6, 1862 and January 6, 1862 [incorrectly dated 1861], both in Garfield Papers, LC; *O.R.*, VII, 23; see copy of petition of Ohio Senate to President Lincoln, February 3, 1862 in Garfield Papers, LC.

40. *Cleveland Herald*, January 16, 1862; other newspaper comments collected by J. H. Rhodes and cited in letter to Garfield, January 20, 1862, Garfield Papers, LC. As the legend of the battle grew, even more fanciful accounts were elaborated until it became (in print at least) one of the major engagements of the war. As one chronicler declared: "It was a wonderful battle. In the history of the late war there is not another like it. Measured by the forces engaged, the valor displayed, and the results that followed, it throws into the shade the achievements of even the mighty hosts which saved the nation. Eleven hundred footsore and weary men, without cannon, charged up a rocky hill, over stumps, over stones, over fallen trees, over high entrenchments, right into the face of five thousand fresh troops, with twelve pieces of artillery!" Kirke, *On the Border*, p. 256.

41. *O.R.*, VII, 56; see also 46-48, 55-57; Johnson and Buel, *Battles and Leaders*, I, 396.

42. *O.R.*, VII, 48-50.

43. *Ibid.*, 57-58; Marshall to Alexander Stephens, February 22, 1862, Marshall Papers, Filson Club.

44. Mason, *42nd Ohio*, pp. 88-89; Garfield to J. H. Rhodes, February 12, 1862, Garfield Papers, LC; Coulter, *Civil War in Kentucky*, pp. 139-46.

45. Garfield to J. H. Rhodes, February 12, 1862, Garfield Papers, LC. This incident forms the basis of a novel by Richard Schuster, *The Selfish and the Strong*.

630

46. *O.R.*, X, pt. 2, 68; Proclamation in *O.R.*, VII, 33.
47. Garfield to J. H. Rhodes, February 12, 1862, Garfield Papers, LC.
48. Garfield to his wife, January 26, 1862, *ibid.* The Kentucky troops did not share in the general enthusiasm for Garfield. Resentful of his apparent preference for Ohio soldiers, these Kentuckians had quite different notions of his doings hereafter, as can be gathered from a toast popular at their gatherings: "Gen. Garfield and Major Pardee—May their souls be in Hell together." Unsigned note dated April 16, 1862, *ibid.*
49. Garfield to J. H. Rhodes, February 12, 1862, *ibid.*
50. Garfield to his wife, January 26, 1862, *ibid.*; see also Mason, *42nd Ohio*, pp. 78-79.
51. Garfield to his wife, February 15 and February 23, 1862, Garfield Papers, LC; Mason, *42nd Ohio*, pp. 82-83; *O.R.*, VII, 663.
52. Garfield to his wife, February 23, 1862, Garfield Papers, LC.
53. *Ibid.*, March 10, 1862; Henry, *Captain Henry*, p. 121.
54. Donald, *Inside Lincoln's Cabinet*, 159-60; Garfield to J. H. Rhodes, March 3, 1862, Garfield Papers, LC.
55. Garfield to Rhodes, *ibid.*; to J. Q. Smith, February 15, 1862; to his wife, February 12, 1862, all in the Garfield Papers, LC.
56. Mason, *42nd Ohio*, pp. 80-86; Bond, *Under the Flag*, pp. 20-23; *O.R.*, X, pt. 1, 33-34; Garfield to his wife, March 19, 1862, Garfield Papers, LC.
57. *O.R.*, X, pt. 1, 34; Mason, *42nd Ohio*, p. 86; Garfield to his wife, March 19, 1862, Garfield Papers, LC.
58. *O.R.*, X, pt. 1, 34-36, 41-42.
59. *Ibid.*, pt. 2, 59; Mason, *42nd Ohio*, p. 90.

8. AT THE FRONT

1. Garfield to F. A. Williams, April 16, in Norris and Martin, "Three Letters," p. 250.
2. Hinman, *Sherman Brigade*, p. 135. Harker would soon win his chance to exercise leadership. After Garfield left the 20th Brigade, Harker resumed command, leading the brigade with distinction until he fell at Kenesaw Mountain. See, Reid, *Ohio in the War*, I, 917-18.
3. Garfield to F. A. Williams, April 16, 1862, in Norris and Martin, "Three Letters," p. 250; Garfield to his wife, April 4, 1862, in Smith, *Life and Letters of Garfield*, I, 206.
4. Hinman, *Sherman Brigade*, pp. 136-39; Wm. M. Farrar to Garfield, April 5, 1879, Garfield Papers, LC.
5. Hinman, *Sherman Brigade*, p. 145.
6. Garfield to F. A. Williams, April 16, 1862, in Norris and Martin, "Three Letters," p. 250.
7. Hinman, *Sherman Brigade*, pp. 146-49, 161; Garfield to his mother, May 6, 1862, Garfield Papers, LC.
8. Hinman, *Sherman Brigade*, p. 205.
9. Garfield to F. A. Williams, July 2, 1862, in Norris and Martin,

"Three Letters," p. 251; see also, Garfield to J. H. Rhodes, June 10, 1862, Garfield Papers, LC.

10. Garfield to J. H. Rhodes, October 5 and May 1, 1862, Garfield Papers, LC.

11. Garfield to F. A. Williams, July 2, 1862, in Norris and Martin, "Three Letters," p. 251.

12. Garfield to J. H. Rhodes, May 1, 1862, Garfield Papers, LC.

13. J. H. Rhodes to Garfield, May 9 and 26, 1862, *ibid.*

14. Garfield to his wife, July 5, 1862; Garfield to J. H. Rhodes, June 10, 1862; see also Garfield to Harmon Austin, June 25, 1862, all in the Garfield Papers, LC.

15. Garfield to J. H. Rhodes, May 28 and June 10, 1862, Garfield Papers, LC.

16. Garfield to his wife, July 5, 1862; to J. H. Rhodes, May 19 and June 10, 1862; to Harmon Austin, June 25, 1862, all in the Garfield Papers, LC.

17. Letter from "P" in *Ashtabula Weekly Telegraph*, July 19, 1862; J. H. Rhodes to Garfield [July 1862 ?]; Garfield to J. H. Rhodes, July 24, 1862, both in Garfield Papers, LC.

18. Garfield to J. H. Rhodes, June 10, 1862, *ibid.*; T. H. Williams, *Beauregard*, p. 196; Hinman, *Sherman Brigade*, pp. 205-33.

19. Garfield to D. G. Swaim, July 20, 1862, WRHS; Garfield to his wife, July 15, 1862, Garfield Papers, LC.

20. Garfield to his wife, July 5, 1862, Garfield Papers, LC; Memoirs of Thomas C. Donaldson, March 31, 1879 (typed copy), HML.

21. *Cong. Globe*, 38 Cong., 1 sess., 846; Fleming, *Civil War in Alabama*, p. 83; Garfield to J. H. Rhodes, May 1, 1862, Garfield Papers, LC.

22. Garfield to Harmon Austin, June 25, 1862, Garfield Papers, LC.

23. Garfield to his wife, June 23, 1862. Garfield sent one of these contraband to Hiram to be a house servant, but he could not adjust to Ohio and eventually returned to the South.

24. Garfield to Harmon Austin, June 25, 1862, *ibid.* According to Garfield, he was the first Union commander to refuse to obey such an order. See, Reid, *Ohio in the War*, I, 762.

25. Garfield to J. H. Rhodes, July 9, 1862, in Smith, *Life and Letters of Garfield*, I, 228; for the Turchin court martial see, *O.R.*, XVI, pt. 2, 273-78; Turchin's explanation is in Garfield to his wife, July 17, 1862, Garfield Papers, LC. Thanks to Lincoln, Turchin escaped the consequences of his dismissal. The President appointed him Brigadier of Volunteers, effective the day before the trial. Turchin thus not only circumvented dismissal, but received a promotion to boot. See Keifer, *Slavery and Four Years of War*, I, 280-81.

26. Garfield to C. E. Fuller, September 5, 1862, Fuller, *Reminiscences*, p. 330; see also a medical report dated August 4, 1862 in the Garfield Papers, LC. A medical acquaintance has suggested to me that Garfield's ailment was probably infectious hepatitis. Bed rest, he says, is the only remedy, but even after thorough rest the disease could conceivably linger

for years, recurring during times of stress. This could explain Garfield's chronic ill-health in later years.

27. Garfield to his wife, September 27, 1862, Garfield Papers, LC.

28. Garfield to his mother, September 2, 1862, *ibid.* Strictly speaking, this was a Union Party, rather than a Republican, convention. But in the 19th Ohio ("The old Giddings' district," as newspapers still called it years after Giddings's death), the antislavery tradition was so strong that even the Union Party wore a radical guise. The call for the Garrettsville convention lacked the compromising spirit which usually characterized Union party pronouncements in 1862. It summoned "all who regard the preservation of the Government as of more importance than the preservation of slavery," and urged the confiscation of rebel property and the liberation of their slaves. See *Ashtabula Weekly Telegraph*, August 9, 1862.

29. Garfield to Ralph Plumb, September 2, 1862, Smith, *Life and Letters of Garfield*, I, 234.

30. *Portage County Democrat*, September 10, 1862; Garfield to C. E. Fuller, September 5, 1862, in Fuller, *Reminiscences*, p. 330.

31. *Portage County Democrat*, September 17, October 8 and 29, 1862; *Ashtabula Weekly Telegraph*, October 4, 1862; Porter, "Ohio Politics During the Civil War," p. 108. The vote by counties was:

County	Garfield	Woods
Trumbull	3,382	1,800
Ashtabula	3,358	764
Portage	2,420	1,753
Mahoning	2,187	2,075
Geauga	1,941	371
	13,288	6,763

32. Garfield to Ralph Plumb, September 2, 1862; Smith, *Life and Letters of Garfield*, I, 234.

9. AT THE CAPITAL

1. Ames, *Ten Years in Washington*, p. 67; Brooks, *Washington*, p. 14; Leech, *Reveille in Washington*, p. 121.

2. Garfield to his wife, September 20, 1862, Garfield Papers, LC; Garfield to J. H. Rhodes, October 5, 1862, in Smith, *Life and Letters of Garfield*, I, 240.

3. Donald, *Inside Lincoln's Cabinet*, pp. 101-02; Garfield to J. H. Rhodes, September 22, 1862, Garfield Papers, LC.

4. Donald, *Inside Lincoln's Cabinet*, pp. 159-60; Wade cited in Dennet, *Diaries and Letters of John Hay*, p. 53; Garfield to his wife, September 20, 1862, Garfield Papers, LC.

5. Donald, *Inside Lincoln's Cabinet*, pp. 167-68; Garfield to J. H. Rhodes, September 26, 1862, Garfield Papers, LC.

6. Garfield to B. A. Hinsdale, October 13, 1862, Garfield Papers, WRHS.

7. Garfield to his wife, September 27, 1862, Garfield Papers, LC.

8. *Ibid.*, January 2, 1863 [incorrectly dated 1862]; Speech of July 25, 1870, Garfield, *Works*, I, 596-97.

9. Garfield to B. A. Hinsdale, October 30, 1862, Garfield Papers, WRHS.

10. Garfield to J. H. Rhodes, September 26, 1862, Garfield Papers, LC.

11. *Ibid.*, October 5, 1862; Garfield to J. W. Schuckers, April 20, 1874; Garfield to his wife, October 12 and November 16, 1862, all in the Garfield Papers, LC.

12. J. W. Schuckers to Garfield, October 19, 1873; Garfield to Schuckers, April 20, 1874, *ibid.*

13. Garfield to J. H. Rhodes, November 2, December 7 and 14, 1862, *ibid.*

14. Chase cited in Sharkey, *Money, Class, and Party*, p. 20; Garfield to J. W. Schuckers, April 20, 1874, Garfield Papers, LC.

15. Garfield to his wife, October 3, 1862, Garfield Papers, LC; Garfield to R. Plumb, October 8, 1862, in Smith, *Life and Letters of Garfield*, I, 248.

16. Garfield to his wife, September 27, 1862, Garfield Papers, LC; Donald, *Inside Lincoln's Cabinet*, pp. 161-62.

17. Garfield to H. Austin, October 14, 1862, Garfield Papers, LC.

18. *Ibid.*, September 25, 1862; Garfield to B. A. Hinsdale, October 13, 1862, Garfield Papers, WRHS; Oberholtzer, *Jay Cooke*, I, 437-38.

19. Garfield to R. Plumb, October 8, 1862, Smith, *Life and Letters of Garfield*, I, 248; Garfield to his wife, October 3, 1862; Garfield to J. H. Rhodes, October 26, 1862, both in the Garfield Papers, LC.

20. Garfield to his wife, October 19, 24, November 5, 1862, Garfield Papers, LC.

21. That the affair with Mrs. Calhoun took place at this time and in this fashion is a supposition on my part based on hints in the Garfield papers. Only in October of 1862, it would seem, did Garfield have both the motive and the opportunity. In 1867 Garfield recovered all the incriminating papers on the matter and presumably destroyed them. Although he cautiously avoided discussing the subject overtly in his correspondence, allusions can be found in letters to his wife of July 7, 8 and December 2, 1867.

22. Lucretia to James Garfield, July 7, 1867; Garfield to his wife, December 26, 1862, January 6, 1863, Garfield Papers, LC.

23. Garfield to B. A. Hinsdale, October 30, 1862, Garfield Papers, WRHS; Garfield to his wife, October 24, 1862, Garfield Papers, LC.

24. Garfield to his wife, October 7, 12 and 31, 1862, Garfield Papers, LC.

25. *Ibid.*, November 5, 1862.

26. Garfield to J. H. Rhodes, November 10, 1862; see also Garfield to his wife, November 7, 1862, both in Garfield Papers, LC.

27. Garfield to his wife, November 16 and 21, 1862, Garfield Papers,

LC; Garfield to B. A. Hinsdale, December 1, 1862, Garfield Papers, WRHS; Hay cited in Eisenschiml, *Case of Fitz-John Porter*, p. 241.

28. Garfield to J. H. Rhodes, December 24, 1862, Garfield Papers, LC.

29. Garfield to his wife, October 3, 1862, *ibid.*

30. Eisenschiml, *Case of Fitz-John Porter*, p. 73; Porter cited in Nevins, *Ordeal of the Union*, VI, 173. One West Pointer, General W. W. Morris of the regular army, was originally named to the court but he was quickly replaced with a volunteer officer.

31. Ed. P. Brooks to Garfield, April 15, 1878; Benj. Prentiss to Garfield, February 11, 1880, Garfield Papers, LC.

32. Garfield to John Pope, December 22, 1869, *ibid.* Porter's subsequent bitterness towards Garfield can be gauged by a story, believed by the Porter family for generations, to the effect that during the trial Garfield threw his arm around Porter's shoulder and assured him he had no need to worry. Eisenschiml, *Case of Fitz-John Porter*, pp. 309-10.

33. Benj. Prentiss to Garfield, February 11, 1880, Garfield Papers, LC.

34. Garfield to J. H. Rhodes, December 14, 1862, *ibid.*

35. Garfield to B. A. Hinsdale, December 16, 1862, Garfield Papers, WRHS.

36. Preface to Garfield's unpublished edition of Frederick the Great's works, in Smith, *Life and Letters of Garfield*, I, 267; Garfield to B. A. Hinsdale, January 6, 1863, Garfield Papers, WRHS; Garfield to J. H. Rhodes, December 14, 1862; Garfield to his wife, January 9, 1863, both in the Garfield Papers, LC.

37. Garfield to his wife, December 19 and December 26, 1862, Garfield Papers, LC.

38. *Ibid.*, January 6 and 9, 1863; Garfield to Chase, January 14, 1863, unidentified newspaper clipping in Garfield Papers, LC.

10. BOBBING AROUND

1. Garfield to his wife, January 25, 1863, Garfield Papers, LC; Reid, *Ohio in the War*, I, 347; Nicolay and Hay, *Works of Lincoln*, IX, 107; VIII, 173.

2. Villard, *Memoirs*, II, 66; Reid, *Ohio in the War*, I, 349; Kirke, *Down in Tennessee*, p. 12; Dana, *Recollections*, p. 128; H. A. Alden to Garfield, March 7, 1876, Garfield Papers, LC.

3. Garfield to his wife, January 25 and 26, 1863, Garfield Papers, LC.

4. *Ibid.*, February 13, 1863; Gilmore, *Personal Recollections*, p. 123.

5. Garfield to J. H. Rhodes, January 27, 1863; to his wife, January 26, 1863; to his mother, March 22, 1863, all in the Garfield Papers, LC.

6. Garfield to J. H. Rhodes, February 14, January 27, 1863; Garfield to his wife, February 1, 1863, *ibid.*

7. Garfield to S. P. Chase, February 15, 1863, unidentified newspaper clipping in *ibid.*; see also Smith, *Life and Letters of Garfield*, I, 276.

8. Garfield to W. S. Rosecrans, March 1864, in Lamers, *Edge of Glory,* p. 418; Garfield to his wife, February 22, 1863, Garfield Papers, LC.

9. Garfield to J. H. Rhodes, February 14, 1863, Garfield Papers, LC.

10. Garfield to R. Plumb, September 2, 1863, in Smith, *Life and Letters of Garfield,* I, 234.

11. Garfield to H. Austin, September 25, 1862, *ibid.,* p. 276; B. F. Wade to Garfield, February 20, 1863; Edward Bates to Garfield, February 21, 1863; Garfield to his wife, February 22, 1863, Garfield Papers, LC.

12. L. A. Sheldon to Garfield, November 14, 1863; Garfield to his wife, February 26, 1863, both in the Garfield Papers, LC.

13. Beatty, *Memoirs,* pp. 176, 191, 193-96; [Fitch], *Annals of Army of the Cumberland,* pp. 257-63; Reid, *Ohio in the War,* I, 347n; Gilmore, *Personal Recollections,* p. 118; Villard, *Memoirs,* II, 66.

14. Kirke, *Down in Tennessee,* p. 198.

15. Beatty, *Memoirs,* pp. 169, 239; Stanley, *Personal Memoirs,* pp. 135-37, 158-59.

16. Garfield to C. E. Fuller, May 4, 1863, in Fuller, *Reminiscences,* p. 336.

17. Garfield to his wife, February 1, 1863, Garfield Papers, LC; Reid, *Ohio in the War,* I, 751-52, 806-09; Beatty, *Memoirs,* pp. 176, 218.

18. "Bobbing" in Tucker, *Chickamauga,* p. 31; Garfield to S. P. Chase, April 12, 1863, unidentified newspaper clipping, Garfield Papers, LC.

19. S. P. Chase to Garfield, May 31, 1863, Garfield Papers, LC; Garfield to James R. Gilmore, June 17, 1863, in McMurty, "Jaquess-Gilmore Mission," p. 20.

20. Gilmore, *Personal Recollections,* 100-03, 145-46. Albert Gallatin Riddle, in his *Life of Jas. A. Garfield* (p. 69), tells a different story—that Gilmore first approached Garfield with Greeley's plan to make Rosecrans president and that Garfield "gave it such emphatic discouragement that it is believed no whisper of it ever reached Rosecrans. . . ." According to Riddle, Garfield argued "that it would be ruinous to the usefulness of his general; that it could not succeed; that it ought not to. Kirk [Gilmore] was convinced, and the idea was abandoned." As a general rule, Riddle's word is more reliable than Gilmore's but in this instance I have chosen to follow Gilmore for these reasons: (1) Gilmore was there; Riddle received the story from Garfield at second hand. (2) Riddle heard the story many years later; Gilmore claimed his version was based on notes taken down within half an hour of the incident. (3) Gilmore's version is consistent with Garfield's attitudes and later activities on behalf of Rosecrans. In 1864 Garfield would urge Rosecrans's name for the vice-presidential nomination. Rosecrans would refuse, as he generally refused political bids, including a later nomination for governor of Ohio. (4) It seems highly unlikely that Gilmore would abandon a mission assigned him by his employer on nothing more substantial than the objections of a brigadier general. He was sent to sound out Rosecrans for the presidency; he could not very well return without having done just that.

21. Ridpath, *Life of Garfield*, p. 127; J. Vallandingham, *Life of Clement Vallandingham*, pp. 297-300; Garfield to B. A. Hinsdale, May 26, 1863, in M. Hinsdale, *Garfield-Hinsdale Letters*, pp. 67-68.

22. Garfield to B. A. Hinsdale, September 12, 1862, in Smith, *Life and Letters of Garfield*, I, 237. For essays on the influence of Jomini, see T. H. Williams, "Military Leadership of North and South," in Donald, *Why the North Won the Civil War*, and Donald, "Refighting the Civil War," in *Lincoln Reconsidered*.

23. Garfield to S. P. Chase, May 3, 1863, unidentified newspaper clipping, Garfield Papers, LC; Garfield to C. E. Fuller, May 4, 1863, Fuller, *Reminiscences*, p. 337.

24. K. P. Williams, *Lincoln Finds a General*, V, 143, 209, 211; Reid, *Ohio in the War*, I, 335-37.

25. Garfield to his wife, May 12, 1863; Garfield to H. Austin, March 25, 1863, both in the Garfield Papers, LC.

26. Garfield to S. P. Chase, May 3, 1863, unidentified newspaper clipping, *ibid.*; K. P. Williams, *Lincoln Finds a General*, V, 184-94; *O.R.*, XXIII, pt. 1, 285-93; Lincoln to Chase, May 12, 1863, Warden, *Chase*, p. 528; Stanley, *Personal Memoirs*, pp. 131-32.

27. Villard, *Memoirs*, II, 66-68.

28. Garfield to J. H. Rhodes, June 11, 1863; Garfield to his wife, June 14, 1863, both in the Garfield Papers, LC; Garfield to S. P. Chase, July 27, 1863, in Garfield, *Works*, I, 773 (letter reprinted from *New York Sun*, June 12, 1882).

29. Garfield to J. H. Rhodes, June 11, 1863, Garfield Papers, LC.

30. Garfield to his wife, June 14, 1863, *ibid.*; Villard, *Memoirs*, II, 70.

31. A reasonably accurate estimate. Bragg himself calculated that his troops numbered 46,665, Johnson and Buel, *Battles and Leaders*, III, 635.

32. Garfield's report can be found in Reid, *Ohio in the War*, I, 753-56.

33. Stanley, *Personal Memoirs*, p. 142; Crittenden cited in Reid, *Ohio in the War*, I, 756; for objections of General Wood, see *O.R.*, XXIII, pt. 1, 433-34.

11. To the River of Death

1. Garfield to S. P. Chase, July 27, 1863, in Garfield, *Works*, I, 773.

2. Garfield to his wife, July 18 and August 23, 1863, Garfield Papers, LC; Rosecrans cited in *O.R.*, XXIII, pt. 1, 40. The parallels between the Tullahoma campaign and the Sandy Valley campaign were suggested by Mr. Richard Shuster.

3. Garfield to his wife, June 29, 1863, Garfield Papers, LC; *O.R.*, XXIII, pt. 1, 621-22.

4. K. P. Williams, *Lincoln Finds a General*, V, 231, 233; Garfield to S. P. Chase, July 27, 1863, in Garfield, *Works*, I, 773.

5. Garfield to his wife, July 18, 1863, Garfield Papers, LC; Reid,

Ohio in the War, I, 756, 337; McKinney, *Education in Violence*, p. 224. A full account of the Tullahoma campaign can be found in K. P. Williams, *Lincoln Finds a General*, V, 216-38. In contrast, the description in Johnson and Buel, *Battles and Leaders*, III, 635-37, although short, contains more than its share of errors.

6. Garfield to his wife, August 1, 1863; W. S. Rosecrans to Garfield, April 1, 1880; Garfield to J. H. Rhodes, August 11, 1863, all in the Garfield Papers, LC.

7. Garfield to S. P. Chase, July 27, 1863, in Garfield, *Works*, I, 773.

8. Rosecrans cited in Smith, *Life and Letters of Garfield*, II, 869; Stanley, *Personal Memoirs*, p. 159.

9. In K. P. Williams, *Lincoln Finds a General*, V, 240.

10. Johnson and Buel, *Battles and Leaders*, III, 641n.

11. Tucker, *Chickamauga*, p. 16; Beatty, *Memoirs*, pp. 229, 231; Garfield to his wife, August 23, September 1, 1863, Garfield Papers, LC.

12. Garfield to his wife, August 23, 1863, Garfield Papers, LC; Beatty, *Memoirs*, p. 230.

13. Garfield to R. Plumb, September 3, 1863, in Smith, *Life and Letters of Garfield*, I, 318; Hazen, *Narrative*, p. 120; Hill cited in Johnson and Buel, *Battles and Leaders*, III, 643.

14. Gracie, *Truth About Chickamauga*, p. 150; Granger cited in Lamers, *Edge of Glory*, p. 443; Dana, *Recollections*, pp. 107-09.

15. Garfield to J. H. Rhodes, September 13, 1863; Garfield to his wife, September 16, 1863, both in the Garfield Papers, LC; McKinney, *Education in Violence*, p. 225. A less prophetic, more prosaic translation of Chickamauga might be "stagnant waters," Tucker, *Chickamauga*, p. 122.

16. Dana, *Recollections*, p. 111; *New York Herald*, September 29, 1863, in Smith, *Life and Letters of Garfield*, I, 324; Tucker, *Chickamauga*, pp. 123-25; Dana's report in *O.R.*, XXX, pt. 1, 191.

17. Dana, *Recollections*, pp. 111-13.

18. K. P. Williams, *Lincoln Finds a General*, V, 255-57; Tucker, *Chickamauga*, pp. 211-17; Lamers, *Edge of Glory*, pp. 336-37.

19. Garfield later said that the order to Wood was the only order from headquarters issued during the battle that he did not write, Smith, *Life and Letters of Garfield*, II, 961, but a glance at the *O.R.*, e.g., XXX, pt. 1, 139, demonstrates that his memory was faulty.

20. Granger cited in K. P. Williams, *Lincoln Finds a General*, V, 202; *O.R.*, XXX, pt. 1, 103, 983-84.

21. Garfield to J. H. Rhodes, May 1, 1862, Garfield Papers, LC; *O.R.*, XXX, pt. 1, 103.

22. *O.R.*, XXX, pt. 1, 647; Dana, *Recollections*, p. 115; Cox, *Military Reminiscences*, II, 9-10.

23. Fiske, *Mississippi Valley in the Civil War*, p. 277n.

24. Dennett, *Diaries and Letters of John Hay*, p. 110; Cox, *Military Reminiscences*, II, 10. Rosecrans told a very different story. In sworn testimony before a congressional committee in 1865, he implied that he was

aware that Thomas still held his ground and that he sent Garfield to the front, while he went to Chattanooga, only because the business at Chattanooga was too complex for Garfield to handle. Sen. Doc. # 142, 38 Cong., 2 sess., pt. iii, 31-32.

In later years his memory grew even more specific and he was able to recall the exact conversation held twenty-five years earlier. According to his account, *Rosecrans told Garfield*, "By the sound of battle we hold our own," and he ordered him to Chattanooga. Garfield protested, claiming that he was unable to deal with all the complicated orders Rosecrans gave him, and so Rosecrans had to deliver them himself, sending Garfield to transact the simpler business at the front. Smith, *Life and Letters of Garfield*, II, 874. The implication was that Garfield was not only incompetent but that he tricked his chief out of the glory that was properly due him.

Garfield never contradicted his chief publicly, but he did tell his story in various private conversations, and it is this version which I have followed. See: Villard, *Memoirs*, II, 157, 185-86; Cox, *Military Reminiscences*, II, 9-10; Dennett, *Diaries and Letters of John Hay*, p. 109-10; Nicolay and Hay, *Lincoln*, VIII, 102; and *Harper's Pictorial History*, II, 548-49, which contains a vivid description based on Garfield's own testimony, as can be inferred from a letter from its author, H. A. Alden, to Garfield, March 7, 1864, Garfield Papers, LC.

Rosecrans's version is compared with Garfield's and convincingly refuted by T. C. Smith in his *Life and Letters of Garfield*, II, 845-85. See also his monograph, "General Garfield at Chickamauga," pp. 268-80.

25. This account of Garfield's ride is based on that in Ridpath, *Life and Work of Garfield*, pp. 155-57. Support for all but the most romantic details of the ride can be found in T. J. McCall to Garfield, January 20, 1881, Garfield Papers, LC. McCall was Garfield's orderly.

26. *Harper's Pictorial History*, II, 548-49; Garfield, *Works*, I, 663; W. H. Forbes to Garfield, n.d.; Garfield to D. G. Swaim, April 11, 1870, letterbook copy, both in Garfield Papers, LC.

27. Beatty, *Memoirs*, pp. 253-54; *O.R.*, XXX, pt. 1, 144-45, 78.

28. Beatty, *Memoirs*, p. 256.

29. Garfield to his wife, September 23, 1863, Garfield Papers, LC. With one child ill and another on the way, Lucretia's feelings upon reading this letter can only be imagined. It seems to betray a certain insensitivity on Garfield's part.

30. Garfield to S. P. Chase, 11:23 a.m., September 23, 1863, unidentified newspaper clipping, Garfield Papers, LC; Warden, *Chase*, pp. 550-51; Thomas and Hyman, *Stanton*, pp. 285-89.

31. Johnson and Buel, *Battles and Leaders*, III, 634; Beatty, *Memoirs*, pp. 256, 258; Nicolay and Hay, *Works of Lincoln*, IX, 132; Dana, *Recollections*, p. 121.

32. *O.R.*, XXX, pt. 1, 201; pt. 4, 249; Villard, *Memoirs*, II, 185-86; Lamers, *Edge of Glory*, p. 387. A touch of sloppiness seems to have crept

into headquarters during the last few weeks of Garfield's tenure as chief of staff. When Garfield left Chattanooga, General Hazen noted with approval, "the method and style of headquarters was at once revolutionized. The floors were scrubbed, whisky-bottles put out of sight, business was done by daylight, and every one became hopeful." Hazen, *Narrative*, p. 151.

33. Smith, *Life and Letters of Garfield*, II, 881; Garfield to Rosecrans, October 23, 1863, in Lamers, *Edge of Glory*, p. 412; Rosecrans to Garfield, November 9, 1863, Garfield Papers, LC; Dennett, *Letters and Diaries of John Hay*, p. 115. See also Garfield to Rosecrans, December 14, 1863, in Lamers, *Edge of Glory*, p. 413, which shows that even while Rosecrans was blaming Stanton he knew that the decison to remove him had been made by Grant.

34. Dana made a similar charge in 1874, see Smith, *Life and Letters of Garfield*, II, 863-64. Rosecrans to Garfield, February 3, 1880, December 20, 1879; Garfield to Rosecrans, January 19, 1880, clipping from *New York Herald*, n.d., in letterbook, Garfield Papers, LC.

35. Rosecrans to Garfield, February 3, 1880, *ibid.*; Smith, *Life and Letters of Garfield*, II, 869-72. Representative of the more extreme of these attacks on Garfield's character arising from the Rosecrans affair was this by Donn Piatt (who disliked Garfield for other reasons even before the Rosecrans scandal): "General Garfield was a soldierly looking man with a genial manner that won the confidence of the unwary. . . . With an oily tongue he wound his way into the affections of a man whose one great defect was his credulous trust in men about him. . . . James A. Garfield was a man of intensely selfish nature, morally without courage, of an impulsive nature, uncontrolled by principle, with a continuous trend in the direction of wrong." Piatt, "The General Who Heard Mass," Part I, 35-36.

36. Montgomery Blair to Dana, March 18, 1882, Schuckers Papers, LC; see also Smith, *Life and Letters of Garfield*, II, 872.

37. Montgomery Blair to Rosecrans, September 21, 1880, in Lamers, *Edge of Glory*, pp. 412-13; Montgomery Blair to Dana, March 18, 1882, Schuckers Papers, LC; Riddle, *Life of Jas. A. Garfield*, p. 68.

38. *Toledo Commercial*, November 22, 1870; *O.R.*, XXX, pt. 1, 201-05, 218-19, 221; Dana, *Recollections*, pp. 124, 128, 132-33.

39. Garfield to R. Smith, October 5, 1874, in Smith, *Life and Letters of Garfield*, II, 864; Stanton to Watson, October 21, 1863, in Lamers, *Edge of Glory*, p. 411.

40. Garfield to Rosecrans, January 19, 1880, clipping from *New York Herald*, n.d., in letterbook, Garfield Papers, LC; Lamers, *Edge of Glory*, pp. 411-12; Dennett, *Letters and Diaries of John Hay*, pp. 109-10; see also Cox, *Military Reminiscences*, II, 8-9.

41. Baltimore speech in *Portage County Democrat*, November 18, 1863; Garfield to his wife, October 30, 1863, Garfield Papers, LC.

42. *Cincinnati Gazette*, in *Portage County Democrat*, November 11, 1863.

43. Garfield to his wife, January 6, 1863, Garfield Papers, LC; Gar-

field to C. E. Fuller, September 5, 1862, Fuller, *Reminiscences*, p. 330; Lucretia Garfield cited in Smith, *Life and Letters of Garfield*, II, 894.

44. Garfield to his wife, December 6, 1863, Garfield Papers, LC; Montgomery Blair to Rosecrans, September 21, 1880, in Lamers, *Edge of Glory*, p. 412; Garfield to Mark Hopkins [December, 1863], in Smith, *Life and Letters of Garfield*, I, 355; Brooks, *Washington*, p. 29.

12. PUSHING LINCOLN

1. Viator, *Washington Sketch Book*, p. 146; Brooks, *Washington*, p. 21; Ames, *Ten Years in Washington*, p. 110.

2. *Cong. Globe*, 41 Cong., 2 sess., 557, 3068. January 18 and April 28, 1870.

3. Garfield cited in Perry, *Williamstown*, p. 826; *Portage County Democrat* [July 1866], scrapbook clipping, Garfield Papers, LC.

4. Garfield to his wife, December 6, 1863, Garfield Papers, LC; Alexander, *History of the House of Representatives*, pp. 39-40. For details of the opening-day plot, see Dennett, *Diaries and Letters of John Hay*, p. 109.

5. Blaine, *Twenty Years of Congress*, I, 499; Garfield on Davis cited in Brooks, *Washington*, p. 28.

6. Brooks, *Washington*, p. 30; *Chicago Evening Journal*, n.d., scrapbook clipping in Garfield Papers, LC; Perry, *Williamstown*, pp. 825-26.

7. Biographical Notes, dictated by Garfield in June of 1880, Garfield Papers, LC; *Cong. Globe*, 38 Cong., 1 sess., 27, 109. December 21, 1863 and January 6, 1864. Before the bounty vote was announced another congressman did change his vote, making the total 112 yeas, 2 noes.

8. *Portage County Democrat*, January 13, 1864; *Cincinnati Commercial*, n.d., scrapbook clipping, Garfield Papers, LC.

9. Biographical Notes; Diary, September 6, 1850, both in Garfield Papers, LC; *Cong. Globe*, 38 Cong., 1 sess., 428. February 1, 1864.

10. *Cong. Globe*, 38 Cong., 1 sess., 285 (January 20, 1864); 2472 (May 25, 1864); 478; 574; *ibid.*, 2 sess., 1075 (February 24, 1865); Garfield, *Works*, I, 3-5; see also Rhodes, *History of the United States*, V, 263-73.

11. Garfield to B. A. Hinsdale, February 18, 1864, Garfield Papers, WRHS; *Cong. Globe*, 38 Cong., 2 sess., 1153-54; 1258.

12. Morse, *Diary of Gideon Welles*, II, 247 (February 22, 1865); Garfield to D. Gordon, April 19, 1872, letterbook copy, Garfield Papers, LC.

13. Garfield to his wife, December 6, 1863, Garfield Papers, LC; *Chicago Evening Journal*, n.d., scrapbook clipping, *ibid.*; Riddle, *Recollection of War Times*, pp. 253-54.

14. Garfield to his wife, December 21, 1863, Garfield Papers, LC; Garfield to D. G. Swaim, December 15, 1863, Garfield-Swaim Papers, WRHS.

15. Biographical Notes, Garfield Papers, LC.

16. Garfield to Harmon Austin, March 25, 1863, Garfield Papers, LC.

17. *Ibid.*, March 24, 1865; Garfield to S.E.M. Kneeland, *et al.*, April 7, 1865, Garfield Papers, WRHS.

18. Remonstrance of S.E.M. Kneeland and twenty others of Freedom, Ohio to Garfield, March 17, 1865, in *ibid.*; Garfield, *Works*, I, 31; *Cong. Globe*, 38 Cong., 1 sess., 3148. June 21, 1864.

19. Biographical Notes, Garfield Papers, LC; see also Robertson, "Lincoln and Congress."

20. Garfield, *Works*, I, 30-31; Garfield to W. C. Howells, June 18, 1864, Garfield Papers, LC.

'21. Garfield, *Works*, I, 12-13, 15.

22. *Ibid.*, 1-18.

23. Garfield to his wife, May 29, 1864, Garfield Papers, LC; *Cong. Globe*, 38 Cong., 2 sess., 617.

24. Garfield, *Works*, I, 4, 37; *Cong. Record*, 45 Cong., 2 sess., 3406. May 11, 1878.

25. Garfield, *Works*, I, 44, 59-60.

26. Garfield to his wife, April 8, 1864, Garfield Papers, LC. Long's speech is in the *Cong. Globe*, 38 Cong., 1 sess., 1499-1503; Garfield's reply is on pages 1503-04. Further elaborations concerning the fraudulent charges against the Indiana Democrats can be found on pages 1733-34 and 2091-95. Garfield wrote to D. G. Swaim on April 23 and May 21, 1864 to authenticate the charges, but to no avail, Garfield-Swaim Papers, WRHS; see also Robertson, "Lincoln and Congress," pp. 348-51.

27. Garfield to his wife, January 2, 1863 [misdated 1862], Garfield Papers, LC; Cox, *Military Reminiscences*, II, 396-98; Rhodes, *History of the United States*, V, 51*n*; Garfield on prospect of Lincoln's reelection in Smith, *Life and Letters of Garfield*, I, 375.

28. M. C. Canfield to Garfield, February 9, 1864; J. H. Rhodes to Garfield, February 4, 1864; E. B. Taylor to Garfield, December 13, 1864, all in the Garfield Papers, LC.

29. Garfield to Harmon Austin, March 4, 1864; to Col. Dumars, February 25, 1864, both in *ibid.*

30. *Cong. Globe*, 38 Cong., 1 sess., 878 (February 29, 1864); see also: Dennett, *Diaries and Letters of John Hay*, p. 112; Kendrick, *Lincoln's Cabinet*, pp. 493-509.

31. Garfield to D. G. Swaim, May 21, 1864, Garfield-Swaim Papers, WRHS; Garfield to J. H. Rhodes, April 28 and May 9, 1864, both in the Garfield Papers, LC.

32. Garfield to J. H. Rhodes, April 28, 1864, Garfield Papers, LC.

33. Lamers, *Edge of Glory*, p. 413; *Cong. Globe*, 38 Cong., 1 sess., 197, 711-12; 2 sess., 617; Rosecrans to Garfield, March 12, 1864, Garfield Papers, LC; Garfield to D. G. Swaim, March 29, 1865, Garfield-Swaim Papers, WRHS.

34. Lamers, in *Edge of Glory*, 424-25, maintains that Garfield never received Rosecrans's reply, presumably because Secretary of War Stanton used his control of the telegraph lines to suppress it, thereby dooming the

Rosecrans movement. However, a copy of this telegram does exist in the Garfield Papers, LC, dated June 7, 1864, and bearing a comment on the back dated the following September. This clearly indicates that if Garfield did not receive Rosecrans's wire in June he must have seen it quite soon thereafter. Since he nowhere betrays any irritation at having his telegrams intercepted and, in fact, never indicated that there was any irregularity at all, it seems reasonable to assume that it was delivered on time and that Rosecrans lost the nomination on his own merits and not through the machinations of Stanton.

35.   Garfield to D. G. Swaim, April 27, 1865 and August 13, 1864, both in the Garfield-Swaim Papers, WRHS.

36.   Garfield to J. H. Rhodes, April 28, 1864, Garfield Papers, LC.

37.   New York *Tribune*, August 5, 1864, in Commager, *Documents*, I, 439-40; Brooks, *Washington*, 155.

38.   Garfield to Harmon Austin, May 1, 1864, Garfield Papers, LC.

39.   Garfield to D. G. Swaim, August 13, 1864, Garfield-Swaim Papers, WRHS.

40.   *Ashtabula Sentinel*, August 24, 1864, in Smith, *Life and Letters of Garfield*, I, 378-79; Tod cited in *Cleveland Herald*, August 21, 1878; see also, Riddle, *Life of Garfield*, pp. 76-77.

41.   Garfield to his wife, October 6 and 8, 1864, both in the Garfield Papers, LC.

42.   Garfield to Ross, September 15, 1864; Garfield to his wife, October 8, 1864, both in the Garfield Papers, LC. The Ashtabula anecdote is found in Boykin, *Wit and Wisdom of Congress*. It is doubtful whether the story could stand close examination.

43.   The total vote was:

County	Garfield	Moses
Ashtabula	5,268	877
Geauga	2,603	123
Mahoning	2,681	1,992
Portage	3,153	1,714
Trumbull	4,381	1,609
	18,086	6,315

Smith, *Life and Letters of Garfield*, I, 380.

44.   Biographical Notes, Garfield Papers, LC.

45.   Garfield to B. A. Hinsdale, January 22, 1865, in M. L. Hinsdale, *Garfield-Hinsdale Letters*, p. 73; Garfield, *Works*, I, 73-84.

46.   Garfield to his wife, February 3, 1864, Garfield Papers, LC; Garfield to H. Boynton, December 14, 1865, unidentified clipping filed in letterbook for February 23, 1874, *ibid.*

47.   A. G. Riddle to Garfield, July 22, 1864, *ibid.*; *Chicago Evening Journal*, n.d. [approx. July 1, 1864] in scrapbook, *ibid.*; *Cleveland Herald*, n.d., in *Portage County Democrat*, March 2, 1864.

48.   B. A. Hinsdale to Garfield, March 27, 1865, Garfield Papers, WRHS; Cox cited in Brooks, *Washington*, pp. 29-30; Garfield to B. A.

Hinsdale, January 22, 1865, in M. L. Hinsdale, *Garfield-Hinsdale Letters*, p. 73; Reid, *Ohio in the War*, I, 758-59; C. R. Williams, *Diary of Rutherford B. Hayes*, III, 7 (December 1, 1865); J. G. Blaine to Israel Washburn, December 21, 1863, in Hunt, *Israel . . . Washburn*, p. 111.

49. J. H. Rhodes to Garfield, January 26, 1865; H. Austin to Garfield, May 7, 1865, both in the Garfield Papers, LC.

50. There were times when Garfield did enjoy doing a favor for a constituent. One such occasion was when he was able to help William Dean Howells stay on as consul at Venice. Garfield recognized young Howells's literary talents and told his father that he was "very anxious that the Tennysonian mind of your son shall have full range over the fine materials open before him in the old world." Garfield to W. C. Howells, February 9, 1865, Garfield Papers, LC.

51. Garfield to his wife, April 24, 1864, *ibid.*

52. Isaac Errett to Garfield, March 27 and May 7, 1865, *ibid.*

53. Garfield to his wife, April 10, 1865; Memo of April 10, 1865, both in *ibid.*

54. Wm. Bascom to Garfield, February 13 and 25, 1865, both in *ibid.*

55. Biographical Notes; Garfield to his wife, April 10, 1865, both in *ibid.*

56. Garfield to R. Plumb, February 3, 1865, in Smith, *Life and Letters of Garfield*, II, 822; Plumb to Garfield, February 12, 1865; January 26, 1865, February 22, 1865; April 5, 1865 [misdated 1864], all in the Garfield Papers, LC.

57. Garfield to his wife, May 31, 1865; April 17, 1865, both in the Garfield Papers, LC.

58. Ridpath, *Life and Work of Garfield*, pp. 270-72.

59. New York *Herald*, April 16, 1865; New York *Tribune*, April 17, 1865; G. N. Cole to Harry Garfield, December 23, 1924; Harry Garfield to L. S. Burchard, September 16, 1933; L. S. Burchard to Harry Garfield, July 18, 1933, all in the Harry Garfield Papers, LC; Depew, *My Memories*, p. 108. Bartlett's *Familiar Quotations* (13th edition, 1955) judges only two Garfield phrases as worthy to be included. One is "God reigns, etc.," and the other is Garfield's tribute to Mark Hopkins and the log. The authenticity of both is suspect. (See Chapter 3, note 3, *supra.*) Phrasemaking was not one of Garfield's gifts.

13. TRYING TO BE A RADICAL . . .

1. Diary, April 26 and December 16, 1876, Garfield Papers, LC. Garfield's retreat from radicalism is statistically documented in Benedict's *Compromise of Principle*. According to the tables on pages 339-77, which are based on roll-call analyses, Garfield began his congressional career in the 38th Congress as an "Extreme Radical." By the second session of the 39th Congress he is voting with the "Centrists," and by the 40th Congress,

he is securely in the ranks of the "Conservative Republicans" on roll calls dealing with Reconstruction matters.

2. Garfield to B. A. Hinsdale, January 1, 1867, in Mary Hinsdale, *Garfield-Hinsdale Letters*, p. 88.

3. Garfield to R. C. Schenck, July 14, 1865; Garfield to his wife, May 12, 1865; Garfield to C. E. Fuller, letterbook copy, all in the Garfield Papers, LC.

4. Garfield to D. G. Swaim, July 26, 1865, Garfield-Swaim Papers, WRHS.

5. Garfield, *Works*, I, 86-88.

6. *Cleveland Herald*, September 1, 1865, in Cochran, "Political Experiences of Cox," II, 905.

7. J. D. Cox to Garfield, January 1, 1866; July 30, 1865; August 7, 1865; Garfield to Cox, August 5, 1865, all in the Garfield Papers, LC; Garfield to R. C. Schenck, August 5 and 19, 1865, Schenck Papers; for Cox's Oberlin Letter, see Moore, "Ohio in National Politics," pp. 235-36.

8. J. D. Cox to Garfield, January 1, 1866, Garfield Papers, LC; Cochran, "Political Experiences of Cox," II, 923.

9. Garfield to D. G. Swaim, September 23, 1865, Garfield-Swaim Papers, WRHS; Garfield to Mrs. Helen Atkins, September 13, 1865; Garfield to Andrew Johnson, September 13, 1865, both in the Garfield Papers, LC; Garfield, *Works*, I, 30.

10. Garfield to R. C. Schenck, August 5, 1865, Schenck Papers; Garfield to C. E. Fuller, October 3, 1865, in Fuller, *Reminiscences*, p. 392.

11. Garfield to D. G. Swaim, September 23, 1865, Garfield-Swaim Papers, WRHS. For evidence that Garfield's suspicions of Johnson were not entirely unfounded, see Cox and Cox, *Politics, Principle, and Prejudice*.

12. Garfield to D. G. Swaim, December 11, 1865, Garfield-Swaim Papers, WRHS; Garfield to his wife, December 3, 1865; Garfield to H. Austin, December 13, 1865, both in the Garfield Papers, LC; Garfield to B. A. Hinsdale, December 11, 1865, Garfield Papers, WRHS.

13. Garfield to J. D. Cox, n.d., in Cochran, "Political Experiences of Cox," II, 920; Garfield to B. A. Hinsdale, December 11, 1865, Garfield Papers, WRHS; Garfield to his wife, December 17, 1865, Garfield Papers, LC.

14. Garfield to B. A. Hinsdale, February 13, 1865, in Mary Hinsdale, *Garfield-Hinsdale Letters*, p. 79; Garfield to J. M. Comly, February 14, 1866, Comly Papers, OHS.

15. Garfield to C. E. Fuller, February 15, 1866, Fuller, *Reminiscences*, p. 398.

16. Garfield, *Works*, I, 103, 111.

17. Garfield to B. A. Hinsdale, February 13, 1866, in Mary Hinsdale, *Garfield-Hinsdale Letters*, pp. 78-79; Garfield to J. M. Comly, February 14, 1866, Comly Papers, OHS; Garfield to D. G. Swaim, February 20,

1866, Garfield-Swaim Papers, WRHS; Garfield to N. L. Chafee, March 24, 1866, Garfield Papers, WRHS.

18. Lucretia Garfield to Eliza Garfield, April 8, 1866; Speech at Hagerstown, unmarked scrapbook clipping; W. C. Howells to Garfield, March 26, 1866, all in the Garfield Papers, LC.

19. Diary, May 12, 1875, Garfield Papers, LC.

20. Garfield to H. Austin, December 13, 1865; Biographical Notes, Garfield Papers, LC.

21. Garfield, *Works*, I, 195.

22. *Ibid.*, 197, 544, 201; Garfield to B. A. Hinsdale, December 15, 1867, in Mary Hinsdale, *Garfield-Hinsdale Letters*, p. 122.

23. B. A. Hinsdale to Garfield, December 9, 1867, *ibid.*, p. 119; Garfield, *Works*, I, 197.

24. Garfield to ?, March 2, 1869; Garfield to H. N. Eldridge, December 14, 1869, both letterbook copies in the Garfield Papers, LC.

25. Warren *Chronicle*, April 17, 1867; Lyman W. Hall to Garfield, December 28, 1867; Garfield to Judge Kinsman, February 9, 1867, both in the Garfield Papers, LC.

26. Garfield to B. A. Hinsdale, December 15 and December 5, 1867, in Mary Hinsdale, *Garfield-Hinsdale Letters*, pp. 122, 118; Garfield to E. Atkinson, May 17, 1868, Garfield Papers, LC.

27. Hinsdale, *Garfield and Education*, pp. 85, 96-98; Monroe, *Oberlin Lectures*, pp. 323-29; Garfield to A. J. White, August 6, 1868, letterbook copy, Garfield Papers, LC.

28. Garfield to M. Maury, May 21, 1868, letterbook copy, Garfield Papers, LC; see also Unger, *Greenback Era*,

29. Garfield, *Works*, I, 200; Garfield to B. A. Hinsdale, November 15, 1869, in Mary Hinsdale, *Garfield-Hinsdale Letters*, p. 144.

30. Biographical Notes; Garfield to H. Austin, January 18, 1866, Garfield Papers, LC.

31. Biographical Notes; R. M. Montgomery to Garfield, July 2, 1866; E. J. Hiatt to Garfield, February 15, 1878, all in the Garfield Papers, LC; Garfield to D. J. Beardsley, May 5, 1866, Garfield Papers, WRHS; *Cong. Globe*, 39 Cong., 1 sess., 1300, 3517; *ibid.*, 2 sess., 1602; Hunsberger, "Garfield and the Tariff," pp. 73-76.

32. *Cong. Globe*, 39 Cong., 2 sess., 1615 (February 27, 1867); Garfield to J. D. Cox, February 3, 1869, letterbook copy, Garfield Papers, LC.

33. Garfield, *Works*, I, 208, 233.

34. Biographical Notes, Garfield Papers, LC.

35. J. H. Rhodes to Garfield, December 20, 1866, Garfield Papers, LC.

36. *Cong. Globe*, 39 Cong., 1 sess., 1940-41. Copies of the correspondence between Garfield and the Phillips brothers from February 14 to June 2, 1866 dealing with the matter are filed separately in Volume 93, part 2 of the Garfield Papers, LC.

37. Harmon Austin to Garfield, May 7, 1868; Garfield to E. Newton, July 25, 1868, letterbook copy, both in the Garfield Papers, LC.

38. *Cong. Globe*, 40 Cong., 2 sess., 233.

39. R. Plumb to Garfield, February 15 and March 1, 1866, Garfield Papers, LC; *Past and Present of La Salle Co.*, pp. 323-24.

40. Memo of American Central RR Directors, February 10, 1866, Schenck Papers; R. Plumb to Garfield, April 14, 1866; June 16, 1866, Garfield Papers, LC.

41. Biographical Notes, Garfield Papers, LC.

42. Clayton, *Reminiscences of J. S. Black*, p. 137.

43. Diary, June 8, 1853; Garfield to J. H. Rhodes, December 7, 1862, both in Garfield Papers, LC; Garfield to his wife, December 9, 1862, in Smith, *Life and Letters of Garfield*, I, 824-25.

44. Biographical Notes, Garfield Papers, LC.

45. *Cong. Globe*, 38 Cong., 2 sess., 320 (January 18, 1865); see also *ibid.*, 1 sess., 1466 (April 7, 1864); Garfield to B. A. Hinsdale, May 26, 1863, in Mary Hinsdale, *Garfield-Hinsdale Letters*, p. 67.

46. Garfield to D. G. Swaim, March 10, 1866, Garfield-Swaim Papers, WRHS; for Garfield's argument, see Klaus, *Milligan Case*, pp. 93-120; Black's argument can be found on pp. 121-47.

47. Warren, *Supreme Court*, II, 433; *Cong. Globe*, 40 Cong., 2 sess., 489.

48. Garfield to L. P. Milligan, July 13, 1871; to D. W. Voorhees, March 18, 1874, letterbook copies, Garfield Papers, LC.

49. Garfield to W. Ford, May 21, 1866, Garfield Papers, OHS; S. P. Chase to daughter Nettie, May 20, 1866, Chase Papers, LC.

50. S. A. Northway to Garfield, May 7, 1866; Garfield to R. C. Schenck, July 14, 1865, typed copy, both in Garfield Papers, LC; Garfield to Schenck, August 19, 1865; V. E. Smalley to Schenck, January 1, 1866, both in the Schenck Papers; Garfield to B. A. Hinsdale, February 19, 1866, in Mary Hinsdale, *Garfield-Hinsdale Letters*, p. 80.

51. J. H. Rhodes to Garfield, July 6, 1866; June 13, 1866, both in Garfield Papers, LC; B. A. Hinsdale to Garfield, July 7, 1866, Garfield Papers, WRHS.

52. Garfield to B. A. Hinsdale, June 11, 1866; Hinsdale to Garfield, March 21, 1865, Garfield Papers, WRHS; H. Austin to Garfield, March 31, 1865 and June 12, 1866, Garfield Papers, LC; see also editorial in Mahoning *Courier*, n.d., clipping in scrapbook, Garfield Papers, LC; Garfield to S.E.M. Kneeland, *et al.*, April 7, 1865, Garfield Papers, WRHS.

53. Garfield to B. A. Hinsdale, January 1, 1867, in Mary Hinsdale, *Garfield-Hinsdale Letters*, p. 88; Harmon Austin to Garfield, July 2, 1866, Garfield Papers, LC.

54. V. E. Smalley to Garfield, May 6, 1866; W. J. Ford to Garfield, May 6, 1866, both in Garfield Papers, LC; *Cong. Globe*, 39 Cong., 1 sess., 2903.

55. Garfield to B. A. Hinsdale, June 11, 1866, Garfield Papers, WRHS; Garfield to W. T. Spear, July 24, 1868, letterbook copy, Garfield Papers, LC.

56. J. H. Rhodes to Garfield, March 13, 1862; Garfield to his wife, May 22, 1865; H. Austin to Garfield, June 12 and 19, 1866, all in the Garfield Papers, LC.

57. H. Austin to Garfield, May 27, 1866; H. Hall to Garfield, August 13, 1866; Diary, August 16, 1866, all in the Garfield Papers, LC.

58. Speech at Warren, Ohio, September 1, 1866, in Garfield, *Works*, I, 216-42.

59. The total vote was:

County	Garfield	Coolman
Ashtabula	5,001	931
Geauga	2,488	401
Mahoning	2,933	2,275
Portage	3,342	1,982
Trumbull	4,598	1,787
Total	18,362	7,376

60. Garfield to B. A. Hinsdale, January 1, 1867 and January 20, 1867, in Mary Hinsdale, *Garfield-Hinsdale Letters*, pp. 88-89, 94.

61. *Anti-slavery Standard* [July 1867 ?], scrapbook clipping; Garfield to W. C. Howells, May 15, 1866, both in Garfield Papers, LC; Garfield, *Works*, I, 249; Garfield to B. A. Hinsdale, January 1, 1867, in Mary Hinsdale, *Garfield-Hinsdale Letters*, p. 88.

62. Garfield, *Works*, I, 248-49, 254.

63. L. W. Hall to Garfield, February 18, 1867; Garfield to W. C. Howells, May 5, 1867; Garfield to H. Austin, April 22, 1867, all in the Garfield Papers, LC.

64. Garfield to H. C. Carey, March 21, 1867, photostatic copy, Garfield Papers, LC.

65. Garfield to his wife, July 8 and December 2, 1867; Lucretia to James Garfield, July 7, 1867, all in the Garfield Papers, LC.

66. Diary, July 17, 1867, Garfield Papers, LC.

67. *Ibid.*, July 28; August 8, 1867.

68. *Ibid.*, August 11, 1867.

69. *Ibid.*, September 26, 1867.

70. *Ibid.*, October 20, 1867; November 5, 1867.

14. . . . And Not a Fool

1. R. C. Schenck to daughter Julia, February 10, 1868, Schenck Papers; B. A. Hinsdale to Garfield, October 22, 1867, in Mary Hinsdale, *Garfield-Hinsdale Letters*, p. 112.

2. Garfield to his wife, November 24 and November 27, 1867, Garfield Papers, LC; Garfield to B. A. Hinsdale, December 5, 1867, in Mary Hinsdale, *Garfield-Hinsdale Letters*, p. 117.

3. L. Sheldon to Garfield, April 22, 1868, Garfield Papers, LC; Garfield, *Works*, I, 261-62; Garfield to B. A. Hinsdale, February 2, 1869, in Mary Hinsdale, *Garfield-Hinsdale Letters*, p. 130.

4. Garfield, *Works*, I, 261; *Cong. Globe*, 40 Cong., 2 sess., 1560 (February 29, 1868); Garfield to J. H. Rhodes, November 25, 1867, Garfield Papers, LC.

5. Garfield to B. A. Hinsdale, December 5, 1867, in Mary Hinsdale, *Garfield-Hinsdale Letters*, p. 117.

6. B. A. Hinsdale to Garfield, December 9, 1867, *ibid.*, p. 119; Garfield to B. A. Hinsdale, February 2, 1868, *ibid.*, p. 130; Garfield, *Works*, I, 255.

7. *Cong. Globe*, 41 Cong., 1 sess., 316 (March 26, 1869); see also *ibid.*, 39 Cong., 2 sess., 24; 40 Cong., 2 sess., 1560.

8. "A Century of Congress," Garfield, *Works*, II, 483; Garfield to B. A. Hinsdale, April 4, 1881, in Mary Hinsdale, *Garfield-Hinsdale Letters*, p. 489.

9. *Cong. Globe*, 40 Cong., 2 sess., 1560 (February 29, 1868); Garfield to Hinsdale, March 8, 1868, in Mary Hinsdale, *Garfield-Hinsdale Letters*, p. 489.

10. Garfield to B. A. Hinsdale, March 6, 1868, Garfield Papers, WRHS; A. Campbell to Garfield, March 14, 1868, Garfield Papers, LC; Riddle, *Life of Garfield*, pp. 366-71.

11. Garfield to N. L. Chafee, March 4, 1868, Garfield Papers, WRHS; *Cong. Globe*, 40 Cong., 2 sess., 1909; Garfield to H. Boynton, March 20, 1868, in *Cleveland News*, November 11, 1959.

12. Garfield to J. H. Rhodes, May 7, 1868, letterbook copy, Garfield Papers, LC.

13. *Ibid.*, April 28, 1868; Halsey Hall to Garfield, [April ?] 1868, filed with "Fragments," Garfield Papers, LC.

14. Garfield to B. A. Hinsdale, May 3, 1868, in Mary Hinsdale, *Garfield-Hinsdale Letters*, p. 135.

15. Garfield to J. H. Rhodes, April 28, 1868, Garfield Papers, LC.

16. *Ibid.*, May 18 and May 20, 1868.

17. *Ibid.*, May 18, 1868; *Cong. Globe*, 40 Cong., 2 sess., 1083; Garfield, *Works*, I, 438.

18. "The Currency," Garfield, *Works*, I, 284-321. (A curious feature of this speech is Garfield's use of the term, "the industrial revolution," some thirty years before it was supposedly coined.); Diary, September 17, 1875, Garfield Papers, LC; Garfield to B. A. Hinsdale, July 12, 1865, Garfield Papers, WRHS; Ingalls, *Writings*, pp. 398-99; Monroe, *Oberlin Lectures*, pp. 326-28.

19. Garfield to J. H. Rhodes, May 18 and May 7, 1868, letterbook copies; E. L. Godkin to E. Atkinson, May 27, 1868, all in the Garfield Papers, LC.

20. Smith, *Life and Letters of Garfield*, I, 442; Nugent, *The Money Question*, p. 54n.

21. E. R. Hoar to Garfield, June 13, 1868 (photostatic copy); Henry Fassett to Garfield, May 9, 1868, both in the Garfield Papers, LC.

22. V. E. Smalley to Garfield, June 12, 1868; H. Fassett to Garfield,

February 11, 1868; Garfield to L. W. Hall, January 10, 1868; to J. Bruff, June 6, 1868, letterbook copies, all in the Garfield Papers, LC.

23. Garfield to B. A. Hinsdale, August 5, 1868, Garfield Papers, WRHS; E. Newton to Garfield, June 25, 1868; J. Bruff to Garfield, June 25, 1868; J. H. Rhodes to Garfield, June 25, 1868, latter three items all in the Garfield Papers, LC.

24. Garfield to J. Bruff [July 1868 ?], letterbook copy; Garfield to E. R. Hoar, June 19, 1868, letterbook copy, both in the Garfield Papers, LC.

25. Garfield to W. T. Spear, June 24, 1868, letterbook copy, *ibid.*

26. Petition to Hon. M. Sutliff, July 4, 1868; T. W. Sanderson to Garfield, July 29, 1868, both in Garfield Papers, LC; Garfield to ?, August 8, 1868, in Smith, *Life and Letters of Garfield*, I, 438.

27. Garfield to his wife, August 24, 1868, Garfield Papers, LC; Garfield to D. G. Swaim, September 3, 1868, Garfield-Swaim Papers, WRHS.

28. H. Fassett to Garfield, February 11, 1868, Garfield Papers, LC. The vote, by Garfield's tabulation, was:

County	Garfield	McEwan
Ashtabula	5,758	1,510
Geauga	2,783	683
Mahoning	3,191	2,785
Portage	3,461	2,402
Trumbull	4,994	2,379
Total	20,187	9,759

Diary, November 3, 1868, Garfield Papers, LC.

29. Riddle, *Life of Garfield*, pp. 117, 120; Garfield, *Works*, I, 202-04.

30. Reid, *Ohio in the War*, I, 759; Mark Hopkins to Garfield, June 26, 1868; Garfield to G. A. Townsend, August 2, 1870; to M. Hopkins, July 24, 1868, letterbook copies, all in the Garfield Papers, LC.

31. *Cong. Globe*, 39 Cong., 1 sess., 3207-08. June 16, 1868.

32. *Ibid.*, 42 Cong., 2 sess., 3973; *Cong. Record*, 43 Cong., 1 sess., 4966; 43 Cong., 2 sess., 152.

33. Speech at Warren, August 16, 1866, unidentified scrapbook clipping, Garfield Papers, LC.

34. *Cong. Globe*, 39 Cong., 1 sess., 60; Garfield to Parke Godwin, March 30, 1872, in Smith, *Life and Letters of Garfield*, II, 786.

35. Garfield, *Works*, I, 127, 130-31; *Cong. Globe*, 39 Cong., 1 sess., 2968-70, 3047.

36. *Cong. Globe*, 39 Cong., 1 sess., 3051, 3207; 40 Cong., 2 sess., 1141.

37. H. Barnard to Garfield, February 28, 1867, Garfield Papers, LC; see also: Steiner, *Life of Barnard*; Mayo, "Henry Barnard, as First U.S. Commissioner of Education" 891-901; Mayo, "Henry Barnard," 769-801; Curti, *Social Ideas of Educators*, pp. 139-68; Peskin, "Short, Unhappy Life of First Department of Education."

38. Steiner, *Life of Barnard*, p. 111; Harris, "Establishment of the Commissioner of Education," p. 905; *Cong. Globe*, 40 Cong., 2 sess., 1139,

1141, 3704; 42 Cong., 3 sess., 420; Garfield to B. A. Hinsdale, January 27, 1869, Garfield Papers, WRHS; Garfield to E. E. White, July 26, 1868, January 26, 1869, letterbook copies, Garfield Papers, LC.

39. Garfield, *Works*, I, 369; *Cong. Globe*, 40 Cong., 3 sess., 17-18, 20, 880-81, 968-71, 1706.

40. Garfield to J. D. Cox, August 6, 1870, letterbook copy, Garfield Papers, LC; *Cong. Globe*, 41 Cong., 3 sess., 734; 42 Cong., 2 sess., 718; *Cong. Record*, 43 Cong., 1 sess., 2107; 44 Cong., 1 sess., 2672-73; 45 Cong., 3 sess., 1133.

41. *Cong. Globe*, 40 Cong., 3 sess., 47-48. December 10, 1868.

42. Garfield, *Works*, I, 409-29; Ambrose, *Upton*, pp. 114-21.

43. Garfield to W. B. Hazen, August 1, 1868, in Smith, *Life and Letters of Garfield*, I, 420-21; *Cong. Globe*, 40 Cong., 2 sess., 3882, 3948-53, 3968-74, 3982, 4493; *Ibid.*, 3 sess., 926.

44. *Cong. Globe*, 40 Cong., 3 sess., 968-71. There was a certain amount of logic in coupling the two measures. Transfer of Indian affairs to the War Department would provide surplus officers with employment. This consideration might explain Garfield's attachment to his Indian bill.

45. *Ibid.*, 1338; 1891.

46. J. G. Blaine to Garfield, November 10, 1868; Garfield to L. Sheldon, December 17, 1868, letterbook copy, both in the Garfield Papers, LC; Garfield to Wallace Ford, December 2, 1868, Garfield Papers, OHS.

47. J. G. Blaine to Sam Bowles, April 10, 1869; H. L. Dawes to Bowles, April 18, 1869, both in the Bowles Papers, Yale College Library. These items were brought to my attention through the courtesy of Professor Fred Nicklason.

48. Garfield to J. G. Blaine, March 11, 1869, Garfield Papers, LC. Although this item is in the Letterbook, it is not a letter-press copy but the original note tipped into the letterbook. This unusual arrangement led T. C. Smith to conclude that it was never sent. That he was mistaken is evidenced by the fact that Blaine replied to the note the next day. The reply, however, was misfiled ten days early in the Garfield Papers, which probably accounts for Smith's confusion. Evidently Blaine returned Garfield's note with his reply.

49. J. G. Blaine to Garfield, March 12, 1869. This letter is misfiled in the Garfield Papers under March 1.

15. RULING ELDER

1. Biographical Notes; Garfield to D. G. Swaim, August 10, 1868; Garfield to W. H. Hudson, November 24, 1873, letterbook copies; Garfield to his wife, May 30, 1869, all in the Garfield Papers, LC.

2. Garfield to B. A. Hinsdale, December 10, 1869, in Mary Hinsdale, *Garfield-Hinsdale Letters*, p. 149; Garfield to S. Colfax, November 12, 1869; Garfield to W. C. Howells, December 22, 1869; Garfield to H. Wilson, December 13, 1869; Garfield to R. B. Hayes, December 1, 1880, letterbook

copies; D. G. Swaim to J. R. Gilmore, July 26, 1880; D. G. Swaim to Garfield, September 6, 1877, all in the Garfield Papers, LC; Garfield to D. G. Swaim, April 9, 1867, February 13 and 23, 1872, Garfield-Swaim Papers, WRHS.

3. Memo of J. Stanley-Brown, January 23, 1885, Garfield Papers, LC. I am grateful to Professor Harry Brown for helping to unravel the code in which this memo was couched. See also, Henry, *Captain Henry*, pp. 527-28.

4. *Cong. Globe*, 41 Cong., 2 sess., 1491; Garfield, *Works*, I, 445, 452-76; New York *Times*, December 8, 1869.

5. Garfield to his wife, June 9, 1869; Edwin W. Snow to Garfield, December 9, 1869, both in Garfield Papers, LC; Garfield to B. A. Hinsdale, December 17, 1869, Garfield Papers, WRHS; *Cong. Globe*, 41 Cong., 2 sess., 36-38, 1148; Garfield, *Works*, I, 451.

6. Garfield to C. H. Hill, July 24, 1869, letterbook copy, Garfield Papers, LC; Hesseltine, *U.S. Grant*, p. 190.

7. W. S. Rosecrans to Garfield, November 16, 1867; Garfield to D. Tilden, February 12, 1869, letterbook copy; D. G. Wells to Garfield, March 10, 1881, all in the Garfield Papers, LC; see also, Peskin, "The Little Man on Horseback. . . ."

8. Garfield to J. D. Converse, January 9, 1869, letterbook copy; Garfield to R. Plumb, March 27, 1869, typed copy; Garfield to J. Sherman, March 18, 1869; Garfield to E. P. Brainard, April 8, 1869; Diary, June 24, 1881, all in the Garfield Papers, LC.

9. Garfield to R. Plumb, March 27, 1869, typed copy; Garfield to J. H. Rhodes, December 7, 1869, letterbook copy, both in the Garfield Papers, LC.

10. *Cong. Globe*, 42 Cong., 2 sess., 1270; 41 Cong., 2 sess., 76.

11. Garfield to B. A. Hinsdale, January 10, 1870, in Mary Hinsdale, *Garfield-Hinsdale Letters*, p. 157; C. A. Dana to Garfield, January 24, 1870; Henry Adams to Garfield, December 30, 1869; Garfield to Irvin McDowell, January 18, 1870, letterbook copy, Garfield Papers, LC.

12. *Cong. Globe*, 41 Cong., 2 sess., 367; Garfield to J. H. Rhodes, January 25, 1870; Garfield to Wm. Ritezel, June 20, 1870, letterbook copies; J. D. Cox to Garfield, February 1, 1870, Garfield Papers, LC.

13. "Gold Panic Investigation," 14, 18-20; *Cong. Globe*, 40 Cong., 3 sess., 881; Jay Gould to Garfield, January 13, 1872, Garfield Papers, LC.

14. Garfield, *Works*, I, 543-92; Knox, *History of Banking*, pp. 106-10, 138-39; Unger, *Greenback Era*, pp. 60-67.

15. E. Atkinson to Garfield, June 7, 1870, telegram, Garfield Papers, LC; *New York Commercial Advertiser*, June 9, 1870.

16. *Cong. Globe*, 41 Cong., 2 sess., 4264-66.

17. *Ibid.*, 4949-50, 4963-64; Garfield to Wm. Ritezel, July 12, 1870, letterbook copy, Garfield Papers, LC; Garfield, *Works*, I, 584-85; Smalley, "Characteristics of Garfield."

18. H. R. Hurlburt to Garfield, August 23, 1869; J. G. Butler to Gar-

field, January 3, 1870, Garfield Papers, LC; *Mahoning Courier*, May 4, 1870, editorial.

19. H. Austin to Garfield, January 23, 1870; Garfield to Austin, January 31, 1870, letterbook copy; Garfield to J. H. Rhodes, January 25, 1870, letterbook copy; Diary, February 19, 1872, all in the Garfield Papers, LC.

20. Garfield, *Works*, I, 520-42; Cox in *Cong. Globe*, 41 Cong., 2 sess., 2768 and *ibid.*, 42 Cong., 1 sess., 741.

21. W. Reid to Garfield, April 5, 1870, Garfield Papers, LC; *Mahoning Courier*, May 4, 1870, editorial.

22. C. E. Henry to Garfield, June 5, 1870; Garfield to W. Reid, July 9, 1870; Garfield to H. R. W. Hall, June 30, 1870, both letterbook copies; F. G. Servis to Garfield, June 18, 1870, all in the Garfield Papers, LC.

23. Garfield to A. W. Stiles, May 23, 1870, letterbook copy, *ibid.*; B. A. Hinsdale to Garfield, December 24, 1869, Garfield Papers, WRHS.

24. Garfield to C. E. Henry, December 28, 1869; Garfield to W. C. Howells, December 23, 1869, letterbook copies, Garfield Papers, LC; Garfield to B. A. Hinsdale, December 10, 1869, in Mary Hinsdale, *Garfield-Hinsdale Letters*, pp. 149-50.

25. Garfield to C. E. Henry, December 28, 1869, letterbook copy; C. E. Henry to Garfield, February 2 and June 5, 1870, all in the Garfield Papers, LC.

26. W. C. Howells to Garfield, July 2, 1870; J. P. Tillston to Garfield, July 9, 1870; Garfield to W. C. Howells, July 29, 1870, all in *ibid.*; Garfield to W. Ford, October 7, 1870, Garfield Papers, OHS.

27. Garfield, *Works*, I, 610-31; Garfield to J. R. Sherwood, July 30, 1870, letterbook copy; speech at Ridgeway, Ohio, September 30, 1869, unidentified newspaper clipping, Garfield Papers, LC.

28. Speech at Mansfield, Ohio, August 27, 1870, in Garfield, *Works*, I, 631; R. D. Harrison to Garfield, October 15, 1870; Garfield to W. C. Howells, October 21, 1870, both in the Garfield Papers, LC.

29. The total vote was:

County	Garfield	Howard
Ashtabula	3,276	965
Geauga	1,688	379
Mahoning	2,382	2,320
Portage	2,547	1,885
Trumbull	3,645	1,714
Total	13,538	7,263

Smith, *Life and Letters of Garfield*, I, 460.

30. R. C. Schenck to Garfield, October 29, 1870, Garfield Papers, LC.

31. Garfield to J. M. Comly, February 24, 1871, Comly Papers, OHS; Garfield to J. D. Cox, December 23, 1870, letterbook copy; D. A. Wells to Garfield, February 28, 1871; J. D. Cox to Garfield, March 20, 1871; Sam Bowles to Garfield, March 29, 1871, all in the Garfield Papers, LC.

32. Garfield to H. Austin, January 21, 1871; Garfield to Wm. Ritezel, December 22, 1870; Garfield to R. P. Cannon, March 24, 1871, all letter-

book copies; Garfield to E. Cowles, typed copy, n.d. [c. July 30, 1877], all in the Garfield Papers, LC.

33. Garfield to D. A. Wells, March 3, 1871, letterbook copy; D. A. Wells to Garfield, October 28, 1870; February 28, 1871, all in *ibid.*

34. Garfield to J. D. Cox, March 23, 1871; Garfield to Sam Bowles, March 31, 1871, letterbook copies; D. G. Swaim to Garfield, March 26, 1871, all in *ibid.*; Hamilton, *Blaine,* p. 250.

35. *Springfield Republican,* March 30, 1871.

36. Cater, *Henry Adams and His Friends,* pp. 49-51; White, *Lyman Trumbull,* p. 354; Brinkerhoff, *Recollections,* pp. 205-06.

37. Ed. Atkinson to J. G. Blaine, September 21, 1871; D. A. Wells to Garfield, August 18, 1871, both in the Garfield Papers, LC.

38. J. D. Cox to Garfield, November 21, 1871, *ibid.,* Brinkerhoff, *Recollections,* pp. 209-10; H. Dawes to J. G. Blaine, December 3, 1871, Dawes Papers, LC. I am grateful to Dr. James Kitson for bringing this, and much of the above information, to my attention.

39. Garfield to B. A. Hinsdale, December 3, 1871, in Mary Hinsdale, *Garfield-Hinsdale Letters,* p. 175; Donn Piatt to Garfield, December 4, 1871, Garfield Papers, LC.

40. C. E. Henry to Garfield, November 9, 1880, *ibid.,* Henry, *Captain Henry,* p. 305n.

41. Garfield to B. A. Hinsdale, December 3, 1871, in Mary Hinsdale, *Garfield-Hinsdale Letters,* p. 175; Garfield to J. M. Comly, December 12, 1871, Comly Papers, OHS; Garfield to H. Hall, December 7, 1871; Garfield to J. Medill, December 9, 1871, both letterbook copies in the Garfield Papers, LC; Hamilton, *Blaine,* pp. 228-29.

42. Garfield, *Works,* II, 2, 130; *Cong. Record,* 43 Cong., 1 sess., 214; *Cong. Globe,* 42 Cong., 2 sess., 73-78.

43. Pensions; Legislative, Executive and Judicial; Consular and Diplomatic; Army; Navy; Military Academy; Post Office; Fortifications; Indian; Sundry Civil; Rivers and Harbors; Deficiency Appropriations.

44. Diary, January 8, 1872, Garfield Papers, LC; Riddle, *Life of Garfield,* pp. 196-97.

45. Garfield to J. H. Rhodes, April 23, 1872; Garfield to H. Hall, December 7, 1871, both letterbook copies; Diary, May 23, 1872, Garfield Papers, LC; Garfield to B. A. Hinsdale, April 11, 1872, Garfield Papers, WRHS.

46. Hinsdale, *Garfield and Education,* p. 85; Diary, January 19, 1872; Biographical Notes, Garfield Papers, LC.

47. Garfield, *Works,* II, 741; 6-7.

48. White, *Republican Era,* Chapter II; Wilmerding, *The Spending Power*; *Cong. Record,* 43 Cong., 1 sess., 2110ff.

49. *Cong. Record,* 43 Cong., 1 sess., 5435; Dawes in *ibid.,* 1459; *ibid.,* 2 sess., 107; Garfield, *Works,* II, 740-52.

50. J. Medill to Garfield, December 6, 1871, Garfield Papers, LC; Garfield, *Works,* II, 97.

51. See Diary for March of 1872, Garfield Papers, LC.

52. *Ibid.*, May 26, 1874; Smalley, "Characteristics of Garfield," p. 168; Garfield, *Works*, II, 752.

53. *Cong. Record*, 43 Cong., 1 sess., 628.

16. STANDING BY THE OLD SHIP

1. Garfield to J. D. Cox, February 3, 1869; Garfield to L. Hall, April 6, 1872, letterbook copies, Garfield Papers, LC.

2. Garfield to A. S. Lathrop, December 26, 1871; Garfield to H. R. W. Hall, December 26, 1871; Garfield to R. Schenck, April 30, 1872; Garfield to R. D. Harrison, March 7, 1870, *ibid.*; *Cong. Globe*, 41 Cong., 3 sess., 1453.

3. *Cong. Globe*, 41 Cong., 2 sess., 39 (December 8, 1869); Garfield, *Works*, I, 735.

4. Garfield, *Works*, I, 122-25; *Cong. Globe*, 40 Cong., 2 sess., 233; 41 Cong., 3 sess., 1470; 42 Cong., 2 sess., 3827ff.; C. C. Washburn to Garfield, April 8, 1871; Garfield to W. E. Ives, June 17, 1870; Garfield to J. Worth, January [3?], 1871, both letterbook copies; Diary, February 29, March 22, April 23, May 6, 1872, Garfield Papers, LC.

5. E. L. Godkin to Garfield, January 11, 1871; Garfield to E. L. Godkin, January 16, 1871; Garfield to P. Lee, January 25, 1869, both letterbook copies; Diary, May 7, 1872, Garfield Papers, LC; *Cong. Globe*, 40 Cong., 2 sess., 1933.

6. Garfield to R. Folger, April 18, 1870, letterbook copy, Garfield Papers, LC.

7. J. D. Cox to Garfield, April 11, 1871, *ibid.*; Garfield to B. A. Hinsdale, March 30, 1871, Garfield Papers, WRHS; *Cong. Globe*, 41 Cong., 2 sess., 1485.

8. Ku Klux Klan speech in Garfield, *Works*, I, 703-31; Garfield to B. A. Hinsdale, March 30, 1871, Garfield Papers, WRHS; Garfield to H. Austin, April 11, 1871; Garfield to J. D. Cox, April 8, 1871, letterbook copy, Garfield Papers, LC.

9. Garfield to J. M. Comly, December 5, 1872, Comly Papers, OHS. Garfield did not, however, take part in the debate or even show up for the vote on February 6, 1867 when an early civil service reform proposal was narrowly defeated. *Cong. Globe*, 39 Cong., 2 sess., 1034-36.

10. Henry Adams to Garfield, May 12, 1870; Garfield to his wife, December 4, 1864; Diary, October 17, November 28, 1872, Garfield Papers, LC; Garfield, *Works*, I, 502-03; *Cong. Globe*, 38 Cong., 1 sess., 1325.

11. Garfield to S. Hayward, May 28, 1872; Garfield to O. Morgan, February 23, 1871, letterbook copies, Garfield Papers, LC.

12. Garfield, *Works*, I, 505, II, 33; Garfield to J. M. Comly, December 5, 1872, Comly Papers, OHS.

13. See Hoogenboom, *Outlawing the Spoils*, pp. 212-14.

14. J. D. Cox to Garfield, October 24, 1870, Garfield Papers, LC.

15. Garfield to J. D. Cox, October 26, 1870, letterbook copy; J. D. Cox to Garfield, December 6, 1870, *ibid.*

16. Diary, April 18 and 19, 1872, *ibid.*; *Cong. Globe*, 41 Cong., 3 sess., 1935; 42 Cong., 2 sess., 2396, 2584-85; 3 sess., 1635; Garfield to B. A. Hinsdale, April 22, 1872, Garfield Papers, WRHS.

17. *Cong. Globe*, 42 Cong., 2 sess., 2584 (April 19, 1872); see W. S. Young to Garfield, August 10, 1872, Garfield Papers, LC.

18. Garfield, *Works*, II, 3-4, 320; Garfield to B. A. Hinsdale, January 12, 1871, Garfield Papers, WRHS; Garfield to I. N. Demmon, December 30, 1870; Garfield to T. J. McLain, March 11, 1871, both letterbook copies; Garfield to Francis Lieber, March 11, 1871; Garfield to W. C. Howells, March 18, 1871, Garfield Papers, LC.

19. Diary, June 12, 1872, *ibid.*

20. Garfield to J. D. Cox, March 23, 1871, letterbook copy, *ibid.*; Garfield to B. A. Hinsdale, March 23, 1871, in Mary Hinsdale, *Garfield-Hinsdale Letters*, p. 172.

21. J. D. Cox to Garfield, March 20, 1871; Diary, February 16, 1872; Garfield to W. C. Howells, April 10, 1872, Garfield Papers, LC.

22. Garfield to H. Austin, December 14, 1872; Garfield to J. R. Conrad, January 3, 1872; Garfield to D. A. Wells, August 14, 1871, all letterbook copies, *ibid.*

23. Garfield to W. C. Howells, December 18, 1871, *ibid.*; see also Moore, "Ohio in National Politics," p. 272.

24. Diary, January 4, 1872, Garfield Papers, LC; Garfield to B. A. Hinsdale, January 11, 1872, in Mary Hinsdale, *Garfield-Hinsdale Letters*, p. 185; R. B. Hayes, *Diary and Letters*, III, 186, 192-93; Moore, "Ohio in National Politics," pp. 272-73.

25. Garfield to L. Hall, April 6, 1872; Garfield to W. C. Howells, April 10, 1872; Garfield to R. C. Schenck, April 30, 1872, Garfield to H. R. W. Hall, December 26, 1871, all letterbook copies; Diary, June 5, 1872, Garfield Papers, LC.

26. Diary, January 8, 1873, *ibid.*

27. *Ibid.*, December 30, 1872; Garfield to A. F. Rockwell, December 16, 1872, letterbook copy, Garfield Papers, LC.

28. Riddle, *Life of Garfield*, p. 283.

29. *Ibid.*, pp. 283-88.

30. Garfield to B. A. Hinsdale, January 3, 1871, in Mary Hinsdale, *Garfield-Hinsdale Letters*, p. 166; Diary, March 24, 1873; Garfield to D. G. Swaim, December 16, 1872, letterbook copy, Garfield Papers, LC; Ingalls, *Writings*, p. 398.

31. A. B. Nettleton to Garfield, November 9 and 25, 1871, January 9, 1872; Harmon Austin to Garfield, November 16, 1871, Garfield Papers, LC.

32. Garfield to D. G. Swaim, December 11, 1871, Garfield-Swaim Papers, WRHS; Diary, October 13, 1875; H. Austin to Garfield, October 31, 1875, Garfield Papers, LC.

33. Diary, October 14, October 19, December 31, 1872; Garfield to J. H. Rhodes, January 5, 1871, letterbook copy, Garfield Papers, LC.

34. Diary, April 19, 1873, November 11, 1875; Garfield to his wife, November 24, 1867; May 29, 1874, Garfield Papers, LC. Garfield's hard-won domestic serenity accounts for his antipathy to the women's-rights movement. This was one reform he could not abide. This "aetheistic" movement, he argued, "must logically result in the utter annihilation of marriage and the family." (Garfield to Isaac Errett, January 18, 1872, letterbook copy, Garfield Papers, LC). Even dress reform seemed to him only another sinister wing of "the free love army whose doctrines I detest," and he saw in their proposals "an assault on the marriage contract." His wife shared his views (Diary, September 3, 1874, *ibid.*).

35. See the Garfield Diary for 1872-1874. The valuable index in the printed edition edited by Brown and Williams has greatly simplified these calculations.

36. Diary, February 10, May 1, 1872; January 23, 1874; February 17, 1876; Wm. Evarts to Garfield, February 25, 1871, Garfield Papers, LC; R. C. Schenck to daughter Sally, March 11, 1868, Schenck Papers.

37. Ingalls, *Writings*, p. 398; F. A. Henry, *Captain Henry*, p. 235.

38. J. D. Cox to Garfield, March 22 and May 10, 1872; Diary, April 27, 1872; Garfield to B. A. Hinsdale, May 17, 1872, Garfield Papers, LC.

39. Garfield to W. C. Howells, July 11, 1872; Garfield to J. B. Burrows, July 29, 1872, letterbook copy; Diary, October 9, 1872, *ibid.*; Smith, *Life and Letters of Garfield*, I, 495.

40. Garfield to W. C. Howells, May 17, 1872; H. L. Dawes to Garfield, July 5, 1872; Diary October 7, 1872, Garfield Papers, LC; Garfield to D. G. Swaim, September 30, 1872, Garfield-Swaim Papers, WRHS.

41. Diary, July 17, October 19, November 6, 1872, Garfield Papers, LC; Garfield to B. A. Hinsdale, December 31, 1872, in Mary Hinsdale, *Garfield-Hinsdale Letters*, p. 202.

42. Garfield to W. C. Howells, March 1 and 25, 1872, Garfield Papers, LC; Garfield, *Works*, II, 30-45. The total vote was:

County	Garfield	Sutliff
Ashtabula	5,430	1,717
Geauga	2,609	639
Lake	2,619	1,021
Portage	3,306	2,592
Trumbull	5,225	2,285
Total	19,189	8,254

Smith, *Life and Letters of Garfield*, I, 496.

43. Garfield to Oakes Ames, July 27, 1871, letterbook copy; Diary, August 1-21, 1872, Garfield Papers, LC.

44. Diary, August 22-26, 1872; *Cong. Globe*, 40 Cong., 3 sess., 1706. For an analysis of the Flathead mission, see the unusually full footnotes on this subject in the Brown and Williams edition of the Garfield *Diary*, volume II.

45. Diary, September 9, 1872, Garfield Papers, LC.

17. Anno Diaboli

1. *Cong. Globe*, 42 Cong., 3 sess., 1724; Kirkland, *Industry Comes of Age*, p. 54.

2. Poland Committee Report, pp. 4-7.

3. *Cincinnati Gazette*, September 16, 1872.

4. J. S. Black to Garfield, September 29, 1872, Black Papers, LC.

5. *Ibid.*; J. S. Black to J. G. Blaine [February 15, 1873], copy with printer's instructions; Garfield to Harmon Austin, February 12, 1873, letterbook copy, both in Garfield Papers, LC.

6. Garfield, *Review of the Crédit Mobilier*, p. 16; Smith, *Life and Letters of Garfield*, I, 534; B. A. Hinsdale to Garfield, January 20, 1873, in Mary Hinsdale, *Garfield-Hinsdale Letters*, p. 209.

7. J. G. Blaine to Garfield, November 7, 1872 [misdated 1873], Black Papers, LC; *ibid.*, November 26, 1872, Garfield Papers, LC; Garfield, *Review of the Crédit Mobilier*, p. 23.

8. Poland Committee Report, pp. 28, 128-31.

9. Garfield to J. S. Black, January 25, 1873; Garfield to J. P. Robison, January 30, 1873; Garfield to E. Cowles, February 7, 1873, all letterbook copies; Diary, January 22, 1873, Garfield Papers, LC.

10. Garfield, *Review of the Crédit Mobilier*, pp. 18-23.

11. Garfield to B. A. Hinsdale, February 8, 1873, in Mary Hinsdale, *Garfield-Hinsdale Letters*, p. 212; Smith, *Life and Letters of Garfield*, I, 546; Garfield to W. Reid, March 6, 1873, typed copy; Garfield to H. Austin, February 17, 1873; W. Reid to Garfield, March 11, 1873; Diary, January 14, 1873, Garfield Papers, LC.

12. Brigance, *Jeremiah Sullivan Black*, p. 216; *Cong. Globe*, 42 Cong., 3 sess., 1816f., 1826.

13. Garfield to J. P. Robison, January 30, 1873, letterbook copy, Garfield Papers, LC.

14. Garfield, *Review of the Crédit Mobilier*, p. 16.

15. Garfield to B. A. Hinsdale, December 31, 1873, in Mary Hinsdale, *Garfield-Hinsdale Letters*, p. 202; *Cong. Globe*, 42 Cong., 3 sess., 1463.

16. Garfield, *Review of the Crédit Mobilier*, p. 25; H. Austin to Garfield, February 17, 1873; W. J. Ford to Garfield, January 2, 1868, both in the Garfield Papers, LC; Garfield to W. J. Ford, April 8, 1868, Garfield Papers, OHS.

17. J. S. Black to J. G. Blaine [February 15, 1873], copy in Garfield Papers, LC; *Springfield Republican*, May 28, 1873; Trottman, *Union Pacific*, pp. 71-72; Caldwell, *Garfield*, p. 229n.; C. F. Adams, "Railroad Inflation," 130-64; H. Adams to Garfield, January 22, 1869, Garfield Papers, LC.

18. *New York Tribune*, February 19, 1873; *Cong. Globe*, 42 Cong., 3 sess., 1129; Garfield to D. G. Swaim, February 8, 1873, Garfield-Swaim Papers, WRHS.

19. *Cong. Globe*, 42 Cong., 3 sess., 1674; *Cong. Record*, 44 Cong., 1 sess., 2208.

20. Diary, March 29, 1873; Garfield to Dr. [J. P. Robison?], February 6, 1873, letterbook copy, Garfield Papers, LC.

21. Eugene Hale to Garfield, July 10, 1874; Garfield to H. Austin, March 12, 1873, *ibid.*

22. Diary, March 2, 1873; Garfield to H. Austin, March 12 and 22, 1873, letterbook copy, *ibid.*; *Cong. Globe*, 42 Cong., 3 sess., 2100-01.

23. Garfield to B. F. Potts, March 5, 1873, letterbook copy; Diary, March 19, 1873; T. J. McLain to Garfield, March 24, 1873; H. Austin to Garfield, March 4, 1873, all in the Garfield Papers, LC; Garfield to D. G. Swaim, April 21, 1873, Garfield-Swaim Papers, WRHS; B. A. Hinsdale to Garfield, March 30, 1873, in Mary Hinsdale, *Garfield-Hinsdale Letters*, p. 225; Garfield to B. A. Hinsdale, April 4, 1873, in *ibid.*, p. 232.

24. Garfield to Hinsdale, April 4, 1873, *ibid.*, p. 232; Diary, April 12 and 21, 1873; Garfield to C. E. Fuller, June 11, 1873, letterbook copy; Garfield to his wife, March 9, 1873, all in the Garfield Papers, LC.

25. Garfield to T. G. Servis, May 19, 1873; Garfield to H. Austin, March 31, 1873; Garfield to Samuel Shellabarger, August 9, 1873, all letterbook copies in the Garfield Papers, LC.

26. Diary, April 2, 1873; H. Austin to Garfield, March 27, 1873; Garfield to T. G. Servis, letterbook copy, *ibid.*; Garfield to D. G. Swaim, April 1, 1873, Garfield-Swaim Papers, WRHS.

27. T. J. McLain to Garfield, March 24, 1873; Garfield to W. C. Howells, July 12, 1873; Garfield to his wife, April 26, 1873; Garfield to F. E. Spinner, June 13, 1873, all in the Garfield Papers, LC; B. A. Hinsdale to Garfield, May 24, 1873, in Mary Hinsdale, *Garfield-Hinsdale Letters*, p. 243.

28. Garfield to his wife, April 24, 1873, Garfield Papers, LC.

29. Garfield, *Works*, II, 46-69.

30. Garfield to J. Q. Smith, August 5, 1873, letterbook copy; Diary, August 22, September 25, October 20, 1873; O. Morgan to Garfield, August 20, 1873; H. Austin to Garfield, September 10, 1873; Garfield to H. Austin, October 21, 1873, letterbook copy; J. F. Scofield to Garfield, September 25, 1873; Garfield to H. Austin, November 19, 1873, all in the Garfield Papers, LC.

31. Glenni Schofield to Garfield, September 27, 1873; Sam Bowles to D. A. Wells, November 3, 1873, both in *ibid.*; Garfield to D. G. Swaim, September 19, 1873, Garfield-Swaim Papers, WRHS; Garfield to D. A. Wells, November 14, 1873, Bowles Papers, Yale University Library. This item was brought to my attention through the courtesy of Professor Fred Nicklason.

32. Diary, November 30 and December 5, 1873, Garfield Papers, LC; Garfield to B. A. Hinsdale, November 24, 1873, in Mary Hinsdale, *Garfield-Hinsdale Letters*, pp. 252-53.

33. Garfield to B. A. Hinsdale, December 4, 1873, *ibid.*, 258; *Cong.*

Record, 43 Cong., 1 sess., 154-55; Garfield to J. S. Black, March 14, 1873, letterbook copy; Diary, December 11, 13 and 17, 1873, Garfield Papers, LC.

34. B. A. Hinsdale to Garfield, November 26, 1873, in Mary Hinsdale, *Garfield-Hinsdale Letters*, p. 254; Garfield to Hinsdale, November 24, 1873, *ibid.*, p. 252; Garfield to J. P. Robison, November 24, 1873, letterbook copy, Garfield Papers, LC.

35. Diary, November 12, 1873, Garfield Papers, LC; *Cong. Record*, 43 Cong., 2 sess., 25-26.

36. Garfield, *Works*, II, 183; B. H. Bristow to Garfield, November 24, 1873; Garfield to J. P. Robison, November 24, 1873, letterbook copy; Garfield to H. B. Payne, December 5, 1874, typed copy in letterbook; Diary, December 4, 1874, all in the Garfield Papers, LC; Garfield to B. A. Hinsdale, December 8, 1874, in Mary Hinsdale, *Garfield-Hinsdale Letters*, p. 300.

37. Garfield to B. A. Hinsdale, March 26 and April 2, 1874, Garfield Papers, WRHS; Garfield to H. Austin, February 4, 1874, letterbook copy, Garfield Papers, LC.

38. Garfield to B. A. Hinsdale, April 8, 1874, Garfield Papers, WRHS; Diary, December 31, 1873, Garfield Papers, LC; Garfield to B. A. Hinsdale, January 2, 1874, in Mary Hinsdale, *Garfield-Hinsdale Letters*, pp. 267-68.

39. Diary, February 23, 1874; March 12, 1874; May 1874 [this entry is inserted on a blank space under the entry for May 22, 1873]; Garfield to R. P. Cannon, February 25, 1874, letterbook copy, all in the Garfield Papers, LC.

40. Diary, November 18, 1873; April 23, 1874; Garfield to H. Stone, April 8, 1874, letterbook copy, all in the Garfield Papers, LC; Garfield to B. A. Hinsdale, April 23, 1874, in Mary Hinsdale, *Garfield-Hinsdale Letters*, p. 286.

41. Diary, December 15, 1873, Garfield Papers, LC; *Cong. Record*, 43 Cong., 1 sess., 4650, 5435-39; 2 sess., 25-26; *Chicago Times*, undated scrapbook clipping, Garfield Papers, LC.

42. Garfield to H. Austin, February 4, 1874, letterbook copy; C. E. Henry to Garfield, January 17, 1874, both in the Garfield Papers, LC.

43. H. Austin to Garfield, December 17, 1873 [two letters of same date]; January 18, 1874, Garfield Papers, LC; Garfield to H. Austin, January 27, 1874, in Smith, *Life and Letters of Garfield*, I, 565.

44. C. E. Henry to Garfield, January 26, 1874, Garfield Papers, LC.

45. E. P. Brainard to Garfield, February 13, 1874; H. R. W. Hall to Garfield, February 19, 1874; C. E. Henry to Garfield, January 14, 1874; Garfield to H. R. W. Hall, June 10, 1874, letterbook copy; Diary, March 3, 1874, all in the Garfield Papers, LC.

46. Diary, March 3, 1874; H. Austin to Garfield, March 9, 1873 and February 25, 1874; Garfield to H. Austin, February 28, 1874; Garfield to W. C. Howells, June 11, 1874, both letterbook copies; C. E. Henry to Garfield, January 7, 1874, all in *ibid.*

47. *Cleveland Herald*, March 19, 1879; Garfield to G. S. Hubbard, April 16, 1874, letterbook copy, Garfield Papers, LC. Despite the impressive testimonials as to their durability, these wooden pavements quickly rotted. See Green, *Washington*, I, 359.

48. *New York Independent*, July 30, 1880, in Smith, *Life and Letters of Garfield*, I, 566; Diary, April 15, 1874; Garfield to J. H. Rhodes, April 17, 1874; Garfield to G. S. Hubbard, April 16, 1874, letterbook copies, Garfield Papers, LC.

49. Garfield, *Tested and Sustained*, p. 11; Green, *Washington*, I, 348-49.

50. *Cong. Globe*, 42 Cong., 2 sess., 3657; 3 sess., 230; D. G. Swaim to Garfield, April 7, 1873, January 4, 1874; Garfield to D. G. Swaim, May 21, 1873, Garfield Papers, LC.

51. Chittenden cited in Caldwell, *Garfield*, p. 241; Riddle, *Life of Garfield*, pp. 274-75; *New York World*, October 30, 1880; Garfield, *Tested and Sustained*, p. 10.

52. B. A. Hinsdale to Garfield, June 4, 1874, in Mary Hinsdale, *Garfield-Hinsdale Letters*, p. 293; Garfield to J. A. Howells, July 20, 1874; H. Austin to Garfield, June 29, 1874; Diary, July 31, 1874, all in the Garfield Papers, LC.

53. Diary, July 21, 1874; Garfield to W. C. Howells, June 11, 1874; G. W. Wilson to Garfield, July 21, 1874; Garfield to D. W. Canfield, June 4, 1868, letterbook copy; Diary, July 27, 1874; August 4, 1874, all in the Garfield Papers, LC; Garfield to N. L. Chafee, March 4, 1868, Garfield Papers, WRHS; Garfield to B. A. Hinsdale, August 6, 1874, in Mary Hinsdale, *Garfield-Hinsdale Letters*, p. 297. Canfield later tried to explain his behavior as a ruse designed to head off the opposition. Garfield was not convinced. See Diary, August 19, 1874, Garfield Papers, LC.

54. B. A. Hinsdale to Garfield, August 10, 1874, in Mary Hinsdale, *Garfield-Hinsdale Letters*, p. 298; *Warren Chronicle*, August 12, 1874; Diary, August 10 and 11, 1874; Garfield to H. Austin, August 10, 1874, Garfield Papers, LC.

55. Garfield to W. C. Howells, October 30, 1874; Garfield to his wife, September 11 and October 1, 1874; Diary, September 21 and October 11, 1874; *Niles Home Record*, unmarked scrapbook clipping, all in the Garfield Papers, LC; see Garfield to Richard Smith, October 5, 1874, in Smith, *Life and Letters of Garfield*, I, 575.

56. W. E. Niblack to Garfield, August 21, 1874; Garfield to Allen Thurman, September 18, 1873, letterbook copy; W. E. Chandler to Garfield, October 7, 1874, all in the Garfield Papers, LC; *Cincinnati Gazette*, January 15, 1880; Sherman, *Recollections*, I, 505-06.

57. Garfield to his wife, October 1, 1874, Garfield Papers, LC.

58. Diary, September 19 and October 6, 1874; Garfield to his wife, October 7, 1874, Garfield Papers, LC. For a transcript of the question-and-answer session see the *Painesville Advertiser*, October 10, 1874.

59. Diary, October 13, 1874; Garfield to his wife, October 13, 1874, both in Garfield Papers, LC; Garfield to I. N. Demmon, October 19, 1874, in Smith, *Life and Letters of Garfield*, I, 581.

60. The total vote was:

County	Garfield	Hurlburt	Woods
Ashtabula	3,478	1,273	755
Geauga	1,798	645	284
Lake	1,925	551	634
Portage	2,543	222	2,340
Trumbull	2,847	736	2,232
Total	12,591	3,427	6,245

Smith, *Life and Letters of Garfield*, I, 579.

61. Garfield to J. H. Paine, November 9, 1874, letterbook copy, Garfield Papers, LC; Garfield to C. E. Henry, November 4, 1874, Henry Papers, Hiram College Library.

62. Garfield to W. C. Howells, October 30, 1874; Diary, October 14, 1874, both in Garfield Papers, LC.

18. In the Bear Garden

1. Garfield to B. A. Hinsdale, January 4, 1875, in Mary Hinsdale, *Garfield-Hinsdale Letters*, p. 307; Diary, November 19, 1875, Garfield Papers, LC.

2. Garfield to W. C. Allen, January 7, 1875; Garfield to S. Shellabarger, August 9, 1873, letterbook copies; Diary, August 20, 1873; June 27, 1873, Garfield Papers, LC; Speech at Hudson, Ohio, July 2, 1873 in, Garfield, *Works*, II, 54.

3. Diary, August 17, 1874, Garfield Papers, LC; Garfield to B. A. Hinsdale, January 21, 1875, in Mary Hinsdale, *Garfield-Hinsdale Letters*, p. 314. In the same breath, Garfield deplored the disenfranchisement of Southern Negroes.

4. Garfield to his wife, April 5, 1875; Diary, April 4, 1875; August 14, 1874, Garfield Papers, LC; Garfield to B. A. Hinsdale, February 11, 1875, in Mary Hinsdale, *Garfield-Hinsdale Letters*, p. 317.

5. Garfield to W. C. Howells, December 29, 1873; Diary, February 4, 1875, Garfield Papers, LC; Garfield, *Works*, II, 487.

6. Garfield to B. A. Hinsdale, January 7, 1875, in Mary Hinsdale, *Garfield-Hinsdale Letters*, p. 309; Diary, May 24, 1873; Garfield to Irvin McDowell, January 8, 1875, letterbook copy, Garfield Papers, LC.

7. Diary, January 7 and 8, 1875; Garfield to W. C. Howells, January 17, 1875, Garfield Papers, LC; Garfield to B. A. Hinsdale, January 7, 1875, in Mary Hinsdale, *Garfield-Hinsdale Letters*, p. 309.

8. *Cong. Record*, 43 Cong., 2 sess., 1005 (February 4, 1875); Garfield to J. O. Converse, January 21, 1875, letterbook copy; Garfield to W. C. Howells, January 17, 1875; Diary, January 7, 1875, Garfield Papers, LC.

9. Diary, December 26 and 27, 1875, Garfield Papers, LC; Garfield to B. A. Hinsdale, December 29, 1874, in Mary Hinsdale, *Garfield-Hinsdale Letters*, p. 301; Garfield to H. Boynton, February 11, 1875, in *Cleveland News*, November 11, 1959.

10. Garfield to J. C. Grubb, December 1, 1874, letterbook copy; Diary, January 8, 1875, Garfield Papers, LC.

11. Jay Gould to Garfield, April 17, 1875, telegram; Garfield to his children, April 19, 1875, both in the Garfield Papers, LC.

12. Cited in Smith, *Life and Letters of Garfield*, II, 766.

13. Garfield to his wife, May 10, 1875, Garfield Papers, LC; Garfield to B. A. Hinsdale, July 8 and 27, 1875, Garfield Papers, WRHS; Boswell reference in unidentified scrapbook clipping, Garfield Papers, LC.

14. Diary, July 27 and December 20, 1875; Garfield to H. Austin, December 22, 1875; Garfield to W. C. Howells, January 17, 1875, all in the Garfield Papers, LC.

15. B. A. Hinsdale to Garfield, January 4, 1876, in Mary Hinsdale, *Garfield-Hinsdale Letters*, p. 326; Garfield to H. Austin, January 16, 1876, Garfield Papers, LC.

16. Garfield, *Works*, II, 245; Garfield to H. Austin, January 16, 1876; Biographical Notes, both in the Garfield Papers, LC.

17. W. B. Hazen to Garfield, February 23, 1872; Garfield to W. B. Hazen, February 16, 1872, letterbook copy; Garfield to J. Coburn, April 8, 1876, unidentified scrapbook clipping, all in the Garfield Papers, LC; *Cong. Globe*, 42 Cong., 2 sess., 3822 (May 24, 1872).

18. Diary, March 2, 1876; J. Coburn to Garfield, April 5, 1876; Garfield to Coburn, April 8, 1876, scrapbook clipping, all in the Garfield Papers, LC; Oberholtzer, *History of the United States*, III, 165.

19. Diary, March 3, 1876, Garfield Papers, LC.

20. Garfield to his wife, March 10, 1876; Garfield to J. Q. Smith, April 16, 1875, letterbook copy; Diary, June 8, 1876, all in the Garfield Papers, LC; Garfield to B. A. Hinsdale, April 4, 1876, Garfield Papers, WRHS.

21. Garfield to B. A. Hinsdale, June 8, 1876, in Mary Hinsdale, *Garfield-Hinsdale Letters*, p. 334; Mrs. J. G. Blaine to Emmons Blaine, May 17, 1881, in Harriet Beale, *Letters of Mrs. Blaine*, I, 201; Diary, April 26, 1876, Garfield Papers, LC.

22. Garfield to E. Hale, June 26, 1874, letterbook copy; J. G. Blaine to Garfield, July [6?], 1876, "Confidential—Strictly. Burn when read," both in the Garfield Papers, LC; Garfield to B. A. Hinsdale, April 4, 1876, Garfield Papers, WRHS.

23. Garfield to B. A. Hinsdale, June 8, 1876, in Mary Hinsdale, *Garfield-Hinsdale Letters*, p. 334; R. B. Hayes to Garfield, March 4, 1876, in C. R. Williams, *Diary and Letters of Hayes*, III, 306-07; C. E. Henry to Garfield, January 22, 1876, Garfield Papers, LC.

24. Garfield to R. B. Hayes, March 2, 1876, in C. R. Williams, *Life of Hayes*, I, 428-29; C. R. Williams, *Diary and Letters of Hayes*, IV, 318-19; Garfield to F. H. Mason, February 5, 1876, letterbook copy; Garfield to H. Austin, January 24, 1876; F. Thorp to Garfield, January 24, 1876, all in the Garfield Papers, LC; Garfield to C. E. Henry, January 27, 1876, Henry Papers, Hiram College.

25. Diary, November 28, 1872; March 16, 1875; February 23, 1876, Garfield Papers, LC.

26. *Ibid.*, April 18, 1876; see also Garfield's memorandum of a conversation of the same date, in the Garfield Papers, LC.

27. *Ibid.*, June 4 and 5, 1876; see also, Muzzey, *Blaine*, pp. 83-99.

28. See note of Garfield's attached to letter of C. E. Henry to B. A. Hinsdale, October 1, 1874, Garfield Papers, WRHS.

29. Garfield to C. E. Henry, May 31, 1876, Henry Papers, Hiram College; Diary, June 11, 12 and 13, 1876, Garfield Papers, LC.

30. Garfield to R. B. Hayes, [July 1?] 1876, letterbook copy; Diary, July 10, 1876; Garfield to H. Austin, July 20, 1876; R. B. Hayes to Garfield, August 4, 1876, all in the Garfield Papers, LC; *Cong. Record*, 43 Cong., 1 sess., 5384; Vatican reference in unmarked scrapbook clipping, c. August, 1875, in Garfield Papers, LC.

31. Diary, November 1, 1876; Garfield to Judge Kinsman, March 28, 1876, Garfield Papers, LC; *Geauga Republican*, March 22, 1876.

32. Garfield to H. Austin, August 6, 1876; Garfield to his wife, August 3, 1876; Biographical Notes; Diary, August 4, 1876, all in the Garfield Papers, LC; Garfield, *Works*, II, 351-87; Garfield to B. A. Hinsdale, August 9, 1876, in Mary Hinsdale, *Garfield-Hinsdale Letters*, p. 338.

33. Garfield to H. Austin, August 6, 1876; Garfield to his wife, August 6, 1876; Luke Poland to Garfield, October 8, 1876; Garfield to his mother, August 11, 1876, letterbook copy; R. B. Hayes to Garfield, August 5, 1876, all in the Garfield Papers, LC; B. A. Hinsdale to Garfield, March 29, 1876, Garfield Papers, WRHS; R. B. Hayes to J. G. Blaine, September 14, 1876, in Hamilton, *Biography of Blaine*, p. 422.

34. Garfield to Wm. Wheeler, July 5, 1876, letterbook copy; Garfield to H. Austin, July 1 and July 4, 1876; Diary, January 18, 1875; June 23 and July 1, 1876, all in the Garfield Papers, LC.

35. *Cleveland Leader*, undated scrapbook clipping; Garfield to his wife, July 27, 1876; Harmon Austin to Garfield, August 6, 1876, all in the Garfield Papers, LC.

36. Painesville resolution cited in Smith, *Life and Letters of Garfield*, I, 611; Diary, August 22, 1876; D. T. Davis to Garfield, September 10, 1876; Garfield to his wife, September 8, 1876; Casement's platform in *Cincinnati Gazette*, undated scrapbook clipping; A. S. Beecher to Garfield, September 28, 1876, all in the Garfield Papers, LC.

37. Diary, September 19, 1876, Garfield Papers, LC; Garfield to B. A. Hinsdale, October 16, 1876, Garfield Papers, WRHS; Garfield to C. E. Fuller, November 9, 1876, in Fuller, *Reminiscences*, p. 423.

38. The total vote was:

County	Garfield	Casement
Ashtabula	5,893	2,547
Geauga	2,641	905
Lake	2,562	1,376
Portage	3,508	2,960
Trumbull	5,408	3,562
Total	20,012	11,349

Smith, *Life and Letters of Garfield*, I, 612.

39. Diary, October 22, 24 and 25, 1876; Garfield to W. C. Howells,

November 11, 1876, Garfield Papers, LC; "Life Book," Harry A. Garfield Papers, LC.

40. Diary, October 28, November 7, 1876; Garfield to his wife, October 21, 1876, Garfield Papers, LC; Garfield to B. A. Hinsdale, October 16, 1876, Garfield Papers, WRHS.

19. RETRIEVING THE IRRETRIEVABLE CALAMITY

1. Garfield to C. E. Fuller, November 9, 1876, in Fuller, *Reminiscences*, p. 423.

2. U.S. Grant to Garfield, November 10, 1876; Diary, November 10, 1876, both in the Garfield Papers, LC; Garfield to B. A. Hinsdale, November 11, 1876, in Mary Hinsdale, *Garfield-Hinsdale Letters*, p. 341.

3. Garfield to his wife, November 16, 1876, Garfield Papers, LC; Garfield to B. A. Hinsdale, December 4, 1876, in Mary Hinsdale, *Garfield-Hinsdale Letters*, p. 345. Sheldon did, however, try to make the best of his bad situation. During the subsequent electoral crisis he would continually pester Garfield for inside information so that he could speculate on Louisiana state bonds. Curiously enough, he expected that the value of these bonds would drop if the Republicans retained control of the state. See L. A. Sheldon to Garfield, January 17, 1877 and January 22, 1877 [misdated 1876], Garfield Papers, LC.

4. Garfield to J. H. Rhodes, November 18, 1876 [misdated 1875]; Garfield to his wife, November 19 and November 20, 1876, all in the Garfield Papers, LC; Garfield to B. A. Hinsdale, December 4, 1876, in Mary Hinsdale, *Garfield-Hinsdale Letters*, p. 344.

5. Garfield to his wife, November 27, 1876, Garfield Papers, LC; Garfield to B. A. Hinsdale, December 4, 1876, in Mary Hinsdale, *Garfield-Hinsdale Letters*, p. 344.

6. See draft of a letter from Garfield and Sherman to the editors of the *Cincinnati Daily Democrat*, February 9, 1877, in letterbook, Garfield Papers, LC.

7. See the following government documents: *H.R.R. #156*, 44 Cong., 2 sess., 81-92; *Sen. Exec. Doc. #2*, 44 Cong., 2 sess., 10-17. [This section of the report was written by Garfield.]; *H.R. Misc. Doc. #31*, 45 Cong., 3 sess., 789-92.

8. Garfield to his wife, November 27, 1876, Garfield Papers, LC.

9. Haworth, *The Hayes-Tilden Disputed Election*, p. 169; Morgan, *From Hayes to McKinley*, p. 3; A. W. Stiles to Garfield, November 13, 1876; A. A. House to Garfield, December 14, 1876, both in the Garfield Papers, LC.

10. Garfield to C. E. Henry, December 18, 1876, Henry Papers, Hiram College; Garfield to his wife, November 27, 1876; L. Q. C. Lamar to Garfield, December 6, 1876; Diary, December 7, 10 and 11, 1876, all in the Garfield Papers, LC.

11. Garfield to R. B. Hayes, December 13, 1876, letterbook copy; R. B. Hayes to Garfield, December 16, 1876, both in the Garfield Papers, LC. It is this proposed rapprochment between Northern Republicans and conservative Whiggish Southerners which C. V. Woodward sees as the key to the resolution of the electoral crisis. I disagree, and the controversy on this question, for those who care to pursue it, can be found in the June 1973 issue of the *Journal of American History.* Cf. Peskin, "Was there a Compromise of 1877?" and Woodward, "Yes, there was a Compromise of 1877."

12. *Cong. Record,* 44 Cong., 2 sess., 298-99; J. M. Comly to R. B. Hayes, January 8, 1877, typed copy, HML; Diary, December 20, 1876, Garfield Papers, LC.

13. Garfield to H. Austin, February 9, 1876; Diary, February 12, 1876, both in the Garfield Papers, LC; J. M. Comly to R. B. Hayes, January 8, 1877; Wm. Henry Smith to R. B. Hayes, February 17, 1877, both typed copies at HML.

14. Diary, December 18, 1876, Garfield Papers, LC; *H.R.R. #139,* 44 Cong., 2 sess., Part III.

15. Diary, December 8 and 11, 1876, Garfield Papers, LC; Garfield to B. A. Hinsdale, November 11, 1876, in Mary Hinsdale, *Garfield-Hinsdale Letters,* pp. 339-40; *Cong. Globe,* 40 Cong., 2 sess., 2083 (March 24, 1868); Garfield to R. B. Hayes, January 19, 1877, in C. R. Williams, *Hayes Diary and Letters,* III, 408-09.

16. Garfield to W. C. Howells, December 18, 1876; Diary, January 4, 1877, both in the Garfield Papers, LC; Garfield to R. B. Hayes, January 19, 1877, in C. R. Williams, *Hayes Diary and Letters,* III, 408-09; Whitelaw Reid to J. G. Blaine, January 10, 1877, Reid Papers, LC; Garfield to R. B. Hayes, December 9, 1876, typed copy, HML.

17. Diary, January 5 and 18, 1877, Garfield Papers, LC; Garfield to R. B. Hayes, January 19, 1877, in C. R. Williams, *Hayes Diary and Letters,* III, 408-09; Garfield, *Works,* II, 405, 420.

18. Biographical Notes, Garfield Papers, LC. For an explanation of David Davis's election to the Senate see, Polakoff, *Politics of Inertia,* pp. 280-83.

19. Garfield to Whitelaw Reid, January 29, 1877, typed copy, Garfield Papers, LC.

20. Garfield to Harmon Austin, February 16, 1876; Diary, January 31 and February 16, 1877; Garfield to W. C. Howells, February 17, 1877, all in the Garfield Papers, LC.

21. Diary, January 19, January 20, February 26, 1877, *ibid.;* see W. E. Chandler's testimony before the Potter Committee, *House H.R. Misc. Doc. #31,* 45 Cong., 3 sess., 536.

22. Diary, March 1, 1877, Garfield Papers, LC.

23. Garfield to his wife, undated note [1875?]; Diary, October 18, 1876; March 5, 1877, all in *ibid.*

20. PARTY PACIFICATOR

1. Garfield to B. A. Hinsdale, March 10, 1877, in Mary Hinsdale, *Garfield-Hinsdale Letters*, p. 368; T. J. McLain to Garfield, February 20 and 22, March 8, 1877; Diary, March 10, 1877, Garfield Papers, LC; Riddle, *Life of Garfield*, pp. 75-76. Garfield and his wife were both struck by the accuracy of Riddle's analysis. See Diary, October 12 and 13, 1878, Garfield Papers, LC.

2. Diary, February 17, 1877, Garfield Papers, LC.

3. *Ibid.*, March 5 and 6, 1877; Garfield to B. A. Hinsdale, March 10, 1877, in Mary Hinsdale, *Garfield-Hinsdale Letters*, p. 368; Garfield to T. J. McLain, March 11, 1877 (misdated March 1), letterbook copy; "Senatorship in the hand" found in unidentified scrapbook clipping; Garfield to H. Austin, March 21, 1877, all in the Garfield Papers, LC.

4. Diary, March 14 and November 24, 1877, Garfield Papers, LC.

5. *Ibid.*, December 15, 1877, January 19, 1878; Garfield to R. B. Hayes, n.d., letterbook copy, Garfield Papers, LC.

6. Garfield to E. Wadsworth, February 5, 1878, letterbook copy; C. E. Henry to Garfield, May 8, 1877, both in the Garfield Papers, LC.

7. Diary, March 29, 1877; May 11, 1880, Garfield Papers, LC.

8. *Ibid.*, March 24, 1878; March 7, 1877.

9. Garfield to J. R. Conrad, January 3, 1872, letterbook copy; Garfield to B. A. Hinsdale, March 10, 1877, in Mary Hinsdale, *Garfield-Hinsdale Letters*, p. 368.

10. Diary, March 6, 1877, Garfield Papers, LC.

11. Garfield to J. D. Cox [July ? 1877], typed copy in letterbook, *ibid.*

12. Garfield to his wife, May 29, 1877; Diary, March 4, 1878, *ibid.*; Garfield to B. A. Hinsdale, September 10, 1877, in Mary Hinsdale, *Garfield-Hinsdale Letters*, p. 377.

13. Diary, February 17, April 4 and 6, 1877; Garfield to W. Reid, March 14, 1877, typed copy; J. B. Brown to Garfield, May 9 and October 1, 1877, all in the Garfield Papers, LC; Wm. H. Smith to R. B. Hayes, February 17, 1877, typed copy, HML.

14. Sinkler, "Race: Principles of Hayes," p. 164; Diary, April 3 and March 11, 1877, Garfield Papers, LC.

15. *New Orleans Democrat*, April 22, 1877.

16. J. DeFrees to Garfield, April 17, 1877. A group of Pennsylvania Republicans headed, oddly enough, by Russell Errett, the brother of Garfield's friend Isaac Errett, abstained rather than vote for Garfield for Speaker. They were put off by his membership in the Cobden Club and his alleged low-tariff sympathies.

17. Garfield to L. Sheldon, February 13, 1878, letterbook copy; H. R. W. Hall to Garfield, May 22, 1878; Diary, October 13 and 26, 1877; April 19, 1878, all in the Garfield Papers, LC.

18. Biographical Notes; Garfield to W. C. Howells, March 1, 1878, *ibid.*

19. Diary, March 3, 1878; Biographical Notes, *ibid.*

20. Garfield to his wife, September 2, 1878; Diary, March 1, 1878; July 22, 1877, *ibid.*; Garfield, *Works*, II, 550, 591-92.

21. Garfield to Judge F. Kinsman, December 12, 1877, Garfield Papers, WRHS; Diary, March 5, 1878, Garfield Papers, LC; Harry A. Garfield to Frances Garfield, March 13, 1939, Harry Garfield Papers, LC.

22. C. A. Adams to Garfield, April 28, 1878; Garfield to W. C. Howells, August 11, 1876, letterbook copy, both in the Garfield Papers, LC; Garfield, *Works*, II, 343.

23. Garfield to B. A. Hinsdale, September 10, 1877, in Mary Hinsdale, *Garfield-Hinsdale Letters*, pp. 376-78; B. A. Hinsdale to Garfield, November 6, 1878, in *ibid.*, 389; Diary, December 4, 1875; D. G. Swaim to Garfield, September 6 and November 5, 1877, Garfield Papers, LC.

24. On the other hand, a leading Democrat, the wealthy New Yorker, August Belmont, gave Garfield money to distribute his antisilver speeches. A. Belmont to Garfield, February 1, 1878, Garfield Papers, LC.

25. Diary, February 28, 1878, *ibid.*

26. *Ibid.*, September 17, 1878; *Cleveland Herald*, August 21, 1878; Garfield to John Curtis, June 15, 1878, Garfield Papers, LC.

27. A. R. Seagrave to Garfield, May 25, 1878, Garfield Papers, LC.

28. The total vote was:

County	Garfield (Republican)	Hubbard (Dem.)	Tuttle (Greenback)
Ashtabula	4,916	1,566	386
Geauga	2,208	441	247
Lake	2,161	757	528
Mahoning	3,592	2,647	1,181
Trumbull	4,289	2,142	806
Total	17,166	7,553	3,148

Smith, *Life and Letters of Garfield*, II, 671.

29. Diary, October 31, 1876; April 14, 16 and 17, 1877, Garfield Papers, LC; *Geneva Times*, May 24, 1877; *Cleveland Leader*, March 12, 1879.

30. Diary, April 21, 1877; June 23, 1878, Garfield Papers, LC.

31. *Ibid.*, February 11, 1874; "The Day's Doings: Copy of Notes Taken in Conversation with Mrs. James A. Garfield at Mentor. Probably in 1915" and "Life Book," April 15, 1884, both in the Harry A. Garfield Papers, LC.

32. Diary, November 1, 1873; May 15 and November 29, 1874; Lucretia Garfield to J. A. Garfield, April 20, 1873 and October 12, 1875; M. Mays to Garfield, June 5, 1877, all in the Garfield Papers, LC; B. A. Hinsdale to Garfield, January 4, 1881, in Mary Hinsdale, *Garfield-Hinsdale Letters*, p. 472.

33. Garfield's unpopularity referred to in an unmarked scrapbook

clipping, Garfield Papers, LC; Alexander, *History of the House of Representatives*, pp. 296-97.

34. "Helpless as a child" from an interview with Warren Keifer in an unmarked scrapbook clipping, Garfield Papers, LC; *Cong. Record*, 45 Cong., 3 sess., 1209. On one occasion, Garfield insisted, quite without justification, that a motion to adjourn took precedence over a motion to adjourn to a specific day. He stubbornly held to this elementary error until the Speaker had the rule book read to him. *Cong. Record*, 46 Cong., 1 sess., 1860.

35. Garfield to B. A. Hinsdale, January 30, 1879, in Mary Hinsdale, *Garfield-Hinsdale Letters*, p. 398; Diary, January 23 and 24, 1879, Garfield Papers, LC.

36. Garfield to B. A. Hinsdale, January 30, 1879, in Mary Hinsdale, *Garfield-Hinsdale Letters*, p. 398; Diary, February 23 and 24, 1879, Garfield Papers, LC; *Cong. Record*, 45 Cong., 2 sess., 800.

37. Garfield to J. M. Comly, December 14, 1878, Comly Papers, OHS; Diary, January 19, May 21 and 24, 1878; Garfield to H. Austin, May 18, 1878, Garfield Papers, LC.

38. *Cong. Record*, 45 Cong., 3 sess., 44-46; Diary, February 20, 1879, Garfield Papers, LC.

39. *Cong. Record*, 45 Cong., 3 sess., 1617.

40. Diary, March 4 and 6, 1879; Biographical Notes, Garfield Papers, LC.

41. Alexander, *History of the House of Representatives*, p. 298.

42. *Chicago Inter Ocean*, January 3, 1879; Andrew D. White cited in Smith, *Life and Letters of Garfield*, II, 710.

43. Unidentified newspaper clipping in Garfield Papers, LC.

44. Garfield, *Works*, II, 655-72.

45. *Cincinnati Commercial*, March 30, 1879; *Cincinnati Daily Enquirer*, March 30, 1879; J. A. Hill to Garfield, March 31, 1879; H. R. McCalmont to Garfield, March 30, 1879, both in the Garfield Papers, LC; B. A. Hinsdale to Garfield [August 27, 1879], in Mary Hinsdale, *Garfield-Hinsdale Letters*, p. 408; McKinley's comment in Memoirs of Thomas C. Donaldson, March 31, 1879, typed copy, HML.

46. Memoir of T. C. Donaldson, May 28, 1879; Memo of Wm. Henry Smith, May 25, 1879, both typed copies, HML; R. B. Hayes to A. Snead, February 21, 1883, in C. R. Williams, *Diary and Letters of Hayes*, IV, 110.

47. B. A. Hinsdale to G. F. Hoar, February 3, 1899, Hinsdale Papers, WRHS; Monroe, *Oberlin Lectures*, p. 327; Diary, February 25, 1879, Garfield Papers, LC.

48. Memo of Wm. Henry Smith, May 25, 1879, typed copy, HML.

49. Garfield to his wife, June 12, 1879, Garfield Papers, LC; *Cong. Record*, 46 Cong., 1 sess., 2283-84, 2441-42; Garfield to B. A. Hinsdale, July 7, 1879, in Mary Hinsdale, *Garfield-Hinsdale Letters*, p. 429; White, *Republican Era*, pp. 35-38.

50. Garfield to B. A. Hinsdale, July 7, 1879, in Mary Hinsdale, *Garfield-Hinsdale Letters*, p. 429; Diary, January 2, 1880; Garfield to his wife, May 10, 1879, both in the Garfield Papers, LC.

51. Diary, July 25 and November 19, 1879, Garfield Papers, LC; Garfield to B. A. Hinsdale, December 20, 1879 and January 28, 1880, in Mary Hinsdale, *Garfield-Hinsdale Letters*, pp. 431, 439.

52. Diary, July 23, 1878; March 18 and 20, 1879; Garfield to H. Austin, March 28, 1879; Garfield to his wife, September 16, 1879, all in the Garfield Papers, LC.

53. J. P. Robison to Garfield, September 18, 1879; Diary, September 25 and 30, 1879, *ibid.*

54. J. Mason to Garfield, September 24, 1879; J. S. Robison to Garfield, September 19, 1879; Diary, October 25 and 29, 1879; C. E. Henry to Garfield, December 10, 1879, *ibid.*

55. F. Thorp to Garfield, March 28, 1879; Diary, July 1 and November 23, 1879; H. Austin to Garfield, May 17, 1879; H. W. Elliot to Garfield, October 24, 1879, *ibid.*

56. Garfield to H. Austin, November 14 and December 14, 1879; C. E. Henry to Garfield, November 6 and December 6, 1879; Diary, December 31, 1879, *ibid.*

57. C. E. Henry to Garfield, October 17, 1879; Garfield to H. Austin, November 14, 1879; F. D. Mussey to Charles Foster, December 16, 1879; F. Thorp to Garfield, January 7, 1880 [misdated 1879], all in *ibid.*; C. E. Henry to Garfield, January 6, 1880, in Norris and Schaffer, *Politics and Patronage*, p. 262.

58. *Ohio State Journal*, January 7, 1880.

59. Diary, January 5 and 6, 1880; Garfield to H. Austin, January 11, 1880; F. Thorp to Garfield, January 7, 1880 [misdated 1879]; C. E. Henry to Garfield, January 18, 1880, all in the Garfield Papers, LC.

60. *Cincinnati Gazette*, January 15, 1880.

61. C. E. Henry to F. A. Henry, October 9, 1904, in F. A. Henry, *Captain Henry*, p. 291; Garfield to B. A. Hinsdale, January 28, 1880, in Mary Hinsdale, *Garfield-Hinsdale Letters*, p. 437.

21. The Put-up Job

1. T. M. Nichol to Garfield, January 9, 1879; J. Rusk to Garfield, May 27, 1881, both in the Garfield Papers, LC; Casson, *"Uncle Jerry,"* pp. 98-99.

2. T. M. Nichol to Garfield, June 20, 1879; H. E. Knox to Garfield, February 24, 1881, both in the Garfield Papers, LC.

3. Hay cited in T. M. Nichol to Garfield, December 20, 1880, *ibid.*

4. Diary, October 30, 1878, *ibid.*; Morgan, *From Hayes to McKinley*, p. 37.

5. Diary, May 23, 1880, Garfield Papers, LC; Curran, *Life of Patrick Collins*, p. 82.

6. L. Sheldon to Garfield, April 7, 1879, Garfield Papers, LC; Matthews statement in *Cincinnati Gazette*, January 29, 1879.

7. Garfield to H. Austin, April 26, 1879; Diary, February 5, 1879; March 16, 1875; J. Atkins to Garfield, February 4, 1879, all in the Garfield Papers, LC.

8. Evans, "Wharton Barker," p. 37; Barker, "Secret History," p. 435.

9. L. Sheldon to Garfield, January 30, 1880; Garfield to R. A. Horr, January 26, 1880, letterbook copy; Garfield to C. E. Henry, January 26, 1880, typed copy, all in the Garfield Papers, LC.

10. B. D. Fearing to Warner Bateman, March 21, 1880; E. Baltley to Bateman, March 23, 1880, both in the Bateman Papers, WRHS; J. Rusk to Garfield, May 27, 1881; T. Nichol to Garfield, March 6 and April 30, 1880; Diary, February 11, 1880, all in the Garfield Papers, LC.

11. Barker, "Secret History," pp. 438-39; W. Barker to Garfield, April 6 and 19, May 7, 1880; Diary, February 18 and May 7, 1880, all in the Garfield Papers, LC.

12. Ingalls, *Writings*, p. 400; Lucretia Garfield to James Garfield, April 25, 1875; C. E. Henry to Garfield, January 31, 1880; Garfield to H. Austin, April 16, 1880, all in the Garfield Papers, LC.

13. "Plainest Saxon" in *Pittsburgh Commercial Gazette*, March 3, 1880; C. E. Henry to Garfield, March 8, 1880; Garfield to H. Austin, February 14, 1880; Diary, February 17 and 27, 1880; C. Foster to Garfield, February 13, 1880; J. Beatty to Garfield, May 3, 1880; L. Sheldon to Garfield, January 30, 1880, all in the Garfield Papers, LC.

14. B. A. Hinsdale to Garfield, April 23, 1880, in Mary Hinsdale, *Garfield-Hinsdale Letters*, p. 451; Barker, "Secret History," p. 439; J. Sherman to W. Bateman, April 25, 1880, Bateman Papers, WRHS; Garfield to H. Austin, April 16, 1880; F. Thorp to Garfield, May 11, 1879; Diary, February 18, 1880, Garfield Papers, LC.

15. C. Foster to Garfield, February 13 and April 17, 1880, Garfield Papers, LC; Sherman, *Recollections*, II, 778.

16. Ingersoll quoted in *New York Daily Tribune*, May 18, 1880; J. Sherman to W. Bateman, May 24, 1880, Bateman Papers, WRHS; Diary, May 23, 1880, Garfield Papers, LC; Garfield to C. E. Henry, March 12, 1880, Henry Papers, Hiram College; *Cincinnati Enquirer*, April 17, 1880.

17. *Cong. Record*, 46 Cong., 2 sess., 3765; Diary, May 25, 1880, Garfield Papers, LC. For examples of Garfield's earlier criticisms of Sherman see: Garfield to J. H. Rhodes, April 21, 1871; Garfield to D. A. Wells, August 14, 1871; Garfield to J. R. Conrad, January 3, 1872, all letterbook copies; Garfield to J. Q. Smith, January 9, 1879, all in the Garfield Papers, LC; Garfield to B. A. Hinsdale, January 8, 1879, in Mary Hinsdale, *Garfield-Hinsdale Letters*, p. 395.

18. Diary, May 28, 1880, Garfield Papers, LC; Wm. W. Crape to Harry Garfield, September 8, 1911, Harry Garfield Papers, LC.

19. G. F. Hoar, *Autobiography*, pp. 390-93; *Cleveland Herald*, May 28 and June 1, 1880; Diary, May 29 and June 1, 1880, Garfield Papers, LC.

20. Barker, "Secret History," p. 440; *New York Weekly Sun*, July 18, 1883; W. Bateman to J. Sherman, June 12, 1880, Bateman Papers, WRHS.

21. W. Bateman to J. Sherman, June 12, 21 and 23, 1880; Mary Fields to Bateman, July 14, 1880, all in the Bateman Papers, WRHS.

22. *Cincinnati Commercial*, undated scrapbook clipping, Garfield Papers, LC; *Cleveland Herald*, May 31, 1880.

23. *Cleveland Herald*, May 31, June 1 and 3, 1880; Garfield to his wife, May 31, June 3 and 4, 1880, Garfield Papers, LC.

24. *Proceedings of the Republican Convention*, p. 31; Barker, "Secret History," p. 444.

25. C. W. Clarke to B. A. Hinsdale, October 28, 1881, Hinsdale Papers, WRHS. The official *Proceedings* of the convention tones down Garfield's remarks to the more innocuous: "I fear this Convention is about to commit a great error." (p. 40).

26. Roscoe Conkling to Garfield, n.d., Garfield Papers, LC; Barker, "Secret History," p. 444.

27. *Cleveland Herald*, May 31 and June 5, 1880; Wm. Henry Smith to R. B. Hayes, June 15, 1880, typed copy, HML; Garfield to his wife, June 6, 1880, Garfield Papers, LC; Barker, "Secret History," pp. 441-42.

28. Garfield to his wife, June 3, 1880; J. B. Cassoday to Garfield, June 30, 1880, both in the Garfield Papers, LC.

29. *Proceedings of the Republican Convention*, pp. 160-65.

30. *Cleveland Herald*, June 4 and 5, 1880; R. B. Hayes Diary, June 5, 1880, in C. R. Williams, *Diary and Letters of Hayes*, III, 600.

31. *Proceedings of the Republican Convention*, pp. 175-77; Depew, *My Memories*, p. 121.

32. C. W. Clarke to B. A. Hinsdale, October 28, 1881, Hinsdale Papers, WRHS; *Cincinnati Commercial*, June 6, 1880; *Proceedings of the Republican Convention*, pp. 179-82.

33. Garfield to his wife, June 2 and 6, 1880, Garfield Papers, LC. Garfield's earlier use of this image can be found in the *Cong. Record*, 42 Cong., 1 sess., 154 (December 11, 1873). His preceptor, Henry Winter Davis had used this same metaphor even earlier.

34. Garfield, *Works*, II, 777-81; G. F. Hoar to B. A. Hinsdale, September 28, 1881, Hinsdale Papers, WRHS; Lincoln story in F. A. Henry, *Captain Henry*, pp. 297-98.

35. C. W. Clarke to B. A. Hinsdale, October 28, 1881, Hinsdale Papers, WRHS; Halstead, "Tragedy of Garfield's Administration," p. 272.

36. A. C. French to Garfield, June 6, 1880, Garfield Papers, LC; H. C. Lodge cited in Smith, *Life and Letters of Garfield*, II, 978; Benj. Harrison to B. A. Hinsdale, September 30, 1881, Hinsdale Papers, WRHS.

37. *Cleveland Herald*, June 7, 1880.

38. W. Bateman to J. Sherman, June 16 and 21, 1880, Bateman Papers, WRHS.

39. Barker, "Secret History," p. 440; W. A. Grier to Garfield, November 17, 1880, Garfield Papers, LC; *Cleveland Herald*, June 7, 1880.

40. *Cleveland Herald*, June 12, 1880; W. Bateman to J. Sherman, June 12 and 21, 1880; Bateman Papers, WRHS; Halstead, "Tragedy," p. 273.

41. Clayton, *Reminiscences of J. S. Black*, pp. 192-94.

42. Henry, *Captain Henry*, p. 296; Wm. Henry Smith to R. B. Hayes, June 15, 1880, typed copy, HML; J. Rusk to Garfield, May 27, 1881, Garfield Papers, LC; Connelley, *Preston Plumb*, pp. 245-47.

43. R. G. Ingersoll to Garfield, June 8, 1880; S. Elkins to Garfield, June 8, 1880, both in the Garfield Papers, LC; *Proceedings of the Republican Convention*, p. 261.

44. J. Rusk to Garfield, May 27, 1881; J. B. Cassoday to Garfield, June 30, 1880, both in the Garfield Papers, LC; Campbell, *Wisconsin*, IV, 285-86.

45. W. Bateman to J. Sherman, June 12, 1880, Bateman Papers, WRHS; A. J. Turner cited in Campbell, *Wisconsin*, IV, 286-90; J. B. Cassoday to Garfield, June 30, 1880, Garfield Papers, LC.

46. Campbell, *Wisconsin*, IV, 287; F. A. Henry, *Captain Henry*, 296; Hoar, *Autobiography*, I, 395-97.

47. C. W. Clarke to B. A. Hinsdale, October 28, 1881, Hinsdale Papers, WRHS; J. Spaulding to Garfield, January 15, 1881, Garfield Papers, LC; Smith, "How Conkling Missed Nominating Blaine," p. 3; Campbell, *Wisconsin*, IV, 298.

48. *Cleveland Herald*, June 9, 1880.

49. *Ibid.*, June 8, 1880; E. C. Smith to A. F. Rockwell, June 22, 1880 in unidentified scrapbook clipping, Garfield Papers, LC; *Proceedings of the Republican Convention*, pp. 276-79.

50. Barker, "Secret History," p. 442; G. L. Shoup to Garfield, November 22, 1880; J. B. Cassoday to Garfield, June 30, 1880, both in Garfield Papers, LC; Journal of Wm. Henry Smith, August 9, 1880, typed copy, HML; Turner cited in Campbell, *Wisconsin*, IV, 287.

51. C. W. Clarke to B. A. Hinsdale, October 28, 1881; Benj. Harrison to B. A. Hinsdale, September 30, 1881, both in the Hinsdale Papers, WRHS; J. B. Cassoday to Garfield, June 30, 1880, Garfield Papers, LC; W. Bateman to J. Sherman, June 12, 1880, Bateman Papers, WRHS.

52. Sherman, *Recollections*, II, 807; "Memo of conversation with Justin Morrill, February 12, 1883," Sherman Papers, LC; Hoar, *Autobiography*, I, 396.

53. *Cleveland Herald*, June 9, 1880; *Chicago Daily News*, in Smith, *Life and Letters of Garfield*, II, 981; Fuller, *Reminiscences*, p. 430; Rockwell, "From Mentor to Elberon," p. 431; Lucretia Garfield, Diary, March 1, 1881, typed copy; Benj. Harrison to B. A. Hinsdale, September 30, 1881, Hinsdale Papers, WRHS.

54. F. A. Henry, *Captain Henry*, 296; W. W. Phelps to Garfield, October 22, 1880; Lucretia Garfield to James Garfield, June 4, 1880, both in the Garfield Papers, LC.

55. Diary, December 31, 1880, Garfield Papers, LC; Garfield to C. E. Fuller, February 11, 1855, Fuller, *Reminiscences*, p. 217.

56. *Proceedings of the Republican Convention*, p. 297; W. Bateman to J. Sherman, June 12, 1880, Bateman Papers, WRHS.

57. Warner Bateman to J. Sherman, June 12, 15 and 21, 1880, Bateman Papers, WRHS; D. G. Swaim to Garfield, April 27, 1880, Garfield Papers, LC; Alexander, *Political History of New York*, III, 442-45; McElroy, *Levi Morton*, pp. 105-06.

58. Hudson, *Random Recollections*, pp. 96-99.

59. *Proceedings of the Republican Convention*, p. 293; J. Sherman to J. M. Hoyt, June 12, 1880, in Moore, "Ohio in National Politics," 339n.; J. Sherman to W. Bateman, June 9, 1880; W. E. Chandler to W. Bateman, June 22, 1880, both in the Bateman Papers, WRHS.

60. *Cong. Record*, 45 Cong., 2 sess., 1192; R. B. Hayes to G. W. Jones, June 11, 1880, typed copy, HML; Hudson, *Random Recollections*, p. 104.

22. A BUSY, PLEASANT SUMMER

1. Lucretia Garfield Diary, March 1, 1881, typed copy; *Cleveland Herald*, June 10-12, 1880; Diary, October 11, 1872; M. Jewell to Garfield, July 29, 1880; R. B. Hayes to Garfield, July 26 and August 22, 1880, all in the Garfield Papers, LC.

2. Garfield, *Works*, II, 782-87.

3. J. G. Blaine to Garfield, December 16, 1880, typed copy; Wm. E. Chandler to Garfield, July 24, 1880, both in the Garfield Papers, LC.

4. Garfield to J. G. Blaine, June 29, 1880; Garfield to C. Schurz, July 22, 1880, letterbook copy, both in the Garfield Papers, LC; Garfield to B. A. Hinsdale, July 25, 1880, in Mary Hinsdale, *Garfield-Hinsdale Letters*, 454-55.

5. R. B. Hayes Diary, July 19, 1880, in C. R. Williams, *Diary and Letters of Hayes*, III, 614; M. Jewell to Garfield, July 15, 1880, Garfield Papers, LC; Smith, *Life and Letters of Garfield*, II, 1004.

6. U. S. Grant to Thomas Nast, June 26, 1880, in Paine, *Th. Nast*, p. 432; J. Sherman to W. Bateman, June 29, 1880, Bateman Papers, WRHS; Curran, *Patrick Collins*, pp. 82-83; Memoirs of Th. P. Donaldson, typed copy, HML.

7. A. R. Conkling, *Life of Roscoe Conkling*, p. 629; Garfield to Conkling, June 17, 1880, initial draft; W. Reid to Garfield, June 26, 1880; Garfield to Reid, June 29, 1880, typed copy, all in the Garfield Papers, LC.

8. Hughes, *Letters of John Murray Forbes*, II, 194-97; Richardson, *William E. Chandler*, pp. 258-59; Marcus, *Grand Old Party*, pp. 39-42; J. M. Forbes to ?, June 17, 1880; Garfield to C. Foster, June 29, 1880, letterbook copy; J. M. Forbes to Garfield, July 1, 1880, all in the Garfield Papers, LC.

9. Herndon, *Centennial History of Arkansas*, I, 307; S. C. Boynton to Garfield, July 10, 1880; D. C. Gordon to Garfield, November 27, 1880; T. M. Nichol to Garfield, July 31, 1880, all in the Garfield Papers, LC.

10. S. W. Dorsey to Garfield, July 25, 1880; M. Jewell to Garfield,

July 24, 1880; W. Reid to Garfield, July 30, 1880, all in the Garfield Papers, LC; B. A. Hinsdale to Garfield, July 30, 1880, Garfield Papers, WRHS.

11. Garfield to W. Reid, July 21, 1880; S. W. Dorsey to Garfield, July 25 and 26, 1880; M. Halstead to Garfield, July 4, 1880; W. E. Chandler to Garfield, July 25, 1880; Diary, July 28, 1880, all in the Garfield Papers, LC.

12. *Cleveland Herald*, August 10, 1880; W. Reid to Garfield, July 3, 1880; Diary, August 3 and 4, 1880; Garfield to his wife, August 4, 1880, all in the Garfield Papers, LC.

13. Marcus, *Grand Old Party*, p. 48; McElroy, *Levi Morton*, pp. 109-10; W. Reid to Garfield, August 13, 1880, Garfield Papers, LC; Gorham, *Conkling Vindicated*, p. 11; Halstead, "Tragedy," p. 275.

14. Marcus, *Grand Old Party*, pp. 45-47; W. E. Chandler to Garfield, July 24, 1880; M. Jewell to Garfield, July 25, 1880; W. Reid to Garfield, July 30, 1880; Memo of J. Stanley-Brown, January 23, 1885; Garfield to W. Reid, July 21, 1880; Garfield to R. B. Hayes, July 31, 1880, letterbook copy, Diary, August 5, 1880, all in the Garfield Papers, LC; Platt, *Autobiography*, 130-31.

15. Conkling, *Life of Conkling*, p. 614; Halstead, "Tragedy," pp. 274-75; Platt, *Autobiography*, pp. 132-33; J. G. Blaine to Garfield, July 4, 1880; W. Reid to Garfield, August 13, 1880, both in the Garfield Papers, LC.

16. Diary, August 9, 1880, James R. Garfield Papers, LC; Diary, August 9 and 10; W. Reid to Garfield, July 30, 1880, both in the Garfield Papers, LC; *New York Weekly Sun*, July 18, 1883; C. R. Williams, *Hayes Diary and Letters*, IV, 220; Ogden, *Diaries of Andrew White*, p. 233.

17. Thad. Pound to Garfield, June 19, 1880; J. N. Tyner to Garfield, June 24, 1880, both in the Garfield Papers, LC; Benj. Harrison to W. Bateman, June 28, 1880, Bateman Papers, WRHS.

18. Davenport, *History of the "Morey Letter,"* 6; M. Jewell to Garfield, September 29, 1880; Diary, October 6 and 14, 1880; Garfield to W. Reid, September 2, 1880, all in the Garfield Papers, LC.

19. A. E. Pillsbury to Garfield, September 14, 1880; E. V. Smalley to Garfield, September 4, 1880; J. G. Blaine to Garfield, September 14, 1880, telegram; Garfield to M. D. Leggett, September 15, 1880, all in the Garfield Papers, LC.

20. C. R. Williams, *Hayes Diary and Letters*, III, 600-01; *Cong. Record*, 45 Cong., 3 sess., 75 (December 10, 1878); *Cleveland Herald*, August 10, 1880; F. Haviland to Garfield, August 31, 1880, Garfield Papers, LC.

21. Hudson, *Random Recollections*, p. 112; *The Business Outlook*, July 14, 1880; Paine, *Th. Nast*, p. 438; E. Cowles to Garfield, October 9, 1880, telegram, Garfield Papers, LC. Garfield had called the tariff a local issue in a speech of August 27, 1870, Garfield, *Works*, I, 624; see also, Diary, May 15, 1872, Garfield Papers, LC.

22. M. Jewell to Garfield, July 23 and 24, 1880; Hoar cited in J. M.

Forbes to Garfield, June 10, 1880; W. Reid to Garfield, August 31, 1880; [Ed. McPherson to Garfield, December 23, 1880], all in the Garfield Papers, LC.

23. Hughes, *Letters of John Murray Forbes*, II, 199-200.

24. *Cong. Globe*, 42 Cong., 2 sess., 2584 (April 19, 1872); J. M. McGrew to Garfield, July 29, 1880, Garfield Papers, LC.

25. J. Hubbell to Garfield, June 25, July 8, August 23 and 27, 1880; J. Sherman to Garfield, September 15, 1880, all in the Garfield Papers, LC; Reeves, "Chester Arthur and Campaign Assessments," pp. 573-82.

26. Magrath, *Morrison Waite*, pp. 239-40; M. Jewell to Garfield, August 30, 1880; Whitelaw Reid to Garfield, August 31, 1880; C. Foster to P. Plumb, September 6, 1880, copy by G. U. Rose on Garfield's Mentor stationery; Garfield to W. Reid, September 2, 1880, all in the Garfield Papers, LC.

27. Magrath, *Waite*, pp. 240-42; W. Reid to Garfield, September 6, 14 and 30, 1880; Garfield to Reid, September 15 and 23 (early draft in letterbook), 1880, all in the Garfield Papers, LC.

28. Wharton Barker to Garfield, October 16, 1880, C. Foster to Garfield, September 16, 1880; L. P. Morton to Garfield, September 22 [1880]; L. Wolfe to Garfield, October 2, 1880, telegram, all in the Garfield Papers, LC.

29. Diary, May 27 and August 22, 1880, *ibid.*; Comer, *Harry Garfield*, p. 43.

30. C. E. Henry to Garfield, January 17, 1874; Diary, August 12, 1880, both in the Garfield Papers, LC; B. A. Hinsdale to Garfield, April 19, 1880, in Mary Hinsdale, *Garfield-Hinsdale Letters*, p. 448.

31. T. M. Nichol to W. Bateman, June 28, 1880, Bateman Papers, WRHS; Fuller, *Reminiscences*, pp. 430-31; Garfield to W. C. Howells, August 23, 1880; Diary, August 15 and September 25, 1880, Garfield Papers, LC; F. A. Henry, *Captain Henry*, p. 304.

32. Diary, September 26 and 30, October 18 and 19, 1880, Garfield Papers, LC; *The World* (London), March 9, 1881; J. Stanley-Brown, "My Friend Garfield," pp. 51-52.

33. Conkling, *Roscoe Conkling*, pp. 618, 620n., 626-27; Jordan, *Roscoe Conkling*, p. 356; Garfield to H. Austin, October 6, 1880; Garfield to U. S. Grant, July 26, 1880, letterbook; Grant to Garfield, August 5, 1880; H. Porter to Garfield, October 13, 1880; see various telegrams to Garfield from Perkins, Hanna, McCoy and Cameron, September 28, 1880, all in the Garfield Papers, LC; Garfield to John M. Stull, September 3 and 4, telegrams, Stull Papers, WRHS; J. Stanley-Brown, "My Friend Garfield," pp. 50-51.

34. Platt, *Autobiography*, II, 135; Smith, *Life and Letters of Garfield*, II, 1033; Memo of J. S. Brown, January 23, 1885; Diary, September 28, 1880, both in the Garfield Papers, LC.

35. Garfield to W. Reid, August 30 and September 2, 1880; Diary,

NOTES: CHAPTER 22

September 2 and 3, 1880; P. Plumb to Garfield, September 19, 1880, all in the Garfield Papers, LC.

36. House, "Democratic State Central Committee," pp. 179-86; Garfield to C. A. Arthur, August 30, 1880, letterbook copy, Garfield Papers, LC.

37. Garfield to W. Reid, September 15, 1880; S. W. Dorsey to Garfield, September 17, 1880; Wm. W. Dudley to Garfield, August 10, 1880; L. Sheldon to Garfield, August 11, 1880; Garfield to A. Townsend, September 2, 1880, letterbook copy; A. Townsend to Garfield, September 3, 1880; D. G. Swaim to Garfield, September 5, 1880, all in the Garfield Papers, LC.

38. O. F. Lane to Garfield, June 12, 1880; L. L. Carpenter to Garfield, July 16, 1880, both *ibid.*; B. A. Hinsdale to Garfield, September 26 and November 2, 1880, Garfield Papers, WRHS; *New York Weekly Sun*, July 18, 1883.

39. R. McCormick to Garfield, August 16 and October 5, 1880; L. P. Morton to Garfield, September 6, 1880; M. Jewell to Garfield, September 14 and 18, 1880, all in the Garfield Papers, LC.

40. *New York Weekly Sun*, July 18, 1883; *Harpers Weekly*, XXVIII (November 15, 1884), 748; House, "Democratic State Central Committee," p. 189; S. W. Dorsey to D. G. Swaim, September 1, 1880; S. W. Dorsey to Garfield, September 27, 1880; Garfield to C. A. Arthur, August 30, 1880, letterbook copy; Wm. W. Dudley to Garfield, September 9, 1880; Wm. T. Henderson to S. W. Dorsey, September 12, 1880, all in the Garfield Papers, LC.

41. See, for example, Allen Pinkerton to S. W. Dorsey, September 15, 1880, in "Letters Rec'd by D. G. Swaim, 1880-1881," Garfield Papers, LC. A typical report was that of a Pinkerton agent who spotted a stranger on a ferry who claimed to be on his way to New Albany to visit friends. His suspicions aroused, the Pinkerton man followed the stranger into New Albany and discovered that he was indeed visiting friends.

42. T. M. Nichol to Garfield, July 31, 1880, Garfield Papers, LC; *New York Weekly Sun*, July 18, 1883; B. A. Hinsdale to Garfield, January 8, 1881, in Mary Hinsdale, *Garfield-Hinsdale Letters*, p. 477; R. McCormick to W. E. Chandler, October 5, 1880, Chandler Papers, LC.

43. House, "Democratic State Central Committee," p. 208; R. Ingersoll to Garfield, October 13, 1880, Garfield Papers, LC.

44. M. Jewell to Garfield, October 21 and October 22 (telegram), 1880; H. E. Knox and A. F. Rockwell to Garfield, October 23, 1880, all in the Garfield Papers, LC.

45. Garfield to M. Jewell and S. W. Dorsey, October 22, 1880; J. C. Keiffer to D. G. Swaim, October 22, 1880, telegrams; Diary, October 22, 23, 24 and 31, 1880; M. Jewell to Garfield, October 26, 1880; A. J. Dittenhoefer to Garfield, October 27 and 28, 1880, all *ibid.*; Caldwell, *Garfield*, p. 309.

677

46. Davenport, *History of the "Morey Letter"*; Garfield to M. Jewell, October 23, 1880, telegram; H. E. Knox and A. F. Rockwell to Garfield, October 23, 1880; J. Hart to Garfield, December 9, 1880; A. Hewitt to M. Jewell, February 7, 1881, typed copy, all in the Garfield Papers, LC.

47. Diary, November 2, 1880, Garfield Papers, LC.

48. These figures, and most of those that follow, are drawn from Burnham, *Presidential Ballots*.

49. Hamilton, *Blaine*, p. 525.

50. Garfield to W. N. Hudson, November 8, 1880, in unidentified newspaper clipping in letterbook, Garfield Papers, LC.

51. Smalley, "Characteristics of Garfield," p. 176; Garfield to J. H. Rhodes, November 16, 1880; C. Schurz to Garfield, December 10, 1880; Diary, December 31, 1880, all in the Garfield Papers, LC.

23. JUSTICE AND JUDGMENT

1. Garfield to B. A. Hinsdale, November 17, 1880, Garfield Papers, WRHS; J. Eggerston to Garfield, July 1, 1880; T. P. Stern to Garfield, June 18, 1880; T. Pound to Garfield, December 25, 1880; T. M. Nichol to Garfield, January 3 and 20, 1881; Garfield to his wife, January 21, 1881; Diary, December 16, 1880; J. Hay to Garfield, December 6, 1880, all in the Garfield Papers, LC; Eliza Garfield Diary, January 15, 1881, WRHS.

2. Rockwell, "From Mentor to Elberon," p. 475; Diary, December 11, 1880; Jere. Black to Garfield, June 10, 1880; W. E. Chandler to Garfield, October 15, 1880, all in the Garfield Papers, LC; J. Hay to Whitelaw Reid, October 29, 1880, typed copy, Reid Papers, LC. Black and Garfield were finally reconciled at the dying president's bedside.

3. *Alta Californian*, August 18, 1880; Garfield to W. S. Rosecrans, December 31, 1880, draft in letterbook; Garfield to C. L. Ransom, January 31, 1881, telegram, both in Garfield Papers, LC.

4. Morgan, *From Hayes to McKinley*, p. 13; C. Schurz to Garfield, February 22, 1881; J. G. Blaine to Garfield, December 16, 1880, typed copy, both in the Garfield Papers, LC.

5. Garfield to J. G. Blaine, December 19, 1880, typed copy in letterbook; C. Schurz to Garfield, January 2 and 28, 1881; Diary, December 29, 1880; J. G. Blaine to Garfield, February 16, 1881, all in the Garfield Papers, LC.

6. Benj. Harrison to Garfield, January 28 and February 4, 1881; J. Logan to Garfield, December 20 and 28, 1880; Diary, December 29, 1880; January 23 and February 11, 1881; T. M. Nichol to Garfield, January 20, 1881; D. G. Swaim to Garfield, February 28, 1881, all in *ibid*.

7. C. H. Hill to Garfield, January 1, 1881; Luke Poland to Garfield, January 6, 1881; T. W. Higginson to Garfield, January 12, 1881; J. Sherman to Garfield, January 23, 1881; U. S. Grant to Garfield, January 26, 1881, all in *ibid*.

8. Diary, April 14 and November 27, 1880; J. G. Blaine to Garfield, December 13, 16 (typed copy) and 20, 1880, all in *ibid.*; Smith, *Life and Letters of Garfield*, II, 1049.

9. Garfield to J. G. Blaine, December 23, 1880; W. E. Chandler to Garfield, December 24, 1880, both in the Garfield Papers, LC; Cortissoz, *Whitelaw Reid*, II, 43-44.

10. Diary, November 27 and December 13, 1880; Garfield to J. G. Blaine, January 21, 1881, letterbook copy; S. W. Dorsey to Garfield, December 16, 1880, all in the Garfield Papers, LC; Connery, "Secret History," p. 152; Platt, *Autobiography*, p. 132; *New York Weekly Sun*, July 18, 1883.

11. L. P. Morton to Garfield, January 17, 1881; Diary, November 28, December 13 and 14, 1880; S. W. Dorsey to D. G. Swaim, December 16, 1880; P. Plumb to Garfield, December 20, 1880; T. M. Nichol to Garfield, January 25, 1881; W. B. Allison to Garfield, January 2, 1881; Memo of J. S. Brown, January 23, 1885, all in the Garfield Papers, LC; Crowley, *Echoes from Niagara*, pp. 194-95. In later years, however, Morton did indicate, in a private memorandum, that Garfield had promised to appoint him Secretary of the Treasury. See McElroy, *Levi P. Morton*, p. 121.

12. D. G. Swaim to S. W. Dorsey, December 22, 1880; Garfield to S. W. Dorsey, December 20, 1880; S. W. Dorsey to D. G. Swaim, December 16, 1880; T. M. Nichol to Garfield, January 25, 1881; W. Reid to Garfield, December 10, 1880; P. Plumb to Garfield, December 20, 1880; W. B. Allison to Garfield, January 2, 1881, all in the Garfield Papers, LC.

13. C. E. Henry to Garfield, July 27, 1880; P. Plumb to Garfield, December 22, 1880; W. Reid to Garfield, December 10, 1880; J. Kilpatrick to Garfield, December 27, 1880; Diary, December 13, 1880; M. Jewell to Garfield, December 18, 1880, all in *ibid.*; Crowley, *Echoes of Niagara*, pp. 194-95.

14. Depew, *My Memories*, 111-12; *New York Tribune*, January 3, 1881; Cortissoz, *Whitelaw Reid*, II, 45-47; W. Reid to Wm. W. Phelps, December 31, 1880; W. Reid to Garfield, January 1, 1881; Garfield to W. Reid, January 3, 1881, letterbook copy, all in the Garfield Papers, LC.

15. W. Reid to Garfield, January 16, 1881, Garfield Papers, LC; Cortissoz, *Whitelaw Reid*, II, 50; Depew, *My Memories*, p. 112.

16. W. Reid to J. Hay, n.d., in Cortissoz, *Whitelaw Reid*, II, 51; W. Reid to Garfield, February 3, 1881; P. Plumb to Garfield, January 21, 1881; L. P. Morton to Garfield, January 17, 1881, all in the Garfield Papers, LC.

17. J. G. Blaine to Garfield, December 24, 1880, January 28 and February 5, 1881; G. W. Allen to Garfield, December 18, 1880; Diary, January 16, 1881, all in the Garfield Papers, LC.

18. J. Sherman to Garfield, January 23, 1881; J. B. Belford to Garfield, January 17, 1881; T. M. Nichol to Garfield, January 25, 1881; U. S. Grant to Garfield, January 26, 1881; S. W. Dorsey to Garfield, February 24, 1881; J. G. Blaine to Garfield, January 30, 1881, all in *ibid.*

19. J. G. Blaine to Garfield, January 30 and February 18, 1881; Garfield to Blaine, February 21, 1881, letterbook copy, all in *ibid.*
20. W. E. Chandler to Garfield, January 26, 1881; W. Reid to Garfield, January 26, 1881; Garfield to J. G. Blaine, January 31, 1881, letterbook copy; [J. G. Blaine] to Garfield, February [4], 1881, all in *ibid.*
21. Garfield to J. G. Blaine, December 23, 1880, typed copy; W. Reid to Garfield, January 9, 1881; Lucretia Garfield to J. A. Garfield, January 21, 1881, all in *ibid.*
22. J. G. Blaine to Garfield, January 28 and 30, February 13, 1881, *ibid.*
23. Roscoe Conkling to Garfield, February 8, 1881; Diary, February 16 and 19, 1881; Garfield to J. G. Blaine, February 18, 1881, letterbook copy, all in *ibid.*; Garfield to B. A. Hinsdale, February 18, 1881, in Mary Hinsdale, *Garfield-Hinsdale Letters*, p. 481; Connery, "Secret History," pp. 151-52; Crowley, *Echoes of Niagara*, p. 204.
24. [J. G. Blaine] to Garfield, February [4] and 20, 1881; W. E. Chandler to Garfield, February 19, 1881; W. Reid to Garfield, January 31 and February 2, 1881; Diary, February 19, 1881; C. J. Folger to Garfield, February 21, 1881, all in the Garfield Papers, LC. During the Arthur administration, Folger would be appointed Secretary of the Treasury. He served his term without disgracing either himself or the country.
25. Diary, June 21 and 22, 1873; January 17 and 27, February 10, 1881, *ibid.*
26. For devotees of psychohistory, here is the entire dream as remembered by Garfield the next morning: "Last night I dreamed that Gen. Arthur, Maj. Swaim and I were on an excursion to attend some great ceremonial. We were on a canal packet during the night. A heavy rainstorm came on, and in the gray of the morning Swaim and I awoke just as the packet was passing a point to enter a deep broad basin. We leaped ashore, and on looking back saw that the packet was sinking. Just as it was sinking I noticed Gen. Arthur lying on a couch very pale, and apparently very ill. In an instant more the packet sank with all on board. I started to plunge into the water to save Arthur, but Swaim held me, and said he cannot be saved, and you will perish if you attempt it. It appeared that we were naked and alone in the wild storm, and that the country was hostile. I felt that nakedness was a disguise which would avoid identification. In this dream, for the first time in a dream, I knew I was Pres. Elect. After a long and tangled journey we entered a house, and an old negro woman took me into her arms and nursed me as though I was a sick child. At this point I awoke." Memorandum, January 21, 1881, Garfield Papers, LC.
27. J. D. Cox to Garfield, February 10, 1881; Garfield to R. T. Lincoln, February 28, 1881; Garfield to W. McVeagh, February 28, 1881, letterbook copies; R. T. Lincoln to Garfield, March 2, 1881; W. McVeagh to Garfield, March 2, 1861, all in *ibid.*

28. Garfield to W. B. Allison, February 28, 1881, letterbook copy; W. B. Allison to Garfield, March 1, 1881, both in *ibid.*

29. R. B. Hayes to Garfield, December 16, 1880; January 28, 1881; Garfield to John Hay, 1881; Garfield to J. G. Blaine, January 25, 1881, letterbook copy; Memo of February 27, 1881, all in *ibid.*

30. J. G. Blaine to Garfield, February 24, 1881; Garfield to Wm. Windom, February 28, 1881, letterbook copy; Garfield to L. P. Morton, February 26, 1881, letterbook copy; L. P. Morton to Garfield, February 28, 1881, all in *ibid.*; W. Reid to E. Mills, March 1, 1881, in Cortissoz, *Whitelaw Reid*, II, 54.

31. Garfield to H. Austin, February 7, 1881, Garfield Papers, LC; *Painesville Telegraph*, March 3, 1881.

32. W. Reid to E. Mills, March 1 and 2, 1881, in Cortissoz, *Whitelaw Reid*, II, 54-55; J. G. Blaine to Garfield, March 1, 1881; Diary, March 1, 1881, both in the Garfield Papers, LC.

33. Connery, "Secret History," pp. 152-53; L. P. Morton to Garfield, March 2, 1881; Diary, March 2, 1881, both in the Garfield Papers, LC. Morton would ultimately reap his reward for patient obedience as vice-president in the Harrison administration.

34. W. Reid to E. Mills, March 2 and 3, 1881, in Cortissoz, *Whitelaw Reid*, II, 55-56; Fowler, *Cabinet Politician*, pp. 168-69; Garfield to J. G. Blaine, January 21, 1881, letterbook copy; J. G. Blaine to Garfield, February 5, 1881; Diary, March 2 and 3, 1881, all in the Garfield Papers, LC. Despite his wide political connections, Garfield had not even met three of his seven cabinet members until after they had been appointed: James, Hunt and Lincoln.

35. *Brooklyn Daily Eagle*, March 8, 1885, in Smith, *Life and Letters of Garfield*, II, 1093-94; Diary, March 3, 1881, Garfield Papers, LC.

36. Diary, November 1, 1875; March 1 and 4, 1881; W. B. Allison to Garfield, March 4, 1881; Sage, *William B. Allison*, pp. 166-70.

37. J. G. Blaine to Garfield [March 4, 1881]; Garfield to J. G. Blaine, March 4, 1881, letterbook copy; Diary, March 4, 1881, all in the Garfield Papers, LC; W. Reid to E. Mills, March 4, 1881, in Cortissoz, *Whitelaw Reid*, II, 56-57.

38. *Springfield* [Mass.] *Republican*, March 4, 1881, *New York Herald*, March 5, 1881; Memoirs of Thos. Donaldson, March 4, 1881, typed copy, HML.

39. *New York Times*, March 5, 1881; *Cincinnati Enquirer*, March 5, 1881; Lucretia Garfield Diary, March 4, 1881, typed copy; Barnard, *Rutherford B. Hayes*, pp. 496, 500.

40. *Cincinnati Enquirer*, March 5, 1881; *New York Herald*, March 5, 1881; Lucretia Garfield Diary, March 4, 1881, typed copy; R. B. Hayes to Garfield, March 6, 1881, Garfield Papers, LC; *London Telegraph*, undated scrapbook clipping in Garfield Papers, LC; Garfield, *Works*, II, 788-95.

41. Garfield to R. B. Hayes, March 11, 1881, Garfield Papers, LC;

New York Herald, March 5, 1881; Riddle, *Recollections of War Times*, p. 330n.; Memoirs of Thos. G. Donaldson, March 4, 1881, typed copy, HML.

42. *Washington Republican*, March 5, 1881; *New York Herald*, March 5, 1881; *Cincinnati Enquirer*, March 5, 1881; Colman, *White House Gossip*, p. 131.

43. Diary, March 4 and 5, 1881, Garfield Papers, LC; Lucretia Garfield Diary, March 5, 1881, typed copy.

24. THE PORCUPINE ADMINISTRATION

1. J. Hay to Garfield, December 6 and 13, 1880, Garfield Papers, LC; Dangerfield, *Era of Good Feelings*, p. 332.

2. Garfield to ?, March 2, 1869, letterbook copy; Diary, March 10, 1875, both in the Garfield Papers, LC; Speech at Warren, Ohio, July 31, 1872, in Garfield, *Works*, II, 32-33.

3. Diary, March 14, 1881, Garfield Papers, LC; Peskin, "President Garfield and the Rating Game."

4. Davison, *Presidency of Hayes*, p. 82.

5. Eliza Garfield Diary, March 2, 1881; Mollie Garfield to J. F. King, March 17, 1881, xerox copy, both at WRHS; *Cincinnati Gazette*, undated scrapbook clipping, Garfield Papers, LC; Lucretia Garfield Diary, March 26, 1881, typed copy; Crook, *Memories of the White House*, pp. 142-46; "Life Book," December 1883, Harry Garfield Papers, LC.

6. Lucretia Garfield Diary, March 17, 19, 21, 22 and 26, 1881, typed copy; A. Snead to R. B. Hayes, April 23, 1881, HML; C. R. Williams, *Diary and Letters of Hayes*, III, 638-40.

7. B. A. Hinsdale to Garfield, November 9, 1880, in Mary Hinsdale, *Garfield-Hinsdale Letters*, p. 464-65; F. Willard to Garfield, June 10, 1880; Diary, August 28, 1880; January 9 and 23, 1881, Garfield Papers, LC.

8. J. G. Blaine to Garfield, December 15, 1880, Garfield Papers, LC; Arthur cited in Morgan, *Hayes to McKinley*, p. 148; *Washington Star*, undated scrapbook clipping, Garfield Papers, LC.

9. Lucretia Garfield Diary, March 12, 1881, typed copy; Memoirs of Thos. M. Donaldson, May 17, 1880 and June 14, 1881, typed copies, HML; W. T. Crump to "Dear Sir," April 18, [18??], Garfield Papers, LC.

10. Davison, *Presidency of Hayes*, pp. 80-81; J. Bushman to A. F. Rockwell, April 8, 1881, Garfield Papers, LC.

11. Wm. J. Sedwick to Garfield, May 24, 1881; J. R. Dillon to Garfield, June 15, 1881, telegrams, Garfield Papers, LC.

12. Garfield to W. Reid, December 7, 1880; Garfield to J. Hay, December 20, 1880, letterbook copy; J. Hay to Garfield, December 25, 1880; Diary, February 4, 1881, all in the Garfield Papers, LC. Hay was already an Assistant Secretary in the State Department, but after he had disappointed Garfield he felt compelled to resign the position and leave the government entirely.

13. G. U. Rose to Garfield, March 15, 1881; T. M. Nichol to Garfield, January 25, 1881, both in *ibid.*

14. Mollie Garfield to J. F. King, March 17 and September 16, 1881, xeroxed copies, WRHS; Diary, March 8, 1881, Garfield Papers, LC; J. Hay to W. Reid, March 23, 1881, typed copy, Reid Papers, LC.

15. Ari Hoogenboom, in *Outlawing the Spoils*, p. 279, computes the total at 107,000.

16. Tocqueville, *Democracy in America*, p. 262; Garfield cited in Smith, *Life and Letters of Garfield*, II, 1151.

17. Hamilton, *Blaine*, p. 514; Diary, March 16 and June 8, 1881, Garfield Papers, LC.

18. Actually, Swaim had been appointed in the last days of the Hayes administration as a favor to Garfield.

19. Henry's appointment caused a minor political storm. Blaine, Albert G. Riddle and others objected to the dismissal of Frederick Douglass, the incumbent marshall, on the grounds that it might be construed as an abandonment of the Negro. To ease these fears, a place in the District was found for Douglass as Recorder of Deeds. For good measure, Blanche K. Bruce was named Register of the Treasury.

20. Neither would enjoy the honor. Nichol's nomination met with opposition from influential Western senators and had to be withdrawn. Rusk, who had expected something more substantial than a minor diplomatic post, spurned the appointment and stayed home to run for governor of Wisconsin instead.

21. Diary, April 17, 19, June 13, 1881; Garfield to L. Wallace, April 19, 1881, letterbook copy, all in the Garfield Papers, LC.

22. Fowler, *Cabinet Politicians*, pp. 168-69, 179. Hayes's First Assistant Postmaster unabashedly boasted of his "untiring efforts to put none but honest men in office anywhere and to trust Democrats only where Republicans cannot be found. And in all cases where positions are sought by Republicans only, I have . . . chosen first those who stood the firmest by the Administration." J. N. Tyner to Garfield, June 23, 1881, Garfield Papers, LC.

23. Diary, November 26 and 28, 1881, Garfield Papers, LC; Hamilton, *Blaine*, pp. 484-85.

24. Unidentified scrapbook clipping, April 21, 1881; undated notes of Blaine to Garfield, both in the Garfield Papers, LC.

25. J. Sherman to Garfield, January 23, 1881; J. G. Blaine to Garfield, n.d., both in *ibid.*; Gerry, *Through Five Administrations*, pp. 262-63.

26. J. G. Blaine to Garfield, February 13, 1881; E. Hale to Garfield, March 16, 1881; M. A. Dodge to Garfield, n.d.; W. E. Chandler to Garfield, October 7, 1874, all in the Garfield Papers, LC; Garfield to B. A. Hinsdale, April 4, 1881, in Mary Hinsdale, *Garfield-Hinsdale Letters*, p. 490.

27. W. E. Chandler to W. Bateman, June 22, 1880, Bateman Papers,

WRHS; Garfield to J. G. Blaine, March 17, 1881, letterbook copy, Garfield Papers, LC.

28. J. G. Blaine to Garfield, n.d.; W. T. Crump to "Dear Sir," April 18, 18[??], both in Garfield Papers, LC.

29. Diary, March 26, 1881; J. G. Blaine to Garfield, n.d., both in the Garfield Papers, LC; Garfield to B. A. Hinsdale, April 4, 1881, in Mary Hinsdale, *Garfield-Hinsdale Letters*, p. 490; Lucretia Garfield Diary, March 29, 1881, typed copy; Richardson, *William E. Chandler*, p. 268.

30. Garfield to Wm. Evarts, February 2, 1881, letterbook copy; J. Sherman to Garfield, January 23, 1881, both in Garfield Papers, LC.

31. Connery, "Secret History," pp. 153-54; Hamilton, *Blaine*, p. 534; Philadelphia *Press*, April 24, 1881, in Smith, *Life and Letters of Garfield*, II, 1120-21; Boutwell, *Reminiscences*, II, 273; Diary, March 20, 1881, Garfield Papers, LC.

32. Merritt, *Recollections*, p. 129; Lucretia Garfield Diary, March 22, 1881, typed copy.

33. Memo of J. S. Brown, January 23, 1885; Diary, March 22, 1881, both in the Garfield Papers, LC; Merritt, *Recollections*, pp. 135-36.

34. Badeau, with characteristic negligence, had not yet gotten around to delivering Grant's letter on his behalf, but its general tone was already known to Blaine. See: U. S. Grant to Garfield, March 16, 1881, Garfield Papers, LC; J. Hay to W. Reid, March 23, 1881, typed copy, Reid Papers, LC; Merritt, *Recollections*, pp. 136-37.

35. Merritt, *Recollections*, pp. 123-24; Blaine to Garfield, March 23, 1881, Garfield Papers, LC.

36. Chidsey, *Gentleman From New York*, p. 332; Platt cited in J. W. Hall to Garfield, March 24, 1881, Garfield Papers, LC; U.S. Grant to A. Badeau, May 7, 1881, in Smith, *Life and Letters of Garfield*, II, 1134.

37. Merritt, *Recollections*, pp. 124-26; Diary, March 25, April 5, 1881; Arthur, Platt, Conkling and James to Garfield, March 25, 1881, all in the Garfield Papers, LC; H. L. Dawes to his wife, May 10, 1881, Dawes Papers, LC.

38. Connery, "Secret History," pp. 154-57; Merritt, *Recollections*, p. 130; Halstead, "Tragedy," pp. 276-77; Garfield to U.S. Grant, May 15, 1881, Garfield Papers, LC.

39. W. Reid to J. Hay, March 27, 1881, telegram, Reid Papers, LC; Diary, April 2, 1881; Garfield to J. Rudolph, April 4, 1881, letterbook copy; J. G. Blaine to Garfield, "Thursday, 7:30 p.m." [April 5, 1881?], all in the Garfield Papers, LC.

40. Garfield to W. Reid, March 30, 1881, Garfield Papers, LC; Merritt, *Recollections*, p. 137; J. Hay to W. Reid, March 28, 1881, typed copy, Reid Papers, LC.

41. Alexander, *Political History of New York*, III, 470; Diary, March 10 and 17, 1875, Garfield Papers, LC; Speech of July 31, 1872 in Garfield, *Works*, II, 33; Garfield to B. A. Hinsdale, April 4, 1881, in Mary Hinsdale, *Garfield-Hinsdale Letters*, p. 490.

42. Garfield to B. A. Hinsdale, December 30, 1880, letterbook copy; B. H. Hill to Chittenden, November 6, 1880, in unidentified scrapbook clipping; B. H. Hill to Garfield, November 7 and December 15, 1880; G. B. Forrester to Garfield, November 10, 1880; Garfield to B. H. Hill, undated draft in letterbook, all in the Garfield Papers, LC; De Santis, *Republicans Face the Southern Question*, p. 141.

43. Garfield to B. A. Hinsdale, December 20, 1879, in Mary Hinsdale, *Garfield-Hinsdale Letters*, p. 431; Diary, December 29, 1880; February 5, 1881; Garfield to W. Reid, December 30, 1880, typed copy; J. D. Brady to Garfield, November 11, 1880, all in the Garfield Papers, LC; W. E. Chandler to Garfield, February 19, 1881, draft copy, Chandler Papers, LC.

44. De Santis, *Republicans Face the Southern Question*, pp. 141-51; Garfield to W. Reid, April 7, 1881, typed copy, Garfield Papers, LC.

45. J. Hay to W. Reid, April 4, 1881, typed copy, Reid Papers, LC; H. L. Dawes to his wife, April 30, 1881, Dawes Papers, LC; Connery, "Secret History," pp. 148-50; Dawes, "Garfield and Conkling," p. 343.

46. Garfield to J. A. Hubbell, August 22, 1880, letterbook copy; Diary, May 3, 1881, both in Garfield Papers, LC; Dawes, "Garfield and Conkling," pp. 343-44; H. L. Dawes to his wife, May 3, 1881, Dawes Papers, LC.

47. H. L. Dawes to his wife, May 18, 1881, Dawes Papers, LC; W. Bateman to J. Sherman, April 25, 1881, Bateman Papers, WRHS; Ingalls, *Writings*, pp. 402-05; Thos. M. Donaldson to R. B. Hayes, June 12, 1881, typed copy, HML.

48. Undated scrapbook clipping from Albany *Journal*; Diary, April 2, 3 and 26, 1881, all in the Garfield Papers, LC; Platt, *Autobiography*, p. 152; Gorham, *Conkling Vindicated*, p. 12.

49. Alexander, *Political History of New York*, III, 475-76; Garfield to H. L. Dawes, May 28, 1881, letterbook copy; Diary, May 4, 1881; J. G. Blaine to Garfield [March 29, 1881 ?] all in the Garfield Papers, LC.

50. Alexander, *Political History of New York*, III, 475; Diary, May 5, 1881; Garfield to J. Hay, May 8, 1881, letterbook copy; J. G. Blaine to Garfield, May 5, 1881, all in the Garfield Papers, LC; Breen, *Thirty Years*, p. 656.

51. Garfield to W. Reid, March 30, 1881; Diary, March 27 and 28, 1881; W. Reid to Garfield, April 11, 1881, all in the Garfield Papers, LC; Platt, *Autobiography*, p. 151; Connery, "Secret History," p. 158.

52. J. Hay to W. Reid, May 26, 1881, typed copy, Reid Papers, LC; H. L. Dawes to his wife, May 16, 1881, Dawes Papers, LC.

53. As Thurlow Weed put it. See Jordan, *Roscoe Conkling*, p. 349n.

54. Garfield to J. D. Cox, May 22, 1881, letterbook copy; J. G. Blaine to Garfield, May 20,1881, both in the Garfield Papers, LC.

55. Connery, "Secret History," p. 161; J. Hay to W. Reid, May 26, 1881, Reid Papers, LC; P. Sheldon to Garfield, December 23, 1880, Garfield Papers, LC.

56. Halstead, "Tragedy," p. 277; W. T. Crump to "Dear Sir," April 18, 18[??]; Diary, May 11 and 31, 1881, all in the Garfield Papers, LC.

57. Davison, *Presidency of Hayes*, p. 207n.; Barrows, *William M. Evarts*, p. 347.

58. Both contemporary observers and subsequent historians have been intrigued by Blaine's diplomacy. For the views of some contemporaries see: Hurlbert, *Atrocious Foreign Policy*; Anon., *Liberal Statesmanship*; Hall, *Mr. Blaine and Foreign Policy*; Romero, "Settlement of the Boundary Question"; and Blaine's own *apologia* in Blaine, "Foreign Policy," and *Political Discussions*. Among more recent accounts see: Tyler, *Foreign Policy of Blaine*; Muzzey, *Blaine*; Pletcher, *Awkward Years*; Bastert, "New Approach"; Peskin, "Blaine, Garfield and Latin America."

59. Blaine, "Foreign Policy " p. 2; J. G. Blaine to P. H. Morgan, June 21, 1881, in *U. S. Foreign Relations, 1881*, pp. 768-70.

60. Tyler, *Foreign Policy of Blaine*, p. 16; Blaine, "Foreign Policy,"; Muzzey, *Blaine*, p. 220n.

61. Blaine, *Political Discussions*, pp. 176-85; Garfield, *Works*, II, 324-28, 571-74; Diary, June 18, 1878,Garfield Papers, LC.

62. *Cong. Globe*, 42 Cong., 2 sess., 1168 (February 21, 1872); Garfield, *Works*, II, 278.

63. *Cong. Record*, 45 Cong., 2 sess., 2127 (February 28, 1879); H. N. Fisher to Garfield, October 28, 1878, Garfield Papers, LC.

64. 47 Cong., 1 sess., *H.R.R. #1790*, "Chile-Peru Investigation," p. 205.

65. Sherman, *Recollections*, II, 815-16; Diary, March 9, 1878; April 12, 1881 *et seq.*; Garfield to W. Windom, March 30, 1881, letterbook copy, Garfield Papers, LC; *Cong. Record*, 45 Cong., 3 sess., 470-71 (January 15, 1879).

66. In Smith, *Life and Letters of Garfield*, II, 1147.

67. J. G. Blaine to Garfield, February 13, 1881; C. E. Henry to H. Austin, June 18, 1881, both in the Garfield Papers, LC.

68. J. G. Blaine to Garfield, January 18, 1881; S. W. Dorsey to Garfield, January 15, 1881, both in *ibid.*; Howe, *Chester A. Arthur*, pp. 129-30; Reeves, *Gentleman Boss*, pp. 213-16.

69. Diary, February 17, 1881; J. G. Blaine to Garfield, February 13, 1881; W. E. Chandler to Garfield, February 17, 1881, all in the Garfield Papers, LC.

70. S. C. Boynton to Garfield, July 10, 1880; D. C. Gordon to Garfield, November 27, 1880; Carl Schurz to Garfield, January 2, 1881; W. B. Allison to Garfield, February 12, 1881; H. E. Knox to Garfield, February 13 and 19, 1881; "A Well Wisher" to Garfield, March 1, 1881, all in *ibid.*

71. Testimony of Thomas James in the Star Route Investigation, cited in Smith, *Life and Letters of Garfield*, II, 1158; C. H. Cramer, *Royal Bob*, p. 201.

72. Diary, April 19, 20, June 6, 1881; C. E. Henry to Garfield, June 20, 1881, Garfield Papers, LC.

73. T. M. Donaldson to R. B. Hayes, August 28, 1881, typed copy, HML; Hayes, *Trial of Guiteau*, pp. 435-36; *U.S. vs. Guiteau*, pp. 692-94.

25. STRANGULATUS PRO REPUBLICA

1. *U.S. vs. Guiteau*, pp. 593, 617ff.; "Autobiography of Guiteau," in Hayes, *Trial of Guiteau*, p. 428.

2. *U.S. vs. Guiteau*, pp. 291-93, 318, 346, 425-26, 463, 499-500, 545, 606.

3. *Ibid.*, pp. 296, 301, 318, 323, 329, 331, 391-92, 448-49, 543, 549, 603, 606.

4. "Married life of Guiteau," in Hayes, *Trial of Guiteau*, pp. 459, 476, 513-14; *U.S. vs. Guiteau*, p. 957.

5. "Married Life of Guiteau," in Hayes, *Trial of Guiteau*, pp. 480, 504-07; "Autobiography of Guiteau," in *ibid.*, pp. 413-18; *U. S. vs. Guiteau*, pp. 303-06, 308, 342-45, 352, 356-62, 369, 468-70, 563-66, 578, 581-84, 677-80, 792-94.

6. C. J. Guiteau to Garfield, March 8, 1881, printed copy, Garfield Papers, LC; *U.S. vs. Guiteau*, pp. 335-37, 584-86, 603, 719, 767.

7. C. J. Guiteau to Garfield, October 16 and December 31, 1880, March 8, 1881, printed copy, Garfield Papers, LC.

8. *U.S. vs. Guiteau*, pp. 222, 444-48, 588-89, 602, 634, 719, 1159; "Autobiography of Guiteau," in Hayes, *Trial of Guiteau*, pp. 424-26.

9. Gerry, *Through Five Administrations*, pp. 266-69; C. J. Guiteau to Garfield, May 16, 1881, printed copy, Garfield Papers, LC; "Autobiography of Guiteau," in Hayes, *Trial of Guiteau*, p. 428.

10. *U.S. vs. Guiteau*, pp. 216, 727, 1108; Charles Guiteau to Garfield, May 23, 1881, printed copy, Garfield Papers, LC.

11. *U.S. vs. Guiteau*, pp. 215-16, 224-25, 638; Garfield to John Sherman, November 16, 1880, in Sherman, *Recollections*, II, 789.

12. "Autobiography of Guiteau," in Hayes, *Trial of Guiteau*, pp. 430-39; *U.S. vs. Guiteau*, pp. 114-15, 198-200, 216, 629, 685-86, 692-94, 698, 704-05.

13. B. Van Horn to Garfield, May 26, 1881; Diary, June 9, 1881, both in the Garfield Papers, LC; Jordan, *Roscoe Conkling*, pp. 404-05.

14. "Life Book," December 1883, Harry A. Garfield Papers, LC; C. R. Williams, *Diary and Letters of Hayes*, IV, 417.

15. Cyrus Field to Garfield, June 29, 1881, Garfield Papers, LC; Ingalls, *Writings*, pp. 406-07.

16. *Cong. Globe*, 42 Cong., 2 sess., 3827 (May 24, 1872); *U.S. vs. Guiteau*, pp. 121-390, 601, 706, 2215.

17. Bliss, "Report," pp. 393-94; *U.S. vs. Guiteau*, p. 172; Brooks, *Our Murdered Presidents*, p. 67; Robert Todd Lincoln cited in Rosenberg, *Trial of the Assassin Guiteau*, p. 4; J. Stanley-Brown. "My Friend Garfield," p. 100.

18. Diary, July 2, 1881, James Rudolph Garfield Papers, LC; Memoir of W. T. Crump; Crump to "Dear Sir," April 18, 18[??], both in the Garfield Papers, LC.

19. Comer, *Harry Garfield*, p. 57; L. S. Bull to Mr. Judd, July 3, 1881, telegram, Garfield Papers, LC.

20. W. T. Crump to "Dear Sir," April 18, 18[??], Garfield Papers, LC; Bliss, "Report," pp. 394-95.

21. Unidentified scrapbook clipping, Garfield Papers, LC; Connery, "Secret History," pp. 146-47; C. R. Williams, *Diary and Letters of Hayes*, IV, 23.

22. Smith, *Life and Letters of Garfield*, II, 1197.

23. W. E. Chandler to J. G. Blaine, July 18, 1881, in Hamilton, *Blaine*, p. 541; R. B. Hayes to J. Hay, July 8, 1881, in C. R. Williams, *Diary and Letters of Hayes*, IV, 25; J. Hastings to Thom. James, July 7, 1881, Garfield Papers, LC.

24. Rockwell, "An Autograph," p. 299; Rockwell, "Mentor to Elberon," p. 437; C. R. Williams, *Diary and Letters of Hayes*, IV, 415.

25. Thom. C. Donaldson to R. B. Hayes, August 28, 1881, typed copy, HML; Gerry, *Through Five Administrations*, pp. 273-74; C. R. Williams, *Diary and Letters of Hayes*, IV, 415; W. T. Crump, "Sick-room Anecdotes"; Lucretia Garfield to M. Austin, July 21, 1881, both in the Garfield Papers, LC.

26. U. S. Navy Department, *Reports on Ventilating and Cooling*.

27. Temkin and Koudelka, "Simon Newcomb and Garfield's Bullet," pp. 393-97; Tindall, "Echoes of Tragedy," pp. 158-59; Brooks, *Our Murdered Presidents*, pp. 88-90; Prichard and Herring, "Problem of President's Bullet," pp. 632-33.

28. *U.S. vs. Guiteau*, p. 1160.

29. The medical literature on Garfield's illness is voluminous and controversial. In addition to the works cited above [Bliss, "Report"; Brooks, *Our Murdered Presidents*; Prichard and Herring, "Problem of President's Bullet"; and Tindall, "Echoes"], I have found the following especially useful: Adams, *Life of Agnew*; Day, "Review of Surgical Treatment"; Fish, "Death of Garfield"; Hammond, et al., "Surgical Treatment of Garfield"; Parker, "Assassination and Wound of Garfield"; Reyburn, "Clinical History"; Vincent, "Presidential Gunshot Wounds."

30. Prichard, "Problem of President's Bullet," p. 632; J. Marion Sims, in Hammond, "Surgical Treatment of Garfield," pp. 596-97.

31. Bliss, "Story," p. 301; Rockwell, "An Autograph," p. 299.

32. C. R. Williams, *Diary and Letters of Hayes*, IV, 115; Howe, *Chester A. Arthur*, p. 153.

33. Brooks, *Our Murdered Presidents*, pp. 577-89; Ridpath, *Life and Work of Garfield*, pp. 509-607.

34. Diary, June 19, 1881, Garfield Papers, LC; Ridpath, *Life and Work of Garfield*, pp. 613-24; Brooks, *Our Murdered Presidents*, pp. 91-95; Bliss, "Story," pp. 302-03.

35. Brooks, *Our Murdered Presidents*, p. 97; Adams, *Life of Agnew*, 247-48.

36. Garfield's last words reported in Lucretia Garfield to J. Warren Keifer, March 12, 1887, letter in possession of William W. Keifer of Springfield, Ohio, who kindly gave me a typed copy. Bliss, "Story," p. 302ff.; Bliss, "Report," pp. 397-98; Brooks, *Our Murdered Presidents*, pp. 98-100; Ridpath, *Life and Work of Garfield*, pp. 632-39.

37. See the autopsy report appended to Bliss, "Report," pp. 394-402. Compare the various points of view expressed in Hammond, "Surgical Treatment of Garfield."

38. Howe, *Chester A. Arthur*, pp. 1-2.

39. Ridpath, *Life and Work of Garfield*, pp. 653-55, 668-72; Diary, September 26, 1881, James Rudolph Garfield Papers, LC.

40. *The Garfield Memorial*. The $225,000 subscribed to build Garfield's tomb was not appreciably smaller than the amount subscribed as a trust fund to sustain his widow and orphans. See, "Garfield Fund Subscribers," Garfield Papers, LC. Cyrus Field provided the inspiration and organization for this fund and insured that it was conservatively invested, yielding an annual income of less than four percent.

41. Wolfe, *From Death to Morning*, p. 121; Bliss, "Story," p. 304; *U.S. vs. Guiteau*, p. 2210.

42. Garfield, *Works*, I, 594; Garfield to J. H. Rhodes, February 14, 1863, Garfield Papers, LC.

SOURCES CITED

A. MANUSCRIPTS

Insofar as possible, I have endeavored to base this biography on Garfield's own viewpoint, unfiltered by second thoughts or postfacto judgments, preferring that readers draw what conclusions they will. This task has been facilitated by the immense and well-organized collection of manuscripts and other private papers Garfield left behind. Unlike some of his contemporaries, such as Blaine, Conkling and Arthur, who either destroyed their papers or censored them for posterity, Garfield was one of the most assiduous hoarders of paper in our nation's history. An indefatigable correspondent, he was well aware of his responsibility to history. No scrap of paper seemed too trivial to be discarded; even overdue library notices were faithfully preserved. Had he not been cut off in his epistolary prime, his papers would undoubtedly surpass in bulk even such mammoth collections as John Sherman's or Booker T. Washington's. Not only are they extensive, they are also remarkably candid and self-searching, resulting in a unique self-portrait that offers the biographer the rare opportunity to see his subject and his subject's times through his subject's eyes.

When I first embarked on this project, the Garfield Papers were scattered: most were at the Library of Congress; a few were still in the possession of the Abram Garfield family at Cleveland, and some, mostly of a personal or private nature, had been lent by the Garfield family to Professors Harry Brown and Frederick Williams of Michigan State University, who were then editing the Garfield diaries. Despite their busy schedule, they graciously put their office at my disposal and allowed me to examine the papers. Since then, the collection has been consolidated at the Library of Congress, and I have so cited it. Since 1973 (too late, unfortunately, to be of asistance to this project), the Garfield Papers have been available on 177 reels of microfilm as part of the Presidents' Papers Series. The letterpress index to these microfilms contains not only a complete description of the collection but also a fascinating history of their provenance in an introductory essay by Kate M. Stewart which is a model of its kind.

Other manuscript collections at the Library of Congress which I have cited in this work include: the Jeremiah Sullivan Black Papers; the William E. Chandler Papers; the Salmon P. Chase Papers; the Henry Dawes Papers; the Harry A. Garfield Papers; the James Rudolph Garfield Papers; the Whitelaw Reid Papers; and the Jacob W. Schuckers Papers.

The Western Reserve Historical Society at Cleveland, Ohio, with its several linear feet of Garfield papers, is the second most useful source for Garfield manuscripts. Of particular interest is the correspondence between Garfield and David G. Swaim. The Society also possesses copies of most of the Garfield-Burke Aaron Hinsdale correspondence. The Garfield side of the correspondence consists of photostat copies; the Hinsdale letters are typed copies. Although the originals are at the Library of Congress, I have cited many of these letters as from the Western Reserve Historical Society, since it was in this form that I first used them. (I have also cited many letters from this same correspondence as they are found in Mary Hinsdale's collection of *Garfield-Hinsdale Letters*, deeming this printed source more easily accessible to most readers.)

Other pertinent collections at the Western Reserve Historical Society include the Burke Aaron Hinsdale Papers and the Warner Bateman Papers, both of which were especially valuable for the 1880 Republican convention; the John M. Stull Papers, useful for the Warren, Ohio "monster" campaign rally; the Eliza Garfield Diary for 1881; and various scattered items.

The Ohio Historical Society at Columbus holds a small but interesting collection of Garfield papers, including a fragment from his diary for 1854. The James M. Comly Papers at the Ohio Historical Society also contains some Garfield items.

The Hayes Memorial Library at Fremont, Ohio, more than compensates for its out-of-the-way location by the unfailing courtesy of its staff and the careful organization of its holdings. The extensive Rutherford B. Hayes Papers and a typed copy of the Memoirs of Thomas C. Donaldson proved especially illuminating.

The Hiram College Library yielded the Charles E. Henry Papers, much of which had already been mined for Henry's biography, but enough of which was fresh to make the trip worthwhile.

The Robert C. Schenck Papers are on deposit at the Miami University Library, Oxford, Ohio. They were made available to me through microfilm copies loaned by the Hayes Memorial Library.

Finally, the Garfield family of Cleveland graciously allowed me to examine their remaining Garfield papers before they were shipped to the Library of Congress. These papers included a typed copy of the Lucretia Garfield Diary, which I have cited in that form.

SOURCES CITED

B. GOVERNMENT DOCUMENTS

Congressional Globe, 38th Congress to 42nd Congress.

Congressional Record, 43rd Congress to 46th Congress.

Foreign Relations of the United States, 1881. Washington, 1882.

House of Representatives Miscellaneous Document #31, 45 Congress, 3 session, "Presidential Election Investigation" [Potter Committee].

House of Representatives Report #31, 41 Congress, 2 session, "Gold Panic Investigation."

House of Representatives Report #77, 42 Congress, 3 session, "Report of the Poland Committee" [Crédit Mobilier Investigation].

House of Representatives Report #156, 44 Congress, 2 session, "The Recent Election in Louisiana."

House of Representatives Report #139, Part II, 44 Congress, 2 session.

House of Representatives Report #1790, 47 Congress, 2 session, "Chile-Peru Investigation."

Library of Congress, *Index to the James A. Garfield Papers.* Washington, 1973.

Navy Department, *Reports of Officers of the Navy on Ventilating and Cooling the Executive Mansion During the Illness of President Garfield.* Washington, 1882.

Report of the Proceedings in the Case of the United States vs. Charles J. Guiteau. . . . 3 vols. Washington, 1882.

Senate Document #142, 38 Congress, 2 session, "Report of the Joint Committee on the Conduct of the War, Part III. Rosecrans's Campaigns."

Senate Executive Document #2, 44 Congress, 2 session.

War of the Rebellion: A Compilation of the Official Records of the Union and Confederate Armies. 128 vols. Washington, 1880-1901.

C. OTHER SOURCES

Adams, Charles Francis, Jr. "Railroad Inflation." *North American Review,* CCXXII (January 1869), 130-64.

Adams, J. Howe. *History of the Life of D. Hayes Agnew, M.D., LL.D.* Philadelphia and London, 1892.

Aldrich, Frederick De Long. "History of Ohio Public School Library Legislation." Unpublished doctoral dissertation at Case Western Reserve University Library (1953).

Alexander, DeAlva Stanwood. *History and Procedure of the House of Representatives.* Boston and New York, 1916.

———. *A Political History of the State of New York.* 4 vols. New York, 1909.

Alger, Horatio. *From Canal Boy to President, or the Boyhood and Manhood of J. A. Garfield.* New York, 1881.

Ambrose, Stephen E. *Upton and the Army.* Baton Rouge, 1964.

Ames, Mary Clemmer. *Ten Years in Washington. Life and Scenes in the National Capital, as a Woman Sees Them.* Hartford, 1875.

Atkinson, Edward. *The Industrial Progress of the Nation. Consumption Limited, Production Unlimited.* New York and London, 1890.

Barker, Wharton. "The Secret History of Garfield's Nomination." *Pearson's Magazine,* XXXV (May 1916), 435-43.

Barnard, Harry. *Rutherford B. Hayes and His America.* Indianapolis and New York, 1954.

Barrows, Chester Leonard. *William M. Evarts: Lawyer, Diplomat, Statesman.* Chapel Hill, 1941.

Bascom, John. *Things Learned by Living.* New York, 1913.

Bastert, Russell H. "A New Approach to the Origins of Blaine's Pan American Policy." *Hispanic American Historical Review,* XXXIX (1959), 375-412.

Beale, Harriet Blaine (ed.). *Letters of Mrs. James G. Blaine.* 2 vols. New York, 1908.

Beale, Howard K. *The Critical Year: A Study of Andrew Johnson and Reconstruction.* New York, 1930.

Beatty, John. *Memoirs of a Volunteer, 1861-1863,* ed. Harvey S. Ford. New York, 1946.

Benedict, Michael Les. *A Compromise of Principle: Congressional Republicans and Reconstruction, 1863-1869.* New York, 1974.

Benjamin, S[amuel] G[reene] W[heeler]. *The Life and Adventures of a Free Lance.* Burlington, Vt., 1914.

Blaine, James G. "Foreign Policy of the Garfield Administration," *Chicago Weekly Magazine,* September 16, 1882.

———. *Political Discussions: Legislative, Diplomatic, and Popular, 1865-1886.* Norwich, Conn., 1887.

———. *Twenty Years of Congress: From Lincoln to Garfield. With a Review of the Events which Led to the Political Revolution of 1860.* 2 vols. Norwich, Conn., 1884.

Bliss, D. W. "Report of the Case of President Garfield." *The Medical Record,* XX (October 8, 1881), 393-402.

———. "The Story of President Garfield's Illness." *Century Magazine,* XXV (1881), 299-305.

Bond, Otto F. (ed.). *Under the Flag of the Nation. Diaries and Letters of a Yankee in the Civil War.* Columbus, 1961.

Boutwell, George S. *Reminiscences of Sixty Years in Public Affairs.* 2 vols. New York, 1902.

Boykin, Edward. *The Wit and Wisdom of Congress.* New York, 1961.

Bratton, Madison. "The Unionist Junket of the Legislatures of Tennessee and Kentucky in January, 1860." *The East Tennessee Historical Society's Publications,* VII (1935), 64-81.

Breen, Matthew P. *Thirty Years of New York Politics, Up to Date.* New York, 1899.

Brigance, William Norwood. *Jeremiah Sullivan Black: A Defender of the Constitution and the Ten Commandments.* Philadelphia, 1934.

694

Brinkerhoff, Roeliff. *Recollections of a Life-time.* Cincinnati, 1900.

Brooks, Noah. *Washington in Lincoln's Time,* ed. Herbert Mitang. New York, 1958.

Brooks, Stewart M. *Our Murdered Presidents: The Medical Story.* New York, 1966.

Brown, Harry James and Frederick D. Williams. *The Diary of James A. Garfield.* 3 vols. to date. East Lansing, 1967-.

Bundy, Jonas Mills. *The Life of James Abram Garfield.* New York, 1880.

Burnham, W. Dean. *Presidential Ballots, 1836-1892.* Baltimore, 1955.

Cabot, James Elliot. *A Memoir of Ralph Waldo Emerson.* 2 vols. Boston and New York, 1895.

Caldwell, Robert Granville. *James A. Garfield, Party Chieftain.* New York, 1931.

Campbell, Henry Colin. *Wisconsin in Three Centuries, 1634-1905.* 4 vols. New York, 1906.

Casson, Henry. *"Uncle Jerry." Life of General Jeremiah M. Rusk: Stage Driver, Farmer, Soldier, Legislator, Governor, Cabinet Officer.* Madison, 1895.

Cater, Harold Dean (ed.). *Henry Adams and His Friends. A Collection of His Unpublished Letters.* Boston, 1947.

Chidsey, Donald Barr. *The Gentleman from New York: A Life of Roscoe Conkling.* New Haven, 1935.

Clayton, Mary Black. *Reminiscences of Jeremiah Sullivan Black.* St. Louis, 1887.

Cochran, William Cox. "Political Experiences of Major General Jacob Dolson Cox." 2 vols. Cincinnati, 1940. Typed copy of unfinished biography deposited in the Oberlin College Library.

Colman, Edna M. *White House Gossip: From Andrew Johnson to Calvin Coolidge.* New York, 1927.

Comer, Lucretia Garfield. *Harry Garfield's First Forty Years. Man of Action in a Troubled World.* New York, 1965.

Commager, Henry Steele (ed.). *Documents of American History.* 2 vols. New York, 1963.

Conkling, Alfred R. *The Life and Letters of Roscoe Conkling, Orator, Statesman, Advocate.* New York, 1889.

Connelley, William Elsey. *The Life of Preston B. Plumb.* Chicago, 1913.

Connery, T. B. "Secret History of the Garfield-Conkling Tragedy." *Cosmopolitan Magazine,* XXIII (1897), 145-62.

Cortissoz, Royal. *The Life of Whitelaw Reid.* 2 vols. New York, 1921.

Coulter, E. Merton. *The Civil War and Readjustment in Kentucky.* Chapel Hill, 1926.

Cox, Jacob Dolson. *Military Reminiscences of the Civil War.* 2 vols. New York, 1900.

————. "Oration on the Youth and Early Manhood of General James A.

695

Garfield," *Society of the Army of the Cumberland: Fourteenth Reunion, 1882.* Cincinnati, 1883.

―――. *Second Battle of Bull Run as Connected with the Fitz John Porter Case.* Cincinnati, 1882.

Cox, John H. and LaWanda Cox. *Politics, Principle and Prejudice, 1865-1866.* New York, 1963.

Cramer, C. H. *Royal Bob. The Life of Robert G. Ingersoll.* Indianapolis and New York, 1952.

Crook, William H. *Memories of the White House,* ed. Henry Rood. Boston, 1911.

Crowley, Mrs. Richard. *Echoes from Niagara: Historical, Political, Personal.* Buffalo, 1890.

Curran, M. P. *Life of Patrick A. Collins.* Norwood, Mass., 1906.

Curti, Merle, *The Social Ideas of American Educators.* New York, 1935.

Dana, Charles A. *Recollections of the Civil War. With the Leaders at Washington and in the Field in the Sixties.* New York and London, 1913.

Dangerfield, George. *The Era of Good Feelings.* New York, 1952.

Davenport, John I. *History of the Forged "Morey Letter".* . . . New York, 1884.

Davis, Harold E. (ed.). *Garfield of Hiram.* Hiram, 1931.

Davison, Kenneth E. *The Presidency of Rutherford B. Hayes.* Westport, Conn., 1972.

Dawes, Henry L. "Garfield and Conkling." *Century Magazine,* XLVII (January 1894), 341-44.

Day, Richard H. "Review of the Surgical Treatment of President Garfield." *New Orleans Medical and Surgical Journal,* X (August 1882), 81-95.

Dennett, Tyler (ed.). *Lincoln and the Civil War in the Diaries and Letters of John Hay.* New York, 1939.

Depew, Chauncey M. *My Memories of Eighty Years.* New York, 1922.

De Santis, Vincent P. *Republicans Face the Southern Question. The New Departure Years, 1877-1897.* Baltimore, 1959.

Donald, David (ed.). *Inside Lincoln's Cabinet: The Civil War Diaries of Salmon P. Chase.* New York, 1954.

―――. *Lincoln Reconsidered. Essays on the Civil War Era.* New York, 1961.

―――. (ed.). *Why the North Won the Civil War.* New York, 1962.

Eaton, Clement. *A History of the Southern Confederacy.* New York, 1961.

Eisenschiml, Otto. *The Celebrated Case of Fitz John Porter, An American Dreyfuss Affair.* Indianapolis and New York, 1950.

Evans, Frank B. "Wharton Barker and the Republican National Convention of 1880." *Pennsylvania History,* XXVII (January 1960), 28-43.

Fish, Stewart A. "The Death of President Garfield." *Bulletin of the History of Medicine,* XXIV (1950), 378-92.

696

Fiske, John. *The Mississippi Valley in the Civil War.* Boston and New York, 1900.

Fitch, John ["An Officer," *pseud.*]. *Annals of the Army of the Cumberland.* Philadelphia, 1863.

Fleming, Walter L. *Civil War and Reconstruction in Alabama.* New York, 1905.

Fowler, Dorothy Ganfield. *The Cabinet Politician: the Postmasters General, 1829-1909.* New York, 1943.

Fuller, Corydon E. *Reminiscences of James A. Garfield.* Cincinnati, 1887.

Garfield, James A. "My Campaign in East Kentucky." *North American Review,* CXLIII (December 1886), 525-35.

———. "My Experience as a Lawyer." *North American Review,* CXLIV (1887), 565-71.

———. *Review of the Transactions of the Crédit Mobilier Company.* Washington, 1873.

———. *Tested and Sustained. Remarks of Hon. James A. Garfield to His Constituents at Warren, Ohio, September 19, 1874, in Reply to Attacks Upon His Official Character.* 1873.

———. *The Works of James Abram Garfield,* ed. Burke Aaron Hinsdale. 2 vols. Boston, 1883.

Garfield Memorial, The. Cleveland, 1894.

Gerry, Margurita Spalding (ed.). *Through Five Administrations. Reminiscences of Colonel William H. Crook.* New York and London, 1910.

Gilmore, James R. [Edmund Kirke, *pseud.*]. *Down in Tennessee, and Back by Way of Richmond.* New York, 1864.

———. [Edmund Kirke, *pseud.*]. *On the Border.* Boston, 1867.

———. *Personal Recollections of Abraham Lincoln and the Civil War.* Boston, 1898.

Gladden, Washington. *Recollections.* Boston and New York, 1909.

Gorham, Geo. C. *Roscoe Conkling Vindicated.* New York, 1888.

Gracie, Archibald. *The Truth About Chickamauga.* Boston and New York, 1911.

Green, Constance McClaughlin. *Washington: Village and Capital, 1800-1878.* 2 vols. Princeton, 1962.

Green, F. M. *Hiram College and Western Reserve Eclectic Institute: Fifty Years of History, 1850-1900.* Cleveland, 1901.

Hall, H. W. *Mr. Blaine and His Foreign Policy.* Boston, 1884.

Halstead, Murat. "The Tragedy of Garfield's Administration. Personal Reminiscences and Records of Conversations." *McClure's Magazine,* VI (1896), 269-78.

Hamilton, Gail [*pseud.* of Mary Abigail Dodge]. *Biography of James G. Blaine.* Norwich, Conn., 1895.

Hammond, William A., *et al.* "The Surgical Treatment of President Garfield," *North American Review,* CXXXIII (1881), 578-610.

697

Harper's Pictorial History of the Great Rebellion. 2 vols. New York, 1868.

Harris, William T. "Establishment of the Office of the Commissioner of Education of the United States, and Henry Barnard's Relation to It." *Report of the Commissioner of Education* (1902).

Hatcher, Harlan. *The Western Reserve: The Story of New Connecticut in Ohio.* Indianapolis, 1949.

Hawley, Zerah. *A Journal of a Tour Through Connecticut, Massachusetts, New York, the North Part of Pennsylvania and Ohio.* New Haven, 1822.

Haworth, Paul Leland. *The Hayes-Tilden Disputed Presidential Election of 1876.* Cleveland, 1906.

Hayden, Amos Sutton. *Early History of the Disciples in the Western Reserve.* Cincinnati, 1875.

Hayes, H. G. and C. J. Hayes. *A Complete History of the Trial of Guiteau.* Philadelphia, 1882. Includes the "Autobiography of Charles Julius Guiteau, Assassin of President Garfield" and "Married Life of Charles Julius Guiteau, by his former Wife, Mrs. Annie J. Dunmire."

Hazen, General W. B. *A Narrative of Military Service.* Boston, 1885.

Henry, Frederick A. *Captain Henry of Geauga: A Family Chronicle.* Cleveland, 1942.

Herndon, Dallas T. *Centennial History of Arkansas.* 3 vols. Little Rock and Chicago, 1922.

Hesseltine, William T. *Ulysses S. Grant, Politician.* New York, 1957.

Hinman, Wilbur F. *The Story of the Sherman Brigade.* n.p., [1897].

Hinsdale, Burke Aaron. *The Eclectic Institute: An Address Delivered at the Jubilee of Hiram College, June 22, 1900.* Ann Arbor, 1900.

———. *President Garfield and Education.* Boston, 1882.

Hinsdale, Mary L. (ed.). *Garfield-Hinsdale Letters: Correspondence Between James Abram Garfield and Burke Aaron Hinsdale.* Ann Arbor, 1949.

Hoar, George Frisbie. *Autobiography of Seventy Years.* 2 vols. New York, 1906.

Hopkins, Mark. *Teaching and Counsels.* New York, 1884.

Hoogenboom, Ari. *Outlawing the Spoils. A History of the Civil Service Reform Movement, 1865-1883.* Urbana, Ill., 1961.

House, Albert V. "The Democratic State Central Committee of Indiana in 1880: A Case Study in Party Tactics and Finance." *Indiana Magazine of History*, LVIII (September 1962), 179-210.

Howe, George Frederick. *Chester A. Arthur: A Quarter-Century of Machine Politics.* New York, 1935.

Howells, William Dean. *Years of My Youth.* New York, 1916.

Hudson, William C. *Random Recollections of an Old Political Reporter.* New York, 1911.

Hughes, Sarah Forbes (ed.). *Letters and Recollections of John Murray Forbes.* 2 vols. Boston and New York, 1899.

Hunsberger, George E. "Garfield and the Tariff." Unpublished Master's Thesis, Oberlin College, 1931.

Hunt, Gaillard. *Israel, Elihu, and Cadwallader Washburn: A Chapter in American Biography.* New York, 1925.

Hurlbert, William Henry. *Atrocious Foreign Policy of Secretary Blaine.* n.p., 1884.

Ingalls, John James. *A Collection of the Writings of John James Ingalls. Essays, Addresses, and Orations.* Kansas City, Mo., 1902.

Johnson, Robert Underwood and Clarence Clough Buel (eds.). *Battles and Leaders of the Civil War.* 4 vols. New York, 1887-1888.

Jordan, David M. *Roscoe Conkling, Voice in the Senate.* Ithaca and London, 1971.

Kaliebe, Jon. "The Big Sandy Campaign." Unpublished paper.

Keifer, Joseph Warren. *Slavery and Four Years of War.* 2 vols. New York, 1900.

Kendrick, Burton J. *Lincoln's War Cabinet.* Garden City, N.Y., 1961 (Dolphin paperback reprint).

Kirkland, Edward C. *Industry Comes of Age: Business, Labor and Public Policy, 1860-1897.* New York, 1961.

Klaus, Samuel (ed.). *The Milligan Case.* New York, 1929.

Knox, John Jay. *A History of Banking in the United States.* New York, 1903.

Lamar, J. S. *Memoirs of Isaac Errett.* 2 vols. Cincinnati, 1893.

Lamers, William S. *The Edge of Glory: A Biography of William S. Rosecrans. U.S.A.* New York, 1961.

Land, Mary. "John Brown's Ohio Environment." *Ohio State Archaelogical and Historical Quarterly*, LVII (1948), 24-47.

Leech, Margaret. *Reveille in Washington, 1860-1865.* New York, 1941.

Lerner, Max (ed.). *The Mind and Faith of Justice Holmes. His Speeches, Essays, Letters and Judicial Opinions.* Boston, 1943.

Liberal Statesmanship. Jews in Russia. Mr. Blaine's Interposition in Their Behalf. n.p., 1884.

McElroy, Robert. *Levi Parsons Morton: Banker, Diplomat and Statesman.* New York and London, 1930.

McKinney, Francis F. *Education in Violence. The Life of George H. Thomas and the History of the Army of the Cumberland.* Detroit, 1961.

McMurty, R. Gerald. "The Jaquess-Gilmore Peace Mission." *Lincoln Herald*, XLIV (February 1942).

Magrath, Peter C. *Morrison R. Waite: The Triumph of Character.* New York, 1963.

Marcus, Robert D. *Grand Old Party. Political Structure in the Gilded Age, 1880-1896.* New York, 1971.

Mason, F. H. *The Forty-Second Ohio Infantry.* Cleveland, 1876.

Mayo, A. D. "Henry Barnard as First United States Commissioner of Education." *Report of the Commissioner of Education* (1902), 891-901.

———. "Henry Barnard." *Report of the Commissioner of Education* (1896-1897), 769-810.

Merritt, Edwin A. *Recollections, 1828-1911.* Albany, 1911.

Monroe, James. *Oberlin Thursday Lectures, Addresses and Essays.* Oberlin, 1897.

Moore, Clifford H. "Ohio in National Politics, 1865-1896." *Ohio Archaeological and Historical Publications,* XXXVII (1928), 220-427.

Morgan, H. Wayne. *From Hayes to McKinley: National Party Politics, 1877-1896.* Syracuse, 1969.

Morse, John T. (ed.). *Diary of Gideon Welles, Secretary of the Navy Under Lincoln and Johnson.* 3 vols. Boston and New York, 1911.

Muzzey, David Saville. *James G. Blaine: A Political Idol of Other Days.* New York, 1934.

Nevins, Allan. *The War for the Union.* 2 vols. New York, 1959-1960.

Nicolay, John G. and John Hay. *Abraham Lincoln: A History.* 10 vols. New York, 1890.

———. *Complete Works of Abraham Lincoln.* 12 vols. Cumberland Gap, Tenn., 1894.

Norris, James D. and James K. Martin (eds.). "Three Civil War Letters of James A. Garfield." *Ohio History,* LXXIV (Autumn 1965), 247-52.

———. and Arthur H. Shaffer (eds.). *Politics and Patronage in the Gilded Age: The Correspondence of James A. Garfield and Charles E. Henry.* Madison, 1970.

Nugent, Walter T. K. *The Money Question During Reconstruction.* New York, 1967.

Oberholtzer, Ellis P. *A History of the United States Since the Civil War.* 5 vols. New York, 1917-1937.

———. *Jay Cooke, Financier of the Civil War.* 2 vols. Philadelphia, 1907.

Ogden, Robert Morris (ed.). *The Diaries of Andrew D. White.* Ithaca, 1959.

Paine, Albert Bigelow. *Th. Nast: His Period and His Pictures.* New York, 1904.

Parker, Owen W. "The Assassination and Gunshot Wound of President James A. Garfield." *Minnesota Medicine,* XXXIV (March 1951), 227-33.

Past and Present of La Salle County, Illinois. Chicago, 1877.

Perry, Arthur Latham. *Williamstown and Williams College.* Norwood, Mass., 1899.

Peskin, Allan. "Blaine, Garfield and Latin America: A New Look." *The Americas*, (1978)

———. "Charles Guiteau of Illinois." *Journal of the Illinois State Historical Society*, LXX (May 1977), 130-39.

———. "From Log Cabin to Oblivion." *American History Illustrated*, XI (May 1976), 24-34.

———. "Garfield and Hayes: Political Leaders of the Gilded Age." *Ohio History*, LXXVII (Spring-Winter-Summer 1968), 111-24.

———. "The Hero of the Sandy Valley: James A. Garfield's Kentucky Campaign of 1861-1862." *Ohio History*, LXXII (January 1963), 3-24; (April 1963), 129-39.

———. "James A. Garfield," *For the Union: Ohio Leaders in the Civil War*, ed. Kenneth Wheeler. Columbus, 1968.

———. "The 'Little Man on Horseback' and the "Literary Fellow": Garfield's Opinions of Grant." *Mid-America*, LV (Oct. 1973), 271-82.

———. "President Garfield and the Rating Game: An Evaluation of a Brief Administration." *The South Atlantic Quarterly*, LXXVI (Winter 1977), 93-102.

———. "The 'Put-up Job': Wisconsin and the Republican National Convention of 1880." *Wisconsin Magazine of History*, LV (Summer 1972), 263-74.

———. "The Short, Unhappy Life of the Federal Department of Education." *Public Administration Review*, XXXIII (November/December 1973), 572-75.

———. "Was There a Compromise of 1877?" *The Journal of American History*, LX (June 1973), 63-75.

Piatt, Donn. "The General Who Heard Mass Before Battle." *The Collector*, LV (January and February 1942).

Pioneer and General History of Geauga County. n.p., 1880.

Platt, Thomas Collier. *The Autobiography of Thomas Collier Platt*. New York, 1910.

Pletcher, David M. *The Awkward Years: American Foreign Relations Under Garfield and Arthur*. Columbia, Mo., 1961.

Polakoff, Keith Ian. *The Politics of Inertia. The Election of 1876 and the End of Reconstruction*. Baton Rouge, 1973.

Porter, George H. "Ohio Politics During the Civil War Period." *Studies in History, Economics and Public Law*, XL, #2 (1911). Edited by the Faculty of Political Science of Columbia University.

Prichard, Robert W. and A. L. Herring, Jr. "The Problem of the President's Bullet," *Surgery, Gynecology and Obstetrics*. XCII, 632-33.

Proceedings of the Republican National Convention Held at Chicago, Illinois . . . 1880. Chicago, 1881.

Reeves, Thomas C. "Chester A. Arthur and Campaign Assessments in the Election of 1880." *The Historian*, XXXI (1969), 573-82.

———. *Gentleman Boss, The Life of Chester Alan Arthur*. New York, 1975.

701

Reid, Whitelaw. *Ohio in the War: Her Statesmen, Generals and Soldiers.* 2 vols. Columbus, 1868.

Reyburn, Robert. "Clinical History of the Case of President Garfield." *Journal of the American Medical Association,* XXII (1894).

Rhodes, James Ford. *Historical Essays.* New York, 1909.

———. *History of the United States from the Compromise of 1850.* 7 vols. New York, 1893-1906.

Richardson, Leon Burr. *William E. Chandler, Republican.* New York, 1940.

Riddle, Albert Gallatin. *Bart Ridgeley: A Story of Northern Ohio.* Boston, 1873.

———. *The Life, Character and Public Services of Jas. A. Garfield.* Philadelphia and New York, 1880.

———. *Recollection of War Times. Reminiscences of Men and Events in Washington, 1860-1865.* New York, 1895.

Ridpath, John Clark. *The Life and Work of James A. Garfield.* n.p., 1882.

Robertson, John Bruce. "Lincoln and Congress" Unpublished doctoral dissertation, University of Wisconsin, 1966.

Rockwell, A. F. "An Autograph of President Garfield." *Century Magazine,* XXV (1881), 298.

———. "From Mentor to Elberon," *Century Magazine,* XXIII (1881), 431-38.

Romero, Matias. "Settlement of the Mexico-Guatemala Boundary Question." *Bulletin of the American Geographical Society,* XXIX (1897), 123-59.

Rose, William Ganson. *Cleveland: The Making of a City.* Cleveland, 1950.

Rosenberg, Charles E. *The Trial of the Assassin Guiteau: Psychiatry and Law in the Gilded Age.* Chicago and London, 1968.

Rudolph, Frederick. *Mark Hopkins and the Log: Williams College, 1836-1872.* New Haven, 1956.

Sage, Leland L. *William Boyd Allison: A Study in Practical Politics.* Iowa City, 1956.

Schuster, Richard. *The Selfish and the Strong.* New York, 1958.

Scudder, Horace E. *Life and Letters of David Coit Scudder, Missionary in Southern India.* New York, 1964.

Sharkey, Robert P. *Money Class and Party. An Economic Study of Civil War and Reconstruction.* Series LXXVII, no. 2 of *The Johns Hopkins Studies in Historical and Political Science.* Baltimore, 1959.

Shaw, Henry K. *Buckeye Disciples. A History of the Disciples of Christ in Ohio.* St. Louis, 1952.

Sherman, John. *John Sherman's Recollections of Forty Years in the House, Senate and Cabinet. An Autobiography.* 2 vols. Chicago, 1895.

Shurtleff, G. W. "A Year with the Rebels." *Sketches of War History 1861-1865. Papers Prepared for the Ohio Commandery of the Loyal Legion of the United States,* Vol. IV (1896), Cincinnati.

702

Sinkler, George. "Race: Principles and Policy of Rutherford B. Hayes." *Ohio History*, LXX (Winter-Spring-Summer 1968), 149-67.

Smalley, E. V. "Characteristics of President Garfield." *Century Illustrated Monthly Magazine*, XXIII (1881-82), 168-76.

Smith, Charles Emory. "How Conkling Missed Nominating Blaine." *Saturday Evening Post*, CLXXIII (June 8, 1901), 2-3.

Smith, Theodore Clarke. "General Garfield at Chickamauga." *Proceedings of the Massachusetts Historical Society*, XLVIII (February 1915), 268-80.

———. *The Life and Letters of James Abram Garfield.* 2 vols. New Haven, 1925.

Squire, Andrew. *A Few Recollections of Hiram, 1861-1932.* Cleveland, 1932.

Stanley, Major General David S. *Personal Memoirs.* Cambridge, Mass., 1917.

Stanley-Brown, Joseph. "My Friend Garfield." *American Heritage*, XXII, #5 (August 1971), 49-53, 100-01.

Steiner, Bernard C. *Life of Henry Barnard, The First United States Commissioner of Education, 1867-1870.* United States Bureau of Education, *Bulletin #8* (1919).

Temkin, Owsei and Janet Koudelka. "Simon Newcomb and the Location of President Garfield's Bullet." *Bulletin of the History of Medicine*, XXIV (1950), 393-97.

Thomas, Benjamin P. and Harold M. Hyman. *Stanton: The Life and Times of Lincoln's Secretary of War.* New York, 1962.

Tindall, Dr. William. "Echoes of a Surgical Tragedy." *Proceedings of the Columbia Historical Society*, XXIII, 147-66.

Tocqueville, Alexis de. *Democracy in America*, ed. Richard D. Heffner. New York, 1956.

Treudley, Mary Bosworth. *Prelude to the Future: The First Hundred Years of Hiram College.* New York, 1950.

Trottman, Nelson. *History of the Union Pacific: A Financial and Economic Survey.* New York, 1966.

Tucker, Glenn. *Chickamauga: Bloody Battle in the West.* Indianapolis, 1961.

Tyler, Alice Felt. *The Foreign Policy of James G. Blaine.* Minneapolis, 1927.

Unger, Irwin. *The Greenback Era. A Social and Political History of American Finance, 1865-1879.* Princeton, 1964.

Vallandingham, James L. *A Life of Clement Vallandingham.* Baltimore, 1872.

Viator [*pseud.* of Joseph B. Varnum, Jr.]. *The Washington Sketch Book.* New York, 1864.

703

Villard, Henry. *Memoirs of Henry Villard, Journalist and Financier, 1835-1900.* 2 vols. Boston and New York, 1904.

Vincent, Esther H. "Presidential Gunshot Wounds." *Surgery, Gynecology and Obstetrics,* XCI (1905), 117-18.

Warden, Robert B. *An Account of the Private Life and Public Services of Salmon Portland Chase.* Cincinnati, 1874.

White, Horace. *The Life of Lyman Trumbull.* Boston and New York, 1913.

White, Leonard. *The Republican Era. A Study in Administrative History, 1869-1901.* New York, 1965.

Wilcox, Alanson. *A History of the Disciples of Christ in Ohio.* Cincinnati, 1918.

Williams, Charles R. (ed.). *Diary and Letters of Rutherford Birchard Hayes.* 5 vols. Columbus, 1925.

———. *The Life of Rutherford Birchard Hayes, Nineteenth President of the United States.* 2 vols. Columbus, 1928.

Williams, Kenneth P. *Lincoln Finds a General. A Military Study of the Civil War.* 5 vols. New York, 1949-1959.

Williams, T. Harry. *P.G.T. Beauregard: Napoleon in Gray,* New York, 1962.

Wilmerding, Lucius, Jr. *The Spending Power. A History of the Efforts of Congress to Control Expenditures.* New Haven, 1943.

Wilson, Carroll A. "Familiar Small College Quotations, II: 'Mark Hopkins and the Log'." *The Colophon,* new series III (1938), 194-209.

Wolfe, Thomas. *From Death to Morning.* New York, 1935.

Woodward, C. Vann. *Reunion and Reaction: The Compromise of 1877 and the End of Reconstruction.* Boston, 1951.

———. "Yes, There Was a Compromise of 1877." *The Journal of American History,* LX (June 1973), 215-23.

INDEX

I am in favor of passing a law that no author shall have a copyright of his book without having an index. It adds immensely to the value of a book and more than doubles its value to the reader.

—James A. Garfield

709

713

Women's rights movement 657
Wormley's House conference 418

Yosemite Valley 391
Young, Brigham 352

Youngstown, O. 292

Zeletherian Society 15
Zollicoffer, Felix 100, 120-21